THE MUSIC OF CENTRAL ASIA

THE MUSIC OF
CENTRAL ASIA

EDITED BY

THEODORE LEVIN

SAIDA DAUKEYEVA

ELMIRA KÖCHÜMKULOVA

INDIANA UNIVERSITY PRESS
BLOOMINGTON AND INDIANAPOLIS

The co-editors and Indiana University Press gratefully acknowledge the support and collaboration of the Aga Khan Music Initiative, a program of the Aga Khan Trust for Culture, in the publication of this volume, whose content has been enriched by the Music Initiative's activities.

AGA KHAN TRUST FOR CULTURE

Music Initiative

This book is a publication of

Indiana University Press

Office of Scholarly Publishing

Herman B Wells Library 350

1320 East 10th Street

Bloomington, Indiana 47405 USA

iupress.indiana.edu

The paper used in this publication meets the minimum requirements of the American
National Standard for Information Sciences—Permanence of Paper for Printed Library
Materials, ANSI Z39.48-1992.

Manufactured in China

Library of Congress Cataloging-in-Publication Data

The music of Central Asia / edited by Theodore Levin, Saida Daukeyeva,
and Elmira Köchümkulova.

pages cm

Includes index.

ISBN 978-0-253-01751-2 (cloth)—ISBN 978-0-253-01764-2 (ebook) 1. Music—Asia,
Central—History and criticism. I. Levin, Theodore Craig, editor. II. Daukeeva,
Saida Diasovna, editor. III. Köchümkulova, Elmira, editor.

ML3758.A783M87 2015

780.958—dc23

2015020867

1 2 3 4 5 21 20 19 18 17 16

Cover illustrations: Sebastian Schutyser. Courtesy of the Aga Khan Music Initiative.

Contents

Preface IX

Acknowledgments XIII

Accessing Music Examples Online XV

A Note on Music Terminology XVII

Guide to Transliteration XIX

Timeline of Central Asian History XXI

Part I. Music and Culture in Central Asia

Chapter 1   Music in Central Asia: An Overview 3
Theodore Levin

Chapter 2   Musical Instruments in Central Asia 26
Theodore Levin

Part II. The Nomadic World

Prologue   Who Are the Nomads of Central Asia? 41
Theodore Levin

Chapter 3   Introduction to Central Asian Epic Traditions 43
Elmira Köchümkulova

Chapter 4   The Kyrgyz Epic *Manas* 52
Elmira Köchümkulova

CHAPTER 5   ORAL EPIC IN KAZAKHSTAN:
                 KÖRUGHLY AND A DYNASTY OF GREAT *JYRAUS*   69
                 Uljan Baibosynova

CHAPTER 6   MUSIC OF THE KARAKALPAKS   79

    PART 1   THE EPIC WORLD OF THE KARAKALPAKS: *JYRAU* AND *BAQSY*   79
                 Frédéric Léotar

    PART 2   *QYSSAKHAN:* PERFORMER OF WRITTEN AND ORAL LITERATURE   88
                 Kalmurza Kurbanov and Saida Daukeyeva

CHAPTER 7   THE ART OF THE TURKMEN *BAGSHY*   109
                 Jamilya Gurbanova

CHAPTER 8   THE TURKMEN *DUTAR*   131
                 David Fossum

CHAPTER 9   KYRGYZ WISDOM SONGS: *TERME YRLARY*   139
                 Elmira Köchümkulova

CHAPTER 10   *AQYNS* AND IMPROVISED POETRY COMPETITIONS AMONG
                 THE KAZAKHS AND KYRGYZ   149
                 Elmira Köchümkulova and Jangül Qojakhmetova

CHAPTER 11   SINGING TRADITIONS OF THE KAZAKHS   179
                 Alma Kunanbaeva

CHAPTER 12   KYRGYZ FUNERAL LAMENTS   198
                 Elmira Köchümkulova

CHAPTER 13   KYRGYZ WEDDING SONGS   217
                 Elmira Köchümkulova

CHAPTER 14   NARRATIVE INSTRUMENTAL MUSIC   234

    PART 1   KAZAKH *KÜI*   235
                 Saida Daukeyeva

    PART 2   KYRGYZ *KÜÜ*   265
                 Nurlanbek Nyshanov

CHAPTER 15   KYRGYZ JAW HARPS   282
                 Nurlanbek Nyshanov

CHAPTER 16   THE KAZAKH *QOBYZ*: BETWEEN TRADITION AND MODERNITY   287
Saida Daukeyeva

CHAPTER 17   *DOMBYRA* PERFORMANCE, MIGRATION, AND MEMORY
AMONG MONGOLIAN KAZAKHS   302
Saida Daukeyeva

PART III. THE WORLD OF SEDENTARY DWELLERS

PROLOGUE   PATTERNS OF CULTURE: SEDENTARY DWELLERS   317
Theodore Levin

CHAPTER 18   *MAQOM* TRADITIONS OF THE TAJIKS AND UZBEKS   320
Will Sumits and Theodore Levin

CHAPTER 19   THE UYGHUR *MUQAM*   344
Rachel Harris

CHAPTER 20   NEW IMAGES OF AZERBAIJANI *MUGHAM* IN THE
TWENTIETH CENTURY   354
Aida Huseynova

CHAPTER 21   POPULAR CLASSICS: TRADITIONAL SINGER-SONGWRITERS
IN UZBEKISTAN AND TAJIKISTAN   367
Theodore Levin

CHAPTER 22   RELIGIOUS MUSIC AND CHANT IN THE CULTURE
OF SEDENTARY DWELLERS   379
Aleksandr Djumaev

CHAPTER 23   SUFISM AND THE CEREMONY OF *ZIKR* IN GHULJA   399
Mukaddas Mijit

CHAPTER 24   *DASTAN* PERFORMANCE AMONG THE UYGHURS   406
Rahile Dawut and Elise Anderson

CHAPTER 25   FEMALE MUSICIANS IN UZBEKISTAN: *OTIN-OY*, *DUTARCHI*,
AND *MAQOMCHI*   421
Razia Sultanova

CHAPTER 26   MUSIC IN THE CITY OF BUKHARA   435
Theodore Levin and Aleksandr Djumaev

CHAPTER 27   MUSIC AND CULTURE IN BADAKHSHAN   461
            Theodore Levin

CHAPTER 28   THE *MADDOH* TRADITION OF BADAKHSHAN   470
            Benjamin D. Koen

CHAPTER 29   *QASOID-KHONĪ* IN THE WAKHAN VALLEY OF BADAKHSHAN 485
            Chorshanbe Goibnazarov

CHAPTER 30   *FALAK:* SPIRITUAL SONGS OF THE MOUNTAIN TAJIKS   504
            Faroghat Azizi

PART IV. CENTRAL ASIAN MUSIC IN THE AGE OF GLOBALIZATION

CHAPTER 31   REVITALIZING MUSICAL TRADITIONS: THE AGA KHAN
            MUSIC INITIATIVE   521
            Theodore Levin

CHAPTER 32   CULTURAL RENEWAL IN KYRGYZSTAN: NEO-TRADITIONALISM
            AND THE NEW ERA IN KYRGYZ MUSIC   541
            Raziya Syrdybaeva

CHAPTER 33   POPULAR MUSIC IN UZBEKISTAN   555
            Kerstin Klenke

CHAPTER 34   INNOVATION IN TRADITION: SOME EXAMPLES FROM MUSIC
            AND THEATER IN UZBEKISTAN   577
            Aleksandr Djumaev

CHAPTER 35   TRADITION-BASED POPULAR MUSIC IN CONTEMPORARY TAJIKISTAN   586
            Federico Spinetti

            MUSICAL INSTRUMENT GLOSSARY   597

            GLOSSARY OF TERMS   609

            INVENTORY OF AUDIO AND VIDEO EXAMPLES   621

            EDITORS   633

            CONTRIBUTORS   637

            INDEX   645

Preface

The Music of Central Asia came to life as part of a larger project with an ambitious objective: to contribute to the revitalization and continuing evolution of musical culture and creativity in Central Asia while bringing the region's rich and diverse musical traditions to the attention of listeners around the world. This project, on-going since 2000, has been spearheaded by the Aga Khan Music Initiative, a non-governmental cultural development program that supports talented musicians and music educators working to preserve, transmit, and cultivate their musical heritage in contemporary forms.[1] *The Music of Central Asia* was envisaged both as a resource for Central Asians to learn about the musical heritage of their own region (translation into local languages is planned for the future) and as an introduction to the region's music and expressive culture for those who live beyond its borders. It can be used as a textbook—read systematically to build comprehensive knowledge about interlinked topics—or approached as a reference work for information on specific musical styles, repertoires, and traditions.

The first part, "Music and Culture in Central Asia," offers an overview of Central Asian music and musical instruments. The second and third parts, "The Nomadic World" and "The World of Sedentary Dwellers," survey musical life in the context of the two major axes of Central Asian civilization—axes that remain influential in our own time. Through a series of chapters devoted to particular musical genres, styles, repertoires, and individual musicians, these sections offer a composite portrait of Central Asia's musical heritage. The fourth section, "Central Asian Music in the Age of Globalization," focuses on what one might call "the future of the past"—how traditional forms of music-making are being adapted, appropriated, transformed, and revitalized by a variety of contemporary actors and stakeholders in the domain of arts and culture. In each section, the aim is to present music and musical heritage not simply as fixed repertoires and traditions inherited from the past, but rather as the continually evolving product of dynamic cultural processes driven by innovative creators, trends in taste and fashion, the exigencies of politics, and forces of social change emanating from near and far.

Deciding which repertoires and traditions to include in *The Music of Central Asia* presented a challenge. First of all, what exactly do we mean by "Central Asia"? The panoply of cultural, physical, and political markers that, in various combinations, have been used to define the region underscores the imprecision of its boundaries (definitions of Central Asia are discussed in the overview in chapter 1). Two areas that many if not most geographers would include as belonging to Central Asia are missing in this book: Afghanistan north of the Hindu Kush Mountains, and Khorasan, which encompasses northeastern Iran and historically covered a much larger territory that includes parts of present-day Afghanistan, Turkmenistan, and Uzbekistan. The reason for the omission is a practical one: excellent and readily accessible materials for the study of music in Khorasan and northern Afghanistan already exist.[2] Meanwhile, if some kinds of Central Asian music are less well described than others, or not described at all, it is not because they are less worthy of attention. Rather the choice of musical topics largely reflects the availability of good documentary materials—audio, video, photos, transcriptions and translations of song texts—and of specialists willing to commit their time and energy to writing about them.

Unlike the typical textbook, which is written by a single author or a small team of authors, this book has twenty-seven contributors from fourteen countries. The rationale for casting such a wide authorial net was to ensure that *The Music of Central Asia* would represent diverse perspectives, and to draw on the expertise of individuals with in-depth knowledge of Central Asia's strikingly varied musical landscape. None of the contributors are "armchair" scholars whose knowledge comes exclusively from written sources, whether primary or secondary. Rather, they are music ethnographers, performers, educators, and cultural entrepreneurs—typically a combination of these—whose experience of music, whether as creators or consumers, has been direct and unmediated. The information and viewpoints expressed in the book represent the wealth of their collective knowledge and experience.

Central Asian musicians performing at the pre-Olympics "River of Music" concert, London, July 2012.
Photo by Louis Wenger.

The diverse perspectives of the contributors are apparent in the different ways they engage with music and musical life through writing. Some chapters frame their subject broadly within the context of social, political, and economic forces that have acted on music and musicians. Others focus more on music itself. Still others offer observations about the social organization of musical traditions or profile a specific musician. Many chapters do some of each. The challenge to the editors has been to preserve this diversity of perspective while ensuring that each chapter conforms to a few core stylistic criteria. Foremost among these is accessibility. All contributors have endeavored to illuminate their topic to readers who are presumed to have no background either in music or in the study of Central Asia. The book is designed to provide all the information that readers need to understand and work with the material. Specialized music terms are compiled and defined in a glossary at the end of the book. Song texts in Central Asian languages are transliterated in the Latin alphabet and translated into English. Most important, the book's 189 musical examples are represented through audio and video recordings. These recorded music examples comprise the very core of the book. Descriptions or listening guides are included with the examples, which in most cases are followed by study questions.

Descriptions, listening guides, and study questions focus on aspects of the music examples that a chapter's author considers noteworthy, or that provide useful points of comparison to other examples or to other kinds of music. The aim of these descriptions, guides, and questions, however, is not to tell you, the listener, what any particular musical example expresses, but rather to help you perceive musical form, style, expression, meaning, and affect through your own listening. Indeed, there is never just one way to listen, or one musical quality to listen for. Collectively, the music examples offer an astonishing array of musical sounds and music-making techniques. Experiencing them directly, as sonic material, may well lead you to hitherto unexplored domains of personal interpretation and imagination. At the same time, one goal of this book is to help listeners understand what it would mean to listen to a particular musical example with the ears of a cultural insider who approaches it with intimate familiarity. At stake in such listening is not whether you end up *liking* this or that piece of music, but whether you come to *understand* the ways in which it is meaningful and affective for its creators, and for a community of listeners close to its source. The key point: whatever your approach to the music examples, please listen to them! Information about accessing the examples, which are all available on a dedicated website, is provided below.

NOTES

1. For more information on the Music Initiative, see http://www.akdn.org/aktc_music.asp.
2. See "Further Reading, Listening, and Viewing" on the *Music of Central Asia* website.

Acknowledgments

Writing, editing, and producing *The Music of Central Asia* and its companion website has been a lengthy process that has drawn on the knowledge, skills, and talents of a great many individuals. First and foremost, the editors express heartfelt thanks to all the authors who accepted invitations to contribute to this book, and who worked conscientiously to meet deadlines, respond to requests for revisions, and supply photos, video clips, and audio recordings. We also express gratitude to the many musicians who made special audio or video recordings for use in the book, or allowed us to use pre-existing recordings, and we thank all the other rights holders of audio and video recordings and photographs who agreed to license them for use in this project. Credits for recordings and photos appear both in the text and in the list of music examples at the end of the book. The absence of a credit indicates that a recording or photo was provided by a chapter's author(s).

We are particularly indebted to the gifted designer of a pilot edition of *The Music of Central Asia,* the late Sonya Cohen Cramer, whose vivid layout and design contributed strongly to the book's overall coherence and clarity. We also extend our gratitude to Mary Blizzard, who intrepidly took over the design and layout of the present edition and to Pam Rude, who finalized the cover based on a design by Sonya Cramer. Filmmaker Saodat Ismailova took on the daunting task of assembling, editing, and subtitling the audio and video examples—many of which she filmed herself in her capacity as principal videographer for *Music of Central Asia,* a ten-volume CD-DVD anthology co-produced by the Aga Khan Music Initiative and Smithsonian Folkways Recordings, from which numerous music examples in the present work have been drawn. We are grateful to both organizations for allowing the extensive use of audio tracks and video excerpts from the anthology. We are also grateful to Sangwolk "Sunny" Nam, technical director of Dartmouth College's Bregman Digital Music Studio, for the expertise he generously contributed in mastering specific audio and video recordings that presented intimidating technical challenges.

For scrupulous reading and listening, followed by detailed comments on the earlier pilot edition of this work, we acknowledge the generous contribution of Richard Wolf, Professor of Music at Harvard University. We are equally grateful for the insightful comments of Mark Slobin, Professor of Music at Wesleyan University, who critically read and commented on the pilot edition on behalf of our publisher, Indiana University Press. We also thank Kazakh ethnomusicologist Aijan Berdibai for advice, and for valuable feedback on the pilot edition.

Iranian literary scholar Saghi Gazerani made the Persian-language poetry presented in several chapters come radiantly alive in English through her vigorous translations. For Russian-English translations of a number of articles written by authors from Central Asia, we thank Munira Chudoba and Aida Huseynova. We also thank contributors David Fossum and Kalmurza Kurbanov for generous editorial assistance with chapters other than their own.

Louis Wenger, now a graduate student in ethnomusicology at Brown University, provided crucial editorial and production assistance for both the pilot and final edition, and also contributed the historical timeline. The pilot edition, which served as a try-out for the present volume in several university courses in Central Asia, benefited from the administrative support of Nasreen Dhanani, former Director of Research at the University of Central Asia, and was fastidiously copyedited by Carla Borden. Cartographer Nathalie Héricourt provided the specially commissioned maps used throughout the book, and Kirill Kuzmin expertly photographed musical instruments from Tajikistan in the collection of Dushanbe's Gurminj Museum. Rebecca Guillaume, working on behalf of the Aga Khan Music Initiative, assured the smooth handling of honoraria for authors, musicians, and licensors of audio and video recordings.

At Indiana University Press, the enthusiasm and deft project coordination of sponsoring editor Raina Polivka and project manager Michelle Sybert, and the high professionalism of the Press's Editorial, Design, and Production Department, under the direction of Bernadette Zoss, provided gratifying reassurance as this complex project gradually came together over months and years. We are also grateful to freelance editor Lindsey Alexander for her exceptionally thorough and careful copyediting of the entire manuscript.

Finally, we thank Luis Monreal, general manager of the Aga Khan Trust for Culture, and Bohdan Krawchenko, director general of the University of Central Asia, who supported the project from its inception. Special thanks and gratitude go to Fairouz Nishanova, director of the Aga Khan Music Initiative, a program of the Trust for Culture, whose unflinching belief in the value of writing this book and spirited encouragement throughout the process of producing it both stimulated and soothed sometimes weary writers and editors. In all our work, the abiding institutional support of the Music Initiative and Trust for Culture, and of their visionary parent organization, the Aga Khan Development Network, founded and guided by His Highness the Aga Khan, played a crucial role in making this book the best that it could be.

ACCESSING MUSIC EXAMPLES ONLINE

The Music of Central Asia has a companion website that includes all music examples discussed in the book. The website address is: http://www.musicofcentralasia.org.

The website also includes a section titled "Further Reading, Listening, and Viewing," which offers an extensive guide to resources classified by topic.

In viewing and listening to the music examples, readers should keep in mind that the majority of these examples were recorded in the field—most of them by music ethnographers using audio and video equipment available to them at the time. The quality of this equipment varies, and older recordings in particular betray the technical limitations of some of the equipment that was used. Nonetheless, older recordings have been included where the material they present is historically important. Part of the goal of listening to such recordings is to be able to "extract" the music itself from the technical limitations of its mediated reproduction.

A Note on Music Terminology

Any thorough account of music in Central Asia must draw on a welter of specialized terminology in the region's local languages as well as in Persian, Arabic, Russian, and Chinese—all of which, in various times and places, have served as meta-languages of Central Asian music theory and history. Indeed, many musical terms in local languages are derived or borrowed from Persian and Arabic, though the same term—often with a slightly different pronunciation and spelling—may have a variety of particularized local meanings in different parts of Central Asia. An example is the term *maqom-muqam-mugham-maqām,* which refers to systems or suites of melodic modes as well as to these modes themselves and is discussed in different cultural contexts in quite a few chapters in the book. Variant pronunciations and spellings, however, need not always imply differences of reference or meaning. Particularly in the case of Turkic languages, cognate words that differ slightly in pronunciation or spelling may have an identical meaning, for example the words *aitys* (Kazakh) and *aitysh* (Kyrgyz), both of which refer to oral poetry competitions. Readers are encouraged to refer to the book's glossary to clarify whether distinctive spellings of cognate terms reflect merely a difference of local pronunciation (e.g., *aitys-aitysh*) or whether such orthographic differences reflect distinctions of meaning (e.g., *muqam-mugham*).

Guide to Transliteration

The many languages and dialects represented in transcriptions of personal names, music terms, performed texts, and bibliographic citations each have international conventions for transliteration into the Latin alphabet. The editors have chosen to follow these conventions up to a point, but have eliminated many diacritical marks used in standard scholarly transliteration systems and have consolidated others in an effort to make the English text as accessible as possible to nonspecialist readers. The pronunciation of most letters will be intuitive to English speakers, but the following pronunciation guide is provided for diacritical marks that appear in the book, as well as for a few letters and letter combinations with more than one possible English pronunciation:

Letter(s)	Sound	Example
ā	"a" as in "father"	*maqām* (Arabic: melodic mode) The long ā sound in Persian and Tajik is transliterated as "o" (*maqom*) with the exception of transliterations that have become conventional in English, e.g., *rubā'ī, Bukhara.*
ä	"e" as in "bend"	*tämbur* (Uyghur: long-necked lute)
ī	"ee" as in "deem"	Navo'i (Uzbek: name of Timurid poet)
ö	"u" as in "purse"	*tökpe* (Kazakh: style of *dombyra* playing)
o'	"u" as in "purse"	O'zbeknavo (Uzbek: name of state concert agency)
ü	"u" as in "tutor"	*kün* (Kyrgyz: day)
ū	"oo" as in "typhoon"	*rūz* (Tajik: day)
y	"i" as in "lit"	*baqsy* (Karakalpak: bard)
		For transliteration of Kyrgyz, "y" also represents the sound "yi"
ý	"y" as in "yacht"	*ýatmak* (Turkmen: to sleep)
ç	"ch" as in "check"	*çeşme* (Turkmen: spring)
gh (also g')	"ch" as in "loch,"	*ghijak* (Tajik/Uzbek: spike fiddle)
	but voiced to sound like "logh"	G'ayrat (name of Karakalpak performer)
j	"j" as in "joke"	*jon* (Tajik: soul)

kh	"ch" as in "loch"	*khalfa* (Uzbek: female wedding entertainer)
ň	"ng" as in "lung"	*seniň* (Turkmen: your)
q	"c" as in "cot"	*qairaq* (Uzbek: clackers)
ş	"sh" as in "shop"	*baş* (Turkmen: beginning)

TIMELINE OF CENTRAL ASIAN HISTORY

3500–3000 BCE
On the Central Asian steppe and grasslands, tribesmen tame, breed, and eventually ride horses.

2200–2000 BCE
Emergence of oasis and riverine urban centers that engage in trade and exchange with pastoralists.

— ZOROASTER (C. 1000 BCE)

— GAUTAMA BUDDHA (C. 6TH–5TH CENTURY BCE)

550–515 BCE
Persian Achaemenid armies under Cyrus the Great and Darius I invade Central Asia.

329 BCE
Alexander the Great's army invades Central Asia.

— ALEXANDER THE GREAT (356–323 BCE)

140 CE
Chinese military power extends to Central Asia under the Han dynasty.

500s
Göktürks establish Turkic khaganate that exercises control over Silk Road trade.

— MUHAMMAD (570–632)

657
Tang dynasty asserts power over Central Asia.

— XUANZANG (C. 602–664)

751
Arabs defeat Tang army at the Battle of Talas and introduce Islam to the region.

— AL-FARABI (C. 870–950)

900s
Samanids transform Bukhara into a center of Iranian culture.

— IBN SINA (AVICENNA) (980–1037)
— NASIR KHUSROW (C. 1004–1088)
— MAHMUD AL-KASHGARI (1005–1102?)
— OMAR KHAYYAM (1048–1131)
— AHMAD YASSAWI (1093–1166)

1210–1221
Mongol armies invade and conquer Central Asia.

— GENGHIS KHAN (1162–1227)
— JALAL AD-DIN RUMI (1207–1273)
— MARCO POLO (1254–1324)
— BAHAUDDIN NAQSHBAND (1317–1388)

1370–1405
Timur's military conquests establish Timurid Empire.

— HAFEZ (1325/26–1389/90)
— TIMUR (TAMERLANE) (1336–1405)
— ABD AL-QADIR AL-MARAGHI (1353–1435)

1400s
Decline of Silk Road overland trade due to new emphasis on trade by sea.

— ULUGH BEG (1394–1449)
— HUSAYN BAYQARA (1438–1506)
— ALI-SHIR NAVO'I (1441–1501)

1465
Kazakh khanate founded in Jetisu (Seven rivers) area south of Lake Balkhash.

— BABUR (1483–1530)

TIMELINE OF CENTRAL ASIAN HISTORY (CONTINUED)

1500–1507
Uzbeks under Muhammed Shaybani conquer Samarkand and Herat and found Khanate of Bukhara.

BOBORAHIM MASHRAB (1653–1711)
(Sufi poet)

MAGTYMGULY PYRAGY (1724–1807?)
(Turkmen poet and spiritual leader)

1644–1912
Qing dynasty reasserts China's control over eastern Central Asia.

QURMANGHAZY SAGHYRBAIULY (1818–1889)
(Kazakh *dombyra* player and composer)

SHOQAN VALIKHANOV (1835–1865)
(Kazakh ethnographer)

Early 1800s–1907
The "Great Game": British and Russian Empires vie for control of Central Asia.

ABAI (IBRAHIM) QUNANBAEV (1845–1904)
(Kazakh philosopher, poet, and songwriter)

1900s–1920s
Jadid enlightenment movement promotes educational reform and growth of publishing, print media, and literature in Central Asia.

VASILY BARTOLD (1869–1930)
(Historian of Central Asia)

SADRIDDIN AYNI (1878–1954)
(Tajik poet, writer, and intellectual)

1917–1922
Bolshevik Revolution in Russia and creation of Union of Soviet Socialist Republics.

ABDURAUF FITRAT (1886–1938)
(Uzbek Jadid and writer)

1924–1936
Soviet Socialist Republics of Kazakhstan, Kirghizia, Tajikistan, Turkmenia, and Uzbekistan established in Central Asia.

CHO'LPON (ABDULHAMID SULAYMON O'G'LI YUNUSOV) (1893–1938)
(Uzbek poet, playwright, novelist)

1930s
Soviet ideological, nationalities, cultural, and economic policies, including collectivization, are implemented throughout Central Asia.

TAMARA KHANUM (1906–1991)
(Uzbek dancer of Armenian origin)

1991
Breakup of the Soviet Union and founding of post-Soviet nations of Central Asia.

CHINGIZ AITMATOV (1928–2008)
(Kyrgyz writer)

1996
Creation of Shanghai Five intergovernmental organization by leaders of China, Kazakhstan, Kyrgyzstan, Russia, and Tajikistan; in 2001, with the addition of Uzbekistan, the name is changed to Shanghai Cooperation Organization.

ROZA OTUNBAYEVA (1950–)
(first female president of a Central Asian nation [Kyrgyzstan, 2010–2011])

THE MUSIC OF CENTRAL ASIA

PART I.
MUSIC AND CULTURE
IN CENTRAL ASIA

CHAPTER 1

Music in Central Asia
AN OVERVIEW

THEODORE LEVIN

GEOGRAPHICAL AND CULTURAL BOUNDARIES

Central Asia suggests by its very name a region with imprecise borders. What constitutes the "central" portion of the huge Asian landmass? And "central" viewed from whose perspective? Indeed, the notion of Central Asia as a coherent geo-cultural region is a European invention, and a relatively recent one at that. (It first appeared in the title of a book published in 1843 by the German explorer and scientist Alexander von Humboldt.[1]) Indigenous inhabitants had their own mosaic of names for the territories in which they lived, and the Russian, British, and Chinese imperial powers that jousted for control of the region in the nineteenth and twentieth centuries used still

Central Asia is a region defined by a mixture of geographical, political, and cultural boundaries.

other names: Turkestan, Tartary, Transoxania, Xinjiang. Today, no people goes by the ethnonym "Central Asian," and linguists have not posited a language group called the "Central Asian" languages. Rather, the peoples, languages, and territories of Central Asia represent identities whose domains are both larger and smaller than the region itself, however it is defined. One fascinating aspect of Central Asia is the multitude of overlapping ways in which its inhabitants have identified themselves and the way these identities have been perpetually in flux as a response to historical events and social change.

Central Asia as commonly understood at the beginning of the twenty-first century is a region defined by a mixture of geographical, political, and cultural boundaries. Most definitions of the region would place its western extreme at the shore of the Caspian Sea, a geographical demarcation. In the southwest, however, the conventional boundary is a political one: the border between Iran and Turkmenistan. By contrast, in the east, the distinct political border represented by the

As a coherent cultural zone, Greater Central Asia arguably spans all or part of 11 countries, from Azerbaijan in the west to China in the east.

Chinese frontier is often disregarded in favor of an imagined cultural boundary farther to the east that crosses into China's Xinjiang Uyghur Autonomous Region, the traditional territory of the Uyghurs, a Muslim, Turkic-speaking people.

The northern and southern flanks of Central Asia are the most problematic. In the south, cultural coherence would argue for the inclusion of Afghanistan north of the Hindu Kush Mountains. However, the geographical boundary formed by the Amu Darya, the river that also serves as a political frontier between Afghanistan and its northern neighbors Uzbekistan and Tajikistan, is frequently given priority, thus excluding Afghanistan altogether. In the north, the political border between Kazakhstan and Russia is a commonly used demarcation, but from a demographic point of view, the north of Kazakhstan, with its considerable Russian population, many of whom are first- or second-generation citizens of Kazakhstan, seems much like an extension of the Siberian frontier. Conversely, the Altai region of southern Siberia, which lies northeast of Kazakhstan and whose indigenous population speaks Turkic languages such as Tuvan, Khakas, and Altai, has strong ethnolinguistic links to Central Asia. Finally, Tatarstan, the autonomous republic within Russia situated north of the Caspian Sea that is the traditional territory of the Turkic-speaking Tatars, has never been included in geographic or political definitions of Central Asia, but on the basis of ethnolinguistic and cultural ties, perhaps it should be.

Even if Central Asia's conventional boundaries vary in type, and though there is not consensus about their location, the region itself displays four kinds of broad coherence and commonality that represent defining features of society and culture. First, over many centuries, Central Asia has developed along two great axes of civilization that, while preserving their own trajectories, have maintained a close and symbiotic relationship. One of these axes represents the culture of nomads, and the other, the culture of settled peoples, or sedentary dwellers, who live in cities, towns, and rural villages or settlements. The interaction between nomads and sedentary dwellers has been shaped over time by a complex of geographic, environmental, economic, cultural, and political factors, which in turn have influenced the development of music and musical life in Central Asia.

A second kind of coherence is that an overwhelming majority of the population identifies Islam as its active religious practice, cultural legacy, worldview that informs everyday social life, or all of these. Most Central Asian Muslims trace their lineage to the Sunni branch of Islam, while Shiʿa Muslims comprise a small minority represented principally by Ismailis, a Shiʿa sect and community that established settlements in the mountainous Badakhshan region of Tajikistan and Afghanistan beginning in the eleventh century. Islamic tradition in Central Asia has incorporated a range of local practices and beliefs—many of them concerned with the veneration of spirits—that have interacted over centuries with more classical or normative interpretations of Islam. The pervasive presence of such practices and beliefs, shared by both nomads and sedentary dwellers, reinforces the specific regional character and cultural framework of Central Asian Islam.

A third kind of coherence concerns language. Just as the near ubiquity of Arabic bolsters social cohesion throughout the Middle East and North Africa, Turkic languages serve as a unifying force in Central Asia. Unlike Arabic, however, which despite its many spoken dialects and local forms is identified at least nominally as a single language, the Turkic dialect continuum in Central Asia has been fractured into a spectrum of closely related languages. Some 90 percent of the region's autochthonous population identify themselves with a Turkic ethnicity and speak a Turkic language as their native tongue. Most of the remaining 10 percent identify themselves with an Iranian ethnicity and speak an Iranian language, although many can communicate in a Turkic language as well. Excluded from these figures are Russian-speaking Slavs who began to populate Central Asia after the czarist conquests in the latter half of the nineteenth century and who, during the Soviet era, constituted 50 percent or more of the population of the region's major cities. Since the breakup of the Soviet Union in 1991, many Slavs have left Central Asia and resettled in Russia and Ukraine.

Finally, a fourth kind of coherence stems from political history. The Russian conquest of Central Asia not only brought Russian-speaking colonizers to the region, but under the administration of the czars, and particularly under the centralized rule of the Soviet Union, Russian and European cultural models were imposed on indigenous societies with the aim of modernizing what the colonizers viewed as "backward" Asian peoples.

PATTERNS OF SETTLEMENT: THE STEPPE AND THE CITY

Historians have called Central Asia a "double periphery." This term expresses the idea that historically Central Asia formed the northeastern periphery of Persian civilization, whose highest cultural aspirations arose from an urban sensibility at the same time that it formed the southwestern periphery of the steppe empires built by Turkic and Mongolian nomads, whose expressive culture reflects the physical, material, and spiritual world of pastoralists. While pastoralism was sharply curtailed during the Soviet era, the cultural memory of nomadic life remains strong among historically nomadic peoples.

The Kyrgyz ensemble
Tengir-Too.
Photo by Katherine Vincent. Courtesy of
Aga Khan Music Initiative.

Steppe and city have produced distinctive forms of music making. Nomadic music reflects a direct sensory experience of the natural world that forms the nomadic habitat. Nomadic expressive culture includes not only various kinds of singing and instrumental music but a rich tradition of oral poetry. Best-known in this genre is the epic. For nomads—"mobile pastoralists" in the parlance of anthropology—mobility makes books and written documents impractical. In place of writing, nomads have historically privileged orality and memory as means of documenting, transmitting, and archiving history, genealogy, and cultural mores.

The ability of certain individuals to recite long epic tales with complex plots and subplots signals not only a talent but what nomadic tradition interprets as a gift bestowed by spirits. This tradition imbues the world with the power of spirits in myriad forms: ancestor spirits that underscore the enduring ties of kinship; spirit-masters and spirit-protectors that inhabit and animate natural phenomena such as rivers and mountains, caves and springs, birds and animals; and, most centrally, the sky deity, known in Turkic languages as Tengri, who is paramount in the pantheon of deities that populate the spirit world of the pastoralists. The cult of the sky deity has ancient roots in Turkic civilizations, which arose in Inner Asia as early as the first centuries CE. It is mentioned in inscriptions written on stone monuments in the Orkhon script, a writing system used by Turkic nomadic clans from the eighth to tenth centuries CE. In post-Soviet Central Asia and Siberia, the cult of Tengri has been revitalized in the form of a spiritual practice known as Tengrism or Tengrianism (Turkic: *Tengrichilik, Tängirshilik*).

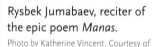

Rysbek Jumabaev, reciter of the epic poem *Manas*.
Photo by Katherine Vincent. Courtesy of Aga Khan Music Initiative.

Humans endowed with a special ability to contact the spirit world can summon and exploit the powers of both benevolent and malevolent spirits for practical ends. Such specially endowed individuals exist in many cultures and are known by a variety of local names, but the word "shaman," borrowed from an indigenous Siberian language, has become widespread as a cross-cultural term to describe them. Among Central Asian and Siberian pastoralists, shamans have been important carriers of many kinds of traditional knowledge, including how to use sound and music for healing purposes.

In contrast to the ancestor spirits and nature spirits that compose the spiritual world of nomads, the spiritual culture of sedentary dwellers has been fundamentally shaped by Islam and Islamic tradition. At once pervasive, variable, and culturally specific, Islamic influences are best understood in the context of particular times, places, ruling dynasties, and social practices. The intersection

Far left: Shamans in Tuva hold a *dunggur,* the shamanic drum, 1998.

Left: A Khakas shaman prepares for a purification ritual, 2000.

Central Asian Cities Old and New

Central Asia claims some of the world's oldest inhabited cities. Bukhara, Samarkand, Kashgar, Herat, Andijan, Khujand, Shahrisabz—all were at one time cosmopolitan crossroads of commerce and culture nourished by the trans-Eurasian trade routes collectively known as the Silk Road. Their populations were multi-ethnic, multi-lingual, and represented a variety of religious faiths. They were the birthplace of kings, conquerors, poets, philosophers, scholars, and musicians. Over the centuries, their fortunes have waxed and waned, with periods of efflorescence followed by decline or destruction, and eventually by rebirth and revitalization.

These days, the largest cities in Central Asia are not the oldest. Beginning in the 19th century and continuing through the 20th, newly founded or greatly expanded cities such as Tashkent, Dushanbe, Ashgabat, Bishkek, Almaty, and Urumchi became the principal centers of commerce, culture, and administration. The most recent major city to rise in Central Asia is Astana, the capital of Kazakhstan, which, beginning in the mid-1990s, grew from the small, northern provincial center of Akmola into a thriving metropolis of more than 700,000.

Below left: Mir-i-Arab Madrasah and surrounding city fabric of Bukhara. Photo by Reha Günay. Courtesy of Aga Khan Award for Architecture/Archnet.

Below: New apartment buildings rise in Astana, Kazakhstan.

of Central Asia's two civilizational axes—one sedentary, Islamic, and Persianate; the other nomadic, animist, and Turkic-Mongolian—has contributed to the rich diversity of Central Asian expressive culture. After millennia of intermingling, Turkic, Mongolian, and Iranian cultural traditions have become so tightly inter-woven that in many cases it is all but impossible—and perhaps pointless—to try to distinguish their ethnic or geographical origin. Yet despite myriad forms of cultural hybridization that have tended to merge the two currents of influence, broad distinctions remain between the cultural world of sedentary dwellers and that of nomads or historically nomadic groups. These distinctions in worldview are expressed through music in many different ways: choice of musical instruments; types of musical performers; typical musical genres and repertoires; characteristic vocal styles; style and genre of poetic texts; methods of setting texts to music; and use of musical scales and rhythms, among others.

ISLAM IN CENTRAL ASIAN CULTURE

Within a decade of the death of Muhammad, the prophet of Islam, in 632 CE, Arab armies loyal to the caliphs who succeeded Muhammad as leader of the *umma,* or

Islamic community, pushed out of the Arabian Peninsula and began a series of assaults on neighboring lands to the west (North Africa), north (Syria, Palestine, Iraq), and northeast (Persia). Over the next century, the scope of these military campaigns expanded significantly, bringing Arab armies eastward into Central Asia as far as the borderlands of China, then ruled by the Tang dynasty. In 751, Arab and Tang armies fought a decisive battle in the valley of the Talas River, near the boundary of present-day Kazakhstan and Kyrgyzstan, in which the Tang forces were defeated. The Battle of Talas marked the end of the Tang dynasty's westward expansion into Central Asia, while also marking the effective end of Islam's expansion toward the northeast periphery of Central Asia.

When Arab armies defeated the Tang forces at the Battle of Talas, they did not impose Islamic beliefs and practices on the nomadic Turkic clans whose territories they had invaded. Rather, the deeply rooted spiritual culture of the pastoralists remained a powerful force. Meanwhile, in the oasis cities and settlements that stretched along the trans-Eurasian trade routes known as the Silk Road, many people continued to practice Zoroastrianism, the state religion of Persia's Sassanian Empire (224–651 CE), which at its peak included much of Central Asia. Others practiced Manichaeism, another Iranian religion that flourished along the Silk Road; Nestorian Christianity; and Buddhism, which was carried to Central Asia and China from its birthplace in India. These religious practices were not exclusive to sedentary dwellers, but permeated the porous boundaries of spiritual culture to find adherents among nomads as well.

The Islamization of Central Asia took place gradually, over many centuries, and proceeded with varying degrees of acceptance and resistance among different social groups and in different geographic regions. Broadly speaking, Islam was established more quickly and more deeply among sedentary dwellers than among nomadic pastoralists. Moreover, among nomads, and to a lesser extent among sedentary dwellers, Islamic practices and beliefs merged with pre-Islamic practices and beliefs. Such merged practices have remained strongly reflected in the social contexts and uses of music and other forms of expressive culture in Central Asia.

Islamization came about in two different ways, one principally political and administrative,

A mosque in Karakol, Kyrgyzstan, shows Chinese architectural influences and was built to serve a local population of Dungan, or Hui Muslims who immigrated from China.

The Silk Road in Central Asia

The term "Silk Road" was coined in the late 19th century by the German explorer and scientist Ferdinand von Richthofen to refer to the network of trade routes that crisscrossed Eurasia from around 200 BCE to around 1500 CE, linking East Asia, South Asia, and Central Asia with Persia, the Middle East, and Europe. Von Richthofen actually used the term "Silk Roads" (*Seidenstrassen*, in German), an acknowledgment of the multiple land and sea routes over which east-west trade flowed.

The caravans that carried silk and other luxury goods along the trans-Eurasian trade routes facilitated not only commerce but cultural exchange. Religious beliefs, technological innovations, scientific ideas, and artistic practices flowed into Central Asia from both east and west. At the same time, Central Asia's own achievements in the arts and sciences were disseminated broadly throughout Eurasia.

and the other principally cultural and spiritual. In the first case, the process was top-down, through the conversion of ruling elites, and in response to the imposition of administrative edicts and taxation policies that made conversion to Islam advantageous on a civic level. In the second case, Islamization proceeded through the arena of popular culture, where a range of performers used music, poetry, storytelling, and theater as a means of disseminating Islamic values, mores, customs, and beliefs. Popular Islam engaged a broad cross-section of Central Asian urban society through the appeal of performers who were at once entertainers and preachers. These performers included figures such as wandering dervishes who gathered street crowds to perform didactic spiritual songs for alms, and itinerant bards who

The mausoleum of Sultan Uways, in Karakalpakstan, serves as a site of *ziyārat*— spiritual pilgrimage to the tomb of a saint.

recited moralistic stories and chanted excerpts from the Qur'an and hadiths—accounts of the teachings, sayings, and deeds of Muhammad, the prophet of Islam (see chapter 22).

Another potent force in the Islamization of sedentary dwellers was Sufism. Sufism—also known by its Arabic name *tasawwuf*, "mysticism"—is broadly understood as the mystical or esoteric dimension of Islam. Sufi practices and beliefs were historically transmitted through brotherhoods of initiates founded or inspired by a renowned spiritual teacher, and a number of influential Sufi brotherhoods arose in Central Asia. These include, most notably, the Yassawiyya, founded in the twelfth century by Khoja Ahmad Yassawi, and the Naqshbandiyya, created in the fourteenth century by Bahauddin Naqshband, who lived in Bukhara.

Sufi practices such as rhythmic chanting, whirling, and other ritualized body movements that can lead practitioners to a state of spiritual ecstasy may have been adapted from older practices rooted in shamanism. Though this proposed link is speculative, it is persistent, and underscores the symbiotic relationship between nomads and sedentary dwellers. At the same time that shamanism may have shaped certain Sufi practices, elements of popular Sufism found their way into the culture of nomads in the form of spiritual, homiletic, and didactic songs.

Islam and Music

Islam has generated a range of views about the legal and moral status of music while firmly distinguishing sacred chant, considered "non-music," from all other kinds of sound-making. Most central to the category of "non-music" is the intoned chanting of the Qur'an (Arabic: *tajwīd*) and of the Call to Prayer (*adhān*) by specially trained reciters.[2] While a beautiful voice chanting the Qur'an or the Call to Prayer indeed sounds "musical" according to most definitions of music, to call such chanting "music" (*mūsīqī*) within the context of Islamic practice would be considered by some a form of blasphemy owing to the cultural associations of this Greek-derived term with secular music making.

If the chanting of the Qur'an and the Call to Prayer is not "music," then what is it from a sonic perspective? Islamic tradition has not yielded a term that subsumes the various kinds of sacred "non-music" into a single category.[3] Seeking such a term, which, as a precondition, must not include the word "music," American ethnomusicologist Lois al-Faruqi proposed *handasat al-ṣawt,* a neologism whose literal meaning in Arabic is "sound engineering." Decades after its introduction, however, the use of this term remains limited.

While the "non-musical" chanting of the Qur'an and the Call to Prayer is unequivocally accepted within diverse forms of Islamic practice as a legitimate form of religious piety, other forms and genres of sound-making—"music" by any other name—occupy a more equivocal status within Islamic tradition. The possibility for diverse interpretations of Islamic tradition regarding the status of music rests on the absence in the Qur'an of either explicit proscription or explicit endorsement of any particular practice of sound-making. As a consequence, the legal and moral status of music has been discussed within the framework of Islamic jurisprudence (*fiqh*) based on interpretations of divine law (shari'a) as revealed in the Qur'an, and sunna—the customary practice of Islam, exemplified by the life of the Prophet Muhammad and recorded in hadiths. Islamic jurisprudence divides human actions into those that are obligatory (*wājib*), desirable (*mustaḥabb*), permissible (*ḥalāl* or *mubāḥ*), undesirable (*makrūh*), and forbidden (*ḥarām*). A long succession of Muslim jurists, rulers, and philosophers has placed various styles, genres, and repertoires of music at different points along this moral continuum. Broadly speaking, music associated with piety and devotion that may help performers and listeners achieve a state of openness to the presence of the Divine has been regarded more favorably than music that is overtly sensuous, or associated with revelry or debauchery. Sufism, in particular, has drawn on the power of ritualized singing, collective chanting, and instrumental music to lead practitioners toward a state of mystical union with a Divine presence. Such musical practices, however, are dismissed as haram by certain orthodox interpretations of Islamic tradition and jurisprudence. In the most extreme cases—for example, under the rule of the Taliban in Afghanistan—listening to and performing music has been strictly forbidden. The era of Taliban rule, however, was a recent aberration in the history of a religious tradition that has produced a rich and diverse musical legacy. In other parts of Central Asia, both historically nomadic and historically sedentary, the cultivation and performance of music that lies within the cultural norms of social life and custom has generally found favor among rulers, philosophers, and Islamic jurists.

SOCIAL CONTEXTS OF MUSICAL PERFORMANCE

Bukharan dancer Muhiniso Mujitova.
Photo by Pidz.

While twenty-first-century music lovers can use portable electronic devices to ensconce themselves in a personal sound world of their own choosing wherever and whenever they please, music worldwide has historically been a social phenomenon performed and consumed in the context of particular social institutions and social spaces. These institutions and spaces, which today may be digital as well as physical, are created and shaped by a variety of forces: local custom and social practice, religious tradition, commercial or mercantile interests, the vision of a patron, ideologies or political agendas introduced by state and non-state actors, and others. Such forces do not work in isolation; on the contrary, they frequently merge and overlap in the way they shape social contexts for music making and listening.

In Central Asia, the most ubiquitous social context for musical performance among both historically nomadic peoples and sedentary dwellers has traditionally been festive gatherings, generically called *toy*, to mark life-cycle events—first and foremost marriage, but also the birth of a child, a boy's circumcision, or a birthday. Lesser occasions—a child's first day at school, a boy's first haircut, or, in former times, the first veiling of a girl—are observed in smaller family gatherings. Other occasions for festivity include harvest celebrations, like the Uyghur *mäshräp*, traditional secular holidays—most notably Nowruz, the Persian New Year that coincides with the spring equinox; and Muslim holidays such as 'Īd al-Fiṭr, or Ait, which marks the end of Ramadan, the Islamic month of fasting. Among nomadic peoples, festivity and celebration are also associated with various kinds of contests and competitions: horse racing, wrestling, and games; poetry contests in which contestants compete in verbal agility and creativity; and musical competitions that pit virtuoso performers against one another.

At the opposite extreme from popular festivity and celebration, performances for elite audiences have flourished under the patronage of noble rulers and leaders, aristocrats, and wealthy individuals. A rich tradition of miniature painting and illuminated manuscripts documents the historical role of musicians as entertainers in the courts, palaces, and gardens of the nobility in many parts of the Muslim world, including Central Asia, where certain noble rulers of the city-states of Bukhara and Khiva patronized performers of local repertoires of classical music (see chapter 18). Singers, instrumentalists, and dancers entertained the family and

Stiltwalkers entertain at a celebration near Urgench, Uzbekistan, 1994.

guests of the Bukharan emirs and Khivan khans, and also performed outside of the noble courts for intimate gatherings of musical connoisseurs. This tradition of individual patronage continues today, with businessmen, oligarchs, and political leaders taking the place of the erstwhile feudal nobility.

During the Soviet era, arts patronage was monopolized by the state, which created its own constellation of cultural institutions and spaces for musical performance: conservatories and music schools, community arts centers and concert halls, radio and television stations, and festivals and national holidays. All of these institutions effectively served the aims of Soviet cultural and nationalities policies, as explained later in this chapter. After the breakup of the Soviet Union, many existing cultural institutions continued to receive state support from the newly independent nations of Central Asia. At the same time, new contexts and institutions appeared, supported by a variety of non-state actors: international non-governmental organizations (NGOs); intergovernmental organizations—in particular, UNESCO (United Nations Educational, Scientific, and Cultural Organization); embassies and development agencies of foreign governments; newly founded universities funded by foreign governments and organizations; and individual philanthropists, both local and international. In the twenty-first century, social contexts for musical performance are diverse, and to a certain extent, serve as proxies for the organizational missions of their sponsors (see chapter 31).

MUSIC AND GENDER

Throughout Central Asia, local interpretations of Islamic tradition and social institutions have shaped gender roles in music making and musical performance. Among sedentary dwellers, a key influence in the gendering of musical life is the tradition of dividing festive and celebratory events into separate spaces for men and women. This separation may be represented by different physical locations for male and female celebration, by the use of different parts of a house or family compound, or by distinctive types of events for men and women, like the Euro-American bridal shower (female only) and bachelor party (men only). Gendered festivity and celebration represents an extension of the traditionally separate male and female social worlds that have been a defining feature of social life among sedentary dwellers in Central Asia. By contrast, festivity and celebration among nomads and historically nomadic groups reflects the daily intermingling of men and women that is both unavoidable and essential in the physically

The men's part of a wedding celebration, northern Tajikistan, 1992.

rigorous conditions of pastoralism. And while the quintessential nomadic performance art—oral poetry—has been historically the province of male bards, these days some of the most accomplished bards are women.

The appropriation of male-dominated musical traditions by female musicians was spurred by the social policies of the Soviet era, which, throughout the vast territory of the USSR, strove to integrate women not only into the workforce but into areas of the performing arts from which they had been excluded by local tradition. The effects of Soviet gender politics reverberated strongly in Central Asia (see chapter 25). Yet even before the establishment of Soviet power, maverick women challenged gender taboos in musical performance. Kazakh folklore has preserved the details of a famous singing contest (*aitys*) that took place around 1870 between Birjan-sal, a renowned male bard, and a talented young female bard named Sara Tastanbekqyzy. Birjan-sal won the contest, but in taking on the famous singer and composer, Sara gained her own honored place in Kazakh music history. Her courageous example encouraged younger generations of Kazakh women to perform musical genres once reserved for men (see chapter 5).

Among sedentary dwellers, female performers have traditionally entertained at women's festivities, and male performers have traditionally entertained at men's festivities. In recent years, European-style celebrations that include both men and women have become increasingly common, yet they often supplement rather than supplant the older style of gendered celebrations.

Musical instruments may also have strong gender associations. While some instruments, for example, the *dutar* (two-stringed lute), jaw harp, and *doira* (frame drum) are commonly played by women as well as men, other instruments are rarely played by women—notably the *tanbur,* a long-necked lute traditionally used to accompany singers of classical *maqom* music; and the *surnai* (oboe) and *karnai* (trumpet), which are both loud instruments that create a joyous sound for open-air festivity and celebration. (For illustrations of instruments, see "Musical Instrument Glossary.")

Islamic tradition has not only shaped gender roles in musical performance but dictated the social background from which particular kinds of performers are typically drawn. Examples are the traditional female wedding entertainers known as *sozanda* in Bukhara and Samarkand, and *khalfa* (from Arabic *khalīfa:* "caliph") in the Khorezm region of northwest Uzbekistan. Both types of performers have traditionally come from marginalized social groups: until recently, *sozanda*s were overwhelmingly Bukharan Jews, and *khalfa*s were typically blind, crippled, or from families of an undistinguished lineage (see chapter 26).

The social marginalization of entertainers reflects the moral ambiguity that Islamic cultural tradition has ascribed to their profession. While marriage itself

Bukharan entertainer Tohfakhon with her troupe of *sozandas*, 1957.
Courtesy of Tohfakhon Pinkhasova.

is imbued with the sense of sacred duty, the revelry associated with weddings has been morally suspect. Wedding entertainers, as purveyors of dance music, even among men and women separately, have drawn fundamentalist pronouncements against celebration. Under certain strict Muslim rulers, particularly in Bukhara, known popularly as "the dome of Islam," public celebration was prohibited.

Music and dancing have also been a feature of men's celebration. Performers alive at the end of the twentieth century recounted seeing boy dancers called *bacha*s who wore women's dresses and painted their lips and eyebrows. Under Soviet rule, *bacha*s were illegal, but while their number diminished, their tradition did not end. Other wedding entertainment was provided by a male singer-dancer called *mavrigikhon* (*mavrigi*: "from Merv"). Like socially marginalized female entertainers, the typical *mavrigikhon* has belonged to a marginalized social group, in this case, the minority Shi'a population of Bukhara, known as Bukharan Irani or Farsi, who trace their ancestry to slaves captured in Iran by Turkmen and brought via Merv to Bukhara.

A *bacha* dancer in Samarkand, between 1905–1915.
Courtesy of Library of Congress, Prints and Photographs Division, Prokudin-Gorskii Collection, reproduction no. LC-DIG-prok-02309.

MUSIC AND ISLAMIC ART

Islamic influences on music in Central Asia are not limited to social traditions and contexts that shape musical performance, but shape aspects of music itself. These aspects include the form of vocal and instrumental pieces, melodic and rhythmic structures, acoustic and affective qualities of musical sound, and thematic content and style of poetic texts set to music. Song texts, for example, are often drawn from Sufi-inspired poetry whose lyrical descriptions of earthly pleasure and beauty serve as an allegory for spiritual ascent toward the perfection of the Divine. In some musical genres, the way a melody unfolds also exemplifies an Islamic aesthetic sensibility. This sensibility is most evident in the musical culture of sedentary dwellers, in particular in repertoires of sophisticated urban art song, often described as "classical music" or "court music," which evolved under the patronage of local Muslim rulers. These repertoires have assumed a variety of local forms and names, but are generically known as *maqom* (from Arabic *maqām*: "place," "position," "station"). *Maqom* in Central Asia forms one branch of a transnational *maqom* (or *maqām*) tradition that has evolved over at least a millennium in a variety of local and regional "dialects" in the Eastern Mediterranean, Iraq, Iran, Azerbaijan, North Africa, and Central Asia. Geographically diverse but musically kindred, these traditions share broadly cognate features of musical form, melodic and rhythmic structure, aesthetics, affect, and terminology.

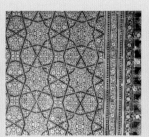

All photos courtesy of Aga Khan Music Initiative.

Above photo by Katherine Vincent.

Ornament in Islamic Art

From the tiled facades of mosques, minarets, and madrasahs to textiles, ceramics, woodcarving, furniture-making, and other applied arts, ornament and decoration are ubiquitous in art from the Islamic world. Intricate patterns are created from the repetition and combination of motifs that represent plants and animals, often mixed with elemental geometric forms. The abstract ornamental designs produced by the manipulation of such forms and motifs provide a visual analogue to the mosaic-like melodic patterns of some kinds of music from Central Asia—in particular the classical *maqom* repertoire.

In Central Asian *maqom* repertoires, as well as in related local vocal genres, a broadly unifying principle is the gradual ascent of the melodic line through a series of discrete pitch areas to a melodic culmination, called *awj. Awj* means "apogee," and indeed, the term is borrowed from Islamic astronomy, providing a cosmic and, by extension, metaphysical connotation to the moment of highest melodic ascent and greatest emotional tension.

Shashmaqom master Abduvali Abdurashidov in the 17th-century Madrasah-i Nav in Hissar, Tajikistan.

Photo by Sebastian Schutyser. Courtesy of Aga Khan Music Initiative.

The *maqom* repertoires also illustrate the filigree embellishment and ornamentation of melody that might be considered a sonic parallel to the ornamental motifs that pervade Islamic visual culture. The language of ornament in Islamic art and architecture has a highly developed vocabulary of patterns, forms, and designs, and to a certain extent, their sonic analogues can be found in music. For example, in *maqom,* melodies typically have a modular, mosaic quality characterized by the systematic sequencing and repetition of conventional patterns and motifs. Certain instrumental pieces in the *maqom* repertoire called Shashmaqom, which was cultivated in the city of Bukhara, are formally structured according to a clearly audible algebra (A + BA + CBA + DCBA) that is loosely analogous to the symmetrical repetition and variation of pattern and motif in Bukharan carpets, and in the decorative ceramic tile surfaces of Bukhara's mosques and minarets.

Sonic ornament is also expressed in the way performers of *maqom* habitually decorate lyrical melodies. Here the appropriate analogue in Islamic visual arts might be calligraphy—the art of beautiful writing using Arabic characters. Just as the calligrapher transforms writing into an art object in its own right, vocalists and instrumentalists transform melody—at root, a rhythmically organized linear sequence of pitches—into musical art. Through sinuous embellishments that both ornament individual pitches and link one pitch to the next, musicians express the lyrical character of *maqom* and the Sufi-inspired poetry that typically provides the texts for *maqom* compositions.

Structural aspects of melody and rhythm in *maqom* are extensively described and analyzed in a tradition of music theory that extends back more than a millennium to the writings of medieval Muslim scholars who, following the model of

Below: Page from a mid-sixteenth-century copy of the *Risāla al-sharafiyya* of Safi al-Din al-Urmawi, written around 1267. The schematic illustrates different combinations of intervals within tetrachords and pentachords.

Courtesy of Adilnor Collection, Sweden.

The Medieval Science of Music

In Baghdad, the capital of the 'Abbasid Dynasty and the cultural center of the medieval Muslim world, Syriac and Arabic translations of Plato, Aristotle, and other ancient philosophers provided the foundation for a flowering of intellectual creativity, invention, and discovery in what has come to be known as the Golden Age of Islam. Many of the leading luminaries of Baghdad's intellectual establishment were of Central Asian origin and spoke Iranian and Turkic languages as well as Arabic, the lingua franca of Islamicate science and scholarship. The most renowned of these medieval polymaths was Abu Nasr Muhammad al-Farabi (c. 870–950), who was born in Farab—now the city of Otrar in southern Kazakhstan. Al-Farabi made important contributions to epistemology, logic, mathematics, physics, metaphysics, political theory, psychology, and music theory. Adopting Plato's model of the liberal arts, which classified music as a mathematical science

together with arithmetic, geometry, and astronomy in what was later called the quadrivium, al-Farabi approached music through a systematic numerical analysis of musical intervals, tetrachords, and scales, and explored their practical application to tuning and positioning frets on stringed instruments. He also analyzed rhythm, described a range of musical instruments current in the Middle East and Central Asia during his time, and, like the ancient Greeks, addressed music's aesthetic and ethical affect and its relation to the universal order of things. The scope and systematic rigor of al-Farabi's *Kitāb al-mūsīqī al-kabīr* (Great Book of Music) in turn inspired a succession of polymaths writing in Arabic and Persian, notably Muhammad al-Khwarizmi (active in the last quarter of the 10th century) and Ibn Sina, known in Europe as Avicenna (980–1037), who were originally from Khorasan and Transoxania. The works of these great philosophers and music theorists created a basis for the subsequent study of

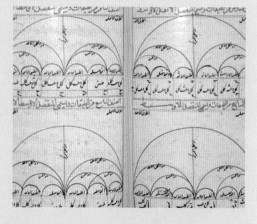

the *maqom* system developed by scholars called the Systematists. Major figures in the Systematist tradition included Safi al-Din al-Urmawi (c. 1216–1294), the author of the influential treatise *Kitāb al-adwār* (Book of Cycles), who came from Urmia in present-day Azerbaijan; and his followers, Qutb al-Din al-Shirazi (1236–1311) and Abd al-Qadir al-Maraghi (1353–1435). Aspects of *maqom* theory and practice were later discussed in the writings of distinguished musicians and scholars from the 16th and 17th centuries, such as the Bukharan-born Najm al-Din al-Kawkabi and Darvish Ali Changi.

ancient Greek philosophy, viewed music as a science. In Arabic, this tradition is known as *'ilm al-mūsīqī*: "the science of music." Erudite treatises on various aspects of the science of music placed music firmly within a broader intellectual domain that included mathematics, medicine, poetry, and philosophy.

CENTRAL ASIAN MUSIC IN THE SOVIET ERA

Russia's conquest of Central Asia began in the middle of the nineteenth century and was formally completed in 1920, when the last of the region's feudal rulers— the Emir of Bukhara and the Khan of Khiva—were deposed. Through the 1920s, the erstwhile colonial territory of Russian Turkestan and the feudal city-states of Bukhara and Khiva were politically and culturally transformed into Soviet Central

Pioneers of Central Asian Music Ethnography

Kazakh ethnographer Shoqan Valikhanov.
Photographer unknown.

Shoqan Valikhanov Monument, Almaty, Kazakhstan.

Central Asia has lured generations of notable explorers and adventurers: Xuanzang, Marco Polo, Ibn Battuta, Alexander von Humboldt, Nikolai Przhevalsky, Pyotr Semenov-Tyan-Shansky, Ármin Vámbéry, Aurel Stein, and scores of others. Unfortunately for students of music, however, the chronicles of these famous travelers have little to say about Central Asia's sound world. Only in the nineteenth century did academically trained ethnographers, linguists, and folklorists begin systematic documentation of the region's music and other forms of expressive culture. Their work was part of the Russian Empire's project to assemble geographic and scientific knowledge about its vast territory and diverse peoples. This work continued during the early Soviet era, spurred by a political agenda that sought to establish a "national" cultural heritage for the USSR's myriad ethnolinguistic groups as well as by the personal curiosity and initiative of researchers themselves.

Pioneers in the documentation and collection of traditional music and oral epic in Central Asia include Shoqan Valikhanov (1835–1865) and Vasily Radlov (1837–1918), who documented oral literature among the Kazakhs, Kyrgyz, and Siberian Turkic peoples (Valikhanov was the first to transcribe portions of the Kyrgyz epic *Manas*); Aleksandr Zatayevich (1869–1936), who notated collections of one thousand songs and five hundred songs and instrumental tunes of the Kazakhs; Viktor Uspenskii (1879–1949) and Viktor Beliaev (1888–1968), authors of the fastidiously transcribed and annotated *Turkmen Music*; Yelena Romanovskaya (1890–1947) and Nikolai Mironov (1870–1952), leading collectors and scholars of Uzbek and Tajik folk music; and Viktor Vinogradov (1899–1992), who researched and wrote about Kyrgyz and Azeri music. The publications of these ethnographic pioneers led the way for subsequent generations of folklorists and musical ethnographers, including the contributors to this book.

Far left: Emir Said Mir Mohammad Alim Khan, the Emir of Bukhara, ca. 1910.
Courtesy of Library of Congress, Prints and Photographs Division, Prokudin-Gorskii Collection, reproduction no. LC-DIG-prok-21887.

Left: Isfendiyar, Khan of Khiva, 1910–1918.
Courtesy of Library of Congress, Prints and Photographs Division, Prokudin-Gorskii Collection, reproduction no. LC-DIG-prok-20106.

Asia. From the earliest years of Soviet rule, ideologically motivated cultural policies irrevocably changed local music and musical life. Soviet culture policy strove to break up ethnolinguistic and cultural continuities with the goal of forging separate national identities centered around five Soviet republics: Kazakhstan, Kirghizia (now Kyrgyzstan), Tajikistan, Turkmenia (now Turkmenistan), and Uzbekistan. Soviet cultural strategy in the region mirrored Soviet political strategy: *divisa et imperiam*—"divide and conquer." Rather than reinforcing ethnolinguistic and cultural continuities throughout Central Asia, Soviet policy worked to undermine them.

Fearing the potential threat to Soviet power of an Islamist, pan-Turkic political alliance, Soviet cultural strategists stressed distinctions between one Central Asian people and another. And where these distinctions were not marked enough, Soviet culture policy manipulated language, literature, music, and other aspects of expressive culture to make them more apparent. Soviet publications on Central Asian music, for example the authoritative work of Victor Beliaev translated into English as *Central Asian Music,* neatly correlated music culture with then-extant Soviet political entities.[4] Musical repertoires or genres that did not correspond with political boundaries were assigned, in any event, to a single republic. Soviet culture policy had a low tolerance for ambiguity.

As was the case throughout the Soviet Union, culture policy directed at Central Asia reflected Marxist-Leninist ideals concerning the role of art in socialist society: Art should realistically reflect the lives of the proletariat—the leading class of society—and it should do so in artistic languages accessible to the working class. Furthermore, works of art should depict and celebrate the bright future of workers in societies that had evolved from feudalism and capitalism to socialism and communism.

At an operational level, cultural strategists addressed the challenges of modernizing a region whose culture, like its politics, was officially viewed as backward and despotic. Following both the spirit and the letter of Joseph Stalin's exhortation that the Soviet Union's diverse cultures should develop along lines that were "national in form and socialist in content," composers and musicians throughout the Soviet Union set to the task of adapting local music to express socialist themes. A common approach was to set old folk song melodies to new lyrics that proclaimed the glories of collective farms and five-year economic plans. An example is the Uzbek song "Pakhtachilik yashnasin" (Let cotton-growing flourish), which was transcribed from rural singers by Uzbek folklorists in the 1950s and published in volume 7 (*Songs of Khorezm*) of the multivolume anthology *Uzbek Folk Music* (*Özbek khalq muzikasi*).[5]

Kolkhoz, sovkhoz a'zolari, dehqonlar	Members of collective farms, farmers,
Ghairat qiling pakhtachilik yashnasin.	Be energetic, let cotton-growing flourish.
Hasrat cheksin sizga qarshi bolganlar,	Let those who are opposed to us come to grief,
Ghairat qiling pakhtachilik yashnasin.	Be energetic, let cotton-growing flourish.
Birlashdingiz bu sevikli vatanda,	Joining together in this beloved homeland,
Kecha-kunduz yashang boghu chamanda.	Live day and night in the gardens and flowerbeds!
Hama örtoq bölib jondek bir tanda,	Become friends, everyone, like the soul of a single body,
Tolmai ishlang pakhtachilik yashnasin.	Toil without tiring, let cotton-growing flourish.
Rahbarimiz Kommunistlar partiyasi,	Our leader is the Communist Party,
Töghri yöl körsatur bizga barchasi	It shows us the true path,
Haddan oshsin Özbekiston pakhtasi,	Let there be an abundance of cotton in Uzbekistan,
Ishlang pukhta pakhtachilik yashnasin.	Work seriously, let cotton-growing flourish.

More disruptive to traditional music was the introduction of European cultural models for musical composition, performance, and pedagogy whose aim was to promote cultural enlightenment among indigenous Central Asian peoples. These models included musical notation, large ensembles such as orchestras and choirs, and a tuning system like that of the piano, which made it possible to play complex chords and harmonies. The Soviet Ministry of Culture created a network of specialized music primary schools and high schools, while conservatories and institutes of art research were opened in the capital cities of each Central Asian republic. The conservatories trained composers as well as performers, and composers were frequently commissioned to write symphonic or chamber music compositions that drew on local folk music as the basis of their melodies and rhythms.

The adoption of European cultural models wreaked havoc on traditional Central Asian forms of musical performance and pedagogy. The introduction of notation and its use in music schools undermined the authority of orality as a method of transmission rooted in the relationship of master and disciple (*ustod* and *shogird*). Moreover, where oral transmission nourished the creative process through which disciples learned eventually to extemporize their own performance versions of songs and melodies, musical notation served as an impediment to this process, resulting in the "freezing" of many songs and melodies in the form in which they were notated, published, and disseminated to music schools. Orchestras of reconstructed folk instruments masked the subtle ornamentation and austere melodic style of folk song.

An amateur choral group performs in a rural house of culture in Tuva, a small autonomous republic in the Altai region of south Siberia, 1987.
Photo by Karen Sherlock.

Old musical scales, legacies of Persian and Arabic cultural influences, were rejected for their ties to "feudalism" and Islam, and replaced by the standard pitches of European major and minor scales.

From the perspective of the post-Soviet era, Soviet interventions in Central Asian musical life may well seem like a form of benighted Orientalism, yet many artists and intellectuals—both Slavs and representatives of indigenous peoples—became deeply committed to the project of building a cultural bridge between East and West. Operating within ideological strictures that to a large extent prescribed the style, form, and content of their artistic production, at least some composers, visual artists, and writers in Central Asia created works of considerable artistic integrity that have retrospectively earned respectful critical assessment, both inside and outside Central Asia.[6]

Following the breakup of the Soviet Union, official cultural policies in Kazakhstan, Kyrgyzstan, Tajikistan, Turkmenistan and Uzbekistan supported the continuation of Soviet-inspired hybrids such as orchestras of folk instruments and so-called *estrada* ensembles, which use a combination of European and indigenous instruments to transform local songs and tunes into vaudeville-like popular music (see chapter 33). European models of musical composition and music theory continue to play a prominent role in music education, and European classical music remains highly visible in state-sponsored cultural life. Meanwhile, a rising generation of musicians from Central Asia has begun to explore diverse contemporary musical languages and compositional techniques with the aim of linking themselves to international artistic communities and networks, while simultaneously striving to retain a sense of place and tradition that is uniquely theirs.

CENTRAL ASIA IN THE AGE OF GLOBALIZATION

In the twenty-first century, cultural continuities and boundaries both within Central Asia and with respect to contiguous and historically related regions of Eurasia are being actively reimagined by diverse stakeholders: national governments,

Far left: Alim Qasimov teaching his daughter, Fargana.
Photo by Katherine Vincent. Courtesy of Aga Khan Music Initiative.

Left: Zainiddin Imanaliev mentors a student.
Photo by Sebastian Schutyser. Courtesy of Aga Khan Music Initiative.

From Master to Apprentice: Transmitting Tradition

In Central Asia, musicians, along with practitioners of other arts and skilled trades, have traditionally acquired knowledge not through formal schooling but through apprenticeship to a master. This master-apprentice system is known by its Persian name, *ustod-shogird*. (Local variants in the different Central Asian languages and dialects differ slightly, for example, *ustat-shakirt* in Kyrgyz and *ustaz-shäkirt* in Kazakh.) Apprentices frequently become part of their master's household, doing household chores in exchange for knowledge and know-how. During the Soviet era, traditional master-apprentice pedagogy declined as official educational credentials became increasingly important in artistic practices as well as trades. In the post-Soviet era, master-apprentice training programs in music are being selectively revived, thus providing an alternative or supplement to state-run conservatories and music schools.

non-governmental and intergovernmental organizations, regional and world powers, cultural operators and educational institutions, individual artists and musicians, and, of course, the residents of Central Asia themselves. These stakeholders each have their own version of Central Eurasian geography. For some, it is expressed through patterns of political and economic activity or the routing of oil and natural gas pipelines. For others, it is expressed by linguistic, cultural, or religious markers. And for still others, it is expressed through the cultivation of values, beliefs, and practices that create conceptual, symbolic, or metaphoric connections between culture and society in Central Asia and in other parts of the world. Different means of expression notwithstanding, what these geographies all have in common is that they are projections. That is, they do not simply map extant features of physical, social, and cultural landscapes. Rather they are products of geographical imagination—an attempt to map Central Asia not as it is, but as it might be in one or another version of a possible future.

Central Asia, like other regions of the world, has many claimants not only to the future but to the past. In a region where tradition has played such an important role in social life, it is not surprising that the "future of the past" is contested. Music plays a key role in imagining Central Asia's possible futures, as is spelled out through several case studies in part IV, "Central Asian Music in the Age of Globalization."

One version of the "future of the past" is exemplified by culture policies implemented by both individual nations and intergovernmental organizations that prioritize the preservation and revitalization of national cultural heritage. These policies are carried out through the construction and preservation of historical monuments; the publication of epic literature; the staging of cultural festivals and celebrations; the production of museum exhibitions, films, public sculpture, and architecture; and the canonization of national performance traditions in music, theater, and dance. Many such canonical performance traditions now enjoy the cachet of support from UNESCO through inscription as Masterpieces of the Oral and Intangible Heritage of Humanity in UNESCO's Convention for the Safeguarding of the Intangible Cultural Heritage, adopted in 2003. As an agency of the United Nations whose membership is open only to UN member nations, UNESCO receives nominations for inscription into the Convention from national UNESCO committees appointed by the governments of member nations. Nominations of intangible cultural heritage traditions from Central Asia have been controversial in cases where more than one nation lays claim to cultural rights in a particular tradition. For example, in 2009, the Kyrgyz epic *Manas* was nominated for inscription in the UNESCO Convention not by Kyrgyzstan but by China, leading to protests in Kyrgyzstan, where *Manas* is widely viewed as a sacred symbol of Kyrgyz nationhood. China justified its nomination on the basis of a small population of ethnic Kyrgyz that resides in China's Xinjiang Uyghur Autonomous Region. Similarly, Uzbekistan's nomination of Shashmaqom, the indigenous classical music of Bukhara, raised consternation in Tajikistan, which also claims cultural ownership of Shashmaqom.

Poster for a concert at the Théâtre de la Ville in Paris, organized in collaboration with the Aga Khan Music Initiative.

While the preservation of intangible cultural heritage glossed as "national" is a cornerstone of state culture policy in all the countries of Central Asia, other cultural currents are pushing the region toward greater integration into global musical flows, which is to say, toward cultural globalization. These global flows consist overwhelmingly of music conceived, produced, and marketed as a commercial commodity. The inflow of such music to Central Asia from Russia, Europe, North America, and South Asia is enormous. By contrast, the outflow of music from Central Asia to the rest of the world is modest, consisting of, on the one hand, a small number of pop musicians who have built careers beyond Central Asia, such as the Uzbek singers Yulduz Usmanova and Sevara Nazarkhan, and the Kazakh rock group Roksanaki, and, on the other hand, musicians performing various kinds of traditional and tradition-based music that has been promoted and disseminated by international foundations, embassies, cultural exchanges, and cultural development programs (see chapter 31). Such programs have successfully introduced music from Central Asia to audiences in other parts of the world, but it is surely too soon to measure their long-term impact on the trajectory of cultural life in Central Asia itself.

Emigration spurred by the breakup of the Soviet Union has also changed the face of musical life in Central Asia. Fearing the consequences of nativism and nationalism, many Russian and other European-identified residents, including a sizable number of musicians, left the region after 1991. And beginning in the late 1970s, Bukharan Jews, who lived in Bukhara, Samarkand, and other Central Asian cities for over a millennium and made important contributions to urban performance traditions, emigrated en masse to Israel and the United States. At the beginning of the twenty-first century, Bukharan Jewish communities in Tel Aviv and Queens, New York, boast an active and diverse musical life nourished by outstanding performers of classical *maqom*, lighter popular music, and Jewish liturgical and para-liturgical chant and song. The diasporic music making of Bukharan Jews is only one among many examples worldwide of artistic communities separated from their geographical source that replicate, revitalize, and recirculate their cultural heritage in new forms.

Students welcome Nowruz, the beginning of spring, at a school in Almaty, Kazakhstan. In 2009 Nowruz was inscribed on UNESCO's Representative List of the Intangible Cultural Heritage of Humanity on behalf of seven countries.

Central Asia's shifting political alignments and alliances, both among its own states and peoples, and with the great powers that surround it, have all resonated in music and musical life. Successive eras of conquest, devastation, détente, and renascence have produced a remarkable accretion of musical forms and influences. Some older traditions have disappeared, but more commonly, they have been reimagined in new forms. The intricacy and richness of Central Asia's musical landscape is not unlike a kind of living tapestry that seamlessly merges repetition and variation into an unending pattern, at once familiar and yet endlessly provocative.

NOTES

A proto-version of this chapter was published as "Central Asia: Overview" in *The Middle East*, vol. 6 of *The Garland Encyclopedia of World Music*, ed. Virginia Danielson, Scott Marcus, and Dwight Reynolds, 895–906 (Routledge, 2002).

1. Alexander von Humboldt. *Asie centrale: Recherches sur les chaînes des montagnes et la climatologie comparée* [Central Asia: Research on mountain ranges and comparative climatology] (Paris: Gide, 1843).

2. Throughout Central Asia, *adhān* is typically pronounced *azan*. The Call to Prayer is also commonly known as *bang-i namāz*—literally "call to prayer" in Persian.

3. In addition to the Qur'an and the Call to Prayer, sources of "non-music" typically include texts chanted during the hajj to Mecca (*taḥlīl*), and eulogies in praise of the life and deeds of the Prophet Muhammad (*madḥ, na'at*).

4. Viktor M. Beliaev, *Central Asian Music: Essays in the History of The Music of the Peoples of the U.S.S.R.,* ed. Mark Slobin, trans. Mark and Greta Slobin (Middletown, Connecticut: Wesleyan University Press, 1976). Abridged English translation from the first volume of *Ocherki po istorii muzyki narodov SSSR* (Moscow: Gosudarstvennoe muzykal'noe izdatel'stvo, 1962).

5. I. A. Akbarov, ed., *Özbek khalq muzikasi* [Uzbek folk music], collected and transcribed by M. Yusupov (Tashkent: Gosudarstvennoe izdatel'stvo khudozhestvennoi literatury Uzbekskoi SSR, 1960), 477–479.

6. Examples from music include works by Russian composers Nikolai Roslavets (1881–1944) and Alexander Mosolov (1900–1973), who both wrote a number of pieces based on Turkmen and Uzbek folk music; Alexei Kozlovsky (1905–1977), a Russian composer who developed a deep knowledge of Uzbek music that is reflected in many of his compositions; and Mutavaqqil Burkhanov (1916–2002), an Uzbek composer who worked in a variety of classical genres including chamber music, choral music, and opera.

The *ghijak* is a roundbodied spike fiddle with three or four metal strings used by Uzbeks, Tajiks, Turkmen, and Karakalpaks.
Photo by Katherine Vincent. Courtesy of Aga Khan Music Initiative.

CHAPTER 2 Musical Instruments in Central Asia

THEODORE LEVIN

Musical instruments can be studied from many different perspectives: art and craftsmanship, physics and psychoacoustics, history and iconography, classification and typology, social practice and political aesthetics. All of these perspectives offer productive ways to approach Central Asia's exceptionally diverse world of musical instruments. This section outlines some of the ways that musical instruments articulate with broader patterns of culture in the region: the symbiotic relationship between pastoralists and sedentary dwellers, the abiding historical influences of neighboring civilizations, and the deeply rooted traditions of spirituality that flow through Central Asian expressive culture. Musical instruments are also the focus of several other chapters in this book (chapters 8, 15, and 16). An illustrated musical instrument glossary at the end of the book includes photographs and physical descriptions of the most widely used instruments from Central Asia.

Legends about the origins of musical instruments abound in Central Asia. In historically nomadic cultures, such legends have a shamanic quality, often attributing the invention of instruments to a mythical figure who created the instrument from the parts of animals and endowed it with magical properties. One such figure is Kambar, also known as Kambar-ata (Kambar-father), whom Kyrgyz regard as the creator of the *komuz,* a three-stringed lute, and whom Turkmen (who know him as Baba Gambar—"grandfather Gambar") regard as the creator of the two-stringed lute, the *dutar.* Nurak Abdyrakhmanov (1946–2014), a Kyrgyz musician who was also an amateur historian, recounted the creation legend as follows:

> Kambar was a hunter, and once when he went to the forest, a monkey fell as he jumped from one tree to another. The monkey's stomach became impaled on a sharp twig and burst open, and his intestine got stretched out between a high tree branch and the ground. When it dried,

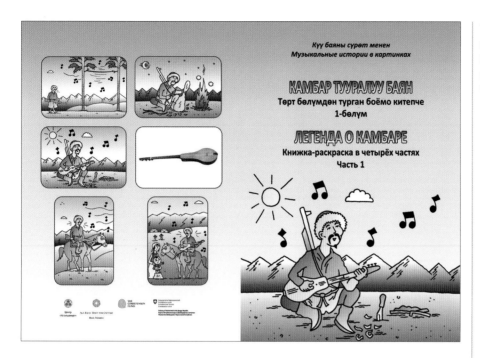

"The Legend of Kambar," a new picture book for Kyrgyz schoolchildren.

Cover art by Ruslan Valitov. Courtesy of Centre Ustatshakirt, Bishkek.

a wind came up, and the intestine emitted a magical sound. Kambar realized that the sound was coming from the monkey's intestine, and he got the idea of using that intestine to make an instrument. He took a piece of wood, curved it, and fixed the intestine tightly over it. That's how he invented the komuz.

Though there is no evidence that monkeys ever lived in what is now Kyrgyzstan, terracotta statues of monkey-musicians dating back almost two thousand years have been unearthed in various parts of Central Asia. A variant of the legend recounted by Nurak Abdyrakhmanov was also known in India, where it turns up in fourteenth century literary sources, underscoring historical links between Central Asia and the subcontinent. An analogous legendary musical instrument inventor is Qorqyt, or Qorqyt-ata, whom Kazakhs regard as the inventor of the two-stringed fiddle, the *qobyz*. (The story of Qorqyt's creation of the *qobyz* is told in chapter 16.)

In the culture of sedentary dwellers, legends about the origin of instruments often reflect the influence of Islamic thought, ascribing mystical rather than magical powers to the instrument. For example, in a legend about the origin of the Pamiri *rubab,* the *rubab* "descends from heaven as a gift from God, is modeled after human form, and uses the skin and gut of a sacrificial lamb for the face and strings of the instrument," as author Benjamin D. Koen explains in chapter 28. Koen adds

Terracotta monkey playing a lute, 2nd–3rd century CE, excavated in the Khotan oasis, south of the Taklamakan Desert.

The State Hermitage Museum, St. Petersburg, Inv. no. GA-2427.

The Iconography of Musical Instruments

The depiction of musical instruments in works of art offers a rich resource for the study of music history. In various epochs, musicians and musical instruments associated with Central Asia have been portrayed in myriad artistic media: petroglyphs, sculpture, ceramics, jewelry, stone sarcophagi, metalwork, frescoes, bas-relief, book arts, miniature painting, and, during the Soviet era, realist oil paintings with socialist themes. Important schools of miniature painting flourished in late Timurid Herat at the court of Sultan Husayn Bayqara (ruled 1469–1506), in 16th- and 17th-century Safavid Persia, and, beginning in the 16th century, in Mughal India. Typically commissioned by noble patrons, miniature paintings depicted courtly life, illustrated important literary works, and portrayed individuals in portraits. Scenes of courtly festivity and entertainment often include musicians. Though represented through stylized and idealized painterly conventions of form and subject, images of music making often depict musical instruments in striking detail, providing pictorial evidence for how musical fashion and taste—at least among the nobility—circulated and developed in Central Asia, West Asia, and South Asia.[1]

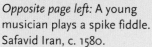

Opposite page left: A young musician plays a spike fiddle. Safavid Iran, c. 1580.

From the Collection of Princess Catherine Aleya Aga Khan.

Opposite page right: A young bearded prince sits under a canopy on a terrace, surrounded by companions and servants and serenaded by musicians. The large, round, decorated bowl of the lute tapers to a short neck with a graceful curved scroll at the end. Illustration from the *Diwan* of Sultan Ibrahim Mirza. Mashhad, Iran. Late 16th century. Opaque watercolor, ink, gold, and silver on paper.

Courtesy of Aga Khan Museum.

Above left: A young musician sits in a tree and plucks an ornately decorated three-stringed long-necked lute accompanied

by a tambourine player while servants attend a prince and his companions in a bucolic garden. From an illustrated manuscript of the Turkish and Persian poetry of Sultan Ibrahim Mirza (d. 1577), an important connoisseur of the arts, and nephew of the Safavid ruler, Shah Tahmasp. Mashhad, Iran, late 16th century.

Courtesy of Aga Khan Museum.

Above middle: A youth playing a five-stringed long-necked lute. The upper part of the instrument's bowl is covered with wood, while the lower part is covered with animal skin—a form still found in the long-necked lutes of Badakhshan (eastern Tajikistan and northeastern Afghanistan). The right hand position, with the thumb and index finger held stiffly apart and the other three fingers curled down, suggests that the player is plucking

the strings rather than playing with a plectrum. Khorasan, northeastern Iran, c. 1580–1590. Opaque watercolor, ink and gold on paper.

Courtesy of Aga Khan Museum.

Above right: Man playing a *kamancha*, c. 1600. A spike fiddle (so-called because of the protruding spike that supports the instrument), the *kamancha* is played in Iran and the Caucasus region and is closely related to the Central Asian *ghijak*. The bowl of the instrument depicted in the painting has a broad, flat deck, in contrast to present-day *kamancha*s and *ghijak*s, which are more spherical. The depiction of the player's right hand shows how he applies variable tension to the bow using the index and middle fingers. Opaque watercolor, ink and gold on paper.

Courtesy of Aga Khan Museum.

that in the legend, "the instrument is played by angels and is meant to be used for singing praises to God. The *rubab* often has prayers carved out of the middle section of the instrument or written on the skin that covers the body or resonance chamber. Thus the *rubab* is viewed as being in a perpetual state of prayer in which it sings its own praises."

CLASSIFICATION AND CONSTRUCTION OF MUSICAL INSTRUMENTS

Musical instruments from around the world are commonly classified according to the way that players produce sound on them—for example, by causing an air stream to vibrate (aerophones); bowing, strumming, or plucking a stretched string (chordophones); causing a stretched membrane to vibrate (membranophones); causing the substance of the instrument itself to vibrate without the use of membranes or strings (idiophones); or using electrically driven oscillators (electrophones). A standard system of classifying musical instruments according to these different sound-generating categories was codified at the beginning of the twentieth century by two music scholars, Curt Sachs (1881–1959) and Erich von Hornbostel (1877–1935), and is known as the Hornbostel-Sachs system (the electrophone

Far left: Luthier Abdughafar Abdusamadov planes a Kashgar *rubab*, Khujand, Tajikistan.

Left: Abdul Azim Qaderi makes an Afghan *rubab* in his workshop in Kabul.
Photo by Mirwaiss Sidiqi.

Instrument-Making

Instrument-making has traditionally been the purview of skilled artisans who require years of training—typically through apprenticeship to a master. Most instrument makers specialize in a particular instrument or a family of related instruments. Whatever the instrument, the craftsman must consider materials, construction techniques, and decorations in order to create a finished product that is both functional and aesthetically pleasing. Today, the profession is endangered due to the growing popularity of factory-made instruments, which can be produced at far lower cost than instruments crafted by hand. In Central Asia, high-quality handcrafted instruments continue to be produced by only a small number of artisans, and apprentices are rare.

category was added by Sachs in 1940). While the Hornbostel-Sachs system is useful for grouping instruments based on their physical properties of sound making, it makes no attempt to link these physical properties to the cultural and social context in which the instruments are used. These links are multifaceted and are shaped by the interaction of many different cultural and historical forces. Complexities aside, however, a few basic connections between instruments and their cultural and social milieu are readily apparent.

First, musical instruments are constructed from physical materials available to instrument makers, either locally or through import. Almost all instrument makers are dependent on a network of suppliers and traders for at least a portion of raw or manufactured materials, and for the tools and technology necessary to render raw materials into finished products. For example, a luthier (builder of stringed instruments) in the city of Bukhara who makes fine long-necked lutes must acquire aged mulberry wood for the body of the instrument, silk or gut to fabricate strings (or the strings themselves), mother-of-pearl or ivory to make decorative inlays for the fingerboard, lacquer and glue to seal the wood, and cloth to sew a carrying case. In addition, the luthier needs woodworking tools—chisels, files, saws, clamps, and so on.

Second, building musical instruments requires specialized knowledge of the intricacies of materials and, with the exception of the simplest instruments made from found objects, knowledge of technologies for rendering the look and sound of an instrument as close as possible to a culturally determined physical and sonic ideal. For example, makers of metal jaw harps, which have ancient roots in Central Asia and Siberia, strive to create instruments that produce not simply the generic "twanging" sound characteristic of jaw harps, but a twang with a particular timbre and sonority that corresponds to the sonic ideal of one or another specific regional style of jaw harp. Doing so requires knowledge of metallurgy; tools to forge, bend, and cut pieces of iron; and expertise in honing and modifying the various metal components until the instrument produces just the right twang. Likewise, two-stringed long-necked lutes are ubiquitous in Central Asia, but each local or regional variety has its own characteristic sonic ideal. A luthier's challenge is to produce instruments that approximate that ideal as closely as possible.

Third, the evolution of musical instruments, like other aspects of culture, responds to trends in taste and fashion. Instruments that are not modified in a way that responds to changes in musical taste and fashion will eventually become obsolete. How many readers of this book have seen or listened to a *barbat*? A theorbo? A rebec? All of these instruments—now confined to museums or replicated by contemporary luthiers for performers of so-called period instruments—were once widely popular in their own cultural milieu.[2] By contrast, musical instruments that ride a fashion trend can attract large numbers of players, resulting in a high demand for instruments and strong economic incentive to introduce technical

The *temir komuz*, or metal jaw harp, was traditionally played by nomadic peoples.

Qobyz player, 1871–1872.
From Turkestan Album, Ethnographic
Part, vol. 1, 1871–1872, Library of
Congress.

The Chinese *pipa*, above,
along with the European
lute and the Middle Eastern
oud, is thought to be a
descendent of the Central
Asian short-necked lute
called the *barbat*.

improvements and innovations. Such was the case with the piano in the nineteenth century, the electric guitar in the mid-twentieth century, and electronic synthesizers in the early twenty-first century.

Fourth, musical instruments may achieve popularity not only on account of their appeal to individual taste but because a political or cultural authority has invested them with cultural esteem as symbols of tradition or identity for a nation or sub-national region, an ethnic group, or other forms of community. For example, in Kazakhstan, the *dombyra,* a two-stringed long-necked lute, is widely viewed as the Kazakh national instrument, synonymous with Kazakh cultural identity. Similarly, the *morin khuur,* a two-stringed horse-head fiddle, enjoys special status in Mongolia as a symbol of Mongolian national identity.

These examples illustrate some of the ways that musical instruments can be understood not only as aesthetic objects that are products of skilled craftsmanship but as cultural artifacts that may hold symbolic meaning, represent taste or fashion, and evoke feelings of connection to place and people. Tradition, taste, technology, territoriality—these are the driving forces behind the evolution and dissemination of musical instruments.

MUSICAL INSTRUMENTS AMONG NOMADS AND SEDENTARY DWELLERS

In Central Asia, it is not surprising that the cultural divide between nomads and sedentary dwellers described in chapter 1 extends to the domain of musical instruments. Indeed, this divide is apparent in the technologies that support the construction of instruments, the techniques used to play them, the way that instrumental performance is configured (for solo, duo or trio, small or large ensemble), and the way that playing instruments serves as a communal activity or, by contrast, a demonstration of individual virtuosity.

The following comparative table illustrates some of the most conspicuous contrasts between musical instruments linked to nomadic or historically nomadic cultures and musical instruments linked to the historically sedentary-dwelling populations of cities, towns, and villages engaged primarily in agriculture.

The title of table 2.1, "Tendencies and Typologies in Central Asian Musical Instruments," indicates that the terse generalizations it contains are precisely that—generalizations. Moreover, the table does not account for the fluid way in which instruments have migrated from the realm of nomads to the realm of sedentary dwellers or vice versa, in the process undergoing adaptation or transformation. The vertical line in the table dividing the attributes of nomadic and historically nomadic groups from sedentary dwellers and agriculturalists represents a porous

TABLE 2.1. TENDENCIES AND TYPOLOGIES IN CENTRAL ASIAN MUSICAL INSTRUMENTS

NOMADIC/HISTORICALLY NOMADIC GROUPS	SEDENTARY DWELLERS/AGRICULTURALISTS
Ancient source of bowed fiddles	Ancient source of long-necked lutes
Lutes are frequently fretless	Lutes are typically fretted
Scales based on diatonic intervals	Non-diatonic intervals such as microtones and neutral thirds are a structural feature of modes and scales
Instrument strings made of animal gut	Instrument strings made of metal or silk
Lutes strummed or plucked with fingers	Lutes played with a metal or wooden plectrum
Lutes typically have 2–3 strings	Many lutes include several drone strings or sympathetic strings
Percussion is peripheral to central musical repertoires	Frame drums or other percussion instruments are central to music making
Virtuosic instrumental soloist is a central figure in musical life	Small vocal-instrumental ensembles are central to musical life
Music and musical instruments are non-gendered (both genders play the same instruments)	Music and musical instruments are gendered ("male" music / "female" music)

and permeable cultural boundary, not a cultural fire wall. The millennia-old coexistence of nomads and sedentary dwellers in Central Asia is evident in myriad aspects of material, expressive, spiritual, and economic culture, including music and musical life. The Silk Road—the ancient network of trade routes that crisscrossed Eurasia, joining China with Central Asia, the Middle East, and Europe—facilitated exchange in all of these dimensions of culture not only between East and West but in Central Asia itself, between nomads and sedentary dwellers.

It may well have been along the Silk Road that some of the first "world music" jam sessions took place, for music and musical instruments were transported across Eurasia along with silk, jade, porcelain, and other luxury goods. For nomadic caravan drivers and the urban merchants whose precious goods they transported, the sound of unfamiliar instruments must have had an appeal not unlike the visual allure of exotic textiles, ceramics, and glass. Curious musicians and innovative luthiers adapted these unfamiliar instruments to perform the music of their own locale and at the same time introduced new rhythmic patterns, scales, and performance techniques imported from elsewhere. Before the Crusades, numerous instruments from the Middle East and Central Asia had already reached Europe: lutes, viols, oboes, zithers, drums, and percussion. Following trade routes, many of these instruments also turned up in China, Japan, India, and Indonesia. For example, the *barbat,* a Central Asian short-necked lute, is considered to be the ancestor of the Middle Eastern oud and European lute, the Japanese *biwa,* and the Chinese *pipa*—an instrument that Chinese documents record as belonging to the "northern barbarians," which is to say nomads. Turkic and Mongolian horsemen from Inner Asia were probably Eurasia's earliest fiddlers. Upright fiddles strung with horsehair strings, played with horsehair bows, and often featuring a carved horse's head at the end of the neck have an archaic history among the nomadic peoples of Inner Asia and are closely linked to shamanism and spirit worship. Such instruments may have inspired the round-bodied spike fiddles played in West Asia (*kamancha, ghijak*) and Indonesia (*rebab*) and the carved fiddles of the subcontinent (*sorud, sarinda, sarangi*), which are strung with metal strings. Loud oboes called *surnai* in Central Asia became the *shahnai* in India, *suona* in China, and *zurna* in Anatolia. Central Asia in turn imported musical instruments from both East and West: plucked and struck zithers, which have old roots in China and Mongolia as well as in Iran, and, in more recent times, European violins—played upright, like a spike fiddle—and various types of accordions, introduced to Central Asia by Slavic colonizers.

Though the origin and early migration of lutes predates the historical record, the many kinds of lutes that are played today in Central Asia most likely originated in the ancient Middle East. In Central Asia, they have evolved along different trajectories that reflect adaptation to the different musical styles and tastes of nomads and sedentary peoples. Lutes that belong to the musical traditions of sedentary dwellers are typically fretted, which allows players to create the precise, mathematically based intervals prescribed by the sophisticated tradition of music theory that was an important element of medieval Islamic science and scholarship. Moreover, fretted instruments make it easy for a group of performers to play the same interval—a useful technology for the musical traditions of sedentary dwellers, in which small instrumental ensembles play a prominent role. By contrast, in nomadic cultures, where solo performance is preeminent, lutes tend to be unfretted, thus allowing intervals to be fluid and individualized.

Another distinction between the music of nomads and sedentary dwellers concerns rhythm and the way it is expressed—or not expressed—on drums and other percussion instruments. Among sedentary dwellers, rhythmic patterns in many if not most musical genres are articulated on frame drums—single-headed drums played with the hands rather than struck with sticks. These rhythms represent a rational, mathematical approach to dividing identical units of time into recurring patterns of strong and weak beats. In the music of sedentary cultures, meter and rhythm are highly theorized constructs expressed in the form of rhythmic cycles, or regularly recurring metro-rhythmic patterns, called *usul* ("procedure," "principle"). Among musicians in sedentary cultures, *usul* is also a general name for the metro-rhythmic dimension of music, analogous, for example, to the meaning of *tala* in the classical raga tradition of India.

The frame drum (*doira* or *daf*) is used in many kinds of folk and classical music throughout Central Asia.

Nomadic musicians, by contrast, do not speak about *usul,* nor does music in nomadic cultures typically include percussion instruments, with the exception of drums used for ritual or ceremonial purposes, such as the shaman's drum. This paucity of percussion does not mean that music in nomadic cultures lacks rhythmic sophistication. On the contrary, nomadic rhythm can be expressed through subtle nuance or bold virtuosity by the plucking, strumming, bowing, blowing, or twanging of lutenists, fiddlers, flautists, and jaw harp players. Many rhythms in nomadic music are mimetic—that is, they represent or imitate rhythmic patterns imported from the real world, some rhythmically symmetrical, like the gallop of a horse, and others irregular, like the lope of a camel. The long-necked lutes of the nomadic instrumentarium are all played with the bare fingers of the right hand rather than with a plectrum, as are lutes played by sedentary dwellers. Strumming or plucking strings with bare fingers offers a player access to a palette of subtly contrasting timbres that are produced by using different parts of the finger, different fingers, and different gestural movements of the hand. These gestural movements can also produce subtle variations in rhythm. By contrast, performers who use a plectrum can strike a string with great rhythmic precision, creating the regular metrical patterns that constitute an *usul* in the music of sedentary dwellers.[3]

Referring again to table 2.1, "Tendencies and Typologies," let us consider the last row in the table, which generalizes about the gendering of musical instruments among sedentary dwellers as opposed to the non-gendering of instruments in nomadic and historically nomadic cultures in Central Asia. The gendering of musical instruments is common in many cultures—and it is typically women rather than men who are restricted from playing and, in certain cases, even seeing particular instruments. For example, among the Kuikuro, an indigenous group that live along the southern tributaries of the Xingu River in the southern Amazonia region of Brazil, women are forbidden to touch or see the *kagutu* flutes played by men. For the Kuikuro, *kagutu* flutes represent the voices of spirit-animals, and are considered sacred and dangerous. But one need not go as far as the Upper Xingu to find gender divisions in the playing of instruments. International classical and

From the Mongolian *Morin Khuur* to the Modern Cello

At the beginning of a concert in New York's legendary Carnegie Hall, the great cellist Yo-Yo Ma walked out on the stage holding his musical instrument. But he wasn't holding a cello. He was holding a *morin khuur*—the two-stringed "horsehead" fiddle that is considered the national instrument of Mongolia. Maestro Ma was about to perform a piece written by a Mongolian composer specially for his multicultural Silk Road Ensemble, which is based in the United States and presents concerts around the world. Pointing to the *morin khuur*, Ma said with excitement, "The instrument I am holding is the distant ancestor of the cello!"

Indeed, Turkic and Mongolian horsemen from Inner Asia were among the world's earliest fiddle players. Two-stringed fiddles like the Mongolian *morin khuur*, Tuvan *igil*, Kyrgyz *kyl-kiak*, and Kazakh *qyl-qobyz* all share a common ancestry rooted in the life of steppe pastoralism. Nomads require musical instruments that are light, easily portable, and constructed from readily available materials. Fiddles handily fulfill all three criteria.

At root, all fiddles can be built from two kinds of material: wood and animal products. Bows are made from horsehair, strings from sinew, the sounding box and neck from wood, the deck or face of the instrument from wood or hide, and the pegs from wood or bone. On fiddles from Inner Asia, a horse's head is often carved into the scroll at the end of the instrument's neck, symbolizing the spirit of the horse that is believed to animate or enliven the music performed on the instrument. Fiddle players are experts at representing the spirits, sounds, and behavior of animals through their instrument, and this close connection to the animal world has endowed the fiddle and its players with special powers. Shamans, epic reciters, and musicians who are "close to the spirits" have traditionally used the fiddle to summon the spirits of animals and ancestors.

During the era of the great steppe empires, fiddles migrated both west and south as the culture of nomads became increasingly intertwined with those of sedentary dwellers. And even before the Crusades of the European Middle Ages, fiddles and other instruments from Asia had reached the cultural capitals of Europe. Medieval fiddles like the rebec (derived from Arabic: *rabab* or *rebab*) evolved into many varieties of viols that were a cornerstone of sacred and secular music during the Renaissance and Baroque. The best known of these is the viola da gamba

A horsehead fiddle (*igil*) from Tuva (Tyva), which shares a border with Mongolia.

(leg viol), the direct ancestor of the modern cello. The violin, viola, and double bass are also descendants of the viol family.

These days, the music played on bowed fiddles is as diverse as music itself. Rock and pop, blues and jazz, country music, Gypsy romances, South Indian classical ragas, and Irish dance tunes are only a few of the many kinds of music performed just on the violin. But notwithstanding their many migrations and transformations, fiddles preserve a strong vestige of their archaic spiritual power. The violin is still regarded in the folk cultures of Europe and the Americas as "the devil's instrument." If you're in a small town in the southern United States or eastern Canada where the Protestant religious traditions of early settlers remain strong, don't ask a fiddler to play on a Sunday. On the Lord's Day, the fiddle—the instrument of the devil—represents unwelcome competition.

concert music culture has its own gendering tendencies. For example, female tuba, trombone, and percussion players, while not unknown, are considerably less common than male players, while conversely, female flautists and harp players are more common than males.

In Central Asia, the gendering of both music and musical instruments is more common among sedentary dwellers than among nomads or historically nomadic groups. Some of these gendered traditions are discussed in chapter 1. While the social legacy of the Soviet Union's campaign to integrate women into economic, social, and artistic life brought an entire generation of talented female singers, dancers, and instrumentalists into the public view, female *tanbur* players and *ghijak* players are still rare in the urban *maqom* traditions of Uzbekistan and Tajikistan. Other instruments—*dutar* and frame drums—have long been played by women, but primarily in social contexts where both performers and listeners are women (see chapter 25).

By contrast, in nomadic and historically nomadic cultures, where men and women share the work of herding animals and frequently spend evenings crowded together inside a yurt listening to music and the recitation of oral poetry, performance culture has been more egalitarian. In present-day Kazakhstan and Kyrgyzstan, the ranks of the most highly regarded performers on the *dombyra* and *komuz* lutes and on two-stringed upright fiddles—*kyl-kiyak* and *qyl-qobyz*—include more or less equal numbers of women and men. Yet, while musical instruments may themselves be non-gendered, certain performance traditions and genres retain traditional gender boundaries. Kyrgyz reciters of the epic poem *Manas*—which is traditionally performed without the accompaniment of an instrument—are almost always men. Likewise, Kazakh epic reciters (*jyrau*s) who accompany themselves on the *dombyra* have traditionally been men, although women are beginning to challenge this gender boundary (see chapter 5). As a manifestation of spiritual and expressive culture rooted in tenacious traditions with old roots, the gendering of music and musical instruments may linger long after gender boundaries have softened or disappeared in other domains of society and culture.

ACTIVITY ———————————————————————————————

Look through the musical instrument glossary at the back of the book and familiarize yourself with the instruments. The names of these instruments will come up repeatedly throughout the book—in particular, in the descriptions of audio and video examples. Can you see physical similarities between Central Asian instruments and European instruments? Between Central Asian instruments and Chinese, Indian, or Iranian instruments?

NOTES

1. For a detailed study of musical instruments in miniature painting, see Bonnie C. Wade, *Imagining Sound: An Ethnomusicological Study of Music, Art, and Culture in Mughal India* (Chicago: University of Chicago Press: 1998).

2. The *barbat* is a lute that was popular in the courts of Sassanian Persia, which included parts of Central Asia. The theorbo is a type of lute that achieved popularity in late 16th-century Europe. The rebec is a medieval European fiddle that evolved from the Arabic bowed *rabab*.

3. Contrasts between the music and musical worldview of nomads and sedentary dwellers are illuminatingly explored in Elie During and Jean During, "De l'espace lisse au temps troué: à propos des musiques nomades" ["From smooth space to time with holes: On nomad music"]. In Pascale Criton and Jean-Marc Chovel, *Gilles Deleuze, la pensée-musique* [Gilles Deleuze, thought on music] (Paris: Centre de documentation de la musique contemporaine, 2015).

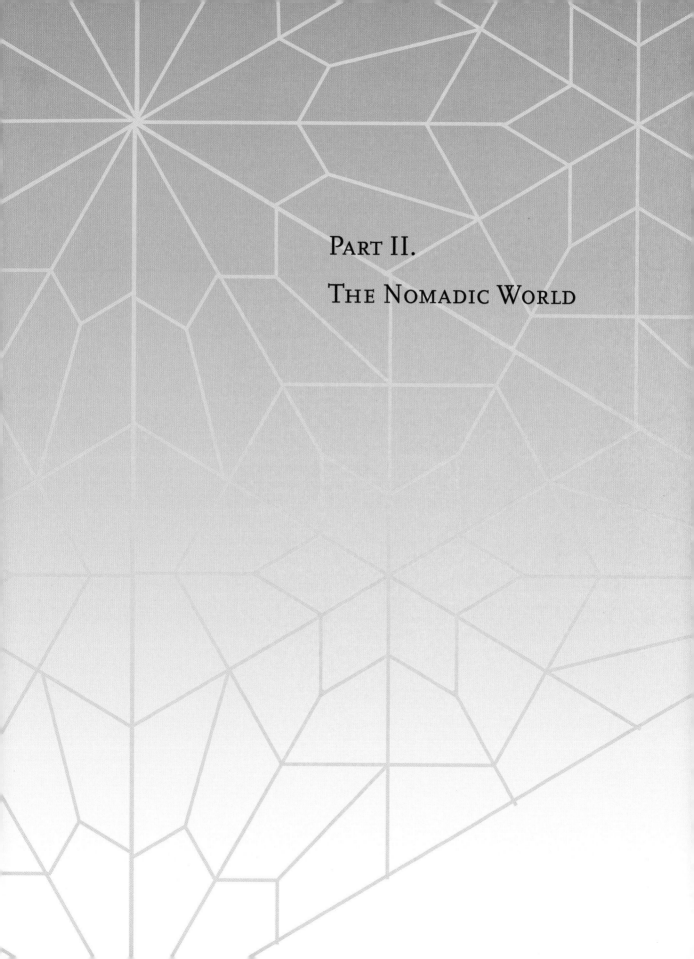

PART II.

THE NOMADIC WORLD

Who Are the Nomads of Central Asia?

THEODORE LEVIN

Nomadism is closely connected to the natural environment of the arid zones that constitute one-quarter of the earth's surface. With annual precipitation of 200–400 mm, these regions of steppe, desert, semi-desert, and mountains are inhospitable to agriculture, and the only economically viable source of livelihood is nomadic stockbreeding ("nomad" derives from Greek *nomos:* "pasture"). These days, an estimated forty million people in more than thirty countries still practice some form of nomadism. An additional thirty million who live in the huge expanse of Eurasia that extends from the west of China almost to the Black Sea can trace their ancestry to nomads who lived as recently as one or two centuries ago.

A portable yurt in Tuva (Tyva), in the Altai region of south Siberia, is home to a herding family during spring, summer, and fall.
Photo by Karen Sherlock.

Since ancient times, nomads and nomadism have played an integral role in the development of material, expressive, and spiritual culture in Central Asia, and in the larger region of Central Eurasia often known as Inner Asia. From Siberian reindeer herders and Mongolian horse breeders to Turkmen shepherds and Tibetan yak drivers, modern-day pastoralists preserve a way of life that embodies some of Inner Asia's most time-tested and ingenious inventions: movable dwellings, clothing suitable for riding horseback, felt and leather utensils, and the equine harness. Nomads invented *koumiss* (fermented mare's milk), the art of hunting with birds of prey, and bowed stringed instruments that are the ancestors of the cello and violin.

Marking the frontiers of the great civilizations of China, Iran, India, and Greece, the historical borders of the nomadic world have been indefinite and diffuse. Nomadic and sedentary peoples have coexisted in Central Asia for millennia,

Above: Grasslands in the west of Mongolia.

Above right: A Mongolian herding family takes down a yurt in preparation for moving to a new campsite.

and their relationship has not always been an easy one. In the thirteenth century, for example, Genghis Khan's nomadic armies laid waste to Central Asia's cities, while in the twentieth century, the Soviet Union, an empire built on the power of industry and agriculture, tried forcibly to sedentarize some of Inner Asia's last nomads. Yet despite periods of hostility, pastoralists and sedentary dwellers have both relied on an intricate commercial and cultural symbiosis that is one of the hallmarks of Inner Asian civilization.

Despite the current rapid pace of urbanization in Central Asia, vestiges of nomadic traditions remain strong. For example, yurts—the circular felt tents that provide sturdy housing in remote pasturages—have become a symbol of nomadic heritage, and are often erected at festivals and celebrations in urban and suburban areas. In urban apartments, the place of honor in the living room is opposite the entrance, just as in a yurt. Rituals of nomadic hospitality are alive and well, as is the art of nomadic cuisine. Traditional nomadic dress has influenced modern fashion and the choice of fabric colors. And, most important for the study of Central Asian music, forms of expressive culture rooted in the traditions of nomadism—oral epic recitation, poetry competitions, marionette theater, music composition and improvisation, and solo virtuosic performance on a musical instrument—have successfully transitioned from the rural cultural context of the nomadic past to the urban cultural context that will surely be the locus of the nomadic future. The chapters that follow offer a survey of some of these remarkable art forms and show how, as living traditions, they are being adapted to the cultural, social, and political conditions of contemporary Central Asia.

CHAPTER 3   Introduction to Central Asian Epic Traditions

Elmira Köchümkulova

What Is an Epic?

An epic (from Greek *epikos* and *epos:* "word," "story," "poem") is a long narrative poem that recounts and glorifies the life and heroic deeds of historical and legendary figures whose exploits and adventures typically take on a larger-than-life quality. Narrated by bards or oral poet-singers, epic is one of the oldest and most popular poetic genres in world literature. Epics contain rich and valuable information about the culture and history of particular peoples and social groups. For example, the two most famous epics of Western antiquity, the *Iliad* and the *Odyssey,* blend mythological and historical thought and narrative. In a similar way, the Indian epics *Ramayana* and *Mahabharata* illuminate Indian culture and civilization. The Kyrgyz epic *Manas,* an encyclopedic compendium of Kyrgyz myth, folktales, and legends, describes nomadic culture and interactions between nomads and sedentary dwellers in Central Asia. Many nations whose literary history includes epic narratives consider the heroes of these epics to be the founders or progenitors of their nation. For instance, in Virgil's *Aeneid,* written in Latin in the first century BCE, the legendary character Aeneas, escaping from his native city of Troy after it was decimated by Greek conquerors, sailed to Italy and founded the city of Rome. In the epic *Manas,* the hero Manas is regarded as the progenitor of the Kyrgyz, for he united the region's many scattered tribes into a single nation. In the epic chronicle *Secret History of the Mongols,* Genghis Khan is portrayed as the founder of the Mongol nation.

Karakalpak *jyrau* Jumabai Bazarov holding his *qobyz,* 1991.
Courtesy of Theodore Levin.

43

Epic Heroes

In many epics, the principal heroes are often portrayed as god-like men. In Greek epics, for example, heroes are regarded as the sons of gods and goddesses. Epic heroes uphold morals and principles that are highly valued in their society, such as bravery, generosity, and justice. For example, in the *Secret History of the Mongols,* Genghis Khan is personified as an ideal, strict ruler, but one who is also just and generous. The Mongols revered him almost as a god. He was destined to establish Mongol rule over much of the known world, and in the eyes of his compatriots, the notion that he was protected by divine powers justified his destruction of cities and nations. Like Genghis Khan, the Kyrgyz hero Manas is likened to the image of a mythic god:

> He is created from the beam between the sky and the earth,
> He is created from the light of the moon and the sun,
> He is created from the blend of gold and silver . . .

The Kyrgyz hero Manas is always accompanied and protected by the spirits of powerful animals.

Manas is not an ordinary man but a hero of tremendous power and wrath. When filled with rage, his eyes turn red like fire, and he thirsts for human blood. Even before he is born, he is destined to conquer the world. In addition, Manas is always accompanied and protected by the spirits of powerful animals, such as a black-striped tiger. A lion walks by his side, a giant black bird flies above him, and a dragon marches in front of him. Traditionally, Turkic epic heroes, like Mongolian heroes, fought alone against ogres and giants. When a hero was alone, he had to have supernatural powers to defeat the enemy. However, as time passed, new generations of epic singers enriched the plot of the epic by adding new themes, characters, and heroes. Thus, in versions of the *Manas* epic recorded from singers in the nineteenth and twentieth centuries, the hero Manas is not a solitary hero but has forty companions (*choros*) who help him fight his enemies.

The traditional tasks and deeds of an epic hero include protecting his land and people, waging wars on enemies, pursuing adventures and journeys, and encountering and overcoming obstacles. The hero invariably overcomes all obstacles and reaches his goal by demonstrating both physical strength and mental agility.

Oral Epic Tradition of Central Asia

Oral literature, and especially epic poetry, is widespread and highly cultivated among the Turkic and Mongol nomadic peoples of Central Asia. Beyond Central

Asia, however, only a few of its major epics, such as *Manas* and *Alpamysh*, are widely known. Many other "smaller" epic poems—*Er Töshtük, Janysh-Baiysh, Er Tabyldy, Jangyl Myrza* (Kyrgyz); and *Edige, Koblandy Batyr, Er Targyn, Kozy-Körpes and Bayan Sulu* (Kazakh)—remain less known and less studied in the West. Russian literary scholar A. N. Veselovskii suggested that the composition and transmission of classical Greek epic and the epic songs of medieval Germanic peoples, which survive only in written form, can be better understood through a study of the living epic traditions of Central Asia. Similarly, the American scholars of epic poetry Milman Parry and Albert Bates Lord used the living tradition of South Slavic epic as a model for understanding the compositional process of ancient Greek Homeric epic. While it is no longer possible to find a singer of the *Nibelungenlied* in Germany or a performer of the *Odyssey* in Greece, one can easily find singers of *Manas* among contemporary Kyrgyz, or of *Alpamysh* among Uzbeks, or of *Görogly* among the Turkmen.

The abiding popularity of epic in the oral tradition of Turkic Central Asia is rooted in the social dynamics of nomadic life. The nomadic lifestyle was incompatible with accumulating large numbers of material possessions, including books. Instead of preserving information in books, nomads relied on their memory to archive historical and cultural knowledge and transmit it orally from one generation to the next in the form of genealogies, epic poems, legends, folktales, and instrumental music (*küü*). The renowned Kyrgyz writer Chingiz Aitmatov succinctly characterized this alternative form of cultural memory: "If other peoples and nations displayed their past culture and history in written literature, sculpture, architecture, theater, and art, the Kyrgyz people expressed their worldview, pride and dignity, battles, and their hope for the future in epic songs."[1]

Like the Homeric epics, most Central Asian heroic epics reflect the life conditions of a "heroic age," when tribes and peoples were in need of brave and strong-hearted men to protect them from their enemies. In many Kazakh and Kyrgyz epics, Kalmyks (Mongols) and Chinese are the traditional enemies of the nomadic Kyrgyz and Kazakhs. Epic singers accompanied warriors to battle and, like today's war correspondents, reported on what they saw. But

Bola bakhshy (1899–1994), shown in this photo with Uzbek musicologist Otanazar Matyakubov (*right*), was a well known epic singer from the Khorezm region of northwestern Uzbekistan.
Courtesy of Theodore Levin.

Kyrgyz epic singer
Moldobasan
Musulmankulov, 1883–1961.

instead of writing journalistic accounts, they observed battles and other adventures and described them in poetry and song. In so doing, they glorified the heroic deeds of warriors, often embellishing or hyperbolizing them for dramatic effect. Two such epic singers—Yramandyn yrchy uul and Jaysang yrchy—are mentioned in the Kyrgyz epic *Manas.*

Some Central Asian heroic epics—*Manas* among them—are thought to have grown out of a *koshok,* or funerary lament song, for a deceased person. In a *koshok,* the wife, daughter, mother, or sister of the deceased expresses her grief and praises the deceased by describing his or her personality and good deeds, family, and ancestors. When well-known heroes, khans, or tribal leaders died, oral poets were hired or invited to publicly lament them. As improvising oral poets, bards were able to compose long poems in which they recounted the life story of the great heroes and khans. And just as in their epic accounts of living heroes, bards glorified the good deeds and valiant character of deceased heroes. If the deceased was a well-known person, the *koshok* dedicated to him eventually developed through continual retelling into a well-structured epic poem with a clear plot.

Epic Themes

Stories about major historical events and heroic deeds traveled from person to person over great distances and considerable periods of time. As epic tales spread and evolved over time, they became intertwined with epic tales from other cultures, resulting in the development of common themes, motifs, and features in epic traditions of the world. Although major world epics have been narrated or written in different languages—the *Iliad* and *Odyssey* in Greek, *Ramayana* and *Mahabharata* in Sanskrit, *Beowulf* in Old English, *Manas* in Kyrgyz, and many other Turkic epics in various Turkic languages—they all have common features. The most common epic themes and motifs are raids, single combat of heroes against their enemies, the theft of large herds, revenge and counterattack, the story of childless old parents and parents' unusual dreams foretelling a future hero's birth, a hero's unusual birth and remarkable childhood, winning a bride, horse racing, archery, wrestling, and journeys and adventures. In the Kyrgyz epic *Manas* and the Mongol epic chronicle *Secret History of the Mongols,* the heroes Manas and Temüjin (the birth name of Genghis Khan) were both born holding a clot of blood the size of a knuckle bone in their right hand. The blood signifies the child's desire to conquer and rule the world when he grows up. Another theme that the two epics share is a dream motif that foretells the arrival or birth of a future hero who will take over the entire world. In the *Secret History,* Temüjin's future father-in-law, Dei Sechen, has a dream and tells it to Temüjin and his father, Yesügin, when they come in search of a bride: "This is thy son, he is a son with fire in his eyes, with light in his face. *Quda* Yesügei, I, this night, dreamed a dream.[2] A white gyre falcon, holding both sun and moon, flew hither and is lighted into my hand."[3]

In the *Manas* epic, the father of Manas, Jakyp, also has a dream before his son is born that bears a strong similarity to Dei Sechen's dream about Temüjin:

> In last night's dream,
> I settled down on the upper Ala-Too
> And caught a young eagle.
> When I took him hunting,
> The sound of his flapping wings was heard.
> Unable to withstand his wrath,
> All the animals fell over in fright.[4]
>
> . . .
>
> Reaching with my right hand,
> I grasped the sun for myself.
> Reaching with my left hand,
> I caught the moon for myself.
> My right hand held the sun,
> My left hand held the moon,
> I took the sun
> And put it in place of the moon,
> I took the moon
> And put it in place of the sun.
> Together with the sun and moon,
> I flew high into the sky.[5]

Another common motif in epics is the return of the hero from a long journey. This is the central motif in Homer's *Odyssey,* and it is also found in Central Asian Turkic epics such as *Alpamysh* (Kazakh, Uzbek, Karakalpak) and *Janysh-Baiysh* (Kyrgyz). In the *Odyssey,* the central character, the Greek hero Odysseus, faces a succession of obstacles, impediments, dangers, and detours as he tries to return to his native city of Ithaca. Finally, with the help of his protector, the goddess Athena, he overcomes all the obstacles and is reunited with his family and people. The "return of the hero" motif lends itself to myriad sub-plots, which reflect the particular historical and cultural conditions in which the epic narrative unfolds. In Central Asian epics, for example, the hero may be kept captive in a dungeon in the enemy's land but finally escapes with the help of his horse, who usually speaks the hero's language, or the enemy's daughter falls in love with the hero. As is the case in the *Odyssey,* when the hero returns home, his family may not at first recognize him. In Central Asian epics, the hero can return disguised as a beggar or shepherd, and, once his identity is confirmed, he may take revenge on enemies in his homeland.

EPIC LANGUAGE

Since heroic epics deal with wars and raids, and glorify bravery and justice, they employ powerful and hyperbolic or elevated language, especially when describing battle scenes and the physical appearance and strength of heroes, as well as their horses and armor. Simile, epithet, formulaic speech, and repetition are important literary features of epic poetry. Similes make language more vivid through comparison, as in the following lines from the *Manas:*

> With a face like wheat smeared with oil,
> With his eyes glowering like an evening fog,
> And looking like a hungry lion,
> The famous Manas khan will appear.

Uzbek bard Kahar Rahimov.
Courtesy of Theodore Levin.

An epithet is a word or phrase that is repeatedly and consistently used to describe a character or a thing in an epic. In Homer's *Iliad,* for example, the inhabitants of Achaea are always referred to as "flowing-haired" or "bronze-armored." In the Kyrgyz epic *Manas,* traditional epithets for the hero Manas are "generous" (*ayköl*), "panther" (*kabylan*), "lion" (*arstan*), "blue-maned" (*kökjal*), and "bloodthirsty" (*kankor*).

Formulaic speech in Kyrgyz epics consists of one to six verse lines (depending on a performer's improvisational skill) that appear in similar narrative contexts with minimal variation, as in the following two-line formula from the *Manas:*

> Carrying red, crescent-shaped flags and banners
> And making a shrill hue and cry,

> Carrying gray-white flags and red banners
> And making a great hue and cry . . .

Repetition of the same group of lines, sometimes with slight variations, occurs throughout the *Manas* epic whenever the hero Manas is ready to attack his enemy:

> The black-striped tiger
> Stood ready to attack.
> When he set out towards his enemy,
> A lion with a short, gray mane
> Stood ready to attack behind him,
> Being a companion to the hero.

Like all other genres of Kyrgyz oral poetry, Kyrgyz epics strictly maintain seven or eight syllables in each verse line. Verse lines are composed with initial and internal alliterations and end rhyme. Kazakh and Uzbek epics may have seven- or eight-syllable lines or, alternatively, eleven- or twelve-syllable lines. The latter occur in lyrical-romantic epics and reflect the influence of Persian poetic traditions.

PERFORMANCE

Epic performance is still a living tradition in many parts of Central Asia, especially among the historically nomadic Kazakhs, Kyrgyz, Turkmen, and Karakalpaks, who preserve rich oral traditions. Until the early twentieth century, the performance of epic was an important part of social life. Reciting epic poems required considerable time and, sometimes, special events. Kyrgyz and Kazakh bards performed parts of their epics at large gatherings and feasts such as *ash,* a memorial feast marking the one-year anniversary of a death, and wedding festivities that included many kinds of equestrian games. The singing of longer epics such as *Manas* could last for weeks. *Olonkho,* the central epic of the Sakha (Yakut) people, might require up to seven nights. Kyrgyz epic singers did not recite an entire epic from memory but improvised new verse lines without changing the main plot and sequence of stories. Every time they sang, the text was a little different. Depending on the time available and the taste and composition of the audience, singers shortened or lengthened some parts of their text. A master Kyrgyz *manaschy* such as Sayakbay Karala uulu (1894–1971) would have needed more than a month to recite the full *Manas,* consisting of three cycles (*Manas, Semetey, Seytek*) and around five hundred thousand poetic verse lines.

EPIC SINGERS

Peoples around the world use their own local terms for "epic" and "epic singer." Traditional terms that mean "epic" in Central and Inner Asia are *jomok* (Kyrgyz), *jyr* (Kazakh), *dastan* (Uzbek, Uyghur), *dessan* (Turkmen), and *olonkho* (Yakut). Kazakhs call their epic singers *jyrau,* while Uzbeks call them *bakhshi,* Uyghurs use the terms *dastanchi or mäddah,* and Turkmen use *bagshy.* Karakalpaks use both *jyrau* and *baqsy* as well as another term, *qyssakhan,* to designate different kinds of epic singers. In the past, Kyrgyz called their epic singers *jomokchu*: "storyteller." During the Soviet period Kyrgyz scholars mostly focused on the recording and study of the epic *Manas* and introduced a new term, *manaschy* (singer of the epic *Manas*), to describe oral poets who recited this particular epic. Among Kyrgyz epics, *Manas* is the only one that is traditionally recited without the accompaniment of a musical instrument, though nowadays, younger performers have begun to perform *Manas* with instrumental accompaniment. All other Kyrgyz epics are sung to the

accompaniment of the *komuz,* a three-stringed plucked lute. Among the Kazakhs, *jyrau*s perform epic verse to the accompaniment of the *dombyra,* a two-stringed long-necked lute.

It is said that in the past, there was no distinction between an epic singer and a shaman or *bakshy.* Nowadays the word *bakshy* (and its cognates, *bakhshi, bagshy, baqsy*) has two different meanings among Central Asian Turkic peoples. Among the Kyrgyz and Kazakhs, a *bakshy* or *baqsy* is a traditional healer (also a fortune-teller) who heals with the help of spirits and neither sings epic songs nor performs any other musical repertoire. Among the Uzbeks and Karakalpaks, the primary meaning of *bakhshi/baqsy* is just the opposite: an epic singer, not a healer. Over time, two separate professions, singer and healer, developed from the same cultural practice. The initiatory dreams and visions common among both epic singers and healers in Eurasia affirm the original connection. Both epic singers and *bakhshy*s claim that they received their original inspiration for singing and healing from a spiritual power. Before becoming a singer or healer, both kinds of practitioners typically experience some kind of psychological or physical illness from which they cannot find relief. Relief comes in the form of a dream in which they are called by an elder sage or epic hero (in the case of epic singers), or by the spirit-masters of animals, fire, rivers, mountains, and so on (for shamans), to either sing an epic or take up a healing practice. Another element that links epic singers and shamans is the practice of going into "trance" during performance. Scholars have noted that despite epic singers' claims of receiving a spiritual calling from above, all bards train and practice before they perform in front of an audience.[6] Mastery of epic performance arts evidently requires a felicitous combination of innate talent, strong inspiration offered by older performers or mentors, and, like all performance arts, practice and experience in front of a live audience.

NOTES

1. *Kojojash* (Bishkek: Sham Press, 1996), 6.

2. *Quda* is a Turkic and Mongol traditional term of address used for and between the fathers of a married couple.

3. Francis Woodman Cleaves, tr. and ed., *The Secret History of the Mongols* (London; Cambridge, Mass.: Harvard University Press, 1982), 15.

4. *Manas: Kyrgyz elinin baatyrdyk eposu. Sayakbay Karalaevdin varianty boiuncha* [*Manas: The heroic epic of the Kyrgyz people. Version by Sayakbay Karalaev*], 4 vols. (Bishkek: "Kyrgyzstan" basmasy, 1995), vol. 1: 105–106.

5. Ibid., 108.

6. Theodore Levin with Valentina Süzükei, *Where Rivers and Mountains Sing: Sound, Music, and Nomadism in Tuva and Beyond* (Bloomington: Indiana University Press, 2006), 171.

CHAPTER 4   The Kyrgyz Epic *Manas*

ELMIRA KÖCHÜMKULOVA

Kyrgyz widely view the monumental epic *Manas* as the most treasured expression of their national heritage.[1] Composed entirely in oral form by generations of bards both well known and anonymous, *Manas* represents the epitome of Kyrgyz oral creativity and the summit of the Kyrgyz spiritual world.[2] The origins of *Manas* are unknown, but scholars have proposed that the oldest layers of the epic are rooted in traditional funeral laments (*koshok*) that glorified the life and deeds of heroes (see chapter 12). Some Kyrgyz scholars believe that a singer named Yramandyn Yrchy uul (the singer son of Yraman), who serves as one of the forty companions of the hero Manas in certain episodes of the epic, might have composed such a lament for a well-known historical hero whose life story and heroic deeds later became the contents of an epic song, and eventually developed into the epic *Manas*.[3]

THE *MANAS* TRILOGY

Manas is a biographical cycle that chronicles three generations of heroes: Manas, his son Semetey, and his grandson Seytek. Some sixty versions of the *Manas* trilogy, recorded from various epic singers and oral poets, exist at present. The longest version of the trilogy, at five hundred thousand poetic lines, is almost twenty times longer than *The Iliad* (15,693 lines) and *The Odyssey* (12,110 lines) together, and two and a half times as long as the Indian epic *Mahabharata*.[4] *Manas* should not only be recognized for its vast size but valued for its exceptionally vivid poetic language and rich content. The size of the epic reflects the compositional process of extemporization, which is the main creative tool of Kyrgyz poets and epic singers. Oral composition and extemporized performance allow singers to add their own poetic verse lines without changing the main plot of the story. One singer may describe a battle scene in fifty verse lines while another singer describes the same scene in a hundred or more lines, depending on the extent of his historical and cultural knowledge, improvisational skill, and the reaction of his audience. For this reason, the sixty-odd versions of *Manas* are all different lengths.

The plot of the *Manas* trilogy consists of the following principal episodes:

I. *Manas*
- Birth of Manas and his childhood
- First heroic deeds
- Marriage to Kanykey
- Military campaign against Beijing
- Death of Manas; destruction of his achievements

II. *Semetey*
- Kanykey's flight to Bukhara
- Semetey's childhood and his heroic deeds
- Semetey's return to Talas
- Semetey's marriage to Aychürök
- Semetey's battle against Kongurbay
- Semetey's death or mysterious disappearance

III. *Seytek*
- Destruction of Semetey's family; capture of Aychürök and Külchoro
- Seytek's upbringing in Kyiaz's palace
- Battles against internal enemies
- Seytek's marriage
- Seytek's defeat of external enemies and his own death[5]

The birth of Manas.

Illustration by Theodore Herzen for an edition of the *Manas* published in the late 1950s.

THE HERO *MANAS*

Medieval accounts of Central Asian history written in Persian, Chinese, Mongolian, and Old Uyghur chronicle many wars and battles between the Kyrgyz and other nomadic groups, as well as between the Kyrgyz and their sedentary-dwelling neighbors. The Kyrgyz regarded Kalmyks, Mongols, Manchus, and Chinese as traditional enemies. In difficult times, when the Kyrgyz were defeated by their enemies and exiled to faraway lands, people longed for a hero (*baatyr*) to reunite and protect them. Manas represents an archetype of such a hero. The archetype, however, is purely a literary creation, since no credible

Manas, the archetypal hero.

Illustration by Theodore Herzen for an edition of the *Manas* published in the late 1950s.

evidence of his historical existence has ever been found. Some Kyrgyz scholars, however, claim Genghis Khan to be a prototype of Manas. The Mongolian epic chronicle *The Secret History of the Mongols* contains one of the traditional themes of heroic epic song, the birth of the hero, Genghis Khan: "At the moment when he was born, he was holding in his right hand a clot of blood the size of a knuckle bone."[6] A similar theme is found in *Manas,* where the baby Manas is also born with a clot of blood in his hand. The wise man Akbalta brings the happy news to Manas's father, Jakyp, and describes Manas's birth:

> When your Manas came out [from the womb]
> He landed straight on his feet!
> In his right hand, khan Manas
> Came out holding a clot of black blood . . .

HISTORICAL SIGNIFICANCE

The rich interweaving of sociocultural and historical realities in *Manas* makes it difficult to divide the events of the epic into historical periods. According to Kyrgyz scholars who contributed to the *Manas Encyclopedia,* published in 1995, some of the motifs and themes, as well as the human characters, in the epic seem to have already been established in the Old Turkic period, i.e., fifth to eighth centuries CE, and reflect religious beliefs and customs of that time.[7] However, the epic also

The core geographical region in *Manas* is the territory of present-day Kazakhstan, Kyrgyzstan, the Altai Mountains, and western China.

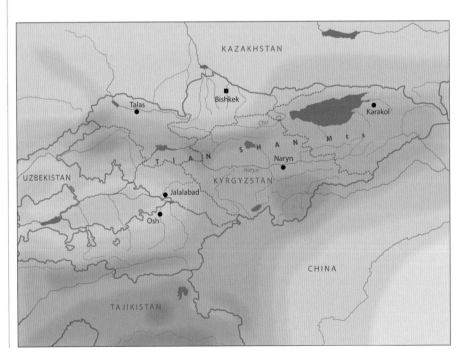

chronicles wars and battles between nomadic Turks and Kalmyks in the sixteenth and seventeenth centuries; indeed, the Kalmyks are depicted as traditional enemies in all Central Asian Turkic epics. *Manas* contains significant historical and sociocultural information about both the Kyrgyz and the nomadic and sedentary neighbors, tribes, states, and empires with which they historically interacted. We learn a great deal about the religious beliefs and practices of the Chinese, Kalmyks, and Manchus as well as about their military dress, arms, and strategies.

GEOGRAPHIC SCOPE OF *MANAS*

The geography covered in *Manas* is vast. The epic encompasses the entire Eurasian continent, extending all the way from the Caucasus and Crimea to Japan.[8] Tibet, the Himalayas, India, Mecca, and various North African countries all appear in the epic. The core geographical regions in *Manas,* however, are the territories of present-day Kazakhstan, the Altai Mountains, China, and Inner Asia.[9] Reciters not only mention these places but describe in some detail their flora and fauna. The version of *Manas* recorded from Sagymbay Orozbak uulu (1867–1930) contains over five hundred geographical place names and the names of over a hundred ethnic groups, most of which have been historically documented. Epic singers were also knowledgeable about geological events and demographic shifts, and recount such phenomena in *Manas:*

> The mountains fell apart, turning into ravines,
> Ravines shook, turning into mountains.
> Many seas became extinct
> Leaving only their names behind.
> Every fifty years, people were new,
> Every hundred years the earth was renewed.

DOCUMENTING *MANAS*

Modern scholarly documentation of Kyrgyz oral literature began in the second half of the nineteenth century with the Kazakh ethnographer Shoqan Valikhanov, who traveled among the Issyk-Kul Kyrgyz in the 1850s. Documentation continued with the work of German-Russian scholar Vasily Radlov, who conducted ethnographic research among the Kyrgyz in the 1860s. These two men recorded some of the main episodes of *Manas* and published them in Russian and German. In 1903, as part of the scholarly expeditions carried out by members of the Russian Geographical Society, several Russian scholars came to the Kyrgyz, recorded episodes from the *Manas* trilogy, and published their translations in a Russian-language prose edition.

Intensive documentation of Kyrgyz folklore, especially epic songs, dates from the early 1920s, when the new Soviet government began to implement policies that developed distinct national identities rooted in local languages and cultures for non-Russian peoples throughout the Soviet Union. A long version of *Manas* was transcribed from the recitation of Sagymbay Orozbak uulu, and the first sound recording of a *Manas* reciter was made after World War II. Transcription of the five-hundred-thousand–line version of *Manas* performed by Sayakbay Karala uulu began in 1936 and ended in 1947. By that time, as the singer himself noted, he could no longer recite the epic as well as he had in his younger years. The original text of Sayakbay's version was never fully published during the Soviet period, and when eventually it was, in 1995, the editors omitted many repetitions, stories, and perceived shortcomings.[10]

RECITATION STYLE OF *MANAS*

In contrast to other Kyrgyz and Turkic epic songs, *Manas* is not sung, but recited—primarily by men—without musical accompaniment.[11] The absence of an instrumental accompaniment in *Manas* recitation must be related to the fact that the singers use their hands to make all kinds of gestures and movements, and their hands must be free for that purpose. The Kyrgyz do not say that they "sing" *Manas* (*Manas yrda*) but rather that they "recite" *Manas* (*Manas ayt*). Moreover, the recitation of *Manas* involves not only reciting but acting. If the reciter describes a battle, he vividly recreates that scene for his audience. If he describes a horse race, he tries to give a sense of the race with his body movements and hand gestures. If he depicts a tragic scene—for example, the death of a hero—he expresses that by singing laments and crying, sometimes with actual tears. In other words, the reciter acts out the epic by speaking in the voice of each character.

All singers, including epic singers, were traditionally called *yrchy* (derived from *yr*: "song"). The term *jomokchu,* "storyteller" (derived from *jomok,* "story" or "folktale") was also applied to epic singers. Such singers typically had a broad repertory that included folktales, wisdom poetry, improvised poems performed in the context of an *aitysh* (improvised poetry contest), and epic songs and *dastan*s (long poems) sung to the accompaniment of a *komuz*. In Soviet times, the development and professionalization of Kyrgyz folk music resulted in the emergence of different types of musicians, such as the *tökmö aqyn* or *yrchy* (improvising oral poet and singer), *aqyn* (poet who writes poetry), *dastanchy* (singer of *dastan*s), and *manaschy* (reciter of *Manas* or the *Manas* trilogy).[12] Their exclusive focus on *Manas* was a result of the strong national overtones that came to be associated with the epic.

Master performers of *Manas* traditionally had their own apprentice. Apprentices typically memorized a few episodes from the main stories. Later, if they possessed the gift of improvisation, they added their own words and innovations. In the conventional performance practice of *Manas,* singers do not recite the entire epic. Rather, they recite separate episodes, such as the "Birth and Childhood of Manas," "Manas's Marriage to Kanykey," "Kanykey's Horse Race on Taytoru," "The Great Campaign to Beijing," and so on.

> **WATCH** **Example 4.1.** Urkash Mambetaliev recites the episode "Chong Kazat" (The Great Campaign) from *Manas.* Filmed by Nurlanbek Nyshanov, Bishkek, Kyrgyzstan, 2011.

This video clip presents Urkash Mambetaliev (1935–2011), one of the last of the older generation of *manaschy*s in Kyrgyzstan.[13] Here, he recites an excerpt from a major episode in the epic *Manas,* "Chong Kazat" (The Great Campaign), in which the hero Manas leads his troops to Beijing to fight against the Chinese and their ruler-hero, Kongurbay. The warriors fight many days and many nights, and Manas and Kongurbay engage in a spear fight (*er saiysh*) in which each man tries to knock the other off his horse and kill him. The video excerpt begins where the hero Manas spots the enemy leader, Kongurbay Khan, trying to escape by crossing a river on his horse Algara.

Urkash Mambetaliev.
Courtesy of Urkash Mambetaliev.

Manas reaches Kongurbay and rips off Algara's tail as Kongurbay crosses the river. Humiliated without his tail, the horse Algara wants to die heroically and tells Kongurbay to fight back against Manas. The two men test their strength by vying to see who can smash a giant rock.

The text for this example is available on the companion website.

STUDY QUESTIONS

How would you describe the performance style of *manaschy* Urkash Mambetaliev?

1. What techniques does the performer use to hold his audience's interest?

2. Most *manaschys* go into a deep trance state during their performance. Did you observe such a state in the performance of Urkash Mambetaliev?

3. Without the English translation, would you have been able to guess from the singer's gestures, facial expressions, emotions, and tone what kind of stories and scenes he is describing?

MANASCHYS AND THEIR VISIONARY DREAM

Great *manaschy*s such as Sayakbay Karala uulu usually did not acknowledge that they learned *Manas* by serving as an apprentice to a master reciter. What was important for *manaschy*s was the spiritual transformation that came as a result of a visionary dream (*tüsh* or *ayan*) in which the *manaschy* was visited by the hero Manas himself, or by other main characters in the epic. In the case of Sayakbay, the visionary dream came when he was in his early twenties. The transformational role of a dream in initiating the career of *manaschy*s resonates with the accounts of *bakshy*s or shamans who frequently speak of having experienced episodes of debilitating physical illness or psychological trauma that led to treatments by traditional healers or doctors. In these accounts, the treatments are unsuccessful and the illness persists until the future *bakshy* has an unusual dream that provides a sign to take up the "profession" of shamanizing in order to effect a cure. Having overcome his or her own illness, the *bakshy* tacitly accepts a responsibility to heal others. Following is a summary of the initiatic dream of *manaschy* Sayakbay Karala uulu that appears in the *Manas Encyclopedia:*

> On his way from Semiz-Bel to Orto-Tokoy, Sayakbay saw a white yurt where there used to be an old big black rock. He became frightened from a loud noise that came from the sky, and fainted. He then woke up and entered the yurt, where he was offered food by Kanykey, the wife of Manas. When he came out from the yurt he met a man who told Sayakbay that he was happy that he and his companions had encountered him on their way to Beijing:

> Causing a great calamity in the world,
> With about forty or fifty *tümön*[14] of an army
> We are going on a war campaign
> To far away and hazy Beijing.

He then told Sayakbay: "I am Bakay, who finds his way in the dark and comes up with words of wisdom when they're needed. I want to give you the *gülazyk*[15] of Manas. Open your mouth." He then introduced some of the forty companions of Manas. Bakay's putting food in Sayakbay's mouth signifies the idea of receiving the gift of singing from the wise man, Bakay.[16]

A contemporary example of a *manaschy* who traces his poetic inspiration to dreams is Rysbek Jumabaev. In Rysbek's account, visionary dreams were connected to episodes of illness. Becoming a reciter of *Manas* cured his illness and gave him a way to respond to the visions in his dreams. Rysbek described these occurrences in a 2003 interview with Theodore Levin.

WATCH **Example 4.2.** Rysbek Jumabaev recites from *Manas*. Filmed by Saodat Ismailova and Carlos Casas, 2004.

It all began when I was eleven and had a dream in which the famous *manaschy* Sayakbay recited the *Manas*. My father knew some episodes from the *Manas,* and when I was four years old, Sayakbay came to my house and blessed me so that I would become a *manaschy*. I started performing at small gatherings when I was sixteen. Then, in 1983, I started having stomachaches. I couldn't eat, I couldn't sleep. I went to various doctors and they gave me drugs, but nothing helped. I had stopped reciting *Manas* because there weren't any invitations. Finally, I went to a clairvoyant who lives in Karakol—his name is Mirbek—and asked why I had fallen into this state. Mirbek said that I had become ill because I had stopped reciting. He told me that I had to go to an ancient poplar tree near my home, slaughter a sheep as an offering, spend the night there, and rededicate myself to *Manas*. I took seven people with me. We slaughtered a lamb and boiled it. During the night, while I slept, my companions were awakened by a tremendous whooshing noise coming from the mountains. They woke me up, and I heard it, too. I couldn't believe my ears. My companions said that it was the sound of a spirit. I don't know, it was some kind of sign from God that a road was being opened. Soon after that, a film crew came and filmed me. And I had more dreams in which I saw Sayakbay reciting *Manas* in a beautiful form—one of the largest parts of *Manas*—and in the dream, Manas's forty knights came to me. I married and had children. I had three girls, and after I started to recite, I had a son. I answered the call of God and was rewarded. I named my son Syrghak, one of the main characters in the epic.[17]

Rysbek Jumabaev became a reciter of *Manas* to cure his illness and to respond to the visions in his dreams.
Courtesy of Theodore Levin.

STUDY QUESTIONS

1. What aspects of theater do you see in Rysbek's performance?
2. In what ways is it similar to and different from the performance style of Urkash Mambetaliev?

Sayakbay Manaschy, the "Homer of the Twentieth Century"

Kyrgyz epic singer Sayakbay Karala uulu, 1894–1971.

Sayakbay Karala uulu (1894–1971), whom the Kyrgyz call the "Homer of the twentieth century," was one of the last great *manaschy*s from whom the *Manas* trilogy—*Manas, Semetey,* and *Seytek*—was recorded. Altogether, Sayakbay's individual performance of the trilogy contained half a million verse lines. Sayakbay was born in the Issyk-Kul region of northern Kyrgyzstan. His family was poor, and they had to work for wealthy Kyrgyz to earn their living. Sayakbay began reciting *Manas* when he was around sixteen. Sayakbay heard the main stories of *Manas* from his grandmother, who probably narrated the epic in prose mixed with poetry.[18] People, including foreigners, who saw and listened to Sayakbay's recitation of *Manas* were very moved by his powerful spirit and great artistic talent. During his recitation, Sayakbay made his listeners cry and laugh. Listeners recounted that "while he was singing, we not only saw him before us, but pictured the epic's characters as well."[19] Chingiz Aitmatov compared Sayakbay's singing to a symphony orchestra: "Sayakbay was not only an oral poet, but a great artist and composer. Like a symphony orchestra, he varied and changed his voice a thousand times. He moved from tragedy to lyrical songs, from lyrics he moved to drama, then within a short time he burst into tears, then became joyful, then tired, then became energetic again. Sometimes he sounded like a teeming army of soldiers, sometimes he became as calm as a lake, and sometimes he became like a fast and strong wind, and rushed like a river."[20]

Watch

Example 4.3. Sayakbay Karala uulu recites excerpts from *Manas*. Filmed by Melis Ubukeev, around 1970.

These short excerpts from Sayakbay's recitation give you a chance to see his performance style, which he varies according the theme of the story he is telling. Here Sayakbay recites the episode where the hero Manas returns from one of his battles against the Chinese without his close companions, who were killed in the battle. According to Kyrgyz custom, Manas approaches the yurt of one of the deceased men by crying aloud (*oküruü*) to give the men's wives a sign that their husbands are dead.

Ayash,	Ayash,[21]
Kötörböskö chara jok.	You have no choice but to accept your fate.
Kok jaldardan ayrylyp,	I lost my brave men [in the battle].
Kongülsüz kalgan beybaktyn,	You, the grief-stricken widow,
Köt jakta erkek bala jok.	Carry no child-son from him in your womb.
Toodogu jylky toguz san,	Herds of mares consisting of great gallopers and amateur racing horses
Toburchak buudan aralash.	Are now left on their own on the mountains.
Toburchak külük beesi jok,	Now, these stallions will go astray
Tosup ele alar eesi jok.	Without an owner who waits for them.
Adyrda jylky alty san,	Herds of mares consisting of great gallopers and amateur racing horses
Argymak buudan aralash.	Are now left on their own on the hills.
Argymak külük beesi jok,	Now, these stallions and racing horses will go astray,
Aydap ele koyor eesi jok.	Without an owner who looks after them.
Karangy tün boldu,	A dark night fell upon us.
Emne degen kün boldu?	What will we do now [without him]?
Dep oshondo chyrkyrap,	The widows began crying and screaming.
Eki aiym yilap burkurap,	Shedding tears
Kosho chykty kök jalga,	The two ladies approached the gray-maned [Manas].
Atangdyn körü dünüyö,	Damn this world, the grave of your father.[22]
Ayashjan,	Dear ayash,
Belesi biyik Beejindi	We know that you had warned us that Beijing was far away and difficult to reach.
Besh künchülük jol deding,	You had told us that it was a five-day journey
Beejindin jaiy kor deding.	And that Beijing was a dangerous place to go.
Baygambar baspas Beejindin,	We learned about this land where the feet of the Prophet [Muhammad] had not walked
Kazyp koygon orlorun,	And the dungeons that they had dug
Kaynatyluu shorlorun,	To make their captives suffer.
Ulamadan uladym.	We learned these things from a learned religious man.
Kayguulga baryp kelipsing,	You came back from the battle,
Janyngda jürgön jarandy	Leaving the men who went with you,
Jandashyp jürgön karaandy	Who always accompanied you
Kaynap atkan Kakanga, ayash	To the teeming Kakans [Chinese], ayash,
Belekke karmap beripsing	As a gift
Berenim, ayashjan, esen kelipsing.	My dear, brave ayash, you returned home safely.

1. How would you compare Sayakbay's recitation style with that of Urkash Mambetaliev in example 4.1 and Rysbek Jumabaev in example 4.2?

2. From Sayakbay's tone, gestures, and emotions, can you guess the theme of the story he is narrating?

3. Identify the poetic features of his verse lines by underlining the initial and internal alliterations and end rhyme.

MANAS IN CONTEMPORARY KYRGYZSTAN

A statue in front of Bishkek's Philharmonic Hall presents Manas holding a sword and accompanied by a dragon, the hero's guardian during his military campaigns.

Courtesy of Theodore Levin.

During the Soviet era, official culture policy portrayed the heroic epics of non-Russian peoples as a potential threat to the Soviet system, because they glorified the history of these peoples and carried powerful messages that could awaken people's pride in their national identity, history, and culture. As was the case with many other non-Russian heroic epics, *Manas* was condemned as "bourgeois-nationalist" and "religious" in its content. All of the published texts of *Manas* that appeared during the Soviet period were heavily edited and sanitized redactions designed to conform to the ideological mandate of Soviet nationalities policy and Socialist Realist aesthetics: to develop art, music, and literature that was "nationalist in form and socialist in content."

Following the breakup of the Soviet Union, Kyrgyzstan's first president, Askar Akaev (1991–2005), used some of the central ideas of *Manas* as a basis for building a new national ideology for independent Kyrgyzstan.[23] This ideology promoted a national awakening and cultural revival in which *Manas* played a leading role. Since independence, *Manas* has been taught in schools and universities, and children as young as four and five—typically boys but sometimes girls as well—recite from memory dozens of lines from popular episodes such as "The Childhood of Manas" or the miraculous "Birth of Manas." Some have become *manaschy*s themselves, whether amateur or professional, and major national celebrations of Kyrgyz culture often feature performances by young *manaschy*s. The Kyrgyz Ministry of Culture organizes annual *manaschy* competitions in Bishkek with the aim of discovering, supporting, and motivating new talent as well as preserving the oral transmission of the epic. Several talented and dedicated *manaschy*s, such as Rysbay Isakov and Samat Köchörbaev, each with his own particular recitation style, have performed abroad with other Kyrgyz musicians, including in the United States. Today's *manaschy*s are building on existing oral tradition by adapting it to a new social context and to contemporary musical tastes. Examples 4.4 and 4.5 show two young *manaschy*s. Rysbay Isakov performs not in the traditional style of a cappella solo recitation but with an instrumental background provided by an ensemble. Samat Köchörbaev has a charismatic style that has become popular among young audiences.

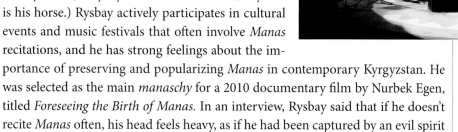

WATCH **Example 4.4.** Rysbay Isakov recites excerpts from *Manas* with music by Ensemble Ordo-Sakhna. Recording courtesy of Ensemble Ordo-Sakhna.

Rysbay Isakov and Ensemble Ordo-Sakhna.
Courtesy of Ordo-Sakhna.

This example shows a recitation by *manaschy* Rysbay Isakov (b. 1975) within the context of a concert performance in Bishkek by the folk-ethnographic ensemble Ordo-Sakhna. Rysbay has a distinctive recitation style, high vocal tone, and clear voice. In 2007, he won first prize in the national *Manas* recitation competition in Kyrgyzstan by reciting the popular episode "Kanikey's Long-distance Horse Race on Taytoru" (Kanykey is the wife of Manas; Taytoru is his horse.) Rysbay actively participates in cultural events and music festivals that often involve *Manas* recitations, and he has strong feelings about the importance of preserving and popularizing *Manas* in contemporary Kyrgyzstan. He was selected as the main *manaschy* for a 2010 documentary film by Nurbek Egen, titled *Foreseeing the Birth of Manas*. In an interview, Rysbay said that if he doesn't recite *Manas* often, his head feels heavy, as if he had been captured by an evil spirit (*jin*), and that he feels better after reciting *Manas*.

Since 2005, Rysbay has made three visits to the United States with Ensemble Ordo-Sakhna. Created in 1999 and directed by Shamil Japarov, Ordo-Sakhna aims to revive traditional forms of Kyrgyz folk art and music and adapt them to contemporary styles and tastes. Rysbay's recitation of "Kanykey's Long-distance Horse Race on Taytoru" has been a highlight of Ordo-Sakhna's concert program.

Upon the death of the hero Manas, Kanykey, Manas's wife, flees to Bukhara with her baby son, Semetey, and her old mother-in-law, Chyiyrdy, to live with her

1. In your view, how successful is Rysbay Isakov and Ordo-Sakhna's adaptation of *Manas* recitation to performance by an ensemble? Does Ordo-Sakhna's musical accompaniment enhance the performance or distract from the narrative and the *manaschy* himself?

2. *Manaschys* were not traditionally accompanied by drums. Do you view Ordo-Sakhna's use of drumming as an interesting innovation, or is it artistically gratuitous?

WATCH

Example 4.5. Samat Köchörbaev recites the episode "Semetey's Encounter with Sary Taz" from the epic *Semetey* in the *Manas* trilogy. Filmed by Nurlanbek Nyshanov, Bishkek, Kyrgyzstan, 2011.

Samat Köchörbaev.
Courtesy of Samat Köchörbaev.

father, Temirkhan. Little Semetey grows up in Bukhara without knowing the true story of his father and fatherland, Talas, until he reaches the age of twelve. One day, the twelve-year-old Semetey, while hunting with birds, encounters a coal miner named Sary Taz in the forest. When Semetey throws his falcon to capture a pheasant, the pheasant escapes into Sary Taz's small tent. Following the pheasant, the falcon flies into the tent. Semetey rudely asks Sary Taz to hand his falcon over to him. Sary Taz grows angry at Semetey's rude behavior and tells him that he does not belong there and that he should go to his own people and land in Talas.

Tokoyung talaa jer emes,	This forest is not a field for you to play,
Atang Manas kök jaldyn	I'm not Kongurbay kalcha who killed
Öpkösün jaryp öltürgön,	Your gray-maned father Manas
Kongurbay Kalcha men emes.	By smashing his lung.
Belingdi bekem buup al,	Tie your waist tight [be strong and ready]
Beren bolsong sen jetim,	If you are brave, you, the orphan,
Atangdyn moysop tashtagan	Take the revenge of your father's blood
Kara kytay kan Kongur	From Kongurbay of the Kara Kytay [Chinese]
Oshondon kunung kuup al.	Who killed your father.
O, atangdyn körü dünüyö,	Oh, damn this world!
Bu tokoy saga jer emes,	This forest is not your land and
Enekengdin emchegin	I'm not Abyke and Köbösh
Jara chaap kachyrgan	Who made your mother flee
Abyke, Köbösh men emes.	By slashing her breast.
Temirge belong bump al	Tie your waist tight like an iron,
Tentigen maga katylbay,	You, the vagabond, don't dare to hurt me!
Kara kytay Kongurbay	Instead, take your father's blood revenge

	From Kongurbay of the Kara Kytay [Chinese].
Oshondun kunung kuup al.	Damn this world!
Atangdyn körü dünüyö,	There is no other thing than a breeze
Shamal jokto temingen	That blows when there is no wind.
Jeldey baykush bar beken?	There is no unfortunate person like yourself,
Enesin ejem dep jürgön,	Who is the adopted son of Temirkhan and
Temirkandyn bakmasy,	Who calls his own mother a sister.
Sendey baykush bar beken?	Damn this world!
Atangdyn körü dünüyö,	There is no one like me,
Kömürchü bolup sendelip,	A destitute coal miner
Körüngöndön til ukkan,	Who is reproached by everyone.
Mendey baykush bar beken?	You, who calls his mother a sister,
Enesin ejem dep jürgön	The adopted son of Temirkhan,
Temirkandyn bakmasy	Damn you, the slave-orphan!
Atangdyn körü jetim kul,	Oh, no!
A, kokuy,	There is no unfortunate person like yourself.
Sendey gana baykush	
bar beken, uuuuu.	
Sary Tazdan kep ugup,	Hearing these words from Sary Taz
Myna oshondo bereging,	At that moment,
Jering Talas dep ugup,	Learning that his land is Talas,
Ugup alyp sabylyp,	He was shaken,
Közünün jashy on talaa.	Tears poured from his eyes,
Myna oshondo bereging,	At that moment,
Kömürchügo jalynyp,	He begged the coal miner:
Aylanaiyn Sary aba,	Dear uncle Sary,
Emne deding balaga?	What did you just say to me, the boy?
Tuybagandy tuyguzdung,	You told me what I didn't know.
Tuura janym sadaga.	I'm ready to die for you.
Kel abake kolungdu,	Give me your hand
Ushul sözüng chyn bolso,	If these words of yours are indeed true,
Körgözömün közüngö,	I will show you
Kishi körbös sonundu.	Great things that no man has seen before.
A düynö ketken sher Manas,	The lion Manas, who left for the other world,
Ata ekeni chyn bolso,	If he is indeed my father,
Baykush katyn Kanykey,	The poor woman, Kanykey,
Ene ekeni chyn bolso,	If she is indeed my mother,
Esen körsöm Talasty,	If I get to see Talas
Argyn menen kyrgyzga,	I will hold a great feast
Shang kötörüp alamyn.	For the Argyn and Kyrgyz [people] there.
Atamday körüp abake,	I will treat you like my father and
Kalyng kyrgyz kalkyna,	Elect you a khan
Kan kötörüp alamyn.	For all the Kyrgyz people.
Aytkanymdy kylbasam,	If I don't carry out what I have told,

Töbösü achyk Kök ursun!	May I be cursed by the Blue Sky which has an open top!
Töshü tuktüü Jer ursun!	May I be cursed by the Earth with a hairy chest!
Atagy ursun Talastyn!	May I be cursed by the fame of Talas!
Arbagy ursun Manastyn!	May I be cursed by the spirit of Manas!

STUDY QUESTIONS

1. How would you compare Samat Köchörbaev's recitation to the recitations of the two older *manaschys* in video examples 4.1 and 4.2?

2. What aspect of his performance style do you find particularly interesting?

3. What difference would it have made for Samat if the recitation had been performed before a live audience?

4. Some people find the *Manas* recitation boring and thus cannot listen to it for too long. Could you share your experiences of listening to these or other recitations of *Manas* by various *manaschys*?

WATCH

Example 4.6. Kulmat Sydykov recites the episode "Kanykeydin Taytorunu chapkany" (Kanykey's horse race on Taytoru) from *Manas*. Filmed by Nurlanbek Nyshanov, Bishkek, Kyrgyzstan, 2011.

Kulmat Sydykov.
Courtesy of Kulmat Sydykov.

This example, recited by the young *manaschy* Kulmat Sydykov, presents one of the popular episodes of *Manas* called "Kanykeydin Taytorunu chapkany" (Kanykey's long-distance horse race on Taytoru). Kulmat is best known in Kyrgyzstan as a *dastanchy*—a singer of *dastans*—since his repertoire consists mainly of Kyrgyz long poems (*dastan*s) and he sings to the accompaniment of a *komuz*. Like Rysbay Isakov he has a distinctive voice, and he likes to recite this popular episode from the *Manas*.

The episode takes place after Manas's death, upon which his widow Kanykey flees to Bukhara with her baby Semetey and mother-in-law Chyiyrdy. Once in Bukhara, Kanykey decides to participate in a major long-distance horse race and feast organized by her father Temirkhan, the ruler of Bukhara, in honor of twelve-year-old Semetey.[24] Semetey grows up in Bukhara with his maternal grandfather Temirkhan without knowing the identity of his real father and mother. Kanykey, whom Semetey calls a sister, waits until Semetey reaches the age of twelve to tell him the truth. She risks her and Manas's dignity by committing her old horse Taytoru to the race with the intention that, if Taytoru wins, she will tell Semetey the truth about his father and fatherland, Talas.

Long-distance horse races were a central feature of traditional life among the nomadic Kyrgyz, with the horses ridden by young boys and sometimes girls. All the praise and fame, however, usually went to the owner and trainer of the race-horses. As the owner of Taytoru, Kanykey waits desperately for the horses to reach the finish line, watching the horses from a distance through binoculars to see how Taytoru is placing in the race.

The text for this example is available on the companion website.

NOTES

This chapter first appeared in a somewhat different form on the website of the The Silkroad Foundation (http://www.silkroadfoundation.org/toc/index.html) and in *ECI Cultural Magazine* (www.ecieco.org) 2 (Fall/Winter 2006–2007): 58–61.

1. The epic *Manas* is also found among ethnic Kyrgyz living in China's Xinjiang Uyghur Autonomous Region, and a version of the epic has been published in a Chinese translation. In 2009, UNESCO inscribed the epic *Manas* in the Representative List of the Intangible Cultural Heritage of Humanity on behalf of the People's Republic of China. China's initiative provoked protests in Kyrgyzstan, whose Ministry of Culture petitioned UNESCO to reconsider the inscription.

2. In summer 1995, with the support of UNESCO, Kyrgyzstan celebrated the one thousandth anniversary of Manas in the northern mountainous region of Talas, which is believed to be the homeland of the eponymous legendary hero. The government of Kyrgyzstan proudly presented nomadic history and culture to their guests by mounting a grand, open-air theatrical show that displayed the main scenes from the epic. It was the first, and remains the largest, national celebration that has taken place in Kyrgyzstan since its independence.

3. S. Musaev, *Epos Manas: nauchnopopuliarnyi ocherk* [The epic *Manas*: A scholarly-popular essay] (Frunze: Ilim, 1984), 117.

4. Ibid., 98.

5. *Manas: Kyrgyz elinin baatyrdyk eposu*. Sayakbay Karalayevdin variyanty boyuncha [*Manas*: The heroic epic of the Kyrgyz people. Version by Sayakbay Karalaev], 4 vols. (Bishkek: "Kyrgyzstan" basmasy, 1995), vol. 1: 11.

6. The 13th-century Mongolian epic chronicle *The Secret History of the Mongols* recounts the origin and history of the Mongols and builds stories around the life of Genghis Khan and his empire.

7. *Manas Entsiklopediyasy* [The *Manas* encyclopedia] (Bishkek: Izd-vo Glavnoi redaktsii Kyrgyzskoi entsiklopedii, 1995), 9.

8. Ibid., 16.

9. Ibid., 432.

10. Karalaev, 6.

11. There have been some female singers, for example, Seyde ene, from whom some episodes were recorded during the Soviet period.

12. Some performers recited only the stories of the epic *Semetey*, the second part of the *Manas* trilogy. They were called *semeteychi* (reciter of *Semetey*).

13. In 2010, Urkash Mambetaliev published his own version of the *Semetey* epic.

14. *Tümön:* a military unit consisting of ten thousand warriors.

15. *Gülazyk:* a traditional food especially prepared to take on a long journey, such as a war campaign. The equivalent of pemmican, it was made from the meat of a horse, sheep, or deer, and it kept for a long time without spoiling.

16. *Manas Entsiklopediyasy,* 185.

17. Adapted from Theodore Levin with Valentina Süzükei, *Where Rivers and Mountains Sing: Sound, Music, and Nomadism in Tuva and Beyond* (Bloomington: Indiana University Press, 2006), 189–191.

18. *Manas Entsiklopediyasy,* 185.

19. Ibid., 186

20. Ibid.

21. *Ayash:* a term of address used toward the wife or husband of a close friend.

22. This is a popular Kyrgyz curse or swearword used by men to express anger. Epic singers often insert the phrase when describing tragic events and scenes.

23. Askar Akaev, *Kyrgyzskaia gosudarstvennost' i narodnyi epos "Manas"* [Kyrgyz statehood and the folk epic *Manas*] (Bishkek: Uchkun, 2002).

24. In *Manas*, Temirkhan is presumed to represent the historical Timur (1336–1405), known in English as Tamerlane, founder of the Timurid dynasty, who traced his ancestry to the Mongol conqueror Genghis Khan.

CHAPTER 5 # Oral Epic in Kazakhstan
KÖRUGHLY AND A DYNASTY OF GREAT *JYRAUS*

ULJAN BAIBOSYNOVA

From early childhood I knew about the existence of a venerable dynasty of bardic performers called *jyrau*s. I always dreamed of becoming a *jyrau* myself, and I had the good fortune to be accepted as an apprentice (*shäkirt*) to a great master (*ustaz*) whose name is Bidas agha.[1] When I first came to my teacher, I asked him a question that had long interested me and that I had kept in the depths of my soul: "Is it true that the epic tradition you belong to is sacred and has a mysterious power?"

The master replied:

> You understand everything correctly. From our very birth, our parents constantly repeated to us: "My light (*Shyraghym*), this is a sacred art. If you do not cherish this tradition, continue it, and transmit your knowledge to the next generation, then the spirit-patron will destroy your life and it will be accompanied by bad luck." Thus, from childhood, we treated our epic art with great seriousness, and my father himself began to teach us this great art. From my father, Rüstembek jyrau, I know that my grandfather, Jienbai, had a mighty animal spirit-patron—the tiger. Once, my grandfather was returning with an entourage from a journey when he met a district governor at a crossroads. This man was older, and had a high rank. Jienbai ceded the road to him, saying: "Please pass me, Mr. Governor." But the governor replied, "No, Jienbai, you go ahead, and I will follow you." When he let Jienbai pass by him, the people who were accompanying the governor asked him: "How is this, sir? Why did you let Jienbai go first when he is younger than you and has a lower rank?" The governor replied, "What do you understand about the situation? You

simply didn't see what was happening. I didn't want to let him pass, but a huge tiger was blocking the path of my horse and I had no choice but to let him go first!"

I once witnessed how the spirit-patron came to my older brother Köshenei. It was late at night and everyone was asleep when we were awakened by a loud cry. I jumped up and saw Köshenei sitting up in bed. Our mother also heard the cry and came running. "Köshpanjan, I heard you cry out. Did something frighten you?" she asked.

"Mother, I had a bad dream. A huge tiger jumped on my back and grabbed me by the shoulders, and I woke up in fear," my brother answered. My mother was upset, but also delighted. "My dear child (*ainalaiyn*), God himself blessed you! The spirit and spiritual power of your grandfather Jienbai has been passed on to you. Congratulations! For you, the path to becoming a *jyrau* is open, and no one can stop you." From that day forward, a notable strength appeared in my brother Köshenei's voice, and he became a master performer who was much celebrated by his community. This is what it means to have a spirit-patron. Our father, Rüstembek, also had an animal spirit protector: the camel.

Only certain people are destined to become *jyrau*s. *Jyraulyq*—the art of being a *jyrau*—is an ancient tradition among many Turkic peoples that was associated with beliefs in animal spirit-patrons and ancestor spirits. The Kazakh *jyrau* was not just a performer of beautiful oral stories, but also someone who could foresee the future and foretell the outcome of events. Beginning in the fifteenth century, when Kazakh statehood was established, *jyrau*s have occupied an important position in society, serving as advisers to khans and sultans, and determining the political direction and fate of the populace. Before military battles, *jyrau*s would summon their spirit-patrons and then lead the armies of the khan to victory.

My teacher's story may seem true to some and like a beautiful fantasy to others. As for me, it offered inspiration, and I didn't want the conversation to stop. "*Agha*, tell me how your grandfather, Jienbai, raised your father, Rüstembek, and how he set him on the path to becoming a *jyrau*," I said. My *ustaz* liked the question and willingly began to recount the whole story.

Jienbai raised his son Rüstembek himself. When Rüstembek was twelve, he achieved the level of a master performer, and grandfather took Rüstembek to a big memorial feast for an important person named Shonai. This memorial feast was a gathering of clans representing all three Kazakh *jüz*.[2] On their journey to the memorial feast, they saw a single yurt standing by itself. An old woman came out and said, "This is the first melon of my new crop. Please try it." They ate the melon, and Jienbai gave his blessing to the entire harvest.

Then Jienbai put Rüstembek on a one-year-old colt and they continued their journey. When they arrived at the memorial feast, they went immediately to the huge guest yurt, where the event's honored guests had assembled. Jienbai said to them, "I want my young stallion to compete in the big competition at the horse races. The assembled guests understood that the great *jyrau* Jienbai wanted to demonstrate his young son's talent.

When Rüstembek began to sing in his ringing voice, everyone was amazed. Surprised by such talent, one of the honored elders said, "Jienbai, you must have fed your son a melon from the new harvest. His voice has incredible power!"

Kazakhs believed that the first fruits of a new harvest have special qualities—that they imbue a person with the powerful strength and energy of the awakening earth. Thus began the first performance of the twelve-year-old *jyrau,* who sang until dawn. Only as day dawned did he begin to tire. Jienbai took the *dombyra*[3] and continued performing the *Körughly* epic that his son had begun.

It seemed as if the mighty voice of Jienbai, like the roar of a camel, had lifted the yurt, and set it aloft. What actually happened was that people who could not fit inside and were sitting around the circumference of the yurt had lifted the huge yurt off the ground and carried it some distance. And that's how the *jyrau* tradition was transmitted from one generation to the next.

I had the feeling that *ustaz* Bidas agha had been carried back to that time, and I did not want to interrupt his mental peregrinations.

"Bidas agha, your father, Rüstembek, not only kept this great tradition alive, but also passed on to you a priceless heritage, didn't he?" I asked. My teacher's face glowed at my question, because he realized how deep my desire was to learn about this tradition. My *ustaz* continued his story:

Yes, *ainalaiyn,* in the same way that my grandfather Jienbai raised his son Rüstembek, my father opened the road for me and set me on this great path. When my brother Köshenei and I were children, our father taught us *maqams.*[4] He often repeated to us that we must avoid making any mistakes in the lyrics and must perform *maqams* properly. "If you do not know or are not sure of yourself, it is better not to sing at all. Do not deceive people. Remember my words," he said. I've remembered those words all my life, and that's why I've always tried to be a real *jyrau,* as my father wanted.

Far right: Bidas with Uljan Baibosynova.

Right: Bidas Rüstembekov holds a *dombyra*.

"Bidas agha, tell me about what it was like to be a *jyrau* in those days, and how people responded to your father's performances."

I often saw my father perform in front of large audiences. He was like a free-spirited falcon. One could see his proud character even from the way he sat—it seemed as if he had a higher seat than anyone else. He would put a pillow under one leg and lean on the other leg. My father sang for hours, never hunching over or getting tired. He sang one *dastan* after another. Sometimes people asked him to perform certain stories, such as *Raua banu*, *Saduaqas saqi*, *Kedei*, *Qobylandy*, and *Körughly*. It seemed as if there was hardly any epic that my father did not know.

The *jyrau* and his audience formed one single energy field, in which a martial spirit prevailed. The *jyrau* would sing, and listeners would cheer: "Go on, Rüsteke, go! Oh, well done! God has willed it (*Oi, bärekeldi! Mashallah!*)" One can easily imagine both the high professional level of the bard and the erudition of the listeners.

At long last, my teacher was ready to begin his conversation about the *Körughly* epic: "I remember my mother's stories," Bidas agha recounted, "about how my grandfather traveled and performed among the settlements (*auyl*s) of the peoples who are closely related to us—Karakalpaks, Uzbeks, and Turkmen. Jienbai ata[5] often performed together with their bards, and sang a multitude of *dastan*s, but best of all was his performance of *Körughly* (Son of the Grave). His performance had a quality of its own. Jienbai composed his own melodies (*maqam*s) for each part of the epic. At the age of twelve, in a matter of one week, my father learned the entire epic. I grew up listening to *Körughly* from earliest childhood, learned it from my father, and, when I was still a boy, tried singing it."

"Bidas agha, it makes me very happy to hear the epic from your mouth."

"It's quite a long story, but I'll tell you what I know." Modestly and slowly, my teacher began the narrative.

In medieval times, Kazakhs called the Persians Qyzylbas.[6] The king of the Persians was Shah Shaghdat, and once the shah asked his soldiers, "Is there a people on earth that is stronger and more powerful than my state?"

One of the soldiers replied, "There's a people called the Turkmen. Their country is ruled by Khan Tolybai, who is greatly respected by all the Turkmen. The people worship him like a God."

Hearing these words, Shah Shaghdat grew angry and said, "Can there really be a more powerful ruler than me!" The shah gave an order to destroy the country of the Turkmen, and sent forty thousand troops. They quickly captured the peacefully dwelling Turkmen, and seized Raushanbek, the son of Khan Tolybai.

That same night Shah Shaghdat had a dream. A strong hurricane threw him from the throne and his crown flew away with the wind. The shah awoke in fear, and gave an order to gather the entire populace. Shah Shaghdat recounted his dream and said, "If you cannot reveal the meaning of my dream, I shall have everyone put to death." The people began searching for someone who could do this, and finally they found an old woman who had lived "three-times-seventy" years. People were frightened not only by her terrible appearance, but by her predictions. The old woman proclaimed: "Raushanbek, whom you have taken captive, will have a son and that child will destroy the power of Shah Shaghdat." Terrified, Shah Shaghdat gave the order to have Raushanbek put to death, but one of the soldiers advised him: "Your Majesty, your country is so great and powerful, and your power is unassailable. Can you not abide one captive Turkmen? Sell him into slavery and get a large ransom. And in any event, how can a slave have descendants? Let him drink a cup of grief to the very bottom!" The shah agreed and ordered that Raushanbek be sold into slavery. Here is how the *dastan* recounts the selling of Raushanbek into slavery:

Raushanbekti bazar ishigä salady.	They brought Raushanbek to the market.
Qul degen song jurttyng bäri qamady.	People gathered to gaze at the slave.
Myngda bes jüz dillä deidi baghasyn,	A thousand and five-hundred *dilla* was his price,
Eshkim almai bazar tarap barady.	Nobody bought him, because the price was too high.
Berse qudai qiyn emes kisige.	God is generous and great.
Qarangyzdar sebep bolghan isine.	Look at his acts.
Jalghyz üili Türkmen jigit bar edi,	For a long time there had lived in that town,
Köpten beri sol shahardyng ishinde.	The only young married Turkmen man [Ghajdenbek].
Ol kelgeli köp bop edi elinen.	Many years had passed since he left his homeland.
Asyl tegi Türkmen elding beginen.	He was of noble birth among the Turkmen.

Jüretin edi öz eline kete almai,	He could not return to his homeland,
Maghrur bolyp dünie maldyng köbinen.	His wealth held him back.
Jylqysynyng esebimen sany joq.	He had countless horses in his herd.
Basqa dünie aqshasymen taghy köp.	He had immeasurable wealth.
Ajal jetip öle ketse mangynan,	If death overtook him,
Eshkim jürmes Qyzylbastyng maly dep.	No one would be there to receive his inheritance.
Raushanbekti bazar saldy taghy da.	Once again, Raushanbek was put up for sale.
Ghajdenbekti dushar qyldy baghyna.	Luckily for him, Ghajdenbek appeared.
Nazar salyp asylyn baiqap qarasa,	He looked at the man.
Uqsatady Türkmen elding zadyna.	The man reminded him of a man of noble Turkmen birth.
Birte-birte jaqyn bardy qasyna.	Slowly [Ghajdenbek] stepped closer to him.
Baiqap tursa Türkpen elding asylyna.	Looking again at the slave,
öz süiegin tanyghan song jany ashyp,	He reminded [Ghajdenbek] of his people.
Rahimy keldi közden aqqan jasyna.	Tears rolled down his cheeks and joy rushed back to him.
Oilap tursam qaida qalghan aghaiyn.	"Where are my people, my relatives?
Körip edim dünie maldyng talaiyn.	I am full of wealth and live in prosperity.
Köp bolghanda bir jyl paidam shyghynda,	The price for this slave is only one annual revenue.
Qazynasynan kem qylmasyn qudaiym.	May God not diminish my assets.
Elden shyghyp kelip edim jasymda.	I was young when I left my homeland.
Jalghyzdyqtyng bar qaighysy basymda.	The grief of loneliness stole my joy.
Osy dünie azdyq qylmas özime,	May the wealth that I have collected become less.
Joldas bolyp jürsin deidi qasymda.	I'll buy him and my heart will be full of joy."
Alaiyn dep jetip bardy deldalgha.	To buy, he approached the seller.
Bul qulyngdy artyq aityp puldama.	Sell me the poor slave, he said to the seller.
Deldalmenen olai bylai söilesip,	In agreeing with the seller,
Satyp aldy myngda üsh jüz dillagha.	He bought him for one thousand and three hundred *dilla*, lowering the price.

At that time Ghajdenbek was the only Turkmen living among the Qyzylbas. Ghajdenbek had a wife named Küläiim and a daughter, Aqanai. He also had a slave named Babaly. However, he had no son to continue his family lineage. Rejoicing, Ghajdenbek wed his only daughter to Raushanbek.

Once Ghajdenbek and Raushanbek went to the bazaar to look at horses. On the way to the bazaar, Raushanbek saw a horse skull on the road and stopped. Taking the skull into his hands, he wept and said, "Who could tell that once you were a real racehorse? And who could tell that I am Tolybai Khan's son? Now I am a slave in a foreign land."

One of Shah Shaghadat's viziers overheard Raushanbek say these words and quickly rushed to deliver the news to the shah. "The slave whom you sold is a real seer," said the vizier. After hearing these words, the shah ordered that Raushanbek be brought to the court, shown the shah's racehorses, and ordered to pick out the true racers. Shah Shaghdat had 250 racehorses. Raushanbek looked over the herd, but couldn't find a single horse worth racing. Suddenly he saw a poor dervish riding a long-maned bay horse (*jalbyr tory*). He said to the shah, "Here is a real racer. You can give the poor dervish all your 250 horses for a horse like his!"

The shah got very angry at Raushanbek. "Are you trying to make fun of me? You are my enemy! Gouge out the eyes that couldn't see a real racehorse in my herd," ordered the shah. With great difficulty Ghajdenbek brought Raushanbek home. Seeing the blind Raushanbek, Küläiim and Aqanai said, "Instead of enduring such humiliation from enemies, it would be better for the two of you to return to your homeland." Ghajdenbek and Raushanbek started to prepare for their journey when Raushanbek asked Ghajdenbek to take him once more to the bazaar to choose a good horse for his long journey. While walking through the market, Raushanbek heard the sound of clomping hooves and immediately recognized it as the sound of the poor dervish's long-maned bay horse. They bargained and Ghajdenbek and Raushanbek bought that horse. For forty days, Ghajdenbek looked after it. On the fortieth day, he brought the horse to Raushanbek. He stroked the horse's mane and said, "Now this horse is ready for a race." Raushanbek asked Ghajdenbek, "Please check if the horse can jump over seven barriers seven meters wide and eleven meters high that the shah built for his horses." Ghajdenbek put the horse through its paces at night, under moonlight. The horse easily jumped all the barriers. Ghajdenbek was happy to give this news to Raushanbek. Ghajdenbek and Raushanbek traveled home on their horse. As for Aqanai and Küläiim, they stayed behind and lived among the Qyzylbas, and Babaly was instructed to look after them.

Aqanai was expecting a child. The time for delivery was approaching when one day she had a dream. There were forty saints who came to see her, who predicted that forty days before giving birth she would die, and her child would be born inside the grave. Exactly as the saints predicted, Aqanai went to the other world. Her mother Küläiim and her slave, Babaly, mourned and lamented as they buried her. Forty days later, Aqanai, lying in her grave, gave birth to a baby boy. Forty saints surrounded Aqanai's grave and took the baby. They named him Körughly—Son of the Grave. Körughly grew not by the day, but by the hour. He ran around his mother's tomb and drank milk from her desiccated breasts.

Once, Babaly went to pray at Aqanai's grave. Near the grave, he saw traces of a child's footprints. The footprints led to the grave and there they

Uljan Baibosynova.
Photo by Katherine Vincent.
Courtesy of Aga Khan Music
Initiative.

disappeared. He realized that it was Aqanai's child. He ran to Küläiim to tell her the happy news about what he had seen. Küläiim did not know how to bring Aqanai's child home. Then she had a dream in which the forty saints suggested to her, "Sprinkle different sweet fruits along the path from the grave. The child will see the sweet food, pick it up and eat it, and forget about everything. In this way your wish will be fulfilled." Everything the saints told Küläiim to do she accomplished with the help of Babaly. The child came out of the grave and began to gather the fruit. When he had walked far enough away, Babaly quietly approached him from behind. As Babaly was ready to catch him, the child saw him and ran back to the grave. When he reached the grave of his mother, the entrance closed up, and Babaly and Küläiim captured the child. They took him home, and Küläiim raised him there as her own child until the age of six without allowing anyone outside the household to see him.

Once Körughly went into town and challenged a Persian boy to a game of *asyq*.[7] He beat the boy and they started fighting. The Persian boy was upset and said, "Who asked you to come out of the grave? If I tell my father how spoiled you are, you'll be thrown out of the city!" Körughly started to cry and ran to Küläiim.

"A boy insulted me," said Körughly. "Tell me who my parents are! Where do I come from? My soul is filled with sorrow. Mother, please, tell me the truth." Küläiim told him everything exactly as it had happened. She told him about the humiliation by the Qyzylbas they'd had to endure. Körughly leaped up and said, "I shall defeat our enemies and shall take revenge for all the humiliation. But first I will go back to my motherland and find my grandfather and my father." He received a blessing from Küläiim and set off in search of his homeland. Time passed and Körughly matured and gained heroic virtue. When he returned to the land of the Qyzylbas, he conquered their country and avenged the fate of his father and grandfather at the hands of the Qyzylbas.

This is how the *Körughly* epic begins. This is only the first part of the miraculous birth of the epic hero. The birth of Körughly from his dead mother illustrates his relationship with supernatural forces that make him invulnerable and undefeatable. He establishes a new order and new justice in the land of the Qyzylbas. The motif of a hero's birth in the grave or on mountain cliffs also exists in ancient Scythian, Greek, Indian, and Nart myths. The figure of Körughly can be correlated with ancient mythological archetypes, and many archaic features are preserved in the Körughly epic. Ancient legends and myths are closely intertwined, and there are fabulous figures such as witches, fairies, jinns, and giants.

A Word about the *Körughly* Epic

Körughly belongs to the group of early Turkic epics whose origins are linked to the Oghuz Khanate of the tenth and eleventh centuries. *Körughly* reflects the history of the twenty-four tribes of the medieval Oghuz state. In the Kazakh version of the epic, Körughly belongs to the Teke-Jäumit (Yomut) lineage. (Teke and Yomut are distinct tribal groups among the Turkmen, who trace their ancestry to the Oghuz Turks.) Thus, the historical memory of the many wars between the Turkmen and Persians that occurred through the centuries was not forgotten. The epic contains different chronological layers, ranging from mythological time to specific historical events of the sixteenth and seventeenth centuries. *Körughly* is an important epic among the Turkmen (Turkmen: *Görogly*) as well as in the Caucasus region (Azerbaijani: *Koroğlu*), and also has a performance tradition among the Tajiks, who speak an eastern dialect of Persian.

Körughly becomes a real knight, a fearless fighter, a marksman, and a skilled rider. He possesses extraordinary strength and is protected by saints. In his early youth he becomes the owner of a horse named Ghirat and a miraculous sword forged from a heavenly metal, which was bestowed on him by his spirit-patrons. As an epic hero, Körughly is distinguished by a baleful war cry, a monstrous appetite, and the ability to fall into a deep slumber after accomplishing heroic deeds.

As I listened to Bidas agha, I understood that he was the guardian of a great artistic tradition. To become a real *jyrau,* you need to be endowed with the gift of great talent, and to be exceptionally honest and fair. *Jyrau*s were teachers of moral values. They established norms of community life and morality and brought people to a high level of spirituality and purity.

I've often asked myself whether I was really prepared to take on this kind of responsibility. As I sat with my teacher, he looked at me, read my thoughts, and answered: "Yes, my dear, you can. I shall pass on to you my knowledge, but you must convey it to the next generation as the precious heritage of our ancestors. Now it is your sacred duty!" I was in seventh heaven with joy, but in the depth of my heart I knew what a huge responsibility I had taken on, and that it wouldn't be easy.

WATCH **Example 5.1.** Uljan Baibosynova with her *ustaz,* Bidas agha Rüstembekov, 2010.

NOTES

1. *Agha* means "brother," but when it is used after a personal name, it serves as a token of respect for an older person.

2. Tribal confederations.

3. Two-stringed lute.

4. *Maqam:* in Kazakh usage, a traditional tune or melody used by epic reciters. Many *jyrau*s had their own *maqam*s. For other meanings of *maqam/maqom,* see chapter 18.

5. Grandfather.

6. Qyzylbas (more commonly written "Qizilbash" or "Kizilbash") literally means "red head" in Turkic languages, and is a name given to Shi'a warriors—many of them Turkmen—who wore distinctive red headgear identifying them as soldiers loyal to the sheikhs of the Safaviyeh Sufi order that founded the Safavid dynasty of Iran at the beginning of the sixteenth century.

7. An ancient game played with the bones of a sheep or goat.

CHAPTER 6 ## Music of the Karakalpaks

PART 1. The Epic World of the Karakalpaks:
Jyrau and *Baqsy*

FRÉDÉRIC LÉOTAR

Music among the Karakalpaks exemplifies the distinctive syncretism of nomadic and sedentary culture that has been an abiding theme in Karakalpak history. The Karakalpaks are Turkic-speaking agro-pastoralists who live mostly in the Republic of Karakalpakstan (also transliterated as Qaraqalpaqstan). Karakalpakstan is politically a part of Uzbekistan, and occupies the arid and sparsely inhabited northwest region of the country. Karakalpakstan's total population is around 1.5 million, of which roughly a third identify as ethnically Karakalpak. Uzbeks and Kazakhs comprise most of the remaining two-thirds.

Contemporary Karakalpaks are the descendants of Turkic tribes—Qytai, Qongyrat, Kipchak, Keneges, Manghyt, Müiten—that formed a confederacy at the end of the fifteenth century and settled along the lower part of the Syr Darya River, in what is now Kazakhstan. Later they migrated south toward the Aral Sea, following the delta of the Amu Darya to reach their current territory. The historical proximity of Karakalpaks and Kazakhs is reflected in the close relationship between their languages and cultures.

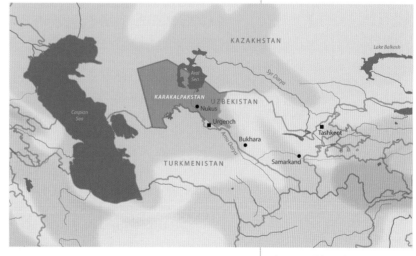

The Republic of Karakalpakstan within Uzbekistan.

Top: A Karakalpak village in the Shymbai Region.

Above: Detail of a Karakalpak yurt.

Karakalpakstan includes large regions of desert and steppe. Since the 1960s, the climate has suffered the catastrophic consequences of the desiccation of the Aral Sea, which resulted from Soviet-era agricultural practices that siphoned off the waters of the Amu Darya and Syr Darya Rivers to irrigate thirsty cotton fields. This disaster has had a major impact on the economy of Karakalpakstan, which is based on stockbreeding, agriculture, and fishing. These three activities have historically been closely intertwined. Karakalpak stockbreeders are nomadic and share many features of their nomadic culture with other Turkic and Turko-Mongol groups. The central cultural role of horses, both in the everyday world and the mythical world, and the vibrant traditional imagery and mythology of hero figures are two such features. Karakalpak farmers represent a sedentary lifestyle that is the legacy of ancient Khorezmian civilizations and Arabo-Persian culture. Finally, industrial fishing and large-scale agriculture, notably cotton growing, are modern developments linked to the period of Russian and Soviet rule in Central Asia. In our own time, these patterns of culture comingle, with the strength of each varying according to geography, demographics, family history, and individual desire. Karakalpak musical traditions are rooted in the lives and lore of nomadic stockbreeders and sedentary farmers. Indeed, music, and in particular the tradition of oral epic (*dästan*), embodies essential aspects of Karakalpak identity.

Epic poetry is at the core of traditional Karakalpak expressive culture, and many of the epics in the repertory of Karakalpak bards—*Görughly, Ghärip Ashyq, Sayatkhan Hämire,* and *Yusip-Akhmet,* among others—are also widely performed in other parts of Central and West Asia (see chapter 3).

Bards traditionally played a key role in Karakalpak society. Through epic, they transmitted knowledge, wisdom, moral guidance, and accounts of historical events intertwined with myths and imaginary elements. Epics were performed in the courts of rulers and local nobility and, more commonly, during weddings. Weddings lasted many days and could include hundreds of guests. At nightfall, a large fire would be lit and the bard would prepare himself. When the bard felt that everyone was ready, the eldest and most prestigious person (*aqsaqal*) in the group asked which epic the assembly wanted to hear. When everyone agreed on a particular epic, the bard started to sing.

In times past, bards knew a large number of epics, each of which could have between five thousand and twenty thousand lines. Each bard had his own version of these epics, with personal affects, expressions, gestures, and poses, all in order to maintain the listener's attention for hours at a time. It often happened that as night turned to dawn, the bard would still be reciting the epic, and in such cases he would continue the following evening or during a future gathering or wedding.

Nowadays, the role and perceived value of bards within Karakalpak society has been significantly weakened because of television, cell phones, social networking, and a secondary education system that does not sufficiently prepare younger pupils to appreciate epic as a central element of cultural heritage. Fortunately, present-day bards are working diligently to revitalize the social tradition of epic performance.

JYRAU BARDS

Karakalpaks distinguish between two principal types of epic bard, *jyrau* and *baqsy*. Of these, the *jyrau* has historically older roots. The term *jyrau*, which also exists in Kazakh, derives from the old Turkic word *iyr* or *yr* (song). *Jyrau* thus means "singer." *Jyraus* mostly sing heroic epics, that is, epics that prominently feature tales about the courage and bravery of a hero in his fight against tyranny and injustice. As a prelude to heroic epics, *jyraus* typically perform shorter historical and didactic songs (*terme, tolghau*), which provide a way for the bard to warm up his voice and begin to focus the attention of listeners. *Jyraus* sing in a guttural voice rich in overtones. This type of singing exists among historically nomadic Turkic and Mongol cultures in various parts of Central Asia (southern Kazakhstan, southern Uzbekistan), South Siberia (Tuva, Khakassia, Altai Republic), and Mongolia. *Jyraus* accompany their singing with a *qobyz*—the upright fiddle that, in a variety of forms, was once widespread in Turkic pastoralist cultures. The *qobyz* is typically fabricated from two pieces of wood joined by a piece of metal. Its two strings are made of horsehair, and its resonating chamber is partially covered by a membrane made of camel hide. In the past, the *qobyz* was the instrument par excellence of shamans, although Karakalpak bards alive today do not recall this. Nonetheless, the performance style of the *jyrau* refers implicitly to Turkic-Mongolian shamanic traditions with their guttural vocal timbres, two-string fiddles, and spirit-imbued sound world, and present-day *jyraus* consider the raspy, guttural vocal timbre they use in the recitation of epic to be an imitation of the sound of the *qobyz*. Some *jyraus* claim that this timbre confers on them strength, memory, and a vision of what they must sing. The heroic epics most commonly performed by Karakalpak *jyraus* are *Edige, Qoblan, Shäryar, Qyryq qyz*, and *Alpamys*, but the historical repertory of epic tales from which these are drawn is considerably larger.

During the second half of the twentieth century, the performance of epic steadily declined. Present-day bards sing only excerpts of epics, sometimes performing them at weddings, though pop singers and recorded music have largely replaced *jyraus* at wedding festivities. The principal venue for epic performance has become concerts, contests, and festivals—events that do not lend themselves to the performance of an entire epic. In these venues, *jyraus* nonetheless preserve the theatrical character of their performance by using sound and visual effects to act out the various scenes of an epic. In doing so, they perpetuate a long-standing tradition of combining poetry and prose in oral composition and performance. For example,

Karakalpak *qobyz*.

when a *jyrau* declaims text in prose, he uses exaggerated facial expressions or eye movements as well as particular postures and gestures. These theatrical expressions prepare his audience for the next lines of poetry and maintain a listener's interest.

Among contemporary *jyrau*s, the leading exponent of the traditional performance style is Baqbergen Syrymbetov, who is both an active performer and a teacher of epic performance at the Pedagogical Institute in Nukus, the capital of Karakalpakstan.

WATCH **Example 6.1. Excerpt from epic *Alpamys*, performed by Baqbergen jyrau, 2010.**

In this excerpt, the hero Alpamys chooses Baishubar, the horse that will help him accomplish his heroic deeds. Note the guttural tone of the *jyrau*'s voice that imitates the sound of the fiddle. Exaggerated facial expressions during the performance of the epic are only one way in which the *jyrau* tries to sustain the attention of his audience. He also changes the tempo of his singing from slower to faster, taking only a few breaths, and sustains notes from which he produces amplified overtones.

STUDY QUESTIONS

1. What happens when the voice of the singer sustains the same note for a long time?
2. What is the role of the fiddle compared to the role of the vocal part?

ANSWERS TO QUESTIONS

1. The voice imitates the timbre of the fiddle.
2. The fiddle plays the melodic lines when there is no singing. It punctuates the spoken narrative, plays in unison with the voice during a song, and supports long notes when the fiddler bows the same note as the voice.

BAQSY BARDS

The other principal type of Karakalpak bard is the *baqsy*. Among the Karakalpaks, *baqsy* bards emerged in the nineteenth century. The term *baqsy* in slightly different pronunciations and with different meanings is also used by the Kazakhs (*baqsy*), Kyrgyz (*bakshy*), Turkmen (*bagshy*), Uyghurs and Uzbeks (*bakhshi*). In Uzbek, *bakhshi* has a dual meaning—it may signify both a bard and a shaman. Karakalpak, by contrast, has a separate word for "shaman" (*porkhan*), while *baqsy* refers to a bard who specializes in singing lyric epics to the accompaniment of the *dutar* and performing narrative instrumental melodies. One such melody, popular among Karakalpaks, is "Qara jorgha," reproduced in example 6.2.

LISTEN **Example 6.2. "Qara jorgha" (Pacer horse), performed by G'ayrat O'temuratov on the *dutar*.**

Baqsy G'ayrat O'temuratov performs "Qara jorgha" on the *dutar*,[1] the local variety of long-necked two-stringed lute (see "Musical Instrument Glossary"). As is fitting in a society where horses traditionally play a key role, the melody of "Qara jorgha" describes a horse race. In the melodic narrative, the performer begins by calling the horses to the starting line (0:00–0:08). The race begins at 0:09 and continues until 2:40. The piece ends when everyone—both winner and pursuers—has crossed the finish line (2:41–3:00). Each part of the race brings a new musical image, although the performer does not always indicate it clearly. Indeed, during the race, numerous images are used and repeated, for example:

G'ayrat O'temuratov.

0:13–0:22	A motif portraying two horses fiercely trying to pass each other is repeated four times. One horse passes the other, and is then passed in turn.
0:23–0:43	The motif reproduces the gallop of a horse.
0:44–0:50	At this point, the *jorgha* (pacing) starts, i.e., a fast and pleasant running speed. Karakalpaks say that at this speed, a rider can hold a cup of tea without spilling a single drop.

These images are framed according to a metrical structure that features alternating cycles of twelve and eight beats, as demonstrated in the following table (the first number in each row represents the number of repetitions of the eight-beat or twelve-beat cycle):

Time code	Number of cycles
0:01	1×12 (or 4×3)
0:08	4×8
0:27	1×12 (or 4×3)
0:34	2×8
0:46	1×12 (or 4×3)
0:51	1×8

0:55	2 × 12 (or 4 × 6)
1:09	8 × 8
1:45	1 × 12
1:52	1 × 8
1:57	2 × 12 (or 4 × 6)
2:10	7 × 8
2:42	[non-measured]

Gülnara Allambergenova, one of the most talented *baqsy*s of Karakalpakstan.

Among the large number of *baqsy*s who traveled from wedding to wedding, a few iconic figures are still talked about today, some of whom were performing as far back as the 1850s. At that time, Aqymbet, the most famous Karakalpak bard, who is considered the founder of the Karakalpak *baqsy* style, created a vibrant school of epic performance and became known all over the right bank of the Amu Darya. Around the same time, a bard of Turkmen origin named Süyew baqsy lived on the left bank of the Amu Darya. Süyew had a major influence on Karakalpak bards by introducing pieces that are now a standard part of the Karakalpak repertory. Today, pieces such as "Ylghal," "Irani," and "Baghlar" are considered to be part of the Karakalpak Süyew school. They are traditionally performed by an ensemble consisting of *girjek* (spike fiddle), *balaman* (clarinet), and *doira* (frame drum) in contrast to the solo practice of other *baqsy* bards, who typically accompanied themselves on the *dutar*.

Alongside epics, contemporary *baqsy*s perform melodies set to lyrics by well-known poets such as Magtymguly Pyragy (1724–1807), Berdaq Gharghabai uly (1827–1900), Äjiniyaz Qosybai uly (1824–1878), and Ibraiym Yusupov (1929–2008). Traditionally, the profession of *baqsy* was restricted to men, but nowadays, female *baqsy*s perform with increasing regularity. Female *baqsy*s garner warm applause during festivals and contests, and often win these contests. Among the best known are Gülnara Allambergenova, Ziyada Sheripova, Gülbähär Aqymbetova, and the young Miyasar Jumatova.

WATCH **Example 6.3.** "Sarbinaz" (Cypress), performed by Gülnara Allambergenova (*dutar* and vocal) and lnjigül Saburova (*girjek*), 2012.

In this excerpt from the epic *Ghärip Ashyq*, Ghärip, who has been driven out of his country, weeps for his beloved Shasänem, whom he has not seen for seven years. The song is intended for Aisänem, who has fallen in love with Ghärip. The strong vocal performance by Gülnara Allambergenova illustrates the principal

Above: Injigül Saburova (*left*) and Ziyada Sheripova.
Photo by Katherine Vincent. Courtesy of Aga Khan Music Initiative.

Right: Gülbähär Aqymbetova, a student of G'ayrat O'temuratov.

stylistic conventions observed by *baqsy*s, whether male or female: a reverberant voice (*ashyq dawys*), wide vocal register (*lapyzy bar*), and frequent use of specific vocal effects. Among these, small undulations (*yrghaq*) within particular syllables are highly appreciated by listeners. The melody of "Särbinaz" (Cypress) is well known, and is set to texts from various epics as well as to its own unique song lyrics.

As you watch the video, follow the transcription of the text, transliterated and translated below, and identify the syllables where the singer uses the *yrghaq* effect. In the first line only, these syllables are boldfaced.

Men saghan aytaiyn gül jüzli janan,	Let me tell you something, dearest face like a rose,
Saghan kewil bersem, wonda yar jylar	If I give you my heart, my beloved will cry.
Alypsan sabyrymdy gül jüzli janan,	You severely put my patience to the test, dearest face like a rose,
Saghan kewil bersem, wonda yar jylar.	If I give you my heart, my beloved will cry.
Häsiret oty menen janyn daghlaghan,	The fire of grief is tormenting my soul,
Ashyqlyq isine belin bailaghan.	And you fell in love with me.
Jeti jyldur, jolgha qarap jylaghan,	For seven years, she has been tearfully waiting for me,
Saghan kewil bersem, wonda yar jylar.	If I give you my heart, my beloved will cry.

Folk Songs

Music making among the Karakalpaks has not been limited to *baqsy*s and *jyrau*s. In addition to the epic repertories, Karakalpaks traditionally sang a wide variety of songs in the course of their daily lives. These songs often mix together worldly lyrics with references to Allah and spirits, both good (*pir*) and bad (*jawyz ruwkh*). Texts of lullabies (*häyyiw*) that a mother sings to lull an infant to sleep exemplify this mixture. These texts convey old views suggesting that spirits can be detrimental to people, and particularly to newborns and their young mothers. Such songs reveal a deep bond between music, human activity, and spirits that was much more prominent in the past. These days, the lullaby repertory includes older melodies as well as recently composed songs such as the one reproduced in example 6.4, composed in 2002. In this video, note how the baby smiles in response to the lullaby and, later, how the song as well as the rocking of the mother induce sleep.

WATCH

Example 6.4. "Lullaby," composed by J. Allambergenov, performed by Gülzabira Mambetnazarova to her four-month-old daughter, Hürliman. Video, text, and translation courtesy of Buda Records.[2]

Aimalasam aidan artyq,	My sweet one, more beautiful than the moon,
Kütken künim keldi qaityp,	At last the day has come that I have waited for so long,
Quwanarman sony aityp,	This being said, I am happy,
Häyyiw, häyyiw, ai balam-aw,	*Häyyiw, häyyiw,* my moon, my son,
Endi kewlim jai balam-aw.	Now my soul is at ease.
Aimalasam aidan jaqsy,	My sweet one, more beautiful than the moon,
Toigha barsa bala baqsy,	You are an apprentice bard at weddings,
Qyzlardyng kewlining naghysy,	All young maids are flocking around you,
Häyyiw, häyyiw, ai balam-aw,	*Häyyiw, häyyiw,* my moon, my son,
Endi kewlim jai balam-a.	Now my soul is at ease.
Qusym desem pärwazynga,	I say, "My bird," seeing you soar,
Köz tiktim üirek ghazyna,	I have looked at the young of your age,
Toilarda shertken sazyna,	I have listened to your music at weddings,
Häyyiw, häyyiw, ai balam-aw,	*Häyyiw, häyyiw,* my moon, my son,
Endi kewlim jai balam-a.	Now my soul is at ease.
Aibatly qus-qyranymsang,	You are my fearsome falcon,
Ghärezsizlik uranymsang,	You are my independent watchword,
Jainap-jasnar baghymsang,	My garden in flowers,

Häyyiw, häyyiw, ai balam-aw,	*Häyyiw, häyyiw,* my moon, my son,
Endi kewlim jai balam-aw.	Now my soul is at ease.
Uiqylai-ghoi, janym, sen balam-aw,	Sleep, my little one, my darling,
Endi kewlim jai balam-aw.	Now my soul is at ease.

STUDY QUESTION

1. How would you characterize the vocal style of a lullaby as opposed to that of an epic using the categories in the table below:

TABLE 6.1.

RESONANT VOICE (*ASHYQ DAWYS*)	EXTENDED REGISTER (*LAPYZ*)	VOCAL ORNAMENTATION (*YRGHAQ*)
yes/no	less/more	yes/no

PART 2. *Qyssakhan:*
Performer of Written and Oral Literature
KALMURZA KURBANOV AND SAIDA DAUKEYEVA

The first part of this chapter focuses on two kinds of bards—*jyrau* and *baqsy*—whose animated performances of different genres of oral poetry remain an active form of artistic practice in present-day Karakalpakstan. In the past, however, one of the main channels for transmitting epic and lyric poetry was provided by another type of bard, called *qyssakhan,* a storyteller who recited or sang unaccompanied written and oral literature in verse and prose. The practice of *qyssakhan*s continues to a limited extent today: there are people who perform in the manner of *qyssakhan*s (*qyssa joly*), and their performance tradition, called *qyssakhanshylyq,* represents an important element of Karakalpak literary and musical culture. Regrettably, young generations of Karakalpaks know little about this distinctive tradition. How did it begin, and why has it faded away?

ORIGINS

Beginning in the mid-eighteenth century, nomadic and semi-nomadic Karakalpak clans who had migrated from the Syr Darya region to the delta of the Amu Darya River came into contact with the sedentary civilization of the Khorezm oasis. In Khorezm's principal city, Khiva, as well as in the cities of Samarkand and Bukhara, which lie to the southwest, across the sands of the Kyzyl Kum Desert, Karakalpaks encountered a range of written literature from the Middle East, notably the classical works of Arab and Persian medieval writers and poets, such as *Kalila wa Dimna* by Ibn al-Muqaffaʻ, *Shahname* by Ferdowsi, *Gulistan and Bustan* by Saʻadi, *Yusuf-Zuleikha* by Jami, and *Khamsa* by Nizami. Karakalpak youth started to study at Islamic religious centers in Khorezm's cities and at Muslim schools (*maktab*s) and seminaries (madrasahs), which proliferated in the Amu Darya delta. Here they learned to read, write, and recite the Qur'an, and became acquainted with religious and scholarly writings as well as prose and poetry in Arabic, Persian, and Turkic languages. Books in these languages were printed in Russian cities, such as Kazan and Orenburg, as well as in Central Asian cities, such as Tashkent, Samarkand, Kokand, and Khiva.

Rising awareness of Middle Eastern literary traditions provided an impetus for the development of the Karakalpaks' own written literature. Yet, in the early nineteenth century, printed books were a luxury—the domain of the clergy and educated people from privileged social groups. Responding to the rising demand for access to written literature among the largely uneducated population, some students and graduates of Islamic schools and seminaries started to copy books by hand and disseminate them orally by reading aloud from manuscripts, or reciting from memory. With the aim of creating an artistic presentation of the text, these performers embellished their recitation by intoning it musically. Such performers of written and oral literature came to be called *qyssakhan*s—tellers of stories and tales, from Arabic *qyssa:* "history," "story," "tale," "romance," and Persian *khan:* "recite," "sing." Storytellers who composed poetry and poets (*shaiyr*s) who recited and sang their own poems were both known as *shaiyr-qyssakhan*s (poet-storytellers).[3]

REPERTORY: LITERARY GENRES AND MUSICAL SETTING

The repertory of *qyssakhan*s was diverse. While *jyrau*s specialized in the repertory of heroic epics and didactic poetry, and *baqsy*s sang romantic epics and poems by classical and contemporary poets, *qyssakhan*s did not confine themselves to any particular literary genre. They could perform various kinds of literature, whether folk or of known authorship, verse (*qosyq*) or prose (*nasr, qara söz*), written or orally transmitted. The repertory of *qyssakhan*s thus overlapped with the repertory of both *jyrau*s and *baqsy*s, and typically included the following elements:

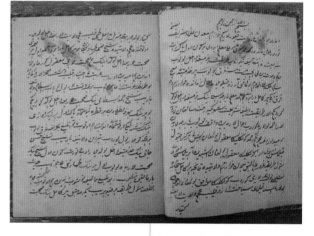

Manuscript of *Khorezmname.*
Photo from the Foundation Library of the Karakalpak branch of the Uzbekistan Academy of Sciences.

1. Middle Eastern religious literature and chronicles brought from the Middle East to Khorezm in written form and recited by *qyssakhan*s to educated audiences in the original languages—Persian, Arabic, or Turkic. Examples include stories and legends from the lives of prophets (*Qisa al-Anbiya* by Nasir ibn Burhan Rabghuzi), Sufi dervishes and saints (*Ibrahim ibn Adham, Ahtam Sahaba, Sultan Uways al-Qarani*), and famous historical figures (*Abu Muslim*).

2. Middle Eastern romantic and heroic epics, originally transmitted in written form in Arabic and Persian and adopted in local Turkic poetic or prose versions that incorporated Arabic and Persian vocabulary and combined *barmaq* and *aruz* poetic meters. Like religious literature and chronicles, these epics were performed for educated people and became known as *qyssa*. Well-known examples include *Yusuf-Zuleikha, Dilaram, Zeynel-Arab, Zufunun, Baba Raushan, Khorezmname,* and Ferdowsi's *Shahname.*

3. Turkic romantic epics—a repertory shared with *baqsy*s that *qyssakhan*s learned in oral or written form directly in Central Asian Turkic languages, such as Chagatai (a late medieval form of proto-Uzbek), Uzbek, and Turkmen, and performed in specially adapted local versions to distinctive melodies. These epics became popular among uneducated people who referred to them as *dästan*, or *ashyqlyq dästanlary* (love epics), rather than *qyssa*. Examples include *Ghärip Ashyq, Yusip-Akhmet, Sayatkhan-Hämire, Zäwre-Taiyr, Gül-Sänewber, Bäzirgen,* and *Khyrmandäli* from the epic cycle *Görughly.*

4. Turkic heroic epics—a repertory shared with *jyrau*s that was learned orally and performed in the syllabic *barmaq* poetic meters to tunes used by *jyrau*s. Subsequently *qyssakhan*s produced their own written versions of the epics modeled on Middle Eastern poetry. For example, the Turkic epic *Edige* became known as *Edige ibn Tükli Aziz* (Edige, the son of Tükli Aziz) and *Shäryar* was renamed *Darapshah* after its main hero. This repertory, called *qaharmanlyq dästanlary* (heroic epics), was performed mainly among uneducated people.

5. Poetry by nineteenth-century and early twentieth-century authors, such as the classical Karakalpak poets Künkhoja Ibraiym uly (1799–1880), Äjiniyaz Qosybai uly (1824–1878), Berdaq Gharghabai uly (1827–1900), Ötesh Alshynbai uly (1828–1902), Omar Süyirbek uly (1879–1922), and Ayapbergen Musa uly (1880–1936).

*Qyssakhan*s usually set the scene for a recitation of *qyssa*s or *dästan*s by performing their own poetry or shorter poems composed by contemporary poets. The two most popular genres of such contemporary poems were *täriyp* and *aitys.* *Täriyp* (from Arabic *ta'rīf*: "introduction," "presentation"), sometimes referred to as *maqtau* or *tengeu* (praise, eulogy), was a form of panegyric verse dedicated to the homeland, one's tribe, a warrior's prowess, a girl's beauty, a horse's fine points, and so on. The genre developed from panegyric verses in folk heroic epics. Its distinguishing feature was the use of the word *täriyp* in the poem, especially in its initial lines, e.g. *"Begler täriyp etsem qalpaq yurtyny"* (Sirs! If I sing a praise to the Karakalpak people), *"Täriypini bayan etsem yaranlar"* (If I recite a eulogy, friends), *"Täriyp etsem bir gözzaldy"* (If I sing a praise to a beautiful girl). An ability to compose or extemporize a *täriyp* on a specific topic was a measure of a poet-storyteller's mastery. Many samples of *täriyp*s have come down to us in *qyssakhan*s' manuscripts from the nineteenth and early twentieth centuries. These traditional *täriyp*s were not captured in sound but have been preserved as poetic texts. A typical example of this genre is a *täriyp* by the poet-bard Ayapbergen Musa uly, composed in 1909–1910.[4]

Arjaq-berjaq bolyp eki san bolghan,

Bölim-bölim eller qaraqalpaqtady.

Gharqyldasyp üirek ushyp, ghaz qonghan,
Aidyn-aidyn köller qaraqalpaqtady.

Sharwalary köship, ataw jailaghan,
Biye sawyp, qatar qulyn bailaghan.
Qulan-kiyikleri sekirip oinaghan,

Qiya-qiya shöller qaraqalpaqtady.

Danyshmand, xosh sözli, faham-idrakly,
Urysta bir özi mynggha derekli.
Görughly haibatly, Rustem yürekli,
Belli-belli jigit qaraqalpaqtady.

Jigitleri el gezer qyznyng qastynda,
Gülleri ashylghan bähär paslynda.
Alma közli, ärebi atlar astynda,
Märt ghoshshaq jigitler qaraqalpaqtady.

Qyzlary bar qiya-qiya qaslary,
Iynin jabar örim-örim shashlary.
Shashbawynda gäwhar hasyl taslary,

Hür-periyzat qyzlar qaraqalpaqtady.

Bir qyldan näzikdur qypsha belleri,
Buwyn-buwyn tarqynaly älleri,
Shekerden mazaly shiyrin tilleri,
Taza näwjawanlar qaraqalpaqtady.

Laghly-marjan—haqiyq ne hasyl zatlar,

Shäkirtler ustazdan alyp irshadlar,
Nar tüye, doinaqly dal bedew atlar,
Ändamly narbuwdan qaraqalpaqtady.

Sahrada seyil etip jyiyn baslaghan,
Qarshygha, aq tuighyn, lashyn qus salghan,

This bank and the other [of the Amu Darya River]
    make two parts [of a whole].
There are several distinct peoples among the
    Karakalpaks.
Squawking ducks are flying, geese are settling,
There are broad lakes between the Karakalpaks.

Herders, migrating, settle on islands,
Milk mares and rope stallions in a row.
Wild asses and saiga antelopes are leaping
    playfully,
There are wide steppes between the Karakalpaks.

Wise, well spoken, smart,
In combat one equals a thousand.
Mighty like Görughly, cordial like Rustem,
There are glorious young men among the Kar-
    akalpaks.

Young men are roaming in search of brides,
Their flowers are blooming at their prime.
With apple-like eyes, astride Arab horses,
There are brave and spirited young men among the
    Karakalpaks.

Girls have curved eyebrows,
Their shoulders are covered with braided hair.
Diamonds, precious stones are on their hair
    bands,
There are fairy-like girls among the Karakalpaks.

Their waists are thinner than a strand of hair,
Their hands are slender and delicate,
Their tongues are sweeter than sugar,
There are pure newlywed lasses among the
    Karakalpaks.

Rubies and corals—what truly precious things are
    these,
Pupils are acquiring knowledge from masters,
One-humped dromedaries, racing horses,
There are great camels among the Karakalpaks.

In the steppe festivities and gatherings are held,
Hawk, white hawk, peregrine falcon,

Aq-qara bas sona, süylin uslaghan,	Black- and white-headed wild ducks and pheasants are chased,
Qus salghan qälpeler qaraqalpaqtady.	There are bird-hunting hawkers among the Karakalpaks.
Mereke-mäjliste, aity-toiynda,	At feasts and gatherings, religious festivals and celebrations,
At shawyp, maiyrghan kökmar oiynda,	Horses are torn apart in *kökmar.*[5]
Sawyn bairaq alghan ully jyiynda,	The winner gets the prize of a cow before a great assembly,
Belli shabandozlar qaraqalpaqtady.	There are many valiant horsemen among the Karakalpaks.
Ghärip aitar, ötti neshshe jahanger,	Says Ghärip,[6] so many conquerors have passed away,
Härkim elin jaman demes, jaqsy der,	Everybody praises his people rather than finding fault,
Mir-Alisher, Jiyrenshege taqabbil,	Like Mir-Alisher [Navo'i] and Jiyrenshe,
Ataqly shaiyrlar qaraqalpaqtady.	There are famous poets among the Karakalpaks.

The other popular genre of *qyssakhan* performance was recitation of texts from poetic competitions, called *aitys*. These competitions took the form of poetic dialogues either composed impromptu before an audience, or exchanged in letters (*sälem khat arqaly aitysyw*) over time and at a distance. In the latter case, the geographical distance between competing poets could be considerable. One poetic contest from the second half of the nineteenth century, recaptured by *qyssakhans*, was an *aitys* between the Karakalpak poet Qulymbet, who lived near the town of Qongyrat between the Amu Darya and the Usturt plateau, and the Kazakh *aqyn* Abu-Bakir Kerderi, who lived near Orenburg in the south Urals.[7] Abu-Bakir was already known among Karakalpaks for his poetic competition with a Nogai mullah, and Qulymbet sent him a letter expressing a wish to make his acquaintance. In a reciprocal letter Abu-Bakir decided to test Qulymbet's knowledge of history and geography by asking him questions about the seven spheres of the universe, the origins of the Turkic peoples, and the inhabitants of Khorezm and neighboring territories. Qulymbet, in his next letter, answered these questions, but Abu-Bakir was apparently not satisfied with his answers, and in his response, which arrived five years later, he answered them himself and expressed his willingness to continue a dialogue with Qulymbet. Apart from the usual contests between poets (*shaiyrlar aitysy*), forms of *aitys* popular among *qyssakhans* included a fable contest (*tymsal-aitys*) and a riddle competition (*jumbaq-aitys*). Like *täriyp*, these have come down to us merely as poetic texts, not having been recorded in sound either before or during the twentieth century, when the tradition of *qyssakhans* performing *aitys* declined.

Qyssakhanshylyq was thus a musically enriched rendering of various kinds of written and oral literature. Although a *qyssakhan* was appreciated above all for his storytelling skill, eloquence, and richness of language, musical aspects of performance played a key role in communicating a narrative.

As is evident from oral tradition, ethnographic accounts, and sound recordings of *qyssakhan*s made in the twentieth century, the musical setting of texts in earlier *qyssakhan* performance encompassed a continuum that extended from recitation to singing, with prose narrative, passages of rhymed declamation, and sung strophic verses interweaving and complementing one another. In contrast to both *jyrau*s and *baqsy*s who accompanied their singing on the *qobyz* and *dutar* respectively, *qyssakhan*s recited epic and lyric poems without instrumental accompaniment. Their vocal style also differed from that of the other two kinds of bards. Unlike *jyrau*s, who performed in a distinctive guttural singing style, *qyssakhan*s sang in a natural, or "open" voice (*ashyq dawys*). And in contrast to *baqsy*s, their singing was less virtuosic and elaborate, and their melodic repertory less varied. Each *qyssakhan* employed two or three characteristic melodies of limited range (within the interval of a fourth or a fifth), which were performed in a strophic form and repetitive pattern resembling lyrical folk songs. When performing a heroic epic, a *qyssakhan* could borrow the tunes of *jyrau*s, while singing them in a distinctive way.

*Qyssakhan*s projected their voices less powerfully and dynamically than *jyrau*s and *baqsy*s. Their manner of recitation, with its clear and resonant enunciation, narrow range, and homogenous pattern of melodies, bore some resemblance to Qur'anic chant, owing to the fact that many *qyssakhan*s received a religious education and were adept at reciting the Qur'an. Although *qyssakhan*s' performance did not match that of *jyrau*s and *baqsy*s in musical versatility and sophistication, talented performers could make an impact on listeners by reciting with expression and artistic skill. The aesthetic dimension of their performance was thus equally valued by their audience, and the art of *qyssakhanshylyq* had its own connoisseurs.

PERFORMANCE AND TRANSMISSION

*Qyssakhan*s performed on festive occasions and at home gatherings, usually before smaller, more intimate audiences, than *jyrau*s and *baqsy*s. Performing without the support of instrumental accompaniment, they seldom appeared at large-scale events like weddings, the speciality of *jyrau*s and *baqsy*s. Typically *qyssakhan*s were invited to conduct the ceremony of *betashar,* "unveiling the bride's face," like Kazakh and Kyrgyz *aqyn*s (see chapter 10). In cities they read poetry among educated people concentrated around madrasahs. In rural areas they wandered around villages (*awyl*s), reciting stories to entertain those who could not read.

On winter evenings, when people had leisure time free from agricultural labor, they would go to homes offering their services. Sometimes they were specially invited to recite from books or manuscripts at small gatherings of friends, acquaintances, and neighbors, such as *geshtek*—male get-togethers. *Qyssakhan*s were also commissioned to compose and sing *täriyp*s eulogizing a native place, a clan, or a daughter. In all these circumstances they were rewarded, often in kind, with food or livestock.

The heyday of *qyssakhanshylyq* as a professional performance art occurred in the last quarter of the nineteenth century and the early twentieth century. During that time, several eminent *shaiyr-qyssakhan*s emerged, giving rise to poetic communities or distinct schools of performance.[8] It is known that some of these *qyssakhan*s roamed with their pupils, reciting *qyssa*s in chorus monophonically.[9] One of the earliest and most significant of these schools is associated with *shaiyr* Qorazbek Razbek uly (1855–1914), a master of *täriyp* who graduated from a Bukharan madrasah and became known under the pen name (*takhallus*) Ghärip (strange, destitute), after the name of the eponymous hero of *Ghärip Ashyq* (The Wandering *Ashyq*), the Karakalpak version of the popular Turkic love epic.[10] In addition to reciting epics and other poetry, his followers copied by hand poems in Karakalpak and translated works by classical Persian- and Turkic-speaking authors, such as Navo'i, Fuzuli, and Magtymguly Pyragy. Some famous *shaiyr-qyssakhan*s belonged to this school; for example, Ayapbergen Musa uly, whose *täriyp* was cited earlier.

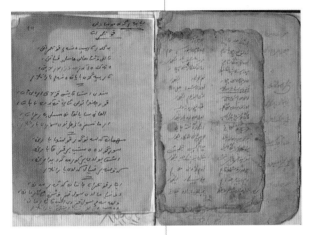

Manuscript collection of poems by Ayapbergen Musa uly.

Photo from the Foundation Library of the Karakalpak branch of the Uzbekistan Academy of Sciences.

Subsequently followers of Qorazbek Razbek uly's school branched into other distinct schools, such as that of Mawdit Bekmukhammed uly (1885–1950), popularly known as Qazy Mawlik. Qazy Mawlik served for a time as a *qazy* (judge) in the city of Shymbai, then the administrative and cultural center of Karakalpak territories, and was known both for his popular *täriyp*s about Shymbai, and for his part in a famous riddle competition (*jumbaq-aitys*) with another *shaiyr-qyssakhan*, Seifulghabit Majitov. He was the first to open a bookstore in Shymbai, for which he obtained books from caravans passing through from the Middle East. Qazy Mawlik's students copied these books and made them widely available. This promoted the development of *qyssakhan* performance. One of Qazy Mawlik's pupils, *qyssakhan* Qäwender bala (Qäwender boy) Khojaniyaz uly (1895–1917), is said to have had a beautiful voice and outstanding performance skills, unmatched among his contemporaries. Despite his short life, he passed on his knowledge to many followers, who carried it into the twentieth century.

QYSSAKHANSHYLYQ IN THE SOVIET ERA

The majority of documented historical information about earlier epic practice and the few extant sound recordings of traditional *qyssakhan* performance are of twentieth-century provenance. *Qyssakhan*s who gained prominence during the first half of the century were remarkable in that their life paths and creative work spanned different eras in the history of the Karakalpaks. Having learned the skills of *qyssakhanshylyq* from past masters, such as Qazy Mawlik and Qäwender bala, and developed as performers prior to the Soviet period, they came to the fore in cultural life and achieved public recognition under the new political regime.[11] The contemporary image of *qyssakhanshylyq* is shaped by three such *qyssakhan* bards— intermediate figures who stood at the interface of the two historical and cultural eras, and whose poetic output and performance style are regarded as classical today: Abbaz Dabylov (1898–1970), Sadyq Nurymbetov (1900–1972), and Rambergen Khojambergenov (1915–1984), known as Ram shaiyr (Ram the poet).

*Qyssakhan*s Sadyq Nurymbetov and Abbaz Dabylov.

Courtesy of Abbaz Dabylov's son, Murat Dabylov.

Although they continued to perform in the customary social contexts linked to everyday life and to compose poetry on conventional subjects, they also became involved in new state-organized cultural projects that served to disseminate socialist ideology and ideals. Along with other bards and musicians, *qyssakhan*s were sent to perform for laborers in the fields, canal builders, and workers on building sites both to provide cultural leisure and to stimulate productivity. During the Second World War, they performed as part of agitprop brigades to urge conscription to the war effort, raise patriotic sentiments, and awaken a combative spirit. In peacetime they were featured at official state events, such as days of culture, festivals, and governmental conventions, promoting socialist ideas and celebrating the people's achievements under Soviet rule. The repertory composed for and performed by *qyssakhan*s at such events, though new in theme and intent, drew upon traditional poetic genres and musical devices. The three above-named *qyssakhan*s, captured on recordings and remembered by those who heard them perform live, exemplify different performance styles.

RAMBERGEN KHOJAMBERGENOV (RAM SHAIYR)

Ram shaiyr's recitation resembles folk songs. His tunes are narrow in range, short and repetitive, and his vocal technique is similar to that of folk singing. The example below features Ram shaiyr's performance of an excerpt from the *dästan Ghärip Ashyq*. The excerpt is based on the poetic form *mukhammas* ("fivefold"), a Middle Eastern verse form that became popular in Karakalpak poetry. The standard *mukhammas* consists of five lines, four of which have an identical end rhyme, which changes from one stanza to the next, while the fifth line has a different rhyme maintained throughout the poem: aaaab ccccb ddddb, and so on. In the excerpt from *Ghärip Ashyq,* however, with the exception of the first stanza, *mukhammas* consists of six lines. The first four of these lines constitute a quatrain with a single end rhyme that changes from one stanza to the next, while the final two lines share a different end rhyme that remains constant throughout the poem, as shown in the following schematic: aaaab ccccbb ddddbb, etc. Each line contains fourteen syllables grouped into two seven-syllable hemistichs. Listen to Ram shaiyr's performance of the poetic fragment and note its stylistic features and the way the verse is set to music.

Example 6.5. "Aman jetker yarymny" (Deliver my lover safe and sound), excerpt from the *dästan Ghärip Ashyq,* performed by Rambergen Khojambergenov, Nukus, 1965. Recording from the archive of the Karakalpakstan Television and Radio Broadcasting Company.

LISTEN

The *dästan* tells a Sufi-inspired story of love between Shasänem, the daughter of a khan, and Ghärip, the son of his vizier, who becomes a hermit and wandering singer-poet (*ashyq*). Betrothed before birth, the lovers are separated by circumstances of fortune but reunited at the end of the poem. In this excerpt, taken from the last part of the *dästan,* Ghärip finds himself at the wedding of Shasänem. Hearing his voice, she recognizes him and throws herself down to him from the top of a tower. As he sees Shasänem fall, Ghärip sings a song praying to God to deliver his lover safely.

Rähim etip halyma, egam özing ber mädat,
Ayar bolsang bärhabar, rähming köptur biyadat,

Häm hazyryw-nazyrsang, ully patsham, ya ahad,
Oshbu etken nalamny, därgahyngnan qylma rad,
Ijabat äilep duwamny, aman etker yarymny.

Oiyn qurghan kepterdei, awdanglap keler asmanda,

Aman keler-kelmesi, bolyp turur gümanda,
Tänimde joq taqatym, mening oshbu zamanda,
Rähim etip ya-ghappar, özing tutqyl amanda,
Qarab etme halymny, aman jetker yarymny.

Yarymdy-aw aman jetkerip-aw, yrzaman alsang janymny.

Jel ushyrghan qaghazdai, köz ushynda keladur,

Gäha astyn, gä üstin, gä särnigün boladur,
Sol kelisten tüsse-aw jerge, anyng ne jany qaladur,

Saqlamasang ilaiym, til tartmastan öledur,

Özing bolyp mädetkar, aman jetker yarymny.
Yar jolynda tärk äileyin, bisatymda barymny.

Mu'allaq atyp hawadan, äilep keler dawamat,

Syghynurman biyribar, ishim ahyw-nädamat,
Özing ully patshasang, jollaryngyz ädalat,
Ädalatly patshahym, qyl duwamny ijabat,
Eshitip ahyw-zarymny, aman jetker yarymny.
Yaqmaghyl otqa tiriklei, tändegi shiyrin janymny.

Shasänem atly yaryma, ilahym özing ber mädat,
Syghyndym sanga sättarym, qylarma dep rähmat,

Take pity on me, my Lord, and give me strength,
If you have mercy on me, Omniscient one, your mercy is boundless,
You, Omnipresent one, great ruler, oh, the One,
Do not reject this, my lament,
Fulfilling my prayer, deliver my lover safe and sound.

Like a playful dove, she comes, fluttering in the sky,
Will she or will she not come safely to me, I wonder.
I have lost my patience now,
Show your mercy, oh, All-Forgiving one, keep her safe,
Do not leave me desolate, deliver my lover safe and sound.
If you bring my lover safe and sound, I consent to your taking my soul.

Like paper carried away by the wind, she is flying almost out of sight,
Now upward, now downward, now head downward,
If she falls to the ground from this descent, what will happen to her,
If you do not save her, my God, she will die without a word,
Being a protector, deliver my lover safe and sound,
For the sake of my lover, I am ready to give up all I have.

Turning around in the air, she has flown for a long time,
I am praying to God, my soul is full of anxiety,
You are a great ruler, your path is just,
Just ruler, fulfill my prayer,
Hearing my anguish, deliver my lover safe and sound,
Do not burn the tender soul in my body alive in the fire.

To my lover Shasänem, my God, give strength,
I am paying homage to you, my Forgiving one, and trusting in your mercy,

Özing rähim qylmasang, boldy-aw bizge qiyanat,	If you do not render your mercy, we suffer a betrayal,
Yar kiyatyr asmannan, bul ne degen älamat,	A lover is falling from the sky, what kind of fate is this,
Özing äilep salamat, aman jetker yarymny.	Keep her in good health, and deliver my lover safe and sound,
	Lord of all the world, hear my lament.
Igasy gülli älamnyng, eshite-gör zarymny.	
	My two eyes are on my lover, I look neither to the right nor to the left,
Ekki közim yarymda, baqman saghyw-solyma,	My Lord, do not let me encounter warriors of sorrow on my way,
Gham läshkerin ilahym, jolyqtyrma jolyma,	Perch a nightingale in love on my open flower,
Qondyr shaida bülbilni, taza ashylghan gülime,	Deliver my lover unhurt into my hands,
Qawyshtyrghyl salamat, säwer yardy qolyma,	Save her from danger and bring my lover safe and sound,
Saqlap qäwpi-qäterden, aman jetker yarymny.	Do not destroy me by not delivering her safely.
Yardy aman jetkermei-aw, qarap etme halymny.	
	To the Almighty I have prayed, imploring you only,
Qädirim dep syghyndym, bir özinge yalbaryp,	Seeing my lover's state, my eyes are turning sallow,
Awhalyn körip yarymnyng, jolynda közim sarghaiyp,	Hoping that she arrives safely, I cry, raising my hands,
Jetkerer dep salamat, iyghlap turman qol jaiyp,	Gazing in hope, here stands this Ghärip,
Tigilip tur telmirip, ümit etip bul Ghärip,	Harken to my prayer, deliver my lover safe and sound,
Mustajab qylyp duwamny, aman jetker yarymny.	Accept my supplication, bring my lover safe and sound.
Qabul äilep nalamny, aman jetker yarymny.	

STUDY QUESTIONS

1. How is the poetic meter of *mukhammas* reflected in the rhythmic pattern of the sung melody?

2. In what ways does the evolving melodic pattern of the song correspond to its poetic language and reflect the hero's state of mind?

3. How would you characterize the style of Ram shaiyr's recitation? Could the *qyssakhan*'s performance style be compared with any types of unaccompanied sung storytelling in other cultures of the world?

SADYQ NURYMBETOV

Sadyq Nurymbetov's recitation lends itself to musically articulated declamation in which the verbal element assumes a primary role. He has a small melodic repertory, using the same tunes for verses in different meters with eight and eleven syllables. The following example presents Sadyq Nurymbetov's performance of his own poem, "Dawytköl." The poem is composed in the eleven-syllable *barmaq* meter with the conventional aaba rhyme structure, which varies in each stanza (bbcb, ccdc, dded, etc.). Listen to "Dawytköl" and compare Sadyq Nurymbetov's recitation style with that of Ram shaiyr in the preceding example.

Composed by Nurymbetov in 1919, this poem tells of the hardships and miseries suffered by the Karakalpaks in the years following the Russian Revolution of 1917. During this period of unrest and famine, the people gathered around Lake Dawytköl between the Kegeili and Shymbai regions in the north of present-day Karakalpakstan in the hope of surviving on fishing, but were overtaken by a severe winter.

Sadyq Nurymbetov.

Painting by Nikolai Kornilov from the album *My Karakalpakiya*.

LISTEN

Example 6.6. "Dawytköl," composed and performed by Sadyq Nurymbetov, Nukus, 1970. Recording from the archive of the Karakalpakstan Television and Radio Broadcasting Company.

Qublangyz Qyrantaw, arqang Naghalai,

Your south is Qyrantaw [mountains], your north is [Lake] Naghalai,

Elim köshti Dawytköldi jaghalai,
Ighbalyna balyq, shabaq shyqpady,
Taghy bajban qondyrmady, bul qalai?

My people migrated to the shores of Dawytköl,
But by bad luck there were hardly any fish,
And the forest guard did not let us stay overnight, how is that?

Jutym ushyn bul ne degen daghdarys,
Taryqqanda tabylmady bir tanys,

What misery because of a morsel of food,
At the time of need there was no acquaintance to be found,

Men de keldim Dawytköldi panalap,
Qursaghym ash, tek qosyghym aldanysh.

I, too, came to Dawytköl seeking shelter,
I was starving, only my poetry gave me pleasure.

Ashlyq bizing äpshimizdi quwyrdy,
Köp adamlar jeken tamyr suwyrdy,
Bir-birewden tabylmady shäpaat,
Sepkil betler köz jas penen juwyldy.

Famine withered our faces,
Many people gathered roots of *jeken*,[12]
Nobody helped anyone else,
Sunburned faces were bathed in tears.

Äwelinde isengening Dawytköl,
Qyiyn boldy bunnan balyq tawyp jer,
Härkim özi kömeshine kül tartqan,
Baspana joq ashyrqady kewip el.

We believed in Dawytköl at first,
It was difficult to find fish in this place,
Each one fought for himself,
We had no shelter, hunger-shriveled people.

Qal jawradyq jalang ayaq qar basyp,
Öitip-büitip kün keshirdik tarmasyp,

We were freezing and trod barefoot on snow,
Barely endured days, clinging to [life],

Talshybyqtai tawlanysqan jananlar,	Beautiful girls thin as cane
Bir batpan tarygha ketti almasyp.	We exchanged for a *batpan*[13] of millet.
Qashan umyt bolar eken kün usy,	When will these days ever be forgotten,
Jalynsang-da bailardyng joq jughysy,	However much you beg, there is no help from men of wealth,
Bir jylgha-da bola almady dalalat,	Not for a single year did it give us protection,
Tunjyraghan Dawytkölding türi usy.	This dreary-looking Dawytköl.

STUDY QUESTIONS

1. Describe the relationship between text and melody in Sadyq Nurymbetov's performance. Does each syllable correspond to a separate musical note? Does the same melodic sequence repeat in each successive quatrain? Does the musical rhythm reflect the text rhythm?

2. In what ways is Sadyq Nurymbetov's recitation style different from or similar to the style of Ram shaiyr in example 6.5?

3. Does the fact that Sadyq Nurymbetov performs his own poem while Ram shaiyr performs a traditional folk epic lead to differences in the performance styles of the two *qyssakhan*s?

ABBAZ DABYLOV

Of the three traditional *qyssakhan*s from the twentieth century—Abbaz Dabylov, Sadyq Nurymbetov, and Rambergen Khojambergenov (Ram shaiyr)—it is arguably Abbaz Dabylov whose legacy remains the strongest. A pupil of Qäwender bala and follower of the school of Qazy Mawlik, he recollected his emerging interest in *qyssakhan* performance: "I was dreaming about being familiar with literacy and learning how to read *qyssa*s. After I had learned how to write, I couldn't find a good *qyssa* book. I didn't have money to go to the bazaar and buy a book. In addition to day labor, I reaped hempweed, collected it, and stripped off its fiber. In those days hemp fiber was used for making thick rope. So I would carry twenty-five bundles of hemp fiber from the banks of the Quwanyshjarma to Shymbai bazaar for sale.[14] With the money I earned, I bought one *qyssa* book, *Ghärip Ashyq*, from a man called Qazy Mawlik, who ran his own bookstore in Shymbai bazaar. At that time it was very difficult to find a book even for money. Qazy Mawlik probably sensed my interest in literature or realized that I didn't have any more money and decided to help me: he gave me the *qyssa Ghärip Ashyq* at twenty coins (*tiyin*) cheaper. That gave me a great pleasure then."[15]

Subsequently, Abbaz Dabylov engaged in *qyssakhanshylyq* professionally. He traveled around villages and made a living performing the *qyssakhan* repertory. In 1933, during his travels in Karakalpakstan, he was recorded performing a *täriyp* of Qorazbek Razbek uly by members of a folklore expedition organized under the auspices of the Karakalpak Research Institute of the Uzbekistan Academy of Sciences. The *täriyp* consisted of 328 verse lines and, according to contemporaries, was one of the most popular examples of this genre at the time.

Under Soviet rule, Abbaz shaiyr became an active advocate for socialist ideas. Together with Sadyq Nurymbetov, another eminent *qyssakhan* favored by the authorities, he traveled around the republic and performed on radio and television propagating the new ideology through traditional folk repertory (*qyssa, dästan, täriyp, aitys*) and his own epic and lyric poems. In 1939, he was granted membership in the Writers Union of Karakalpakstan and, as part of a delegation of cultural workers from the Republic, visited Moscow for the first time. His impressions of that trip are captured in his *täriyp* about Moscow, "Körip keldim" (I saw), composed in the form of a traditional panegyric ode. In this form, strophes of four lines have the following pattern of end rhyme: aaaa, bbba, ccca, ddda, and so on. Each line consists of eight syllables—an example of the widely used Turkic *barmaq* meter described earlier in this chapter.

Abbaz Dabylov performs his poems on stage during "Ten Days of the Culture of Karakalpakstan" in Moscow in 1939.

Courtesy of Murat Dabylov.

The full text for this example is available on the companion website.

Example 6.7. "Körip keldim" (I saw), a *täriyp* composed and performed by Abbaz Dabylov, Nukus, 1968. Recording from the archive of the Karakalpakstan Television and Radio Broadcasting Company.

LISTEN

Qulaq salyng jan doslarym,	Listen here, my friends,
Moskvany körip keldim.	I saw Moscow.
Esitsengiz yar-doslarym,	Harken, my dear friends,
Körip miyrim qanyp keldim.	I saw and enjoyed it with my soul.

Köshe aralap jürgenimdi,	Having walked around the streets,
Közim menen körgenimdi,	What I saw with my eyes,
Öz kewlime bilgenimdi,	What I learned with my heart,
Men sizlerge alyp keldim.	I bring to you.
Barghansha temir jol eken,	While you are on your way, there is a railroad ahead,
Ölmesek ömir mol eken.	While you are alive, there is a long life ahead.
Moskva kätta, zor eken,	That Moscow is powerful and great
Zeinim tanyp bilip keldim.	I knew in my soul.

STUDY QUESTIONS

1. Describe how the *täriyp*'s verse is set to music. Are the poetic and musical structures in sync, or do they diverge?

2. Compare this *täriyp* with the *täriyp* of Ayapbergen Musa uly cited above, and discuss what is conventional and what is new about this panegyric.

Abbaz Dabylov in the sound recording studio at Karakalpak Radio.

Courtesy of Murat Dabylov.

In the 1950s, Abbaz Dabylov composed the *dästan Bahadyr,* in which he addressed the subject of social inequality and struggle. The *dästan* contrasts the hard, oppressed life of the Karakalpak people before the revolution with their happy, liberated life after the revolution. Its hero, Aryslan, a poor and deprived but noble and brave young man, falls in love with a girl, Qyrmyzy, who is promised in marriage to a wealthy man, Artyq. By overcoming obstacles, Aryslan emerges as a leader in the establishment of Soviet authority in Karakalpakstan and, with the help of his poet-musician friend Azat, attains happiness with his lover. Although it treats a contemporary social topic, the epic poem draws upon the poetic and musical traditions of folk *dästan*s, and adopts narrative motifs and character types found in ancient epics: the trials and tribulations of lovers and their struggle for happiness; the antithesis of good and evil in the opposition between the hero and his enemies; and the images of a poor but virtuous young man, his beautiful and loyal bride, devoted friend, and valiant horse.

The following excerpt from Abbaz Dabylov's performance of the *dästan* tells of Aryslan's encounter with Azat. The initial, recited part of the excerpt (up to 00:27) contains passages of rhymed declamation in the seven-to-eight-syllable *barmaq* meter. This is followed by a sung part in a strophic form based on the eight-syllable meter with one rhyme in the first three lines and a different, repeated rhyme in the fourth line. The entire recording, which lasts thirty minutes, is the only extensive sound recording to be preserved of a *qyssakhan* performing an epic poem.

Example 6.8. Excerpt from the *dästan Bahadyr*, composed and performed by Abbaz Dabylov, Nukus, 1959. Recording from the archive of the Karakalpakstan Television and Radio Broadcasting Company.

In contrast with the other two *qyssakhan*s, Abbaz Dabylov's performance is distinguished by a special musicality. His recitation highlights the musical presentation of words. His melodic repertory is more diverse and heterogeneous, comprising five or six tunes, and his singing is more elaborate and ornamented. His idiosyncratic recitation style has become widely known and familiar to contemporary listeners and is perceived nowadays as emblematic of *qyssakhan* performance.

STUDY QUESTIONS

1. Compare Abbaz Dabylov's manner of recitation in the two above examples with the performance style of Ram shaiyr and Sadyq Nurymbetov. In your view, what component of the overall structure, verbal or musical, comes to the fore in each of their performances?

2. Judging from the brief summary of *Bahadyr*'s content and this excerpt, what features of folk *dästan*s would you say the *qyssakhan* adopts in his own epic poem?

TRADITION IN DECLINE

In the 1970s and 1980s, with the passing of the last three *qyssakhan* masters to have practiced this art professionally, the role and significance of the *qyssakhan* in Karakalpak society began to decline. Continuity of knowledge and skills associated with *qyssakhanshylyq* was broken, and performance lost its former appeal in the face of rising literacy, Europeanization of indigenous culture, and the increasing prominence of modern, more sophisticated forms of performance art and entertainment. It was as if the tradition had been shorn of its social and cultural relevance and vitality.

In the early twenty-first century, epic narration and poetic recitation by *qyssakhan*s is no longer a part of everyday life, and techniques of *qyssakhan* performance are not consciously passed down, either through traditional master-pupil lineages or through modern institutional modes of transmission. *Qyssakhanshylyq* as a distinctive, specialized art has effectively disappeared, yet the repertory of *qyssakhan*s continues to be performed by folk musicians and professional singers who specialize in other repertories but can reproduce *qyssakhan*s' melodies. In addition to such performers, a small number of self-trained *qyssakhan*s continue to recite epic poems and their own poetry as a hobby or amateur activity.

In the next example, a professional singer, Biybiraba O'tepbergenova (b. 1946), performs a fragment from the *dästan Alpamys*. Although her main repertory is contemporary Karakalpak songs sung to the accompaniment of a folk instrumental ensemble, she has also learned to sing in the manner of *qyssakhan*s (*qyssa joly*), and is thus one of only a few female performers to have mastered this traditionally male art.[16] Here she sings a song from the popular heroic epic to a tune used by *jyrau*s, as was common in *qyssakhan*s' renditions of *jyrau*s' repertory. The song is based on the seven-to-nine-syllable *barmaq* meter with a different rhyme at the end of each stanza. In her musical rendition, the singer elongates each poetic line to a larger number of rhythmic units, adopting the dramatic singing style of *jyrau*s.

LISTEN

Example 6.9. "Ne körding, qara atym, ne körding?" (What have you seen, my black horse, what have you seen?), excerpt from the *dästan Alpamys,* performed by Biybiraba O'tepbergenova. From Frédéric Léotar, *Karakalpakistan—La Voix des Ancêtres* [Karakalpakstan—The Voice of Ancestors] (CD, DVD, PDF file) (Buda Records/Universal, 2008), track 9.

The song comes from the episode of the epic where Alpamys travels to the land of enemies, the Qalmaqs, to bring back his bride. At the border he encounters a Qalmaq hero, Qarajan batyr. On hearing Alpamys's horse stamp its hooves, Qarajan attempts to ride toward him to prevent him from crossing the border, but the hero's horse stands still, refusing to move forward. Qarajan is angry but tries to calm down and cheer up his horse by singing this song.

Ne körding, qara atym, ne körding?	What have you seen, my black horse, what have you seen?
Keininge qarap sheginding,	Why are you stepping back,
Tört ayaqlap tebinding,	Stamping with your four hooves?
Ne körding, qara atym, ne körding?	What have you seen, my black horse, what have you seen?
Alyp (ta) edim al menen,	I bought you on advice,
Alpys tuwar mal menen,	In exchange for sixty heads of cattle,
Jüirik degen dang menen,	For you were a famous steed,
Ne körding, qara atym, ne körding?	What have you seen, my black horse, what have you seen?
Maqpaldan sailap dorba ildim,	I made a feedbag for you from velvet,
Kishmishten sailap jem berdim,	I fed you with select raisins,
Jemingdi qashan kem berdim?	When have I fed you little?
Ne körding, qara atym, ne körding?	What have you seen, my black horse, what have you seen?

Qäteptei awzyngdy ashpaisang,	You are not opening your mouth like a camel,
Däryadai güwlep taspaisang,	You are not raging like a river,
Aldynga qädem baspaisang,	You are not taking a step forward,
Ne körding, qara atym, ne körding?	What have you seen, my black horse, what have you seen?
Begler qurghan shatyrma?	Is there a tent set up by warriors ahead?
Shatyrda jolbarys jatyrma?	Is there a tiger resting in the tent?
Jatqanlar bizden de batyrma?	Would he be braver than us?
Ne körding, qara atym, ne körding?	What have you seen, my black horse, what have you seen?
Keter me däwran biyqarar?	Will my life pass without glory?
Eglenseng keter yqtyiar,	If you do not move, luck will escape us,
"Shüw," desem nege jürmeiseng?	Why don't you move forward when I say, "Giddy-up"?
Jamanlatqyr jäniwar.	May you catch anthrax, beast.

STUDY QUESTIONS

1. Analyze the verse form and melodic pattern of the song.

2. Does the singer's rendition of the fragment from *Alpamys* share any stylistic features with the performance of the same heroic epic by Baqbergen Syrymbetov (Baqbergen jyrau) in example 6.1?

3. In what ways is Biybiraba O'tepbergenova's manner of singing distinct from the other examples in this chapter?

In summer 2013, in the course of preparing this chapter, Kalmurza Kurbanov set out to recreate the context of male get-togethers (*geshtek*) where, according to oral accounts, *qyssakhan*s used to recite epic poetry. He arranged an informal gathering that brought together people interested in *qyssakhanshylyq* and individuals who perform as *qyssakhan*s on occasion, notably Khalila Dawletnazarov and *baqsy* Kärimbai Tynybayev (b. 1941). During the evening, those present shared their knowledge and memories of *qyssakhan* performance, exchanged stories about old masters, discussed the recitation styles of different *qyssakhan*s, and listened to excerpts of epic poetry. The following video filmed at the *geshtek* shows an excerpt from the *dästan Ghärip Ashyq* read by Khalila Dawletnazarov, and a fragment of conversation about *qyssakhanshylyq* with *baqsy* Kärimbai Tynybayev. Watch the video and notice the styles of *qyssakhan* performance exemplified by Khalila Dawletnazarov and demonstrated by Kärimbai Tynybayev.

The growth of urbanization, the widespread dissemination of globalized mass culture, and the ubiquitous presence of media technologies make the demise of the *qyssakhan* tradition among the Karakalpaks almost inevitable. Vehicles for delivering popular entertainment, such as theater, cinema, television, and the Internet have

Performer Profile: Khalila Dawletnazarov

The only performer who can be said to continue the *qyssakhan* tradition in Karakalpakstan today is Khalila Dawletnazarov (b. 1952). A journalist by profession who completed a musical college course as an opera singer, he never specially studied the art of *qyssakhanshylyq* with a master but considers the poetic and musical atmosphere of his childhood as being crucial in awakening his interest in poetry and *qyssakhan* performance. His maternal uncle was an amateur poet and *qyssakhan*. At weddings in his village, Khalila had a chance to listen to *jyrau, baqsy,* and *qyssakhan* bards. Performances by Ram shaiyr, in particular, made a lasting impression on him. Later he became aware of Abbaz Dabylov, whom he considers his spiritual teacher.

He learned all of Dabylov's tunes by listening to them on radio and television, and subsequently used them for the performance of his own poetry.

But it was Khalila's work as a musical editor at Karakalpak Radio, beginning in 1985, that was decisive in launching him as a *qyssakhan*. After listening to rare recordings of *qyssakhan* performance held in the radio archive and preparing radio programs about *qyssakhans*, he started to perform publicly before large audiences, reciting his own poetry to *qyssakhans'* tunes. Currently chief editor of the literary journal *Amu Darya*, Khalila performs on radio and television and at official state celebrations and holidays, as well as, rarely, at traditional festive occasions, such as weddings or home

Khalila Dawletnazarov recites poetry at a Nawryz celebration in Nukus in 1989.
Courtesy of Khalila Dawletnazarov.

gatherings. Though he does not intentionally transmit his skills to a younger generation, performers who occasionally practice *qyssakhanshylyq*, such as Qädirbai Jumaniyazov and Rawaj Otarbayev, regard him as their master.

WATCH

Example 6.10. *Geshtek* (Male get-together): excerpt from the *dästan Ghärip Ashyq*, performed by Khalila Dawletnazarov, and conversation with Kärimbai Tynybayev, Nukus, 2013. Film courtesy of Kalmurza Kurbanov.

The text for this example is available on the companion website.

STUDY QUESTION

1. Compare the fragments of epic singing featured in this video with all the preceding examples in the chapter. To what extent have contemporary performers preserved or moved away from the earlier *qyssakhan* performance as exemplified by Abbaz Dabylov, Sadyq Nurymbetov, and Ram shaiyr?

---

superseded the live performance of epics, while poetry, formerly transmitted orally, can now be read from books and digital media without recourse to storytellers.

In the face of these realities, state organizations spearheaded by enthusiastic individuals have made attempts to revitalize *qyssakhan* performance and reintroduce it into the cultural life of Karakalpaks. Performances by old *qyssakhan* masters and contemporary performers have been broadcast on radio and television. Epic bards, including performers of the *qyssakhan* repertory, have been involved in a variety of festivals and competitions and featured in concerts of traditional music. In 2007, a festival and competition dedicated to Abbaz Dabylov "Abbaz hawazy—Qaratereng yrghaqlary" (The Voice of Abbaz—Qaratereng's Tunes), was held in Qaratereng, Takhtaköpir, the northernmost region of Karakalpakstan. Following this event, the Karakalpak film company produced a documentary film, *Qyssakhanlar* (*Qyssakhan*s). These and other initiatives aimed at raising awareness of *qyssakhanshylyq* give hope that this idiosyncratic phenomenon in Karakalpak expressive culture will live on and be transmitted to future generations of performers and listeners.

NOTES

1. In the official transliteration system for Karakalpak, *dutar* is written "*duwtar.*" For sake of consistency, *dutar* is used throughout this book.

2. Originally published in *Karakalpakistan—La Voix des Ancêtres* [Karakalpakistan: The voice of ancestors] (Musique du Monde/Music from the World 3017797, 2008). Collection Dominique Buscail, directed by Gilles Fruchaux. Buda Musique: www.budamusique.com.

3. Similar types of storytellers have existed among other Turkic- and Persian-speaking peoples (see, for example, chapter 7). In the Persianate world, the tradition of oral declamation of literary works, including those by the great classical poets, such as Rudaki and Ferdowsi, is said to have a long-standing history going back to the early Middle Ages. See Iosif Braginskii, "Ob Iranskoi skazochnoi entsiklopedii" (On the encyclopedia of Iranian tales), *Iranskaya skazochnaya entsiklopediya* (Encyclopedia of Iranian tales), translated from Persian by A. Dun and Y. Salimova, edited by I. Braginskii (Moscow: Khudozhestvennaya literatura, 1977), 7.

4. Adapted from Ayapbergen Musa uly, *Shygharmalary* [Works], ed. T. Najimov (Nökis: Qaraqalpaq mamleket baspasy, 1960), 107–108.

5. A traditional sport in which horse-mounted players compete to seize a goat carcass from one another.

6. Ghärip is the pen name of Ayapbergen Musa uly.

7. See Näjim Däwqarayev, *Shygharmalarynyng tolyq jiynaghy* [Complete collection of works], vol. 3, ed. T. Najimov (Nökis: Qaraqalpaqstan, 1979), 172.

8. Äbdisaiyt Pakhratdinov, *XIX äsirding aqyry—XX äsirding basyndaghy qaraqalpaq ädebiyaty tariykhy* [The history of Karakalpak literature from the late 19th–early 20th century] (Nökis: Bilim, 1996), 117–118.

9. Qally Aiymbetov, *Khalyq danalyghy* [Folk wisdom] (Nökis: Bilim, 1968), 171.

10. Owing to the epic's popularity, this pen name was adopted by several *shaiyr-qyssakhan*s. This may have signified their affiliation with the same poetic school (see Pakhratdinov, *XIX äsirding aqyry—XX äsirding basyndaghy qaraqalpaq ädebiyaty tariykhy*, 119).

11. Karakalpakstan became part of the Soviet Union in 1924, initially as an autonomous area within Kazakhstan. In 1936, it became part of the Soviet Socialist Republic of Uzbekistan.

12. Perennial marsh plant whose roots contain sugar and starch.

13. Measure of weight equivalent to 20–40 kg.

14. Quwanyshjarma is an irrigation canal supplying water to the northeastern areas of Karakalpakstan, Qaraözek and Takhtaköpir. Shymbai is a region in the north of Karakalpakstan. The distance between the Quwanyshjarma Canal and Shymbai is approximately 20–25 km.

15. Aiymbetov, *Khalyq danalyghy*, 219.

16. For another historical instance of a female *qyssakhan* and *baqsy*, see Aiymbetov, *Khalyq danalyghy*, 167.

CHAPTER 7   # The Art of the Turkmen *Bagshy*

JAMILYA GURBANOVA

"Turkmen" is an old ethnonym in Central Asia that historically has referred to a variety of different social groups spread over a wide geographic territory, as well as to a specific Turkic language. "Turkmen" has also been adopted as a place name for cities and towns, and as a personal surname, not to mention its well-known use as a descriptive term for a type of handwoven carpet (often spelled Turkoman or Turcoman) and a famous breed of horse. Today the Turkmen are the titular ethnic group of the modern nation of Turkmenistan, where they constitute some 85 percent of the total population of around five million. An estimated one million or more ethnic Turkmen live in the northeastern provinces of Iran that border Turkmenistan—Golestan, North Khorasan, and Razavi Khorasan— and another estimated nine hundred thousand Turkmen live in northwestern Afghanistan. All of these areas are encompassed in what historically could be called Greater Khorasan—a Persianate geocultural region that once included parts of present-day Afghanistan, Iran, Turkmenistan, and Uzbekistan. This chapter focuses on the musical traditions of bards, called *bagshy,* in the nation of Turkmenistan, where *bagshy*s occupy a highly respected social and cultural role.

The word "*bagshy,*" in slightly variant pronunciations, has different meanings among different Central Asian peoples. Presently, *bagshy* and its cognate forms have two principal meanings: "bard" and "shaman." For example, in Kazakh *baqsy* means "shaman" while in Turkmen *bagshy* means "bard"—specifically, a bard who sings epics and shorter songs, and also typically plays instrumental music on the two-stringed lute, the *dutar.* (Turkmen musicians who play instrumental music but don't sing are called *sazanda,* which is also a general Turkmen term for "musician.") In the Uzbek language, *bakhshi* may refer both to an epic reciter and a shaman. The persistence of this dual meaning suggests that the functions of epic reciter and shaman were once combined in one and the same individual. Such a dual function

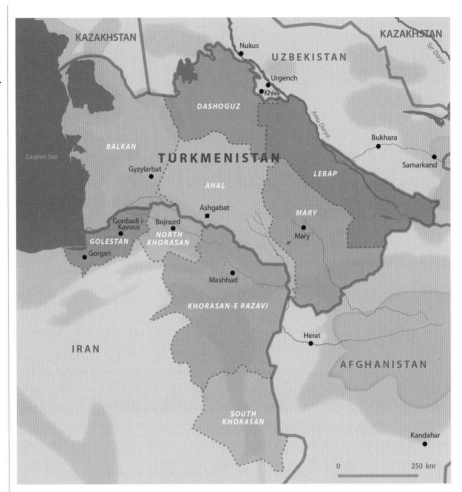

Turkmenistan comprises five provinces. Significant populations of ethnic Turkmen also live in the northeastern provinces of Iran and in northwestern Afghanistan.

is evident in the legendary figure of Dede Korkut (or Qorqyt), the prototypical Turkic bard, who is venerated as the saint-protector of *bagshys* and is the central heroic figure of the eponymous epic tale "The Book of Dede Korkut." In the epic, Dede Korkut is an *ozan,* or shaman-bard, who recounts the history of the pre-Islamic Oghuz group of Turkic clans and tribes—the ancestors of the Turkmen. Dede Korkut is also regarded as the inventor of the *qobyz,* the two-stringed fiddle associated with shamans and shamanic power (see chapter 16).

Scholars have proposed different etymologies for the term *bagshy/bakhshi/baqsy.* One explanation is that it came from Chinese *bóshì,* meaning "Buddhist religious teacher," and was adopted as a loan word in Mongolian, and later, in Uyghur, in the form *bakhshy,* which meant "scribe," and more specifically a "scribe able to write in the Uyghur (or rather Mongolian official) alphabet."[1] Another explanation is that *bagshy* is from the Sanskrit *bhikshu,* "teacher," which was adopted in Central

Asia with the spread of Buddhism and, among the ruling classes, came to refer to Buddhist lamas who could read and write the Uyghur script, while among common people, who continued to worship spirits, it was understood as "shaman." With the advent of Islam in Central Asia, mullahs largely took over the religious function of shamans, and the *bagshy* retained only some attributes of former shamanic practices, notably singing and instrument playing. Thus *bagshy* eventually came to denote a folk singer, musician, and bard.[2] Changes in the social function of the *bagshy* notwithstanding, the magic powers ascribed to shamans continued to be ascribed to *bagshy* bards. These powers include the ability to communicate with spirits and to affect people's psyche through spoken words and verbal eloquence. Like shamans, *bagshy*s traditionally undergo rites of passage—typically an initiatory dream or a serious illness—in order to demonstrate their authenticity and competence.

Monument to Ashyk Aydyn Pir in Dashoguz, northern Turkmenistan.
Courtesy of Turkmenistan State Archive.

LEARNING

The art of the *bagshy,* called *bagshychylyk* in Turkmen, has for centuries been transmitted orally from one generation to the next. Becoming a master required extensive specialized training, achieved through close communication between master (*halypa*) and pupil (*shägirt*). Traditionally, *bagshy*s were overwhelmingly male, though female *bagshy*s were not unknown. During the Soviet era, when women were integrated not only into the workforce but into areas of the performing arts from which they had been excluded by local tradition, many girls and young women became interested in learning *bagshychylyk*. This interest continues today. Leading female *bagshy*s of the post-Soviet era include Almagül Nazarowa (b. 1983), Soltanbagt Rejepowa (b. 1986), and Bibinur Ashyrowa (b. 1984).

Akjagul Myradowa (1924–2004) was a leading representative of the Yomut school of epic performance.
Courtesy of Turkmenistan State Archive.

Traditionally, aspiring *bagshy*s would go on a pilgrimage to the shrines of Ashyk Aydyn Pir and Baba Gambar, the saintly patrons of musicians, whose names appear in a number of Turkmen legends and epics (*dessan*s).

At the shrines, they would make sacrifices, sing, and play the *dutar* in order to receive the saint's blessing in an initiatory dream. Well-known *bagshy*s typically had a small circle of pupils. Over the course of several years, pupils lived with and accompanied their mentor on travels as a way to assimilate performance skills and repertory. As a performing artist, a *bagshy* needed a strong voice, retentive memory, artistic skills, and general proficiency in performance. In addition to offering training in musical aspects of *bagshychylyk,* a master *bagshy* introduced pupils to the history of Turkmen tribes and clans and the genealogy of prominent historical personalities, explained the meaning of popular sayings and maxims, and instructed pupils in religious and everyday traditions and customs. In disclosing the secrets of *bagshychylyk,* the master also passed on a body of professional and ethical canons formed over centuries. When a young *bagshy,* whether primarily a singer of lyric songs or entire epics, attained sufficient mastery of performance techniques and had absorbed and internalized the specialized knowledge of *bagshychylyk,* this knowledge was demonstrated at a public initiatory event. The mentor granted a blessing, and from that moment on, a young *bagshy* could launch an independent performance career.

Nowadays Turkmenistan has a state system of music education for folk performers, in which traditional performance skills are taught alongside staff notation and classical European music history and theory, yet the conventional oral transmission of the *bagshy*'s art continues to flourish in the broader musical milieu. The two systems of transmission—traditional and state institutional—are not mutually exclusive. Young musicians often enter music colleges or the conservatory having already become accomplished *bagshy*s, and teachers in these institutions may have pupils outside their classes who study with them and accompany them to performance events such as weddings and other festivities. Novice *bagshy*s still visit monuments to the saintly patrons Ashyk Aydyn Pir and Baba Gambar as a symbolic act of initiation into the art of *bagshychylyk.* Blessing by a master remains essential in marking the end of a novice's period of apprenticeship, and signals to the public that the student is worthy of the title *bagshy.* The master offers spiritual guidance to the young *bagshy,* who commits to following it. For example, the celebrated bard Magtymguly Garlyýew (1889–1957) offered the following guidance to his pupil Ilaman Annaýew, who later became a renowned epic performer:

> *Meniň kesbi-kärim berilsin, "gum" diýip garbanyň gyzyl bolsun, kesbiňden bereket tap, agzyňdan patrat (erbet) söz çykmasyn. Iki zada gaýym bol: nebsiňe we diliňe. Diliň ötgür, akylyň kesgir bolsun.*

> "May my craft-vocation be passed on to you. May it serve you as a source of inspiration and become a firm support in your life. May your lips not utter strong language. Be attentive to the state of two things: your soul and your tongue. May your tongue be well-honed and your mind sharp."[3]

The guidance given by another epic bard, Jumadurdy Durdyýew (b. 1958), included these tenets: do not rest on one's oars—in art, the sky is the limit; have the courage and willpower to guard against pernicious temptations; be ever more demanding of oneself with the rise of one's recognition; do not mark oneself out from the crowd as someone special.

Performance

A performance by a *bagshy* has always been an integral part of social life among the Turkmen. Before the advent of modern media, the arrival of an itinerant *bagshy* was a significant event that drew large audiences. Arminius (Ármin) Vámbéry, a Hungarian orientalist who traveled around Central Asia in the 1860s disguised as a Muslim dervish, remarked on the popularity of *bagshy*s: "The utmost pleasure for the Turkmen is the coming of *bagshy*s and performance by them on the *dutar* of songs by Görogly and Magtymguly."[4] *Bagshy*s were not only entertainers; they kept abreast of the latest news and circulated it in the course of their travels. In order to listen to a famous *bagshy* sing and narrate stories, legends, and tales, people would flock to the place where he performed from near and far. The most common occasions for performance by a *bagshy* were the various kinds of family celebration known as *toy*. No *toy* was considered complete without a *bagshy*'s singing and storytelling. *Toy*s could feature performances by individual *bagshy*s as well as competitions between two or more performers that displayed their quick-wittedness, sharp memory, and talent for improvisation. *Bagshy*s were, above all, honored guests who were unfailingly welcomed hospitably, encouraged by their audience during a performance, and, upon departure, rewarded with presents in recognition of their talent and mastery. In their classic study *Turkmenskaya Muzyka* (Turkmen music), Russian musical ethnographers Viktor Uspenskii and Viktor Beliaev described the ambiance of a typical *bagshy* performance in the 1920s:

> In the evening . . . in the tent where the visiting *bagshy* has found hospitality, almost the entire *aul* [settlement] gathers together or, better to say, packs in. The *bagshy* sits in the middle. Beside him are a tea-pot and a cup of green tea, with which he quenches his thirst every now and then. All around people are sitting tight in deep concentration and keeping absolute silence. Occasionally somebody exclaims before the beginning, "*Bashlaver!*" (get started), and every so often during the performance people shout out "*Berekella!*" (well done), "*Hai!*" (exclamation of encouragement), "*Chal!*," "*Chalyber!*" (play, strum the strings), "*Sag bol!*" (bless you), "*Ya, Allah*" (oh, my Lord), and others. The music almost always lasts the whole night, moreover, none of the listeners leave before it ends. If two *bagshy*s are playing, they sit close facing each other, sometimes knee to knee, and then the "concert" takes on the form of a musical contest. The mood of performers and listeners continues to rise until it passes into sheer ecstasy; exclamations of approval ring out more

Bagshy Magtymguly Garlyýew.
Courtesy of Turkmenistan State Archive.

and more often; money starts to fly onto the carpet where the *bagshy* is sitting as a reward and a sign of attention from the contented and moved listeners. Due to the hot temperature in the tent, sweat pours from the musicians like hail, even though they've already made themselves as comfortable as possible by even unbuttoning the collar of their shirts.[5]

In contemporary Turkmenistan, performances by *bagshy*s retain their popularity as an essential attribute of *toy*s, both in rural villages and in towns. *Bagshy*s can also be invited to perform outside of a specific festive occasion. Some areas, such as Halach township, in the northeastern region of Lebap, hold regular gatherings (*genesh*) of *bagshy*s in different homes, during which they take turns performing, starting with junior musicians and ending with senior masters.

TYPES OF *BAGSHY*

On the basis of performance style and repertory, Turkmen distinguish three different types of *bagshy,* called *yanamachy, tirmechi,* and *dessanchy.* A *yanamachy bagshy* sings songs generically called *yanama*—a genre defined by its performance style: a solo vocalist is accompanied by an instrumental player who typically plays an end-blown flute called the *gargy tuýduk,* or alternatively, the *dutar.* Singers emulate the *tuýduk*'s distinctive, plangent sound by singing long phrases augmented with grace notes. The art of the *yanamachy bagshy* has old roots, but singing to the accompaniment of *tuýduk* is now rare.

Yanamachy bagshy singing to the accompaniment of *dutar,* played by Durdy Muradow.
Courtesy of Turkmenistan State Archive.

The *tirmechi bagshy,* or performer of *tirme* (songs) emerged in the eighteenth century with the development of Turkmen poetry in the works of Magtymguly Pyragy (c. 1724–1782), the most famous figure in Turkmen literary history, and other contemporaneous poets such as Andalib (1712–1780), Shabende (1720–1800), and Sheýdaýy (c. 1730–1800).[6] These poets composed their poetry in writing at a time when poetry among other historically nomadic Central Asian peoples was overwhelmingly orally composed and transmitted. And in contrast to epic poetry, whose authorship was mostly unattributed, poems by Magtymguly and his contemporaries became popular based on the reputation of their author. *Tirmechi bagshy*s accompany themselves on the *dutar,* supported by a second *dutar* player, or by a duo of *dutar* and *ghijak.*

A *tirmechi* begins a performance with songs in the lower register and, as the performance continues, raises the pitch level of successive songs and increases the emotional intensity of singing, reaching a climax in the final song. Each song is allotted an established position within a performance event. The entire repertory of songs performed by *tirmechi bagshy*s falls into three groups:

1. Opening songs in low register that do not exceed the range of a fourth (*muhannes aýdymlar*)

2. Central songs in middle register with a wider pitch range, more varied structure, and more apparent dynamic development (*orta tap aýdymlar*)

3. Concluding songs in high register (sung in the singer's highest tessitura) that form the climax and conclude the performance (*jemleýji* or *soňlama aýdymlar*)

In addition to setting texts by Turkmen poets to music, *tirmechi bagshy*s also sing lyrical songs drawn from the repertory of epic (*dessan*). Epics consist of prose-narrative (*qyssa*) and poetic sections (*aýdym*). While the former are declaimed, the latter are sung to instrumental accompaniment. Song is an important structural and artistic element in epic. It provides a musical portrayal of an epic hero and reflects the stylistic properties and manner of performance typical of particular *bagshy*s and the epic school they represent. The number of songs performed in the name of a certain character offers a sense of the character's importance in an epic. *Tirmechi bagshy*s do not perform narrative prose sections but may sequence together a series of songs whose texts are drawn from different poetic sections of a single epic, from different epics, or that mix sections of epic with songs that set the lyrics of well-known poets.

In contrast to the *tirmechi, dessanchy bagshy*s specialize in the performance of both prose and poetry sections of *dessan*. A *dessanchy* narrates or declaims the prose sections and sings the poetry sections to the accompaniment of a *dutar,* typically supported by two instrumentalists playing *dutar*s, or *dutar* and *ghijak*. A typical *dessanchy bagshy* repertory comprises various genres of epic poetry that include heroic as well as romantic tales derived both from Turkic oral lore and from classical Arab and Persian literature. While prior to the eighteenth century most epics were transmitted orally as unattributed folk tales, the development of Turkmen literature led to the emergence of written versions of epics created by Turkmen poets, such as Andalib's *Leýli-Mejnun* and *Yusup-Zuleýha,* Shabende's *Gül-Bilbil* and *Shabahrem,* and Sheýdaýy's *Gül-Senuber.* These texts were disseminated by the poets themselves, many of whom assumed the role of *bagshy*s, as well as by literate bards, called *qyssachi,* who recited epic texts in a melodious manner to simple, recurring tunes without instrumental accompaniment (see chapter 6, part 2). At the same time, illiterate *bagshy*s committed *dessan*s to memory and subsequently recited them with musical accompaniment, arranging poetic sections (as opposed to prose narrative) as songs.

The most popular epic in the repertory of *dessanchy bagshy*s is the heroic epic *Görogly* (Son of the grave), which is known in various versions across the Caucasus and Central Asia (see chapter 5). In the Turkmen version, Görogly is not only a skillful singer and musician but an invincible leader of valiant warriors in charge of the Chandybil fortress, who stands against the cruel ruler, Leke shah. *Bagshy*s perform this and other large-scale epic cycles over several successive evenings, or choose individual episodes or fragments from the epics, each of which represents a self-standing *dessan*.

A *dessan* narrative consists of an introduction, the development of narrative incidents, and a final episode. It is woven from a series of motifs, or epic formulae, which depict the birth of the hero, his confrontation with enemies, and various characters and images, such as the hero's horse and yurt (*garaöÿ*). Recreating the story line of a *dessan*, the *bagshy* variously combines these formulae anew for each individual performance. In this way, a performance is never a mere repetition of the epic as heard from a master, but a creative re-assembling of its narrative elements.

The texts of epic songs are usually based on either of two verse forms in seven-, eight-, or eleven-syllable meters: the *murabba'* form is expressed in couplets (ab/cb db/db eb/eb), while *goshgy* is expressed in quatrains, with a recurring end rhyme in the last line (aaab [or abab] cccb dddb). More rarely, epic songs draw on the poetic form of *muhammas*, consisting of five-line stanzas with a rhyming fifth line; or *ghazal*, a love poem in couplets united by an internal rhyme (*qafia*) and a refrain (*radif*). Epic songs are based on a melody repeated at different pitch levels throughout a song's strophic form.

Before performing a *dessan*, *bagshy*s sing ten to twenty introductory songs (*tirme*) unrelated to the epic's main content. This allows performers to warm up their voice and prepare listeners to absorb a complex story many hours long. During a performance, *bagshy*s tighten up the strings of the *dutar* ten to twelve times before reaching the desired pitch level for most effectively "tuning" the emotions of listeners. Listeners not infrequently request a particular song, thus showing their knowledge of the *bagshy*'s repertory. Such interaction, along with encouraging exclamations on the part of an audience, rouse and inspire the performer. Songs within a *dessan* itself are also sequenced according to the principle of pitch rise and increasing dynamic intensity. As the performance progresses, the *bagshy*'s manner of singing and instrumental accompaniment become ever richer and more intense.

LOCAL STYLES AND SCHOOLS OF *BAGSHY* PERFORMANCE

Turkmen society historically consisted of a conglomeration of tribal groups identified with particular geographical territories. In the nineteenth and early twentieth centuries, these tribal groups gave rise to local styles and schools of *bagshy* performance associated with renowned *bagshy*s and their lineages, which came to be known as *bagshychylyk ÿollary*, or "schools of *bagshy* art." The six principal schools were Ahal (or Ahal-Teke), Damana, Ersary, Salyr-Saryk, Yomut-Göklen, and Yomut-Chowdur. While each school (*ÿol*) had its own distinctive features of performance style and repertory, contact with other schools as well as with the

Table 7.1. Tribal-Based Schools and Their Corresponding Contemporary Performance Schools

Tribal-based school (ýol)	Contemporary Performance School	Geographic Region
Ahal (or Ahal-Teke)	Ahal	South-Central
Damana		
Ersary	Lebap (also included influences from Ahal and Salyr-Saryk ýollary)	East
Salyr-Saryk	Mary	Southeast
Yomut-Göklen	Balkan	West
Yomut and Chowdur	Dashoguz	North

musical traditions of other ethnic groups—principally Khorezmi Uzbeks and Karakalpaks—facilitated mutual influence and exchange.

During the Soviet era, tribal-based affiliations were replaced by a new classification of *bagshy* performance schools that linked the principal *bagshy* schools to one of five administrative regions (*welaýatlar;* singular: *welaýat*) of the Turkmen Soviet Socialist Republic, which was established in 1925. In linking each region to a distinct form of musical heritage, Soviet culture policy strove to strengthen the cultural dimension of regional political identities while at the same time undermining the salience of traditional tribal cultural identities. The older tribal-based schools and their corresponding contemporary performance schools are indicated in table 7.1. (Several Soviet-era administrative regions were renamed after Turkmenistan became an independent nation.) Following are brief descriptions of the five contemporary performance schools, accompanied by musical examples.

Ahal

The south-central province of Ahal, which borders Iran, is renowned for idiosyncratic instrumental and singing traditions that evolved among the Teke and other local Turkmen clans. Ahal is particularly known for the sophistication of its *dutar* music, which is characterized by complex playing techniques, richly ornamented melodies, and developed musical structures (see chapter 8). Celebrated masters of the Ahal *dutar* school include Amangeldi Gönibek (1830–1879), Tächmammet Suhangulyýew (1865–1942), Mylly Tächmyradow (1885–1960), Pürli Saryýew (1900–1971), Chary Tächmämmedow (1923–1976), and Ýagmur Nurgeldiýew (1931–1993).

Master *dutar* player Pürli
Saryýew, 1970.
Photo by A. Guseynova.

Ahal *dutar* players
(*left to right*): Mylly
Tächmyradow, Ödeniýaz
Nobatow, Tächmämmet
Suhangulyýew.
Courtesy of Turkmenistan State Archive.

Bagshy Sahy Jepbarow.
Courtesy of Turkmenistan State Archive.

Another important instrumental tradition in Ahal is performance on the *gyjak,* a spike fiddle with a loud, full-bodied sound that is used both as a solo instrument and to accompany singing. Present-day performers play both the traditional three-stringed *gyjak* and a modernized version that has four strings, like a violin or viola. Leading performers on the *gyjak* from Ahal include Ata Ablyýew (1925–2002), Pürli Saryýew (1900–1971), Amangeldi Julgaýew (b. 1929), and Begmyrat Gutlymyradow (1947–2009).

Ahal is also known for its rich tradition of *tirme* songs. The singing tradition of Ahal is associated with the names of *tirmechi bagshy*s Sary bagshy (1871–1934), Sahy Jepbarow (1905–1977), Orazgeldi Ilýasov (1933–1966), Dörtguly Durdyýew (1933–2000), Nurýagdy Baýramow (b. 1938), and Oraznepes Döwletnazarow (b. 1944). The vocal style of Ahal *tirmechi bagshys* is distinguished by expansive breath control, broad vocal range, soaring high notes, wide dynamic gradations, and an abundance of guttural embellishments on alexical, or meaningless, syllables, known as *juk-juk.* These features are readily apparent in the performance of Sahy Jepbarow presented in example 7.1.

LISTEN

Example 7.1. "Näler görüner" (What will you not see), a folk song on a poem by Magtymguly, performed by Sahy Jepbarow (vocal, *dutar*), accompanied by Ýagmur Nurgeldiýew (*dutar*) and Ata Ablyýew (*gyjak*). Recording from the archives of Turkmen National Conservatory; year of recording unknown.

Seýl edeliň bu jahana,	Let us take a walk in the universe,
Jahanda näler görüner.	What will you not see there.
Iskender, Jemşit saldyran	Built by Iskandar[7] and Jamshid,[8]
Beýik binalar görüner.	High palaces you will see.
Çaglan, ýalan dünýä, çaglan!	Imagine, fickle world, picture it!
Ne gülen galar, ne aglan.	There will be no laughing, nor sadness left.
Gar ýagmyrlap, burjy baglan	Snow will fall, a covering of frost,
Kemerli daglar görüner.	Mountain spurs you will see.
Ne watan galar, ne çeten,	There will be no homeland, nor home left,
Senemler seýl edip öten,	Lovers will leave on travels.
Toty, bilbil mesgen tutan,	Only the haunt of nightingales and parrots,
Howaly baglar görüner.	Beautiful gardens you will see.
Magtymguly, kim bar ölmez?	Magtymguly, is there anyone who is immortal?
Ajal doýmaz, zemin dolmaz,	Death is insatiable, earth is fathomless.
Asman inmez, ýer çöwrülmez,	The sky will not fall, the soil will not turn over,
Gün ýörir, aýlar görüner.	The sun will take its course, the moon you will see.

STUDY QUESTIONS

1. What features of this song's performance situate it within the Ahal school?
2. What philosophic meaning does this song express?

A younger performer who traces his musical lineage to the Ahal school but whose own style is more eclectic is Muhammetgeldi Geldinejad (b. 1993). Popularly known as Oglan bagshy, or "boy *bagshy*"—the same nickname given to Ahal *bagshy* Sahy Jepbarow in his youth—Muhammetgeldi is from Gonbad-e Kavus, a city in Iran's Golestan Province with a large Turkmen population. (The poet Magtymguly is believed to have been born in a nearby village). Muhammetgeldi began playing the *dutar* at the age of six, studying with his father, Abdolghaffar Geldinejad, who was himself a student of the Ahal school *gyjak* player Ata Ablyýew. Older *bagshys* bestowed the name Oglan bagshy on Muhammetgeldi in 2002, when he was nine, in recognition of his prodigious talent. Thereafter, Oglan bagshy formed his own group and began his career as a professional performer, presenting concerts and participating in festivals and music competitions in both Iran and Turkmenistan,

Muhammetgeldi Geldinejad, known as *Oglan bagshy* (boy *bagshy*).
Courtesy of Muhammetgeldi Geldinejad.

and later performing in many European cities. In 2013, he graduated from the D. Öwezow Turkmen National Musical Vocational School and began studies for a master's degree at the Mimar Sinan University Conservatory, in Istanbul. Oglan bagshy exemplies a younger generation of musicians who have developed musical professionalism both through the traditional master-apprentice form of oral tradition and through institutional studies based on Western models. Though his *dutar* playing is very much in the tradition of the Ahal school, his repertory of *bagshy* songs draws on music from all over Turkmenistan. As a musical cosmopolitan, Oglan bagshy contributes to strengthening a contemporary Turkmen cultural identity that is at once transnational and transregional.

Watch **Example 7.2.** "Tä men gelinçäm" (Until I return), performed by Muhammetgeldi Geldinejad, *dutar* and voice. Filmed by George Murer, Istanbul, 2014.

Bir gözel alar men sen Öwezjana,	I'll find a beautiful girl for my Öwezjan,
Toý şaýyny tutuň, tä men gelinçäm,	Get everything ready for the wedding before I return,
Bir habar iberiň şaga soltana,	Send the news to the lords and the sultans:
Dursun gullugynda, tä men gelinçäm.	Let them live in prosperity until I return.
Bir habar iberiň, Halaba, Şama,	Send news to Aleppo and to Syria,
Bir toý tutuň, älem galsyn haýrana,	Plan a wedding that will amaze the whole world,
Günde mün guzyny çekiň bir ýana,	Each day pick out a thousand lambs
Iýsin Türkmen ilim, tä men gelinçäm.	And let my Turkmen people feast until I return.

Bize duşman olan Reýhan Arapdyr,	Our enemy Reikhan is from the Arabs,
Pir olmasa merdiň işi harapdyr,	A brave man without a protector is in despair.
Çişde kebap, piýalada şerapdyr,	Kebabs are on the grill and wine is in the cups,
İçibem mes olsun, tä men gelinçäm.	Let everyone drink and be merry until I return.
Görogly beg, sygyn Kadyr Subhana,	Beg Körogly, trust in almighty God,
Gyrat münüp, yglar etsem her ýana.	I'll sit on Gyrat and ride over the whole region.
Günde mün guzyny çekiň bir ýana,	Every day pick out a thousand lambs
İýsin Türkmen ilim,tä men gelinçäm.	And let my Turkmen people feast until I return.

STUDY QUESTIONS

1. Does Muhammetgeldi's performance hold your attention? If so, how? If not, what's missing?

2. Where would you place the vocal style on a continuum between speech and song?

3. What role does *juk-juk* play in the song?

4. What function does the *dutar* principally serve in the performance?

5. What unconventional or "extended" vocal technique do you hear in specific moments?

WATCH **Example 7.3.** "Jan jan" (My soul, my soul), performed by Muhammetgeldi Geldinejad, *dutar* and voice. Filmed by George Murer, Istanbul, 2014.

Sözle (weýeý wey ahaheyy ah jan jan) gurban bolaýyn,	I'm telling you, my beloved, that I'll sacrifice myself,
Janym aldaý jellad gözlerin seniň.	Your ruthless eyes conquered my soul.
Sana gelen derdi satyn alaýyn,	I'll assume the burden of your sadness,
Janym dökdi gara.	You conquered my soul.
Aşyk bolaneý janyndan umydyn,	I'm in love with your soul and your temperament,
Gijeler (weýeý) ýatmaýan nohanlar düzen.	I don't sleep at night, dreaming,
Çeşminiň kölünin garkyllap ýüzereý gel ýüzer	That you're ducking and floating in the springwater of my soul
Ýaşyl baş sonalý ýar.	Like a drake, my beautiful one.

Gözeller (weýeý weý ahaheý) içinde sensiz otaga,	If you're not lovely, then no one is,
Gel ikimiz (weýeý) keşt eýläli bu baga.	Let's take a walk in the garden.
Dünýäniň bar gyzy sana sadaka,	No girl in the world can compare with you,
Janym aldy ah näzleriň.	Your coquetry has captivated me.
Garyp aşygaý gül ýüzliniň zarydyr.	The face of the enraptured Garyp is filled with tears.
Gören aýdaraý olar kimiň ýarydyr, ýörise gözlerine däridir.	Whoever sees her asks whose beloved is this, whose stride is like a tonic for the eyes.
Gadamyňda çykan ah tozlaryň müň gyza degmez ah jan.	Even a thousand virgins aren't worth the dust that arises from your step.

STUDY QUESTIONS

1. How would you describe Muhammetgeldi's vocal style? What different kinds of timbres does he use, and why do you think he alters his vocal timbre? Of the music you know, can you think of any comparable vocal style?

2. Describe the rhythm of the *dutar* in the introductory instrumental section of the song. Does it have a regular meter?

3. What unconventional or "extended" *dutar* techniques do you hear?

4. Compare Muhammetgeldi's demeanor during the performance to the way other musicians comport themselves while they perform. Which of the traditional qualities of a *bagshy* does he exemplify or not exemplify?

BALKAN

The next music example is from the province of Balkan, in the southwest of Turkmenistan, the historical territory of the Yomut and Göklen tribes, who developed their own school of *bagshy* performance, known as Yomut-Göklen *ýoly*. The art of *bagshychylyk* in Balkan is mainly represented by *tirmechi bagshy*s. Their song repertory includes lyrics from classical Turkmen and Persian poetry as well as local poets from the second half of the nineteenth and early twentieth centuries, such as Misgingylych and Döwletmämmet Balgyzyl. Although some of their songs are shared with *tirmechi*s from other regions of Turkmenistan, notably Ahal, the local manner of singing is distinguished by an open, trembling, or "bleating" voice production, both in the main stanzas of a song and in filler phrases embellished with *juk-juk* guttural ornaments.

One of the most renowned performers of the Yomut-Göklen *ẏoly* was Ashyrmämmet Dawudow (1930–2011). The following example features a popular folk song, "Akmeñli," performed by Ashyrmämmet Dawudow together with a *dutar* and *gyjak* player.

Ashyrmämmet Dawudow.
Courtesy of Turkmenistan State Archive.

LISTEN

Example 7.4. "Akmeñli" (female name), a folk song set to a poem by Mämmetweli Kemine (1770–1840), performed by Ashyrmämmet Dawudow (vocal, *dutar*), accompanied by Myratdurdy Hajyẏev (*dutar*) and S. Garajayẏew (*gyjak*). Gazanjyk village, Balkan, 1997.

STUDY QUESTIONS

1. How does Ashyrmämmet Dawudow accommodate the poetic form of "Akmeñli" to a musical form? That is, to what extent does melodic phrasing reflect the form of the poetic lines?

2. What structural roles do the accompanying *gyjak* and *dutar* play in creating the trio's sound?

3. Where does the singer insert *juk-juk* syllables?

LEBAP

Music in Lebap province merges a range of instruments and musical styles that reflect its geographical location as a border region. Influences from Uzbekistan, with which Lebap shares a long border, are particularly prevalent in folk music, and include the use of instruments such as the plucked lutes *tar* and Kashgar *rubab*, frame drum (*doira*), and struck zither (*chang*). Singing by *tirmechi bagshy*s bears a stylistic affinity to the Mary and, to a lesser extent Ahal schools. An indigenous school of *bagshy* performance, called the Ersary school, after the dominant local tribe, was prominent from the eighteenth to the mid-twentieth century. Among contemporary *bagshy*s, one of the most respected is Musaguly Ẏazmyradow (b. 1956), who is featured in example 7.5.

Ensemble of *tuýduk* players, Lebap Province.

Example 7.5. "Ýusup soltanym" (My sultan Yusup), a song (*tirme*) from the heroic *dessan Ýusup-Ahmet,* by Magrupy. Performed by Musaguly Ýazmyradow (vocal, *dutar*), accompanied by Hally Begmämmedow (*gyjak*). Halach village, Lebap, 1997.

LISTEN

Ahmet beg: *Arkamyzdan ýetip geldi ýezitler,*

Maňa rugsat bergin, Ýusup soltanym!
Daglaryň saýyna doldy ýezitler,

Maňa rugsat bergin, Ýusup soltanym!

Ýusup beg: *Ýaş oglan sen, jerahaty görmedik,*

Tomaşany görgün, Ahmet mürzeýim!
Onuň üçin saňa rugsat bermedik,

Tomaşany görgün, Ahmet mürzeýim!

Ahmet beg: *Ahmet beg diýer, meni göze almadyň,*

Öwüt edip, belli jogap bermediň,

Özüň bildiň, meni adam bilmediň,

Ak patany bergin, Ýusup soltanym!

Ahmet bek: The oppressors are breathing down our backs,
Give me permission, my king Yusup!
The tyrants have filled the mountainside,
Give me permission, my king Yusup!

Yusup bek: You are still young, you have not seen life,
Enjoy merriment, my prince Ahmet!
I shall not give you my permission for this,
Enjoy merriment, my prince Ahmet!

Ahmet bek: Ahmet bek says, you have not understood me,
You gave counsel, but have not given a clear response,
You learned yourself, but didn't allow me to learn,
Give me your white blessing, my king Yusup!

Ýusup beg:	*Ýusup beg diýer, bildim, arslan ekeniň,*	**Yusup bek:**	Yusup bek says, I have learned that you are a lion,
	Jahany titreden pälwan ekeniň,		You are a hero shaking the world,
	Boýny ýogyn, gödek oglan ekeniň,		Brave, of mighty stature,
	Barabarda ýörgün, Ahmet mürzeýim!		Be virtuous, my prince Ahmet!

STUDY QUESTIONS

1. Describe how the poetic text is set to music. Where does the emotional climax of the dialogue fall? How is this climax supported by the music?

2. What is the role of the *gyjak* in the performance?

DASHOGUZ

The center of epic performance in Turkmenistan is the northern province of Dashoguz, bordering Karakalpakstan and Kazakhstan, which once lay within the territory of the Khivan khanate. *Dessan* narration developed among two major local tribes: the Yomut, who also inhabit the west of Turkmenistan; and the Chowdur, an indigenous tribe who speak a specific dialect of the Turkmen language. The principal epic school of the Yomut *ýoly* from the eighteenth century to the early twentieth century was founded by Hoja *bagshy* and has been continued by his descendants—son Goch bagshy, grandson Atanazar ogly, great-grandson Ata Hoja, and great-great-grandson Pälwan bagshy Ata ogly (1890–1961). Despite efforts to "reterritorialize" the tribal-based Yomut *ýoly* into the regional Dashoguz school, it remains strongly associated with the Yomut.[9]

In contrast to other regional *bagshychylyk* styles, Dashoguz *dessanchy bagshy*s sing and play the *dutar* accompanied only by a solo *gyjak* player. The role of the *gyjak* is essential, leading the main melodic line of a song and embellishing it with ornaments and grace notes, as if competing with the singer's voice in artistry and virtuosity. The *dutar*, for its part, underscores a song's rhythmic pattern, and provides the cue for the gradual acceleration of tempo typical of epic performance among Dashoguz *bagshy*s. The Dashoguz vocal style is similarly dynamic and vibrant. Epic singers render prose sections of *dessan*s rapidly and explosively, as if sputtering them all out in one breath. Their singing of poetic sections is loud and bold, with a shrill, strained timbre. As a performance progresses, the *dessanchy*'s voice reaches a higher range and gains in emotional intensity. Listeners can guess how close a *dessan* performance is to the end by the height of a *bagshy*'s voice and the degree of emotional intensity. In the following example, Hojamyrat Oraýew, a hereditary *bagshy* from the Yomut *ýoly*, performs an introductory "warm-up" song (*tirme*) of the type that would typically precede the performance of an epic.

Example 7.6. "Hatyja" (female name), a folk song (*tirme*) on a poem by Seýdi, performed by Hojamyrat Oraýew (vocal, *dutar*), accompanied by Baky Rejepow (*gyjak*). Tagta town, Dashoguz, 2001.

Ala gözli ablaksaýat,	Iridescent-eyed, rosy-faced,
Eýlediň bimar, Hatyja.	You made me fall into oblivion, Hatyja.
Ýüregime saldyň ýara,	You left a wound in my heart,
Eýlediň bimar, Hatyja.	You made me fall into oblivion, Hatyja.
Ýatyrdym daň sesine,	I was lying enrapt in the sounds of dawn,
Oýatdyň men jan sesine,	You woke me with the sound of your tender voice,
Ýüregme batan sesine,	Your voice sank into my heart,
Saçlary şamar, Hatyja.	Your dragon braids, Hatyja.
Gözüňe sürme ýaraşar,	Surma suits your eyes,
Saçyňa örme ýaraşar,	Plaiting suits your hair,
Biliňe tirme ýaraşar,	A belt suits your waist,
Saçlary şamar, Hatyja.	Your dragon braids, Hatyja.
Seýdi diýer, bu şertlere,	Seidi says, in these states,
Başladyň köne ýurtlara,	You led me into old lands.
Meni tükenmez dertlere	To eternal torments
Eýlediň duçar, Hatyja.	You subjected me, Hatyja.

STUDY QUESTIONS

1. Describe Hojamyrat Oraýew's vocal style, including his use of guttural ornaments. What distinguishes it from other styles of epic singing?

2. On a continuum ranging from declamatory speech to singing, where would you place this example?

3. Based on the video, what would you guess was the occasion for this performance?

MARY

In contrast to the central role of epic narration among the Yomut and Chowdur of Dashoguz, the *bagshy* tradition of Mary, which takes its name from the ancient oasis city of Merv, has focused on singing and instrumental music. Local *bagshy*s, in addition to mastering a lyrical and plangent vocal style, are typically accomplished *dutar* players, equally skilled in performing both vocal and instrumental versions of a melody. The end-blown flute, *tuýduk,* is also used, both as a solo instrument and to accompany singing and dancing. There are two varieties of *tuýduk:* a long flute, the *gargy tuýduk,* characterized by a husky timbre; and the smaller flute, the *dilli tuýduk,* which has a piercing, bright sound.

The narrative performance of epic in Mary is fairly recent—it developed in the second half of the twentieth century and is most strongly linked to *dessanchy* Gurt Ýakupow (1929–1985) and his son, Chary Ýakup (b. 1962).

Baky Mashakow, a well-known performer of the *gargy tuýduk.*

WATCH

Example 7.7. "Serwi agajy" (On the cypress), from the epic *Gülpam,* performed by Gurt Ýakupow (vocal, *dutar*) accompanied by Ýazgeldy Kuwwadow and Amannazar Ataýew (*dutars*). Ashgabat, around 1984. Video recording from the sound archive of the Center for Folk Music Studies of the Turkmen National Conservatory.

WATCH

Example 7.8. "Serwi agajy" (On the cypress), from the epic *Gülpam,* followed by a section of narrative prose text, performed by Chary Ýakup. Filmed by George Murer, Mary, Turkmenistan, 2014.

Serwi agajyň güli soldy,	A flower on the cypress has withered and fallen,
Bu güli ne etse bolar?	What to do with this flower?
Serwiden tabyt ýasap,	From the cypress a headstone,
Gülden kepen etse bolar.	From the flower a shroud.
Gül berki bir näzik zatdyr,	A flower is a delicate thing,
Ýetmese neýlese bolar?	What to do if you are too late?
Kimhadan kenep ýasap,	Make a winding-cloth,
Gül suwuny sepse bolar.	And sprinkle it with flowery moisture.
Aýp etmegin, şahym, menden,	Do not blame me, my king,
Derdim artdy dembe-demden,	I am ever more troubled.
Döwranyň gitdi jahandan,	Your happy time has left this world,
Patyşahym, ne etse bolar?	My king, what can be done?

Performer Profile: The Ýakupows: Three Generations of Musicians

The Ýakupow family illustrates how musical craft and sensibility were transmitted from one generation to the next over the course of a century. The story begins in the early twentieth century, when a poor laborer with a talent for music and a yearning for knowledge about Turkmen musical and literary traditions learned to read the Arabic script in which Turkmen epics had been written down, and committed many *dessan*s to memory. At the same time, he became an accomplished performer on the *dutar* and *tuýduk* (end-blown flute). This musician was named Ýakup, and his skill on the end-blown flute—also called *nai* in the Mary region—earned him the nickname Ýakup-*naichy*: Ýakup the flute player. As was customary in the early years of the Soviet Union, when indigenous Central Asians widely adopted the Russian convention of using last names, Ýakup's given name

Gurt Ýakupow.
Courtesy of Turkmen State Archive.

became a surname for his family: Ýakupow.

Gurt Ýakupow inherited his father's interests and skills. He learned to read and write Arabic script, explored old Turkic languages, and played melodies he learned from his father on the *dutar* and *tuýduk*. Gurt was also an innovator and introduced his own manner of performing narrative and poetic sections of *dessan*s. He recited prose sections in a low, gruff voice, enunciating the text in an unhurried, emphatic way. His singing was characterized by soft articulation, moderate pace, subdued guttural ornaments, and accentuation of final rhythmic beats in a melodic phrase. Gurt Ýakupow and his followers became known for a vivid manner of storytelling that involves expressive gestures and swaying the body in time with the music.

Gurt Ýakupow transmitted his passion for epic performance to his son, Chary Ýakup, whose name derives from the Persian word for "four," and who is the fourth son in the family (Chary removed the Russified "ow" suffix from his last name, following a trend in post-Soviet Central Asia). Chary was surrounded by music from childhood. His paternal uncles and his siblings sang and played the *dutar*. As a teenager, Chary accompanied his father to performances at weddings, the typical venue for epic, and assimilated the art of the *dessanchy*.

Chary Ýakup narrating the prose portion of an epic, Ashgabat, 2012.

His repertory of *dessan*s, however, is considerably smaller than his father's, consisting at present of around ten epic poems. Among these is the romantic epic *Gülpam* (a woman's name), which is also known under the name *Soltansoýun Baýkara*.

In the following two examples, Gurt Ýakupow and Chary Ýakup each perform a song from the epic *Gülpam*, called "Serwi agajy" (On the cypress). The song recounts a key episode in the epic where, unable to see his beloved wife Gülpam in a state of fatal illness, Sultan Husayn (the historical figure Husayn Bayqara, a descendent of Timur, who ruled Khorasan from 1469 until his death in 1506) goes hunting with his vizier Mirali.[10] In order to tell him the news of Gülpam's death, Mirali sings a song in which he asks, "What to do with a fallen leaf?" Hearing these words, the king realizes what has happened.

Dostum, sen gumlar iýsene,	My friend, depart,
Dynç alaýyn, dost, gaýtsana,	Go away, friend, and leave me in peace,
Ondan "Gül öldi" diýsene,	Better still say, "Gül is dead,"
Mundan yza gaýtsa bolar.	And now we must return.
Ýöräp-ýöräp ýollar aşyp,	Having gone a long way,
Gelip bu menzile düşdük.	We have reached this point.
Gül ölenni sizden eşitdik,	That Gül has died I heard from you yourself,
Soltanym, ne etse bolar?	My king, what can be done?
Her iş geldi işbu sere,	Everything comes to an end,
Geldik ikewmiz bu ýere,	Both of us have come to this land,
Soltan Hüseýn hem Baýkara,	Sultan Husayn and Baykara,
Myndan yza gaýtsa bolar.	And now we have to return.
Myraly, neýleý bu jany,	Mirali, what am I to do with this soul?
Nedersiň pany jahany,	What am I to do in the world?
Goldan aldyrdyň Gülpamy,	I let Gülpam slip from my hands,
Tur, gaýtsaň ki gaýtsaň bolar.	Stand up, we have to return.

STUDY QUESTIONS

1. What similarities and differences can you detect in the performance styles of Gurt Ýakupow and Chary Ýakup? Where does each performer's vocal style fall on a continuum ranging from natural spoken discourse at one extreme to intoned declamation at the other extreme?

2. How extensive a melodic range does Chary Ýakup use in his performance? Can you sing the principal pitches of the melody he sings?

3. How would you compare the vocal style of both Gurt and Chary to other schools of epic performance you have heard?

4. What is distinctive about the instrumental accompaniment that Chary Ýakup uses in "Serwi agajy" relative to instrumental accompaniment in other excerpts of epic and *tirme* songs you have heard?

5. What qualities make both father and son effective performers?

Chary Ýakup is much in demand as an entertainer at *toy*s, where, in addition to performing excerpts from epics, he plays instrumental music on the *dutar*. The following example is a brief excerpt from one such appearance.

WATCH **Example 7.9.** Chary Ýakup performs on the *dutar* at a *toy*. Filmed by George Murer, Mary, Turkmenistan, 2014.

1. How would you describe the mood that Chary Ýakup creates with his *dutar* music?

2. How "present" would you guess Ýakup's music is in the consciousness of listeners? That is, where is it situated on a continuum from background to foreground? What is the social purpose of this kind of music?

NOTES

1. Sir Gerard Clauson, *An Etymological Dictionary of Pre-Thirteenth-Century Turkish* (Oxford: Clarendon Press, 1972), 321.

2. Paraphrased from Viktor Uspenskii and Viktor Beliaev, *Turkmenskaya muzyka* [Turkmen music], ed. Shahym Gullyev, foreword and comm. Eduard Alekseev (Almaty: Soros Foundation-Kazakhstan, 2003), 58.

The same explanation appears in Vasily Bartold's classic work *Turkestan Down to the Mongol Invasion,* 4th ed. (London: Luzac, 1977), 388.

3. Myradow Amanmyrat, *Ilaman bagşy hem-de onuň edebi-folklor mirasy* [Ilaman Bagshy and his literary and folklore heritage] (Ashgabat: Magaryf, 1992), 16.

4. Arminii Vamberi, *Puteshestvie po Srednei Azii. Ocherki i kartiny narodnykh nravov* [Journey in Central Asia. Sketches and descriptions of folkways] (Saint-Petersburg: U.A. Bokram, 1877), 182.

5. Uspenskii and Beliaev, *Turkmenskaya muzyka,* 44–45.

6. Other poets whose works figure in the *tirmechi bagshy* repertory include Magrupi (1734–1810), Seýdi (1775–1836), Kemine (1770–1840), Zelili (1779/80–1846/48), Mollanepes (1810–1862), and Mätäji (1822–1884).

7. "Iskendar" refers to Alexander the Great. Known in Islamic tradition as Dhul-Qarnayn (The two-horned one), Alexander appears in Turkmen folk legends as a powerful and cruel ruler who founded several cities. His name is associated with Merv (formerly Alexandria), an ancient oasis city near today's Mary.

8. One of the first kings of the world in Iranian and Turkmen folklore, whose reign became known as the Golden Age, during which there were no wars, diseases, vice, or deaths. He encouraged innovation in arts and crafts and ordered the construction of public buildings and palaces. According to legend, Jamshid had a magical cup, from which he could derive immortality and observe the universe. The whole world obeyed Jamshid, until he grew proud of his power and his subjects began to rebel. His name epitomizes both royal greatness and perilous vanity.

9. Other leading representatives of the Yomut *ýoly* include Nazar Bagha Morsy ogly (1873–1942), Hekim bagshy (19th century), Magtymguly Garlyýew (1889–1957), Ore Shih (1893–1864), Baýar Baýramow (1908–1974), Ilaman Annaýew (1920–1995), Sülgün Meretgeldiewa (1922–2002), Akjagül Myradowa (1924–2004), Tüli Otuzow (1926), Hojamyrat Oraýew (1928–2010), Pirjan Moşşyýew (1932–1997), Bally Mätgeldiýew (b. 1933) and Bazarbaý Gurbandurdyýew (b. 1946). Celebrated representatives of the Chowdur *ýoly* in the 19th and early 20th century include its founder Petek bagshy, his followers Allanur bagshy and Jumamyrat bagshy, and other bards, such as Soýog bagshy (1850–1917), Sapar Süýrentgi, Mämmetanna bagshy (1884–1944), Palta bagshy Gara ogly (1900–1974), Taganýaz bagshy, Gurt Garlyýew (1901–1986), Jumamyrat bagshy, Täjibaý Gurbanow (1928), and Durdybaý Gurbanow (1950).

10. Mir-Alisher Navo'i (1441–1501), a leading poet of his time who wrote in the proto-Uzbek Chagatay language and who, as vizier to Sultan Husayn Bayqara, became a patron of arts and architecture in Khorasan—in particular, in its capital, Herat.

CHAPTER 8 The Turkmen *Dutar*

DAVID FOSSUM

The most celebrated and best-researched musical figure in modern Turkmenistan is surely the *bagshy,* a folk bard whose art combines poetry, storytelling, singing, and instrumental skill. The *bagshy* accompanies himself—or herself, for women are also represented in the *bagshy* tradition—on a lute called the *dutar.* While the primary focus of the *bagshy*'s performance is vocal music, instrumental proficiency is also an essential skill. In a performance, the *bagshy* both sings and plays, doubling the sung melody on the *dutar.* The *bagshy* is also usually accompanied by an additional *dutar* and, in much of Turkmenistan, by a spike fiddle called *gyjak* (a name that is cognate with *ghijak*—see entry in the musical instrument glossary). Turkmen melodies can be highly ornamented, and in the music associated with two regions of the country, Mary and Ahal, the demand for skilled accompaniment has given rise not only to schools of instrumental specialists but to an entire repertoire of

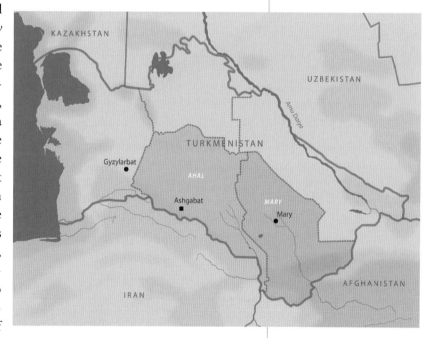

instrumental music. Local listeners tend to focus their attention on the *bagshy,* but virtuosic solo *dutar* players (*dutarchy*) also have admirers who are drawn to their performances of the substantial instrumental repertoire. Vocal music is the preferred entertainment for high-profile occasions such as weddings or circumcision

The provinces of Ahal and Mary are particularly known for performance traditions of instrumental *dutar* music.

celebrations, yet instrumentalists also frequently have their moment in the spotlight at such events. Some twentieth-century virtuosos have even become household names in Turkmenistan after performing for radio or television broadcasts. For the most part, however, instrumental music thrives in smaller, informal gatherings of enthusiasts, among whom the soft, rich tone of the *dutar* is best heard and appreciated. This chapter focuses on *dutar* music from the region of Ahal, or what can be called the Ahal school of solo *dutar* performance.

THE *DUTAR*

The *dutar* is a two-stringed, long-necked lute. *Dutar*s exist in a variety of local forms throughout much of Central Asia, some of which, such as the Uyghur *dutar*, are very long indeed. The Turkmen *dutar*, however, is relatively short. Shorter neck lengths tolerate thinner strings and produce higher pitches, and Turkmen musicians often boast that, thanks to the *dutar*'s fine strings, their music is more delicate, graceful, and ornate than other music. The Turkmen *dutar*'s resonator and soundboard are made of solid mulberry, and the neck of apricot wood. Steel frets are wrapped around the neck. The strings are also made of steel, although in the past they were silk.

Dutar.
Courtesy of Wesleyan University Virtual Instrument Museum.

Turkmen *dutar* technique demands strength and agility in the left hand—usually the fingering hand, and accuracy and quickness in the right hand, usually the strumming hand. Rather than simply playing successive notes in a melody, performers often ornament and embellish the melody by quickly playing one or more neighboring notes on their way to the target note. Most melody notes are played on the upper of the *dutar*'s two strings with the four fingers of the left hand.[1] These are the melody notes that a *bagshy* would sing if the composition were performed as a song rather than as an instrumental piece. Meanwhile, the lower string is stopped by wrapping the thumb around the neck of the instrument.

The two strings are positioned quite close to each other and are almost always strummed simultaneously using a variety of strokes. Turkmen *dutar* players may strum with the index finger only, or with several fingers together, which produces a percussive sound as the fingers scrape across the uneven grains of the *dutar*'s wooden deck. Such full strokes are used sparingly, for emphasis. There are also a few quick, compound strokes involving several fingers successively.

The compound right-hand stroke *gyruw.*

TABLE 8.1. FORMAL STRUCTURE OF "GARRY SALTYK"

TIME CODE	CHARACTERISTICS
0:00–0:12	Rejepow strums the *dutar*'s open (unfretted) strings before playing anything recognizable as "Garry saltyk." In Turkmen, such open-string strumming is called *boş kakuw* (empty striking) or simply *kakuw*. In fact, the *kakuw* isn't completely "open," for Rejepow lightly fingers the lower string. After this, he fingers both strings at the fifth fret before beginning the actual melody of the piece. This is a typical procedure in Turkmen music. The *kakuw* at the opening of a piece can last any reasonable length of time; its purpose is to state the underlying rhythm of the piece and also allow the performer to adjust the tuning of the *dutar* as necessary. You may also notice very brief *kakuw* separating the sections of a piece.
0:12–1:38	The composition alternates between statements of two main ideas, one lower on the *dutar* and one higher.
1:38–2:53	Next, the composition explores some new, complex ideas. One especially interesting moment occurs at 1:58–2:12. This passage highlights the relatively great degree of movement that can occur on the lower string of the Turkmen *dutar*. Here the note on the upper string remains stable, but the note on the lower string shifts up and down.
2:56–3:00	Toward the end, Rejepow plays a descending line of notes using a right-hand technique called *gyruw* in which he strikes downward with the index finger and then immediately upward with the thumb and index finger together, producing a strong, full-sounding strum. *Gyruw* is one of several kinds of compound right-hand strokes.

WATCH   Example 8.1. "Garry saltyk," performed by Ýazmyrat Rejepow.

"Garry saltyk" is one of seven parts of a long instrumental suite called "Saltyklar" (plural of *saltyk*). The piece probably takes its name from the composer to whom it is attributed, although it has presumably undergone many changes as it has been transmitted from one performer to another through oral tradition. The seven parts of "Saltyklar" may be played independently or together. "Garry saltyk" (The old *saltyk*), is the only one that is also sung. The other six are only performed as instrumentals. Watch the video recording of *dutar* player Ýazmyrat Rejepow performing "Garry saltyk" and observe a few of its characteristics.

WATCH   Example 8.2. "Goňurbaş mukamy" performed by Akmyrat Çaryýew.

Akmyrat Çaryÿew and *gyjak* player Baÿrammyrat Söyünow accompany *bagshy* Parahat Şahymow.

"Goñurbaş mukamy," like "Saltyklar," is often referred to as a "folk instrumental" (*halk sazy*) because it is an old piece and the identity of its composer is either unknown or disputed.[2] Some *dutar* players say that "Goñurbaş mukamy" is so called because its melody mimics a field of grain undulating in the wind (*goñurbaş* is a kind of grass on which livestock graze).

"Goñurbaş mukamy" is one of a handful of Turkmen instrumental pieces that *dutar* players describe as *mukam*. Musicians in many parts of the Middle East and Central Asia use a variant of the Arabic word *maqām* as a musical term, although in different genres of music, the word can have different meanings (see chapter 18). The Turkmen variant of *maqām*—*mukam*—can be used in a general sense to mean "melody." It may also be used loosely to refer to any instrumental composition. However, in its strictest sense, it refers to a small set of specialized musical compositions revered by Turkmen *dutar* players.

One feature of this special set of *mukam*s is that they share a similar melodic structure. All of these pieces shift into a distinctive melodic mode in the final section of the composition. This mode includes a lowered second scale degree and a raised third scale degree.[3] If you are not a musician and don't know much about scales, just listen for the way the mood of "Goñurbaş mukamy" changes at 2:30, when the switch to this special mode takes place.

The lowest four pitches of each scale are written in staff notation below. These are the pitches used in the main body of the piece:

By contrast, the lowest four notes in the final *mukam* section are:

Table 8.2 provides an outline of the piece, showing its various sections (A, A', B, etc.) and the time at which each section begins and ends.

The logical structure of this piece exemplifies the structure of many Turkmen songs and instrumental compositions. Within each section (A, A', B, B', C), there are repeated phrases. However, performers keep the music interesting by slightly changing the ornamentation or accenting different notes when they play a phrase a second time. Each section is followed by a refrain, which is also subject to slight variations in each repetition. Additionally, each section centers on a higher note than the previous section. Most of the action in the A and A' sections occurs around

TABLE 8.2. FORMAL STRUCTURE OF "GOÑURBAŞ MUKAMY"

TIME CODE	SECTION
0:00–0:10	*kakuw*
0:11–0:20	A
0:20–0:30	refrain
0:35–0:42	A'
0:43–0:54	refrain
0:58–1:10	B
1:11–1:20	refrain
1:24–1:38	B'
1:38–1:48	refrain
1:51–2:08	C
2:09–2:18	refrain
2:22–3:10	D (final *mukam* section)
3:11–3:20	*kakuw*

the first fret of the *dutar,* while the B section starts around the fifth fret; the B' section is similar to the B section but jumps up a little higher. Finally, in the C section, the melody reaches a climax as the performer plays in the very highest range of the *dutar.* After this, in the final section, the mode changes and the melody drops back down to a lower range. The following schematic illustrates the ascending and descending melodic movement of the composition:

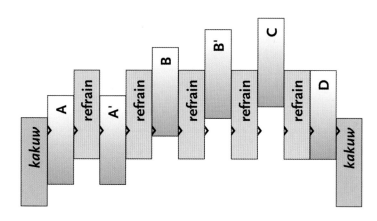

Since the beauty of Turkmen music lies not only in its overall structure but also in its fine ornamentation and rich timbre, it's important to notice some of the details. For example, within the refrain, *dutar* player Charyÿew hammers the second finger of his left hand extremely rapidly on a few of the notes, producing a fluttering sound. While all *dutar* players who play this piece hammer on these same notes in one of a few different ways, Charyÿew's approach requires a truly virtuosic, graceful technique.

"Balsaÿat" holds a special position in both the vocal and instrumental repertoires. In both vocal and instrumental performances, the *bagshy* or *dutarçy* begins playing the *dutar* with slack, low-pitched strings as the voice or fingers warm up. As the recital progresses, the performer gradually tightens the strings to higher and higher pitches. The later songs or pieces are said to be *çekimli* ("tight" or "pulled"). "Balsaÿat" is a *çekimli* song, and if a performer chooses to play it, it will be the last song of the night. Tightly tuned, the strings of the *dutar* produce a particularly rich and loud tone; however, they require more strength to play. Consequently, *dutar* players use the thumb less frequently to stop the lower strings during many *çekimli* songs in order to focus the energy of the hand on playing the melody on the upper string. The lower string simply acts as a drone.

"Balsaÿat" comes from an epic tale (*dessan*) called *Saÿatly Hemra*. *Bagshy*s recite epics in prose interspersed with songs, and "Balsaÿat" is one such song—indeed, a love song about the heroine of the epic, whose name is Saÿat (*bal* means "honey," and thus *Balsaÿat* means something like "sweet Saÿat.")

WATCH | **Examples 8.3 and 8.4.** "Balsaÿat," performed by Ýazmyrat Rejepow (example 8.3) and Akmyrat Charyÿew (example 8.4)

Listen now to the two versions of "Balsaÿat," the first performed by Ýazmyrat Rejepow, and the second by Akmyrat Charyÿew. Rejepow plays Pürli Saryÿew's version of the piece (example 8.3). Charyÿew plays Chary Tächmämmedow's version (example 8.4).

STUDY QUESTIONS

1. What elements of the two performance versions are different?
2. What are the creative skills that *dutar* players need in order to be able to make their own version of an older song or tune?
3. Which version do you prefer, and why?

Can you think of other examples of music in which performers create their own performance versions of well-known songs or tunes?

The Life of a *Dutar* Player (*Dutarçy*)

The repertoire of the *dutarçy* is passed down orally from master (*halypa*) to disciple (*shägirt*). Despite the frequent use of recordings and, increasingly, Western-style notation for learning compositions, the personal instruction of a *halypa* remains crucial to a *dutarçy*'s development. Nowadays, this relationship is often set within the formal context of an official institution.

Ýazmyrat Rejepow, the performer of "Garry saltyk" in the example above, began studying *dutar* at a music school in his hometown of Gyzylarbat (now Serdar), about 200 kilometers west of Ashgabat, Turkmenistan's capital. His first teacher was his father, who was employed at the school. When Rejepow finished school in 1993, he entered the national conservatory, which had opened just that year. Here, under the influence of two masters, he began learning to play in the style of the famous *dutarçy* Pürli Saryýew (1900–1971). Rejepow describes Pürli Saryýew's style as highly developed; Saryýew is broadly admired for his ability to improvise new variations and even entirely new sections of older compositions. When Rejepow begins learning a new piece, he turns to the recordings of Saryýew, and to the guidance of his teachers, who know these versions. If he wants to play something differently, he always discusses it with his teachers before making a change. If he can't find Saryýew's rendition of a given piece, he turns to recordings of other masters.

Ýazmyrat Rejepow.

In 1998, upon finishing his studies at the conservatory, Rejepow stayed on as a music producer, subsequently earned a position in the Department of Turkmen Music Theory, and is currently writing a graduate thesis. He is constantly at work transcribing recordings of old *dutar* masters as an aid to students. He has compiled several books of such transcriptions.

Akmyrat Charyýew is one of the preeminent living masters of the *dutar* in Turkmenistan. He was born in 1947 in a village on the western edge of the Ahal region. After first learning to play *dutar* while participating in an arts enthusiasts club in his hometown, he entered the music academy in Ashgabat in 1965, where his talents were quickly recognized. As a member of the national folk instrumental ensemble, he played alongside master *dutarçys* and learned from them. While he had a number of teachers, including Pürli Saryýew, he considers himself a disciple of Chary Tächmämmedow (1925–1976). He learned to play songs of the *bagshy* repertoire from the great *bagshy* Sahy Jepbarow (1905–1977), with whom he performed in the national ensemble.

Charyýew later became the leader of the national folk instrumental ensemble himself, and he teaches *dutar* at the national conservatory to a number of disciples. In addition to developing a distinctive individual style of playing, he has composed several well-known pieces. He has performed in numerous venues around Europe, Japan, Africa, Iran, Turkey, and the Arab world, although he more frequently accompanies singers at weddings in Turkmenistan.

NOTES

1. The two strings of the *dutar* are called the *ẏokarky kirş* (upper string) and the *aşakky kirş* (lower string). Confusingly, these Turkmen names refer to the physical position of the strings, not their pitch. In my discussion, the *aşakky kirş* is the upper string, because it sounds higher, and the *ẏokarky kirş* is the lower string, because it sounds lower.

2. Turkmen musicologist Shahym Gullyev cites five different scholars who variously attribute this composition to three different 19th-century musicians. See Shahym Gullyev, *Turkmenskaya Muzyka: Nasledie* [Turkmen music: Heritage] (Almaty, Kazakhstan: Soros-Kazakhstan, 2003), 164.

3. Note that a few pieces that are not considered to belong to this special group of *mukams* also make this melodic shift in their final sections.

CHAPTER 9

Kyrgyz Wisdom Songs

TERME YRLARY

ELMIRA KÖCHÜMKULOVA

Terme is didactic and philosophical poetry composed and performed in the form of a song by Kazakh and Kyrgyz improvising poets (*aqyn*s). The word *terme* derives from the Turkic verb *ter* ("to pick," "to collect," "to choose") and denotes a collection of wise and eloquent words about various spiritual and philosophical themes and concepts concerning life and existence. *Terme* are also known in Kyrgyz as "wisdom" or "advice" songs (*sanat-nasyiat yrlary*).

Terme poetry is an example of what has been called "wisdom literature"—a term coined to describe literary works that use poetry, parables, proverbs, tales, and legends to convey moral advice and practical wisdom within the framework of a religious or spiritual tradition. Frequently cited examples of wisdom literature include the biblical psalms; parables attributed to Sufi, Taoist, Zen Buddhist, and Hasidic masters; Native American legends; and African folktales. Like other cultures that have archived wisdom in oral tradition rather than books, the culture of Kazakh and Kyrgyz nomads reserved a place of honor for talented individuals who were the bearers and transmitters of oral history and traditional knowledge. These individuals, called *aqyn*s, developed and practiced unique forms of verbal art, including *terme* poetry. Accompanying their songs on the *komuz* (Kyrgyz) or *dombyra* (Kazakh), Kazakh and Kyrgyz *aqyn*s, *yrchy*s (Kyrgyz), and *jyrau*s (Kazakh) entertained the public at traditional gatherings and feasts with their improvised *terme* on various topics to reinforce social, cultural, and moral values.

Common themes of Kyrgyz *terme* poetry include the world (*dünüyö*); God and the forces of nature (wind, fire, water, the moon, the sun); time (*zaman*) as it relates to the span of a human life; the difference between good and bad people (*jakshy adam, jaman adam*) or a good wife and a bad wife (*jakshy katyn, jaman katyn*); childhood (*balalyk*); youth and old age (*jashtyk, karylyk*); life and death (*ömür, ölüm* or *ajal*); and wealth and poverty (*döölöt/baylyk* and *jokchuluk*). Drawing on common knowledge as well as their own personal experience, knowledge, and worldview, almost all Kyrgyz *aqyn*s of the past composed versions of *terme* songs on these themes. As Islamic practices and beliefs—especially those connected to Sufism, the mystical dimension of Islam—became popular among the nomadic Kyrgyz and Kazakhs in the eighteenth and nineteenth centuries, poets began to incorporate Sufi imagery, ideas, and terminology into their *terme* poetry. Some Kyrgyz poets who learned to read and write Arabic wrote down their poetry in Kyrgyz using Arabic script. People called such poets *moldo* (mullah). Kyrgyz scholars have referred to this group of *aqyn*s as *jazgych aqyn*s—poets who compose poetry in writing as well as through the more customary technique of oral extemporization. Many *terme* songs composed by well-known Kyrgyz *aqyn*s and *yrchy*s of past centuries were revived after Kyrgyzstan gained its independence in 1991. Audiocassettes of *terme* songs, *dastan*s, and folk lyrical songs performed on the *komuz* became commercially available, and several folk music ensembles and individual singers became popular by singing *terme*s and *dastan*s.

WATCH **Example 9.1. "Jalgan düynö" (False world) performed by Elmira Köchümkulova.**

Elmira Köchümkulova
playing the *komuz*.

Listen to "Jalgan düynö"[1] (False world), a *terme* composed by the well-known Kyrgyz poet Korgol Dos uulu (1890–1964). In this religious *terme* song, Korgol praises the omnipotence of God, the power of Mother Earth, and life after death; and, referring to mullahs, affirms the falseness of the world of the living. The original melody of the song in Korgol's own performance was not recorded, but people who have seen him sing this song remembered the melody. Today only one version of the melody exists, and that melody, especially the refrain, resembles the chanting of Kyrgyz traditional healers (*bakshy*s) who used some elements of the Sufi ceremony of *zikr* (remembrance of God) and the chanting of wandering dervishes who traveled among the nomadic Kyrgyz to proselytize Islam. The excerpt from this *terme* is sung by Elmira Köchümkulova, who is a self-taught singer. Note that for a refrain, the song uses the Muslim *shahada*, the declaration of faith in Allah and in His messenger, the Prophet Muhammad, which is repeated at the end of each couplet. Another interesting feature of the song's performance style is the phrase inserted just before the *shahada*, which consists not of words but of vocables: "Ay-diy-diy-diri-diy-diy-diy." Such vocables offer singers a respite from the demands of extemporizing words, and provide an opportunity to express pure emotion in sound.

Ötörbüz da keterbiz, pendem,	People, we will leave this world quickly,
Ölgöndön kiyin bekerbiz.	After we die, we will have no value.
Opol düynö jalgansyng,	Big world, you are false,
Jakshylyk kimge kylgansyng.	You spare no one from death.
Biz emes chyny kara Jer,	Black Earth, you not only took us,
Baabedindi algansyng.	But took Bahauddin [Naqshband].[2]
Paygambardy chalgansyng,	You took the Prophet [Muhammad].
Degi oylop karasam,	When I really think about it,
Ushul düynö jalgansyng.	This world is indeed a false one.
Jalgansyng ey, jalgansyng,	You are false, indeed, yes, you are false.
Ay-diy-diy-diri-diy-diy-diy . . .	Ay-diy-diy-diri-diy-diy-diy . . .
Ilaa-Ilaha il-Allah,	There is no god but God and
Muhammadu-Rasul-Allah,	Muhammad is His messenger.
Kuday özüng bir sakta.	God, please have mercy on us.
Kan Manasty algansyn,	You took the khan Manas,
Kara jer özüng balbansyng.	Black Earth, you are strong.
Jengijoktu algansyng,	You took Jengijok,[3]
Jer enem sen da balbansyng.	Mother Earth, you are brave.
Toktoguldu algansyn,	You took Toktogul,[4]
Togolok jerim balbansyng.	Round Earth, you are brave.
Moldolorum chyn aytat,	The mullahs are right,
Ushul düynö jalgansyng.	This world is a false one.
Jalgansyng ey, jalgansyng,	You are false, yes, you are false.
Ay-diy-diy-diri-diy-diy-diy . . .	Ay-diy-diy-diri-diy-diy-diy . . .
Ilaa-Ilaha il-Allah,	There is no god but God and
Muhammad-u-Rasul-Allah,	Muhammad is His messenger.
Kuday özüng bir sakta.	God, please have mercy on us.
Kashka tish tüshüp eek kalat,	When we get old, our front teeth will fall out, only our lips will remain,
Karylyk bizdi jep salat.	Old age will eat us up.
Karyp kalgan kezingde,	When you get old,
Kyz-kelin kaydan kep salat.	Young girls and women will not talk to you.
Oynop alchy jash chakta,	So enjoy your youth,
Bayagy jigit dep kalat.	Then they will remember you saying, "Oh, that young man."
Etegi jok, jengi jok,	[When we die] we will wear a short dress
Ensiz köynök kiyerbiz.	That has no hem and sleeves.
Eshigi jok törü jok,	We'll go into a dark grave

	That has no door and *tör* [seat of honor inside
Karangy körgö kirerbiz.	the yurt, which is opposite the entrance]
Oynop alchy jash chakta,	So enjoy your youth,
Ölgöndön kiyin bekerbiz.	We will have no value after we die.
Bekerbiz, oo, bekerbiz.	Yes, we will be worthless, yes, worthless.
Ay-diy-diy-diri-diy-diy-diy . . .	Ay-diy-diy-diri-diy-diy-diy . . .
Ilaa-Ilaha il-Allah,	There is no god but God and
Muhammad-u-Rasul-Allah,	Muhammad is His messenger.
Kuday özüng bir sakta.	God, please have mercy on us.

STUDY QUESTIONS

1. How would you characterize the melody of this song? Were you able to follow the transcription?

2. Which elements of the song's performance make it a religious song?

3. What is the function of the initial and internal alliterations and end rhyme in the song lyrics? Try to identify these key poetic features in each couplet and underline them.

POETIC STRUCTURE AND MELODY OF *TERME*

Like all traditional genres of Kyrgyz oral poetry, including the epic poem, *terme* poetry consists of seven or eight syllables in each verse line, which strictly maintains initial and internal alliteration and end rhyme. The key concept in each verse line typically comes at the very end and is contained in a single word: "destitute" (*karyp*), "good" (*jakshy*), "something is indeed so" (*turbayby*). These words may be repeated again and again at the end of successive phrases to build thematic analogies and examples, or can provide a starting point for other rhyming end words. This basic formal principle of the *terme* is illustrated in the text transcribed and translated below. In this *terme*, the poet, a nineteenth-century Kyrgyz *aqyn* named Arstanbek, composed verses on the nature of destitution, leadership, justice, wealth, good and bad men, friends, wives, and horses. As is common in *terme*s, Arstanbek incorporated popular proverbs and sayings and also adapted pithy phrases composed by other poets. Each poet has his own style of improvising, singing, and creating melody. The rhythmic melodic form of oral poetry is specifically designed to allow listeners to concentrate more on the content of the words than on the music.

Maksat Kuluev.
Courtesy of Maksat Kuluev.

Example 9.2. *Terme* of Arstanbek, performed by Maksat Kuluev.

Arstanbek's *terme* is performed in example 9.2 by Maksat Kuluev, a young *aqyn* who presently resides in Bishkek. Note how Maksat ends the last verse line of each thematic section by prolonging the final syllable, thus showing that he is concluding one theme and switching to another.

The text for this example is available on the companion website.

As the song text makes clear, this *terme* song does not have a single unifying theme but rather addresses many different themes and issues. The poet improvises rhymed poetry by jumping from one topic to another, thus combining various proverbial sayings and statements whose meanings are not necessarily related. Like many other genres of Kyrgyz oral tradition, *terme* songs were not meant for silent reading but for listening and singing aloud to the accompaniment of a *komuz*. Thus great emphasis is placed on alliteration and euphonious rhyming sounds, which make the poetry easy to memorize and remember, and pleasing to the ear.

Roza Amanova (b. 1973) is a Kyrgyz singer who has contributed to the post-Soviet revival and popularization of *terme* songs. Roza graduated from the Kyrgyz National Conservatory in Bishkek and later received her *Kandidat* degree from the Kazakh National Conservatory named after Qurmanghazy, in Almaty, Kazakhstan. She is also the founder and director of the Saltuu muzyka borboru (Center for [Kyrgyz] Traditional Music) in Bishkek. Her repertoire consists mainly of Kyrgyz *terme* songs and *dastan*s composed and sung by well-known nineteenth- and twentieth-century Kyrgyz oral poets and singers. Philosophical *terme* songs of Jengijok, Barpy, and Toktogul such as "Ala-Too körkkö kelbeyt el bolboso" (Ala-Too is not beautiful without the people), "Yntymak" (Unity), "Dünüyö" (World), and "Akkan-Suu" (Flowing Water) became popular in Roza Amanova's performance. She received the official honorary title "People's Artist of the Kyrgyz Republic" in 2009. Example 9.3 is an excerpt from Roza Amanova's performance of Toktogul aqyn's "Dünüyö" (World), filmed at a solo concert that she performed in Bishkek in 2010.

Note that before starting the song, Roza says, "May the spirit of our father Toktogul [aqyn] be pleased. Let me try singing with this instrument by saying 'Bismilla' (in the name of Allah)." She says this short prayer because she is playing a *komuz* that resembles Toktogul's *komuz*—an instrument she won in a song competition honoring Toktogul aqyn.

Roza Amanova.
Courtesy of Roza Amanova.

Example 9.3. "Dünüyö" (World), performed by Roza Amanova.

Bul dünüyö bekersing,	Life in this world, you are false,
Bir künü ötüp ketersing.	One day, we will leave you.
Opasy jok düynönün,	No one will get to the bottom
Tübünö kiming jetersing.	Of this false life.
Keleringde dünüyö,	When you are coming, this life,
Tolukshup chykkan aydaysyng.	You are like a new beautiful moon.
Keteringde dünüyö,	When you are leaving, this life,
Suu jürbögön saydaysyng.	You are like a streambed without water.
Keleringde dünüyö,	When you are coming, this life,
Asmandagy kündöysüng.	You are like the sun in the sky.
Keteringde dünüyö,	When you are leaving, this life,
Kaygyluu kongül kirdeysing.	You are like a sad feeling in the heart.
Keleringde dünüyö,	When you are coming, this life,
Özongo bütkön taldaysyng.	You are like a poplar tree that grows on a riverbank.
Keteringde dünüyö,	When you are leaving, this life,
Ölümdön beter aldaysyng.	You deceive us worse than death.
Keleringde dünüyö,	When you are coming, this life,
Mömölüü darak shaktaysyng.	You are like a tree with fruits.
Keteringde dünüyö,	When you are leaving, this life,
Suu jetpegen kaktaysyng.	You are like a thirsty, dried-up tree.
Keleringde dünüyö,	When you are coming, this life,
Almash-örköch löktöysüng,	You are like a camel whose humps are filled with all kinds of goods.
Keteringde dünüyö,	When you are leaving, this life,
Tulpar minseng jetpeysing.	We can't reach you even if we chase you on a stallion.
Keleringde dünüyö,	When you are coming, this life,
Argymak minip oynoysung.	You ride a stallion playfully.
Keteringde dünüyö,	When you are leaving, this life,
Aylanyp uchkan torgoysung.	You are like a lark flying high in the sky.
Keleringde dünüyö,	When you are coming, this life,
Adyrdan sokkon jeldeysing.	You are like a breeze blowing on a hill.
Keteringde dünüyö,	When you are leaving, this life,
Kol jetpes aska beldeysing.	You are like a high, unreachable cliff.

Keleringde dünüyö,	When you are coming, this life,
Ay menen kündöy jaryksyng.	You are as bright as the moon and the sun.
Keteringde dünüyö,	When you are leaving, this life,
Tamany tüshkön charyksyng. . .	You are like a leather shoe without a sole.

STUDY QUESTIONS

1. How would you compare this *terme's* melody, poetic structure, and content to the previous *terme* songs, especially "False World," performed by Elmira Köchümkulova?

2. How is this singer's performance style similar to or different from the performance style of the other *terme* singers you have listened to?

3. Were you able to follow the end rhyme in the song? Identify and underline the rhyming words.

4. Compose your own *terme* poem of 10–20 verse lines on the theme of "this world," using Roza Amanova's poem as a model for the poetic style and the rhyme pattern.

CONTEMPORARY *TERME* SONGS

Today, the middle and younger generations of Kyrgyz *aqyn*s continue the tradition of composing their own individual *terme* songs. The themes of these songs are diverse, but the form in each case follows the traditional syllabic structure of oral poetry, with its verse lines of seven to eight syllables. Like *aqyn*s in the past, contemporary *aqyn*s also address major socio-cultural, political, and religious issues and developments of their own time. For example, influenced by the post-Soviet Islamic revival, some younger Kyrgyz *aqyn*s composed religious *terme* poetry praising Islam and the Prophet Muhammad, calling people to be faithful (*yimanduuluk*) and to observe the five pillars of Islam, and condemning immoral elements of modern Western popular culture. Other common topics of contemporary Kyrgyz *terme* poetry include Kyrgyzstan's Tulip Revolution of March 2005, which ousted the first president, Askar Akaev, and replaced him with Kurmanbek Bakiev; the second "revolution" that overthrew Bakiev in April 2010, and took the lives of over eighty young men; and the subsequent tragic events in southern Kyrgyzstan in June 2010, which caused a major interethnic conflict between Kyrgyz and Uzbek residents in the cities of Osh and Jalal-Abad.

Terme poetry continues to play an important role in the social and political culture of contemporary Kyrgyzstan. People enjoy listening to caustic improvised poetry composed and sung in the style of traditional *terme* songs. A Kyrgyz aphorism states, "May *aqyn*s speak the truth" (*Akyndar akty süylösö*), and indeed, people expect *aqyn*s to speak openly about wrongdoings of the government and politicians, or, if it is warranted, to acknowledge their good work and public service. In other words, the *terme* poetic genre provides a platform for *aqyn*s to openly express their individual and public opinions on important social and political issues. However, not all *aqyn*s have had the courage to criticize government leadership. The older generation of *aqyn*s who lived and worked during the Soviet period tends to be more cautious in what they say at large public gatherings and concerts and tries to avoid touching on political issues. However, as another popular Kyrgyz aphorism states, "A pupil should best his teacher" (*Ustattan shakirt ötüptür*). This advice seems true in the case of *aqyn*s, for the post-Soviet generation of Kyrgyz *aqyn*s appears to have a stronger sense of national identity and trenchant language than the preceding generation. Some of these younger *aqyn*s did not hesitate to criticize the former Kyrgyz presidents Askar Akaev and Kurmanbek Bakiev while they were still in power (1991–2005 and 2005–2010, respectively). *Aqyn*s enjoy a tacit freedom of poetic speech, relying on the broad popular support of their listeners to defend them against censorial actions by those they criticize.

Example 9.4. "Kalk armany" (The people's lament/misfortune), performed by Jengishbek Toktobekov.

"Kalk armany" (The people's lament/misfortune) is a new *terme* composed by a thirty-nine-year-old *aqyn,* Jengishbek Toktobekov, who is also known by the stage name Avtomat (Machine gun). In addition to improvising poetry orally and participating in *aitysh* poetry contests, Jengishbek, as a practicing, pious Muslim, writes poetry with religious content. However, unlike traditional improvised poetry, his written poetry consists of eleven-syllable lines, making it difficult to sing with the traditional rhythmic melody that is used for poetry of seven- or eight-syllable verse lines. Thus instead of singing his written poetry, he recites these poems without the accompaniment of *komuz.*

Jengishbek's *terme* poem, "Kalk armany," was composed after the events of April 2010 that resulted in the ousting of the second Kyrgyz president, Kurmanbek Bakiev. Like other young *aqyn*s as well as the majority of citizens of Kyrgyzstan, Jengishbek had been a strong opponent of Bakiev's political regime and family rule. In this *terme,* he talks about *zaman* (time), a popular theme in the verse of eighteenth- and nineteenth-century Kyrgyz poets who sang about the changes and problems of their own time. He begins the poem by giving a short summary of the socio-political situation in Kyrgyzstan since its independence and recollecting the first happy years following the Soviet collapse in 1991: Askar Akaev's election as the first president of independent Kyrgyzstan; the adoption of new national symbols such as the flag, state emblem, and Kyrgyz national currency (*som*); the major

Jengishbek Toktobekov.

public celebration of the one-thousand-year anniversary of the epic *Manas* in 1995; and the promotion of an open society by increasing use of the Internet. He then talks about how Akaev became corrupt. He sold Kyrgyz land to the Chinese and natural resources such as gold to a Canadian mining company; ordered soldiers to shoot at peaceful protesters from the Aksy region in 2002; and presided over a 2005 parliamentary election in which his daughter and son were candidates and which many observers considered to have been tainted by fraud. Finally, he was ousted from power and fled to Moscow in March 2005. In a similar way, he goes on to describe how the second president, Kurmanbek Bakiev, came to power, what went wrong with his leadership, how opposition leaders were persecuted, and how the brave crowd of young Kyrgyz men put an end to his regime on April 7, 2010, by sacrificing their lives in the hope of creating a better future for the country. Jengishbek ends his *terme* by calling the Kyrgyz people to unite as one nation; he condemns those who divide the people into "northern" (*tündük*) and "southern" (*tüshtük*), and warns the new interim government that replaced Bakiev that a similar fate might await them if they repeat the selfish mistakes of past leaders.

The text for this example is available on the companion website.

STUDY QUESTIONS AND ACTIVITIES

1. *Terme* denotes a collection of wise and eloquent words on various themes. Identify and compare the themes in the four *terme* poems in examples 9.1–9.4.

2. Do you find Kyrgyz wisdom poetry composed in the eighteenth and nineteenth centuries relevant to values and wisdom in contemporary society?

3. What do you think about the content of Jengishbek's "Kalk armany" *terme* and his verbal skill? Why do you think he is known by the stage name "Machine Gun"?

4. Some people compare the Kazakh and Kyrgyz *aqyns* and their improvisational skill to that of rappers. In what ways are *terme* and rap similar and different?

5. Compare the poetic structure of the Kyrgyz *terme* texts transcribed above and identify the key poetic features, such as initial and internal alliteration and end rhyme.

6. Poetic exercise: Write a short poem with seven or eight syllables in each verse line on a particular theme (in the form of advice or wisdom), in English or in your own native language, with initial alliteration and end rhyme. You can share your poems in class and discuss the challenges you experienced in writing or improvising the verse lines. This exercise will help you test your own verbal skill as well as appreciate the unique verbal skill of Kyrgyz and Kazakh *aqyns* who can extemporize hundreds of verse lines in front of an audience.

7. How would you compare the melodies of the three *terme* songs (examples 9.1–9.3)? Do they sound different or similar in terms of the pace, style, and use of *komuz*? Also, how would you compare the melody of these *terme* songs to the recitation of *Manas*?

NOTES

1. The song is also known as "Opsuz düynö" (Temporary world).

2. Bahauddin Naqshband is the name of a 14th-century Sufi master who is revered as the founder of the Sufi brotherhood that bears his name, the Naqshbandiyya. The Naqshbandiyya became one of the principal Sufi orders of Central Asia. The shrine of Bahauddin is located near the city of Bukhara, Uzbekistan. Many Central Asians regard him as a saint, and consider a pilgrimage to his grave as a substitute for the Hajj pilgrimage to Mecca.

3. Jengijok is a well-known Kyrgyz *aqyn* from the Aksy region of southern Kyrgyzstan.

4. Toktogul is a well-known Kyrgyz *aqyn* from the Ketmen-Töbö region (now known as the Toktogul region) of central Kyrgyzstan.

CHAPTER 10 *Aqyn*s and Improvised Poetry Competitions among the Kazakhs and Kyrgyz

ELMIRA KÖCHÜMKULOVA AND
JANGÜL QOJAKHMETOVA

There's a popular Kyrgyz saying, "A red tongue (eloquence) is the best skill of all" (*Önör aldy—kyzyl til*). Indeed, the nomadic Kyrgyz and Kazakhs have long placed a high value on rhetorical skill (Kyrgyz: *chechendik;* Kazakh: *sheshendik*) and developed sophisticated forms of verbal art that are displayed in public competitions of improvised poetry, called *aitysh* (Kyrgyz) or *aitys* (Kazakh). Vasily Radlov, a Russian scholar who collected oral literature among the nomadic Kyrgyz in the nineteenth century, noted that the ordinary speech of the Kyrgyz sounds like poetry, and that they consider rhythmic speech to be the highest form of verbal art. Similarly, the Russian orientalist, writer, and diplomat, Petr Pashino, who visited Turkestan in the second half of the nineteenth century, observed that the Kazakhs constantly sing and improvise at the same time.

Kazakh and Kyrgyz oral tradition is intimately linked with the nomadic way of life that has provided a livelihood for myriad Turkic and Mongolian groups in the vast grasslands, mountain ranges, and steppe country of Central Eurasia. Beginning in the early 1930s, Soviet economic and cultural policies prescribed that nomads be resettled in villages, towns, and cities. Yet even in the conditions of sedentary life, nomadic heritage and oral tradition continue to be integral elements of national identity and culture. These elements have become increasingly important in the decades since 1991, when Kazakhstan and Kyrgyzstan became independent nations. Before the twentieth century, Kyrgyz and Kazakh nomads did not generally practice writing in their everyday lives, or carry books when traveling from

Posters of *aqyn*s from the Soviet period.

pasture to pasture with their livestock. Instead, they had "living books" in the form of epic singers (Kyrgyz: *yrchy*s; Kazakh: *jyrshy*s, *jyrau*s), oral poets (*aqyn*s) who extemporized verse during the course of performance, and storytellers (*jomokchu*s; *ängimeshi*s) who were able to preserve traditional wisdom, cultural knowledge, history, and tribal genealogy in poetry, epic poems, songs, and instrumental music.

MASTERS OF ORAL POETRY AND MUSIC PERFORMANCE: YRCHY/JYRSHY, JYRAU, AND AQYN

Both the Kyrgyz and Kazakh languages—which are very similar—have the old word *yr/jyr* which derives from the Turkic *iyr*: "song," "epic song." Cognate with this word are the terms *yrchy/jyrshy* and *jyrau,* meaning "oral poet," "singer," "musician," "bard," or "epic singer," which refer to masters of oral poetry and music performance. Kyrgyz *yrchy*s and Kazakh *jyrshy*s sang improvised as well as pre-composed poetry in a variety of lyric and smaller epic genres and participated in oral poetry competitions, *aitysh* and *aitys,* accompanying themselves on the *komuz* (Kyrgyz three-stringed long-necked lute) and *dombyra* (Kazakh two-stringed long-necked lute). The Kazakh *jyrau*s, as distinct from *jyrshy*s, specialized in the performance and composition of large-scale epic poems and originally accompanied their recitation on the *qobyz* (Kazakh two-stringed fiddle), later transferring to the *dombyra.* (See chapters 5 and 11.)

In the nineteenth century, in response to broad social and musical change, the Kazakhs and Kyrgyz acquired a new term to designate an oral poet and musician: *aqyn.* This term, according to a commonly accepted opinion, derived from the Persian *ākhūn* ("preacher," "orator," "tutor") and was adopted in Turkic languages under the influence of Persian language and literature and disseminated among the nomads with the spread of Islam.[1] An alternative etymological explanation offered by Kazakh scholars interprets *aqyn* as an originally Turkic word. According to this interpretation, it derives from the word *aqin* ("flow," "stream," "torrent"), alluding to the nature of *aqyn*s' oral improvisation associated with torrential flow, and its cognate words meaning "attack," "strike," "incursion," which reflect the traditional understanding of *aqyn*s' performance in poetic contests as combat with an opponent representing a different clan, and a defense of one's own clan.[2] *Aqyn*s have overwhelmingly been male, but there were also female bards who challenged male contenders in improvised poetry competitions. Although *aqyn*s primarily performed lyric poetry and participated in *aitysh/aitys,* they could also perform epic genres and were versatile oral poets and singers who accompanied themselves on musical instruments—typically the *komuz* (Kyrgyz) and *dombyra* (Kazakh). Kazakh *aqyn*s also used the *qobyz* and button accordion (*syrnai*) to accompany singing. In addition to composing orally, some *aqyn*s who received a Muslim

A group of Kazakh *aqyn*s with their instruments.

Courtesy of the Central State Archive of Film, Photography, and Sound Recordings of the Republic of Kazakhstan.

education and learned the Arabic script also wrote down their poetry and therefore came to be called *jazgych* (Kyrgyz) or *jazba* (Kazakh) *aqyn*s (from *jaz*: "to write").[3]

During the Soviet period, with the spread of literacy in the Latin and, later, the Cyrillic alphabet and the rising significance of written literature, a new group of poets emerged who composed poetry in writing (examples include the Kyrgyz poets Aaly Tokombaev and Alykul Osmonov, and the Kazakh poets Mayasar Japaqov and Isa Baizakov). These poets addressed new themes and adopted some of the literary norms and styles of Russian and Soviet poetic traditions. And while they did not compose or perform music, nor participate in *aitysh/aitys,* they did retain the name *aqyn*. In order to distinguish this new group of *aqyn*s from traditional oral poets and singers, Kyrgyz and Kazakh scholars divided *aqyn*s into three categories:

- *tökmö/tökpe* (from *tök-:* "to pour," "to spill out words") or *suyryp salma* (Kazakh: "here-and-now," "on the spot") *aqyn*s: improvising oral poets;
- *jazgych/jazba aqyn*s: eighteenth- and nineteenth-century poets who wrote down their poetry;
- *aqyn*s: Soviet and post-Soviet poets who have composed poetry in writing.

Today most improvising oral poets can also compose written poetry. Meanwhile, the term *yrchy/jyrshy,* which formerly designated individuals who both composed and performed poetic texts, has come to refer exclusively to performers. In this chapter, we will focus on *tökmö/suyryp salma aqyn*s (or *yrchy*s/*jyrshy*s in the older, pre-Soviet sense of the term), and on the improvisatory verse performed at poetry competitions, *aitysh/aitys.*

THE ART OF *AQYNS: AQYNDYQ*

In Kyrgyz and Kazakh nomadic societies, the art of improvising oral poets (Kyrgyz: *aqyndyq, yrchylik, tökmölük önör;* Kazakh: *aqyndyq, jyrshylyq öner*) was closely interwoven with everyday life. People very much enjoyed improvised music and poetry and invited performers to a variety of traditional ceremonies and festivities (Kyrgyz: *ash, toy;* Kazakh: *as, toy*), such as a celebration for a newborn child (*jeentek toy/ shildekhana*), a circumcision feast (*sünnöt/sündet toy*), weddings (*üylönüü/üilenu toy*), funerals and memorial feasts (in particular, the one-year anniversary of the dead, *ash/as*), and community gatherings (*jiyn*). Within these festivities, an *aqyn* often acted as a master of ceremonies (*jarchi/jarshy*) who was in charge of the feast's entertainment "program" and conducted important life-cycle rituals that involved singing. These included the performance of a special wedding song (*betashar*) that accompanied the unveiling of a bride's face, and the performance of mourning laments (*koshok, joktoo/joqtau*) at funerals and memorial feasts (see chapter 12).

The repertory of *aqyns* included a variety of poetic and musical genres: storytelling (*jomok/ängime*) and epic narration (*jyr, dastan, qissa*); lyric (*qara öleng*), didactic, and wisdom poetry (*terme, jeldirme, tolghau*); wedding songs (*betashar, toy bastar*) and funeral lamentations (*koshok, joktoo/joqtau*); songs dedicated to particular themes (*arnau*) and instrumental music (*küü/küi*). In their youth, *aqyns* composed love songs (*ashyktyk yrlary/ghashyqtyq jyrlary*) and, as they became older, they composed and sang philosophical and religious poetry that reinforced social mores and spiritual values.

Through their multifarious engagement in family and community affairs, *aqyns* and *yrchys/jyrshys* played important roles in nomadic society, facilitating communication and exchange, perpetuating memory and identity, and validating socially established customs and norms. Far from being just entertainers, they were highly esteemed bearers and transmitters of historical and cultural knowledge, traditional values, wisdom, and oral musical traditions. Such poets and singers assumed an elevated social status and high moral obligations before their community. The nineteenth-century Kyrgyz *yrchy* Arstanbek eloquently describes what kind of person an *yrchy* should be and what kind of roles he should play in society in an impromptu song that he sang to his pupil Jengijok:

Oo, balam,	Oh, my son,
Yrchylik jaiyn aytaiyn,	Let me tell you about being an *yrchy:*
Yrchy bolsong synchy bol.	If you want to be an *yrchy,* be a *synchy,*[4]
Argymak mingen baatyr bol.	Be a brave man who rides on a stallion,
Külük mingen küchtüü bol,	Be a strong man who rides on a racehorse,

Küydürgügö mizdüü bol.	Be a sharp knife to one who's obnoxious,
Jetimderge kömök bol,	Be a help for orphans,
Jesirlerge jölök bol,	Be the support for widows,
Kankorlorgo kasap bol,	Be the butcher to bloodsuckers,
Kalp aytkanga mazak bol.	Be the mocker to liars,
Ashta, toydo myrza bol,	Be the gentleman at feasts,
Akyndarga nuska bol.	Be an example for *aqyn*s,
Karözgöy bolboy kalys bol,	Be just and not wicked,
Koshomattan alys bol.	Stay away from ingratiation,
Eregish chyksa elchi bol,	Be the conciliator during a fight,
El-jurtungdun kenchi bol.	Be the treasure of your people,
Kalktyn zaryn zardap öt,	Sing the sorrows of people with sorrow,
Kachanky yryn yrdap öt.	Sing the old songs that they like,
Kalk köngülün chalkytyp,	Bring joy to people's hearts, and
Kaniet alyp jyrgap öt.	Lead a grateful and joyful life.
Balam,	My son,
Synchylardyn synyn uk,	Learn the skills of *synchy*s,
Yrchylardyn yryn uk,	Learn the songs of singers,
Jomokchunu izdep uk,	Listen to the storytellers by chasing after them,
Ushakchyny uktap uk,	Learn from gossipers in your sleep,
Akylmandy angdap uk,	Learn well the wisdom of the wise,
Duduktardy jandap uk.	Learn from the deaf by going close to them,
Chechenderdin sözün uk,	Learn the words of eloquent men,
Kösömdördün köchün uk,	Learn the wisdom of wise men,
Komuzchunun küüsün uk,	Learn the melodies of *komuz* players attentively,
Kiyakchyny kyldat uk,	Learn the melodies of *kiyak* players clearly,
Choorchunu chordop uk,	Learn the music of *choor* [flute] players cheerfully,
Temir komuz termeltet,	The *temir komuz* [jaw harp] makes one swing,
Nazar salyp taasyn uk.	Pay attention and learn it proficiently,
Adebi jok yrchydan,	Behind an ill-mannered singer
Artynda jaman söz kalat.	Only bad words will remain.
Anyk nuska yrchydan	Behind a real singer,
Aalamga ketchü kep kalat.[5]	Words of wisdom will live forever!

In addition to its social role, the art of *aqyn*s and *yrchy*s/*jyrshy*s was understood to have sacred significance. Like shamans (*bakshy*s/*baqsy*s) and epic bards (*manaschy*s/*jyrau*s), bearers of *aqyndyq* were believed to have their poetic and musical gift bestowed by supernatural powers, usually through a visionary dream (*ayan*) in which they were visited by a messenger, such as a saint, a sage, or the spirit of a famous late singer and poet-improviser. Their poetic improvisation and singing were thus imbued with magical qualities, and their performance at

Elmirbek aqyn.
Courtesy of Elmirbek Imanaliev.

life-cycle rituals and community festivities was understood to facilitate mediation between humans and the world of ancestor-spirits.

MASTER-APPRENTICE TRAINING

Notwithstanding the belief in an otherwordly source for the *aqyn*'s gift, the path to gaining mastery in *aqyndyq,* whether in the past or nowadays, is not an easy one. Becoming a master *aqyn* involves both self-learning and training with a master (*ustat/ustaz*) in a variety of domains: verbal improvisation and musical skills, knowledge of local history and culture, and an ability to storytell and entertain. An amateur oral poet among the Kyrgyz is called *jamakchy* (from *jamak:* "patch"). As the term suggests, *jamakchy*s learn to patch together words and improvise verse lines with simple rhymes and alliterations. *Jamakchy* singers are typically young and have not yet gained enough knowledge, wisdom, and life experience to feel confident about their verbal improvisational skills. They would not be competitive in *aitysh* contests but test their verbal skill at smaller feasts and parties. Mastering verbal arts to the professional level expected of a *tökmö/tökpe* or *suyryp salma aqyn* requires practice, training, and exposure to the public, as well as traveling, communicating, and socializing. In addition to artistic talent and a good knowledge of history and culture, *tökmö aqyn*s need an excellent memory and strong listening skills (*kuyma kulak/quima qulaq*) in order to memorize the songs of other *aqyn*s as well as the wise words of elders.

A young person who wants to become an *aqyn* first identifies a teacher or master (*ustat/ustaz*) willing to transmit wisdom along with the craft of performance: improvising and rhyming verse lines, singing, playing the *komuz* or *dombyra,* and becoming an engaging storyteller and entertainer. Like athletes who undertake daily training regimes, amateur *aqyn*s must train their mind, language skills, and voice. Serving as an apprentice (*shakirt/shäkirt*) to a master over a certain period of time, they acquire a subtle command of the art of improvisation, and toward the end of their study, they receive a spiritual and artistic valediction, or blessing (*bata*), from the master in which he offers words of advice for the *aqyn*'s future life. The well-known Kyrgyz *aqyn* Kalyk (1883–1953), gave the following advice to his pupil Osmonkul: "If one does not train, feed and take care of one's skill (*önör*) like a racehorse, it will get dull like a rusty knife. Thus one must constantly sharpen it. People need singers like us to tell their sorrows, to entertain them, and to express their thoughts and ideas in eloquent words."[6] Another Kyrgyz *aqyn,* Barpy, said: "The essence of good words lies in song. The more one sings the more words will be composed. There are many different songs and they must be sung at the right place and time. Singers have a great responsibility depending on their fame and talent."[7] Some poets gave their advice in poetry.

For example, the Kyrgyz poet Korgol gave the following precepts to one of his students, Altymysh:

Yr chykpayt balam oylonboy	Words will come out without thinking,
Kurch sözdü taap yrdagyn,	Find sharp words to put together
Kirpich kynap koygondoy.	Like evenly stacked bricks,
Kyialyng daana ergisin,	Let your mind think clearly,
Karyia atang Korgoldoy.[8]	Like your old father Korgol.

And to his student Tuuganbay, Korgol said:

Badaldyn körkü shagynda,	The beauty of a bush is in its branches,
Baltanyn küchü sabynda.	The beauty of an ax is in its handle,
Bal koshkondoy söz aytyp,	Sing words as sweet as honey and
Bargan jerge jangy yrda.	New songs at every place you go.
Buchkakka töönü chapkanday,	Like a camel rider hitting a camel on the shin,
Buydalbastan shar yrda!	Sing fast without stumbling.
Oymoktoy oozung shok bolso,	If you have a bad mouth,
Oyungda yryng jok bolso,	If you have no good songs,
Köpchülükkö jakpasang,	If people do not like you,
Köröngöngö taarynba![9]	Don't complain about your ineptitude!

The great nineteenth-century Kazakh *aqyn* Süiinbai Aronuly gave this blessing to his pupil, Jambyl Jabaev (1846–1945), who subsequently became a famous *aqyn* in his own right:

O, Jambyl, bata deding—berdim saghan,	Oh, Jambyl, you asked for a blessing, and I give it to you,
Baqytty, ömirli bol, jürgin aman.	Be happy, live long, and keep well.
Batasyn at ornyna berdi ghoi dep,	Don't blame me,
Qoimaghyn bylai shyghyp kinä maghan.	Saying I gave you a blessing instead of a horse.
Songynan Süiinbaidyng ornyn basyp,	As you follow in my footsteps,
Tilingnen balyng tamsyn sorghalaghan.	May the honey [of your words] flow from your tongue like a stream.
Japagha riza bolsyn aita barghyn,	May people be content with what you say,
Osymen ökpelemei jürsin aman.[10]	May they not be upset by it and keep well.

The master's blessing initiates young *aqyn*s into independent practice as professional performers, after which they further develop and refine their verbal and musical skills. In the past, depending on their personal characteristics, voice, and

Jambyl Jabaev.
Courtesy of the Central State Archive of Film, Photography, and Sound Recordings of the Republic of Kazakhstan.

oral-poetic improvisational skills, *aqyn*s often acquired a "stage name" in the form of an epithet, such as *ak tangday* (white palate), *jez tangday* (copper palate), *too bulbulu* (mountain nightingale), *kara jaak* (black/sharp jaw), and *tökmö* (torrential rain). The titles were usually attached to the *aqyn*'s first name—for example, "Kara jaak Kalmyrza" (Black-jawed Kalmyrza), "Too bulbulu Toktogul" (Toktogul the Mountain Nightingale), "Jez tangday akyn Jengijok" (Jengijok with a Copper Palate), "Alymkul tökmö" (Alymkul, the Torrential [Rain]), "Eshmambet tulgara" (Eshmanbet the Black Horse), and "Okeanday Osmonkul" (Oceanic Osmonkul). Similar epithets are also used among contemporary *aqyn*s. For example, the Kyrgyz *aqyn* Jengishbek Toktobekov is called "Avtomat" (Machine Gun) because he improvises verse lines as if shooting bullets from a machine gun. Another *aqyn*, Amantay Kutmanaliev, is nicknamed "Sary kashka" (Horse with a Yellow Spot on its Forehead) because he is fair-skinned, and Elmirbek Imanaliev is known as "Ak jaiyk" (Wide Pasture) on account of his calm personality, chubby body, and mellow voice.

Through gaining experience in performance, an *aqyn* prepares himself for participation in *aitysh/aitys,* the highest form of improvisatory verbal art.

ORAL POETRY COMPETITIONS: *AITYSH/AITYS*

The word *aitysh/aitys* is derived from the Turkic verb *ait* ("to tell," "to say") and means "verbal duel," "quarrel," or "dispute." Although unique as a sophisticated type of improvised poetry contest, it is by no means the only dialogic art form among the Kazakhs and Kyrgyz. The competitive tradition has old historical origins in the cultures of Central Asian nomads, and is rooted in ritualized rivalry between different tribes and clans in tribal societies. Elements of competitiveness permeated various spheres of nomadic social and cultural life, including sports and martial arts, poetry and music. They found expression in wrestling (Kazakh: *qazaqsha küres;* Kyrgyz: *kürösh*), horse racing (Kazakh: *at jarys, bäige;* Kyrgyz: *at chabysh, bayge*), and horsemanship games, such as polo played with a goat carcass (Kazakh: *kökpar;* Kyrgyz: *kök börü, ulak*) and contests in archery (Kazakh: *jamby atu;* Kyrgyz: *jamby atmay*). They have also manifested themselves in sung poetic exchanges in ritual practice and in everyday life, such as dialogic incantations against livestock diseases (*bädik aitys*) performed by a shaman or by groups of young men and women, the wedding song (*jar-jar*) performed in alternation by friends of the groom and girlfriends of the bride at her farewell ceremony, and verses on various topics (*qara öleng*) exchanged impromptu by amateur performers (Kazakh: *qaiymdasu, qaiym aitys;* Kyrgyz: *kaiym aitysh, alym sabak aitysh*).

Competitions could also take place between masters of rhetoric and jurists (*sheshen*s, *bii*s), epic performers (*yrchy*s/*jyrshy*s, *jyrau*s), and, among Kazakhs, instrumental virtuosi (*dombyra* players) who competed in the performance of

An *aitys* of Kazakh *aqyns*.
Courtesy of the Central State Archive of Film, Photography, and Sound Recordings of the Republic of Kazakhstan.

narrative pieces, *küi*s (*tartys*).[11] In contrast to ritual and everyday dialogic forms of singing, these forms of competitions all provided an arena for accomplished master performers. *Aitysh/aitys* presented the most challenging platform for *aqyn*s, putting their intellect, knowledge, outlook, eloquence, wit, and oral poetic skill to the test before a live audience and determining a performer's eminence as a poet-improviser.

Traditionally, participants in *aitysh/aitys* or similar contests between master performers performed on behalf of different clans. A competition was forbidden between members of the same clan or distant paternal relatives. During the competition, they had to praise their own clans and find fault with their opponents' clans. Poetic and musical contests were therefore the highlight of large intertribal festivities, such as a memorial feast to mark the one-year anniversary of a person's death, a wedding, or a community gathering. Such festivities took place in mountain pastures (*jayloo/jailau*) during summer and autumn when fermented mare's milk (*qymyz*) was plentiful and animals had grown fat enough to be consumed. In addition to *aitysh/aitys,* these festivities also featured competitive play and games, such as wrestling and horse racing. Large memorial feasts were planned far in advance, and people waited eagerly to listen to songs sung by well-known entertainers. An *aqyn* appointed as a master of ceremony would welcome guests, accompanying himself on the *komuz* or *dombyra,* and introduce the various singers, musicians, wrestlers, and horsemen. Memorial feasts lasted for several days so that people who came on horseback from long distances could rest and enjoy one another's company, share meals, watch horse games, and listen to the music and poetry of *aqyn*s, especially to their *aitysh/aitys.* Many *aqyn*s earned their living by singing, and as a sign of appreciation, wealthy hosts and clan leaders presented *aqyn*s with gifts, such as horses, sheep, fur coats and hats, or money.

In the twentieth century, following the transformations in Kyrgyz and Kazakh societies that came about as a consequence of Soviet nationalities and cultural policies, the social connotation and content of *aitysh/aitys* changed: oral poet-improvisers started to perform not as representatives of particular clans and tribes but on behalf of their home regions and areas. The context of *aitysh/aitys* also changed, with performances typically relegated to a stage in a theater or concert hall as part of a state-supported event or as a specially organized and publicly attended spectacle. These changes notwithstanding, contemporary *aitysh/aitys* has maintained much of its traditional character and form, and it remains widely popular among connoisseurs of poetic eloquence and improvisation, providing a measure of an *aqyn*'s mastery and ingenuity. The following sections outline the types, form, and poetic and musical structure of the Kyrgyz *aitysh* and Kazakh *aitys.*

TYPES OF COMPETITION

Based on form and content, Kyrgyz *aqyn*s distinguish six principal types of *aitysh:*

- *alym sabak aitysh:* short exchange of poetic words
- *tabyshmak aitysh:* riddle *aitysh*
- *sanat aitysh:* wisdom *aitysh*
- *chechendik aitysh:* eloquence *aitysh*
- *kordoo aitysh:* insult *aitysh*
- *tamalashaluu aitysh:* entertainment *aitysh*

Alym sabak is the most interesting and difficult form of *aitysh,* and only master *aqyn*s possess the requisite quick-wittedness and improvisational rhyming skills to compete in it successfully. *Alym sabak* is also one of the main methods that master *aqyn*s use to train and test their students. In the *alym sabak aitysh,* two and sometimes three *aqyn*s engage in a lively poetic dialogue by improvising short two- or four-line verses on a specific theme or topic. The main feature of this *aitysh* is the principle that contestants carry on the thought or idea initiated by an opponent using the same initial alliteration and end rhyme provided by the opponent. The goal is not so much to beat one's opponents as to entertain the audience while at the same time learning about the improvisatory methods of other *aqyn*s.

WATCH | **Example 10.1.** *Alym sabak aitysh* between senior master *aqyn* Tuuganbay and his pupil, Aaly aqyn.

Watch the *alym sabak aitysh* between senior master *aqyn* Tuuganbay Abdiyev (1937–2008) and his pupil, Aaly aqyn. The key principle of this type of poetic contest is to reply to one's opponent using the same number of syllables in a verse line and the same rhyming pattern as one's opponent. An *aqyn* who is not able to come up with a quick and correct response using a rhyming word is considered a loser in the contest.

The text for this example is available on the companion website.

STUDY QUESTIONS AND ACTIVITY

1. What does the *aitysh* reveal about the relationship between the two *aqyn*s?

2. How would you evaluate the two men's poetic improvising skills? Do they observe the rule of the competition by maintaining alliteration and end rhyme? Whom would you select as the winner in this contest?

3. What kind of verbal skills do you think a person needs to be able to improvise one- or two-line verses with alliteration and rhyme within two or three seconds?

4. Oral poetry composition exercise: Test your verbal skill and wit by improvising short verse lines using similar themes and structures to those used by *aqyn*s. You can make up a simple melody to fit your rhythmic template and try to sing and compete with a classmate, who, as your opponent, will have to respond to you in the same rhyming pattern.

The *tabyshmak aitysh* is performed in the form of a riddle. One of the *aqyn*s begins the *aitysh* by asking riddle-like questions in poetry, and the opponent gives the answer, also in poetry. Only a few accounts of such *aitysh* survive in Kyrgyz oral tradition. The best-known *tabyshmak aitysh* is one that took place between a young woman, Talym kyz, and a man named Köbök in the mid-nineteenth century. Talym decides to choose her future husband by engaging men in an *aitysh* that tests their knowledge and verbal skill. She promises to marry the one who comes up with the answer to her riddle, which is about nature, human beings, animals, and moral values.

LISTEN **Example 10.2.** *Tabyshmak aitysh,* **a riddle** *aitysh* **performed by Azamat Bolgonbaev.**

This riddle *aitysh* between two Kyrgyz *yrchy*s named Chongdu and Arstanbek, which took place in the mid-nineteenth century, has been preserved in oral tradition. In example 10.2, Azamat Bolgonbaev (b. 1983), sings the texts of both Chongdu and Arstanbek.

The text for this example is available on the companion website.

STUDY QUESTIONS AND ACTIVITY

1. How would you compare the riddle *aitysh* to the preceding *alym sabak aitysh* with regard to the time span, poetic structure, performance style, and function of the *komuz*?

2. As represented in the performance of Azamat Bolgonbaev, how would you compare the verbal skills of the two poets in terms of their use of alliteration and end rhyme?

3. What kind of wisdom does the song contain about family relations in nomadic Kyrgyz society?

4. How do the two poets represented by the performer see the specific identity, image, role, and status of each family member?

5. Compose a short riddle poem about the significance of people or things in your family and life using the same poetic structure as in this poem. Try to use initial alliteration and end rhyme.

Kazakh *aitys* can similarly be divided into several types according to various distinguishing features. With regard to content, these include riddle (*jumbaq*), fable (*ötirik*), joke (*äzil*), and religious (*dini*) *aitys,* as well as *aitys* on a given topic or dedicated to a particular occasion. With regard to number, type, and gender of performers, they include *aitys* between individual *aqyn*s or between several performers, between amateurs or professional *aqyn*s, and between male or female *aqyn*s, or between a young man and a girl (*qyz ben jigit aitysy*). There are also instances of *aitys* in which an *aqyn* competes with an animal (e.g., a horse) or an inanimate object (e.g., a *dombyra*), extemporizing verses both on his or her own behalf and on behalf of the opponent.

With regard to form, Kazakh *aqyn*s distinguish two main types of *aitys: türe* and *süre.* In *türe aitys* (from *türe söileu,* "to speak concisely, succinctly"), two or more *aqyn*s exchange short, two- or four-line verses. In *süre aitys* ("long," "full-length" *aitys*), each of two opponents improvises at length in an effort to display intelligence, sharpness of mind, and skill at improvisation.[12] Whereas *türe aitys* can be performed by amateur, less skillful, and less experienced *aqyn*s, participants in *süre aitys* are necessarily master poet-improvisers who have a broad knowledge of the history of Kazakh tribes and clans, biographies of major historical personalities, and a range of topics relating to Kazakh culture, society, and politics.

WATCH

Example 10.3. *Süre aitys* between Köken Shäkeev and Qonysbai Äbilov (excerpt), Almaty, Kazakhstan, 1985. From Jürsin Erman, *Aitys 4. Torghai—Kökshetau oblystary aqyn-jyrshylarynyng öner saiysy* [Competition between the art of *aqyn*s and *jyrshy*s from the Torghai and Kökshetau regions], Almaty: Studiya Dastan, 2006.

Watch an excerpt from a *süre aitys* between Köken Shäkeev (1926–1999), an acclaimed senior *aqyn* from the Kökshetau region in northern Kazakhstan, and Qonysbai Äbilov (b. 1954), a junior *aqyn* from the neighboring Torghai district of the northern region of Qostanai. As the excerpt shows, each *aqyn* performs an extended poetic utterance in which he develops ideas about the social and cultural significance of *aitys* among the Kazakhs and demonstrates his knowledge of the history and culture of the opponent's home region. The poetic dialogue reveals the *aqyn*s' high regard for the art of *aitys* and the regions they represent, as well as a respectful attitude toward each other in accordance with notions of age and seniority. It is an example of high poetic improvisation.

The text for this example is available on the companion website.

STUDY QUESTIONS AND ACTIVITY

1. On the basis of this example, how would you describe the content and the poetic and musical structure of the Kazakh *süre aitys*? What, in your view, distinguishes this type of Kazakh *aitys* from, or makes it similar to, the types of Kyrgyz *aitysh* illustrated above?

2. In what ways do the two *aqyn*s speak of the art of *aitys*?

3. What literary devices do they use to describe their homelands, Kökshetau and Torghai?

4. What do we learn about the relationship between the two *aqyn*s from their form of address and communication with each other?

5. Analyze the rhyme structure used by each *aqyn* and explain how the verse is set to music.

Form of an *Aitysh/Aitys*

An *aitysh/aitys* has a prescribed format. A competition begins with the *aqyn*s greeting spectators and one another. If the contestants vary in age, they perform in order of seniority. In the past, following the greetings, *aqyn*s necessarily introduced their tribe and clan background and home region. Here, for example, are the initial verse lines of the introduction (*tanystyru*) from an *aitys* between the nineteenth-century Kazakh *aqyn*s Janaq and Tübek:

Janaq:	*Uranymdy surasang arghyn, naiman,*	If you, Naiman, ask about my clan,[13] it is Arghyn.
	Kedei Janaq deseng de ar qylmaimyn.	Even if you say, poor man Janaq, I shall not be disgraced.
Tübek:	*Arghyn bolsang qaiteiin naimandaimyn,*	I am Naiman, so what if you are Arghyn,
	Küäm bar qai sertingnen taighandaimyn.[14]	I have evidence of what oath you have broken.

Present-day *aqyn*s do not necessarily mention their tribe and clan origins. They can likewise identify themselves and their opponents with reference to their home region (for example, "a child of the west," *Batystyng balasy,* or "the cream of Syr Darya," *Syrdyng sümeui*) and characterize it by mentioning historical personalities—heroes, poets, musicians—who came from there. Thus, an *aqyn* from the Semei (Semipalatinsk) region in eastern Kazakhstan can be addressed as "a young colt reared in Abai's homeland" (*Abai tughan öngirding töl qulyny*), with reference to Abai Qunanbaev (1845–1904), the great philosopher, poet, and composer born in this region.

After the greetings and introduction, *aqyn*s begin to challenge each other by teasing, joking, or insulting. Their form of address reflects traditional notions of age, seniority, and gender, though contestants are also allowed to speak in ways that depart from the socially accepted modes of discourse. The following excerpt is from a nineteenth-century *aitysh* that took place in Talas between two well-known Kyrgyz *aqyn*s. As the senior *aqyn*, Esenaman begins the *aitysh*:

Amanby balam Jengijok,	Greetings, my son, Jengijok!
Abangdyn senden kemi jok.	Your uncle is not less than you.[15]
Ak kalpaktuu kyrgyzdan,	Among the white *kalpak*[16] Kyrgyz
Aitysharga tengi jok.	There is no one to compete with you.
Alaman yrchy köp jüröt,	There are many so-called *yrchys*,
Aytkanynyn ebi jok . . .	But their words do not make much sense . . .

*Aqyn*s compare themselves to a nightingale, cuckoo, skylark, or eagle. Thus, Esenaman praises himself with the following words:

| Torusumun jylkynyn, | I am the bay one among the horses, |
| Torgoyumun yrchynyn. | I am the skylark among the singers. |

His opponent Jengijok replies:

Torusu bolsong jylkynyn,	If you are the bay among the horses,
Tokmoktop toygo minbeybi?	A man will beat and ride you at feasts.
Torgoyu bolson yrchynyn,	If you are the lark among the singers,
Too jagalmay ilbeybi?	A mountain hawk will seize you,
Tobokelchil Jengijok	I, the risk-taking Jengijok,
Töbösü jok kak bashty	You bastard with no head,
Tomsortorun bilbeybi?	I'll put you down like this!

It is the spectators who judge the *aqyns*' verbal skill and determine the winner. Formerly, *aqyns* themselves would stop the contest when they felt they were losing to their opponent, and the loser or the *aqyns*' pupils subsequently disseminated the *aitys* orally. Today, formal *aitysh/aitys* competitions organized for special occasions have a predetermined time limit, and they are judged by a group of judges (Kyrgyz: *kalystar tobu*; Kazakh: *qazylar alqasy*) consisting of five to ten people who are knowledgeable about Kyrgyz and Kazakh oral traditions. The judges usually include senior master poets, singers, folklorists, writers, and journalists. They evaluate the contestants according to several criteria. In an interview, the Kyrgyz *aqyn* Aaly Tutkuchev explained these criteria as they apply to both a traditional and a contemporary *aitysh*:

> The main criteria for judging an *aqyn* are the content, use of words, and rhyme of their song. Then of course their *komuz*, whether it matches their voice. Then they look at how you conduct yourself on stage. The last thing is your costume—whether it has a national flavor. You can't just wear a black suit. Also, in the past *aqyns* could sing as long as they wanted to. Today, the judges give us twenty minutes and interrupt us after the time is up. In the past, *aqyns* competed until one of them withdrew from the contest. People would notice who was losing and who was winning, and they would identify the winner. Today, it's difficult to identify the winner in twenty minutes, and that's why it takes at least ten judges to evaluate the *aqyns* fairly.

Of key importance in *aitysh/aitys* is the reaction and disposition of the audience. Many *aqyns* of the past and present age have pointed out that the enthusiastic response of listeners, true connoiseurs of this art, is a prerequisite for creative inspiration that allows talent and improvisational flair to shine. A good *aqyn*'s performance is usually punctuated by bursts of applause, supportive cries, and exclamations of admiration and delight (Kyrgyz: "*Bali! Barakelde!*" [Good for you!], "*Azamat!*" [Good job!], "*Söz emes beken!*" [Nicely said!] "*Ak söz!*" [That is true!]; Kazakh: "*Oi, de!*" [Oh, say!], "*Ei*," "*Ua-u*," "*Shirkin-ai*," "*Pai-pai*"). Such cries and exclamations usually mark ends of verse lines and are uttered in response to the *aqyns'* jokes and witticisms. They create an atmosphere of joyfulness and excitement, spurring the *aqyns* to further banter and wordplay.

POETIC AND MUSICAL STRUCTURE

Verbal and musical elements of *aitysh/aitys* are closely interrelated. Oral poetic improvisation is carried out on the basis of a recurrent vocal tune or melody called *obon* in Kyrgyz and *saryn* or *maqam* in Kazakh.[17] Every *aqyn* has in his repertory one or several personal or borrowed tunes that provide a musical framework for verbal extemporization, facilitate articulation of a text's meaning, and enhance its impact on listeners.

Kazakh *aqyns* often begin their *saryns* from an opening cry on a held note sung in the middle or high register ("A," "Ou," "Ei," "Ua-u"), which serves to attract the audience's attention and helps an *aqyn* prepare to face a rival. Contemporary Kazakh *aqyns* explain the purpose of such exclamations as "the summoning of an *aqyn's* inspiration."[18] Scholars also suggest that it may have served as a means of establishing a connection with spirit-protectors.[19]

Vocal tunes of the Kazakh *aitys* can be of two main types: song (*än*) and recitative or tirade (*jyr*). Song tunes have a strophic form in which four lines of verse, or a strophe, sung in an eleven-syllable poetic meter (*qara öleng*) with a common end rhyme in lines 1, 2, and 4 (aaba), compose a single musical unit. By contrast, the musical form of tirade tunes encompasses a succession of poetic lines in the seven-to-eight–syllable (*jyr*) or, less commonly, eleven-syllable meter that may or may not rhyme, though they are perceived as a unified poetic and melodic utterance. Song tunes are used in both amateur and professional types of *aitys,* while tirade tunes are more typical of the professional *aitys.* In the course of poetic and musical dialogue, contestants may improvise on the same tune (as in the examples of Kyrgyz *aitysh* provided earlier in the chapter) or exchange different tunes of the same or different type (song or tirade). Their choice determines the overall musical arrangement of the competition.

Instrumental accompaniment also plays an important role in *aitysh/aitys.* In addition to facilitating a better delivery of the *aqyn's* vocal tune, accompaniment on the *komuz* or *dombyra* stimulates poetic improvisation by helping create an emotional and psychological atmosphere that enables an *aqyn* to focus his mind and come up with a stream of improvised verses. Many *aqyns* have linked instrumental accompaniment to poetic inspiration. The Kazakh *aqyn* Köken Shäkeev succinctly summarized the role of the *dombyra* in an *aitys:*

Köken Shäkeev.
Courtesy of Köken Shäkeev's family.

Dombyra sharshy topta qolgha tise,	When I hold the *dombyra* in my hands before a large crowd,
Özimdi ustai almai jeligemin.	I cannot restrain myself from getting excited.[20]

*Aqyn*s from different regions of Kazakhstan and Kyrgyzstan can be identified by local stylistic features in their music. For example, *aqyn*s from the central, northern, and eastern areas of Kazakhstan known as Saryarqa, or Arqa, sing in the style of local folk and art songs (*än*) in a strophic form usually set to the eleven-syllable meter (*qara öleng*), accompanying themselves on the *dombyra* by plucking the strings with individual fingers in the performance style of eastern Kazakhstan known as *shertpe*. By contrast, *aqyn*s from western Kazakhstan tend to sing in a recitative or tirade style (*jyr*) based on the seven-to-eight–syllable meter, and accompany themselves by strumming, rather than plucking, the *dombyra,* in the style of western Kazakhstan known as *tökpe* (see chapters 11 and 14). These stylistic differences shape the character of a musical performance: while *aqyn*s from Arqa tend to perform in a measured, lyrical manner, singing out their tunes and sustaining notes, performances of *aqyn*s from western Kazakhstan are typically fast, dynamic, and impetuous.

WATCH

Example 10.4. *Aitys* between Amanjol Ältaev and Mels Qosymbaev (excerpt), Almaty, Kazakhstan, 1990. From Jürsin Erman, *Aitys* 5 (VHS cassette) (Almaty: Center Records, 2002).

This excerpt of an *aitys* between Amanjol Ältaev (b. 1971), a well-known *aqyn* from the Qaraghandy region in central Kazakhstan, and Mels Qosymbaev (b. 1970), an *aqyn* from the city of Oral in western Kazakhstan, illustrates regional stylistic differences in the performance of *aqyn*s.

The text for this example is available on the companion website.

STUDY QUESTIONS AND ACTIVITY

1. How do the two *aqyn*s address the audience and each other? What expressions, metaphors, and figures of speech do they use, and what meanings do these carry?

2. Listen to the exclamation on a held note that opens Mels Qosymbaev's performance (3:20–3:26). What, in your view, is the meaning and artistic function of this opening?

3. Which of the two types of *saryn*—the song type or tirade type—do each of the *aqyn*s adopt in their performance?

4. Compare the structure of the *aqyn*s' poetic improvisation, their singing style and manner of instrumental playing, as well as the overall character of their respective performances, and explain how they exemplify the styles of Arqa and western Kazakhstan.

5. Note the spectators' reaction to the *aqyn*s' performance. At what points can you hear them cry out in response to the *aqyn*s' words, and what do these exclamations express?

The Role of *Aqyns* in Society and Politics, Past and Present

*Aqyn*s have always played an important role and enjoyed a high status in Kazakh and Kyrgyz culture and society. Before adopting a sedentary life in the 1930s, male *aqyn*s traveled freely from one mountain pasture to another to sing at various traditional festivities and events. Believed to be connected with spirits and endowed with knowledge and wisdom, they served as advisors to tribal leaders and khans on social and political issues, such as solving intertribal matters and disputes, in addition to acting as performers. Brave *aqyn*s who wielded a sharp mind and caustic language dared to publicly criticize leaders for their wrongdoings and injustices, and for not taking care of their own people, especially the poor and needy. *Aqyn*s spoke on behalf of people who expected and valued justice and generosity in a ruler.

During the Soviet period, well-known *aqyn*s played an important role in the preservation, continuity, and development of Kazakh and Kyrgyz oral traditions. They did so by adapting their singing to the new context of Soviet social and cultural life and thus contributing to the early establishment of Soviet rule among the nomads, and to the cultural development of Soviet Kazakhstan and Kirghizia [Kyrgyzstan]. Together with other musicians, *aqyn*s traveled to remote steppe and mountain villages (*auyl*s) to give concerts at which *aitysh/aitys* competitions were the highlight of the program. A younger generation of *aqyn*s worked at theaters and philharmonic societies in Almaty and Bishkek (then Frunze) as well as at provincial and district Houses of Culture, which served as centers for community arts activities. Amid strict ideological censorship, *aqyn*s were subject to orders from government authorities concerning what to sing and what not to sing. Songs from the Soviet era frequently glorified communism, the Soviet Union, its leaders, and its politically mandated "friendship among peoples." The topic of religion, namely Islam, as well as spiritual values and sentiments related to the status of the Kazakh and Kyrgyz languages and national culture were taboo and thus excluded from the repertory. Aside from merely complying with the current ideology and voicing politically sanctioned topics, however, many *aqyn*s genuinely supported the social and cultural changes implemented by the new political regime. They sang about Soviet achievements in industry, agriculture, and livestock production in Central Asia, and praised the "heroes of Soviet socialist labor" and "culture workers." They expressed their feeling of gratitude for "the great father Lenin" (*uluu Lenin atabyz*) and "great Russian older brothers" (*uluu orus agabyz*) for bringing the "dawn of the October Revolution of 1917" to the "backward and poor" Central Asian peoples. During the Second World War (known in the Soviet Union as the Great Patriotic War), they raised patriotic spirits and called for civic courage in songs that achieved nationwide fame, for example, "My Leningrad's Young Children" (*Leningradtyq örenim*) by the Kazakh *aqyn* Jambyl Jabaev, which was addressed to the blockaded residents of Leningrad, and "Farewell, Ala-Too Mountains! Your Son Left for the Battlefield!" (*Kosh Ala-Too, uulung ketti maydanga*) by the Kyrgyz *aqyn* Joomart Bökönbaev (1910–1944). To recognize their contribution to national culture-building, the state bestowed on them honorary titles and awards. The Kazakh *aqyn* Jambyl Jabaev was awarded the Stalin Prize, and appointed a member of the Supreme Council of the Kazakh Soviet Socialist Republic (SSR). Another renowned *aqyn*, Kenen Äzirbaev, was granted the title Honored Artist and People's *Aqyn* as well as membership in the Writers and Composers Unions of the Kazakh SSR. Two well-known Kyrgyz *aqyn*s, Alymkul Üsönbaev and Estebes Tursunaliev, were designated People's Artists of the USSR and appointed as deputies in the Supreme Council of the Kyrgyz SSR.

Estebes Tursunaliev.

Classically trained composers of the Soviet era in Kazakhstan drew on the theatrical dimension of *aitys* as a resource for opera. Large scenes of *aitys* in which opera-singers perform a scored, pre-composed poetic and musical contest to the accompaniment of an orchestra are central to the dramaturgy of a number of Kazakh operas, such as "Aiman–Sholpan" (1938) by Evgenii Brusilovskii, "Abai" (1944) by Akhmet Jubanov and Latyf Khamidi, and, most notably, "Birjan–Sara" (1946) by Muqan Tölebaev, whose plot is based on the legendary nineteenth-century *aitys* between the well-known male and female *aqyn*s, Birjan sal Qojaghululy and Sara Tastanbekqyzy.

Kenen Äzirbaev.
Courtesy of the Central State Archive of Film, Photography, and Sound Recordings of the Republic of Kazakhstan.

In the 1980s, a period in which Russian language and culture became dominant in Central Asia, especially in the major cities of Kazakhstan and Kyrgyzstan, Kazakh and Kyrgyz intellectuals, including *aqyn*s, feared that their language, traditional values, and oral heritage would be forgotten, since they were not taught in schools and universities, where the main language of instruction was Russian (up to 1991, only one secondary school in the capital city of Bishkek taught all subjects in Kyrgyz). To the surprise of many Kazakhs and Kyrgyz, however, by the

Scene of *aitys* from the opera "Birjan–Sara" by Muqan Tölebaev.

mid-1990s, a group of young, vibrant *aqyn*s endowed with strong national sentiments and pride, sharp tongues, and a diverse poetic repertory began to emerge. This new generation of post-Soviet *aqyn*s often raises sensitive and critical issues such as the lack of state support for preserving and promoting Kazakh and Kyrgyz language and cultural heritage, the continuing dominance of Russian (which is still the official language of Kazakhstan and Kyrgyzstan), corruption in the presidential administration, and more broadly, the problem of immorality and the need for stronger religious values. In Kyrgyzstan, in the run up to the fall 2010 parliamentary election, three well-known young *aqyn*s showed their political activism by joining one of the newly established political parties.

Present-day *aqyn*s have spoken forcefully about the importance of maintaining the traditional role of *aqyn*s as bardic political advisors and pundits. During an interview for this chapter, one Kyrgyz *aqyn,* Jengishbek Toktobekov, put it as follows: "Since *aqyn*s are close to their people, it would be best if the president heard what is happening among his people from the mouth of *aqyn*s, because truth

Kyrgyz *aqyn*s on stage.

does not always reach our leader. We would tell him about who is who and what they are doing. Even without having an *aitysh* he could invite us to his office and say: 'OK, sing to me about what is happening in society.' We speak the truth, and no one can shut our mouths. We are freethinkers, like an eagle that flies freely. As the saying goes, 'One can cut the head, but not the tongue' (*Bash kesmek bar, til kesmek jok*). We are ready to speak on the people's behalf." Another *aqyn,* Aaly Tutkuchev, spoke about the influential role of *aqyn*s in neighboring Kazakhstan: "[President] Nazarbaev once said, 'I hear about which governor is doing what from the mouth of *aqyn*s.' Recently, when we were in Kazakhstan, one of the district governors looked at the twenty-six *aqyn*s [standing on the stage] and said, 'Dear *aqyn*s, please sing carefully. As a result of your constant critique, I had to replace my seven vice-governors!'"

AITYS/AITYSH TODAY

In contemporary Kazakhstan and Kyrgyzstan, *aitys/aitysh* poetry competitions have achieved new popularity. Nowadays they rarely take place within traditional ceremonies and festivities but have turned into autonomous staged spectacles that serve as major social and artistic events, attracting large audiences who flock to watch a younger generation of master improvisers compete in verbally pyrotechnic poetry duels. The popularity of poetry competitions has been fueled by the emergence of televised *aitys/aitysh* that capture a staged contest or are filmed in a television studio, as well as by the dissemination of video recordings of contests on the Internet and through social media. Since the 1990s, following independence, *aitys/aitysh* has been actively promoted by the Kazakh and Kyrgyz governments. Contemporary poetry contests are often dedicated to specific themes, such as the revival of national culture and language, traditions and customs, the problems of rural communities (*auyl*s), ecology, health, education, or, in Kazakhstan, the repatriation of Kazakhs living abroad. Many contests are organized on the occasion of important historical and official dates and anniversaries, like those that recognize the birthdays of famous historical personalities, the creation of administrative regions, and (somewhat arbitrarily) the genesis of national epics, such as the Kyrgyz *Manas* or Kazakh *Qozy-Körpesh–Bayan-Sulu.*

WATCH **Example 10.5.** *Aitys* between Didar Qamiev and Ainur Tursunbaeva (excerpt), Shieli, Qyzylorda region, Kazakhstan, 2009. Video courtesy of Didar Qamiev.

This *aitys* between a male *aqyn* from Qaraghandy, Didar Qamiev, and a female bard from the city of Taraz, Ainur Tursunbaeva, took place in 2009 in the town of Shieli in the Qyzylorda region of southern Kazakhstan, and was dedicated to the eightieth anniversary of the Shieli district, the one hundredth anniversary of its native poet and playwright, Äbdilda Täjibaev, and the one hundred fiftieth anniversary of the great *aqyn* from the nineteenth and early-twentieth century, Imanjüsip Qutpanuly.

The text for this example is available on the companion website.

STUDY QUESTIONS

1. How does the *aitys* reflect the *aqyn*s' notions of identity and relation to one another with regard to age and gender? How does the fact that it is a cross-gender contest (*qyz ben jigit aitysy*) impact its content and the contestants' form of address?

2. How is the theme of the occasion developed in the *aqyn*s' verses? How do they play with the name of the commemorated district, Shieli (from *shie:* "cherry")?

3. Define the type and structure of the *aitys*. In what poetic form and musical style do *aqyn*s perform?

4. Describe the audience's reaction to the performance? What moments in the *aitys* are marked by the spectators' applause and exclamations?

Kazakhs and Kyrgyz have a long-standing tradition of travelling to each other's lands to engage in *aitys/aitysh* competitions at gatherings and festivities. Following this tradition, contemporary Kazakh and Kyrgyz *aqyn*s have also exchanged

Didar Qamiev (*right*).
Courtesy of Didar Qamiev.

invitations to participate in poetry contests dedicated to major national celebrations, such as Independence Day and anniversaries of well-known *aqyns,* cultural luminaries, and cities. Both Kazakh and Kyrgyz spectators enjoy such contests, which address a variety of historical and current cultural and socio-political ties and issues between two peoples and countries that share a common nomadic heritage as well as the experience of seven decades of Soviet rule. The Kazakh government has been promoting international *aitys* competitions on a regular basis by awarding winners significant prizes such as cars and apartments. In Kyrgyzstan, deposed president Kurmanbek Bakiev officially sponsored two *aitysh* competitions between Kazakh and Kyrgyz *aqyn*s in the cities of Bishkek (2008) and Osh (2009), allocating large winners' prizes from his presidential fund.

There are distinct differences in the performance style of Kazakh and Kyrgyz *aqyn*s. They accompany themselves on two different stringed instruments, with different tunings that produce different kinds of melodies and sounds, and typically recite in different poetic meters. Aaly *aqyn* characterizes Kyrgyz and Kazakh songs as follows: "Kyrgyz songs are like their mountain ranges, which go up and down (*oyku-kayky),* whereas the songs of the Kazakhs are like their steppe: they like to stretch their voice 'Ay-goooy!' toward the steppe." One of the main reasons for the growing popularity of Kazakh and Kyrgyz *aitys/aitysh* competitions is related to the open and dynamic nature of the young post-Soviet generation of *aqyn*s, who have a different outlook and understanding of Kazakh-Kyrgyz cultural and historical connections. Most often, contests between Kazakh and Kyrgyz *aqyn*s take the form of an insult *aitysh* (Kyrgyz: *kordoo aitysh*). Insulting and belittling

170   ELMIRA KÖCHÜMKULOVA AND JANGÜL QOJAKHMETOVA

happen on a personal level, as well as on the basis of ethnicity or national identity. Most *aqyn*s take personal insults as a form of humor, which is an acceptable norm of behavior in an *aitys/aitysh*. However, they can be sensitive about issues concerning their national culture, values, land, language, identity, and pride. In the end, however, competing *aqyn*s always express mutual respect and genuine friendship, addressing one another as *"Qyrghyz bauyrlar"* ("Kyrgyz brothers") and *"Kazak boordoshtor"* ("Kazakh brothers"). Since the point of the *aitys/aitysh* is to entertain spectators, *aqyn*s often tease each other by pointing to personal physical features and singing styles. Teasing is more common and interesting in *aitys/aitysh* contests between male and female *aqyn*s.

WATCH | **Example 10.6.** *Aitysh* between Aaly Tutkuchev and Qanysha Raisova (excerpt), Bishkek, Kyrgyzstan, 2008.

This example is taken from an *aitysh* between Aaly Tutkuchev, the young male Kyrgyz *aqyn* from the Talas region of northern Kyrgyzstan, and Qanysha Raisova, a middle-aged female Kazakh *aqyn* from the Jetisu region of southeastern Kazakhstan. Their competition took place within the framework of an "international *aitysh*" between Kazakh and Kyrgyz *aqyn*s sponsored by the former Kyrgyz president Kurmanbek Bakiev, which took place in Bishkek in 2008. Qanysha Raisova was one of two female Kazakh *aqyn*s who came to the *aitysh*. She and her Kyrgyz competitor, Aaly aqyn, became the finalists in the final round contest after being matched by drawing numbers from a hat.

The text for this example is available on the companion website.

STUDY QUESTIONS ————————————————————————————

1. How is the fact that this is a cross-national contest reflected in its content? How do the *aqyn*s' ways of addressing each other conform to traditional notions of age, seniority, and gender?

2. How are the two *aqyn*s similar or different in their performance style, melody, use of instrumental accompaniment, and poetic compositional techniques?

3. What poetic meter do they use? Do they make similar use of alliteration and end rhyme?

4. How do the *aqyn*s engage the audience as well as the judges to win their favor? When and how does the audience react to the singers?

Performer Profiles: Didar Qamiev

JANGÜL QOJAKHMETOVA

Jangül Qojakhmetova (JQ): Tell me about your family background. What brought you to the art of *aqyndyq* and *aitys* performance?

Didar Qamiev (DQ): I was born on December 10, 1988, in Aqbauyr village of Shet district in the Qaraghandy region. My grandfather, Qami, was adept in folk epics (*jyr, dastan, qissa*); he could extemporize a verse and song instantaneously. My grandfather immersed me from the age of five in the culture of folk oral literature. I inherited the *aqyn*'s talent, though, not only from him but also from my grandmother's ancestors; for example, the well-known *aqyn* Jäken Baituov. My father, Janat, played the *dombyra*, guitar, and other musical instruments. He taught me how to play the *dombyra*. My brothers, Aidar and Ulanghasyr, are also artists who have many times performed and won prizes at regional *aqyns*' *aitys*. It is my family environment that brought me to *aqyndyq*. As for *aitys*, I loved to listen to it from childhood.

JQ: Who do you consider to be your master?

DQ: First of all, Amanjol Ältaev. But I also consider all *aqyns* from Arqa to be my teachers. I regard myself as a pupil of all *aityskers* of the older generation with whom I have had a chance to associate. It is they who taught me the art of *aitys*.

JQ: What can you tell about the nature of poetic and musical improvisation (*suyryp salma*)? Do you consider yourself a *suyryp salma aqyn*?

DQ: Mukhtar Äuezov[21] wrote: "One of the great distinctive qualities of the Kazakh people is skill at improvisation, in particular instantaneous improvisation in an *aitys*." This is an impromptu poeticized response to the words of the opponent or a momentary reaction to what is happening around. It is not possible to learn the art of improvisation, since it is passed on from one's ancestors, with one's mother's milk. If an *aqyn* does not master improvisation, he has no right to call himself *aitysker*, because an *aitys aqyn* and improvisation are like twin brothers.

JQ: Are there special techniques of learning and teaching how to improvise? What does improvisation during an *aitys* depend on?

DQ: I think the ability to improvise is a biological quality that is inherited genetically. Teaching it specifically is to no avail. The *aqyn* himself should strive to develop, that is, to broaden his knowledge, erudition, and intellectual capacity. An *aqyn* should be well-versed in the history, clan genealogies, literature, and culture of his people. As for his ability to improvise, it has to do with creative inspiration, with the

Courtesy of Didar Qamiev.

listening audience, and with the tune he chooses.

JQ: In your view, from what age can the art of *aqyndyq* be taught? Are there any special schools for training *aqyns*?

DQ: The art of *aqyndyq* can be introduced to children from school age. In Qaraghandy, we have a school of *aqyns* called "Arqa." There are also *aqyns*' schools in Shymkent and in Astana, at the Gumilyov Eurasian National University. These schools have had considerable influence on the shaping of many contemporary *aqyns* of the young generation.

JQ: From what age can one perform at an *aitys*?

DQ: There are no age limits for performing at an *aitys*. Nowadays *aqyns* perform at an increasingly young age.

Performer Profiles: Didar Qamiev (CONTINUED)

JQ: At what age did you perform at an *aitys* for the first time? What type of *aitys* do you draw on in your performances?

DQ: I first performed at an *aitys* in 1999 during the regional festival "Arqa üni" (Arqa's Melody) against the well-known *aqyn* from Qaraghandy, Tilegen Ädilev. I was eleven years old then. At that time, I usually performed at the *türe aitys*.

JQ: What is the purpose of different tunes (*saryns*) at *aitys*? And what is the role of the *dombyra* accompaniment?

DQ: Different tunes are used to appeal to the listeners and to display the special qualities of the *aqyn*'s voice. The *dombyra* helps the *aqyn* to think during the competition and brings out the expressive nature of the tune and the meaning of the words.

JQ: How do *aqyn*s prepare for an *aitys*?

DQ: An *aqyn* will always be at his best if he is constantly learning. He must be knowledgeable about the people's history, everyday life, and current news.

JQ: In your view, does the art of *aqyn*s' *aitys* have old historical origins?

DQ: *Aqyn*s' *aitys* as a genre of oral literature must have emerged with the Kazakh people. It has very deep historical roots.

JQ: Apart from *aitys*, what other oral poetic genres do you adopt in your creativity?

DQ: I compose and sing in the genres of *arnau* (dedication song), *jyr, dastan, tolghau, qissa, terme,* and others.

JQ: What can you say about the structure and procedure for developing *aitys*?

DQ: Because an *aqyn*s' *aitys* is a dialogic genre, it may have a variety of forms and unfold in many different ways. Each *aqyn* has his own techniques and tactics in *aitys*, and its development also depends on the *aqyn*s' abilities and creative power. One of the common features of an *aqyn*'s performance, though, is the introductory exclamation that serves to summon the *aqyn*'s inspiration.

JQ: Is the tune (*saryn*) on which you base your performance your own or an adopted tune? What is the reason for the "migration" of tunes across the repertories of different *aqyn*s? How many tunes do you use as a basis for improvisation, and why?

DQ: The tune I mainly use for performance is one from Amanjol Ältaev which I once heard and liked. Usually the reason for the "migration" of a tune is that it suits one's manner of poetic improvisation. This is why the same tunes can be used in *aitys* and in other improvisational poetic and musical genres. I mostly improvise on two tunes, as this allows for shifts between poetic meters and helps to hold spectators' attention and raise their spirits.

JQ: How do you see the role of *aqyn* in the social and political life of the people past and present?

DQ: *Aqyn*s have always given heart to the Kazakh people in times of hardship and misery. During the Great Patriotic War, in 1943, in Almaty a republic *aitys* took place at which *aqyn*s raised people's spirits and hopes. Contemporary *aitys* enlighten people and enrich them spiritually.

JQ: What was the biggest prize you ever won at an *aitys*?

DQ: For me there can be no bigger prize than the recognition of my people. It makes me happy if the people are in high spirits, and if they bestow their blessings on me. This is certainly the best prize ever!

Performer Profiles: Aaly Tutkuchev

ELMIRA KÖCHÜMKULOVA

Elmira Köchümkulova (EM): Tell me about yourself—your family and your village.

Aaly Tutkuchev (AT): I was born on December 9, 1983, at 1:00 PM, when all the nurses and doctors were on their lunch break. There were seven children in my family. I have two older sisters, two older brothers, and two younger sisters. I was born into an ordinary family, or as they say into a "poor peasant" family.[22] My mother is a housewife. I come from a small village called Aral (Island) in the Manas district of Talas province [in northern Kyrgyzstan]. The reason it is called Aral is because it is surrounded by mountains. Many well-known *aqyn*s come from the same village, and I am the youngest.

EK: Who is your *ustat* (master), and how did he teach you?

AT: I have not just one *ustat,* but four. People ask me why I have four rather than one. For example, they say that Alymkul[23] learned from Toktogul[24] and therefore that one should learn from just one *ustat.* In the past, when technology wasn't developed, Alymkul had to travel from Talas to Ketmen Töbö to learn from Toktogul, whereas today, I can learn from Esteke [Estebes Tursunaliev] without seeing and meeting him. I can sit at home and listen to him on the radio and watch him on TV. If I sing in Esteke's style, it means that I learned from him. Therefore,

I can say that I learned from four *ustat*s: Estebes Tursunaliev, Ashyraaly Aytaliev, Zamirbek Üsönbaev, and Tuuganbay Abdiev. Three of them are alive today.[25] I have a close relationship with all three. Breaking my relationship with them would be like breaking my relationship with God.

EK: How about techniques of poetic improvisation (*tökmölük*)? Do your *ustat*s also teach you the secrets of their improvising techniques?

AT: Of course! I ask them to share their techniques. However, I used to think that these accomplished *aqyn*s didn't feel nervous when they were on stage. I was wrong. They feel more nervous than I do, because the more famous you become, the greater people's expectations. If these *aqyn*s feel nervous, then the *aqyn*'s art (*önör*) has no limit, I thought, and there is no such thing as total mastery. Indeed, we never stop learning.

EK: On a recent television program, someone asked an interesting question about whether there should be a special school for *aqyn*s.

AT: Yes, we should definitely open a school for *aqyn*s. Last year, the Kyrgyz art of *tökmölük* was recognized by UNESCO as a Masterpiece of Intangible Cultural Heritage. In the past, the Kyrgyz did not know how to write and read, so they preserved their history orally in their language

Courtesy of Aaly Tutkuchev.

and in the *komuz* strings of *aqyn*s. Therefore, it would be very wrong to disregard the great art of our ancestors. To tell the truth, the art of *tökmölük* was a tradition on the verge of disappearing. People were concerned that there would be no *aqyn* after Zamirbek Üsönbaev because during the Soviet period, *aqyn*s and their poetry were strictly controlled. The KGB told them to write down the texts of their poetry before they went out to sing in front of people. Fortunately, the tradition was revived after Independence. Therefore, we should introduce such schools, and all schoolchildren should know about this unique tradition. Some people tell me, "I don't believe that you guys really improvise your poetry!" You see, the Kyrgyz themselves don't know the tradition and history of our ancestors. They don't believe in it, and that is really an example of *mankurtchuluk*.[26] If you clear the source of a spring, the water will flow better. There are

Performer Profiles: Aaly Tutkuchev (CONTINUED)

many interested children, but there is no one who can give them guidance. If one shows and explains to them, once they understand, there will be an interest. For example, at my school in the village, pictures of all the well-known *aqyn*s that I mentioned used to be hanging on the wall. Seeing them, I would feel proud and dream of becoming a great *aqyn* like them and seeing my picture next to theirs. I was in the third grade when I had this wish. Had there been pictures of Karl Marx and Lenin instead of these *aqyn*s, I wouldn't have been so inspired.

EK: At what point does an *aqyn* consider himself a *tökmö aqyn*? Are you a *tökmö aqyn*?

AT: No, I don't consider myself a *tökmö aqyn*. It's journalists who call us *tökmö aqyn*s. If you want an example of a real *tökmö aqyn*, take Alymkul, from whom most of the versions of Kyrgyz *dastan*s were recorded. When Alymkul sang the epic *Kojojash,* at the end of the epic, the hunter [Kojojash] gets stranded on a high cliff. At that moment the Gray Mother Goat (Sur Echki) curses him. It's a very powerful curse that makes you cry. So, when Alymkul sang this part, the people would cry and ask him, "Oh, dear Alymkul! Please don't let Kojojash die [by forcing him to throw himself over the cliff]. Save his life!" And Alymkul was able to change the end of the story

on the spot and make Kojojash live. That means that he was a real *tökmö*. He was able to pour words like rain, and play any melody (*küü*), compose songs, and sing *dastan*s.

EK: Do you consider being an *aqyn* a profession?

AT: I personally consider it my profession, because I earn a living with this skill of mine. In the past, neither Toktogul nor Alymkul earned his living by farming or selling things in the bazaar. They only practiced poetry. They rode their horses and traveled among the people. Just imagine, they sang at five or six places every day. Every time they sang, their bounty grew larger. Today's *aqyn* sings once a month at most, and sometimes we don't sing at all, which means that we have to farm or sell goods to earn money.

EK: Are there special techniques of learning the skills of improvisation?

AT: Yes, but there are two specific environments in which I can't improvise. First, I can't improvise anything when I'm in a recording studio, because there's nothing there except a microphone or a video camera. And second, I can't improvise when five or six professors are examining me. On other occasions, especially when I see people sitting in front of me eagerly waiting to hear what I'm going to say, I have no problem improvising.

How can I disappoint the hope of many people? When you sing before an audience, you should cheer up the audience in the beginning by saying pleasant words. Then the people cheer for you by applauding and exclaiming things like "Oh, Bali!" (Yes! Good job!). These kinds of words make you feel happy, and words just begin coming out of your mouth. But you always have to be thinking on your feet, so that you say the right word at the right moment. While you're singing the first line, your brain must have the next words ready.

EK: People always say that wisdom comes as you get older. Being an *aqyn* requires knowledge of one's own history, culture, and tribal genealogy.

AT: Definitely. However, there's a saying "*Köp jashagan bilbeyt, köptü körgön bilet*" (One who has lived long does not know, but one who has seen a lot knows more). One must read and know a lot. You read more as you get older. Let's say that I'm competing with a Kazakh *aqyn*, and he asks me, "There was a hero called Ormon Khan [among the Kyrgyz],[27] and he had a special military tactic (known as *Ormon opuza*) in beating the Kazakhs. What kind of tactic was it?" It would be shameful for me if I didn't know my own history. So, like journalists, *aqyn*s must have broad knowledge. Unfortunately, today our *aqyn*s lack that knowledge.

Performer Profiles: Aaly Tutkuchev (CONTINUED)

EK: How is the *aqyn* repertory divided up? For example, do individual performers tend to have their own individualized repertories? Do repertories differ from region to region?

AT: Let me talk about one particular difference. Each region has its own *obon,* melody. There is the Talas melody and the southern melody, which are quite different. In the south, *aqyn*s like Barpy[28] sang without the accompaniment of *komuz.* And of course, there are also dialect differences.

We *aqyn*s make a mistake. As the saying goes, "*Koldo bar altyndyn barky jok*" (One does not value the gold in one's own hand). *Aqyn*s who write their poetry immediately write down whatever they compose, even if it's two lines, whereas we do not write it down, thinking that it's ready to perform and there's no need to commit it to writing. This attitude will destroy us. We must write down our poetry, for after we die, our poems will just fly away in the air. If we write them down, they'll be remembered. When I was younger, I used to think that writing down poems would be a shame because people would think that we just memorize and sing instead of improvising. Later I began to understand. If I sing well in a certain place, I remember those lines that I liked, and when I come home, I write them down. Words that aren't particularly meaningful won't be remembered. You usually remember words that make people happy and get a lot of applause. Today's technology is great and handy; sometimes we *aqyn*s record ourselves on our cell phone.

EK: What was the biggest prize you ever won in an *aitysh*?

AT: I won the grand prize in the 2005 *aitysh* that was held in Bishkek among Kyrgyz *aqyn*s. I received five thousand dollars, but it wasn't the money that made me happy. It was having my mother in the audience, who had not seen me sing onstage before that. I had invited her to this *aitysh,* and she was sitting in the audience. I did not expect to win the grand prize at the *aitysh*. People's applause was a big inspiration for me, but my mother's applause with tears running from her eyes meant so much for me. The fact that I was able to make my mother very happy was a big prize for me. I immediately bought a car with that money and said to myself: "It is okay if I am on foot, but may my mother not be on foot." So I presented the car to my older brother, who lives with my mother in the village, and asked him to drive my mother around.

NOTES

1. The word *ākhūn* is said to have been introduced as a title for Muslim clergy, or mullahs (Alkei Marghulan, "O nositelyakh drevnei poeticheskoi kul'tury kazakhskogo naroda" [On the bearers of the ancient poetic culture of the Kazakh people], in *Sbornik k 60-letiu M. O. Auezova* [Collection of articles for the 60th anniversary of the birth of M. O. Äuezov] [Alma-Ata: Izdatel'stvo Akademii Nauk KazSSR, 1959], 78).

2. See Mahmud al-Kashghari, *Diwan Lughat at-Turk,* trans. Zifa-Alua Auezova, (Almaty: Daik-Press, 2005), 110; Marghulan, "O nositelyakh drevnei poeticheskoi kul'tury kazakhskogo naroda"; Edige Tursynov, *Vozniknovenie baqsy, aqynov, seri i jyrau* [The origins of *baqsy*s, *aqyn*s, *seri*s, and *jyrau*s] (Astana: IKF Foliant, 1999), 108–111.

3. Kyrgyz *jazgych aqyn*s are also called *zamanachy aqyn*s (from *zaman*: "time," "period"), for they composed poetry about specific political and socio-cultural changes and problems of contemporary times (such as Russian settlers, land and pasture issues, and the role of Islam) that arose with the arrival of Russians in Central Asia in the 18th and 19th centuries. Kazakh *jazba aqyn*s, in addition to composing individual poems, engaged in written poetry competitions (*jazba aitys*). Early examples of such competitions through correspondence come from the 19th century and include the *jazba aitys* between *aqyn*s Aqan seri and Ismaghul and between Kete Jüsip and Qanly Jüsip.

4. *Synchy* (from *synda-:* "to judge," "to criticize") is a person who possesses the natural skill to judge people, as well as animals, mainly horses, by looking at their behavior, personality, language, and physical appearance.

5. B. Kebekova, comp., *Arstanbek* (Bishkek: Ilim, 1994), 136–139.

6. Abdysalim Obozkanov, *Tökmölüktün bashaty, kalyptanuu etaptary jana sinkrettüü tabiyaty* [The origin, development, and syncretism of *tökmölük*] (Bishkek: Sham, 2006), 60.

7. Ibid., 60.

8. Ibid., 60–61.

9. Ibid., 61.

10. Süiinbai Aronuly, *Shygharmalar: Tolghaular, syn-syqaq ölengder, aitystar* [Works: *Tolghau*s, satirical songs, *aitys*] (Almaty: Jazushy, 1990), 50.

11. Unlike Kazakh *dombyrashy*s, Kyrgyz *komuzchu*s and *aqyn*s did not traditionally engage in *küü* competitions. In recent years, however, among young *komuz* players a form of instrumental contest has developed, known as *küü aitysh.*

12. The term *süre aitys* has been linked with the Arabic word *sura* (Kazakh *süre*) referring to a chapter from the Qur'an. This etymological interpretation highlights the scope and exhaustiveness of verbal utterances in *süre aitys,* as distinct from *türe aitys* (Svetlana Djanseitova, *Kazakhskaya muzykal'naya terminologiya: Uchebnoe posobie* [Kazakh music terminology: Study guide] [Alma-Ata: Almatinskaya gosudarstvennaya konservatoriya imeni Kurmangazy, 1991], 59.)

13. Literally, a clan battle-cry (*uran*).

14. Jangül Qojakhmetova, *Muzyka kazakhskogo aitysa* [Music of the Kazakh *aitys*] (Qaraghandy: Glasir, 2012), 29.

15. Esenaman refers to the younger Jengijok as "my son" and to himself as "your uncle."

16. *Kalpak:* national headdress made of white felt worn by Kyrgyz men.

17. The Turkic word *saryn*—also used among the Kazakhs with reference to ritual, domestic, and epic types of melody—is thought to have old origins as a designation of an *aitys* tune. The Arabic term *maqām,* on the other hand, came to be used more recently, as a loan word from performers of epic through the sharing of repertory between *aqyn* and *jyrshy,* and is more commonly applied in contemporary practice.

18. Qojakhmetova, *Muzyka kazakhskogo aitysa,* 51.

19. Saida Elemanova, *Kazakhskoe traditsionnoe pesennoe iskusstvo: Genezis i semantika* [Kazakh traditional song art: Genesis and semantics] (Almaty: Daik-Press, 2000), 70–71.

20. Köken Shäkeiuly, *Kökshem mening! Öleng, jyrlar men aitystar* [My Kökshe! Songs, epic poems, and *aitys*] (Astana: Elorda, 2001), 100.

21. Mukhtar Äuezov (1897–1961) was an acclaimed Kazakh writer, playwright, and literary scholar who wrote a classic novel about the Kazakh philosopher, poet, and songwriter Abai Qunanbaev, *Abai joly* [The path of Abai].

22. Aaly said this sarcastically, referring to the popular statement used in textbook autobiographies of Soviet poets and writers. In the 1930s, due to Stalin's persecution of kulaks, many poets and writers hid their family background by saying that they came from a *jönököy,* "ordinary," or *kedey-dyikan,* "poor peasant" family.

23. Alymkul Üsönbaev (1896–1963).

24. Toktogul Satylganov (1864–1933).

25. Today, only Zamirbek Üsönbaev (b. 1951) is alive.

26. *Mankurtchuluk* (*mankurtism* in Russian) comes from the word *mankurt*—a person who does not know, or has forgotten, his identity, culture, and language. The term is also used in the epic *Manas,* but it achieved widespread popularity in the Soviet Union in the 1980s after the Kyrgyz writer Chingiz Aitmatov (1928–2008) reintroduced it in his novel *A Day Lasts Longer than a Hundred Years.*

27. Ormon was the khan of the Kyrgyz Sarybagysh tribe in the 19th century. He defeated the Kazakh khan Kenesary in 1847.

28. Barpy Alykulov (1884–1949) was a well-known *aqyn* from southern Kyrgyzstan. He composed many philosophical, religious, and love poems and is known for his specific melodic style, and for singing without the *komuz.*

CHAPTER 11 # Singing Traditions of the Kazakhs

ALMA KUNANBAEVA

Kazakh vocal music can be divided into four broad categories: ritual and ceremonial songs, improvised poetry competitions (*aitys*), lyrical songs (*än*), and epic songs and narration (*jyr*). The first of these categories, ritual and ceremonial songs, is the province of untrained singers. The other three categories each correspond to a cultivated artistic practice that became the domain of specialized performers and acquired the characteristics of a social institution with its own rules and norms of social conduct. The art of improvising oral poets is known as *aqyndyq,* from *aqyn,* a practitioner of this art. *Aqyn*s and *aqyndyq* are addressed in chapter 10. The art of performing *än,* or lyrical songs, is called *änshilik,* and the art of performing epic poems and narration is called *jyraulyq* (discussed in chapter 5 and chapter 6, part 1). Each of these institutions arises from and illuminates a different aspect of Kazakh traditional social life. *Aqyndyq* is linked to the ritualized ceremonies and celebrations cultivated among Kazakh clans and tribes. *Änshilik* is linked to the inner emotional and psychological world of individual community members. *Jyraulyq* synthesizes elements of both *aqyndyq* and *änshilik,* presenting a panoramic view of human existence that is at once narrative, homiletic, and didactic. A principle theme in all three kinds of artistic practice—indeed, a theme that transcends distinctions of musical style, genre, and performance practice—is the fundamental moral question of how to define and distinguish right and wrong. This theme emerges repeatedly in the lyrics and narrative texts of Kazakh songs and epics, which, for listeners who in many cases did not know how to read or write, offered a crystallized form of pragmatic moral philosophy.

RITUAL AND CEREMONIAL SONGS

Ritual and ceremonial songs constitute a repertoire linked mostly to traditional rites performed by women. Prominently featured in this repertoire are wedding songs for the opening of the ceremony (*toy bastar*), unveiling of the bride's face (*betashar*), and introduction of the bride to her new family (*tanysu*), as well as bridal laments (*syngsu*), farewell songs (*qoshtasu*), and the song *jar-jar,* which features dialogue between male and female groups and remains a popular wedding game. Other ritual singing traditions include laments at funerals and annual memorials (*joqtau, dauys*); songs that announce a death (*estirtu*) and offer condolences (*köngil aitu, jubatu*); and calendar songs, in particular, songs connected to Ramadan (*jarapazan:* a type of Ramadan carol). Ritual songs were identified by their specific ritual function rather than as songs in their own right, and became musical symbols of the ritual to which they were linked.

Ritual songs have no refrains, and most possess a formulaic structure in which a stable number of syllables constitutes a syllabic group. For example, an eleven-syllable line has three groups: 3 + 4 + 4, in which each syllable corresponds to one sound and no word is divided between two syllable groups. This constraint means that no word in the song text may have more than four syllables—a significant limitation in Kazakh, an agglutinative language in which multiple syllables may be added to the root of a word to create a grammatical inflection that modifies a word's meaning. The melodic range in ritual songs typically does not exceed an interval of a fifth or sixth (*do-sol* or *do-la*). The following example illustrates one of the quintessential forms of Kazakh ritual song: bridal lament (*syngsu*). Brides traditionally sang a *syngsu* to lament the parting with their own home and family following their wedding, when they moved to the domicile of their new husband, typically in a different settlement (an analogous practice among the Kyrgyz is described in chapter 13). As you listen to the *syngsu,* note the ritualized restraint of emotion in the performance.

LISTEN

Example 11.1. Excerpt from *Syngsu* (Bridal lament), performed by Aitughan. Settlement of Senek, Manghystau region, Kazakhstan, 1997. From János Sipos, *Kazakh Folksongs from the Two Ends of the Steppe* (book and CD) (Budapest: Akadémiai Kiadó, 2001), track 11 (music notation on p. 162).

Bazardan alyp kelgen böz belbeuim,	Bought from the bazaar, my belt of coarse calico,
Jaman-jaqsy bolsa da öz belbeuim,	Good or bad, at least it's my own.
Köp aidan körmegel'au köp kün boldau,	Many days, many months went without seeing you, my kinsfolk,
Aman-esen jürmising köz körgenim.	Are you safe and sound, my relatives?

In traditional Kazakh culture, human life centers around three basic transitional passages: birth, marriage, and death. Through my ethnographic field research in Kazakhstan, I have come to understand that in Kazakh tradition, these passages are perceived as a journey from one state of being to another in the form of recurring metaphorical death and rebirth. For example, an unwed girl must "die" in order to be "reborn" as a married woman. Furthermore, these passages represent crucial moments in which the three worlds of the traditional Kazakh nomadic worldview—the upper world (sky, inhabited by Tengri, the sky god), middle world (earth, inhabited by humans) and underworld (inhabited by spirits)—are open and convergent, and thus, dangerous. Rituals were intended to protect humans.

The author's musical fieldwork in the Qyzylorda region of southern Kazakhstan, July 1977. Standing, second from the left: Bidas Rüstembekov, Alma Kunanbaeva, *jyrau* Sabyt Jusupov.
Photo by Kuat Shildebaev.

As long as people believe in the power of rituals, they continue to exist as a vital practice. Participants all know their place and function in a ritual: who should speak or sing; what should be said or sung; and how and when this should be done. The performance of musical elements of a ritual involves formulaic approaches to melody, rhythm, text, style, and behavior, yet "actors" personalize their own performance through specific qualities of voice and personality, as well through their facility with poetic language.

Many ritual and ceremonial songs are performed in the form of a dialogue among participants, while others, such as wedding and funeral laments, make a clear division between "actors" and audiences. Dialogue songs permeate other genres of Kazakh singing tradition as well, among them *aitys* (song competitions), *qara öleng*—described below, and the professional tradition of lyrical song. *Aitys* ("to talk together"), an exceptionally popular form of dialogical competition between poet-singer-improvisers (*aqyns*), is discussed in chapter 10.

Lyrical songs (*änshilik*) are divided into two distinct subgenres: simple songs (*qara öleng*) performed mainly by women, and songs that, from a musical perspective, are more melodically elaborate and were traditionally performed by professional singers known as *sal* or *seri,* who had a distinguished social status. Women traditionally sang without instrumental accompaniment, while men accompanied their singing on a two-stringed *dombyra.*

Qara öleng grew out of ritual songs and are close to them musically. Like ritual songs, they are not attributed to a specific songwriter, and are based on poetic and melodic formulas that are repeated with a large number of variations. The texts of *qara öleng* typically have no coherent story and their narrative is full of logical gaps. Moreover, they do not have fixed lyrics, and performers are free to change the words as long as the form of the song is maintained. Yet, in contrast to ritual and ceremonial songs, which essentially constitute forms of ritual and ceremonial behavior and are perceived as such, *qara öleng* belong to the world of art, and their performance is evaluated according to aesthetic and artistic criteria: the beauty of a voice, the skill with which a singer embellishes a melody.

Qara öleng can be sung wherever people meet for celebration. Typical occasions include local singing contests *(qaiym öleng)*, social and family gatherings featuring vocal improvisations by guests *(böget öleng)*, mealtimes, and exchanges of riddle songs *(jumbaq öleng)*. Their main function is dialogical interaction—that is, they serve as a means of connecting people through song. The notion of music as a form of social connectivity is apparent in traditional Kazakh discourse, for example, *"auyldyng alty auyzy"* ("sing a song of your *auyl* [settlement]")—a request that a host might ask of a visiting guest from a different locale, or *"qonaq käde"* (guest's debt)—an expression of a guest's "debt" to a host that can be fulfilled by singing a song.

The wide use of *qara öleng* has resulted in a great variety of performance forms and styles, ranging from simple tunes to lavishly embellished melodies. The word *qara*—literally, "black"—can also mean "simple," "ancient," "basic," "mighty," "numerous," and "a song that belongs to everyone." *Qara* is also used to describe the *qara öleng*'s verse form. Unlike ritual songs, whose lines are not grouped into stanzas and which have no refrain, *qara öleng*'s eleven-syllable lines are set in two quatrains, often with a refrain. Usually, such songs have four lines of which the first, second, and fourth rhyme. Their eleven-syllable verses are configured in two distinct versions: 3 + 4 + 4 and 4 + 3 + 4.

While the meaning of *qara öleng* songs seems simple and clear, performing them properly requires deep knowledge of Kazakh poetics since their real meaning is poetically coded. This meaning becomes apparent not through the text itself, but through an understanding of the traditional worldview of which it is a part. Poetic images in the texts are rich in associations. The semantic link between an initial maxim (first two lines) and a subsequent individual statement (second two lines) creates a poetic tension that listeners find both memorable and repeatable. A good example is the *qara öleng* "Top shengel" (Thorny reeds).

Esik aldy qara su balghyn köldi,	At the entrance [of the yurt] there is water, deep as a lake.
Balghyn kölding balyghyn alghym keldi.	I'd like to catch a fish from that lake.
Kishkentaidan birge ösken säulem eding,	We are the same age and grew up together.
Attandyrghan jeringe barghym keldi.	I long to visit the *auyl* [settlement] where you got married.
Qayirmasy:	Refrain:
Esik aldy top shengel,	There is a thicket of thorny reeds at the entrance [of the yurt]

Top shengelge kelseng kel.	If you'd like to come, then do come.
Top shengelge kelgende	If you do come to those thorns,
Özinge özing senseng kel.	Come with confidence in yourself.
Qarayghangha qaraimyn qaban ba dep,	Peering at every shady place, do I not see a wild boar?
Qamshylaymyn atymdy shabam ba dep.	I whip my horse with the hope of galloping.
Ötkennen de suraimyn, ketkennen de,	I ask every passerby,
Qalqataidyng auyly aman ba dep.	"Is everything well in the *auyl* of my sweetheart?"

All of the images in this moving song should be understood not literally but symbolically. For example, the entrance of the yurt symbolizes the boundary between interior and exterior spaces and the point of departure for life journeys into the wide-open world of possibilities and freedom. The suffering of the lyric hero begins at the entrance of his house, which is symbolically shut, barricading his way out forever. The hero is helpless to change his fate: his much-beloved girl has married and moved to her new place of residence from which he cannot bring her back. His inner psychological state is expressed through the images of deep water, the impossibility of catching the desired fish, the thicket of thorny reeds (in reality, inconceivable around a yurt), the wild boar and horse (impossible not only to keep but even to imagine inside a yurt), and the outside world of accidental passersby to whom he dares to address only an indirect question about the *auyl* of his beloved. There is no consistent plot in the song, but the unbearable tragedy of love is obvious for anyone able to read traditional Kazakh imagery.

Qara öleng remain popular in contemporary Kazakhstan. All of their traditional features and stylistic sources are apparent in contemporized performance versions like those of the well-known Kazakh vocalist Indira Rasylkhan, whose performance of "Ädemi qyz," a lyrical *qara öleng* from western Kazakhstan, is presented in example 11.2.

LISTEN

Example 11.2. "Ädemi qyz" (A beautiful girl) performed by Indira Rasylkhan, vocal and *dombyra. Musical Heritage of Kazakhstan,* disc 2, track 10. Produced by PanTerra (Sound Light Stages) and EL Producer Centre.

Aq köilek, qyzyl beshpet ädemi qyz,	White dress, red vest, oh a beauty!
Tigen joq äli eshkimge, ädemi, älegimiz.	For the time being, we didn't cause anyone any trouble.
Birge ösken kishkentaidan qurbym eding,	You were my own age, the one with whom I grew up,
Biz sizden äli künge, ädemi, dämelimiz.	Yet I don't lose hope that you would respond to my feelings.

Qayirmasy:
Säuleli altyn aiymsyng,
Baqytym sensing, barymsyng.
Darigha mynau jalghanda,
Tangdap bir süigen jarymsyng.

Aq köilek, qara qamzol belin bughan,
Jan eding qataryngnan, ädemi, artyq tughan.
Men sizge ghashyqtyktan söz aitamyn,
Ar jaghyn özing tauyp, özing oilan.

Refrain:
My shiny gold moon, my happiness!
You are everything that I have.
In this deluding world,
You're my chosen one, my darling.

White dress, black vest fit your figure snugly,
From birth you were inimitable, unique.
I say this because I'm in love with you,
But what will be next—that is for you to decide.

"Ükili qamshat" (The girl with the beaver-fur hat adorned with eagle-owl feathers) is a *qara öleng* lyrical song from central Kazakhstan that has shed the obvious signs of the genre's origins as a form of ritual song: the repetition of a single melodic motif; the limited melodic range of the melody, and the focus on words over music. The musicality of *qara öleng* is clear in Ardaq Balajanova's eloquent performance of "Ükili qamshat," presented in example 11.3, which draws attention to the purely sonic quality of the lyrics as much as to their semantic meaning. For example, many words begin with the sibilant sound "s," and among these, quite a few use a form of the word *sary,* which means "yellow," "sunny," "golden": *sarghaiyp, sary maidai, Sarygha, sary belden.* The effect is to cast a luminous glow on the entire song (the same phonetically expressed luminous effect arises in English from the "gl" sound in words such as "glow," "glisten," "gleam," "glare"). The drawn-out vowel sounds at the end of each verse line (except in the refrain) provide moments of purely sonic pleasure while also emphasizing the song's end rhyme scheme: aaba.

LISTEN

Example 11.3. "Ükili qamshat" (The girl with a beaver fur hat adorned with eagle-owl feathers) performed by Ardaq Balajanova, vocal and *dombyra*. Recorded by Michael Church, *Songs from the Steppes: Kazakh Music Today* (Topic Records, 2005), track 17.

Sary belden sarghaiyp tang atqanda,
Bidai öngdi aqquba til qatqanda.
Uzaq tanggha er jigit qaityp shydar,
Sari maidai tolyqsyp qyz jatqanda.

At dawn when sunbeams shone from behind the mountain,
When the white-faced girl uttered her word,
How could the young lad contain himself
When his golden butter-like sweetheart is waiting for him.

Qayirmasy:	Refrain:
Ükili qamshat börkingdi-ai,	The beaver-fur hat adorned with the eagle-owl feathers,
Shirkin sening körkingdi-ai.	Your beauty is matchless.
Tolgan aidai tolyqsyp	You're like the full moon,
Bir körein körkingdi-ai.	Allow me to see enough of you.
Sart degizip Sarygha qamshy bastym,	I whipped my light-brown horse
Namazdyger bolghanda belden astym.	And crossed the pass by the time of the evening prayer.
Qudai mening jolymdy ongdaidy eken,	It seems like God Himself blessed my road,
Izdep shyqqan kisime tu jarmastym.	I rushed to the beauty that I've been looking for.
Qayirmasy	Refrain

STUDY QUESTIONS

1. What are the musical differences between ritual lament and *qara öleng?* What do they have in common?

2. What is the effect of the *dombyra* accompaniment on the way you hear the characteristic features of each genre?

3. How would you describe the qualities of the performer's voice in all three examples you've listened to—"Synsu," "Ädemi qyz," and "Ükili qamshat"?

Lyrical *qara öleng* songs like "Ükili qamshat" are not linked to a specific kind of ceremony or celebration, as are ritual songs, nor are they attributed to a specific composer. Rather, such songs represent what might be considered a transitional form that suggests the genetic relationship between folk songs and lyrical songs composed and performed by professional singer-songwriters. The latter constitute a distinct genre in Kazakh musical tradition, and it is to this genre that we now turn.

PROFESSIONAL SINGER-SONGWRITERS: *SAL* AND *SERI*

Lyrical songs performed by professional singer-songwriters—*sal* and *seri*—flourished between the second half of the nineteenth century and the beginning of the twentieth century. The finest examples of professional lyrical singing are from a region in central Kazakhstan known as the Saryarqa, or Golden Steppe. The best-known singers from the region were Aqan seri Qoramsauly (1843–1913); Birjan sal Qojaghululy (1831–1894); Jayau Musa Baijanuly (1835–1929); Ybyrai Sandybaiuly (1860–1932); Mädi Bäpiuly (1880–1921);

Äset Naimanbaiuly (1867–1922); Estai Berkenbaiuly (1874–1946); and Ämre Qashaubaiuly (1888–1934), who became widely known beyond Kazakhstan. Leading twentieth-century followers of the great singer-composers of the past include Manarbek Erjanov (1901–1966), Jüsipbek Elebekov (1904–1977), and Jänibek Kärmenov (1949–1992).

In contrast to *qara öleng* songs, lyrical songs performed by professional singers are attributed to a specific composer who often plays a role in the lyrics of the song, and feature a stable relationship between text and tune, forming what in artistic parlance would be called a musical "work." Composers of such works would also have typically performed them, and thus the contemporary expression "singer-songwriter" is an apt description of the Kazakh *sal* and *seri*. The performance style of *sal* and *seri* was characterized by the so-called steppe bel canto—a reference to the refined and technically challenging vocal style perfected by opera and oratorio singers in eighteenth- and nineteenth-century Italy. In steppe bel canto, singers demonstrated their vocal skills and artistic passion by sustaining notes over long durations in full voice, and by using vocables (meaningless syllables) in the refrains of songs to sing highly ornamented melodic lines. Listeners exclaim to performers specific words of support and encouragement: "*Keremet*" (wonderful!), "*Bar bol*" (go on!), and so on. *Sal* and *seri* accompanied their singing on a special kind of *dombyra* that had a small resonator, relatively short neck with eleven frets, and was plucked rather than strummed, as is typical in other kinds of *dombyra* performance.

The distinctive features of *sal* and *seri* singing appear clearly in the two examples that follow. The first of these is "Balqadisha" (a girl's name), a song composed by Aqan seri that is widely known among Kazakhs.

LISTEN

Example 11.4. "Balqadisha" (A girl's name), composed by Aqan seri, performed by Tileules Qurmanghali, vocal and *dombyra*. *Musical Heritage of Kazakhstan,* disc 2, track 16. Produced by PanTerra (Sound Light Stages) and EL Producer Centre.

Degende . . . Balqadisha, Balqadisha,
Buralghan beling näzik, shirkin-ai, tal Qadisha.
Seksen qyz seruenge shyqqan kezde,
Ishinde qara basyng, shirkin-ai, khan Qadisha.

I say . . . o Balqadisha, Balqadisha
Whose slender build is like a willow trunk, Qadisha!
Among eighty strolling girls
Your head is visible like a queen in the sky.

Qyzy eding Ybykengning Balqadisha,	You were a daughter of Ybeken, Balqadisha.
Esildi örlei bitken, shirkin-ai, tal Qadisha.	Esil's banks are covered with willows.
Bulangdap asau taidai jürgen basyng,	Being free as an untamed two-year-old foal,
Bolarsyng qandai jangha, shirkin-ai, jar Qadisha.	By whose wife would you become what fate has willed?
Basynan Jylandynyng qulaghanym,	I crashed down from the peak of Jylandy (Snake) Mountain
Kekilin Kerbestining, shirkin-ai, sylaghanym.	And stroked the withers of my horse.
Ketti dep Balqadisha estigende,	When I heard that Balqadisha had been given in marriage,[1]
Qushaqtap qus jastyqty, shirkin-ai, jylaghanym.	How I grieved and bitterly wept, embracing the pillow.

Several features of "Balqadisha" readily identify it as belonging to the *sal-seri* repertoire of "professional" lyrical song. These include the dominant role of melody in shaping the form of the song (in contrast to ritual songs, where melody is subservient to text); the melodic ornamentation of the last syllable in each even line (*tal Qadisha, khan Qadisha, jar Qadisha*); the independent importance of musical accompaniment; and, most important, the subject and content that develop through the entire song (in contrast to the texts of *qara öleng* songs, which typically have no coherent story). In "Balqadisha," this story is closely intertwined with legends about the life of Aqan seri, one of the last *seri*s of the steppe, and the tragic events of his life: the early death of his wife; the killing of his favorite horse, Kulager; unrequited love; and the loss of his golden eagle, Qaratorghai, and favorite hound dog, Bazarala. These events all became the topics of songs, which in turn became part of a collective oral narrative of the rough and tumble life of *sal*s and *seri*s that was a central part of Kazakh folklore, perhaps in the same way that the traditional delta blues of the American South, which documents the hard lives of rural blues singers, became central to American folklore.

Among *sal* and *seri* self-portraits in song, one in particular, "Aq qaiyn" (White birch), holds a special place in Kazakh musical culture. It was composed by *sal* Shäshubai Qoshqarbaev (1865–1952), a skillful singer and jongleur who, while participating in trading fairs, used to perform while standing on his moving horse and accompanying himself on the accordion.[2]

> LISTEN
>
> **Example 11.5.** "Aq qaiyn" (White birch), composed by Shäshubai Qoshqarbaev, performed by Qurmash Ibishev, vocal and *dombyra*. Recorded by Michael Church, *Songs from the Steppes: Kazakh Music Today* (Topic Records, 2005), track 8.

Aq qaiyn, qyzyl qaiyn, syrly qaiyn!	White birch, red birch, secret birch!
Balasy Qoshqarbaidyng Shäshubaimyn.	I'm Shäshubai, son of Qoshqarbai.
Ölengning qudai bergen arqasynda	Owing to this song that is given by God
Dabyldy aqaqtantyp elge jaidym!	I play the drum and send a signal to the people!
Qayirmasy:	Refrain:
Qaq. Qaghygha qaq-qaq, qaghygha qaq-qaq-qaq.	Qaq. Qaghygha qaq-qaq, qaghygha qaq-qaq-qaq.
Qaghaghagi ghagi-ghagi ghai-ghai-ghai ghagi-	Qaghaghagi ghagi-ghagi ghai-ghai-ghai ghagi-
ghagi-ei	ghagi-ei.
Aq qaiyn, jalghan-oi, ötting däuren-ai	White birch, deceptive world, the happy time is gone.
Qalqymnyng arasynda saldym sairan!	I create joy and merriment among the people.
Balasy Qoshqarbaidyng Shäshubaimyn	I'm Shäshubai, son of Qoshqarbai,
Bolsam da malgha kedei, änge baimyn!	I'm poor in cattle but rich in songs!
Künine jüzdi berip myngdy alsam da,	Giving away by the hundreds and receiving by the thousands,
Qaltamnyng tübi tesik, baiymaimyn.	I do not grow rich because of the hole in my pocket.
Qayirmasy	Refrain

"Aq qaiyn" displays all the core features of professional lyrical song: attributed authorship, a sustained introductory cry, and a refrain with words that have no semantic meaning. It also includes an enigmatic feature in the refrain: the stylized scream of a bird and shriek of a swan in a quasi-language of vocables. These sounds arouse a subconscious genetic memory in listeners that transports them to the ancient source of Kazakh music: shamanism. The song's symbolic reference to birch trees underscores the connection to shamanism, and in particular, to traditions of Siberian shamanism in which the birch was an important symbol. In the song text, the three different-colored birch trees can be understood as symbolizing the three worlds of the traditional tripartite nomadic worldview described earlier. White birch symbolizes the upper world of the sky god; red birch symbolizes blood and fire, which belong to the middle world that hosts human life; the secret birch symbolizes the underworld—the world of spirits. Many legends from the Altai region of south Siberia speak of secret rituals conducted around birch trees.

Another reference to shamanism is in the fourth line of the song: "I play the drum and send a signal to the people" (*Dabyldy aqaqtantyp elge jaidym*)—a reference to the shaman's drum, here represented by the *dabyl,* a two-headed Kazakh drum that was used as a signaling instrument. The song text also echoes the shamanic prohibition on using one's gift for profit, hence the text speaks of poverty in cattle but richness in songs. Even the name of the singer—Shäshubai, son of

Qoshqarbai—suggests ritual associations: *shashu* means to shower newlyweds with candies or sweets; *qoshqar* refers to a ram whose horns protected people's homes and whose stylized representation is now common in ornaments used in felt carpets and decorations.

SAL AND SERI AS ARTISTS

The word *seri* has a range of meanings: "musician," "artist," "fop," "dandy," and "knight." The word *sal* has an even broader range of meanings and etymologically appears to be much older. In one sense, *seri* means "poet," "composer," "singer," or "person of the arts." The word is also connected to the Kazakh tradition of battue—a method of hunting wherein a hunting party encircles game and then closes the circle, trapping the game in the center. (Battue—French for "beaten"—takes its name from the practice of using the sound of drums or beaters to drive game.) Kazakh battue had a festive and theatrical air, hence words such as *salburyn*—a collective hunt lasting several days that takes place at a distance from the *auyl;* and *än salu*—literally, "to drive a song," "play a song," or "pursue a tune." *Sal* has one more peculiar meaning: coitus. This connotation seems related to the legendary ability of *sal*s to bring about fertility—in humans, animals, and in the earth.

In traditional Kazakh culture, *sal* and *seri* were traveling folk artists who were given wide latitude in social behavior, resulting in behavior that by local norms was anti-social. For example, Aqan seri, the composer of "Balqadisha," was known for sleeping on the ground outside the yurt of a host who had invited him as an honored guest for an evening of feasting and ritualized hospitality. Guests were expected to sleep inside the yurt, and the violation of this pervasive social norm led astonished hosts to believe that Aqan seri had a fairy wife who dragged him away from humans at night.[3] Moreover, *sal*s and *seri*s never had to say good-bye to anyone.

*Sal*s and *seri*s traveled with groups of itinerants that included, in addition to musicians, a humorist or master of wit, a blacksmith or jeweler, and a strongman-wrestler. Members of such troupes metaphorically personified the power of words through their professional activities: blacksmiths *forged* words, jewelers *embellished* words; strongmen and wrestlers unleashed *triumphant, muscular,* and *well-aimed* words. Thus words were both honed in the expression of ideas and embodied in visible acts, and through performance, word and act were allegorically united.

The *sal* and *seri* were not simply bohemians, as their unusual way of life and eccentric clothing might suggest (they wore silk, which was typically associated with women, as well as embroidered cloaks, jewelry, and women's feathered hats). Rather, in the nineteenth century, *sal* and *seri* represented, both literally and figuratively, a historical echo of the archaic institution of shamans, the most ancient bearers of Kazakh folklore, who were not only healers, but ritual mediators who maintained the order of the world.[4] Like shamans, *sal*s and *seri*s were believed to possess magical abilities that were manifested through their voice and musical instrument, and through their touch—for example, they were believed to be able to heal by laying their hands on people. Moreover, the *sal* and *seri* were noble men as well as gifted and skillful artisans who personified the world of beauty and the arts.

Beyond their practical skills in treating human disorders and repairing and restoring order, *sal* and *seri* comprehended and organized the structure of the world, time and space, life and death. In the historical development of this ancient institution of ritual mediators, basic branches gradually diverged: *jyraulyq,* the art of performing epic poetry and tales, came to function as history; *aqyndyq* concentrated on politics (relationships between clans); and *änshilik* specialized in artistry, spirituality, and the soul.

THE RECITATION OF EPIC: *JYRAULYQ*

Jyraulyq has been best preserved in the southwest and west of Kazakhstan, especially in the region that abuts the Aral Sea. In Kazakh culture, epic singers (*jyrau*) are keepers of collective memory that connects oral traditions with shamanic spirituality and nomadic philosophy (see chapter 5 and chapter 6, part 1). From a musical perspective, the performance style for epics in the repertoire of the *jyrau* is similar, whether the subject is heroic, historical, fantastical, or romantic. Where differences exist, they can be attributed to regional stylistic variation, rather than to different performance conventions linked to epic theme or genre.

The vocal style and timbre of the *jyrau* is characterized by dramatic oratorical recitative delivered in a raspy, guttural voice that sets it apart from the voice of other kinds of traditional singers. *Jyrau*s are overwhelmingly male, however, in some local traditions women may also become *jyrau*s. To do so, however, they must possess a specific vocal timbre known as "male voice" (*erkek dauys*). *Jyrau*s accompany themselves on the *dombyra,* and this accompaniment is interwoven with the singing. A "singer of tales" cannot narrate a tale without it. The *jyrau*'s raspy vocal style is reminiscent of the sound of the *qobyz,* the two-stringed bowed lute played by Kazakh shamans (see chapter 16).

The magical power of the *jyrau* extends to his instrument, which is believed to have its own soul, and the ability to bring good or bad fortune. This belief holds that after a bard's death, his instrument must find a new owner; otherwise, it will play itself at night and scare children. For this reason, older *jyrau*s typically seek a new owner for their instrument—an analog to the generational transmission of shamanic power in ancient cultures.

In the context of Kazakh socio-artistic institutions, the perception of epic is bound up with the social status of the *jyrau* as a spokesman for the higher, philosophical dimension of traditional life. *Jyrau*s themselves understand their performance as the creation of a panorama of traditional life with which listeners can empathize. For its part, a traditional audience understands the entire repertoire of the *jyrau*, which includes classical epic tales as well as short philosophical homilies, as a holistic verbal and musical act with complex dramaturgy and dynamics. For such listeners a performance of epic by a *jyrau* constitutes a form of journey, ascension, or rebirth that can be transformative, energizing, and life-affirming.

The repertoire of *jyrau*s includes, in addition to epic tales, works in a cluster of shorter epic genres: didactic songs (*terme*); philosophical reflections (*tolghau*); words of edification spoken by prominent storytellers (*naqyl söz*); oral "letters" associated with words of edification (*khat*); exhortations (*ösiet*); praise-songs (*maqtau*); consolations and condolences (*köngil qos*); dedications and eulogies (*arnau, madaqtau*); and "song-beginnings" (*bastau-än*), which usually precede the performance of lengthy stories and give *jyrau*s an opportunity to invoke inspiration in an audience and enumerate the various legends the *jyrau*s know.

Bidas Rüstembekov (b. 1951), a *jyrau* from the Qyzylorda region of southern Kazakhstan, inherited the tradition of his grandfather, father, and older brother. (For more on Bidas Rüstembekov, see chapter 5.) As Kazakhs say, "Tulpar is born from tulpar." (Tulpar is the legendary winged horse of Turkic mythology, corresponding to the Greek Pegasus.) Bidas's modesty and reserve, intelligent self-awareness, and respect for those around him immediately reveal him as someone exceptional— and very different from the typical portrait of a *sal* or *seri*. One person who knows Bidas well said of him that he is "not of this world." Another person added that he "has a different life inside." As a performer, he has a low voice, rich in overtones, and a rhythmically precise style of recitation, which he accompanies with a resonant *dombyra*. Bidas's style is marked by a virtuosic mastery of the ability to change the way he produces sound, transitioning from an "open" sound to more diverse forms of vibration and vocal tonality. The texts that Bidas performs, which are drawn from all the genres of Kazakh epic tradition, are set to a small repertoire of melodies, all similar in style, some of which are attributed to other *jyrau*s.

Bidas produced his own classification of listeners in order to explain why certain audience members, especially women and children, freely come and go during a performance (doing so tactfully) while others wait until the end to leave or stand up. Women, he says, are occupied with hosting duties such as receiving guests, and are thus outside the periphery of the *jyrau*'s attention. Children, by virtue of traditional social precepts, are not bound by prescribed behavioral norms. Among the remaining listeners, i.e., adult men, Bidas distinguishes the following three subcategories: experts who are themselves storytellers, elders, and guests. It is to these

Bidas Rüstembekov in 1977, when the author met him for the first time.
Photo by Quat Shildebaev.

listeners that Bidas addresses his performance. In some performance situations, he might address one person in particular who is more attuned and responsive than other listeners, and is thus able to influence an entire audience with his attitude. This individual's conduct can determine the sequence of pieces performed, and even the performer's emotional state. During a performance, audience members who are present from the start may move away without drawing attention to themselves while the arrival of unfamiliar people can impede a performance, since *jyrau*s need time to integrate newcomers into their sphere of attention. A *jyrau* who performs more involved, plot-filled stories may not be strongly connected to an audience, but rather fixated on events described in the story. At certain moments, however, a storyteller needs the support of listeners, who express themselves through formulaic exclamations of approval. The storyteller's singing unites all present as the audience is arranged around him in concentric circles, each with its own social group and rules of conduct. In the outer circles are younger people and those whose role is to serve others; elders and honored guests sit in the innermost circle.

In Bidas's words, "The *jyrau* is like a racehorse in a competition; he needs the support of the majority, of the public at large. Any true *jyrau* should not cry out, and should have no need for superfluous shouting. He should just follow the melody, as if following a path, not straying from it, and simply obeying it. One should not 'switch paths' or unnecessarily slide from one path to another. Playing the *dombyra* should also correspond to what one is singing; one must not beat down on the strings, one should play *burap*-style [spiraling in, carefully and gently]."

Performances of Kazakh epic usually contain three main sections: a preface or initial section (*bastau*); a central recitation, performed in a measured rhythmic intonation which tends to repetitions (*uzyn sonar,* "long pursuit" or "hunt"); and a conclusion (*qaiyrma*) or "turning point"; that is, the conclusive break when recitation of a text is replaced by extemporized jubilant singing without a text. This final section is usually performed at a slower tempo in order to provide a break from the vocal pulse of the preceding section.

In the following video example, Bidas Rüstembekov performs "Jienbaidyng termesi" (Jienbai's *terme*), which exemplifies an ancient form of Kazakh epic composition that scholars have described as "tirade." Tirade refers to a verse form in which an indefinite number of lines are joined by a rhyme pattern. Epic tirades consisting of short verses are called *jyr*. Using the tirade form as the basis for a performance allows any number of repetitions of its various components. A sequence of tirades can be interrupted by spoken interludes, which do not disrupt the rapid pace of epic verse.

Bidas Rüstembekov in 1990, Qarmaqshy settlement of Qyzylorda region.
Photo by Sergei Jirkevich.

Example 11.6. "Jienbaidyng termesi" (Jienbai's *terme*), performed by Bidas Rüstembekov, vocal and *dombyra*. Words and music by Jienbai, grandfather of Bidas. Recorded in Qarmaqshy, Qyzylorda region, 2001, and published in *A Journey to Epic Qyzylorda: Three Kazakh Jyraus* (DVD), vol. 4 of *Musical Treasures of The Silk Road House* (Silk Road House, 2013), scene 10.

WATCH

Asyly bir teksiz aqymaqty	You will not make a vagrant fool into
Tekti dep bolmas qur maqtap.	A high-born noble with empty praises.
Pighyly buzyq qarany	You will not make a criminal into
Sara dep bolmas qur aqtap.	A high-minded man with compliments.
Ölmei jürse keledi	Anyone who wants to live
Adamizattyng basyna	Must go through
Üsh türli mysal jortaqtap.	Three stages in life.
Tusang äueli bir küni,	You're born one day
Qatyrei sudan jaralyp,	From a drop of the ocean,
Jan ughlym dese ata-anang,	You hear the words "my son."
Mas bolyp anda jürersing	Drunk on the love of your parents,
Balalyqpen taltaqtap	You totter along like a pigeon.
Aqyl esing kiredi	Your mind will finally reason
Onsegiz jasqa kelgen song.	When you reach eighteen.
Ata-anangnyng aqysy	You'll worry about
Moinynga tüsken bir salmaq.	Your mother and father.
Ylajy joq tutpasqa,	There's no choice
Jürersing äni arqalap.	But to carry that duty.
Byl düniening qamy üshin	You'll start to look down every path,
Oilaidy jigit är talap.	Trying to find your fate.
Bahardyng samal jelindey,	Like a gust of spring wind,
Jigittikting qamaly	Youth will blossom inside you.
Basynga bir kün keledi	Like a galloping horse,
Bäige atyndai alshaqtap.	You'll be anxious then;
Qaiterin bilmei adamizat	Being confused
Bul näubetting kezinde	A human being might lose his path.
Shyghady joldan bultaqtap.	They say that the fever of youth
Qyisaitad deidi ökshesin	Wears down your boots,
Kön etikting bul Jastyq.	So that they'll have no heel.

Osylai eken äseri	Hey, now, you know –
Jigittikting baiqasaq	That's how it is!
Jazghy jaughan jangbyrmen	Women blossom like tulips,
Bäisheshektei türlenip	Tulips in the summer rain.
Jorgadai basar aiaghyn	Even people's gait becomes different,
Erkek äiel shalqaqtap.	Like a confident amble.
Dünie shirkin köshpeli	But the world changes,
Bir jerde turmas turaqtap.	Doesn't stay in one place,
Bir küni aqyry ketedi	And beauty will leave you behind,
Basyngnan osy säuleting.	Will dump you like a girl so cruel
Qoshyrei sulu qyzdai bop	She shoos you away
Eki qolyn bylghaqtap.	With her hands held high.
Erge de keler bir näubet,	The same fate awaits us humans,
Jerge de keler bir näubet.	And the same fate awaits the earth.
Basyngda däuir turganda	While still alive
Söz söile tilim yrghaqtap.	Speak, my tongue, rhythmically.
Baiany joq qurghyrdy,	In this ephemeral world
Uaqtynda shygharmai	Why should I keep it back?
Ne qylaiyn qur saqtap.	Why should I hide it?
Qara jer degen ajdaha,	The earth is a dragon,
Auzyn ashyp jutady	It opens its maw and swallows us
Bir shybyndai janyngdy	Having no mercy
Jürseng de qansha ardaqtap.	On your cherished soul.
Bul düniening mysaly	The symbol of this world
Altaiy tülki sekildi	Is a red fox
Aldyngnan qashqan jaitaqtap.	Running alone in the fresh white snow.
Pändanyng köngili mysyly qus.	Human hopes and human passions
Körgen song qyzyl tülkini	Are like a bird of prey.
Ushyrar qusyn aidaqtap.	Seeing the target it takes off
Qus aiaghy iliner	If luck is on your side,
Ornaiyn dese oghan baq.	It will hook its prey;
Qusy keyin ushady	If it is not,
Ongbaiyn dese ol talap.	It will just fly away.
Atanyng etken joly dep,	With the saying "that's our ancestors' way,"
Dünieni jidyq tyrnaqtap	Misers collect every penny but not words of wisdom.
Arqasymen qalyqtyng,	From now on, my equals,
Qatar tengim jürgen song,	With the backing of the people,
Tai qulyndai oinaqtap.	I will reign like a young spring foal.

—Translation by Scott Bartling

1. How would you describe the performance style of *jyrau* Bidas Rüstembekov? Which feature of his singing attracts your immediate attention?

2. How would you define the theme and the message of the *terme* that Bidas performs? What time frame is captured by the author of the *terme*?

3. Note the last word of the fourth line of the *terme* text: *aqtap*. Now identify at least fifteen other words that occur at the end of a line and rhyme with *aqtap*.

4. Which voiceless consonant is most striking in Bidas's articulation: "t," "p," or "q"? What impression does this sound make on listeners?

Rysbek Ashimov (1955–2014) from Aralsk, in the far west of Kazakhstan, represented a different tradition of *jyraulyq* from that of Bidas Rüstembekov, who comes from southern Kazakhstan. In the following example, Rysbek performs a *bastau* "Qaneki, tilim, söileshi," composed by Nurtughan Kenjeghululy (1889–1930) on a poetic text by the *jyrau* Mysabai (d. 1936).

Example 11.7. "Nurtughannyng termesi" (Nurtughan's *terme*), composed by Nurtughan Kenjeghululy on a text by Mysabai, performed by Rysbek Ashimov, vocal and *dombyra*. Recorded in Qarmaqshy, Qyzylorda region, 2001, and published in *A Journey to Epic Qyzylorda: Three Kazakh Jyraus* (DVD), vol. 4 of *Musical Treasures of The Silk Road House* (Silk Road House, 2013), track 27.

WATCH

Qanekei tilim söileshi	Speak now, my tongue,
Körsetip köpke önerdi.	Show everyone your artistry.
Qyzyl tilim jel sözge	Since birth, my skillful tongue
Tughannan-aq sheberdi.	Has had command of words that fly.
Kim tyngdaidy sözingdi	I ask you: Who will come to listen
Bolmasa äsem mänerli	If the words are unrefined?
Basy puldy bolady	He who has command of art
Bolsa jigit önerli.	Will have command of wealth.
Düniedegi jandynyng	Among those living on this earth,
Biri artyq, biri tömendi.	One is born high, one is born low.
Alma moiyn naz bedeu	The ardent youth, the youth with fire alone
Qumar jigit minedi.	Deserves to mount the supple, purebred horse.

Aruana shalkquiryq	The noble dromedary comes to a gallop
Birden de birge keledi.	At once, with a single stride.
Baldaghy altyn aq irek	The golden eagle flies from his perch
Erden de erge könedi.	In a beeline, straight toward his prey.
Qara jal qulan aqshubar	The black-maned onager, thirsting,
Su tunyghyn biledi.	Will always seek the purest water.
Alqyr bürkit muzbalaq	The mountain eagle, keen and strong,
Asqar tauda tüleidi.	Lives among the snowy heights.
Altaiy qyzyl aq tamaq	The red fox, with his sleek white ruff,
Qia shyngda jüredi.	Conceals himself in the distant plains.
Jigitting artyq abzaly	Those who are noble are confident;
önerine senedi.	They rely upon their own skill.
Näsildi erge mal bitse	The aristocrat with honor
Shygharar ishten shermendi.	Assuages the sorrow of many people.
Näsilsiz erge mal bitse	The aristocrat without honor
Bitken saiyn tömendi.	Falls only into sorrow himself.
Qanekei söile qyzyl til!	So speak now, my tongue,
öneringdi körem dep	Pour out words,
Jinalyp otyr köp endi.	The judges have already gathered.

—TRANSLATION BY SCOTT BARTLING

Nowadays, this song is very popular throughout Kazakhstan, as epic genres are reinterpreted within the framework of popular music (*estrada*) nourished principally by urban-dwelling musicians within the social and commercial framework of urban entertainment.

STUDY QUESTIONS

1. In the text of "Nurtughan's *terme*," can you identify lines that address the "fundamental ethical question of how to define and distinguish right and wrong," which, as mentioned at the beginning of the chapter, is ubiquitous in Kazakh folklore?

2. What is the principal idea conveyed in the *terme*'s lyrics?

3. What do you think that Mysabai jyrau, the author of the *terme*'s lyrics, wants listeners to understand from the terse descriptions of different animals' behavior?

Notes

1. A collection of songs by Aqan seri includes variants of the song with supplementary couplets about an eighty-five-year-old man who becomes the bridegroom of Qadisha, who was taken to him by two sisters-in-law. See Qairolla Jüzbasov, comp. and ed., *Mangmangger* (Almaty: Öner, 1988), 67.

2. For more on Shäshubai Qoshqarbaev, see Akhmet Jubanov, *Zamana bulbuldary* [The era of the nightingales] (Almaty: Jazushy, 1975), 424.

3. Ibid., 457.

4. See Edige Tursynov, *Qazaq auyz ädebietin jasaushylardyng baiyrghy ökilderi* [Ancient creators of Kazakh oral literature] (Almaty: Ghylym, 1976), 122.

CHAPTER 12

Kyrgyz Funeral Laments

ELMIRA KÖCHÜMKULOVA

Tirüünün körkü syi bolot,
Ölüktün körkü yi bolot.

Respect graces the living,
Lamentation graces the dead.

—KYRGYZ PROVERB

The ritual of singing a lament for a deceased person is an essential aspect of funerary practices among many peoples around the world, including the Kyrgyz. Kyrgyz scholars assume that most Turkic heroic epics arose from traditional laments that were orally composed and sung for well-known historical personalities such as rulers (khans), tribal leaders (*biy*s), and heroes (*baatyr*s). In Kyrgyz nomadic society, bearers of traditional and historical knowledge—improvising oral poets (*aqyn*s), singers (*yrchy*s), and women—played an important role in developing, refining, and preserving this genre of folk music. When well-known people died,

Koshok and *Joktoo*

Kyrgyz use two words, *koshok* and *joktoo*, interchangeably for a funeral lament. *Koshok* (*kosh*-, to put two things together, to combine, to add) means "to improvise verse lines," whereas *joktoo* (*jok*, no, it does not exist) means "to lament someone's loss, or death." Kazakhs use the term *joqtau*. The term *koshok* has

a different meaning among the neighboring Uzbeks, who call their lyrical song *qoshiq*. *Qoshiq ayt* in Uzbek means "to sing a song." There are two types of *koshok* among the Kyrgyz: one is a *koshok* sung for a deceased person; the other is a *koshok* sung for a newly married girl by her female relatives (mainly by

her mother, grandmother, sister[s], sister[s]-in-law) at a ceremony held at her home before she leaves for her husband's home. In this text we will discuss the socio-cultural context, poetic structure, and performance style of the funerary *koshok* singing ritual.

*aqyn*s or professional lamenters (*koshokchu*s) were invited to sing *koshok*s. They improvised long lament poems in which they sang about the life of the deceased by employing formulaic language from a pool of existing traditional *koshok*s as well as incorporating elements of a heroic epic poem. The best *koshok* compositions dedicated to a hero or khan entered the collective memory of particular social groups and, as time passed, turned into a long epic story.

Women inside a funeral yurt.

The singing of *koshok*s is still alive among the Kyrgyz, especially in rural areas. In the past, *koshok*s were composed and sung by both men and women, but today *koshok*s are sung primarily by women. It is usually older women who maintain this tradition. Today, few professional *koshokchu*s can improvise new *koshok*s or adapt traditional versions to new social and individual contexts. The diminishing number of professional *koshokchu*s is reflected in the waning social significance of *koshok* singing, especially in urban areas. In villages, it is considered shameful for grown-up Kyrgyz women not to sing a *koshok* at the funeral of their close family members—parents, husband, children, and siblings. One needs a good voice, poetic and musical skills, and an agile memory to sing a *koshok*. Most women memorize several lines from traditional texts of a *koshok* and sing them using a version of a traditional melody. As is broadly true for orally transmitted song repertoires, a single authoritative version of the song—and for that matter, of the text—does not exist. Thus women freely draw lines from a general reserve of traditional *koshok*s and fill in the particulars of names, kinship relations, and other circumstances drawn from the life of the deceased.

In the Aksy region of southern Kyrgyzstan, Kyrgyz mothers who have lost a child often sing the following traditional *koshok*:

Alty arkar jyldyz batkycha,	Until the Aries constellation faded away,
Alty aylanyp emizgem.	I breastfed him six times a day.
Aman soo jashap jürsö dep,	So that he/she grew up healthy,
Arkardyn etin jegizgem.	I fed him/her wild sheep meat.
Jeti arkar jyldyz batkycha,	Until the Aries constellation faded away,
Jeti aylanyp emizgem,	I breastfed him seven times a day.
Jetilip aman jürsö dep,	So that he/she grew up well and sound,
Jeyrendin etin jegizgem.	I fed him/her gazelle meat.

Depending on their ability to improvise, mothers add their own verse lines to the existing texts if they want to say something specific about a beloved son. When an elderly mother lost her forty-eight-year-old son, who had held a government position and thus drove a nice car, she sang the traditional *koshok* excerpted above, and added the two following lines at the end as a way of commenting on his unfulfilled life.

Mashina minding chong jolgo,	You drove a car on a wide road,
Oo, kagylaiyn kulunum!	Oh, my dearest foal,
Jetalbay kaldyng moljolgo.	But you couldn't reach your goal.

Koshok is sung both at funerals and at the memorial feasts that follow a funeral at specified intervals. These include *beyshembilik,* which is offered on the first Thursday after a person's death; *kyrky,* the fortieth-day memorial feast; and *jyldyk* or *ash,* the last feast, offered on or around the one-year anniversary of a death. The final symbolic *koshok* is sung at the *ash* to mark the end of the mourning period and pay last respects to the spirit of the deceased. In the past, when nomadic Kyrgyz moved from one pasture to another, the widow of a recently deceased man would sing a *koshok* while passing other nomadic camps on horseback so that people knew that she was in mourning.

Singing a *koshok* is an effective spiritual tool for comforting mourning family members and easing their pain. The formal constraints of the song form help to channel emotions of grief and sorrow and keep them from becoming physically overwhelming. In her study of Greek laments, Margaret Alexiou notes that wild shouting and wailing as an expression of deep grief may harm a person physically and even cause illness.[1] Many Kyrgyz women agree that singing *koshok* helps them control their emotions, suppress negative feelings of anger and bitterness, and conserve energy. A Kyrgyz woman shared her personal feelings when she sang a *koshok* after her parents died:

> Crying without saying anything is very hard. After crying hard for some time, you begin to lose your voice and also feel tired. You know that you cannot bring them back, and *koshok*s confirm this fact and let you admit God's will. You cry every time new visitors or relatives come to offer condolences. Singing *koshok* helped me to console myself and express what I was feeling inside without crying. I tried to sing those lines that suited my father's life and my feelings. Also, when I sang *koshok,* I felt as if my deceased father and mother [who lay in front of me behind the curtain inside the yurt] heard what I was saying about them in my *koshok.*

She also added that before his death, her father had told her that she should sing a good *koshok* in his honor, as people would be listening to what she said about him. He had also added jokingly: "If you don't sing a *koshok* when I die, I will get up from my deathbed [i.e., come back to life]."

Preservation and Transmission of *Koshok* Singing in Modern Kyrgyz Society

Today, even though most Kyrgyz no longer live in yurts (*boz üy*), their nomadic cultural heritage plays an important role in their social and cultural lives and national identity. It is still customary in all regions of Kyrgyzstan, including urban areas where people live in apartment buildings, to erect a funerary yurt (in cities, the yurt is placed in a courtyard) and place the body of the deceased in it for a day or two before it is taken to the burial ground. The yurt stands at the center of all funeral rituals, both before and after the burial. Close female family members dressed in mourning clothes sing a *koshok* inside the yurt, sitting close to the body. In some regions, women sing a *koshok* facing the wall of the yurt where the body is laid out, while in other regions, they cry and sing a *koshok* facing the entrance of the yurt.

Women lament at the funeral of the author's great uncle, Kyzyl-Jar village, Aksy Region, Jalal-Abad Province, 2010. The body of the deceased lies behind the red curtain drawn across the inside of a yurt.

These days, Kyrgyz women, especially younger women, usually learn to sing a *koshok* by imitating older women at funerals who remember words and melodies of *koshoks* they heard from their mothers, grandmothers, and aunts. This "on-site" learning has come about due to the decline of professional *koshok* singers, and due to a common belief that singing a *koshok* before the person's death is a bad omen. Moreover, many younger people simply do not understand the significance of traditional rituals and practices and thus are not interested in them. Finally, Kyrgyz women and men who embrace forms of Wahhabi Islamic practice imported into Kyrgyzstan from the Arabian Peninsula in the years following the breakup of the Soviet Union condemn the custom of singing *koshok* as well as other culturally important funeral rituals, such as *bidda'h,* on the basis that they represent religious innovations that contradict the norms of Muslim practice.

Principal Features and Poetic Structure of *Koshok*

Koshok melodies vary from region to region in Kyrgyzstan, but they share key common features such as crying-like exhalations and a sad affect, which make them hard to listen to without crying oneself. Those special sounds, which lamenters insert after every one or two verse lines, add to the pathos and give the lamenter time to remember or improvise the next words. These important elements of a *koshok* are difficult to describe or transcribe, and must be experienced in the context of an actual "performance."

In poetic structure and style, *koshok* shares common features with other traditional genres of Kyrgyz oral literature such as love songs, wisdom and didactic poetry, and epic poems. *Koshok* has seven or eight syllables in each verse line and strictly maintains initial and internal alliteration as well as end rhyme. These poetic elements, formulaic language, parallelisms, and metaphors make *koshok* texts

effective and easy to memorize. Moreover, pre-existing formulas can be adapted to fit the gender, life, and personality of any individual. Traditional *koshok*s have a specific structure consisting of opening lines, core, and closing lines, and good lamenters follow that structure. Some *koshok*s begin and end with popular Muslim and Kyrgyz expressions or references to God (Allah, Kuday, or Tengir) and the Qur'an, and mention the fact that death affects both ordinary people and prophets, including the Prophet Muhammad.

WATCH

Example 12.1. *Koshok* sung at a Kyrgyz memorial feast in Aksy region, 2003. Performed by Anash Andeleyeva.

This excerpt from a video of a Kyrgyz memorial feast that took place in the Aksy region of southern Kyrgyzstan in 2003 shows an elderly female lamenter (*koshokchu*) singing a *koshok* at a memorial feast marking the one-year anniversary of a man's death (*jyldyk*). The lamenter sits inside the funerary yurt in the company of other mourning women. The lamenter was asked to sing the final *koshok* to mark the end of the mourning period for the relatives of the deceased. After the last *koshok,* all close female relatives changed out of their mourning dresses (dark or blue colored), which they had been wearing for a year, to white or bright-colored clothes. The following is a transliteration and translation of the *koshok* text.

Asmandap uchkan ak kushka,	One can't feed the white bird
Asmandan jemin beralbayt.	That flew away toward the sky.
Ardaktap bakkan baldaryng,	Your cherished children,
Kagylaiyn kendirim,	Oh, my dear *kendir,*[2]
Senin süylögön sözüng tabalbayt.	Can no longer find your fatherly advice.
Kökölöp uchkan kök kushka,	One can't feed the blue bird
Köktön bir jemin beralbayt.	That flew away toward the sky.
Körkömü sonun tuuganyng,	Your beloved kinsmen
Kagylaiyn kendirim,	Oh, my dear *kendir,*
Senin baskan bir izing tabalbayt.	Can no longer find your footsteps.
Ak jorgo minip duulagan,	You enjoyed life riding on a white trotter, [i.e., white Volga car],
Kendirim kaynim men aytsam,	If I tell about my *kendir,* my *kayni,*[3]
Rais bolup duulagan.	He lived a good life as a *rais.*[4]
Kök alaluu kögüchkön,	Did a bluish pigeon
Köktü bir karay uchtubu?	Fly away toward the blue sky?
Köngülü jakshy kendirim	Did my kind-hearted *kendir*
Jannatka karay syzdyngby?	Fly away toward Heaven?

Kagylaiyn kendirim,	My dear *kendir*,
Jylyng bir senin "kut" bolsun.	"Congratulations" on your one-year memorial feast.
Jannatty karay baskanda	When you walk toward Heaven,
Kagylaiyn kendirim,	My dear *kendir*,
Süylögön sözung jup bolsun.	May your words be intact.
Külüktü minip taptagan,	He rode a race horse and trained him well
Birinchi bolsun külük dep.	So that he would come in first in the race.
Kagylaiyn kendirim,	My dear *kendir*,
Soorunan sylap maktagan.	He praised [his horse] by stroking his hind quarter.
. . . . . .	. . . . . .
Almaluu bakty aralap,	You strolled in the apple garden
Almasyn terip jebeding.	But didn't get to eat its apples.
Ardaktap bakkan baldaryng	You could have enjoyed the respect of your children,
Ubaiyn körüp ölbödüng.	Whom you raised with great love, and then you died.
Aytkan da menen ayla jok,	A profusion of words will not bring you back,
Bu düynödön öttüng sen,	You passed away from this world,
Emi kurandan bashka payda jok.	Nothing helps, except reciting from the Qur'an.

STUDY QUESTIONS

1. What kinds of ritualized behavior are displayed by the individual "actors" in the funerary event?

2. What specific qualities of the lamenter's performance evoke the ritual context of mourning?

3. How does the lamenting affect the listeners? To what extent are they drawn into the ritual action?

4. How do the dress and appearance of the participants reflect the ritual occasion?

5. Rituals always unfold within a circumscribed ritual space. What is the ritual space of the lament? Who is inside the ritual space, and who is outside it?

6. In which ways does the funerary ritual synthesize elements of Islamic and pre-Islamic symbols, beliefs, and practices?

7. Is there something intrinsic to the musical sound that makes it feel sad? Or is the sadness that is evidently being experienced by the participants purely a conventional, learned response to the sound of the lamenter? If you hear "intrinsic sadness," where do you hear it? In which particular kinds of vocal sounds is it embedded, and how would you guess that these sounds act on human listeners?

A yurt erected in a courtyard for a memorial feast.

Men outside a funeral yurt.

Koshok Sung for a Father

The text of the following *koshok* was written down from a Kyrgyz woman named Suusar from the Aksy region of southern Kyrgyzstan. When Suusar's father died, at the age of seventy-four, she sang a *koshok* that represented a synthesis of traditional verse lines and her own improvised lines. She had learned some verse lines from her mother and some from elderly female relatives. The lines she selected from existing traditional lament poetry nicely described the deeds and personality of her father, Süyünaly. In his youth, Süyünaly was a strong horseman and herder who loved playing traditional games on horseback and was also known for his generosity among his kinsmen. He also owned a great deal of livestock and spent his summers in high mountain pastures (*jayloo*s), living in a yurt, and milking mares to make fermented mare's milk (*koumiss*).

Opening lines:

Bysmylda ele sözdün adaly,	Bismillah[5] is the purest of all words,
Ölböy bir adam kalaby.	There is no man who doesn't die.
Ölgönü menen kurusun,	But death is very hard to accept,
Öksütöt eken adamdy.	For it makes one very sad.
Kelme bir sözdün adaly,	Kalima[6] is the purest of all words,
Kemibey adam kalaby.	There is no man who remains alive.
Kemigeni kurusun,	But death is very hard to accept,
Keyitet eken adamdy.	For it makes one sad.

Core: After the opening lines, Suusar proceeds to the main part, lamenting the loss and irreplaceability of her father and describing his life in the mountains, his love of horses and horse games, the fame of his forefathers, and his good deeds and characteristics. Water, sometimes in the form of a lake, often provides a symbolic expression of irreplaceability. Wealth is measured by the quantity of livestock and the quality of a riding horse and yurt. Generosity is described in connection to giving alms to Muslim religious clergy and support of the poor and needy. The choice of metaphors, symbols, and terms of endearment depends on the lamenter's relationship to the deceased. Daughters usually express their love and respect for their father by saying "my dearest father" (*kagylaiyn atakem*), or "my soul-like father" (*jan atam*), "my bazaar" (*bazarym*), or "my garden" (*charbagym*).

Jeti aryktan suu kelse,	Even if seven rivers were to flow together,
Jetkileng köldör tolobu.	They wouldn't be enough to fill the lake.
Jeti bir da jyiyn el kelse,	And even if seven crowds of people gather,
Atakem bir özüngdöy bolobu.	My dear father, they wouldn't be able to fill your place.

Kümüshtön kamchy suy tashtap,	Using a silver-plated whip
Külüktü mingen köch bashtap.	He led the *köch*[7] riding on a galloper.
Altyndan kamchy suy tashtap,	Using a gold-plated whip,
Argymak mingen köch bashtap.	He led the *köch* riding on a stallion.
Chylbyryn salgan bulakka,	He watered his horse from a spring,
Kagylaiyn atakem,	My dear father,
Chyngyryp kirgen ulakka.	Entered the game of *ulak*[8] with great fanfare.
Eshikke ekken gülkaiyr,	He planted hollyhocks in the yard,
Charbagym atam,	My garden-like father,
Eshenge bergen kol kaiyr.	Always gave alms to *ishan*s.[9]
Koroogo ekken gülkaiyr,	He planted hollyhocks in the yard,
Charbagym atam,	My garden-like father,
Kojogo bergen kol kaiyr.	He always gave alms to *khoja*s.[10]
Tündügünön ay ötkön,	The moon shone through his *tündük*,[11]
Bazarym atam,	Oh, my *bazaar* [i.e., generous] father,[12]
Tüpkü atasy bay ötkön.	His forefathers were rich men.
Jabygynan ay ötkön,	The moon shone through his yurt's felt cover,
Bazarym atam,	Oh, my generous father,
Jalpy atasy bay ötkön.	All of his ancestors were rich men.
Koroosun koygo tolturgan,	He filled his corral with sheep,
Koroosunun chetinde	On the side of his corral
Atakem,	My dear father
Kojodoy bolup olturgan.	Sat like a *khoja* [with dignity].
Eshikke koyun tolturgan,	He filled his yard with sheep,
Eshiginin chetinde	On the side of his yard
Atakem,	My dear father
Eshendey bolup olturgan.	Sat like an *ishan* [with dignity].
Küröng bir bee jetelep,	Leading his brown mare to milk,
Atakem,	My dear father
Kyraanga chykkan ertelep.	Headed to the hills early in the morning.
Küröng bir bee kymyzyn	We, your daughters, enjoyed drinking
Kyzdaryng ichken erkelep.	The *koumiss* of your brown mare.
Jeerde bir beeni jetelep,	Leading his chestnut mare to milk,
Jakaga chykkan ertelep.	He headed to the hills early in the morning,
Jeerde bir bee kymyzyn,	Your *jeen*s[13] enjoyed drinking
Jeenderi ichken erkelep.	The *koumiss* of your chestnut mare.

Most often, a lamenter's sad *koshok* is compared to the sad voice of a nightingale or lark. Daughters mention the change in the color of their dress before and after the death of a parent, saying that their bright and colorful silk dress, which they used to wear while their parent was alive, is now replaced by a dark (black or blue) dress, and their laughter with weeping.

Burulushta sayragan,	The voice of a nightingale singing
Bulbuldun ünü mungaiym.	At a bend in the road sounds sad.
Bul düynödön öttüngüz,	You passed away from this world,
Mungduu bir kyldy kudaiym.	God made us sad as well.
Kayrylyshta sayragan,	The voice of a swallow singing
Karlygach ünü mungaiym.	At a bend in the road sounds sad.
Kayran bir közüng ötkön song,	You passed away from this world,
Kaygyluu kyldy kudaiym.	God made us cheerless as well.
Zaar bir tursam shamal jok,	There is no wind when I wake up at dawn,
Kagylaiyn atakem,	Oh, my dearest father,
Sagynyp turam aylam jok.	I miss you in despair. In my grief
Erte bir tursam shamal jok,	There is no wind when I wake up early in the morning,
Kagylaiyn atakem,	Oh, my dearest father,
Ezilip turam aylam jok.	I sob in anguish.
Atakem közü barynda,	When my father was alive,
Külgündön köynök kiychü elem,	I used to wear a colorful dress
Külüp bir oynop jürchü elem,	And laugh a lot and play mirthfully.
Külgündön köynök sögüldü,	After my dear father died,
Atakemdin közü ötüp,	My colorful dress became torn,
Külküm bir jerge tögüldü.	My laughter spilled on the ground.
Atakemdin barynda,	When my dear father was alive,
Shaiydan köynök kiychü elem,	I used to wear a silk dress
Shaani bir menen jürchü elem,	And walk with poise.
Atakemdin közü ötüp,	After my dear father died,
Shaiydan köynök sögüldü,	My silk dress became torn,
Shaanim bir jerge tögüldü.	My poise spilled on the ground.

KOSHOK SUNG BY A DAUGHTER FOR HER DECEASED MOTHER

Traditional *koshok*s sung by daughters for their mothers usually mention the mother's skill in such domains as felt making, quilting, embroidery, cooking, and hospitality, as well as her beauty, respect for her husband's family and kinsmen, and close relationship with her daughter. The following lines mention these good qualities of a mother in beautiful rhythmic poetry characterized by initial and internal alliteration:

Tölbörjün chiyip oydurgan,	She drew the design and made a *törböljün*,[14]
Törünö koyun soydurgan.	She invited guests to sit on the *tör* and killed a sheep in their honor.
Bozpunu közdöy köchköndö,	When moving toward Bozpu[15] [a mountain pasture],
Boz jorgo oozung choydurgan.	She led the *köch*[16] riding on a gray trotter.
Bozpudan uchtu ularym,	My *ular*[17] flew away from Bozpu,
Kagylaiyn enekem,	Oh, my dearest mother,
Bozdop bir yilap turamyn.	I'm left weeping and crying.
Uktabay üch kün koshsom da,	Even if I sing *koshok* for three days without sleeping,
Ukpayt ko emi kulagyng.	You won't hear me.
Altyndan chachpak suy tashtap,	Wearing a golden *chachpak*[18] gracefully,
Argymak mingen köch bashtap.	She led the *köch* riding on an *argymak*.[19]
Kümüshtön chachpak suy tashtap,	Wearing a silver *chachpak* gracefully,
Külük bir mingen köch bashtap.	She led the *köch* riding on a *külük*.[20]
Enekem,	My dear mother
Kyraanga bütkön archaday,	Was like a juniper tree that grew on a mountain ridge,
Kyrk büktölgön barchaday,	And like a *barcha* silk[21] folded forty times.
Beleske bütkön archaday,	She was like a juniper tree that grew on a mountain pass,
Besh büktölgn barchaday.	And like a *barcha* silk folded five times.
Törgö bir kilem tashtagan,	She threw a carpet on the *tör*,
Törödöy uul bashtagan.	And raised a king-like son.
Kapshytka kilem tashtagan	She threw a carpet on the side of the yurt,
Kanyshay kelin bashtagan	And trained a queen-like daughter-in-law.
Enekemdin közü ötüp,	Now that my dear mother passed away,
Tördögü kilem chang boldu,	The carpet on the *tör* became dusty,
Törödöy uul mang boldu.	Her king-like son feels lost.
Kapshytta kilem chang boldu,	The carpet on the side of the yurt became dusty,
Kanyshay kelin mang boldu,	Her queen-like daughter-in-law feels lost.
Sary-Kamysh chyga jaylagan.	She went to Sary-Kamish to summer,
Sarkashka kulun baylagan	And tied a foal with a yellow spot on its forehead [onto a *jele*[22] to make *koumiss*].
Kesege kuygan kymyzym,	You are my *koumiss* poured into a bowl,
Kemibey turgan yrysym.	And my fortune that never ends.
Baytal bir bee bal kymyz	Now, to whom will we offer
Any da kimge sunabyz?	The honey *koumiss* of the *baytal*[23] mare?

Baldan bir shirin sözüngdü	And from whom will we hear,
Enekem,	Dear mother,
Emi bir kimden ugabyz?	Your words as sweet as honey?
Ayagyn juup mis kylgan,	She washed her dishes very clean,
Aylanaiyn enekem,	My dearest mother,
Abysyn köönün kush kylgan.	Pleased her *abysyns*.[24]
Kazanyn juup mis kylgan,	She washed her cauldron very clean,
Kagylaiyn enekem,	My dearest mother,
Kaiyn jurt köönün kush kylgan.	Pleased her *kaiyn jurt*.[25]
Kyzyldan uchuk saptagan,	She used a red thread for a needle,
Kyjymdan töshök kaptagan.	And made sleeping mats from *kyjym*.[26]
Kyzdarym eptüü bolsun dep,	So that her daughters would be skilled,
Kyrgyyek kushtay taptagan.	She trained them like a hawk.

The following lines reveal the close relationship between mother and daughter. In the past, long distances and social and gender restrictions concerning married women kept married daughters from visiting their own parents as often as they wished. When daughters did come home, they were well received and treated with great respect by their family and kinsmen. Mothers were especially happy to see them, and sent them back with nice gifts such as dresses and scarves. The following *koshok* mentions such a special occasion, when a mother shows her love and care for her daughter when the latter visits:

Jaz kelsem jashyl kiygizgen,	She put a green dress on me when I visited her in the spring
Jarygyn ayday tiygizgen.	And shone on me like moonlight.
Küz kelsem külgün kiygizgen,	She put a colorful dress on me when I visited her in autumn
Külpötün kündöy tiygizgen.	And shone on me like the sun.

As the Kyrgyz say, "A mother is a house's fortune" (*Ene-üydün kutu*). This belief makes up one of the popular lines of a traditional *koshok* for a mother and is presented in a poetic combination with the metaphor of a large wooden chest (*sandyk*)—a principal possession that almost every nomadic Kyrgyz family had for storing valuable items.

Ak sandyktun butu eleng,	You were the legs of a white chest,
Ak saray üydün kutu eleng.	And the fortune of a big white yurt.
Enekem közü ötkön song,	After my dear mother died,
Ak sandyktan but ketti,	The legs of the white chest broke,
Ak saray üydön kut ketti.	And the fortune left the big white yurt.

Kök sandyktyn butu eleng,	You were the legs of a blue chest,
Kök saray üydün kutu eleng.	And the fortune of my big gray yurt.
Enekem közü ötkön song,	After my dear mother died,
Kök sandyktan but ketti,	The legs of the big blue chest broke,
Kök saray üydön kut ketti.	And the fortune left the big gray yurt.

Another common metaphor used for a mother is the moon, which in the following lines is combined with the image of a gated city symbolizing comfort and protection. The words for "moon" (*ay*) and "safe haven" (*jay*) also provide a rhyme.

Enekem,	My dear mother
Kashattan chykkan ay ele,	Was the moon rising behind the mountain
Kapkaluu shaar jay ele,	And my safe haven in a gated city.
Enekem közü ötkön song,	Now that my beloved mother passed away,
Kashattan aiym tutuldu,	My moon disappeared behind the mountain,
Kapkaluu shaarym buzuldu.	And my gated city was destroyed.

As a Kyrgyz proverb states, "A poker that stands near the hearth gets burned, a daughter who is closest to the mother burns [cares for her]" (*Otko jakyn shish küyöt, enege jakyn kyz küyöt*). The following lines are sung by daughters for their mothers, whose loss they compare with the moon and sun being covered by a cloud.

Aiymdy bulut chaldyrdym,	A cloud has covered my moon,
Ayarymdy aldyrdym.	I lost the person who sympathized with me.
Künümdü bulut chaldyrdym,	A cloud has covered my sun,
Küyörümdü aldyrdym.	I lost the person who burned [cared] for me.

For a daughter, another common metaphor for losing a mother or father is the loss of a knitting or embroidery needle—an essential tool for a girl in handicraft work:

Saiyp bir koysom iynem jok,	I can't find my needle that I pinned up,
Aylanaiyn enekem,	Oh, my dearest mother,
Sagynyp kelsem üydö jok.	I couldn't find you at home when I came there, missing you.
Ilip bir koysom iynem jok,	I couldn't find my needle that I hung up,
Kagylaiyn enekem,	Oh, my dearest mother,
Izdep bir kelsem üydö jok.	I couldn't find you at home when I came looking for you.

Koshok for a Younger Man

A *koshok* sung for a young married man with children has different content and themes. If a man dies young, leaving his wife and small children behind, his widow sings a *koshok* addressing her husband with the term *jash myrzam,* "my young gentleman," or *arstanym,* "my lion." The widow mentions his horse, yurt, clothes, and personality, and laments the fact that he left this world too early without enjoying life and seeing his children grow up. The widow also expresses how she feels without her husband. Common metaphors are taken from natural surroundings, for example, mountains, hills, stars, the sun, water, ice, birch trees, and animals and birds such as a lion, gray trotter, and white or blue dove.

Kyr-kyrdyn bashyn kün chalat,	The sun shines on hilltops,
Kubargan beebak ün salat,	[I], the pale-faced miserable one sings sadly.
Too-toonun bashyn kün chalat,	The sun shines on mountain tops,
Tomsorgon beebak ün salat.	[I], the unhappy and miserable one sings sadly.
Ak kaiyng tübü bolkuldak,	Like a white birch with loose roots,
Armanda ketting solkuldap.	You died too young.
Kök kaiyng tübü bolkuldak,	Like a green birch with loose roots,
Körünböy ketting solkuldap.	You disappeared too young.
Sazdak bir jerge suu sepsem,	When I sprinkle water on wet ground,
Saymaluu kilem suu bolot.	My embroidered carpet gets wet.
Jash myrzamdy estesem,	When I think of my young gentleman,
Ichken bir ashym uu bolot.	My food tastes like poison [i.e., bitter].
Kumdak bir jer suu sepsem,	When I sprinkle water on sandy ground,
Kurama kilem suu bolot.	My appliqué rug gets wet.
Jash myrzamdy estesem,	When I think of my young gentleman,
Ichken bir chaiym uu bolot.	My tea tastes like poison [i.e., bitter].
Sur jorgo mingen suluu dep,	He rode a dark gray trotter admiring its beauty,
Jash myrzam,	My young gentleman
Sur ichik kiygen jyluu dep.	Wore a dark gray fur coat enjoying its warmth.
Jash myrzam közü öttü ele,	Now that my young gentleman passed away,
Sur jorgo butu tyiyldy,	The legs of the dark gray trotter halted
	[i.e., no one rides him],
Sur ichik jükkö jyiyldy . . .	The dark gray fur coat is put away on the *jük*[27]
	[is no longer worn] . . .
Alty kanat ak üydün,	You dismantled your six-*kanat*[28] yurt
Arkasynan kapshyrdyng.	From its back unexpectedly.
Alpeshtep bakkan baldardyn,	To whom did you leave the lives
Azilin kimge tapshyrdyng?	Of your children whom you raised with great love?
Eshiging aldy mayda tash,	Like small rocks lying in the yard,
Eshikte kaldy mayda bash.	Small heads [children] remain in the yard.

Üyüngdün aldy mayda tash,	Like small rocks lying in front of your yurt,
Üyüngdö kaldy mayda bash.	Small heads remain in the yurt.
Kölökö jerde muz kaldy,	Ice remained unmelted in a shady place,
Kökülün jaykap kyz kaldy.	Your daughter with her flowing forelock remained behind.
Salkyn bir jerde muz kaldy,	Ice remained unmelted in a cool place,
Saamaiyn jaykap kyz kaldy.	Your daughter with her flowing forelock remained behind.

The unfulfilled life of a person is compared to a long road trip or life journey suddenly cut short:

Uzun, uzun, uzun jol,	You wanted to reach the end
Uchuna jetem dechü eleng.	Of a long, long road.
Uulumdun uulun jetelep,	By holding the hand of your son's son,
Ubaiyn köröm dechü eleng.	You hoped to see him grow and prosper.
Kyska, kyska, kyska jol,	You wanted to reach the edge
Kyryna jetem dechü eleng.	Of a short, short road.
Kyzymdyn kyzyn jetelep,	By holding the hand of your daughter's daughter,
Kyzmatyn köröm dechü eleng.	You hoped to see her grow and take care of her grandparents.

The death of a young person is often compared to a bird that's flown away and won't return to its tree:

Tuura bir bütkön butakka,	The merlin won't return and land
Turumtay kelip konalbayt.	On a straight-growing tree branch.
Tuygunday janyng ötkön song,	Once your young soul passes away,
Tuugandar yilap taba albayt.	Your relatives can't find you by crying.
Kayrylyp chykkan butakka,	The hawk won't return and land
Karchyga kelip konalbayt,	On a twisted tree branch.
Kayran bir janyn ötkön song,	Once your noble soul passes away,
Kalgandar yilap tabalbayt.	Those who remain behind can't find you by crying.

When brothers and sisters lose a sibling, they lament, addressing him or her as "my brood mate" (jan uyam), or "my young liver" (jash boorum) or "my only liver" (bir boorum). (The liver was believed to be the seat of a person's vital life force.)

Closing lines: After singing about the good qualities of the deceased, the lamenter acknowledges the inevitable fact that no one can bring the dead back to life. The following expressions have become traditional closing lines in Kyrgyz koshoks, and people use them to console and make peace with themselves. The lamenter wishes the deceased a cool and shady final resting place under a poplar tree, which will protect him or her from the sun. A herd of mares grazing on a green pasture by the bank of a river or lake is a common metaphor for a scene in Heaven. In the final line, the lamenter expresses the Muslim belief that faith in God and reciting the Qur'an for the deceased's spirit is the most righteous response to the death of a loved one:

Saralaluu san jylky,	May a herd of palomino mares
Say boyuna juushasyn.	Graze on the edge of a river.
Sanaasy jakshy atakem,	May my dear, kindhearted father
Salkyn bir jerde uktasyn.	Sleep in a cool place.
Kök alaluu köp jylky,	May a herd of dappled gray mares
Köl boyuna juushasyn.	Graze on the bank of a lake.
Köngülü jumshak atakem,	May my dear, softhearted father
Kölökö jerge uktasyn.	Sleep in a shady place.
Kün tiye turgan jagynga,	May a silvery poplar grow
Kümüshtön terek ornosun.	On the sunny side of your grave.
Kagylaiyn atakem, sizdi,	My dearest father,
Kün tiygizbey korgosun.	May it protect you from the sun.
Ay tiye turgan jagynga,	May a golden poplar grow
Altyn bir terek ornosun.	On the moonlit side of your grave.
Kagylaiyn atakem, sizdi,	My dearest father,
Ay tiygizbey korgosun.	May it protect you from the moon.
Beyishtin törü besh eshik,	May the five doors leading to the *tör* of Heaven
Besh manjang tiybey achylsyn.	Open before your five fingers touch them.
Beyishtegi kyzyl gül,	May the red flowers in Heaven
Beshenenge chachylsyn.	Shower on your forehead as you enter.
Emi yilagan menen arga jok,	Much crying does not help,
Kurandan bashka payda jok.	Other than reciting the Qur'an, there is nothing to be done.

KOSHOK SUNG AT THE GRAVE

As in other Muslim cultures, women do not participate in the burial part of a funeral, but visit the grave before sunrise on the day after burial. Kyrgyz cemeteries are typically in elevated places—usually on a hilltop or mountain slope. As they approach the grave, close relatives become emotional and begin crying aloud. Reaching the grave, they sit close to it and sing a *koshok.* After they stop crying and singing a *koshok,* one of them recites from the Qur'an.

Ak kyiadan chykkanda,	When I come to the white hill,
Ak turpagyng körünör.	I see your grave with a white mound.
Atakem seni estesem,	My dear father, when I think of you,
Alkymdan jashym tögülör.	I choke up with tears.
Kök kyiadan chykkanda,	When I come to the green hill,
Kök turpagyng körünör.	I see your grave with a green mound.
Atakem seni estesem,	My dear father, when I think of you,
Közümdön jashym tögülör.	Tears flow from my eyes.
Bozorgon toonun boorunda,	I see gray larks grazing separately
Boz torgoy ottoyt birikpey.	On a gray mountain slope.
Boz topurak aldynda,	How can you lie alone
Kantip bir jattyng zerikpey.	Underneath the gray soil?
Karaygan toonun boorunda,	I see crows grazing separately
Kargalar ottoyt birikpey.	On a black mountain slope.
Kara bir jerdin aldynda,	How can you lie alone
Kantip bir jattyng zerikpey.	Underneath the black soil?
Kaygy-mung bashka saldyngby,	You put me in deep sorrow and sadness,
Kagylaiyn enekem,	My dear mother,
Kayrylbas jakka bardyngby,	You left for a place from where no one returns,
Syzdatyp tuugan uruktu,	By leaving your kinsmen in grief behind,
Syz jerge jatyp aldyngby,	You went to lie in a damp place.
Tüngültüp uul-kyzyngdy,	By making your sons and daughters lose their hope,
Tübölük uktap kaldyngby.	Did you go to eternal sleep?

Koshok for Chingiz Aitmatov (1928–2008), Renowned Kyrgyz Writer

While it is mainly ordinary Kyrgyz women who preserve the tradition of singing *koshok,* it is male *aqyn*s—oral poets who compose spontaneous rhythmic poetry—and sometimes also female singers who compose and sing *koshok*s when grieving the loss of a well-known public figure, poet, or writer at public gatherings, or on television and radio. The renowned Kyrgyz writer Chingiz Aitmatov died in the summer of 2008, while his country was celebrating his eightieth birthday in the "Year of Chingiz Aitmatov." In Kyrgyzstan, June fourteenth was declared an official mourning day. Aitmatov's state funeral ceremony was held at the Kyrgyz National Philharmonic Hall in Bishkek. The highlight of the public funeral and mourning was the performance of two *koshok*s composed and sung by two Kyrgyz *aqyn*s, Zamirbek Üsönbayev (b. 1952) and Elmirbek Imanaliev (b. 1978). They composed their *koshok*s in traditional poetic form and musical style, but unlike

Elmirbek Imanaliev.
Courtesy of Elmirbek Imanaliev.

Chingiz Aitmatov.
Photo by Janarbek Amankulov for the
Chingiz Aitmatov Foundation.

female lamenters, they accompanied themselves on the *komuz,* as is traditional for male *aqyn*s. The melody of Elmirbek's *koshok* was close to the traditional melody of laments sung by women, with one exception: Elmirbek did not add cry-like sounds at the end of each couplet. The two *koshok*s were aired on Kyrgyz national television and radio for several days and played over and over during the official farewell ceremony. Like many other Kyrgyz oral poets, Elmirbek is also known as a songwriter. However, he surpasses all other contemporary *aqyn*s when it comes to singing a funerary *koshok* or *joktoo,* for he has a pleasant voice, beautiful *koshok* melody, and a very attractive performance style.

Example 12.2. "Chyngyz ölbös bolsochu" (If only Chingiz were immortal), composed and performed by Elmirbek Imanaliev. Film footage compiled by Aytysh Film Co., Bishkek, Kyrgyzstan.

WATCH

This eleven-minute video tribute to Chingiz Aitmatov features Elmirbek Imanaliev's *koshok* "Chyngyz ölbös bolsochu" (If only Chingiz were immortal) as the soundtrack. The video was prepared by the Aytysh film company in Bishkek immediately after Aitmatov's death—it is a Kyrgyz custom to sing *koshok* before the deceased is buried. Visuals in the clip represent a compilation of short excerpts from documentary films about Aitmatov and excerpts from movies based on his literary works.

The text of the *koshok* is partially transliterated and translated on the companion website (0:00–6:00, and 9:50–end). The entire text is subtitled in English in the video.

Note that Elmirbek uses the hero Manas and his death as the main theme of his *koshok*. The lines "Many people in the world mourn your death, even the sky and the earth" are appropriated from the famous lines in the epic *Manas:* "When the hero Manas died, all peoples wept, even the fir trees and poplar trees wept."

Büsaadat Satybaldieva, Sary-Mogol village, Alay region, Osh province, 2013.

STUDY QUESTIONS

1. How would you compare the content and melody of Chingiz Aitmatov's *koshok* with the traditional *koshok* sung by women? Does Elmirbek's *koshok* sound sad? What difference does the *komuz* accompaniment of the song make in the ritual's presentation?

2. Are the metaphors and symbols in the Aitmatov *koshok* different from (or similar to) those of the traditional *koshoks*?

3. How would you compare the Kyrgyz funeral ritual depicted in the video excerpt to funeral events you have personally witnessed in your own family, or in your own community? Which elements are similar, and which elements are different?

As the textual and socio-cultural analyses of Kyrgyz *koshok*s show, nomadic Kyrgyz lived in harmony with the natural world. Most of the themes, symbols, and metaphors used in traditional *koshok*s are drawn from nature (mountains, rivers, trees, animals, birds), the cosmos (sky, sun, moon, stars), and essential attributes and patterns of nomadic life and culture (seasonal movements, yurts, horses, sheep, fermented mare's milk, hospitality, handicraft, wooden chests, warm clothes, silk, gold, and silver). In the past, almost every mature Kyrgyz woman knew what kind of *koshok*s would be fitting to the deceased's gender, age, occupation, and personality, as well as her family and kinship relationship to the deceased. Younger women learned from older, experienced women who taught them "on-site" what to say in their *koshok*. In most cases, women used ready-made formulaic verse lines from a general pool of existing traditional *koshok*s that were appropriate for any death. For funerals of well-known personalities that involved a large number of people, a professional male or female *koshokchu* was invited to compose a new, individualized *koshok* glorying the deceased's life and deeds.

The author interviews Burulay Talasbaeva, Ak-Suu village, Aksy region, Jalal-Abad province, 2011.

In present-day Kyrgyzstan, the metaphors and symbols of traditional *koshok*s are a poor fit for the agrarian world of farmers and the urban lifestyle of businessmen, merchants, teachers, artists, and so on. Contemporary Kyrgyz, especially those living in cities and towns, have distanced themselves from the natural world, and no longer enjoy the daily contact with birds and animals that pervade the texts of old *koshok*s. And these days, few people can compose or improvise their own funerary *koshok*. Despite these changes, however, the singing of *koshok,* even if done symbolically, is still an obligatory ritual for women at a funeral and at subsequent memorial feasts. The tradition is most prevalent in rural areas, where it is also condemned by orthodox Muslim clergy who discourage women from singing *koshok* on the grounds that it violates shariʻa law. It is difficult to predict the future of this ancient and important ritual, believed to be the source of Kyrgyz oral epic songs. But where there is death, there will always be grief and lament, and the ritual of singing *koshok* may well remain a broadly used and effective palliative that brings consolation and solace.

The author transcribes a funeral *koshok* from Meyilkan Myrzabaeva, Kyzyl-Jar village, Aksy region, Jalal-Abad province, 2013.

NOTES

1. Margaret Alexiou, *The Ritual Lament in Greek Tradition* (Cambridge: Cambridge University Press, 1974), 73.

2. *Kendir:* a sturdy rope made from a special type of cotton used for tying a horse. Traditionally, the word is used by a sister-in-law (*jenge*) as a term of endearment for a younger brother of her husband (*kayni*).

3. *Kayni:* a term used by sisters-in-law toward their husband's younger brothers.

4. *Rais:* an Uzbek term for the chief executive of an administrative district.

The author transcribes a funeral *koshok* from Jumakan Döölötbakova, Ak-Terek village, Jeti-Ögüz region, Issyk-Kul province, 2013.

5. "In the name of Allah, the Almighty!" Like all Muslims, Kyrgyz use this expression before beginning to do something, especially before eating.

6. *Kalima shahada:* the first pillar of Islam, the declaration of faith: "I declare that there is no deity but Allah and that Muhammad is His Prophet."

7. *Köch:* a Turkic word for a seasonal nomadic movement of Kyrgyz and Kazakhs from one pasture to another.

8. *Ulak* (goat): The Kyrgyz name for a traditional men's game widely played among nomadic peoples of Central Asia, also known as *kök börü* (gray wolf), as well as in Afghanistan (where it is known as *boz kashi*), in which a group of horsemen try to capture a stuffed goat or calf carcass from one another and carry it across a designated line.

9. *Ishan:* a wandering Sufi.

10. *Khoja:* a Muslim religious teacher.

11. *Tündük:* a round wooden structure at the top of the yurt that allows light to enter and vents smoke.

12. *Bazaar* is used in Kyrgyz to connote endearment, symbolizing wealth, generosity, prosperity, and bounty.

13. *Jeen:* a Turkic kinship term referring to the children of one's daughters and other female relatives.

14. *Törböljün* (Mongolian): another name for *shyrdak,* a colorful appliqué felt carpet.

15. *Bozpu:* the name of a mountain and pasture in the Aksy region of southern Kyrgyzstan.

16. *Köch:* see n. 7. People looked forward to this special event, and women wore their best clothes and rode trotters. The oldest woman in the family led the *köch.*

17. *Ular:* a small wild turkey that lives in high mountains. It has a beautiful singing voice, and its meat is delicious and considered nutritious.

18. *Chachpak:* silver decoration attached to the tips of married women's two braids.

19. *Argymak:* a pure breed of horse.

20. *Külük:* a race horse.

21. *Barcha* designates a valuable kind of sparkly silk textile.

22. *Jele:* a strong, thick rope stretched on the ground and secured on both ends to two sticks. It is used to tie foals when mares are being milked to make *koumiss* in summertime.

23. *Baytal:* a mare that has given birth to a foal.

24. *Abysyn*s: wives of brothers or men within the same clan.

25. *Kaiyn jurt:* a term that refers to the family and kinsmen of a woman's husband, whereas *törkün* is a term for her own family and kinsmen.

26. *Kyjym:* a thick and valuable fabric that comes in various bright colors. Kyrgyz use it for making sleeping mats, blankets, and clothes such as vests and coats.

27. *Jük:* folded-up sleeping mats, blankets, and pillows placed on a large chest, which is located on the *tör,* opposite the yurt's entrance.

28. *Kanat:* a collapsible side wing or frame of a yurt. A medium-sized yurt has six side wings, whereas a large yurt has twelve side frames.

CHAPTER 13   Kyrgyz Wedding Songs

ELMIRA KÖCHÜMKULOVA

In the past, the ritual singing of *koshok,* farewell songs for a bride who is about to leave her home to be married, was an essential part of the wedding tradition of the nomadic Kyrgyz. This old ritual of *koshok* singing was practiced up until the second half of the twentieth century and later largely forgotten as the Kyrgyz adopted a sedentary lifestyle and modern Russian-Soviet marriage practices. The tradition described here is essentially one from the past. In the post-Soviet period, however, some Kyrgyz families and communities in rural areas have attempted to revive the practice of *koshok* singing. This chapter discusses the past and current sociocultural context and significance, poetic structure, themes, melody, and performance style of bridal *koshok (kyz uzatkandagy koshok).*[1] The bridal *koshok* texts used in this chapter were recorded from elderly Kyrgyz women in the Aksy and Alay regions of southern Kyrgyzstan during my fieldwork in 2011 and 2013.

In its poetic composition, melody, and themes, a bridal *koshok* shares many similarities with the funerary lament (*koshok* or *joktoo*). Both types of *koshok* present praise of the departed and departing person. Both employ metaphors drawn from nature, such as animals and birds, and from the essential tools and values of nomadic life and culture. The two kinds of *koshok* also share a sad melodic affect that involves crying, and a common poetic structure consisting of seven or eight syllables in each verse line that follow strict initial and internal alliteration and end rhyme. While in the funerary *koshok* it is the lamenter who sings and cries, it is the bride who cries when a bridal *koshok* is sung to her. The major connecting themes in the two kinds of *koshok* are the theme of departure from one place to another and the expression of farewell words by close family members. While the funerary *koshok* is sung for a deceased person who has left this world permanently, the bridal *koshok* is sung for a girl who is leaving her own home in order to live at her husband's home permanently.

Elmira Köchümkulova leaves her parents' house on horseback, after her husband arrived on horseback with his parents and relatives to fetch her, 1999.

Sociocultural Context

As in many other cultures, marriage in Kyrgyz nomadic culture represented a major turning point in a girl's life, and the singing of *koshok* served as an important ritual to mark that change. It also signaled a girl's separation from her parents and relatives and signified her social transformation from girl to woman or wife (*ayal/katyn*) or daughter-in-law (*kelin*). Sooner or later she would marry and leave her home—thus the popular Kyrgyz proverb, "A daughter is a guest in her own house" (*Kyz-konok*), and the girl's treatment by her family and kinsmen with respect and kindness. In the past, Kyrgyz women married at an early age, and mothers prepared their daughters for marriage by teaching them essential domestic skills such as cooking, milking, embroidering, and felt-making as well as good manners of the sort expected from a daughter-in-law and wife (*ayal*). Through the *koshok* singing ritual, girls were counseled by their mother or grandmother, older sisters, sisters-in-law, and aunts before leaving their parents' home on how to be a good wife and daughter-in-law, and on how to deal with domestic issues. *Koshok* served as a way for older women to express their love and sense of caring for a bride-to-be and their feeling of sadness at her departure, while providing a ritualized way to tell the groom and in-laws to take good care of her.

In clan-based Kyrgyz society, marriage within one's own clan (*uruk*) was and is still prohibited or strongly discouraged up to seven degrees of consanguinity.[2] Marriage between first cousins, which is widely practiced in some Muslim cultures, including Uzbek and Tajik, is nonexistent among the Kyrgyz. Most girls married men from other clans that lived in different mountain villages. After marriage, a girl was considered a member of her husband's family, but kept her own clan identity. In the past, due to the long distance between their parents' and husband's village, married women could not visit their own family as often as they wished. Sending a daughter away to another family from a different clan that lived in a faraway village was a very sad occasion for the parents and relatives.

The singing of *koshok* was the highlight of a Kyrgyz traditional wedding and was done exclusively by women inside the yurt when it was time for the bride to leave with her groom and his parents, who had come to fetch her. Like the funerary *koshok,* the bridal *koshok* song also has a mini-plot with a clear structure consisting of opening lines, core, and ending, and each of these sections is expressed with traditional poetic metaphors and themes.

POETIC STRUCTURE

Terms of address and endearment: As in the funerary *koshok*, special terms of address and endearment are widely used towards the bride. A mother usually addresses her daughter with words such as *ynagym* (my closest one), *chyragym* (my lantern/light), *jan balam* (my soul child). The bride's sister-in-law (*jenge*) addresses her with *biykech*, a term used for a young unmarried woman, and *kyzyke*, a respectful term of endearment used by a sister-in-law (*jenge*) towards the younger sister of her husband (*kaiyn singdi*).

Opening lines: A traditional bridal *koshok* begins with one or two of the following opening lines, which say that raising a daughter and marrying her off is the duty of parents as well as a Kyrgyz custom.

Kyz östürgön ata eken,	It is the father who raises a daughter.
Kyz kögörtkön bata eken.	It is the blessing that makes a girl happy in marriage.
Kyngshylatyp kyz bergen,	Marrying a girl off by making her cry
Kylymdan kalgan salt eken.	Is the custom left from past centuries.
Kyzyldy kiymek kymbat ish,	Wearing a red [dress] shows affluence
Kyzdy da bermek urmat ish.	Marrying off a girl is noble work.
Jashyldy kiymek kymbat ish,	Wearing a green [dress] shows affluence
Jashty da bermek urmat ish.	Marrying off a young [girl] is noble work.
Uluu bir toonun booruna,	The wild turkey came flying and landed
Ular kush kelip konuptur.	On the side of a mighty mountain.
Uluu bir kichüü birigip,	The young and old people came and
Biykechti ele bermek boluptur.	Decided to marry off the maiden.
Kulaaly degen shakta bar,	The buzzard resides on branches,
Kudalashkan narkta bar.	Becoming in-laws is our tradition.
Kyrgyek degen shakta bar,	The little hawk resides on branches,
Kyzdy da bermek narkta bar.	Marrying a girl off is our tradition.

CORE THEMES

The bride's dowry (*sep*) is another important theme of a bridal *koshok*, reflecting the importance of the dowry in Central Asian wedding customs. Among the nomadic Kyrgyz and Kazakhs, the quantity and quality of the bride's dowry usually depended on the amount of bride price (*kalyng*) paid by the groom's parents. However, parents always tried to give more to show their love and care for their daughter as well as to demonstrate the family's wealth. Among the Kyrgyz, wealthy parents gave a dowry in the form of nine sets (*syira*) of each item—for example nine felt carpets (*kiyiz*), nine colorful appliqué carpets (*shyrdak*), nine large blankets (*juurkan*), nine sleep-on mats (*töshök*), and nine sets of pillows (*jazdyk*). A traditional dowry also included two large wooden chests (*sandyk*) for storing valuables, kitchenware, and sets of clothes for the bride and the groom. In other words, the groom's parents provided the yurt, and the bride's parents furnished it with a dowry, which also included the interior and exterior decoration of the yurt. In the following *koshok*, the mother sings about how much of a dowry she is giving to her daughter and why:

Üzügüm boosu jibekten,	My *üzük*'s[3] strings are made from silk,
Uchurdum kyzym tünöktön.	I let my daughter fly away from her home.
Japsarym boosu jibekten,	My *japsar*'s[4] strings are made from silk,
Jönöttüm kyzym tünöktön.	I sent my daughter off from her home.
Kerege boyu sep berdim,	I gave her a dowry reaching the height of *kerege*,[5]
Kyzym	So that my daughter doesn't feel miserable
Keyibey jürsün dep berdim.	[there].
Kara nar jüktöp sep berdim,	I gave her the dowry by loading it onto a black camel,
Kyzym	So that my daughter doesn't feel sad
Kaygyrbay jürsün dep berdim.	[there].

The relationship between mother and daughter is another popular subject of bridal *koshok*. In the following lines a mother expresses her love and affection for her daughter by comparing her to sweet, beautiful, and valuable things in her life, and describes how sharing their secrets and clothes helped them feel close to one another.

Süt üstündö kaymagym,	You're my cream on top of the milk,
Jük üstündö aynegim.	You're my mirror on the *jük*.[6]
Oozumdagy sherbetim,	You're my sherbet in my mouth,
Jakamdagy bermetim.[7]	You're my pearl on my collar.
Bosogogo tülkü ilgenim,	You're my fox fur hanging on the doorjamb,
Bozorgonum bilgenim.	You're one who knows when I feel sad.
Keregege tülkü ilgenim,	You're my fox fur hanging on the *kerege*,
Keyigenim bilgenim.	You're the one who feels when I'm troubled.

As in the funerary *koshok*s, bridal *koshok*s also employ many metaphors about animals and birds. A girl's departure from her home is compared to wild ducks and geese leaving their lake:

Jetimish ördök, jeti kaz,	By shooting with arrows,
Jebelep köldön uchurduk.	We made seventy ducks and seven geese fly away.
Jetkileng baydyn balasy,	We made you move [to the home] of your partner,
Tengtushuna köchürdük.	Who is the son of a wealthy man.
Altymysh ördök, alty kaz,	By scaring them off,
Aydap köldön uchurduk.	We made the sixty ducks and six geese fly away.
Aytyluu baydyn balasy,	We made you move [to the home] of your husband,
Alganyna köchürdük.[8]	Who is a well-known rich man.

Another key theme is the change in a girl's status and identity from girl to married woman. The *koshok* song mentions the hairstyle and type of headdress that a girl wears before and after marriage. In the past, teenage girls wore their hair in multiple braids (*besh kökül* and *kyrk chach*) and a cap with the feather of an owl, parrot, or crane on top to protect them from evil eyes and spirits. After marrying, they wore their hair in only two braids down their back with silver jewelry and a scarf or *elechek* (also called *ileki*), a large, turban-like headdress made from white cloth. The following verse lines have become a formulaic expression of a girl's changed status and identity upon marriage:

Karkyra saiyp kyz kyldyk,	We raised you as a girl by putting a crane's feather on your cap,
Jooluk salyp jat kyldyk.	Now, we're estranging you from us by putting a scarf on your head.
Totu saiyp kyz kyldyk,	We raised you as a girl by putting a parrot feather on your cap,
Ileki salyp jat kyldyk.	Now, we're estranging you from us by putting an *ileki* on your head.
Totunun jünün kayrydyk,	We took the parrot's feather off [your head]
Torko ileki buyruduk.	And put on an *ileki* made from *torko* silk.
Karkyrasyn kayrydyk,	We took the crane feather off [your head]
Kazy ileki buyruduk.	And put a big *elechek* on you.
Karkyra senden jat bolsun,	May the crane feather be estranged from you,
Kazy ileki kut bolsun.	May your goose feather be blessed!
Totu senden jat bolsun,	May the parrot feather be estranged from you,
Torko ileki kut bolsun.[9]	May your silk *ileki* be blessed!

The bride's sister-in-law also mentions that the girl lived a happy and carefree life, which is described by pointing out her laughter, and the fine quality and color of her clothes:

Jay kiygening kulp ele.	In the summer, you wore a colorful dress,
Kysh kiygening tülkü ele.	In the winter, you wore a coat with a fox fur collar.
Oturgan jering kyz biykem,	The places where you sat, my dear maiden
Oyun menen külkü ele.	Were filled with fun and laughter.
Oyun, külkü tyiylar,	Now, the fun and laughter will stop,
Kojo-moldo jyiylar,	Khojas and mullahs will gather and
Kokustan nike kyiylar.[10]	Perform the nikah ceremony.

Praise for the girl's family and kinsmen to raise her value and social status is another important subject of *koshok* songs. For reasons of modesty, praising is usually done by a girl's sister-in-law or distant female relative, or by a professional *koshokchu* who is not closely related to the girl's family:

Et jibekten kanjygang,	Your *kanjyga*,[11] which is made from pure silk,
Engilip atka jarashkan.	Looks very good on your horse.
Enesi narktar kishi dep,	People from two different tribes competed to marry you
Eki uruu elder talashkan.	Knowing that your mother is wise and respected [by people].
Ak kurjun tolo ak mata,	Like a white saddlebag filled with white fabrics,
Kyzykenin,	Our girl's
Aga-inisi baybacha.	Older and younger brothers are rich men.
Kök kurjun tolo kök mata,	Like a blue saddlebag filled with blue fabrics,
Kyzykenin,	Our girl's
Köp inisi baybacha.	Younger brothers are rich men.
Chong atang eldin ulugu,	Your grandfather is the people's leader.
Öz atang suunun tunugu.	Your father is the purest of water.
Abalaryng men aytsam,	If I'm to talk about your uncles,
Altyndan kylgan kupaday,	They're like a horse harness plated with gold and
Ala barchyn shumkarday.	Young freckled falcons.

Another theme is comforting the girl: the mother comforts her daughter by saying that she will be going to a beautiful place and to a family of dignity and tradition:

Üstü takta aldy tash,	You will go to a nice house which has
Barktuu jerge barasyng.	A wooden roof and stone flooring.
Jazynda gülü tögülgön,	You will go to a place which has
Baktuu jerge barasyng.	A flower garden blooming in spring.
Uul üylöp, kyz bergen,	You will go to a respected family
Narktuu jerge barasyng.	That values the marriage tradition.

Another popular theme is that of good versus bad husband. Women warn a girl about what it is like to live with a good husband and a bad husband, and how a good or bad marriage relationship affects her health and well-being. While a husband's love and care for his wife is associated with the wife's wearing of silver earrings (*söykö*) or golden and silver hair decorations (*chachbak*), his mistreatment of his wife is compared to tarnished earrings and the newlywed bride losing her mind.

Alganyng jakshy bolso da,	If the man whom you married is good,
Altyndan chachbak süyrötor,	He will let you wear golden *chachbak* on your braids,
Ayda ele akyl üyrötör.	He will teach you wisdom every month.
Alganyng jakshy bolboso,	If the man whom you married is not good,
Altyndan chachbak chang basat,	Your golden *chachbak* will get dusty,
Ayda akylyng mang basat	You will lose your mind as months pass.
Küyööng jakshy bolsa da,	If your husband is good,
Kümushtön chachbak süyrötör,	He will let you wear silver *chachbak* on your braids,
Kündö ele akyl üyrötör.	He will teach you wisdom every day.
Küyööng jakshy bolboso,	If your husband is not good,
Kümüshtön chachbak chang basat,	Your silver *chachbak* will get dusty,
Kündö akylyng mang basat.	You will lose your mind as days pass.

The theme of advice: Women also give a girl advice on domestic issues and tell her to respect her husband and in-laws, to be nice and respectful, not to get angry, and to take things easy:

Kamyshtan tutkan chiy eken,	Do not step onto the reed mat
Kairyp any baspay jür.	Covering the side walls of the yurt.
Kaynatang saga süylösö,	Do not talk back to your father-in-law
Kayasha sözdü aytpay jür.	When he tells you something.
Kara sakal körünsö,	When you see a man with a black beard,
Kaynagang bolot jaskay jür.	Know that he is your *kaynaga* and show respect to him.[12]
Kayneneng katuu süylösö,	When your mother-in-law scolds you,
Kayrylyp beri kachpay jür.	Do not run away to your [parents' house].
Jelbir-jelbir ot küysö,	If there is a flame,
Eteging menen öchürgün.	Snuff it out with the hem of your dress.
Jaman-jakshy kep uksang,	If you receive criticism,
Külküng menen kechirgin.	Forgive it with your laughter.

Engiltip kamchy saldyrba,	Don't let [your husband] hit you with a horsewhip,
Enenge naalat ayttyrba.	And bring a curse to your mother.
Artyltyp kamchy saldyrba,	Don't let [your husband] hit you with a horsewhip,
Atanga naalat ayttyrba.	And bring a curse to your father.

Finally, after all their advice and messages to a girl, women offer their blessings and wishes. Popular wishes include having a baby in a golden or silver cradle.

Atyndan beshik yrgap öt,	May you rock a golden cradle
Alganyng menen jyrgap öt.	And lead a happy life with your partner.
Kümüshtön beshik yrgap öt,	May you rock a silver cradle
Küyööng menen jyrgap öt.	And lead a happy life with your husband.

Wishes and blessings usually draw on animal metaphors such as a horse (or snake), wild rabbit, deer, or partridge, and the idea of a happy marriage is compared to the shedding of these animals' hair, feathers, or skin. The various names of mountain landscapes—for example, *jylga, koktu, buyga,* and *keri,*[13] where these animals shed—is a clear reflection of the mountain environment in which the nomadic Kyrgyz lived. These words are used quite masterfully and carefully chosen for their alliteration:

Jylgaga jylkynyn jünü chachylsyn,	May the horse's hair fall around a spring-fed pool,
Jylmyshpay baktyng achylsyn.	May you have a happy and smooth life.
Koktuga koyondun tügü chachylsyn,	May the rabbit's hair fall to the bottom of a mountain slope,
Kyzykem, bargan jeringden	My dear girl,
Kozgolboy bagyng achylsyn.	May you find happiness in your new home.
Buygaga bugunun jünü chachylsyn,	May the deer's hair fall in a ravine,
Kyzykem bargan jeringden,	My dear girl,
Bukarday bagyng achylsyn.	May your life be as bountiful as in Bukhara.
Kerige kekilik jünü chachylsyn,	May the partridge's hair fall on the mountain slope,
Keridey baktyng achylsyn.	May you find happiness as big as a mountainside.

After these blessings to the bride, the bride's mother usually tells her daughter's mother-in-law, whom she addresses using the traditional term *kudagyi,* that she should take good care of her daughter, as the girl is still young and grew up being carefree in a good and loving family. This message is expressed indirectly with a metaphor comparing the girl to a palomino or white horse (*sary at/kök at*), a piece of sewing thread (*uchuk*), and an untrained falcon (*shumkar*) to be used for hunting.

Kudagyi,	*Kudagyi,*
Sary atka tumar tagyp al,	Hang a protective charm on this palomino horse,
Salkyn bir jerge bagyp al.	And take good care of her in a cool place.
Salkyn jerge bakpasang,	If you don't take care of her in a cool place,
Sanatyluu malyngdy al.	Take your numerous livestock back [which were given as bride price].
Kök atka tumar tagyp al,	Hang a protective charm on this white horse,
Kudagyi,	*Kudagyi,*
Kölökö jerge bagyp al,	And take good care of her in a shady place.
Kölökö jerge bakpasang,	If you don't take care of her in a shady place,
Köpkö tüshüp malyngdy al.	Take your many livestock back.
Kudagyi,	*Kudagyi,*
Ak uchuk berdim saptap al,	I'm giving you a white piece of thread, Please put it through the needle yourself.
Ak shumkar berdim taptap al.	I'm giving you a white falcon, Please train her well yourself.
Kudagyi,	*Kudagyi,*
Kök uchuk berdim saptap al,	I'm giving you a blue piece of thread, Please put it through the needle yourself.
Kök shumkar berdim taptap al.	I'm giving you a gray falcon, Please train it well yourself.

In some cases, the bride's sister-in-law, who usually mediates between the bride and the groom and accompanies the bride to her husband's house, turns to the groom and tells him to treat her well:

Kaptalga atyn tushasyn,	Let him hobble his horse on the mountain side and
Kapshytka kelip tyngshasyn.	Come and stand outside the yurt and listen attentively to my words.
Kan küyöögö aytkyla,	Tell the groom, the khan
Kan kyzynday jumshasyn.	He should treat her like the daughter of a khan.
Beleske atyn tushasyn,	Let him hobble his horse on the spur of the mountain and

Berireek kelip tyngshasyn.	Come and stand close to the yurt and listen attentively to my words.
Bek küyöögö aytkyla,	Tell the groom, the *bek*[14] that he
Bek kyzynday jumshasyn.	Should treat her like the daughter of a *bek.*

WATCH **Example 13.1.** Bridal *koshok* performed by Kynatai Tashybekova at author Elmira Köchümkulova's wedding, which took place in 1999 in her home in Aksy District of Jalal-Abad Province, southern Kyrgyzstan.

New bride Elmira Köchümkulova sits behind a bridal curtain inside the wedding yurt erected at her husband's house.

According to tradition, the first part of the wedding feast (*toy*) took place in Elmira's home, where her parents organized a big feast by slaughtering a horse and inviting all close and distant relatives and neighbors. The groom and his friends, sisters-in-law, and parents arrived with special gifts (*kiyit,* sets of clothes) to be given to the bride and her parents, grandparents, siblings, and other close relatives. Below is Elmira's own description of the *koshok* singing ritual:

"At my wedding, when it was time for me to leave my parents' house, the groom and his best men, who were sitting with me inside the yurt that had been specially erected in the courtyard of the house, were asked to go outside. The big tablecloth (*dastorkon*) filled with all kinds of food spread in front of us on the floor was put away. All my female relatives, including my grandmother, great-aunts, sisters-in-law, and young cousins, as well as my mother-in-law, came into the yurt. I remained in my seat (*tör*) opposite the entrance, with my dowry folded up behind me on the two big chests. Someone handed me a handkerchief to wipe my tears, because they knew that the bride is expected to cry when a *koshok* is sung to her. I became nervous looking at all the women and children who eagerly waited to hear this long-forgotten ritual. The felt coverings of the yurt were folded up so that those who did not fit in the yurt could watch and listen. I could see people staring through the yurt's frame. We waited for my elderly female relatives who were supposed to perform this ritual. Finally, the four women came into the yurt, their heads adorned with the traditional white headdress worn by elderly women. All of this was being videotaped by my cousin. As a good lamenter (*koshokchu*), my great-aunt Kynatai was given the honor of starting the *koshok.* One of my sisters-in-law made her a comfortable seat by folding one of the traditional mattresses. Aunt Kynatai sat herself in front of me with a handkerchief in her hand to wipe her own tears and began her *koshok* in a sad melody."

Kulaaly degen shakta bar,	The buzzard resides on branches,
Kuda da bolmok narkta bar.	Becoming in-laws is our tradition.
Kyrgyiek degen shakta bar,	The little hawk resides on branches,
Kyzdy da bermek saltta bar.	Marrying a girl off is our tradition.
Ukuruk tiybes kachagan,	Now, you're like a horse that can't be caught with a lasso,
Urugung bashka jasagan.	You're destined to go to another clan.
Kamchy da tiybes kachagan,	Now, you're like a horse that a whip cannot reach,
Kalkyngdy bashka jasagan.	You're destined to go to other people.
Kanatyn kakpay jem jegen,	Is there a bird like the hawk,
Karchygaday kush kayda?	Which eats grain without flapping its wings?
Akyly menen til bilgen,	Is there a maiden like Elmira,
Elmiraday ele kyz kayda?	Who is wise and who knows the language [i.e., English]?
Tumshugun kakpay jem jegen,	Is there a bird like the falcon,
Turumtayday ele kush kayda?	Which eats grain without making its beak messy?
Chet elge baryp til bilgen,	Is there a maiden like Elmira,
Elmiraday ele kyz kayda?	Who studied abroad and learned the foreign language?
Ak kagazdy eey karalap,	You have traveled in a foreign land,
Chet elde gana jürdüng aralap.	By writing on a white paper.
Jazgan kagazyngda kata jok	There is no error in her writing, and
Singdim Aychüröktön kemi jok.	My sister is as beautiful as Aychürök.[15]
Boz torgoy eleng bierde,	You were a gray skylark in your house,
Bolup da berdik tiyerge.	Now we're giving you away to them.
Kashkaldak eleng biyerde,	You were a bald-coot in your home,
Kaalap da berdik tiyerge.	Now we're voluntarily giving you away.
Chong atangdy men aytsam,	If I'm to talk about your grandfather,
Chong atang eldin ulugu.	Your grandfather was a great man,
Öz atang suudun tunugu.	Your own father is the purest of water.
Altyndan kylgan kupaday,	If I'm to talk about your uncles,
Abalaryng men aytsam,	They're like a horse harness plated with gold,
Ala barchyn shumkarday.	They're like eagles turning into hunting birds.
Kümüshtön kylgan kupaday,	If I'm to talk about your uncles,
Abalaryng men aytsam,	They're like a horse harness plated with silver,

Newlyweds Elmira Köchümkulova and Sovetaly Aitkul uulu.

Kök ala tuygun shumkarday.	They're like grayish grouses and gyrfalcons.
Suu tübündö sülüktöy,	If I'm to talk about your brothers,
Akelering men aytsam,	They're like leeches under the water,
Suurulup chykkan külüktöy.	They're like stallions running ahead of the herd,
Köl tübündö sülüktöy,	They are like leeches under the lake.
Akelering men aytsam,	If I'm to talk about your brothers,
Körnöödö chykkan külüktöy.	They are like racing horses that win the race.
Kunduzday kara chachynga,	Your black hair shines like otter's fur,
Chyrmalsyn döölöt bashynga.	May your head [i.e., life] be filled with wealth and prosperity!

"Since the ceremony was a unique experience for many people, after my aunt finished her song, the men and women who were not in the yurt asked us to come outside and sing into the microphone so that everybody could hear the words. My aunt did not mind doing it again outside, but it became a bit noisy because everyone wanted to have a closer look at us. One of my distant uncles was holding the microphone right in front of the singers' mouths, and that made them feel nervous. But they all got the chance to sing a few lines to me. My grandmother was able to sing only several lines, because she could not hold back her tears while singing to me. Here is her short symbolic message to my mother in-law, whom she addresses by the traditional term *kudagyi*."

Kudagyi,	*Kudagyi,*
Sary atka tumar tagyp al,	Hang a protective charm on a yellow horse,
Salkyn bir jerbe bagyp al.	And take good care of her in a cool place.
Kudagyi,	*Kudagyi,*
Kök atka tumar tagyp al,	Hang a protective charm on a gray horse,
Kölökö jerge bagyp al.	And take good care of her in a shady place.
Kudagyi,	*Kudagyi,*
Ak uchuk berem saptap al,	I'm giving you a white piece of thread,
	Put it through the needle yourself,
Ak shumkar berem taptap al.	I'm giving you a white falcon,
	Train her well yourself.

My great-aunt Anarkül also became nervous and sang just a few lines of advice to me:

Jelbir-jelbir ot küysö,	If the flames burn too strong,
Jan balam,	My dear child,
Eteging menen öchürgün.	Smother them with the hem of your dress.

Jaman-jakshy kep uksang,	If you get scolded with bad words,
Jan balam,	My dear child,
Külküng menen kechirgin.	Forgive them with your smile.

In the past, when the Kyrgyz led a nomadic life, the singing of a bridal *koshok* was the most essential ritual of a wedding. But Soviet sedentarization and modernization policies in Central Asia in the first half of the twentieth century brought major changes to traditional values and practices. For example, paying bride price (*kalyng*), which was widely practiced among the nomadic Kyrgyz and Kazakhs, was prohibited by Soviet law. And in urban areas, marriage customs and wedding celebrations were influenced by Russian and Western wedding traditions. Elements of a typical Soviet-style Russian wedding included receiving official state registration, which was required for a marriage certificate; driving the bride and groom around the city in a decorated white Volga car; placing flowers on an eternal flame or unknown soldier's monument; holding an evening party called a "Komsomol evening" at the groom's house ("Komsomol" is a syllabic abbreviation of the name of the Soviet-era youth organization); playing pop music and dancing; wearing Western-style wedding clothes—for the bride, a bridal gown and for the groom, a suit; public kissing between the bride and groom when the wedding guests shout "*gor'ka*" in Russian; and drinking alcohol. Eventually, these practices were also adopted in rural areas. At the same time, many older wedding customs were preserved because they reinforced social and kinship relationships and values.

Recent years have seen attempts to revive and adapt some older wedding practices to contemporary-style wedding ceremonies—the ritual of singing a bridal *koshok* being one example. These days, masters of ceremonies, who are both men and women with good verbal skills and traditional knowledge, often compose new wedding poems in the style of a traditional bridal *koshok*. When the bride's parents are asked to give a speech, some mothers or grandmothers incorporate traditional *koshok* texts into their personal wishes and blessings. Typically they recite the *koshok* like a poem instead of singing it with a sad melody. The bride's mother gives her motherly advice and blessings, not at her own home before she sends her daughter off but at a wedding party that takes place in a restaurant where several hundred invited guests sit at tables filled with all kinds of food and drinks. In rural areas such as the Aksy region, where Elmira's wedding took place, some families have attempted to revive traditional marriage practices by erecting a yurt, displaying the bride's dowry inside the yurt, and singing a symbolic farewell *koshok* to the bride. However, since today all Kyrgyz live a sedentarized life and most marriages occur within a village or between couples from neighboring villages, a newly married girl will be likely to see her parents much more often than in the past.

WATCH

Example 13.2 and 13.3. *Koshok* recited (example 13.2) and sung (example 13.3) by Kunduz Toktomambetova. Jalal-Abad, Kyrgyzstan, 2001.

These two examples present variants of one and the same *koshok,* first recited and then sung by Kunduz Toktomambetova, the author's mother-in-law, who lives in the village of Kyzyl-Jar, in the Aksy region of southern Kyrgyzstan. Kunduz's daughter married a man from a different tribe (*uruu* or *el*) in the city of Jalal-Abad, located some sixty-five miles from Kyzyl-Jar. The groom's parents offered a big party in one of the restaurants in the city, where they also invited the bride's parents and relatives as honored guests. When the bride's mother, Kunduz, was invited to offer a wish to her daughter and son-in-law, she surprised her daughter and guests by reciting a traditional *koshok* poem. According to people who attended the party, everyone was very touched by her *koshok,* as they had not heard such a beautiful poem full of practical advice, symbolic messages and wishes, and rhythmic language. Moreover, she individualized the traditional *koshok* by adding a few lines of her own with initial alliteration: she said to her daughter that by being a good daughter-in-law, she would make her home village and region proud and make people say that she is the daughter of Kyzyl-Jar of the famous Aksy region. The mother, who has a very good voice, knew how to sing the *koshok,* but she did not want to make her daughter cry and feel sad by singing it with a sad melody, and thus recited it.

Later, at the author's request, she agreed to sing, rather than recite, the *koshok* for an audio recording. The transcription and translation provided below follow the sung performance in the audio recording. The recited version uses some of the same lines, sequenced differently, as well as quite a few different lines from those in the recited version.

Kyz östürgön ata eken,	It is the father who raises the daughter.
Kyz kögörtkön bata eken.	It is the blessing which makes the girl happy in marriage.
Kyngshylatyp kyz bergen,	Marrying a girl off by making her cry
Kyrgyzda kylymdan kelgen salt eken.	Is the Kyrgyz custom left from past centuries.
Koktuga koyondun tügü chachylsyn,	May the rabbit's hair fall on the mountainside.
Jan balam, bargan jeringden	My dear child,
Kozgolboy baktyng achylsyn.	May you find happiness in your new home forever.

Jylgaga jylandyn tügü chachylsyn,	May the snake's skin shed around the spring-fed pool.
Jan balam, bargan jeringden	My dear child,
Jylbastan baktyng achylsyn.	May you find happiness in your new home forever.
Amriken maasy butungda	Wearing an American *maasy*,[16]
Jan balam,	My dear child,
Aynybay bargyn jurtunga.	Go to your new home without changing your mind.
Kepich bir maasy butungda,	Wearing a *kepich*[17] and *maasy*,
Jan balam,	My dear child,
Keyibey bargyn jurtunga.	Go to your new home without feeling sad.
Ak kurjun tolgon ak mata,	Like a white saddlebag filled with white fabrics,
Kyzymdyn aga-inisi baybacha.	My daughter's brothers are all wealthy men.
Kök kurjun tolgon kök mata,	Like a blue saddlebag filled with blue fabrics,
Kyzymdin köp inisi baybacha.	My daughter's brothers are many and well off.
Kaynatang kelse eshikten,	When your father-in-law comes,
Kayrylyp baryp eshik ach.	Go and open the door with grace.
Kaadangdy buzbay jan balam,	Follow the tradition, my dear child,
Karsyldatpay sekin bas.	Walk softly without making noise.
Enekeng kelse eshikten,	When your dear mother-in-law comes,
Jan balam,	My dear child,
Engilip baryp eshik ach.	Go and open the door with respect.
Een bash eken degizbey	Don't let people say that you're unruly,
Kyzym,	My daughter,
Elbirip kelip sekin bas.	Walk softly and gracefully.
Engiltip kamchy saldyrba,	Don't let [your husband] hit you with a horsewhip,
Enenge naalat ayttyrba.	And bring a curse to your mother.
Artyltyp kamchy saldyrba,	Don't let [your husband] hit you with a horsewhip,
Atanga naalat ayttyrba.	And bring a curse to your father.
Ak shaiy kiyseng delbirgin,	Wear a white flattering silk dress.
Akyryn süylöp til bilgin.	Speak softly and know what to say.
Atagy ketken alyska,	Let people say proudly that
Jan balam,	You're the daughter of Aksy, whose fame
Aksynyn kyzy dedirgin.	reaches faraway lands.

Kyzyldy kiyseng delbirgin,	Wear a red flattering silk dress.
Kyzykem,	My dearest daughter,
Kymtyna süylöp til bilgin.	Speak carefully and know what to say.
Kylymga ketken atagy,	Let people say proudly that
Kyzyl-Jar kyzy dedirgin.	You're the daughter of Kyzyl-Jar, whose fame lasts for centuries.
Ak uchuk berdim, saptap al,	I gave you a white piece of thread, put it through a needle yourself.
Kudagyi,	*Kudagyi,*
Ak shaiy berdim, taptap al.	I gave you a white silk, use it well yourself.
Kök uchuk berdim, saptap al,	I gave you a blue piece of thread, put it through a needle yourself.
Kudagyi,	*Kudagyi,*
Kök shaiy berdim, taptap al.	I gave you a blue silk, use it well yourself.

STUDY QUESTIONS

1. What is the main purpose of the *koshok* singing ritual for the bride?

2. Identify common themes such as "advice," "praise," "wishes," etc., in the *koshok* texts in Examples 13.2 and 13.3, above.

3. What differences and similarities do the funerary and bridal *koshok*s share in their themes, poetic structure, performance styles, and melodies?

4. Examples 12.1 (*Koshok* sung at a Kyrgyz memorial feast) and 13.1 (excerpt from the author's wedding) both show rituals that take place inside a yurt. Can you observe differences and similarities in the two yurts' interior decorations, in the objects displayed inside, and in women's sitting arrangements and clothes?

5. How would you compare the reaction of listeners to the lamenters' *koshok* in examples 12.1 and 13.1? What kind of atmosphere did the sung *koshok* and the recited *koshok* create?

6. What is intrinsic in the ritual that makes the bride sad to the point where she cries? Is it the melody, the content, or both?

7. What aspects of the bridal *koshok* texts excerpted above reflect Kyrgyz nomadic life, values, and oral tradition? Which metaphors did you like the best, and why?

8. How would you compare Kyrgyz marriage customs, especially the *koshok* singing ritual in the first video excerpt, to marriage rituals in your own culture?

9. How do you understand the role of such traditional practices and rituals in modern Central Asian society? For girls: Would you prefer incorporating traditional marriage rituals, including the bridal *koshok*, into your wedding? Why or why not?

NOTES

1. Another type of female wedding song called *jar-jar* is sung by groups of women, in contrast to the solo form of Kyrgyz *koshok.* Uzbek women perform the same genre of communal wedding song under the generic name *yor-yor.*

2. However, this prohibition is not always followed. In many cases people marry after three or four generations, but that occurs mostly among the children of a brother and sister, because the sister's husband is usually from another clan.

3. *Üzük:* the yurt's exterior felt coverings. The *üzük* has a long string attached to its top and side called *jel boo,* which is used during strong winds to prevent the yurt from collapsing.

4. *Japsar:* a kind of sack made from colorful fabrics. It is hung inside the yurt for storing women's sewing utensils and jewelry.

5. *Kerege:* the collapsible side wing of the yurt.

6. *Jük:* the folded-up sleeping mats and blankets placed on top of the wooden chest inside the yurt.

7. These four lines are from a published collection of *koshoks: Koshoktor,* vol. 21 (Bishkek, Sham Press, 1998), 336.

8. Ibid., 325.

9. Ibid., 336.

10. Ibid., 327.

11. *Kanjyga* is a cord tied to the front side of the horse saddle. It is used for tying lighter loads and bags.

12. The older brother of one's husband.

13. As nomads who lived in the mountains for centuries, Kyrgyz developed many terms and words to describe their mountain environment and landscape. They have many different names for each part of a mountain or valley. In the past, the nomadic Kyrgyz clearly distinguished and used these names in their everyday life.

14. *Bek* is a term used for a tribal leader.

15. The wife of Semetei, son of the hero Manas in the Kyrgyz epic *Manas.*

16. *Maasy:* soft leather boots worn by Central Asian men and women in rural areas. These boots were made by sedentary Uzbeks, who called the shiny leather "American *maasy*" probably to attract customers.

17. *Kepich:* galoshes worn outside the *maasy.*

CHAPTER 14 Narrative Instrumental
Music

INTRODUCTION: MUSIC AND NARRATIVE

At its simplest, narrative refers to the act of telling a story or providing an account of events and experiences. Narration with words, it is safe to say, is a universal attribute of humankind. Whatever their length, form, content, and thematic roots in the human psyche, stories, tales, and oral poetry, sometimes supplemented by gesture, are culturally ubiquitous. In many cultures, oral literature is recited or performed to the accompaniment of music. But the notion of telling stories, relating events, or conveying images exclusively through instrumental music itself without the aid of texts—what in the West would be called "program music"—is a more limited phenomenon.

Narrative instrumental music exists throughout the Inner Asian nomadic realm, but it has reached a particularly high level of professionalism among Kazakh and Kyrgyz musicians who compose and perform closely related repertories called *küi* (Kazakh) and *küü* (Kyrgyz). This chapter is divided into two sections, which address *küi* and *küü,* respectively.

PART 1. Kazakh *Küi*

SAIDA DAUKEYEVA

Küi is a genre of narrative instrumental music that serves as a major vehicle of cultural expression among the Kazakhs. Developed as a sophisticated form of solo performance by folk musicians and master composer-performers (*küishi*s) on a variety of Kazakh musical instruments, it is a versatile medium of narration through sound central to the Kazakhs' social and musical life. The repertory of *küi*s is diverse, and includes pieces for the end-blown flute, *sybyzghy,* traditionally played by shepherds, and the two-stringed bowed lute, *qobyz,* in former times the instrument of shamans and epic bards (see chapter 16). The largest number of *küi*s, however, belongs to the *dombyra,* the two-stringed long-necked lute that is the most widespread Kazakh instrument and came to epitomize Kazakh culture and national identity (see chapter 17). This chapter presents a brief account of the origins and development of *küi* and explores the relationship between music and narrative in *küi* performance, focusing on an examination of *dombyra* performance styles and repertories of *küi*s in the two principal stylistic traditions centered in western and eastern regions of Kazakhstan.

HISTORICAL DEVELOPMENT OF *KÜI* AND THE RELATIONSHIP BETWEEN MUSIC AND NARRATIVE

The origins of the *küi* genre have been traced to instrument playing that formed part of shamanic rituals, singing, and the narration of epics among the Kazakhs' nomadic predecessors in medieval Central Asia. The oldest layer of Kazakh instrumental music deriving from shamanic ritual practice is represented by *qobyz küi*s attributed to Qorqyt, or Qorqyt ata, hero of the Oghuz epic and legendary forefather of Kazakh shamans, epic bards, and musicians, who is thought to have lived around the eighth or ninth century.[1] The earliest *küi*s for the *dombyra* are believed to be those ascribed to the quasi-historical, quasi-legendary *küishi*s, Ketbugha (twelfth to thirteenth century) and Asan qaighy (fourteenth to fifteenth century).[2] The heyday of *küi,* however, came in the nineteenth century, when celebrated *küishi*s from across present-day Kazakhstan created distinctive instrumental styles that became identified with local composition and performance on various instruments, first and foremost, the *dombyra.* These styles and the related repertories of *küi*s—anonymous, or "folk" (*khalyq*), and those of known authorship—have been transmitted down to the present through lineages of

Kazakh *küishi*s and *änshi*s, 1900–1910s.

Courtesy of Central State Archive of Film, Photography, and Sound Recordings of the Republic of Kazakhstan.

students and successors by way of oral tradition and, since the early twentieth century, through notated transcriptions and recordings.

The interrelation between the musical and verbal elements of *küi* evolved in the course of its history. In earlier performance practice, notably in folk *küi*s based on legendary subjects (*khalyq angyz küiler*), music was integrated with the verbal narrative (*angyz-änggime*, legend-story). Performers would alternate their storytelling with brief instrumental interludes or self-standing *küi*s, which served to illustrate, imitate, or elaborate in sound the content of individual narrative episodes. But over time, instrumental performance became structurally and artistically independent from storytelling, assuming the leading role in *küi*. The present-day *küi* is primarily a musical genre. Verbal discourse serves more as an introduction, explaining the origins of the instrumental piece, than as an artistically equal component of performance, and in concert practice *küi*s are commonly performed without their verbal element.

Through its long-term association with the spoken word, however, purely instrumental playing acquired some of the communicative qualities of verbal expression. Both *küi* and the instruments of its performance are regarded in their indigenous milieu as a means of communication between performers and listeners. A common metaphor for *küi* is that of a "speechless" (*tilsiz*) or "wordless language" (*sözsiz tili*) that has the capacity to convey meanings beyond the verbal narrative itself. This concept corresponds to the belief in the narrative, speaking powers of the *dombyra*. Traditionally, *dombyra* players would announce the telling of a story by the instrument and conclude their performance with the words *dedi* or *depti*, meaning "[the *dombyra*] said" or "it seemed to say." The highest acknowledgment of a *dombyra* player's mastery is to say that his *dombyra* "speaks" (*aityp tur*).[3]

Aqyn performs in an *auyl*, accompanying himself on the *dombyra*, 1930s.

Courtesy of Central State Archive of Film, Photography, and Sound Recordings of the Republic of Kazakhstan.

Küi narratives embrace an array of subjects relating to the Kazakhs' social and cultural world: their ways of life, relationship with nature and worldviews, oral lore, traditions and customs, and historical experiences. Folk legend *küi*s (*khalyq angyz küiler*), which are considered to have early origins, depict images of nature, animals, and birds, evoking ancient mythology and animist beliefs among the nomads. *Küi*s attributed to specific composer-performers (*küishi*s) from the eighteenth century onward tend to be biographical, historical, philosophical, or lyrical in content. Many of them reflect particular occurrences in the lives of their creators or important historical events. The genre provenance of *küi*s is accordingly varied. Some draw on particular song genres, for example, songs for opening a celebration (*toy bastar*), farewell (*qoshtasu*), announcement of a death to relatives (*estirtu*), mourning lament (*joqtau*), and contemplation (*tolghau*). Others relate to genres of specifically instrumental origin, such as *aqjeleng* (pieces of vivacious, playful character), *qosbasar* (lyrical or philosophical pieces), and *qongyr* (meditative, sorrowful *küi*s). A group of *küi*s arises from instrumental contests (*tartys*). Another distinct group consists of dedications (*arnau*) to particular images, characters, or personalities.[4]

The musical embodiment of these diverse subjects involves a range of expressive devices, from imitation of the sounds of nature and intonations of human speech to evocation of emotional and psychological experiences. Apart from relating a story, imitating images or recording history, though, each *küi* explores a certain universal state of mind that encapsulates the *küi*'s underlying meaning—for example, joy, elation, melancholy, sorrow, or nostalgia. The depiction of a storyline in *küi* does not involve development or elaboration of its main characters. Narrative images and episodes, even those featuring physical movement, such as a bird's flight or a horse's galloping, are captured in sound as complete and lasting states rather than as a dynamic process. This method of artistic representation is expressed in the name of the genre, *küi*, which literally means "state of mind," or "mood." The capacity of *küi* performance to communicate universal states of mind is rooted in the aesthetics of *küi*—its instrumental "language," compact form, and short duration (typically one to five minutes). Imparting universal states of mind is also central to the artistic purpose of its composition and performance, which lies not in the mere re-creation of a narrative but in revealing an essential meaning or idea at its heart.[5]

An example of the musical representation of narrative is the folk legend *küi* "Aqsaq qulan," which is believed to relate to an early layer of Kazakh instrumental music. This widely known *küi* draws on a legend demonstrating the power of music to tell a story without recourse to words that is found in various versions across Inner Asia. In the Kazakh version, the legend recounts how the only son of Jochi Khan, heir of Genghis Khan and governor of the Golden Horde (thirteenth century), regardless of his father's warnings, went to hunt wild horses (*qulan*), sacred animals whose killing is forbidden among the Kazakhs. During the hunt, he was killed by the leader of a herd, a lame wild horse.[6] Having learned about the disappearance of his son, Jochi Khan announced that anyone who dared to break bad news to him would have molten lead poured down his throat. Nobody had the courage to tell him about his son's death. Eventually a *dombyra* player came before him and performed "Aqsaq qulan," which so vividly narrated the story of the hunt and the death of his son that the khan immediately realized the truth.[7] In his fury, the khan was about to punish the musician, but, perceiving that it was the *dombyra* that had revealed his son's fate, he ordered molten lead to be poured on the instrument's body.[8] Some versions of the legend say this is how the *dombyra* acquired a hole in its soundboard.[9]

"Aqsaq qulan" is known in several variants throughout Kazakhstan. The variant featured here comes from western Kazakhstan, and is performed by a renowned twentieth-century *dombyra* player, Rüstembek Omarov (1919–1988). In musical terms, the piece belongs to the group of folk legend *küi*s presumed to be of early origin. Such *küi*s are commonly intended for a *dombyra* whose two strings are tuned to the interval of a fifth (*teris burau*), and are based on reiterations of simple melodic motifs within a small pitch range. In some of them, the melody is supported by a bass drone produced on the unfretted, or open, lower-sounding string. A common narrative device employed in these *küi*s is instrumental imitation of the sounds and physical traits of the legend's protagonists, in particular, the voices and movements of animals and birds.

"Aqsaq qulan" evolves from the initial motif with a stepwise melody in the lower voice against the main tone ostinato in the upper voice (0:00–0:15). The motif is then transposed and developed in higher registers, and recapitulated at the original pitch. Played throughout with a rapid strumming technique (*qara qaghys*) that produces an agitated rhythmic pulse, the *küi* has an imitative effect: it draws a sonic picture of the hunt and horses galloping in the steppe. Additionally, though, it conveys a sense of disquiet, foreboding the tragic resolution of events. This air of disquiet is created, in particular, by variant reiterations of the stepwise melody that resembles Kazakh mourning laments (*joqtau*). The use of this motif and the overall musical character of the legend *küi* have prompted scholars in Kazakhstan to compare it with the traditional song genre *estirtu* in which Kazakh musicians broke news of a death to relatives of the deceased in a figurative, allegorical form.[10] The *küi*'s message or state of mind is thus encoded by the *dombyra* player in musical "language" and communicated to the listeners—and, in the legend, to the khan—through a confluence of imitative and symbolic means.

LISTEN

Example 14.1. "Aqsaq qulan" (Lame wild horse), folk legend *küi,* performed by Rüstembek Omarov. Courtesy of Central State Archive of Film, Photography, and Sound Recordings of the Republic of Kazakhstan.

DOMBYRA PERFORMANCE STYLES

Dombyra performance, in both its folk and authored forms, encompasses two principal stylistic traditions: *tökpe* and *shertpe*. *Tökpe* is identified with western Kazakhstan, while the roots of *shertpe* are in eastern Kazakhstan. Historically, these stylistic traditions arose among the different Kazakh tribal confederations, or Hordes (*jüz*), that populated these regions. *Tökpe* originated among the Little Horde (*Kishi jüz*) in the western region (Batys), its local sub-traditions evolving

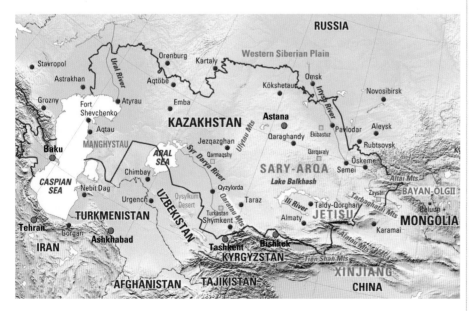

Map of Kazakhstan.

in the northwestern area formerly known as Bökei Orda, in the area of the Aral Sea and Syr Darya River, and on the Manghystau Peninsula.[11] *Shertpe* developed among the people of the Middle (*Orta jüz*) and Great Hordes (*Uly jüz*) in the eastern Kazakh lands, with separate schools in the regions of Saryarqa, or Arqa, Jetisu, and Altai, as well as among some tribes of the Little Horde (*Kishi jüz*), such as the Tama and Tabyn, in the southeastern region of Qaratau.

Across these different localities, two main types of *dombyra* evolved, distinguished by morphology and sound properties. Prevalent in the western region was a *dombyra* with a rounded, pear-shaped body and a long, slender neck with twelve to sixteen frets. In the eastern region, the prevailing instrument was a *dombyra* with a flat body of varying shape—rectangular, shovel-like, or triangular—and a shorter, broad neck with seven to eleven frets.[12] In some areas, notably Arqa, early *dombyra*s were provided with intermediate movable frets called *qashaghan perne* (deviating, deflecting frets) that produced variant pitches of the main scale-degrees.[13] Whereas the western *dombyra* type with the rounded body produced a bright and resonant sound, its eastern counterpart with a flat resonator had a more subdued and mellower voice.[14]

Intended for performance on the different *dombyra* types, *küi*s in the *tökpe* and *shertpe* styles came to differ in playing techniques, structural principles, themes, and narrative devices. These differences, formalized in the classical repertories of western and eastern Kazakhstan from the nineteenth and early twentieth century, were largely maintained in subsequent performance practice, despite the widespread adoption in Kazakhstan, as part of Soviet-initiated musical reforms in the 1930s, of a new, modernized type of *dombyra* with a pear-shaped body and an extended nineteen-fret neck, that differed morphologically and acoustically from the traditional instruments (see chapter 17). The distinction between *tökpe* and *shertpe* styles is not rigid, but takes into account *küi*s' prevalent technical and structural properties.

Tökpe

In the *tökpe* style, the *dombyra* is strummed with a wrist movement of the right hand, using a variety of finger strokes (*qaghys*). Simultaneous strumming across both strings produces a sustained two-voiced heterophony in which the leading and accompanying voices are exchanged between the strings, while precise and strong rhythmic strokes lend *küi*s a percussive effect. These features are reflected in the name of the style, *tökpe,* meaning literally "outpouring, spilling," from *tögu,* "to pour out, spill, scatter, embroider." The distinctive manner of sound production and rhythmic articulation in *tökpe küi*s give them a dynamic quality, which is evident, in particular, in the depiction of epic, dramatic, and philosophical themes and images.

Dombyra from western Kazakhstan attributed to *küishi* Makhambet Ötemisuly (19th c.).
Courtesy of Museum of Kazakh Folk Musical Instruments.

The *tökpe* style is identified with a distinctive structural principle designed to exploit the wide tonal range of the western Kazakhstan *dombyra*. Many *tökpe küi*s are structured as a succession of thematically related sections in progressively higher pitch areas or registers (*buyn*) on the fingerboard of the *dombyra*: the initial section, serving as a refrain, produced in the low pitch area close to the pegboard of the *dombyra* (*bas buyn*); the middle section produced in the middle pitch area of the *dombyra* fingerboard (*orta buyn*); the culminating section of the *küi* marked by attainment of the high pitch area close to the body of the instrument (*sagha*). The area spanning the upper pitches of *bas buyn* and *orta buyn* usually contains salient melodic material that can be perceived as the main theme of the *küi* (*negizgi buyn*). In the course of the instrumental piece, this theme is variably presented in the different registers of the *dombyra* scale, with ascending leaps or passages to mark the onset of new, higher-pitched sections and periodic returns through descending melodic movement to the low-pitched refrain. The culminating section (*sagha*) may comprise two subsections of an increasingly wide range: *birinshi* (first) or *kishi* (small), and *ekinshi* (second) or *ülken* (great) *sagha*. The recurrence and variation of the thematic sections, involving a gradual expansion of tonal range and alteration of the intervallic distance between the two voices, creates a sense of development, while contributing to the structural integrity of the *küi*. The following figure shows the interrelation of the *buyn*s in the structure of *tökpe küi*s, which is known accordingly as *buyndyq* (sectional).[15]

Dombyra from eastern Kazakhstan that belonged to *änshi* Birjan sal Qojaghululy (19th c.).
Courtesy of Museum of Kazakh Folk Musical Instruments.

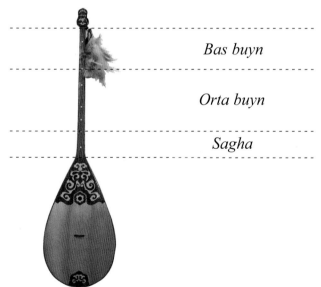

Bas buyn

Orta buyn

Sagha

Some Kazakh scholars have drawn attention to the extra-musical—anthropomorphic, zoomorphic, and metaphysical—connotations of the indigenous terminology for the *dombyra* scale: *bas* (head, beginning), *orta* (middle, center) or *keude* (chest), and *sagha* (estuary), also known as *ayaq* (leg, end). These connotations and the progression of *tökpe küi*s through low, middle, and high pitch areas prompted these scholars to suggest an analogy between the *küi*s' tripartite form and the tripartite structure of the universe in traditional Kazakh cosmology. In this view, the structure of *küi* could represent a shaman's journey to the lower world in the course of a healing ritual.[16]

A leading role in the development of *tökpe* in the nineteenth century was taken by *küishi*s from Bökei Orda, notably the *dombyra* composers and performers Qurmanghazy Saghyrbaiuly (1818–1889) and Däuletkerei Shyghaiuly (1820–1887)—both originally from the Ural region.[17] Qurmanghazy, in particular, is regarded as the founder of a distinctive school of *dombyra* performance. While drawing on conventions of *tökpe* established by his predecessors, including his master, *dombyra* player Uzaq, he extended the scope of theme and genre in *küi* performance and enriched it with new technical and expressive devices. From a poor herder's family, Qurmanghazy clashed with the Kazakh authorities and sympathized with the uprising against the local and czarist administration that took place in western Kazakhstan in the 1830s. Originally from a Kazakh tribe that supported the rebels, he was persecuted and imprisoned, and spent much of his life in exile. Qurmanghazy's *küi*s, accordingly, reflect on themes of struggle, courage, and social injustice, and evoke heroic and dramatic images. In order to convey these themes and images, he used a variety of virtuosic playing techniques, such as a powerful strumming with all fingers of the right hand (*qara qaghys*), tremolo, glissando, and the damping of the instrument's table with the right-hand elbow to create dynamic contrasts. He developed *bas buyn* into a distinct thematic section, and regularized the second *sagha* as a self-standing culmination zone, thereby expanding the tonal range and dimensions of *küi*s and enhancing their dynamic character.

Qurmanghazy Saghyrbaiuly.
Rendering of a portrait by Aigerim Ilip.

Many of Qurmanghazy's *küi*s, such as "Kishkentai," "Balbyrauyn," "Adai," and "Saryarqa," form the core repertory of contemporary *dombyra* players. Among these widely known *küi*s is "Alatau" (Many-colored mountain), in which the image of a mountain serves as a metaphor for expressing philosophical contemplation about life. In the following example, this *küi* is performed by Qali Jantileuov (1902–1993), a successor of Qurmanghazy's school, who passed a number of Qurmanghazy's *küi*s down to the present day. As you watch the video example, try to discern the different sections (*buyn*s), as they appear in the course of the piece. Then listen to the *küi* again, following the time code and description of the *küi*'s structure in table 14.1.

WATCH **Example 14.2.** "Alatau" (Many-colored mountain), composed by Qurmanghazy Saghyrbaiuly, performed by Qali Jantileuov. Fragment from the film *Shabyt* (Inspiration), 1980s. Courtesy of the archive of the Kazakhstan Republic Television and Radio Corporation.

TABLE 14.1. FORMAL STRUCTURE OF "ALATAU"

TIME CODE	SECTION	NAME	CHARACTERISTICS
0:00–0:15	A	*Bas buyn*	Initial section, which recurs later as a refrain. The section comprises a distinct stepwise melody in the lower voice and can be perceived as a salient theme of the *küi*.
0:15–0:33	B	*Negizgi buyn*	Main thematic section, embracing the middle pitch area. The end of the section merges with the beginning of the refrain, contributing to a smooth transition between the sections.
0:33–0:47	A	*Bas buyn*	Refrain
0:47–1:15	C	*Sagha*	Culmination section, introduced with a melodic leap. The section combines two sub-sections, *birinshi* and *ekinshi sagha*, reaching toward the highest tone and the widest interval (two octaves) in the *küi*.
1:15–1:32	B¹	*Negizgi buyn*	A sequential melodic descent from the culmination segues into a variant version of the main theme.
1:32–1:43	A	*Bas buyn*	Refrain
1:44–1:57	D	*Orta buyn*	A new section in the middle pitch area.[A]
1:58–2:14	B¹	*Negizgi buyn*	The version of the theme that appeared previously now follows on from *orta buyn*.
2:14–2:26	A	*Bas buyn*	Refrain

NOTE:
   A. In another variant of the *küi*, this section also appears at the beginning of the *küi*, before the *sagha* section, and is followed by *bas buyn*.

STUDY QUESTIONS

1. How would you describe the overall mental state or affect expressed in "Alatau"? How does the composer convey it in music?

2. What musical means are used in the *küi* to create a sense of development and contrast, and, at the same time, formal coherence?

3. Listening to the *küi*, do you find the analogy, described above, between the progression of *tökpe küis* and a shaman's journey to the underworld persuasive? Can you offer your own interpretation or understanding of the progression of the *küi*'s thematic material through low, middle, and high pitch areas?

Rysbai Ghabdiev.

Courtesy of Central State Archive of Film, Photography, and Sound Recordings of the Republic of Kazakhstan.

In addition to *küi*s structured according to the standard sectional principle, Qurmanghazy's output includes a number of *küi*s that depart from the model described above and exemplified in "Alatau." One of these is "Töremurat," a virtuosic piece whose performance requires a high level of mastery. Töremurat was the name of a Kazakh hero (*batyr*) who broke customary law (*adat*) by marrying a girl, Qyz-Danai, who had already been promised to another man for bridewealth. One day, Töremurat's settlement (*auyl*) was attacked by men from the *auyl* of Qyz-Danai's former fiancé. Qurmanghazy, who was staying as a guest in Töremurat's *auyl,* took an active part in fierce combat for Qyz-Danai and, after the attackers fled without being able to take the girl away, he composed this *küi* depicting Töremurat's fight for Qyz-Danai.[18] The *küi* is unusual in its structure: it does not have a *bas buyn* section, but begins with rapid strumming in the *orta buyn* zone (0:00–0:14) and proceeds into a main thematic section, comprising several distinctive motifs, which move across the pitch area of *orta buyn, birinshi sagha,* and *bas buyn* (0:15–0:52). The culmination section (*ekinshi sagha*), which appears twice (0:53–1:04, 1:49–1:59), is clearly separated from the preceding sections, and rather than being followed by a steady melodic descent, briskly switches to the main theme in the *orta buyn* and *birinshi sagha* zone. Melodic leaps, rapid shifts in pitch and register, rhythmic acceleration and deceleration, and abrupt pauses all contribute to the *küi*'s dynamic and impetuous character and its almost theatrical effect. The example below features a performance of the *küi* by another famous interpreter of *tökpe küi*s, Rysbai Ghabdiev (1936–2004). Watch the example, paying attention to the performer's techniques and the movement of his left hand along the *dombyra* neck in the course of the *küi.*

WATCH

Example 14.3. "Töremurat," composed by Qurmanghazy Saghyrbaiuly, performed by Rysbai Ghabdiev. Fragment from a film, 1983. Courtesy of Central State Archive of Film, Photography, and Sound Recordings of the Republic of Kazakhstan.

STUDY QUESTIONS

1. In your opinion, is the *küi* imitative (i.e., does it create a sonic image of the heroes' fight, horses stamping, and so on), or does it (perhaps additionally) convey a certain composite state of mind or affect?

2. Compare the structure of "Töremurat" with that of "Alatau." In what ways are the two *küi*s different or similar?

3. What qualities of performance, in your view, make Rysbai Ghabdiev a master performer?

A distinctive stylistic branch of *tökpe* developed in the nineteenth century to the southeast of Bökei Orda, in the region of the Aral Sea and Syr Darya River. *Dombyra* performance in this region, which was then part of the Khanate of Khiva, came to be influenced by the local tradition of epic narration (*jyraulyq*) among the Kazakhs and the music of neighboring peoples in the Khorezm oasis—Karakalpaks, Uzbeks, and Turkmen. The most acclaimed representative of this stylistic tradition is Qazanghap Tilepbergenuly (1854–1921), a *küishi* born on the western shores of the Aral Sea, in the present-day Aqtöbe region. Qazanghap's *küi*s, in their character, melodic themes (*äuen*), and structural development, are distinct from *küi*s by Qurmanghazy. Their thematic material, often resembling the tunes of epics (*jyr*), typically unfolds through varied reiteration and elaboration in different registers, which reveal various dimensions of its musical character. The transition between sections is more fluid and flexible than in Qurmanghazy's *küi*s, where sectional divisions tend to be clearcut. Melodic development is centered on the *orta buyn* area and rarely reaches the upper *sagha* zone (*ekinshi sagha*), a prominent structural feature of Qurmanghazy's instrumental style.[19] The composer frequently uses strumming with the index finger (*ilme qaghys*), in contrast to the wrist strumming with all fingers (*qara qaghys*) often used by Qurmanghazy, and embellishes the melodic line with melismas and grace notes that resemble ornamentation in Karakalpak, Uzbek, and Turkmen music.

Among the best known of Qazanghap's *küi*s is a series of pieces under the title "Aqjeleng," which refers to a genre of cyclic *küi*s (*tarmaqty küiler*) in the *tökpe* style distinguished by a joyful, playful character, and often associated with female images. According to oral tradition, a cycle of sixty-two "Aqjeleng" *küi*s ("Alpys eki Aqjeleng") was originally composed and performed by a girl named Aqjeleng, who sought to affect her listeners by opening the pathway of each of their veins (*tamyr*)—traditionally numbered by Kazakhs as sixty-two, causing them to experience a surge of energy and exaltation.[20] A number of western Kazakhstan *küishi*s, including Uzaq, Qurmanghazy, and Däuletkerei, composed "Aqjeleng" *küi*s. Qazanghap is said to have perfected the genre by creating an entire cycle of sixty-two *küi*s comprising distinct groups of pieces of varied character and recognizable musical traits.[21] Performance of this cycle won him victory at a *tartys* among acclaimed *dombyra* players that took place in Kongyrat, in present-day Karakalpakstan, in the late nineteenth century.[22] Only a handful of these *küi*s in various performers' interpretations have come down to us, such as "*Küi* basy Aqjeleng" (Head Aqjeleng *Küi*), "Buranbel Aqjeleng" (Slender Aqjeleng), "Domalatbai Aqjeleng" (Spinning Aqjeleng), and others.

In the following example, a successor and promoter of Qazanghap's musical legacy, *dombyra* player Säduaqas Balmaghambetov (1941–1999), performs one of these remaining *küi*s, "Kerbez Aqjeleng" (Graceful Aqjeleng), which the *küishi* composed in dedication to a girl, Jämi, after being dazzled by her beauty and

Performer Profile: Dina Nurpeisova, *Küishi* and *Dombyra* Tradition Bearer

SAIDA DAUKEYEVA

An outstanding representative of the western Kazakhstan tradition of *dombyra* performance is Dina Nurpeisova (1861–1955), a disciple of Qurmanghazy and the most celebrated female *dombyrashy* and *küishi* ever in the history of Kazakh music.[23] Dina's life and legacy span a transitional period between what is regarded as the "classical" age of Kazakh music in the nineteenth century and the time of transformation and change that occurred during the Soviet era. Born in the Ural region into the family of a herder who was fond of *dombyra* playing and encouraged her early learning of this instrument, she became widely known as a "girl *dombyra* player" (*dombyrashy qyz*) by the age of nine, and when Qurmanghazy visited her father's home to listen to her, she so impressed him that he asked her father's permission to take her with him as his apprentice. Thus began her formative stage as a *dombyra* player: for nine years she frequently met with Qurmanghazy and accompanied him in his travels across the region, absorbing new repertory and playing techniques from him and other performers, and observing and participating in instrumental contests. Although she suspended travel and public performance following her marriage, she had a chance to learn *küis* by renowned *küishis* in western Kazakhstan, among them Uzaq, Eshchan, Baijuma, Balamaisan,

Däuletkerei, and Turkesh. On the advice of her master, she also started composing herself—at first versions of *küis* by well-known composers and then her own instrumental pieces. In the 1920s— years marked by turmoil and famine in Kazakhstan—Dina, then a widow, moved closer to the Caspian Sea in search of a better livelihood and resumed public performances, traveling around *auyls* and playing *küis*.

A major turning point in Dina's life and musical career came in the 1930s when she was invited to Alma-Ata and became involved in state-supported cultural events that were to gain her recognition across and beyond Kazakhstan. In 1937, she had resounding success at the second All-Kazakhstan Rally of Folk Art Workers convened by the People's Commissariat of Enlightenment of the Kazakh SSR. Two years later, she won the Grand Prix at the first All-Union Competition of Performers on Folk Instruments in Moscow, where she led the delegation of musicians from Kazakhstan. Another major appearance for Dina was at the Ten Days of Music of the Republics of Central Asia and Kazakhstan held in Tashkent in 1944. Back in Kazakhstan, she was awarded several prestigious state awards, notably People's Artist of the Republic. She performed and toured actively as an artist of the Philharmonic Society, and trained *dombyra* players from

Courtesy of Central State Archive of Film, Photography, and Sound Recordings of the Republic of Kazakhstan.

the Folk Orchestra named after Qurmanghazy, in this way handing the legacy of traditional *dombyra küis* down to a younger generation of performers.

Living through a period of major upheaval and change in Kazakh society, Dina responded to it in her compositions. Among her well-known *küis* are "On altynshy jyl" (1916), or "Nabor" (Conscription), which chronicles the 1916 uprising in the steppe against mobilization of the male population into labor brigades imposed by the czarist government; "Ana buiryghy" (A mother's command), "Jengis" (Victory), and "Engbek eri" (Worker heroes), which refer to World War II and the postwar reconstruction of people's lives; and " Segizinshi mart" (The 8th of March) and "Toy bastar" (Opening of the celebration), which

Performer Profile: Dina Nurpeisova, *Küishi* and *Dombyra* Tradition Bearer (CONTINUED)

relate to important occasions in the modern history of the Kazakhs, such as International Women's Day and the twentieth anniversary of Soviet Kazakhstan in 1940.

In depicting these contemporary topics, Dina drew on the traditions of western Kazakhstan *dombyra* performance while displaying her unique compositional and performance style. Her renditions of her own *küi*s and interpretations of pieces by other composers became known for their virtuoso, vibrant manner, marked by technical sophistication and rhythmic variation. This was attributed to the extraordinary physical qualities of her hands: a flexible and agile right hand capable of producing a range of articulation techniques, and the long stretch of her left hand that facilitated unusual fingerings on the neck of the *dombyra*. Qurmanghazy reportedly praised Dina's left hand, saying: "If your left hand and my right hand were given to one person, there would not have been a better *dombyra* player in the world."[24]

Many classical *tökpe küi*s, including those by Qurmanghazy and Däuletkerei, have come down to present-day performers in Dina's interpretations. One such *küi* is "Nauysqy," a virtuoso jocular piece that is played with gestural movement of the right hand. The *küi* is variously attributed to Qurmanghazy and to Dina herself. According to one version,

Dina performs *küi*s to a group of young people, Alma-Ata, 1950.

Courtesy of Central State Archive of Film, Photography, and Sound Recordings of the Republic of Kazakhstan.

Qurmanghazy composed it as an impression of a trade fair, using the right-hand gestures as a caricature on gesticulation by people who exchanged goods without knowing each other's languages. It is said that he based the *küi* on the Russian joke song "Chijik-Pyjik" ("Finch-Fawn"), which he heard at the trade fair. The name "Nauysqy" in this version derived from the name of the place where the trade fair supposedly took place. According to another version, the *küi* was composed by Dina herself in response to a performance by Kyrgyz *komuz* players, as a way of demonstrating that their peculiar gestural techniques could also be applied in *dombyra* performance. The word "Nauysqy" thus meant a "parody" or "mimicry."[25] Dina's performance of "Nauysqy" is featured in a short documentary

film made in 1947, the earliest ever to feature a renowned *dombyra* player. In the film, she plays a shorter version of the *küi*, without the *sagha* section, and with only a brief allusion to the song "Chijik-Pyjik" at 1:03–1:05. As you watch the film, note the peculiar gestural movement of Dina's right hand and the techniques of her left hand (for example, at 0:17–0:23 or 0:42–0:46). Note also that the lower-sounding string is often played unfretted, or open. This is a feature of *küi*s for the *dombyra* tuned to the interval of a fifth, which are comparatively fewer in the *tökpe* performance tradition than *küi*s for the *dombyra* tuned to a fourth.

Example 14.4. "Nauysqy," composed by Qurmanghazy Saghyrbaiuly or Dina Nurpeisova, performed by Dina Nurpeisova. Documentary film, 1947. Courtesy of Central State Archive of Film, Photography, and Sound Recordings of the Republic of Kazakhstan.

STUDY QUESTIONS

1. How is "Nauysqy" distinct from the previous examples in the chapter? Is it stylistically or structurally close to the *küi*s by Qurmanghazy you have heard?

2. What, in your view, is the purpose of the performer's right-hand gestural movement? What does it tell you about the *küi*'s character and the image it creates?

3. Based on this historical video, what can you tell about Dina Nurpeisova's musicianship?

grace.[26] Typical of the *aqjeleng* genre, "Kerbez Aqjeleng" evolves from a short, dancelike initial motif (*bas buyn*), which is taken up by a tuneful main theme (*negizgi buyn*) and developed through elaborate melodic interlocking (including a modulation into a new tonality), creating smooth transitions between *buyn*s.

Example 14.5. "Kerbez Aqjeleng" (Graceful Aqjeleng), attributed to Qazanghap Tilepbergenuly, performed by Säduaqas Balmaghambetov. Courtesy of Central State Archive of Film, Photography, and Sound Recordings of the Republic of Kazakhstan.

STUDY QUESTIONS

1. How would you describe the difference in compositional and performance style between Qazanghap's "Kerbez Aqjeleng" and the *küi*s in the previous examples composed by Qurmanghazy?

2. Does the *küi* in any of its musical properties (for example, the nature of thematic material, rhythmic articulation, melodic ornamentation, modal development) seem to you to bear an affinity to epic singing among the Kazakhs, or to Karakalpak, Uzbek, or Turkmen music, in particular, *dutar* performance?

3. Could a *küi* like "Kerbez Aqjeleng" have an emotional and psychological effect on listeners similar to the one attributed to "Alpys eki Aqjeleng" in the story of its origin? If so, what are the musical qualities that contribute to such an effect?

Table 14.2. Formal Structure of "Kerbez Aqjeleng"

Time Code	Section	Name	Characteristics
0:00–0:05	A	*Bas buyn*	Initial section serving as a refrain.
0:06–0:20	B	*Negizgi buyn*	Main theme, taking up the *bas buyn*. The end of the section merges with the beginning of the refrain.
0:20–0:26	A	*Bas buyn*	Refrain
0:27–0:37	C	*Orta buyn*	A section in the middle pitch area: melodic development in the lower voice against the upper voice drone is followed by a variant form of the main theme in the *orta buyn* area.
0:37–0:42			
0:43–0:49	B¹	*Negizgi buyn*	C segues into a shorter repetition of the main theme at the original pitch, which serves as a descent and return to the refrain.
0:49–0:55	A	*Bas buyn*	Refrain
0:56–1:03	D	*Sagha*	A section in the higher pitch area: melodic development in the lower voice against ostinato tones in the upper voice is followed by a modulation of the main theme into a tonality a fifth higher than the main tone. The theme then modulates back to the main tonality through a sequential intervallic descent.
1:04–1:19			
1:20–1:21			
1:22–1:29	B¹	*Negizgi buyn*	D segues into a shorter repetition of the main theme, which serves as a descent and return to the refrain.
1:29–1:34	A	*Bas buyn*	Refrain
1:35–1:52	B²	*Negizgi buyn*	Reiteration of the main theme with an ending from B¹.
1:52–2:00	A	*Bas buyn*	Refrain^A

NOTE:
    A. In a longer variant, the *küi* additionally proceeds into the *orta buyn* section, and concludes with a reiteration of the main theme and refrain.

A further recognizable tradition of *tökpe* originated from the Manghystau Peninsula, a region in the far southwest of present-day Kazakhstan, bordering the Caspian Sea. *Dombyra* performance there, as in the Aral and Syr Darya region, acquired its particular stylistic features through interaction with local epic and singing traditions, and with the instrumental and vocal music of the Turkmen and Karakalpaks.[27] A number of celebrated *küishi*s from Manghystau, notably Öskenbai

Qalmambetuly (1860–1925), became equally well known as epic bards and singers, leading to the circulation in the local *dombyra* repertory of *küi* variants of epics and songs, known, respectively, as *jyr küi* and *än küi*. Many musicians, including Öskenbai and the eminent *küishi*s Abyl Taraquly (1820–1892) and Esir Aishuaquly (1840–1904), were in contact with Turkmen *bagshy*s through performances and competitions at festive events (*toy, as*) that took place in Manghystau as well as in adjacent areas of Khorezm that are now within the borders of the neighboring countries of Turkmenistan and Uzbekistan. Kazakh *dombyra* players and Turkmen *dutar* players often demonstrated their art and challenged each other in displays of musical ingenuity at competitions (*tartys*). Instrumental pieces performed or extemporized during such competitions have been preserved in oral tradition among the Kazakhs as *tartys* or *aitys küi*s. There is, for example, a series of *küi*s arising from a famous *tartys* between Öskenbai and the Turkmen *bagshy* Qulbai, in which the

Murat Öskenbaev.

Courtesy of Central State Archive of Film, Photography, and Sound Recordings of the Republic of Kazakhstan.

Kazakh musician gained the upper hand. Such musical interaction contributed to the popularity of so-called "Turkmen *küi*s" and folk instrumental melodies, called "Nauai," which were widely performed in the southwest of Central Asia. The repertory of Manghystau *dombyra* players currently includes a group of "Nauai" tunes that show similarities to Turkmen and Karakalpak *dutar* music.

In example 14.6, one such tune, "Qaqpaly Nauai" (Nauai with finger strokes), is performed by Murat Öskenbaev (1904–1982), a son of *küishi* Öskenbai and himself a distinguished *dombyra* player, who was also well known in Turkmenistan and Karakalpakstan, and whose repertory included *dombyra* versions of *dutar* pieces. As you watch the example, observe the right-hand finger strokes used by the performer that are referred to in the *küi*'s name (*qaqpaly*). This type of articulation, which creates a peculiar sharp rhythmic pattern, is also found in Turkmen and Karakalpak *dutar* music. Pay attention to the performer's right-hand gestures, or "hand play" (*qol oinatu*). Employed in some *küi*s throughout Kazakhstan (see example 14.4), gesticulation is a prominent feature of local *dombyra* performance in Manghystau, intended to make a performance visually attractive to listeners and, in some cases, to illustrate the images of the *küi*'s narrative or express its general character.

WATCH ▷ **Example 14.6.** "Qaqpaly Nauai" (Nauai with finger strokes), folk *küi*, performed by Murat Öskenbaev. Fragment from a film, 1978. Courtesy of Central State Archive of Film, Photography, and Sound Recordings of the Republic of Kazakhstan.

1. Which musical features of "Qaqpaly Nauai" situate it within the broader *tökpe* tradition of western Kazakhstan, and which features reflect the influence of *dutar* music? Consider the *küi*'s structural organization, playing techniques, rhythmic pattern, melodic ornamentation, and modal shifts.

2. Does the *küi* follow the sectional structural principle found in many *tökpe küis*, i.e., does it progress through the three pitch areas (*bas buyn*, *orta buyn*, and *sagha*), or is it structured differently?

3. How do you interpret the role of the hand gestures in the *küi*? In your view, how do they correlate with the music, both structurally and semantically?

Shertpe

In the *shertpe* style of eastern Kazakhstan, performers pluck the *dombyra* strings with individual fingers of the right hand rather than strum across the strings with a wrist movement, as in the *tökpe* style of western Kazakhstan. The plucking technique, which gave rise to the style's name, *shertpe*, or "plucking, flicking," from *shertu*, "to pluck, flick, snap," includes various methods of sound articulation, ranging from a gentle touch to a sharp touch to a forceful attack with the right-hand fingernails snapping against the instrument's deck. By plucking strings with individual fingers, performers can produce melodies with two separate "voices"—an upper voice that presents the lead melody and a lower voice that accompanies it, lending such *küis* a songlike quality. The finger plucking technique gives players more subtle control over rhythmic and agogic execution than strumming from the wrist, and *küis* in the *shertpe* style are distinguished by intricate, varied rhythmic patterns, sometimes organized in a flexible or free meter. The sound of plucked strings in the *shertpe* style evokes a different kind of sonic imagery than the rhythmic strumming characteristic of *tökpe*. Many *shertpe küis* are devoted to lyrical and psychological subjects, and capture images of nature and the world of human emotional experience.

In structural terms, *shertpe küis* are not unified by any common principle comparable to the sectional (*buyndyq*) form that prevails in *tökpe*. Originally intended for a *dombyra* with a smaller neck than instruments used in the *tökpe* tradition, *küis* in the *shertpe* style, particularly the oldest chronological layer of the repertory, unfold within a more limited tonal range and do not normally involve the gradual tonal expansion and intervallic variation typical of *tökpe küis*. Although they may consist of distinct, repeatable sections, the order and function of these sections are not necessarily determined by the relative position in which they are played on the *dombyra* fingerboard, as is the case in the *tökpe* style. Some *shertpe küis* progress according to an internal melodic logic, or present variations on a theme. Others unfold through a flexible combination of interrelated motifs in what has been described as a "mosaic" or "patchwork" (*quraqtyq*) form, a coinage derived from an indigenous analogy of such *küi*s to a patchwork quilt (*quraq*).[28] The structural heterogeneity of *küi*s in this style can be attributed to the fact that, spread over a large and culturally diverse geographic area extending from central Kazakhstan to the Altai region in the extreme east, the *shertpe* style embraced a variety of distinctive traditions which evolved from local features of *dombyra* performance and other kinds of music making in their respective regions.

The central and most representative tradition of *shertpe* arose in Saryarqa, or Arqa, a steppe region that spans eastern, northern, and central Kazakhstan, stretching from the Tarbaghatai Mountains in the east to Torghai in the west, and from the western Siberian plain in the north to Lake Balkhash in the south. The development of this tradition in the nineteenth century is mainly associated with the creative work of the celebrated *dombyra* player and composer Tättimbet Qazanghapuly (1817–1862). Tättimbet recreated the *shertpe* style that he inherited from his predecessors, notably the *küi* master Baijigit (seventeenth to eighteenth centuries), by assimilating into it elements of the local singing tradition that reached its zenith in the nineteenth century. The descendant of an aristocratic family from central Kazakhstan who were connoisseurs of music and frequently hosted musicians and singers, Tättimbet became known as a virtuoso *dombyra* player, charismatic singer-poet (*änshi*), and artistic personality (*seri*). His *dombyra* performance style thus absorbed some of the lyricism and melodious nature of the song repertory, though elaborated in an instrumental idiom.

In example 14.7, one of Tättimbet's well-known *küi*s, "Sylqyldaq" (Tinkling), is performed by a twentieth-century follower of his style, Äpike Äbenova (1915–1999). According to one version of its origin, the *küi* emerged when Tättimbet, in the late 1840s, migrated with his *auyl* to the lands of the Naiman tribe from the Middle Horde (*Orta jüz*). There he met and engaged in a competition with a remarkable girl nicknamed Erkekshora ("akin to a man"), who was a skillful *dombyra* player and horse rider, and who challenged men in *dombyra* contests and horse racing. It is said that Tättimbet and his female opponent competed for a long time and exchanged many beautiful *küi*s without being able to defeat each other. But Erkekshora stopped after performing thirty-nine *küi*s, whereas Tättimbet went on to play a fortieth *küi* and thus won the competition. This *küi*, which the *küishi* dedicated to his rival, came to be known as "Sylqyldaq" (from *sylqyldau*, "to tinkle," or *sylqyldap külu*, "to laugh sonorously") as a reflection of its joyful character.[29] As you listen to and watch the example, pay attention to the performer's technique and the resultant sound, and note how the *küi*'s musical image unfolds in time.

Tättimbet Qazanghapuly.
Rendering of a photograph by Aigerim Ilip.

WATCH

Example 14.7. "Sylqyldaq" (Tinkling), composed by Tättimbet Qazanghapuly, performed by Äpike Äbenova. Fragment from a film, 1980. Courtesy of Central State Archive of Film, Photography, and Sound Recordings of the Republic of Kazakhstan.

STUDY QUESTIONS

1. How would you characterize differences between the *tökpe* and *shertpe* playing techniques?

2. Based on the example of "Sylqyldaq," how would you define differences between *küi*s in the two styles with regard to the narrative flow of music and the aesthetic quality of the sound, or sound ideal?

3. Describe the structural progression of the *küi*. Does it have a recognizable theme? If so, how is it developed by the composer?

Tättimbet became known as the author of sixty-two *küi*s called "Qosbasar" ("Alpys eki Qosbasar"), a genre of cyclic *küi*s in the *shertpe* style analogous to "Alpys eki Aqjeleng" in the *tökpe* tradition. Oral accounts of the cycle's origin, based on an archetypal legend, link the emergence of Tättimbet's *küi*s to his encounter with Küshikbai, a wealthy man (*bai*) from his tribe, the Arghyn. Küshikbai had lost his only son and heir and, overcome by grief, lay down and decided to starve himself to death. Seeing this, his alarmed relatives asked Tättimbet to make a visit and help save Küshikbai's life. The *küishi* arrived in Küshikbai's *auyl* and, seating himself on the threshold of his yurt, began to play sixty-two tunes on the *dombyra,* one by one.[30] As Tättimbet played, Küshikbai felt relief and regained his will to live. The story goes that when Küshikbai rose from his bed, he was surprised to see before him a young musician, to whom he said, "I thought my grief was the most terrible in the world, but listening to your *küi*s, I realized that there is grief worse than mine, and that a man should continue to live in the face of all adversity. But I thought you were an old wise man, and you are little more than a child. Where does the grief in your *küi*s come from?" To this Tättimbet responded, "Your grief is the grief of one person, while I bear in myself the grief of all people."

Äpike Äbenova.
Courtesy of Central State Archive of Film, Photography, and Sound Recordings of the Republic of Kazakhstan.

Tättimbet's cycle of sixty-two "Qosbasar" (Two-stringed or twofold), a series of reflections on life and death, is said to have consisted of six groups of *küi*s (five groups of ten *küi*s and the sixth of twelve), each expressing a certain emotional state and marking a particular stage in the healing of Küshikbai. The last group of twelve *küi*s was called "Qyrmyzy Qosbasar," *qyrmyzy* (scarlet) being the name of a short-lived steppe flower similar to a dandelion. Explaining the meaning of this group of *küi*s, Tättimbet reportedly said, "A man's life is as ephemeral as a dandelion. Why seek to shorten it still more?"[31] Example 14.8 features a version of "Qyrmyzy Qosbasar" passed down by a leading inheritor of Tättimbet's musical legacy, Äbiken Khasenov (1897–1958). Like other surviving "Qosbasar" *küi*s, it has a prominent melody and a songlike strophic form unified by recurring cadences that reaffirm the main tones. A formal scheme of the *küi* is provided in table 14.3.

LISTEN

Example 14.8. "Qyrmyzy Qosbasar" (Scarlet Qosbasar), composed by Tättimbet Qazanghapuly, performed by Äbiken Khasenov. Courtesy of Central State Archive of Film, Photography, and Sound Recordings of the Republic of Kazakhstan.

Table 14.3. Formal Structure of "Qyrmyzy Qosbasar"

Time Code	Section	Characteristics
0:00–0:19	A	The first melodic motif or phrase akin to the initial verse of a song, followed by a cadence-like repetition of the main melodic interval, a fifth.
0:20–0:28	B	The second melodic phrase akin to the final verse of a song, followed by a cadence. A and B appear to be in a question-answer relationship.
0:29–0:46	A^1	Variant of the first phrase.
0:47–1:00	B^1	Variant of the second phrase.
1:01–1:18	A^2	Another variant of the first phrase. An amplification of the melody with the bass drone at 1:09–1:11 marks the culmination of the *küi*.
1:19–1:33	B^2	Another variant of the second phrase, continuing on from the culmination.
1:34–1:41	B^3	Varied repetition of a passage from B^2, which serves as a coda.

Study Questions

1. In what ways is "Qyrmyzy Qosbasar" structurally distinct from *tökpe küi*s composed according to the sectional principle? Does it show any similarity in its formal organization to "Sylqyldaq" in the previous example?

2. How would you describe the influence of singing traditions in "Qyrmyzy Qosbasar"? Does the *küi* sound songlike? If you hear songlike features, how are they reinterpreted on the *dombyra*?

3. What state of mind is expressed by this *küi*? Does the story of its origin correlate with the image conveyed by the music?

A contrasting example of Tättimbet's compositional style is "Saryjailau" (Golden summer settlement), a large-scale, technically sophisticated, and structurally complex *küi* that is regarded as a masterpiece of Kazakh *dombyra* music. The *küi* paints the idyllic scene of an alpine summer settlement, which has been variously interpreted as a symbol of human life in a perpetual state of mobility, or the promised land (*Jeruiyq*) that was sought by a legendary Kazakh hero, Asan qaighy.[32] This image is musically created through richly melodious thematic material based on two distinct initial themes (0:06–0:15 and 0:19–0:23) and a contrasting section (2:11–2:23). The contrasting section appears after the development of the main themes has reached its climax, and is followed by a new culmination and variant recapitulation of the two themes. The following example presents the version of the *küi* transmitted by Äbiken Khasenov.

Äbiken Khasenov.
Rendering of a photograph by Aigerim Ilip.

LISTEN **Example 14.9.** "Saryjailau" (Golden summer settlement), composed by Tättimbet Qazanghapuly, performed by Äbiken Khasenov. Courtesy of Central State Archive of Film, Photography, and Sound Recordings of the Republic of Kazakhstan.

STUDY QUESTIONS

1. How would you compare "Saryjailau" with the two previously presented *küi*s by Tättimbet? Is it close to either of them in its technical execution and structural development? Does it display any songlike qualities, similar to or distinct from those examples?

2. What can you say about the rhythmic pattern employed by the composer? Is it regular or irregular? What is its role in creating the *küi*'s image, whether it is to be understood in literal or figurative terms?

3. How do you hear the narrative and emotional state communicated by the *küi*? Do you concur with the interpretations referred to above?

In the late nineteenth and early twentieth centuries a new idiosyncratic stylistic trend within the *shertpe* tradition of *dombyra* performance evolved in the southeast of Kazakhstan, in the area that forms the foothills of the Qaratau Mountains. The founder of the Qaratau *dombyra* tradition, Sügir Äliuly

(1882–1961), originally from the Sozaq region of present-day Kazakhstan, was a follower of the Arqa *shertpe* school and an accomplished performer of Tättimbet's *küi*s. He was also a disciple of the great *qobyz* player and composer from Qaratau, Yqylas Dükenuly (1843–1916), and came to master the performance of *qobyz küi*s (see chapter 16). His composition style fused elements of the classical Arqa *shertpe* with the musical language of *qobyz* performance. Additionally, it embraced the technical and structural properties of the *tökpe* style current in the contiguous southwestern region of the Syr Darya River and the Aral Sea. Thus, some of his *dombyra küi*s are distinguished by lyricism and a songlike quality typical of Arqa *küi*s. Others show an affinity to *qobyz* music, having been either adapted from *qobyz* repertory or performed interchangeably on both instruments. Still others are played with the strumming technique (*qara qaghys*) or are structured in a manner similar to the sectional principle of *tökpe küi*s, with specific musical and stylistic devices adapted to the narrative content and character of individual pieces. The intersection of *shertpe* with *tökpe* and *qobyz* performance, which is a hallmark of the Qaratau tradition, with its local musical interconnections and exchange, became possible thanks to its late development in Kazakh instrumental music as the creation of twentieth-century *küishi*s. It thus represents the most recent and stylistically heterogeneous tradition of *shertpe,* and of *dombyra* performance in general.

Maghauiya Khamzin, *shertpe dombyra* player.

The following example of Sügir's *küi*, "Toghyz tarau" (Nine branches), illustrates the fusion of *shertpe* style with *qobyz* performance tradition. The *küi* is thought to belong to the cycle of nine *küi*s of contemplative character and epic genre (*tolghau*) called "Kertolghau." A legendary account of the origins of these *küi*s has it that in old times one *küi* from the cycle would be played before a khan each day of the year, and that nine of these *küi*s were accorded special significance.[33] These cyclic *küi*s have circulated in both *dombyra* and *qobyz* variants. Like other *küi*s in the cycle, "Toghyz tarau" has a principal melody that includes sustained reiterations of the same tones, calling to mind the sound of the *qobyz,* and a recurring cadential motif typical of traditional *qobyz* tunes. Like some *qobyz küi*s, "Toghyz tarau" is intended for a *dombyra* tuned to the interval of a fifth (*teris burau*), and its main theme (D) is played with an open drone string, producing a sound reminiscent of bowing across the *qobyz* strings. In example 14.10, "Toghyz tarau" is performed by the celebrated *dombyra* and *qobyz* player from the Qaratau region, Jappas Qalambaev (1909–1969). The form of the *küi* is shown in table 14.4.

Example 14.10. "Toghyz tarau" (Nine branches), composed by Sügir Äliuly, performed by Jappas Qalambaev. Courtesy of Central State Archive of Film, Photography, and Sound Recordings of the Republic of Kazakhstan.

TABLE 14.4. FORMAL STRUCTURE OF "TOGHYZ TARAU"

TIME CODE	SECTION		
0:00–0:19	A	Introduction	Main motifs develop in the high register, with the widest intervals attained at the outset of the *küi*.
0:20–0:31	B		
0:31–0:47	A		Cadential motif in the low register adopted from the *qobyz* tradition.
0:48–0:57	B		
0:57–1:03	C		
1:04–1:23	D^1	Main part	Melodic development in the high and middle registers against a bass drone, with occasional moves up a fifth and a sixth on the low-sounding string in D^2.
1:24–1:50	D^2		
1:50–2:08	D^3		
2:08–2:33	D^2		The setting begins as D^3 but the bass then moves up a third before returning to the main tone in the conclusion.
2:34–2:55	D^4		

STUDY QUESTIONS

1. Compare this example with the examples of *qobyz küi*s given in chapter 16. How is the sound of this *küi* similar to or distinct from them? What means are employed in *dombyra* performance to represent the sound of the bowed lute, *qobyz*?

2. Would you say that this *küi* is structurally unusual compared to the examples of *shertpe küi*s you have heard earlier?

3. How would you characterize the general emotional mode or affect of the *küi*?

The assimilation of the stylistic features of *tökpe* in the Qaratau *shertpe* tradition can be observed in the *küi* "Saltanat" by a successor of Sügir, the twentieth-century *küishi,* Tölegen Mombekov (1918–1997). "Saltanat" belongs to a series of four

Tölegen Mombekov.
Courtesy of the archive of the
Kazakhstan Republic Television and
Radio Corporation.

biographical *küi*s that he composed as a response to the death of his wife, in 1969. This *küi,* in particular, was dedicated to his young daughter, Saltanat, who missed her mother, and it expressed feelings of loss, sorrow, and nostalgia.[34] Evolving from a songlike tuneful melody and played primarily with a *shertpe* plucking technique, the *küi* progresses according to the sectional principle, with clearly defined sections in increasingly higher pitch areas (*orta buyn, birinshi,* and *ekinshi sagha*) alternating with the refrain. Unusually for a *tökpe küi,* however, each new section is repeated like a strophe in a song, the sectional division thus assuming a strophic form. Example 14.11 features a performance of the *küi* by the composer himself during a recital in Almaty in the 1980s. A formal scheme of the *küi* appears in table 14.5.

WATCH

Example 14.11. "Saltanat," composed and performed by Tölegen Mombekov. Fragment from a film, 1980s. Courtesy of the archive of the Kazakhstan Republic Television and Radio Corporation.

STUDY QUESTIONS

1. Which features distinguish "Saltanat" from "Toghyz tarau," and which features identify both of them as originating from the Qaratau *shertpe* tradition?

2. Compare the structure of "Saltanat" with that of *tökpe küi*s analyzed in this chapter. In what ways is its sectional division dissimilar from them?

3. Discuss Tölegen Mombekov's manner of performance. Does anything in his music or his performance style suggest that he is a twentieth-century composer and performer?

TABLE 14.5. FORMAL STRUCTURE OF "SALTANAT"

TIME CODE	SECTION	NAME	CHARACTERISTICS
0:00–0:17 0:17–0:21	A a	*Orta buyn*	Initial section in the middle pitch area with intonations of the main theme (B), ending with a cadence that recurs later as a refrain.
0:22–0:47	B	*Negizgi buyn*	Main theme in the middle pitch area.
0:48–0:50	a	*Orta buyn*	Refrain
0:51–1:14	B	*Negizgi buyn*	Repetition of the main theme.
1:15–1:20	a	*Orta buyn*	Refrain with strumming across open strings.
1:21–1:51	C	*Birinshi (kishi) sagha*	First culmination section in the lower high register, followed by a descent that segues into the refrain.
1:52–1:54	a	*Orta buyn*	Refrain with strumming across open strings.
1:55–2:21	C	*Birinshi (kishi) sagha*	Repetition of the first culmination section.
2:22–2:24	a	*Orta buyn*	Refrain
2:24–2:48	B	*Negizgi buyn*	Repetition of the main theme.
2:49–2:51	a	*Orta buyn*	Refrain with strumming across open strings.
2:51–3:14	D	*Ekinshi (ülken) sagha*	Second culmination section in the upper high register.
3:14–3:29	C¹	*Birinshi (kishi) sagha*	D segues into a shorter version of the first culmination section in the lower high register, followed by a descent to the refrain.
3:29–3:31	a	*Orta buyn*	Refrain with strumming across open strings.
3:32–3:53	D	*Ekinshi (ülken) sagha*	Repetition of the second culmination section.
3:53–4:08	C¹	*Birinshi (kishi) sagha*	Repetition of the shorter version of the first culmination section.
4:08–4:09	a¹	*Orta buyn*	Variant form of refrain.
4:10–4:35	B	*Negizgi buyn*	Reiteration of the main theme.
4:36–4:38	a	*Orta buyn*	Refrain

Unlike the Qaratau tradition, *dombyra* performance styles arising from the regions of Jetisu and Altai in the southeast and east of Kazakhstan and from neighboring areas populated by Kazakh communities in present-day Chinese Xinjiang, western Mongolia, and the Altai Republic of the Russian Federation, are associated with an early type of Kazakh instrumental music.[35] *Dombyra*s historically current in these regions had a shorter fingerboard than instruments found in central or western Kazakhstan. In Altai, in particular, musicians used a *dombyra* with seven frets and an entirely diatonic scale. Accordingly, local *küi*s, as distinct from many *küi*s in Arqa, Qaratau, or the western region, have a small tonal range and are relatively simple in their melodic and modal organization, rarely including modal shifts or chromatic tones. Many of them are short and built up from reiterations of one tune or melody. Compared to *dombyra* pieces in the other *shertpe* traditions, *küi*s in Jetisu and Altai tend to be less rhythmically complex and variable, and are based on regular rhythmic patterns. In this way, they are like the local songs, many of which have a small melodic range, simple strophic form, and regular rhythmic patterns. A distinctive feature of *dombyra* repertory in Jetisu and especially in Altai is the prevalence of *küi*s whose strings are tuned to the interval of a fifth (*teris burau*)—a less common tuning for *dombyra* performance in the west of Kazakhstan. In such *küi*s the melody develops on the higher-sounding string and is supported by a bass drone produced on the open lower string. Melodic development draws on pitches of the harmonic series, thus linking this stylistic type of *dombyra küi* with other kinds of music making among the Kazakhs and neighboring ethnic groups in the greater Altai region (see chapter 17). Another specific feature of *shertpe* in Jetisu and Altai is the occurrence of *küi*s for the *dombyra* with strings tuned to a fifth or, more rarely, to

a fourth, that are played with basic wrist strumming (*qara qaghys*), either throughout or in alternation with finger plucking, which produces a sustained two-voiced sound or two separate "voices." These features occur, in particular, in folk legend *küi*s ascribed early origins that are prominent in the local repertory.

Example 14.12 presents one such *küi* that is current in Altai, performed by a renowned *dombyra* player and composer originally from western Mongolia, Qabykei Aqmeruly (1927–2012). The *küi* is dedicated to the Kazakh hero (*batyr*) Jänibek, who fought against the Jungars in the eighteenth century. According to the story of its origin recounted by the performer, Jänibek received a call to attack enemies who were approaching the Kazakh lands, and this call was

Qabykei Aqmeruly.

captured by *dombyra* players in a *küi* that articulates the words "*Jänibek, Jänibek, shap*" (Jänibek, Jänibek, strike), while at the same time depicting the galloping of Jänibek's horse, Kök dönen.

Example 14.12. "Jänibek, Jänibek, shap" (Jänibek, Jänibek, strike), or "Kök dönen," folk *küi*, performed by Qabykei Aqmeruly. Aqjar, Taldyqorghan region, Kazakhstan, 2004.

STUDY QUESTIONS

1. How are the words of the call in the legend articulated in music?

2. In what ways is this folk legend *küi* distinct from the spectrum of *küi*s in the two stylistic traditions of *dombyra* performance presented in this chapter?

3. As you listen to the *küi*, do you find the idea of the early origins of the style exemplified in folk legend *küi*s convincing?

Performer Profile: Abdulhamit Raiymbergenov, *Dombyra* Player and Visionary Music Educator
THEODORE LEVIN

Courtesy of Abdulhamit Raiymbergenov.

Abdulhamit Raiymbergenov (b. 1957) is a virtuoso *dombyra* player who has focused his energy not on musical performance but on music education. Raiymbergenov is the founder and director of Kökil College, in Almaty, Kazakhstan, where he launched a pioneering program called "Murager" (Heritage) to provide musical enrichment on a mass scale to Kazakh schoolchildren. Students participating in the program are not specially selected for musical talent, and most do not intend to become professional musicians. Instead, Raiymbergenov's goal is to build audiences for the next generation of traditional musicians under the assumption that their music will not survive unless it is performed within a social milieu that supports it. Raiymbergenov expanded the "Murager" program to schools nationwide, and created curriculum materials and teacher training seminars to support its activities.

Abdulhamit Raiymbergenov was born into a family of musicians in the Aqtöbe region of western Kazakhstan. His great-grandfather was a famous *dombyra* player, his grandfather a mullah and Sufi, and his father a professional musician who worked in a teacher's college and composed many *küi*s and songs. Abdulhamit listened to the music and stories of musicians who gathered in the home of his grandfather, where he heard the lore of their exploits and adventures. From his family and local *dombyra* players he learned about the *küishi* Qazanghap Tilepbergenuly, originally from his home region of Aqtöbe, and became a leading performer, researcher, and promoter of his musical legacy. He also learned about Qurmanghazy Saghyrbaiuly, the eminent *küishi* from the Ural region, and came to master the performance of his *küi*s. Qurmanghazy became one of Abdulhamit's own heroes.

"Qurmanghazy was renowned for his cunning, courage, and skill on the *dombyra*," said Abdulhamit. "He lived at a time when czarist Russia had begun to exert a strong influence

Performer Profile: Abdulhamit Raiymbergenov, *Dombyra* Player and Visionary Music Educator *(CONTINUED)*

on the Kazakhs. He belonged to the Qyzylqurt tribe, and they all became followers of a revolutionary leader named Makhambet who led a revolt against czarist colonization. Qurmanghazy was accused of horse-thieving and czarist soldiers were sent from Orenburg to arrest him. They came to his home and, not finding him there, took away his wife and baby son. That evening when Qurmanghazy returned, people told him what had happened, and Qurmanghazy mounted a horse and rode off to find his wife. In the dark

of night, he spotted a fire burning in uninhabited steppe. Dismounting and scurrying closer, he saw his wife and son sleeping by the fire, and the soldiers asleep nearby. Silently, he crept up and removed the bullets from their rifles, took one rifle for himself, swept up his wife and baby, and ran away.

Later Qurmanghazy composed a *küi* about the incident. The music illustrates the way he ducked down into gullies and crevices in the steppe to avoid detection as he crept up on the soldiers. At one point, he

rolls down a hillock, and the music shows that with a portamento."

In Qurmanghazy's *küi*, the *dombyra* "speaks" the words *"Buqtym, buqtym, saida buqtym"* (I'm ducking, I'm ducking, I'm ducking in a ditch). The performer alternately damps and strums the strings to highlight speech rhythm and articulation. The *küi*'s loping rhythm and abrupt halts convincingly portray Qurmanghazy's jerky movements as he sneaks up on the soldiers' campfire to save his wife and son.

WATCH **Example 14.13.** "Buqtym, buqtym" (I'm ducking, I'm ducking), composed by Qurmanghazy Saghyrbaiuly, performed by Abdulhamit Raiymbergenov. Almaty, Kazakhstan, 2005.

STUDY QUESTIONS

1. How successful is "Buqtym, buqtym" at representing Qurmanghazy's physical movements? If you didn't already know the "program" of the *küi*, would you be able to guess it from the music alone?

2. What is the central element of musical craft for a *dombyra* player? In other words, what is involved in playing the *dombyra* at a level of mastery like that represented by Abdulhamit Raiymbergenov?

Performer Profile: Talasbek Äsemqulov
The Art of *Küi*: "Tengri's Whisper"
SAIDA DAUKEYEVA

"Eight faces, one essence" (*Segiz qyrly, bir syrly*), a popular Kazakh expression that celebrates the cultural ideal of versatility, aptly

describes master *dombyra* player, *küishi*, writer, and music scholar Talasbek Äsemqulov (1955–2014). Äsemqulov represented the *shertpe*

tradition rooted in Saryarqa—the Golden Steppe—and belonged to the lineage of Baijigit, Tättimbet, and their disciples and successors in the

Performer Profile: Talasbek Äsemqulov (CONTINUED)

twentieth century. Äsemqulov was also an accomplished writer and scholar whose works illuminated the significance of *küi* in Kazakh culture and society, both historical and contemporary. Brought up by his maternal grandfather, Jünisbai Stambaev (1891–1973), a renowned *küishi* in the Semei (Semipalatinsk) region of eastern Kazakhstan, Talasbek Äsemqulov immersed himself in the study of *dombyra küi* from an early age, learning under the guidance of his grandfather and other famous *dombyra* players in the region, such as Baghanaly Sayatölekov (1895–1982). Before his grandfather died, he bestowed his blessing on the young Talasbek to follow the path of a *dombyra* player. By the age of eighteen, when he went to Almaty, Talasbek had mastered a large repertory of *shertpe küi*s, and in 1976, he recorded a solo LP of *küi*s by Baijigit on the Soviet Union's Melodiya record label. Offered admission to study at Almaty Conservatory, he followed his grandfather's admonition not to make *dombyra* performance a means of livelihood, and declined the offer, noting that conservatory training departed from the traditional approach to musicianship that he wished to pursue. Instead, Talasbek devoted himself to his other passion, the study of literature. He became a writer and literary critic who wrote on Kazakh culture, history, mythology, literature, and music in both Kazakh and Russian languages in a variety of genres, including stories, novels, film scripts, and articles for newspapers and journals.

Uniquely for a Kazakh musician steeped in tradition, Talasbek Äsemqulov combined qualities of both a cultural insider and outsider. As a pupil of acclaimed *küishi*s from the past and a master performer and composer in his own right, he promoted the transmission and preservation of the old *shertpe* repertory and creatively interpreted the *shertpe* tradition in his own *küi*s. A number of *küi*s by Baijigit, a *küi* by Ketbugha, and a few formerly unknown *küi*s by Tättimbet were rediscovered through his interpretations. At the same time, he offered insight into Kazakh music and *dombyra* performance from the perspective of a music scholar and cultural studies specialist with a panoramic knowledge of Kazakh folklore, poetry, and prose, Western philosophy and theosophy, and Russian, Indian, and Japanese literature. Through his publications on Kazakh music, students and researchers learned about the characteristic features of *dombyra* instrument types in western and eastern Kazakhstan and the related musical terminology, the traditional system of musical transmission from master to disciple, as well as technical, structural, and aesthetic aspects of *shertpe* and *dombyra küi* in general. At a time when the priorities of Soviet cultural policy sidelined the *shertpe* tradition in mainstream performance practice and led to a decline in its homeland of eastern Kazakhstan (see chapter 17), Äsemqulov was one of only a few musicians and music critics who raised awareness

Courtesy of Zira Naurzbaeva.

of this idiosyncratic style and actively promoted it through performances, compositions, and writings. Though Äsemqulov was never able to teach music officially because he lacked a conservatory degree, his musicianship and ideas inspired many performers and scholars as well as a small group of devoted students and followers, who continue his work today.

Talasbek Äsemqulov underscored the spiritual dimension of *dombyra* performance and pedagogy. In an article comparing traditional musical training to the academic education of *dombyra* players in Kazakhstan, he wrote: "The art of *küi* is a path for a mature consciousness imbued with a sense of spiritual quest. The musician revives the art of the past, creates contemporary art, and, if his level permits, shapes [the art of] the future . . . With due training, a person can be taught whatever he

Performer Profile: Talasbek Äsemqulov *(CONTINUED)*

likes, including the order of pressing frets and striking strings. But such a person is not a *küishi,* and what he performs is not *küi* . . . The true art is a high summit. But this summit is not something separate from the human soul and spirituality. Attainment of this summit is the inner state of one who has achieved spiritual maturity."[36] Referring to an old Kazakh expression that reflects an understanding of instrumental music as a sacred, divine art, Äsemqulov called *küi* performance "Tengri's whisper" (*Tängirding kübiri*),[37] or "subtle matter" that has the power to reveal the presence of eternity in transient human life: "*Küi* is Tengri's whisper, the Kazakhs thought, and they venerated *küishi*s capable of hearing the voice of the Almighty inaudible to an ordinary person, the primordial silence from which the world was created."[38]

Another theme that Äsemqulov raises in his work is the expression of grief, anguish, and sorrow in Kazakh music. Interpreting the prevalence of major-sounding modes in the musical depiction of sorrowful images, he linked it with old beliefs among the Kazakh nomads according to which life and death are interrelated phases in the cycle of human existence, with death considered "an apotheosis, a culmination of life."[39] In Äsemqulov's view, the emergence of minor-sounding Kazakh *küi*s dedicated to themes of grief and sorrow in the twentieth century resulted from a change in the understanding of death in that time of political upheaval and cultural modernization in Kazakh society.

The following examples present two *küi*s in the traditional genre *qongyr* (deep-brown)—meditative, sorrowful instrumental pieces that are current in both *shertpe* and *tökpe* stylistic traditions. The first *küi* was composed by the famous twentieth-century *shertpe dombyra* player, Äbiken Khasenov, who is discussed in the present chapter. Various accounts explain the *küi*'s origin as dedicated to tragic events in modern Kazakh history or to the death of a friend, but whatever the case, this plaintive *küi* in a minor mode powerfully evokes a state of distress and anguish. Once, while listening to this *küi* performed by another *dombyra* player, Talasbek Äsemqulov was reminded of the unconventional nature of *qongyr küi*s in minor modes and, as a response (*nazira*) to Äbiken Khasenov, composed a version of this *küi* in a major mode, which he called "Äbikendi jubatu" (Consolation of Äbiken).

LISTEN

Example 14.14. "Qongyr" (Deep-brown), composed and performed by Äbiken Khasenov. Courtesy of Central State Archive of Film, Photography, and Sound Recordings of the Republic of Kazakhstan.

LISTEN

Example 14.15. "Äbikendi jubatu" (Consolation of Äbiken), composed and performed by Talasbek Äsemqulov. Courtesy of Zira Naurzbaeva.

STUDY QUESTIONS

1. How distinct is Talasbek Äsemqulov's version from the original *küi*? Does it seem to you to be a sorrowful *küi*? If not, what state of mind or affect does it communicate?

2. Having listened to these and other *küi*s in the chapter, would you agree with Äsemqulov's perspective on the spiritual significance of *küi* that he called "Tengri's whisper"?

PART 2.   Kyrgyz *Küü*

NURLANBEK NYSHANOV

In Kyrgyz, the term *küü* refers to narrative music traditionally played as a solo on one of a variety of local instruments that include wooden and metal jaw harps, flutes, the two-stringed bowl fiddle *kyl-kiyak,* and the three-stringed lute *komuz.* Analogous narrative musical forms, for example, Kazakh *küi* and Bashkir *kuy,* exist among other Turkic peoples. Kyrgyz *küü*s are typically short, with the longest of them lasting around five minutes.

The traditional performance style of *küü* is based on improvisation, and many *küü*s exist in multiple versions, leading to comparisons with the art of oral poetic improvisation (*tökmölük*) practiced by bards (see chapter 10). Like improvising oral poets, instrumentalists extemporize a specific performance version of a narrative piece while preserving its core contents and key themes. The composition and performance of *küü* underwent a serious decline between the mid-1960s and mid-1980s—a period when Kyrgyz traditional music lost its popularity and Western instruments such as the guitar and accordion replaced indigenous instruments. In the late 1980s and early 1990s, a revival of interest in traditional music stimulated musicians to compose new *küü*s. Many of them were fixed in music notation and designed for performance not by soloists—as was traditional—but by ensembles.

Table 14.6 shows brief characterizations of *küü*s performed on eight different instruments.

*Komuz küü*s constitute the largest portion of the overall *küü* repertory, analogous to the preeminence of *dombyra küi*s in Kazakh music. And just as the *dombyra* is widely regarded in Kazakhstan as the national instrument of the Kazakhs, the *komuz* is viewed within Kyrgyzstan as the national instrument of the Kyrgyz. In both cases, the present-day popularity of the instrument is due in part to the large and virtuosic repertory of instrumental music composed for it beginning in the nineteenth century and extending down to the present.

The repertory of *komuz* music is exceptionally rich. In the twentieth century, more than three hundred *küü*s were recorded from various Kyrgyz *komuz* players. Some of these *küü*s were composed by the players from whom they were recorded, while others were passed down to players from earlier performer-composers. Most *küü*s can be attributed to a specific composer—a striking contrast to many repertories of "folk" music in which the identity of talented composers from the past has been lost.

Gülbara Baigashkaeva
with *komuz.*

Photo by Katherine Vincent. Courtesy of
Aga Khan Music Initiative.

TABLE 14.6. CHARACTERIZATIONS OF *KÜÜS* PERFORMED ON EIGHT DIFFERENT INSTRUMENTS

NAME OF INSTRUMENT	TYPICAL NARRATIVE CONTENT	CHARACTERIZATION OF MUSIC
Jygach ooz komuz (wooden jaw harp)	Descriptions of nature or natural setting, e.g., summer pasture, a yurt, a nightingale	Short and simple
Temir ooz komuz (metal jaw harp)	Descriptions of animals and nature as well as legendary men	Repertory includes traditional songs and *küüs* played on other instruments
Surnai (clarinet)	Mainly played at traditional feasts and on military campaigns	Expressive—had a great impact on animals, including horses
Sybyzgy (side-blown flute)	Descriptions of nature ("Shepherd's *küü*") or people ("Akmaktym"—a girl's name)	Lament-like; repertory includes variants of folk songs
Chopo choor (clay ocarina)	Old laments and *küüs* about nature	Main repertory consists of variants of folk songs
Choor (end-blown reed flute)	Widespread in Kyrgyzstan until the second half of 20th century; rich and diverse repertory including illustrative *küüs* (e.g.,"Flight of the wild mountain turkey"), lament *küüs*, *dastan küüs* (i.e., narratives excerpted from epic songs), lyrical and descriptive songs, functional *küüs* used to accompany handcraft work or *biy* dance	Archaic character, expressive, special timbre
Kyl-kiyak (bowl fiddle)	Group 1: *küüs* originating from songs Group 2: purely instrumental *küüs* that portray images of nature, animals, and traditional customs	Skilled *kyl-kiyak* players can imitate human language, the howl of a wolf, the neighing of a horse
Komuz (three-stringed lute)	Group 1: *küüs* originating from melodies of songs and *dastans* Group 2: *küüs* performed with mimetic hand gestures, typically playful in nature. Group 3: classical *küüs*	Diverse melodic characteristics; see below

*Komuz küü*s can be roughly divided into three categories, listed below. The boundaries between these categories are not rigid, and some *küü*s fall into more than one category.

1. *KÜÜS* DERIVED FROM THE MELODIES OF SONGS AND EPIC POEMS PERFORMED AS SONGS (*DASTANS*)

*Küü*s in this category are sometimes called "*obon küülör*" (song *küü*s). Their name notwithstanding, song *küü*s are performed without words, as purely instrumental music, and constitute a distinct instrumental genre. Some song *küü*s have been refined by skilled musicians who have elevated them to the level of classics. Their subject matter encompasses lyrical, tragic, and historical themes; personalities, and events; for example, Genghis Khan, the subject of the *küü* "Ket Buka," and Attila, the subject of "Shüdüngüt küü."

2. GESTURAL *KÜÜS*, I.E., *KÜÜS* WITH GESTURAL MOVEMENTS OF THE HANDS

These *küü*s require great technical and acting skills from the performer. Before or during a performance, most musicians tell the narrative story of the *küü*. The performer must be at once a musician, actor, narrator, and sometimes a singer. In other words, this genre reflects the theatrical image of a single actor. *Komuz* players of the past century contributed significantly to the development and popularization of gestural *küü*s. Among the greatest of them was Niyazaaly Boroshev (1856–1942).

Niyazaaly was born in the Aksy region of southern Kyrgyzstan, and by the age of fifteen, he had become known as a *komuzchu*. In the past, musicians traveled on horseback from one region to another to meet with other musicians, exchange experiences, and entertain the public. Niyazaaly interacted closely with musicians from the Talas region of northern Kyrgyzstan. The art of playing *komuz* with elaborate hand gestures was widespread in the Talas region, and this tradition had a significant influence on Niyazaaly's music. He was known as a great instrumentalist and left many masterpieces, among them "Arsar küü," "Ker tolgoo," "Niyazaaly's Kambarkan," and "Kara özgöy." Of these *küü*s, "Kara özgöy" (Impudent one) is the most popular. A performance of "Kara özgöy" by Emilbek Ishenbek uulu is reproduced in example 14.16. Emilbek (b. 1993) comes from a musical family, studied at the Ustatshakirt traditional music center in Bishkek, and was a *shakirt* (apprentice) of *küü* master Nurak Abdyrakhmanov (1946–2014).

The *komuz* is a fretless three-stringed long-necked lute.

Niyazaaly Boroshev.

Example 14.16. "Kara özgöy" (Impudent one), composed by Niyazaaly Boroshev, performed by Emilbek Ishenbek uulu. Filmed by Nurlanbek Nyshanov, Bishkek, Kyrgyzstan, 2011.

Emilbek Ishenbek uulu.

According to one contemporary master *komuzchu,* Niyazaaly composed "Kara özgöy" when he went to the forest to collect firewood, and there encountered robbers who tried to kill him. Niyazaaly asked the leader of the robbers to give him a chance to say a few words and play his *komuz.* The leader agreed, and Niyazaaly grabbed his *komuz* and played a lively *küü* using elaborate and swift hand gestures and body movements. The robbers were mesmerized and asked him to play more. He played another *küü,* about his unruly cow, which almost killed his old wife by butting her when she tried to milk her. Last, he played a sad and mellow *küü* and put the robbers to sleep. As he tried to run away, the robbers awoke and ran after him, shouting to him to tell them the name of the first *küü* he played, which had purified them spiritually. They asked Niyazaaly to forgive them for their wickedness and impudence (*kara özgöylük*), and begged him not to tell people about this incident. He forgave them, told them about the power of the *komuz küü* to prevail over evil, and called them to be kind to people and leave their "profession" for good.[40]

STUDY QUESTIONS

1. What musical techniques does the composer use to express or evoke "impudence" in "Kara özgöy"?

2. What does "Kara özgöy" suggest about its composer—about his personality and the nature of his musical creativity?

Atay Ogonbaev.

Another well-known composer-performer of gestural *küüs* was Atay Ogonbaev (1900–1949). Atay, as he is known, was born in the Talas region of northern Kyrgyzstan. He first learned to play *komuz* from his grandfather and from *komuzchus* who lived in his village. He later became the student of the great *komuzchu* Toktogul. Almost all of Atay's *küüs* represent the genre of gestural *küüs.* Among them, "Ak-Tamak—Kök-Tamak" (White-throat—Gray-throat) occupies a special place. Before playing this *küü,* the performer typically tells its story. The plot of the piece involves an argument between two birds, husband and wife, who disagree about whether to stay and nest where they are or fly south in search of warmer weather. The wife, Ak-Tamak, who wants to fly south, proposes that they settle their disagreement by engaging in a singing contest. They do, and Ak-Tamak wins.

The performance of "Ak-Tamak—Kök-Tamak" repro-duced in example 14.17 is by Namazbek Uraliev. Namazbek (b. 1956) grew up in the Issyk-Kul region of northern Kyrgyzstan. He learned to play the *komuz* from his grand-father, Uraaly, and from a relative named Bekbay. For many years, Namazbek worked in the cultural sphere, winning first place at various music contests. He has a rich repertory of *komuz* music and is known as a master *komuzchu* who plays classical *küü*s. He is also a skilled *komuz* maker (*usta*), and many well-known *komuzchu*s value his instruments.

Namazbek Uraliev.
Photo by Katherine Vincent. Courtesy of Aga Khan Music Initiative.

WATCH

Example 14.17. "Ak-Tamak—Kök-Tamak" (White-throat—Gray-throat), composed by Atay Ogonbaev, performed by Namazbek Uraliev. Filmed by Theodore Levin, Semenovka, Kyrgyzstan, 2003.

STUDY QUESTIONS

1. How does Namazbek Uraliev use hand gestures to illustrate the plot of the *küü*? To what extent are his gestures literal and representational or, conversely, symbolic and abstract?

2. Without knowing the story of "Ak-Tamak—Kök-Tamak" in advance, would you have been able to guess its plot based on Namazbek's hand gestures—or, at least, that it concerns birds?

3. CLASSICAL (*ZALKAR*) OR GREAT/LARGE (*KARA*) *KÜÜ*S

*Zalkar küü*s, also known as *kara küü*s, represent the most sophisticated category of *küü* in terms of form and content, and are composed by professional *komuz* players. They include several genres, such as *botoy* ("camel calf"), which are more archaic and generally historical *küü*s; *shyngyrama* ("ringing"), which are basically lyrical, sometimes epic *küü*s played in a high position on the fingerboard of the *komuz; kerbez* ("vanity"), which are facetious *küü*s played in a middle position on the fingerboard of the *komuz;* and *Kambarkan* (the name of the legendary inven-tor of the *komuz*), which are narrative, philosophical *küü*s. Each of these genres is played at a particular fingering position on the neck of the *komuz,* with the in-strument's three strings set in a distinctive tuning. Present-day *komuz* players use eighteen different tunings, four of which are considered to be core tunings. Of the eighteen tunings in current use, some are used for only a single *küü*.

TABLE 14.7. FOUR CORE *KOMUZ* TUNINGS

STRING PITCH	1ST STRING	2ND STRING	3RD STRING
Tuning 1	Mi	La	Mi
Tuning 2	Mi	La	Re
Tuning 3	Re	La	Mi
Tuning 4	Re	La	Re

Toktogul Satylganov.

Table 14.7 shows the four core tunings. The pitch relationships shown in the table are not linked to absolute pitches. Rather, within the physical limits of string length, thickness, and tautness, a *komuz* player can set the "*do*" of his or her instrument to whatever pitch best suits the sound of a particular instrument and the character of the particular *küü* being performed.

Some classical *küü*s do not belong to any of the three genres described above. Among these is the popular *küü* "Toguz kayryk" (Nine variations), composed by the great master *komuz* player and oral poet Toktogul Satylganov (1864–1933). "Toguz kayryk" indeed consists of a series of variations and permutations on a melodic theme; however, the number nine is conventional, and the piece actually has more than nine variations. (In the past, nine was considered to be a sacred number, and was held in great esteem by the Kyrgyz.) Toktogul experienced many difficulties, and "Toguz kayryk" is in some sense about the numerous major and sudden turns in his life.

Toktogul was born in the Ketmen-Töbö region of central Kyrgyzstan. He composed more than fifty *küü*s in almost every genre. Among the *küü*s that were transmitted through his pupils, "Toguz kayryk" became a favorite of contemporary *komuz* players, who play it with great enthusiasm. The following video clip shows *komuz* master Ruslan Jumabaev performing his version of "Toguz kayryk."

WATCH

Example 14.18. "Toguz kayryk" (Nine variations), composed by Toktogul Satylganov, performed by Ruslan Jumabaev. Filmed by Theodore Levin, Bishkek, Kyrgyzstan, 2003.

An autobiographical "program" for "Toguz kayryk" that circulates among contemporary *komuz* players links the *küü* to a dark chapter in Toktogul's life. In 1898, Toktogul participated in a major uprising against Russian administrative rule that took place in the city of Andijan, in the Ferghana Valley. The Russian army put down the uprising, and the leaders, including Toktogul, were exiled to Siberia.[41] Toktogul worked in terrible conditions, cutting wood and mining coal. He finally managed to escape and return home. Upon his return, he told his kinsmen and villagers what he had seen and experienced in that cold and faraway land. He grouped his experiences into nine stories and transformed each one into a *komuz* tune, with its story providing the tune's program. Toktogul himself improvised when he performed the *küü,* often adding more than nine parts, thus the program is best understood in a general rather than literal sense. The serial stories relate Toktogul's experience of exile—of being separated from his family, living in a cold prison where he experienced pain, suffering, and hunger while engaged in forced labor, trying to escape and being caught and punished, and finally escaping and returning home, only to discover that his son had died and his wife had married another man.[42]

Ruslan Jumabaev.
Photo by Katherine Vincent. Courtesy of Aga Khan Music Initiative.

STUDY QUESTIONS

1. How does the use of gesture in "Toguz kayryk" differ from that in "Ak-Tamak—Kök-Tamak"?

2. What musical techniques did Toktogul use to alter the initial melodic motif of "Toguz kayryk" in successive variations? Are these variations discrete, with obvious beginning and ending points, or do they flow together seamlessly into a continuous stream of sound?

3. For some listeners, "Toguz kayryk," with its slowly shifting variations on a short melodic motif, has a very contemporary sound. Does "Toguz kayryk" strike you this way?

Among the genres of classical *küü, Kambarkan küü*s are considered to be the most complex and musically deep. These *küü*s require both great technical skill and intense concentration. Traditionally, *Kambarkan küü*s do not include external effects such as playful hand gestures. A popular Kyrgyz saying links *Kambarkan küü*s to the very origin of *küü*: "*Küünün bashy Kambarkan*" (The origin of *küü* is *Kambarkan.*) The saying stems from a legendary figure named Kambar who is credited with inventing the *komuz* and composing the first *küü*. The legend recounts how, in ancient times, Kambar, a hunter, once heard a pleasant sound coming from the forest. Trying to identify the source of the sound, he saw that it came from a long piece of gut stretched between two branches of a tree. The stretched gut was the result of an accident involving a monkey: attempting to jump from one tree branch to another, the monkey fell and impaled its stomach on a sharp twig. As the poor monkey sailed through the air, its abdomen burst open and its gut was ripped out. Stretched thin in mid-air, the dried gut of the monkey vibrated in the wind, creating a rich sound. Kambar was inspired by his discovery to build a stringed

Toktomambet Orozov, known as Karamoldo.

instrument—the *komuz*—using animal gut for the strings, and on his *komuz,* he composed "Kambarkan." No evidence suggests that monkeys ever lived in what is now Kyrgyzstan, but terra-cotta statues of monkey musicians dating back almost two thousand years have been unearthed in various parts of Central Asia. A variant of the Kambar legend was also known in India, where it turns up in fourteenth-century literary sources, underscoring historical links between Central Asia and the subcontinent.

Komuz players from all Kyrgyz regions know the genre of *Kambarkan,* but the *komuz* players of the Issyk-Kul region contributed the most to its development. The best known of these musicians was the great *komuzchu* Karamoldo (birth name: Toktomambet) Orozov (1883–1960).

Toktomambet Orozov was born in the Issyk-Kul region of northern Kyrgyzstan. As a teenager, he received a religious education, and neighbors nicknamed him "Karamoldo"—"Black Mullah" or "Mullah with Dark Skin." Karamoldo first learned to play the *komuz* from his father, Oroz, and then from other well-known *komuz* players in Issyk-Kul and Naryn regions. He is the author of about thirty *küü*s.

Among the master *komuz* players known for performing Karamoldo's "Kambarkan" was Nurak Abdyrakhmanov (1946–2014) (see the performer profile in this chapter). Nurak Abdyrakhmanov was from the Ak-Talaa region of Naryn province and was considered one of Kyrgyzstan's leading *komuz* players and contemporary composers of *küü.*

Example 14.19. "Kambarkan," composed by Karamoldo, performed by Nurak Abdyrakhmanov. From *Tengir-Too: Mountain Music of Kyrgyzstan,* vol. 1 of *Music of Central Asia* (SFR, 2005), track 17.

STUDY QUESTIONS

1. What musical qualities distinguish "Kambarkan" from the *küü*s in the preceding examples— "Ak-Tamak—Kök-Tamak," "Toguz kayryk," and "Kara özgöy"?

2. Does the performance of Karamoldo's "Kambarkan" suggest a particular narrative program? If so, what is this program? If not, what does the *küü* evoke for you?

3. What is your critical assessment of Nurak Abdyrakhmanov's performance of "Kambarkan"? Is it a good performance? Why or why not?

Komuz Music Today

Komuz music remains popular in twenty-first-century Kyrgyzstan, and many contemporary *komuz* players are composing new *komuz küüs*. Through these new compositions, the tradition preserves its inner vitality, and the *küü* repertory is continually refreshed.

Some of the new *küü* compositions are intended for solo performance, while others are designed for group performance in an ensemble. The need to coordinate precisely the different instrumental parts of an ensemble performance has led to the use of Western staff notation, which represents an innovation in the overwhelmingly oral-aural history of *küü* composition, performance, and transmission.

Working with fellow members of the ensembles Tengir-Too and Ordo-Sakhna, and with students in Bishkek's Center Ustatshakirt, I have made my own contribution to this new repertory of notated *küüs* for two or three *komuz*es (see chapter 32). An example of such a *küü* is "Jol jürüsh" (On the road), reproduced in the following audio example in a performance by members of Tengir-Too. This short *küü* expands on two traditional melodic motifs. Tengir-Too always played it from notation, and it remains a fixed composition in its present form. The initial two motifs are old; the rest of the *küü* is new.

Students of Nurlanbek Nyshanov use sheet music to learn his compositions for *komuz* and other traditional Kyrgyz instruments.
Courtesy of Theodore Levin.

LISTEN **Example 14.20.** "Jol jürüsh" (On the road), composed and arranged by Nurlanbek Nyshanov, performed by members of Ensemble Tengir-Too. From *Tengir-Too: Mountain Music of Kyrgyzstan*, vol. 1 of *Music of Central Asia* (SFR, 2005), track 12.

Study Questions

1. How many *komuz*es are playing in the piece?

2. In what ways is "Jol jürüsh" different from older *küüs*?

3. What images does "Jol jürüsh" create? What kind of "road" and what kind of transport do you imagine when you hear the piece?

4. Do you believe that fixing *küüs* in notation is a good idea, or does notation impede traditional processes of extemporized performance?

Performer Profile: A Conversation with Nurak Abdyrakhmanov

ELMIRA KÖCHÜMKULOVA

Nurak Abdyrakhmanov (1946–2014) was one of the best-known and most versatile musicians in Kyrgyzstan. He was at once a virtuoso performer on the *komuz,* a composer of tradition-based music, a music theorist, historian, philosopher, and educator. My conversation with Nurak took place in fall 2010, in the unique, yurt-shaped guestroom of the house where he lived with his family in a village not far from Bishkek.

Photo by Katherine Vincent. Courtesy of Aga Khan Music Initiative.

Elmira Köchümkulova (EK): How did you learn to play the *komuz?*

Nurak Abdyrakhmanov (NA): Our family lived in an isolated mountainous *jayloo* (pasture) in northern Kyrgyzstan, and I had no children my own age to play with. My brothers and sister were older, and I liked to spend time with my father, who played the *komuz.* He used to make me bite down on the tip of the *komuz*'s neck while he played so that I would feel the vibration of the instrument's strings in my mouth. I was four years old, and he'd take me on his lap and make me play the *komuz* by holding my hand. We did that often, and by the time I was six, I could play quite well. My father knew many *küü*s. Later, when I was already a professional, he would still point out even the smallest flaws in my playing and say: "My son, don't distort the *küü!*"

When I was around eleven, my father sent me to a *komuz* master named Kasymkul Köchörbay uulu. I had to travel four to five hours on horseback to reach his house, and in exchange for his teaching, my father would send along fresh mutton and *koumiss,* fermented horse milk.

As a child, I also learned *küü*s from recordings. When I was in fifth grade, I fell ill, and had to stay in the hospital for more than a month. My father borrowed a portable gramophone—at that time only rich people could afford a gramophone—and brought me records made by well-known *komuz* players. I learned two *küü*s a day by listening to records and trying to play along. I learned more than forty *küü*s while I was in the hospital. People in the region began calling me "*bala komuzchu*"—"the little *komuz* player." At that time, it was rare for small children to play the *komuz.* In 1962, when I was sixteen, I participated in a national music competition and won first place among *komuzchu*s, and I was awarded a diploma and a gold-plated wristwatch. The more I began meeting talented people and performing at public gatherings, the more I became inspired to play the *komuz.* The fingernail of my right index finger would hurt from playing the *komuz* so much, and I'd play it with my middle finger. When my middle finger would start to bleed, I'd use my ring finger. Seeing blood on the top of the *komuz,* my mother made special finger covers

Performer Profile: A Conversation with Nurak Abdyrakhmanov (CONTINUED)

from deerskin that I'd wear on my fingers when I practiced.

In the 1960s, there were a lot of *komuz* players. They had all seen the older generation of master performers. When I played *komuz* for them, they'd get very excited and show me the techniques of the great masters from the past.

EK: What does it take to become a master performer of *küü?*

NA: First of all, you've got to have a gift. This gift is given by God. Second, you must undertake a long journey to come to the point where you understand and feel deeply the secret and power of a *küü.* When my father listened to a master performer, tears would well up in his eyes. Later, I also had the experience of listening to masters perform *küü,* and I understood why my father cried. He was a man of strong personality and mind, and for him, it was highly unusual to show his emotions.

EK: How many *küüs* can you play?

NA: About ninety, of which eighteen are my own compositions.

EK: Where do you draw your inspiration from when you compose a *küü?*

NA: In 1974, I began teaching at a music school, and at that time, there were only a couple of *küüs* suitable for teaching beginners. To enlarge the repertory, I composed a special *küü* called "Kulunchak" (Foal) for

my young students. My students played this *küü* at various music competitions, and people liked it a lot. After that, I developed the self-confidence to compose *küüs.* Not long after, I lost both my parents and my older brother, all within three months, and I experienced real psychological trauma. One night, lying in bed at home, I kept hearing a particular melody in my head. I grabbed my *komuz* and played that tune over and over all night long, and composed a *küü.* The next day, I played this *küü* to my teacher, who had taught me many traditional songs. After listening, he said: "Your father's spirit sent this *küü* to you. You should call it 'Father's Heritage.'" This experience confirmed my belief that inspiration comes from above, or from human spirits. I didn't know that I'd compose this particular *küü;* rather, it came to me from somewhere beyond myself.

EK: You have a powerful voice and a distinct singing style, and your repertory consists of popular Kyrgyz folk songs as well as classical songs that are not easy to sing. Did you learn singing around the same time that you began playing the *komuz,* or did you take up singing later?

NA: As a child, I listened to older men singing in the village. Their singing was quite different. There was a man named Orozobek, who was a friend of my father's. He was in his seventies and had a white beard. When he sang, the mountain cliffs

Photo by Katherine Vincent. Courtesy of Aga Khan Music Initiative.

echoed and accompanied his voice like an orchestra. I was mesmerized by his singing. And there was another man, Kashkary, who was born at the end of the nineteenth century—my father used to say, "When Kashkary sang, all the dogs in the village would stop barking and the sheep would stop bleating. Everyone would stand still and listen to his song." Orozobek had heard Kashkary's singing and sang like him.

In 1986, the Kyrgyz Ministry of Culture was seeking to hire someone who could sing old traditional songs and play the *komuz.* They invited many singers from various regions for an audition. I heard about it and decided to try out. When it was my turn, I sang a song, accompanying myself on the *komuz.* Afterward, the judges, who were well-known singers themselves, got up from their seats, applauding and shouting, "We found him! You're the one! We'll take you!" At that time, I was forty years old, and my beard had begun to turn gray.

Performer Profile: A Conversation with Nurak Abdyrakhmanov (CONTINUED)

The judges all got up to bless me, and one of them said, "Your beard reminds us of those elderly singers (literally 'white beards'—*aksakal*s) from the past. Don't shave your beard. May the spirit of those fathers support you!" And since then, I've had a beard, like an *aksakal*.

EK: How do you see the relation of tradition and innovation in your *küü* repertory?

NA: Tradition and innovation are mixed together in my *küü*s. They're not like traditional or classical *küü*s—especially "Sary-Özök," which has a new melody and a different style. Old *küü*s don't have this kind of melody. You can say that "Sary-Özök" is a contemporary *küü*. My other *küü*s also differ in many ways from traditional *küü*s. This could be a result of my individual artistic style. Sometimes I wonder whether my *küü*s are influenced by other contemporary music that I hear, but I don't really think they are. They're my own innovations.

EK: Is it right to say that if you want to compose a popular *küü* that has a long life, you should take into consideration people's taste?

NA: Of course taste is very important. However, music that is composed solely for the sake of pleasing people is like words that are spoken simply as flattery. Such music may not be very deep, and may have a short life. In other words, when I'm composing my music, I don't think about whether or not people will like it. First, I have to like it myself. This is very important to me. I don't feel bad if people don't understand or don't like one of my compositions. I only hope that they will come to understand it later.

Photo by Katherine Vincent. Courtesy of Aga Khan Music Initiative.

EK: You've invented your own system of notation for transcribing your compositions, and for teaching *komuz* to students. Why is your notation system more effective than European notation?

NA: European notation doesn't work well for the *komuz*. The *komuz*'s three strings are tuned differently for different *küü*s, and thus the position of notes and fingers also changes. When students play different *küü*s, they get confused by the changing positions of the notes on the fingerboard of the

Photo by Katherine Vincent. Courtesy of Aga Khan Music Initiative.

Performer Profile: A Conversation with Nurak Abdyrakhmanov (CONTINUED)

komuz. Other stringed instruments have one fixed tuning, but the *komuz* has eighteen different tunings, which means that learning to play it is like learning eighteen different instruments. In order to make learning easier and eliminate learning barriers, I developed a special notation that uses the old runic letters that were found engraved on stones near the Yenisey River, which flows through present-day Tuva, in south Siberia. That's the region that is believed to be the ancient homeland of the Kyrgyz. Recently, I published a *komuz* method book based on my notation system, which makes my teaching much easier.

EK: You are known as a master luthier who crafts his own instruments. Where did you learn this skill, and how is your *komuz* different from other *komuz* makers' instruments with regard to its shape and sound?

NA: My father used to make *komuz*es, and I learned from him. Well-known *komuz* players such as Karamoldo, Ybyray, and Asylbek Eshmanbetov owned instruments with a wonderful sound, since they traveled extensively and were able to select the best *komuz*es made by master *komuz* makers from different regions. I've been trying to make the ideal *komuz* for the past forty years. In the past, I used to take my tools with me on international tours and work on an instrument while staying in hotels. I use apricot wood because it's the hardest wood. It takes one summer to prepare the wood and two weeks

to make an instrument. The sound of my *komuz*es began to differ from that of other makers' instruments. My *komuz*es have a more delicate sound. Most of the instruments I make are for playing *küü*s, not for accompanying singing, which requires a different tonal quality for female and male singers. In the past, people played one *komuz* for all types of music because they didn't have a choice, and they didn't experiment much with their *komuz.*

EK: What do you see as the future of *komuz* music in Kyrgyzstan?

NA: I used to think that *komuz* music didn't have a future. When I was a child, music teachers who graduated from schools in Leningrad and Moscow used to ask me, "Why are you carrying around a *komuz?*" "The *komuz* is finished," they'd say. "It's for playing folk music, and folk music is dead. Don't waste your time; learn the violin, piano, or accordion." So, in 1966, I learned to play the accordion. It was considered shameful to carry a *komuz* on the streets of big cities

like Bishkek (then called Frunze). Russians would ridicule us. If you were a musician, it was prestigious to carry a balalaika or a guitar. Through the 1970s and 1980s, the once-plentiful number of *komuz* players in villages decreased year by year. I, too, began singing with an accordion. It was only after independence, in 1991, that the revival of the *komuz* began. Later, some music schools began teaching *komuz,* but only five to ten students would graduate each year—in many cases without adequate training to play professionally.

EK: Recently, in recognition of your outstanding talent and contribution to the preservation and development of Kyrgyz music, the government of Kyrgyzstan bestowed on you the honorary title "People's Artist of the Kyrgyz Republic." What does this title mean for musicians, and for you personally?

NA: Over the years, I've twice been honored with the title "People's Artist," but I have to say that for me, it's much more important to have the approval

Performer Profile: A Conversation with Nurak Abdyrakhmanov (CONTINUED)

WATCH

Example 14.21. "Song of Attila Khan," performed by Nurak Abdyrakhmanov, *komuz* and vocal. Filmed by Saodat Ismailova and Carlos Casas, Kyrgyzstan, 2003.

and respect of my listeners than to receive a title from the government. In the end, your legacy as a musician is decided by the people, not the state.

In example 14.21, Nurak Abdyrakhmanov performs his version of a song about Attila the Hun (d. 453 ce), who is known as Adil Baba in Kyrgyz. Nurak offered the following explanation about the origins of the song: "When the Kyrgyz were traveling back from the funeral of Attila (in Europe, where he died), they became lost in the Balkan Mountains. To find the right path, the old women played a melody on the jaw harp: 'Black lark, where are our lands, where is Attila, and where is our river?' They say that a storyteller called Baliq lived in the seventeenth century. He transformed funeral laments about Attila into an epic that described his life and how his people were walking back home after his death, and how funeral songs dedicated to Attila were created. This is one such song."

Balkan, Balkan, Balkan too,	The Balkan, Balkan, Balkan Mountains,
Balkan toogo men chyksam,	I went up to the Balkan Mountains and
Bashynda bar ayry too,	Saw the mountain range from their summit.
Ayry toogo men chyksam,	I went up to the mountain range and
Köldö jatkan köp ördök,	Saw many ducks in the lake there.
Ylaachyn tiyse bölünböy(i)t.	When attacked by a hawk,
Ylaachynday shumkarym,	They stay together.
Atillam senden ayrylyp,	My hawk-like Attila,
Kaygy-mungum bölüügö,	I became separated from you,
El karaany köünböy(i)t,	I do not see any sign of my people
El karaany körünböy(i)t.	Who would share my grief.
Atillam sendey el bakkan,	Oh, my Attila,
Erdi kaydan tabamyn?	Is there a brave man like you
Joonun jerin aralap,	Who cares for his people?
Joldu kaydan tabamyn?	How will I find my way back [home] by
Edil jayyk jaylagan ooy,	Traveling through the lands of enemies?
Eldi kaydan tabamyn?	How will I find my people who
Arstanym senden ayrylyp,	Inhabit the banks of the Edil (Volga) River?
Kiyimdi kaydan kiyemin,	Now, separated from my Lion,
Achtan ölüp ketsem da,	How will I put on my clothes?
Tamakty kaydan ichemin?	How will I eat when I am starving to death?
Atillam sen dep kaygyryp,	Oh, my Attila!
Men armanda ölör bekenmin.	I will die in regret grieving for you.

NOTES

1. See Viktor Zhirmunskii, "Oguzskii geroicheskii epos i 'Kniga Korkuta'" [Oghuz heroic epics and "The book of Korkut"], in *Kniga moego deda Korkuta: Oguzskii geroicheskii epos* [The book of my grandfather Korkut: Oghuz heroic epics], ed. Viktor Zhirmunskii and Andrei Kononov, trans. Vasily Bartold (Moscow and Leningrad: Izdatel'stvo Akademii Nauk SSSR, 1962), 131–258; Qorqyt, *Elim-ai: Küiler* [Oh, my people: *Küi*s], ed. Musabek Jarqynbekov (Alma-Ata: Öner, 1987).

2. See Aqseleu Seidimbek, *Qazaqtyng küi öneri* [The art of Kazakh *küi*] (Astana: Kültegin, 2002).

3. On the narrative dimension of *küi* and its genesis and evolution as a genre, see Bagdaulet Amanov and Asiya Mukhambetova, *Kazakhskaya traditsionnaya muzyka i XX vek* [Kazakh traditional music and the 20th century] (Almaty: Daik-Press, 2002), 119–152.

4. On *küi* genre types, see Tamara Djumalieva and Alma Temirbekova, eds., *Traditsionnaya muzyka kazakhskogo naroda: Pesennaya i instrumental'naya* [Traditional music of the Kazakh people: Sung and instrumental], vol. 1 of *Istoriya kazakhskoi muzyki v 2 tomakh* [History of Kazakh music in two volumes] (Almaty: Ghylym, 2000), 249–300; Amanov and Mukhambetova, *Kazakhskaya traditsionnaya muzyka i XX vek,* 88–92.

5. On the distinctive method of artistic representation in *küi,* see Talghat Sarybaev, "Kui kak kommunikativnoe yavlenie" [*Küi* as a communicative phenomenon], in *Instrumental'naya muzyka kazakhskogo naroda: Stat'i, ocherki* [Instrumental music of the Kazakh people: Articles, essays], ed. Asiya Mukhambetova (Alma-Ata: Öner, 1985), 49–62; Amanov and Mukhambetova, *Kazakhskaya traditsionnaya muzyka i XX vek,* 119–152, 172–186.

6. Images of lame animals and humans frequently found in Kazakh legends have been linked to the cult of ancestor-spirits among the nomads. According to this view, lameness represents a sign of sacredness, with lame legendary heroes acting as bearers of dead souls and mediators between this and the other world. See Abdulhamit Raiymbergenov and Saira Amanova, eds., *Küi qainary: Qobyzgha, sybyzghygha, dombyragha arnalghan küiler* [*Küi* sources: *Küi*s for the *qobyz, sybyzghy,* and *dombyra*] (Almaty: Öner, 1990), 80–81.

7. The legendary *dombyra* player is sometimes identified as Ketbugha (Kerbuqa), the *küi* master and epic bard said to have lived in the 12th–13th century (Seidimbek, *Qazaqtyng küi öneri,* 267–279).

8. The account of the legend is based on: Akhmet Jubanov, *Struny stoletii* [Strings of the centuries] (Almaty: Daik-Press, 2001), 12–13.

9. Amanov and Mukhambetova, *Kazakhskaya traditsionnaya muzyka i XX vek,* 109.

10. See Asiya Mukhambetova, "Narodnaya instrumental'naya muzyka kazakhov: Genezis i programmnost' v svete evolutsii form muzitsirovaniya" [Folk instrumental music of the Kazakhs: Genesis and programmatic nature in light of the evolution of forms of music making], Avtoreferat dissertatsii kandidata iskusstvovedeniya [Abstract of candidate dissertation in art studies] (Leningrad, 1976), 12–13; Djumalieva and Temirbekova, *Traditsionnaya muzyka kazakhskogo naroda,* 260–264.

11. Bökei Orda (Horde) was a Kazakh khanate under the Russian empire north of the Caspian Sea, in the area between the Ural and Volga Rivers, which existed from 1801 to 1876.

12. The *dombyra* could also have three strings. Historically, such *dombyra*s were found in various parts of Kazakhstan, but at present they have been retained only in the eastern region of Semei (Semipalatinsk). In its shape and sound production the three-stringed *dombyra* is close to the eastern Kazakhstan type, with a flat body, broad neck, and *shertpe* playing technique, its

low string serving as a drone. See Bolat Sarybaev, *Kazakhskie muzykal'nye instrumenty* [Kazakh musical instruments] (Almaty: Jalyn, 1978), 26, 103, 105.

13. A particular type of intermediate movable frets known as *Arqa* or *Saryarqa perne* produced neutral thirds, intervals between the standard major and minor third. See Talasbek Äsemqulov, "Dombyragha til bitse: Qazaqtyng baiyrghy muzyqalyq terminologiyasy khaqynda" [If the *dombyra* could speak: On the old Kazakh musical terminology], *Juldyz* [Star] 5 (1989): 186–190; Sarybaev, *Kazakhskie muzykal'nye instrumenty*, 100–101.

14. Ludmila Alekseeva and Jumageldi Najimedenov, *Kazakhskaya dombra i ee akusticheskie osobennosti* [The Kazakh *dombyra* and its acoustic properties] (Almaty: Kazakhskii institut kul'tury i iskusstvoznaniya, 2003), 34–35.

15. Gülzada Omarova and Gülbarshyn Murzaghalieva, *Etnosolfeggio: Ädistemelik qural* [Ethnosolfège: Method manual] (Almaty: T. Jürgenov atyndaghy Qazaq ulttyq öner akademiyasy and P. I. Tchaikovsky atyndaghy Almaty muzykalyq kolledji, 2005), 14–16.

16. See Bagdaulet Amanov, "Kompozitsionnaya terminologiya dombrovykh kuev" [Compositional terminology of *dombyra küi*s], in *Instrumental'naya muzyka kazakhskogo naroda* [Instrumental music of the Kazakh people], ed. Asiya Mukhambetova, 42–44; Amanov and Mukhambetova, *Kazakhskaya traditsionnaya muzyka i XX vek,* 220–223, 249–250, 283–284.

17. Where variant dates for the years of birth and death of *küishi*s circulate in scholarly literature, as they do for Qurmanghazy, the years used in this chapter are those provided by Jubanov, *Struny stoletii.*

18. This *küi* is also known as "Qyz-Danaidyng Qyrghyny" [The fight for Qyz-Danai]. See Jubanov, *Struny stoletii,* 54.

19. Qazanghap, *Aqjeleng: Küiler* [Aqjeleng: *Küi*s], ed. Abdulhamit Raiymbergenov (Alma-Ata: Öner, 1984), 7, 10.

20. Amanov and Mukhambetova, *Kazakhskaya traditsionnaya muzyka i XX vek,* 107–108.

21. Säduaqas Balmaghambetov, *Saz zergeri Qazanghap* [The master of music Qazanghap], ed. Aitjan Toqtaghan and Murat Äbughazy (Almaty: Baspa, 2001), 3.

22. Qazanghap, *Aqjeleng,* 9–10.

23. This account of Dina Nurpeisova's biography is based on essays from Jubanov, *Struny stoletii,* 114–139, and Seidimbek, *Qazaqtyng küi öneri,* 615–622.

24. Jubanov, *Struny stoletii,* 133; Seidimbek, *Qazaqtyng küi öneri,* 616.

25. Pernebek Shegebaev, "Zhanrovye osobennosti kuya 'Nauysqy': Komicheskoe v dombrovoi muzyke" [Genre properties of the *küi* "Nauysqy": The comic in *dombyra* music], in *Instrumental'naya muzyka kazakhskogo naroda* [Instrumental music of the Kazakh people], ed. Asiya Mukhambetova, 106.

26. Balmaghambetov, *Saz zergeri Qazanghap,* 5.

27. See Saule Utegalieva, *Manghystauskaya dombrovaya traditsiya* [Manghystau *dombyra* tradition] (Almaty: Almatinskaya gosudarstvennaya konservatoriya imeni Kurmangazy, 1997).

28. Omarova and Murzaghalieva, *Etnosolfeggio,* 18. For an alternative interpretation of *küi* structure in both *shertpe* and *tökpe* stylistic traditions, see Äsemqulov, "Dombyragha til bitse."

29. Jubanov, *Struny stoletii,* 170–172.

30. Talasbek Äsemqulov, who passed down this version of the cycle's origin, points to a symbolism of the image of the musician playing *küi*s while sitting on the threshold of the yurt. In Kazakh tradition, it has been taboo to sit or stand on the threshold, perceived to be a boundary between the inner and outer world and between life and death. Accordingly, in

Äsemqulov's interpretation, the musician sitting on the threshold was akin to a shaman or the legendary Greek hero Orpheus descending to the underworld in order to lead out and bring back a human soul to this world (see Talasbek Asemqulov, "Vse prekrasnoe imeet edinyi istok" [Everything beautiful has one source], 2004, trans. Zira Naurzbaeva, accessed December 18, 2014, www.otuken.kz). He thereby occupied the liminal status of an intermediary between life and death.

31. Äsemqulov, "Dombyragha til bitse."

32. Äsemqulov, "Dombyragha til bitse"; Aitjan Toqtaghan and Murat Äbughazy, eds., *Tättimbet jäne Arqa küileri* [Tättimbet and Arqa *küis*] (Almaty: Bilim, 2005), 176.

33. Aitjan Toqtaghan, Gülperizat Ultarakhova, and Murat Äbughazy, eds., *Sügir: Qaratau shertpesi* [Sügir: Qaratau *shertpe*] (Almaty: Atamura, 2006), 89. The numbers nine and sixty-two in the *dombyra küi* cycles are considered sacred numbers among the Kazakhs.

34. Tölegen Mombekov, *Saltanat: Küiler* [Saltanat: *Küis*], ed. Biläl Ysqaqov (Almaty: Öner, 1995), 10.

35. Bazaraly Müptekeev, "Jetisudyng dombyra küilerining stildik erekshelikteri" [Stylistic properties of Jetisu *dombyra küi*s], in *Traditsionnaya muzyka Azii: Problemy i materialy* [Traditional music of Asia: Issues and materials], ed. Saule Utegalieva, (Almaty: Daik-Press, 1996), 64–75; Saida Daukeyeva, "*Dombyra* Performance, Meaning and Memory among Mongolian Kazakhs." PhD Dissertation, School of Oriental and African Studies, University of London, 2010.

36. Talasbek Asemqulov, "Budushee iskusstva kuya" [The future of the art of *küi*], *Ruh-Miras* [Spiritual heritage] 2, no. 5 (2005): 86–87.

37. Tengri (*Tängir*) is the name of the sky deity and, more generally, an appellation for a supreme being in ancient nomadic beliefs.

38. Zira Naurzbaeva, "Sotvorennye iz ognya (o kinopovesti T. Asemqulova 'Smert' Kokbalaka')" [Created from fire (On the film-essay "The death of Kökbalak" by T. Äsemqulov)], accessed December 18, 2014, www.otuken.kz.

39. Talasbek Asemqulov, "Tema gorya, stradaniya i pechali v traditsionnom kazakhskom iskusstve" [The theme of grief, suffering, and sorrow in Kazakh traditional art], trans. Zira Naurzbaeva, accessed December 18, 2014, www.otuken.kz.

40. Adapted from Asan Kaybyldaev, *Kyrgyz küülörü: Iliktöölör, oyrlor, pikirler* [Kyrgyz *küis*: analysis, thoughts, and opinions], ed. Elmira Köchümkulova (Bishkek: University of Central Asia, 2011), vol. 1: 542–543.

41. Soviet literary books and school textbooks gave a different version of Toktogul's exile to Siberia: he was a great democratic poet who sang against the rich men and tribal leaders (*bay-manap*) who exploited the poor. The rich men in Toktogul's village sent him to Siberia when he criticized their unjust rule.

42. Adapted from Kaybyldaev, *Kyrgyz küülörü,* 456–457.

CHAPTER 15 Kyrgyz Jaw Harps

NURLANBEK NYSHANOV

Kyrgyz metal jaw harp
(*temir ooz komuz*).

The jaw harp (also called Jew's harp), one of the world's most archaic musical instruments, has long been a part of the musical cultures of Eurasia, with indigenous jaw harp traditions spanning the continent from China to Western Europe, and from northern Siberia to southern India. Jaw harp traditions have developed with particular virtuosity and variety in Inner Asia, and since ancient times, jaw harps have been favorite musical instruments of the Kyrgyz. Kyrgyz jaw harps consist of two varieties: wooden jaw harps (*jygach ooz komuz*) and metal jaw harps (*temir ooz komuz*). Wooden jaw harps are mainly played by Kyrgyz who live in certain specific regions, while metal jaw harps are played in all regions of Kyrgyz settlement.

Different theories have been advanced to explain the origin of the jaw harp, but the only incontrovertible fact about its origin is that no one knows when and where the first jaw harp player lived. Certain kinds of simply constructed jaw harps still in use today, however, may provide clues about the earliest instruments. In Tuva, a small republic in the Altai region of south Siberia, simple wooden jaw harps (Tuvan: *iyash khomus*) are made from a Y-shaped stick without the need for any tool. The playing technique is analogous to that for other jaw harps: the player grips the single end of the stick in the mouth while firmly holding one branch of the "Y" and vibrating the other branch of the "Y" with the fingers of the free hand. Kyrgyz wooden jaw harps most likely evolved from the simple stick jaw harp into two closely related forms:

1. The tongue is vibrated by plucking it with a finger. This form is also widespread in Southeast Asia.

2. The tongue is vibrated by pulling a thread attached to it. This is the form currently used in Kyrgyz traditional musical culture.

Tuvan wooden jaw harp
(*iyash khomus*).

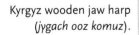

Kyrgyz wooden jaw harp
(*jygach ooz komuz*).

Among the Kyrgyz and among some Siberian peoples, such as the Nivkh and Ket, "thread-vibrated" wooden jaw harps were traditionally made from the branches of a hardwood bush or from animal bones. Nowadays bone jaw harps are no longer made or played. Kyrgyz musicians play *küü*s (narrative instrumental pieces) on the wooden jaw harp as well as on other instruments. Different pitches are produced by widening or narrowing the oral cavity and closing or opening the throat. Since the range of the wooden jaw harp is not large, *küü*s played on the instrument tend to be short and simple. Such *küü*s mostly represent birds and animals, e.g., "Kükük" (Cuckoo) and "Jorgo" (Pacer horse), or describe patterns of nomadic lifestyle, e.g., "Boz üydo" (In a yurt) and "Jailoodo" (In a pasture).

WATCH **Example 15.1.** "Kükük" (Cuckoo), traditional *küü*, performed by Nurlanbek Nyshanov (wooden jaw harp).

STUDY QUESTIONS

1. How is the image of a cuckoo bird expressed in the *küü*?
2. How successful is the *küü* in representing the cuckoo bird?
3. What cultural and social forces might either promote or impede the use of the wooden jaw harp in the future?

Metal jaw harps are also ancient and are a testament to the sophisticated metallurgy of the Iron Age. In the most common kind of metal jaw harp, a flexible tongue and frame are made separately, and the tongue is fixed at one end to the frame.

To produce a sound, the player grips the round portion of the frame between the front teeth and plucks the tongue with a finger. The resultant sound is rich in harmonics, or overtones, which can be selectively amplified by precise movements of the player's mouth. In the past, both wooden and metal jaw harps were popular among Kyrgyz women and children, and women played a key role in the development of jaw harp music. Burulcha Osmonbek kyzy, a great female musician of the nineteenth century, said, "A child who grows up listening to a metal jaw harp will develop good verbal skills." Her linking of music and verbal skills shows that people in the past had a deep understanding of music's value in childhood education and development.[1]

In the twentieth century, men also began to play metal jaw harps, and jaw harp ensembles became popular. Many jaw harp melodies were recorded and notated.

Kutmanaaly Sultanbekov playing a wooden jaw harp.

Yakut metal jaw harp.

Different types of compositions were written for the instrument, and metal jaw harp melodies were played with the accompaniment of an orchestra. In the second half of the twentieth century, due to the spread of European musical instruments in Kyrgyz cultural life, people's interest in jaw harps as well as in other traditional instruments decreased. This situation lasted until the end of the 1980s. Then, influenced by perestroika and independence, interest in jaw harps as well as in other traditional instruments was revived.

The metal jaw harp has a wider range than the wooden jaw harp, and, as a result, its repertoire is richer and more diverse. The metal jaw harp repertoire can be divided into three groups:

1. Variations on songs—mostly themes of old traditional songs

2. *Küüs* that represent nature and animals, e.g., "Karacha torgoi" (Black lark), "Turumtai" (Hawk), "Erkin too" (Free mountain), "Ker özön" (Wide valley)

3. *Küüs* that narrate personal stories, e.g., "Kojojash mergen" (Kojojash the hunter), "Eselbai"

Some contemporary metal jaw harp players perform old *küüs* in a new style, creating their own versions in ways that do not contradict Kyrgyz musical tradition. Variation and improvisation are characteristic of Kyrgyz music. In the following audio example, the performer plays a traditional *küü*, gradually accelerating the tempo, then adding a second traditional theme and improvising on it.

WATCH **Example 15.2.** "Ala too jazy" (Spring in the Ala Too mountains) and "Erkin too" (Free mountain), performed by Nurlanbek Nyshanov (metal jaw harp).

STUDY QUESTIONS

1. How do the two *küüs* that compose this medley convey an image of their subject matter?

2. How would you characterize the differences between the technical capacity of the metal jaw harp and that of the wooden jaw harp?

3. How successful is the juxtaposition of the two *küüs*? Do they go together well, or does the transition to the second *küü* seem incongruous?

Hand gestures are sometimes incorporated into a performance to create a beautiful visual effect. The performer, generally a woman, gently plucks the tongue of the jaw harp with the fingers of both hands while making smooth, sweeping gestures of the hands and arms, as illustrated in the following example by Gülbara Baigashkaeva.

WATCH **Example 15.3.** "Tagyldyr too" (Mountain where an orphan baby deer lives), composed by Adamkaliy Baybatyrov, performed by Gülbara Baigashkaeva (metal jaw harp).

STUDY QUESTIONS

1. Does the *küü* succeed in portraying an image of mountains? If so, through what means?

2. In your view, are the hand gestures abstract, or do they represent something in particular? In either case, could they be considered a form of dance?

Today, interest in jaw harps is growing, and young performer-composers in Kyrgyzstan are creating new music for the instrument. Kyrgyz musicians have performed this new repertory not only in Kyrgyzstan but internationally (see example 32.4). The majority of new *küüs* for metal jaw harp are being composed for ensemble performance, and are notated in Western staff notation. One such composition is presented in the following audio example. The piece, called "Jangylyk" (Novelty), features a wooden jaw harp and two metal jaw harps tuned a fourth apart

The Tengir-Too junior ensemble playing jaw harps.

(the difference between the scale degrees *mi* and *la)*. In "Jangylyk," the players try to extract all possible overtones from their instruments—overtones that aren't typically used in jaw harp music. "Jangylyk"—which is one of my own compositions—reflects my conservatory training in counterpoint: there are canons and melodic motifs in contrary motion. The performers learned the piece from musical notation and play it from a score, even though it has the feeling of an improvised jam session.

Watch

Example 15.4. "Jangylyk" (Novelty), composed by Nurlanbek Nyshanov, performed by Kambar Kalendarov (metal jaw harp in A), Kutmanaaly Sultanbekov (wooden jaw harp in A), and Gülbara Baigashkaeva (metal jaw harp in E).

STUDY QUESTIONS

1. What clues reveal that "Jangylyk" is a recently composed *küü*?

2. How are the three jaw harps integrated in the piece? Does each one have a specific role (e.g., melody, accompaniment, rhythm), or do they switch roles and each play different roles?

3. How does the musical content of "Jangylyk" represent or refer to its title?

4. Do you see a musical future for the metal jaw harp? If so, how do you see it developing? What kind of music might be written for jaw harp(s) by future composers?

NOTE

1. The link between early musical training and verbal skills has been underscored by recent research in neuroscience. See, for example, Nina Kraus et al., "Music Enrichment Programs Improve the Neural Encoding of Speech in At-Risk Children," *The Journal of Neuroscience,* (September 3, 2014): 11913–11918.

CHAPTER 16 The Kazakh *Qobyz*

BETWEEN TRADITION
AND MODERNITY

SAIDA DAUKEYEVA

The *qobyz*, a two-stringed bowed lute, has a special status and significance among the Kazakhs as a sacred (*kieli*) instrument deeply rooted in their traditional culture and spirituality that is believed to aid mediation with ancestor-spirits. Distinguished by a versatile imitative and expressive sound, the *qobyz* was originally used as an accompaniment to shamanic ritual and epic narration, and was later adopted in the performance of narrative instrumental pieces (*küis*) as a form of art music. Its subsequent history, from the cultural transformations of the Soviet era to the years following Kazakhstan's independence, has seen a marked change in the identity of the instrument, the role and musicianship of the *qobyz* master (*qobyzshy*), and the context and style of *qobyz* performance. This chapter chronicles the history of the *qobyz* and examines its multifaceted performance tradition against the backdrop of political and social change, and in relation to evolving ideologies and concepts of identity among the Kazakhs.

ORIGINS

The Kazakh *qobyz* is a lute hollowed out from a whole piece of wood in a ladle-like shape, with an open resonator whose lower part is covered with a camel-skin sound table.[1] It has two horsehair strings tuned a fourth or a fifth apart and played with an arched horsehair bow (in the compound name of the instrument, *qyl-qobyz, qyl* means "horsehair"). The *qobyz* belongs to a family of Central Asian fiddles with horsehair strings and bow that includes the Karakalpak *qobyz,* Kyrgyz *kiyak,* and Mongolian *khuur,* from which bowing is thought to originate.[2]

In oral tradition the invention of the *qobyz* is associated with Qorqyt, or Qorqyt ata, a legendary hero among Turkic peoples who is the protagonist of the Oghuz

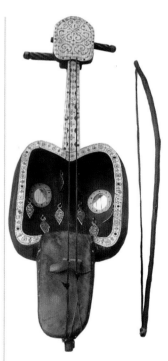

Small mirrors and metal pendants in the soundbox of this highly ornamented *qobyz* were believed to attract protecting spirits.

Courtesy of Museum of Kazakh Folk Musical Instruments.

The instrument's bridge is set on a sound table made of camel skin.

Kazakh shaman with the *qobyz*. In the rituals of shamans (*baqsy*), playing and singing to the accompaniment of the *qobyz* was a means of mediating with spirits, healing patients, and soothsaying.

epic *Dede Korkut Kitabi* (The book of grandfather Korkut), and whom Kazakhs regard as their first shaman, epic bard, and musician. According to a popular legend in the corpus of *küi*s attributed to Qorqyt, the hero devised the instrument on the shores of the Syr Darya River to escape death. In search of immortality, he visited all four parts of the world. But wherever he appeared, death would meet him in a different guise. Then he returned to his homeland, the shore of the Syr Darya River, and made the *qobyz,* covering it with the skin of his sacrificed she-camel, Jelmaya ("Fast-as-the-Wind"). Thinking that death would not reach him on the waters of the Syr Darya, he spread out a carpet on the river's waves and came to play the *qobyz* day and night. His playing attracted all earthly creatures who gathered by the river drawn by the music, and as long as Qorqyt played, death could not approach him to take his soul. But one day, when Qorqyt put down his *qobyz* to take a drink of water, he was bitten by a poisonous snake, and died. Thus Qorqyt became the patron (*pir*) of *qobyz* players.

Belief in the magic powers of the *qobyz* as a medium between the human and spiritual worlds, and between life and death, in which capacity it offered protection from evil and misfortune and helped maintain equilibrium in the universe, permeated the original context of its performance. In the rituals of shamans (*baqsy*s), playing and singing to the accompaniment of the *qobyz* was a means of mediating with spirits, healing patients, and soothsaying. In narrations of epic poems and tales by bards (*jyrau*s), who acted as spiritual leaders and advisers to the khans, *qobyz* playing served to protect and guide the community, and to foretell the outcome of important events, such as battles and military campaigns.

While little is currently known about musical dimensions of early epic performance, ethnographic accounts of shamanic rituals from the nineteenth and early twentieth centuries recapture the original context of the rituals and tell us about the role of music in them. According to these accounts, shamans played the *qobyz* several times during the course of a ritual, typically to accompany singing. At the beginning of the ritual, the *qobyz* served as a means of calling the shaman's spirit-protectors and entering a state of trance. One account of a shamanic ritual from the end of the nineteenth century offered the following description: "During the séance the *baqsy* does not stop playing his *qobyz,* and his calling [to the spirits] is interrupted only with the coming of complete exhaustion."[3] After the ecstatic actions or "play" (*oiyn*) believed to be conducted under the spell of spirits, the shaman would resume playing the *qobyz* in order to receive their answers and advice: "[The *baqsy*] began to play the *qobyz* again, but more calmly. . . . This time he was not singing and, listening to his own playing, he rocked from side to side. With the assurance of Oken [*baqsy*] himself, at this point the spirits gave answers to his questions, advice and cures for illness."[4] Finally, playing the *qobyz* would bring to an end the ritual of "letting go the spirits": "Concluding his séance with the words 'it is all over,' the *baqsy* takes up the *qobyz* again and begins to play and sing for the jinns [ancestor-spirits] a 'letting go' song."[5]

The perception of the *qobyz* as a medium for contacting the spiritual world arose from its peculiar shape and sound properties. Kazakhs associated the *qobyz* with images of totemic animals—the camel, horse, and swan. This association supported the idea of the instrument as a vehicle for transporting the shaman during healing séances to the mythical upper, middle, and lower worlds in search of a patient's soul seized by evil spirits. In oral accounts, the *qobyz* was depicted as a living creature able to walk, ride, fly, and produce sounds of its own accord. The usual attributes of the shamanic *qobyz*—a mirror set within the soundbox and metal pendants and bells hanging from its head—were believed to attract protecting spirits.

The instrument's sound suited its ritual purpose. The *qobyz* is distinguished by a peculiar raspy sound amplified by harmonics—the series of high-frequency, acoustically related tones generated by a fundamental tone sounded on a string, or in a reverberant space such as a hollow tube. Strings made of horsehair are particularly rich in harmonics when excited by the friction of a horsehair bow drawn across the strings, and when fingered lightly instead of being pressed down hard against the neck of the instrument (a technique known as *flageoletto* in Western musical practice). In shamanic rituals the harmonics and melodic ornaments combined with sound effects produced by ringing metal pendants and tinkling bells created a complex resonating soundscape. This soundscape was described in ethnographic accounts as "mystical, mysterious, and unearthly, evoking a state of mesmerization . . . well matched with the shamans' incantations and conjurations."[6] Listen to the use of harmonics in the *küi* "Qongyr" (Deep-brown), whose composition is attributed to Qorqyt, and particularly to the harmonic amplification of the second motif in the upper register (1:19–1:35).

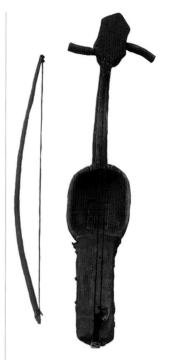

An old *qobyz*. The carved out section in the middle of the sound box originally held a mirror.

Courtesy of Museum of Kazakh Folk Musical Instruments.

LISTEN

Example 16.1. "Qongyr" (Deep-brown), attributed to Qorqyt, performed by Jappas Qalambaev. Courtesy of Kündiz Qalambaeva.

STUDY QUESTIONS

1. In your own words, how would you describe the sounds of the harmonics at 1:19–1:35? Do you agree with the characterization of the ethnographic account quoted above?

2. What about the rest of the melody? How would you describe its character and rhythmic flow?

3. Listen for the use of double-stops, in which the performer plays on both strings at once. Where in the piece do you hear double-stops? If you are a musician, can you identify the intervals made by the two strings? What do you think is the purpose of double-stops in the music?

Along with the use of harmonics, another powerful device in ritualized *qobyz* performance is the imitation of sounds made by animals and birds that are associated with the shamans' helping spirits. The well-known folk legend *küi* "Aqqu" (White swan) offers a vivid imitation of the voice and movements of the swan, a totemic bird and the embodiment of an ancestor-spirit among the Kazakhs.

WATCH

Example 16.2. "Aqqu" (White swan), folk *küi*, performed by Raushan Orazbaeva. Filmed by Saodat Ismailova, 2014.

STUDY QUESTIONS

1. How does Raushan Orazbaeva represent the swan on her *qobyz*? What sounds associated with the swan does she evoke in her performance, and by what playing techniques?

2. What else, beyond imitation, does this music express? Could one say that, apart from representation, it has an abstract expressive quality?

Raushan Orazbaeva.
Courtesy of Saodat Ismailova.

The imitation of totemic animals served to express the "language of spirits" or "alien voices" that marked the stage of the ritual when the shaman had already been possessed. In the hands of the shaman, the *qobyz* would be transformed into the instrument of the spirits, transmitting the music of the other world. This instrumental onomatopoeia corresponded in its purpose and meaning to vocal imitations performed by the shaman. According to an ethnographic account, "The *baqsy* accompanies his conjurations by sudden remote soft whistling . . . guttural and hissing sounds in which one can pick up imitation of the cries of birds, beasts, and domestic animals."[7] Thus the production of both harmonics and onomatopoeia served a mediatory and transformative role, inducing a trance-like state in the shaman and exerting a powerful effect on participants in the ritual.

Some accounts, corroborated by musicological studies, point further to shamans' use of recurrent personal tunes (*saryns*) either inspired by spirits or passed down through a *baqsy*'s hereditary lineage. Consisting of repetitive motifs and/or a refrain, these tunes were believed to have magic, conjuring, and healing properties and, like the *qobyz* itself, were not played outside a ritual setting.

The experience of listeners during a shamanic ritual at the end of the nineteenth century is evoked in the ethnographic account of Nevolnik: "Suddenly Oken with masterly skill and power passed the bow over the *qobyz* strings and began to play. Lamentably heart-breaking sounds began to flow among the crowd holding their breath. . . . For a moment one could hear in the *baqsy*'s playing a rending stream of subconscious grief and yearning of a people migrating across the monotonous dreary steppe; the Kazakhs, lulled to sleep, as it were, held their breath and plunged into thought. . . . Everyone was transfixed in an almost blissful ecstasy."[8]

DECLINE OF THE EPIC TRADITION

Whereas the shamanic practice of the *baqsy* continued into the early twentieth century, the epic performance tradition of the *jyrau* had already begun to fade away in the late eighteenth century. The decline of epic performance came as a response to transformations in nomadic society under the increasing political and economic influence of the czarist empire in Central Eurasia. This influence led to the subjugation of the Kazakh tribal confederations, or Hordes (*jüz*); the disruption of traditional social organization; and the elimination of the power of the ruling khans. The epic bard Bukhar jyrau Qalqamanuly (1688–1787), adviser to Ablai, the khan of the Middle Horde (*Orta jüz*), is said to have been the last great *jyrau*. The epic tradition continued in the form of smaller epic genres performed by bards (*jyrshy*) who accompanied themselves on the *dombyra,* the two-stringed plucked lute that from the nineteenth century onward would gain widespread currency among Kazakhs.

The decline of epic performance, as some historical sources suggest, was also a consequence of the changing ideology brought about by the proselytizing of Islam as part of czarist colonial policy. The Kazakh ethnographer Shoqan Valikhanov, writing in the mid-nineteenth century, observed that under the influence of this policy, "Our national character increasingly takes on a general Muslim type . . . , and our bards, instead of folk epics, sing Muslim apocryphal stories set to folk verses."[9] In another work, Valikhanov specifically points to the decline of the epic tradition and *qobyz* performance among *jyraus* as parallel to the rise of the poet-improviser (*aqyn*) and singer (*ölengshi*): "Although at the present time . . . *aqyn* (or *ölengshi*)[10] in the steppe are many, they are mostly improvisers, while ancient *jyrs*, being yet more incomprehensible to the new generation, are falling out of use year by year, and very few of their experts remain."[11] He further indicates that "the form of *jyr,* like the *qobyz* itself, remained now solely the property of *baqsys*.[12] Only they still preserve this form of verse, using it during the conjuration of jinns."[13]

The continuity of shamanic ritual practice in the face of the new ideological influences noted by Valikhanov could be explained by the fact that it was embedded in everyday life, and in indigenous syncretic beliefs that combined elements of shamanism and Islam. This allowed for the integration of *qobyz* performance into Muslim devotional practice, particularly Sufi rituals of "remembrance" (*zikr*). Historical accounts support the inference that such an integration came about through the ecstatic nature of both shamanic and Sufi practices and their mutual aim of achieving spiritual transformation and trance. While the practice of "shamanic *zikr*" (*baqsynyng zikiri*) must have existed prior to the twentieth century, firm evidence comes from the mid-twentieth century. The writer Tanash Däurenbekov cites an account of such a ritual, as related by an observer, which was held secretly in Syr Darya district of Qyzylorda region in the south of Kazakhstan in 1943: "He [the *baqsy*] took the *qobyz* and began to play on it . . . His sad melody pierced me through; I felt tingles all over my body. . . . One of the old men . . . began to make movements corresponding to the rhythm of the melody. The *qobyz* resounded with a new power. 'Stand up!' said Bekbergen [the *baqsy*]. The sharp voice sounded imperatively. Everybody stood up from their places. . . . 'Do *zikr!*' All the old men began together: '*La ilaha illa lla! La ilaha illa lla!*' ['There is no god but God! There is no god but God!']"[14]

Küi Performance

In the nineteenth century, the *qobyz* began to be played outside the ritual context, in the form of narrative instrumental pieces accompanied by storytelling (*küis*). These pieces were an example of "program music"—that is, music that tells a story, represents images and events, or conveys emotions and states of mind. The shift in *qobyz* performance from ritual to art music is associated with the name of Yqylas Dükenuly (1843–1916), a *qobyz* player and *küi* master (*küishi*) who came from the present-day Shymkent region of southern Kazakhstan. Relatively few accounts of his life and the circumstances in which he composed his *küis* have been passed down to us, and these were subject to adjustment under ideological censorship during the Soviet era. Yet it is known that Yqylas descended from several generations of *qobyzshy* and *baqsy;* that his instrument, inherited from his shaman father, Düken, was believed to possess magic healing and mediatory powers;[15] and that his performance had a powerful effect on listeners, akin to that experienced by participants in shamanic rituals.

The small body of *küis* attributed to Yqylas that have come down to the present day—about ten out of approximately fifty he is thought to have composed—are elaborate instrumental pieces. Compared to the shamanic *saryns* and *küis* attributed to Qorqyt, they encompass a wider pitch range, employ more advanced playing techniques, and are characterized by developed musical forms not found in the folk *qobyz* repertory. In their imagery, genres, and musical language, *küis* by Yqylas nevertheless reveal continuity with older forms of music making on the *qobyz*.

Onomatopoeia and the use of recurrent motifs (*saryns*) typical of epic and ritual *qobyz* performance are distinctive features of Yqylas's *küis*. In these *küis*, the

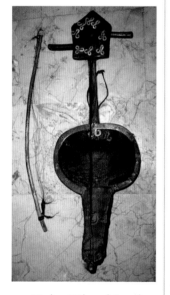

Yqylas Dükenuly's *qobyz*.
Courtesy of Aqnar Shäripbaeva.

sound of the *qobyz* represents episodes and images in the narrative, or "speaks" in a human voice. Thus, in the *küi* "Shyngyrau" (Abyss), which Yqylas composed after witnessing a snake about to swallow defenseless nesting birds, each character in the story is introduced by a distinctive motif. The *küi* "Erden," improvised on the occasion of the death of the son of Erden, a district governor, is based on a lament-like tune similar to a shamanic *saryn*. The *küi* expresses sentiments of grief and sorrow and, according to one version of its narrative, musically articulates the words "*Beu! Ainalaiyn qaraghym-ai*" (Oh! My dear, beloved), which deeply moved Erden and his grieving family.[16] Listen to the performance of "Erden" in example 16.3. As you listen, focus in particular on the lament theme, amplified through the use of harmonics at its second appearance (from 0:21), and on the evocative imitation of the spoken phrase (1:21–1:40).

LISTEN

Example 16.3. "Erden," composed by Yqylas Dükenuly, performed by Smatai Umbetbaev. From Xavier and Saoulé Hallez, *Kazakhstan: The Kobyz, The Ancient Viol of the Shamans* (France: INEDIT Maison des Cultures du Monde, 2004), track 1.

STUDY QUESTIONS

1. What happens in the music at 1:21–1:40 to evoke the imitation of the spoken phrase described above?

2. What qualities in the performance contribute to the musical affect of the *küi*?

The effect of Yqylas's music on contemporary listeners is tellingly captured in the reminiscences of the Kazakh poet, writer, and statesman Säken Seifullin (1894–1938), who described Yqylas's performance of an unknown *küi* during a ceremony to commemorate the death of Säken's son: "Yqylas, tuning, pulled tight the *qobyz* strings and began to run his bow. From under his fingertips there began to flow a groaning, sorrowful *küi* that tugged at one's heartstrings. My heart began to palpitate. . . . It was as if the crying *küi* was flowing from somewhere above, from the sky. People in the yurt were motionless. The *qobyz* was yearning, lamenting, sobbing. Having come to myself from a deep numbness, I raised my eyes to Yqylas and saw the head of his *qobyz* as if rooted to Yqylas's temples. While making the *qobyz* sob with both his hands, Yqylas himself was crying together with the *küi*. Tears were flowing over his cheeks and small beard. . . . I did not dare to stir. Yqylas abruptly broke off the tearful sobbing of the *qobyz*. . . . People sat long in a deep silence."[17]

Suppression and Transformation

With the rise of the Soviet era in Kazakhstan, the *qobyz* and its performance practice underwent a profound change and decline.[18] In the 1920s, the instrument, closely associated with shamanic practice, was declared "a vestige of the dark feudal past" and was widely banned and suppressed. Aleksandr Zatayevich (1869–1936), a Russian musicologist, music critic, and composer who collected Kazakh musical folklore in the 1920s and 1930s, wrote about the imminent disappearance of shamanic practices as follows: "*Baqsy*s are, undoubtedly, a remnant of the dark past and nowadays are bound for extinction. So even more one is made to regret that their interesting magical music remains unrecorded."[19] While some shamans and musicians continued to play the *qobyz* secretly, others stopped practicing for fear of persecution.[20]

At the same time, however, modified versions of the *qobyz* were assimilated into official cultural life. In 1934, the first orchestra of folk instruments (later named after Qurmanghazy) was established in Almaty—a major enterprise that came to epitomize the music of Soviet Kazakhstan. The creation of such an orchestra entailed both reconstructing traditional Kazakh instruments for orchestral playing and adapting the traditional performance culture of Kazakh music to the new social venue of concert halls. Master luthiers attached to the Music and Drama College (later Conservatory) in Almaty were instructed to modify the *qobyz,* and set to work under the supervision of the orchestra's artistic director, music scholar, and composer Akhmet Jubanov (1906–1968).

The first "improved" version of the traditional instrument, called *prima-qobyz,* was produced in 1936, and underwent further adjustments in subsequent years. The *prima-qobyz* was modeled on the violin and, like the violin, served as the lead melodic instrument in the orchestra. Though still fashioned in a ladle-like shape, it was covered with a wooden sound table over its open resonator, strung with two gut strings and one metal string tuned a fifth apart, and played with a violin bow. *Qobyz* players, seated in chairs on a concert stage, held their instruments in an upright position between the knees, with the instrument's neck resting against the performer's chest. This position represented a departure from the way traditional performers played their instrument: kneeling or sitting on the ground, with the *qobyz* held away from the body, resting against the knee or ankle.

Though it was different from the traditional *qyl-qobyz,* the *prima-qobyz* retained aspects of its physical form and playing techniques. For example, the strings of the *prima-qobyz* were placed high above the instrument's neck, allowing players to press their fingernails against the strings sideways, as on the *qyl-qobyz.* The gut and metal strings of the *prima-qobyz* deadened the harmonics that were a distinctive feature of the *qyl-qobyz,* but the gut strings and skin table lent it a warm, velvety

Jappas Qalambaev with the first modified *prima-qobyz.*

Courtesy of Central State Archive of Film, Photography, and Sound Recordings of the Republic of Kazakhstan.

timbre that resembled a human voice. On balance, however, the limited range and subdued sound of the *prima-qobyz* were inconsistent with the brightness and clarity needed to perform the new solo, ensemble, and orchestral repertory, and to make the instrument audible amid the ever-expanding orchestral forces, which later included both Kazakh and European wind and percussion instruments.

These shortcomings led to further modification of the *prima-qobyz*. The second modified version, introduced in 1954, represented a closer imitation of the violin, with four metal strings, tuned to fifths, and a shortened fingerboard fabricated according to violin measurements. After a series of experiments with the shape of the instrument and material of the sound table, the *prima-qobyz* acquired a violin-like, figured body and an entirely wooden table. Following the introduction of the modified *prima-qobyz,* the other instruments in the *qobyz* consort were also superseded by their four-stringed, short-necked counterparts. The consort was now a quintet analogous to the string section of a symphony orchestra: *prima-qobyz* 1 and 2 (1st and 2nd violin), *alto-qobyz* (viola), *bass-qobyz* (cello), and *double bass-qobyz* (contrabass).

The new type of violin-like *qobyz,* strung with metal strings and played with a taut bow, could not produce the rich field of harmonics and other sound effects that were such a vital part of older performance techniques. Its repertory now centered on folk orchestra arrangements of Kazakh songs and solo *küi*s, on European classics, and on new works by modern composers from Kazakhstan. An example of the latter is "Aria" by Akhmet Jubanov.

The *qobyz* group of the Qurmanghazy Orchestra in the 1950s. Seated in the front row from left to right are performers on the *prima-qobyz* 1, *qyl-qobyz* (playing the *alto* part), *bass-qobyz*, another *qyl-qobyz*, and *prima-qobyz* 2. The *double bass-qobyz* player is outside the picture, standing at the back of the orchestra.

Courtesy of Central State Archive of Film, Photography, and Sound Recordings of the Republic of Kazakhstan.

LISTEN

Example 16.4. "Aria" for *prima-qobyz* and piano accompaniment, composed by Akhmet Jubanov, performed by Ghaliya Moldakarimova. Courtesy of Ghaliya Moldakarimova.

STUDY QUESTIONS

1. How would you describe the style of "Aria"? What is Kazakh about it? What is European?

2. What kind of European music would you guess serves as the model for the style of the piece?

3. What is the difference between the sound of the *prima-qobyz* and the sound of the violin?

Present-day *qobyz* group of the Qurmanghazy Orchestra: *prima-qobyz* and *double bass-qobyz* players.

The new aesthetics of *qobyz* playing reflected a reimagined sound ideal influenced by Western classical music and a broader cultural trend toward modernization, urbanization, and the adoption of European standards in Kazakhstan. This trend emerged not so much from state policy as from changes in cultural values, aspirations, and notions of identity, and musicians welcomed it with interest and enthusiasm. In Kazakhstan's mainstream music scene, the Europeanized *qobyz* displaced the traditional *qobyz*, propelled by a perception that it was a more advanced instrument that symbolized dynamic change and progress in society. Over time the general public began to view it as a bona fide substitute for the *qyl-qobyz*.

Meanwhile, the older form of *qyl-qobyz* was marginalized throughout much of the Soviet period. Only two traditionally trained *qobyz* players—both followers of the school of Yqylas Dükenuly—continued to work within the institutional framework of the Kazakh State Philharmonic Society and the Orchestra of Folk Instruments: Däulet Myqtybaev (1905–1976) and Jappas Qalambaev (1909–1969), who performs the *küi* "Qongyr" in example 16.1. Their *qyl-qobyz* playing in the orchestra, though, was merely a timbral addition to the sound of the reconstructed instruments, serving as humble evidence that such an instrument still existed among the Kazakhs.

REVIVAL

This situation changed in the 1960s, the time of the political "thaw" in the Soviet Union, when, against the backdrop of a changing ideological climate and broad resurgence of interest in the origins of Kazakh ethnicity and culture, musicians, music scholars, and cultural activists began to study and restore traditional instruments, including the *qobyz*. In 1968, the original *qobyz* was reintroduced into the curriculum of the Kazakh National Conservatory in Almaty. However, the way in which *qobyz* training and performance were carried out reflected the influence of contemporary music practice and education, which by that time had already been profoundly Europeanized. One master performer, Däulet Myqtybaev, taught students in the traditional master-apprentice method in which students memorized *küi*s aurally from the playing of their teacher. Another teacher, Bolat Sarybaev, offered instruction in basic playing techniques on one of the orchestral versions of the *qobyz*—the *bass-qobyz*, a diminished replica of the cello. Däulet Myqtybaev's teaching facilitated the transmission of a number of traditional *qobyz küi*s, including both anonymous folk compositions and compositions attributed to Qorqyt and Yqylas. These compositions were subsequently transcribed and published, and have become part of the repertory of present-day performers. But the type of *qobyz* player shaped through the dual approaches of traditional and Europeanized training differed from that exemplified by the former *qobyzshy*.

Däulet Myqtybaev performing on the *qyl-qobyz*. Courtesy of Central State Archive of Film, Photography, and Sound Recordings of the Republic of Kazakhstan.

This becomes apparent when comparing video recordings of performances by Däulet Myqtybaev and one of his pupils made in the 1970s (examples 16.5 and 16.6). These recordings reveal differences in the posture of the two performers, the way they hold the instrument, bowing and fingering techniques, and the quality of the *qobyz* sound. Whereas Myqtybaev holds the *qobyz* away from the body, his student rests it on his chest in a cello-like position. Even though both performers use a violin bow, the master holds it from underneath, in a traditional way, while the pupil holds it from above, like a cello player. Consequently, the trajectory of bowing and the distribution of the hand's weight on the strings are different in the two cases. The master's left-hand fingers are positioned tight against each other, and sound is mainly produced by the index and third fingers, which frequently slide down the string to reach out to different pitches, generating a fluctuating intonation. The student, by contrast, uses a cello fingering with a wide finger-stretch to distribute tone production, and the resulting intonation is clearer and more stable. In contrast to his student, the master uses ornaments and harmonics liberally, which produces a different quality of sound. The perception of time is also distinct in the two cases: the master plays in a flexible manner, whereas the pupil keeps to a more rigid metric structure. These observations attest to the student's assimilation of European technical and aesthetic norms of performance in his interpretation of a *qobyz küi* learned through training with a traditional master.

Examples 16.5 and 16.6. "Qongyr" (Deep-brown), attributed to Qorqyt, performed by Däulet Myqtybaev. "Qorqyt," attributed to Qorqyt, performed by Bazarkhan Qosbasarov. Fragments from films, 1970s. Courtesy of the archive of the Kazakhstan Republic Television and Radio Corporation.

STUDY QUESTIONS

1. Compare the performances of master and pupil. What, in your opinion, distinguishes their interpretations of the traditional *küis*?

2. How would you characterize the aesthetics and sound ideal of *qobyz* playing as reflected in the two performances?

3. How, in your view, did the aesthetic and semantic shift in *qobyz* performance exemplified by these interpretations of *küis* relate to changes in Kazakh society that took place during the 1960s–1970s?

NEO-TRADITION

The most recent phase in the evolution of the *qobyz* began in the years prior to and following Kazakhstan's emergence as an independent state in 1991. In post-Soviet Kazakhstan, the traditional *qyl-qobyz* has been revitalized and reintroduced in mainstream performance as well as in the curricula of music schools and the national conservatory. *Qobyz* students and researchers have sought out performers who acquired their skills by studying with traditional masters or through a hereditary lineage. One such traditional master is Smatai Umbetbaev (b. 1949), whose performance of Yqylas's "Erden" is presented in example 16.3.

The *qyl-qobyz* has also been taken up by healers in the context of neo-shamanic practices, and by neo-epic singers attempting to re-create the older style of epic singing to the accompaniment of the *qobyz* inferred to have been practiced by Kazakh bards of the fourteenth to eighteenth centuries. The *qyl-qobyz* is featured frequently at concerts, festivals, and folk music competitions. Its sound is heard in the media and on recent sound recordings such as the CD anthologies of Kazakh *küi*—"Eternal Melody" (*Mänggilik saryn*) and "1000 Traditional Kazakh *Küis*" (*Qazaqtyng dästürli 1000 küii*)—produced within the state-supported program "Cultural Heritage" (*Mädeni mura*). State promotion of the *qyl-qobyz* as an attribute of traditional Kazakh culture and spirituality contributes to its visibility in the public domain.

The survival of a small traditional *küi* repertory in a European-influenced world of contemporary music in Kazakhstan has led to a lively discourse on the nature of "tradition" and "authenticity" in *qobyz* performance. While some present-day musicians define traditionalism as the restoration of old repertory and playing techniques derived from early recordings and performances by the few living masters, other musicians understand the essence of the *qobyz* tradition as a performer's ability to mediate with supernatural powers and transform listeners emotionally and spiritually. Central to this discourse is the special quality of the *qobyz* sound, which for some musicians lies in the style of playing and for others in its transformative effect.

Contemporary *qobyz* music ranges from arrangements of European classical music for the *prima-qobyz* to popular adaptations of traditional tunes, to innovative creativity that explores aesthetic and spiritual dimensions of older *qobyz* performance styles by reproducing their idiomatic musical language on the cello or the *prima-qobyz*. An example of one such piece is "Oyanu" (Awakening) by the *prima-qobyz* player and composer Güljan Amanjol. In the words of the composer, "Oyanu" evokes "the awakening of the soul to a new spiritual realm, its liberation from matter and opening up to new spaces of light." The piece can be understood to reproduce the progress of a shamanic ritual, with a dynamic buildup toward an ecstatic climax, followed by a lyrical melody (c. 1:53) taken up in the performer's singing (2:45), which finally dissolves into *prima-qobyz* playing, rich in harmonics and sound effects. "Oyanu," with its imaginative mixture of innovation and older influences, serves as an apt metaphor for Kazakhstan's contemporary music scene—a meeting point of the local and the global, tradition and modernity.

Güljan Amanjol.

LISTEN

Example 16.7. "Oyanu" (Awakening), composed and performed by Güljan Amanjol. Recorded by Bakhtiyar Amanjol.

STUDY QUESTIONS

1. What elements of traditional *qobyz* playing do you hear in "Oyanu"?

2. What about the piece makes it contemporary?

3. As a piece of contemporary music, how would you assess and critique "Oyanu"?

NOTES

1. The name *qobyz* is related to a cluster of words in Turkic and Mongolian languages that mean "hollowed-out object," "container," "gourd," and "drinking cup," including those objects hollowed out for the purposes of making the resonator of a stringed instrument. See Gerard Clauson, *An Etymological Dictionary of Pre-Thirteenth-Century Turkish* (Oxford: Clarendon Press, 1972), 582–583; Gerhard Doerfer, *Türkische und Mongolische Elemente im Neupersischen* (Wiesbaden: Franz Steiner Verlag GMBH, 1967), 1419.

2. The term *qobyz*, in different phonetic variants and with different prefixes, figures in the names of other Central Asian instruments, in particular, varieties of jaw harp (*shang qobyz, jygach ooz komuz, temir ooz komuz*).

3. Abubekir A. Divaev, "Baqsa" [Baqsy], *Etnograficheskoe obozrenie* [Ethnographic review] 4 (1907): 23.

4. Nevolnik, "Vo mrake nevezhestva" [In the darkness of ignorance], *Turgaiskaya gazeta* [Turghai newspaper] (Orenburg, 1896), 77; Quoted in Saida Elemanova, *Kazakhskoe traditsionnoe pesennoe iskusstvo: Genezis i semantika* [Kazakh traditional song art: Genesis and semantics] (Almaty: Daik-Press, 2000), 21.

5. Abubekir A. Divaev, "Iz oblasti kyrghyzskikh verovanii: Baqsy kak lekar' i koldun" [From the realm of Kyrghyz (Kazakh) beliefs: *Baqsy* as a healer and magician], *Izvestiya Obshchestva arkheologii, istorii i etnografii pri Imperatorskom Kazanskom universitete* [Proceedings of the society of archeology, history and ethnography at the Imperial Kazan University] 15, no. 3 (1899): 56.

6. Ibid., 58.

7. I. A. Chekaninski, "Baqsylyq: Sledy drevnikh verovanii kazakhov [*Baqsylyq*: Traces of the Kazakhs' ancient beliefs], *Zapiski Semipalatinskogo Otdela Obshchestva izucheniya Kazakhstana* [Proceedings of the Semipalatinsk branch of the society for the study of Kazakhstan] 1, no. 18 (1929): 81–82.

8. Nevolnik, quoted in Elemanova, *Kazakhskoe traditsionnoe pesennoe iskusstvo*, 22. The author uses the ethnonym "Kyrghyz" to describe Kazakhs, as was the custom of the time.

9. Shoqan Valikhanov, "O musul'manstve v stepi" [On muslimness in the steppe], in *Sobranie sochinenii v pyati tomakh* [Collected works in five volumes], ed. Alkei Marghulan et al., vol. 4 (Alma-Ata: Glavnaya redaktsiya Kazakhskoi Sovetskoi Entsiklopedii, 1985), 71. Valikhanov uses the Russian words *bayan* for "bard," and *bylina* for "epic."

10. Valikhanov uses the word *akhun* and the Arabic transliteration of *ölengshi*, "singer."

11. Shoqan Valikhanov, "O formakh kazakhskoi narodnoi poezii" [On the forms of Kazakh folk poetry], in *Sobranie sochinenii v pyati tomakh* [Collected works in five volumes], ed. Alkei Marghulan et al., vol. 1 (Alma-Ata: Glavnaya redaktsiya Kazakhskoi Sovetskoi Entsiklopedii, 1984), 286.

12. *Jyr* here refers to the seven- and eight-syllable poetic meter typical of epic recitation.

13. Valikhanov, "O formakh kazakhskoi narodnoi poezii," 281. In the opinion of the ethnographer Älkei Marghulan, "Shoqan's assumptions about the disappearance of the singers of epic poetry relate to the Kazakhs of the Middle Horde, but do not reflect the state of affairs in the other two hordes, where epic poetry was in its heyday." See Alkei Marghulan, "O nositelyakh drevnei poeticheskoi kul'tury kazakhskogo naroda" [On the bearers of the ancient poetic culture of the Kazakh people], in *Sbornik k 60-letiu M. O. Auezova* [Collection of articles for the 60th anniversary of the birth of M. O. Äuezov] (Alma-Ata: Izdatel'stvo Akademii Nauk KazSSR, 1959), 77.

14. Jaqau Däurenbekov and Edige Tursynov, eds., *Qazaq baqsy-balgerleri* [Kazakh shamans and healers] (Almaty: Ana tili, 1993), 205; quoted in Elemanova, *Kazakhskoe traditsionnoe pesennoe iskusstvo,* 34–35. This account and other relevant information point to a more widespread use of the *qobyz* and a greater continuity of its traditional performance into the 20th century in the south of Kazakhstan, the legendary birthplace of the instrument, compared with other regions.

15. According to Akhmet Jubanov, Düken's *qobyz* aided childbirth by expelling evil spirits, and was "invariably hung at the threshold of the yurt where childbirth was taking place." See Akhmet Jubanov, *Struny stoletii* [Strings of the centuries] (Almaty: Daik-Press, 2001), 231.

16. Bazarkhan Qosbasarov, *Qobyz öneri: Muzyka oqu oryndarynyng oqytushylary men studentterine arnalghan oqu quraly* [The art of the *qobyz*: Textbook for students and teachers at music institutions] (Almaty: Sanat, 2001), 21.

17. Boris G. Erzakovich, *U istokov kazakhskogo muzykoznaniya: Po materialam russkikh uchenykh XIX veka* [At the sources of Kazakh musicology: Based on materials of 19th-century Russian scholars] (Alma-Ata: Nauka, 1987), 23–24.

18. Kazakhstan became an autonomous republic of the USSR in 1920, and a constituent republic (Kazakh SSR) in 1936.

19. Aleksandr V. Zatayevich, *1000 pesen kirgizskogo naroda: Napevy i melodii* [1000 songs of the Kyrgyz (Kazakh) people: Tunes and melodies] (Orenburg: Gosudarstvennoe muzykal'noe izdatel'stvo, 1963), 469. Zatayevich himself never witnessed a live shamanic ritual; the few tunes of *baqsy*s published in his collection were performed outside the ritual context.

20. Since any association with the *qobyz* could lead to persecution as an "enemy of the people," the instrument was often hidden, or even buried according to Muslim custom.

CHAPTER 17 # *Dombyra* Performance, Migration, and Memory among Mongolian Kazakhs

SAIDA DAUKEYEVA

Map of Bayan-Ölgii and the surrounding area.

The Altai Mountain range, which straddles northwestern China, western Mongolia, southeastern Russia, and eastern Kazakhstan, has long offered a home and a site of migration to nomadic Kazakh communities. In the eighteenth century, Kazakhs sought refuge in the Altai region in response to the occupation of their lands by the Jungars, a confederation of Western Mongol (Oirat) tribes. The subsequent annexation of Kazakh lands by czarist Russia and, in the twentieth century, the rise of Soviet Kazakhstan also led to a large influx of Kazakh nomads into the Altai region.

Among these nomads were tribal groups originally from northeastern and central Kazakhstan, notably the Kerei, Naiman, and Uaq, which belonged to the *Orta jüz* (Middle Horde), one of the three Kazakh tribal confederations that has existed since the seventeenth century. These groups resettled in the Xinjiang region of northwest China, and subsequently in the west of the territory then known as Outer Mongolia. From the 1860s, a Kazakh diaspora community began to form in the Khovd region of western Mongolia. This community gained relative autonomy in 1940 when the Mongolian People's Republic, as Mongolia was known from 1924 to 1992, established a new province (*aimag*) called Bayan-Ölgii.

Outnumbering other inhabitants of Bayan-Ölgii, such as Oirat Mongols, Tuvans, and Uyghurs, the Kazakhs became the largest ethnic minority in Mongolia and were granted high political status in the state. But the economic crisis that followed the collapse of the socialist system in 1990 and the announcement of a repatriation program for ethnic Kazakhs by the government of Kazakhstan impelled many Kazakhs to emigrate to what had become, in 1991, the independent Republic of Kazakhstan. About sixty thousand people, or half the Kazakh population of Bayan-Ölgii, moved to Kazakhstan in the early 1990s. Some of these migrants, known as "returnees" (*oralmandar*) in their new place of residence, have since re-migrated to Mongolia, after finding it difficult to reintegrate socially and culturally in their historic homeland. Though Kazakhs still form the majority (around 90 percent) of Bayan-Ölgii's population, the outflow to Kazakhstan continues to this day.

Through their complex migratory history, the Kazakhs of Mongolia have maintained their language and social practices, which are linked to a mobile pastoral way of life. They have taken their musical traditions along the path of their migration, reinventing them along the way in response to new political circumstances and cultural agendas. This process can be traced in the way Mongolia's Kazakhs perform on the *dombyra,* the two-stringed plucked lute that is widely regarded as a cultural symbol of Kazakhs. *Dombyra* performance in the genre of narrative instrumental pieces, *küi*s, is central to the musical life of the diaspora community. In its evolving contexts, forms, and style, it has reflected the Kazakhs' experiences of migration, social transformation, and changing notions of memory and identity.

This chapter follows the evolution of *dombyra* performance among Mongolian Kazakhs through a brief look at the lives and repertory of three *dombyra* players. These players are all descended from a single clan, the Tölek, within the tribal group Kerei, formerly known as the "*Dombyra* Community" (*Qalaqshanyng auyly*). Their musical careers span the three major periods in the community's history: the pre-socialist period when Mongolia was part of the Qing Empire of China, the socialist period of the Mongolian People's Republic, and the post-socialist period of independent Mongolia. The trajectory of the three musicians' lives can be seen as broadly representing the dynamic of social and cultural processes among the Kazakh diaspora in Mongolia.

Dombyra stele on the road to Ölgii.

FORMATION OF THE DIASPORA AND EARLY *DOMBYRA* PERFORMANCE: BERDIBAI MATAIULY

The emergence of the "*Dombyra* Community" (*Qalaqshanyng auyly*) is related to the late nineteenth century when the Tölek clan, along with other Kazakh

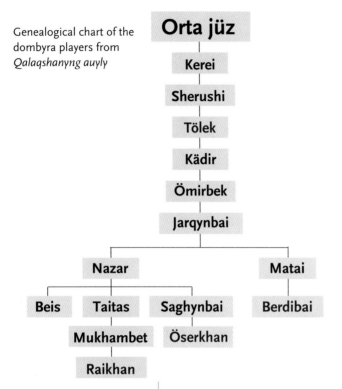

Genealogical chart of the dombyra players from *Qalaqshanyng auyly*

Orta jüz

Kerei

Sherushi

Tölek

Kädir

Ömirbek

Jarqynbai

Nazar · Matai

Beis · Taitas · Saghynbai · Berdibai

Mukhambet · Öserkhan

Raikhan

communities, driven by political instability and economic hardships in Xinjiang, followed their migration routes over the Altai Mountains into the valley of the Khovd River, which, together with Xinjiang, formed a single administrative region under the Qing dynasty. The leader of the clan, Beis Nazaruly (1848–1921), is said to have encouraged music making in the community and supported its musicians. He invited and hosted performers from across the Altai and Khovd, and sent local musicians to perform at intertribal gatherings and celebrations (*toy*s) and to learn new repertory.[1] One of the celebrated early *dombyra* players from the "*Dombyra* Community" was Berdibai Mataiuly (1867–1940). Berdibai gained his musical knowledge by studying with renowned masters such as Beisenbi Dönenbaiuly (1825–1898), originally from the Buyrshyn (Burqin) area in Altai. It was through Berdibai and other local performers that Beisenbi's *küi*s, first and foremost "Kenges" (Council), became known in western Mongolia.[2]

Musical contacts between Xinjiang and Altai remained active in the early twentieth century, as Kazakh tribes continued to move between the southern and northern sides of the Altai Mountains amid border disputes and changes of political control in Xinjiang and Mongolia.[3] Musicians from Altai and Khovd still traveled to community events, the usual sites of musical performances and contests (*saiy*s). At one such contest at a commemorative celebration (*as*) that took place in Khovd in 1927 and attracted musicians from both sides of the Altai, Berdibai defeated a performer from Xinjiang after dexterously performing a hundred *küi*s.[4] After his victory, Berdibai received a blessing (*bata*) from a well-known master, who bestowed on him the honorific title of "*dombyra* player" (*dombyrashy*). It was not until the 1940s that the hardening of political borders between China and the newly established Mongolian People's Republic halted cross-border travel and migration by the Kazakh community that remained in western Mongolia. The result was a lessening of musical interchange with Xinjiang.

The Kazakhs' migration to western Mongolia following a mass loss of livestock (*jut*) and famine in Xinjiang is commemorated in the *küi* "Zar zaman" (The time of sorrow) by Berdibai Mataiuly. According to the story of its origin passed down through oral tradition, Berdibai composed the *küi* during a journey over the Altai Mountains, when he and his family, destitute after the *jut,* were stopped on the border by Chinese tax collectors or couriers, who took away their last horses. One of the couriers, seeing Berdibai's *dombyra,* asked to hear him play. In response, Berdibai improvised "Zar zaman," which so moved the couriers that they inquired about its meaning. Berdibai explained that the music depicted the sorrowful time when the nomads were deprived of their horses and forced to migrate on foot. Hearing this, the couriers returned the horses, and Berdibai was able to reach the Khovd Valley and join his fellow clansmen.

Example 17.1. "Zar zaman" (The time of sorrow), composed by Berdibai Mataiuly, performed by Öserkhan Saghynbaiuly. Ulaankhus, Bayan-Ölgii, Mongolia, 1978. Courtesy of Mels Öserkhanuly.

LISTEN

Though documenting a specific episode in the life of its creator, "Zar zaman" came to epitomize more generally the time of hardship and misery in the early history of Mongolian Kazakhs. One unusual musical feature of the *küi* is the occasional unexpected rhythmic suspensions that disturb the otherwise regular pulse (e.g., at 0:11, 0:14, 0:21, 0:24, 0:32). Evoking an image of the labored or faltering step of someone struggling over a mountain pass on foot, this feature is interpreted by present-day *dombyra* players, descendants of the "*Dombyra* Community," as an expression of uncertainty and void experienced by somebody crossing the boundary between a wretched past and an obscure future—a musical metaphor of the "sorrowful time."

Stylistically "Zar zaman" is typical of the traditional Mongolian Kazakh repertory, known as *Kerei küi*s, and of *küi*s by early masters in Chinese Altai, notably Beisenbi. Played in the *shertpe* style, that is, by "plucking" or "flicking" the strings with individual fingers, it is designed to be performed on a *dombyra* with a flat, shovel-shaped resonator and a short, broad neck with seven to nine frets (see chapter 14). This type of *dombyra,* brought by migrants from their homeland in eastern and central Kazakhstan, became popularly known as *qalaq* or *qalaqsha*—literally "spoon" or "shovel"—hence the name of the *dombyra*-playing community, *Qalaqshanyng auyly. Kerei küi*s are simpler in structure than the classical *shertpe* repertory, typically repeating a single tune in a regular rhythmic pattern. Most of these *küi*s are intended for a *dombyra* with the two strings tuned to the interval of a fifth. A distinctive feature of such *küi*s is that the melody is performed on the higher of the *dombyra*'s strings against the background of the unfretted, or "open," lower string, which produces a constant pitch, or drone.

The harmonic series is a series of pitches that represent integral multiples (1x, 2x, 3x, etc.) of the frequency of a fundamental pitch "x." Harmonics, or overtones, are present in almost all sounds but usually are not heard as distinct pitches. Rather, they contribute to the timbre, or "color," of a fundamental pitch. In particular styles of vocal and instrumental music, however, harmonics are selectively amplified, and may be used to create pitch sequences that listeners perceive as melodies.

In this style, the principal melodic pitches are those of the harmonic series. The resulting sound is close to that of the end-blown flute *sybyzghy,* whose low-pitched drone, voiced by the player, provides the basis for the instrumental melody, consisting of amplified harmonic pitches, or overtones. This affinity indeed arises from the in-

terrelated history of the *sybyzghy* and the *dombyra* among the Mongolian Kazakhs, and is strengthened by the prevalence of drone-overtone music making in the Altai region both on end-blown flutes (*sybyzghy, shoor, tsuur*) and in the vocal practice generically known as "throat-singing." Thus, some *küis* can be played either on *dombyra* or *sybyzghy,* while others migrated from one instrument to the other in the course of performance practice.

WATCH

Example 17.2. "Beijin sary atan" (The golden camel of Beijing), performed by Näsiretkhan Qambaruly. Ölgii, Bayan-Ölgii, Mongolia, 2004.

Socialist Times: Öserkhan Saghynbaiuly

The arrival of the socialist era in Mongolia was marked by the establishment of Party-administered cultural centers, such as mobile Brigades of Art and Propaganda, Red Yurts, and more permanent Corners, which were set up to spread the new ideology among nomadic people through a campaign of "cultural enlightenment." These centers presented "voluntary art" productions performed by musicians—now redefined as "artists"—who were recruited from among local people. Such musicians performed revolutionary songs and tunes on imported instruments such as the mandolin and accordion, alongside older repertories of local music.

In Bayan-Ölgii, one of the best known of the early socialist-era "artists" was the *dombyra* player Öserkhan Saghynbaiuly (1918–1994). Öserkhan belonged to the Tölek clan, which migrated mainly within the region of Ulaankhus, a rural center for trade and small enterprises that became an official district (*sum*) of Bayan-Ölgii in 1940. A talented performer, Öserkhan learned from masters of the "*Dombyra* Community" and gained the title of "*dombyra* player" (*dombyrashy*) at the age of fifteen. In 1936, he became involved in the work of a Communist Party Brigade of Art and Propaganda and, together with musicians from Ulaanbaatar, toured western Mongolia, giving concerts in district centers and in the countryside at which he performed traditional *küi*s.[5]

As socialism took root in Mongolia, the early mobile Art Brigades and Red Yurts were upgraded to permanent Clubs and Houses of Culture that staged concerts on the occasion of significant official events. These included Communist Party assemblies, anniversaries of the founding of provinces (*aimag*s) and districts (*sum*s), and special "art days," when musicians from a district would perform in the provincial center, or musicians from across the province would perform in the capital, Ulaanbaatar. The designation of Bayan-Ölgii as an autonomous province (*aimag*) intended mainly for Mongolia's Kazakh and Altai Uriankhai minority populations ensured that Kazakh music would be well represented at such cultural events.

These events frequently featured instrumental and singing contests (*saiys* and *aitys*), which complied with the spirit of socialist competition promoted by the state. Though different from the original contests in their social connotations—with performers brought together to compete on behalf of districts and brigades rather than, as in the past, on behalf of tribes and clans—the contests retained much of their traditional function: to provide a venue for musicians from across the province to display their skills and share repertory. Winners of these contests were awarded state prizes and the title of *Aimag dombyra* player (*Aimaqtyq dombyrashy*), and their *küi*s were later included in the programs of concerts in the *aimag* and in Ulaanbaatar.

A number of locally acclaimed *dombyra* players gained state recognition through such contests. Öserkhan was awarded the title *Aimaqtyq dombyrashy* at a contest marking the tenth anniversary of Bayan-Ölgii, in 1950, where he performed his newly composed *küi* "Beibitshilik" (Peace), also known as "Beibitshilik qusy" (The bird of peace). The *küi* was celebrated during the socialist era as a symbolic depiction of a peaceful and prosperous life under the new order after years of misery and unrest, and became a popular number in concert programs in the province. Öserkhan composed his *kui* in the local stylistic idiom, in which the strings of the traditional *qalaqsha dombyra* were tuned to the interval of a fifth, and the melody was supported by a bass drone.

> **LISTEN**
>
> **Example 17.3.** "Beibitshilik" (Peace), composed and performed by Öserkhan Saghynbaiuly. Ulaankhus, Bayan-Ölgii, Mongolia, 1978. Courtesy of Mels Öserkhanuly.

STUDY QUESTIONS

1. Which performance techniques and elements of musical structure situate this piece within the Mongolian Kazakh stylistic tradition of *dombyra* performance?

2. How do you perceive the character of the *küi*? Can you see how this piece could be interpreted in light of the ideology of the socialist era? Does it express any other meaning for you?

Later interpretations of the *küi* reflected changes in local *dombyra* performance that occurred as a result of broader social and cultural developments in Bayan-Ölgii. In 1956, as part of the widening network of cultural and educational institutions that were being built across the country, a Music and Drama Theater was opened in the town of Ölgii. To assist the development of the new enterprise in the Kazakh-dominated province, musicians from Kazakhstan—performers, tutors, conductors, and an instrument maker working at the Almaty Conservatory—were assigned to Bayan-Ölgii within a program of cultural exchange between Mongolia and the Soviet Union. Musical reforms that took place at the theater thus followed the course of reforms that had taken place in Kazakhstan two decades earlier. A central focus of these reforms was the establishment of an orchestra of folk instruments—a local counterpart of the Orchestra named after Qurmanghazy, founded at the Almaty Conservatory in 1934.

The establishment of the theater's Folk Orchestra led quickly to changes in the musical instruments that orchestra members played. The old *qalaqsha dombyra* was soon replaced by a modified version of the instrument developed in Kazakhstan, which had an enlarged, pear-shaped resonator, an extended neck with nineteen fixed frets, and nylon strings in place of the gut strings used on older instruments. The modified instrument had a larger tonal range, a chromatic scale, higher-pitched tuning, and a more intense and resonant sound that was suitable for staged orchestral performances. Initially played by members of the orchestra, it was soon adopted throughout Bayan-Ölgii, following the importation of mass-produced *dombyra*s from Kazakhstan and the establishment of *dombyra* manufacturing in Ölgii in the 1960s. Widespread use of the new kind of *dombyra* led in turn to changes and reinterpretations in *dombyra* music itself. Such a reinterpretation took place in the performance of Öserkhan's well-known *küi* "Beibitshilik," which was arranged for the Folk Orchestra and later rearranged for solo *dombyra*. The rearrangement replaced the sustained drone featured in Öserkhan's own rendition with a melody line elaborated and replicated in the lower register.

Bayan-Ölgii Music and Drama Theater.

WATCH **Example 17.4.** "Beibitshilik qusy" (The bird of peace), composed by Öserkhan Saghynbaiuly, performed by Turymtai Müsirbaiuly. Qalbatau, Semei region, Kazakhstan, 2006.

STUDY QUESTIONS

1. What, in your opinion, distinguishes this piece from the original *küi* by Öserkhan in example 17.3?

2. How does the movement of the performer's hand along the *dombyra*'s neck correspond with the melodic progression and form of the piece?

LATE SOCIALIST AND INDEPENDENCE PERIOD: RAIKHAN MUKHAMBETULY

In 1990 and 1991, in the wake of the breakup of the Soviet Union, Mongolia and Kazakhstan became independent nation-states. These political events and the ensuing social transformations spurred new patterns of movement and migration among Mongolian Kazakhs. Some residents of rural areas moved to the provincial center, Ölgii, or the capital, Ulaanbaatar. Others went to study or work in Kazakhstan, Russia, or other former socialist bloc countries before ultimately returning to Bayan-Ölgii. Still others left Mongolia for Kazakhstan, settling in its eastern and central regions, the ancestral lands of Mongolian Kazakh tribal communities.

These processes affected *dombyra* performance among Mongolian Kazakhs, including descendants of the "*Dombyra* Community." Although this instrument and the genre of *küi* remain prominent in the community, diffusion of its previously cohesive social and musical milieu, as well as the rising influence and prestige of institutional musical training and concert performance, have disrupted the transmission of knowledge, skills, and repertory inherent in the local instrumental tradition. The modified *dombyra* is now widespread in western Mongolia, and a style distinct from that of *Kerei küi*s has gained currency among the diaspora community and returnees in Kazakhstan.

These trends can be seen in the life path and musical career of *dombyra* player Raikhan Mukhambetuly (b. 1936). A nephew of Öserkhan and son of the performer and *küi* master Mukhambet Saghynbaiuly, Raikhan took to the *dombyra* at an early age and soon became known in Ulaankhus and Ölgii through his virtuoso performances of local *küi*s. In 1958, Raikhan, along with other talented youngsters from across the province, was invited to audition for the Folk Orchestra and was awarded a place as a performer. He played clarinet before being transferred to the *dombyra* in 1959 and becoming leader of a *dombyra* group and a soloist in the orchestra.

Under the supervision of musicians from Kazakhstan, members of the Folk Orchestra learned musical notation, selected European classics, and traditional and modern compositions from Kazakhstan. In the early stages of Ölgii's Music and Drama Theater, though, the re-training of local musicians was not rigorous and relied mainly on oral means. Raikhan recalled that performers, unaccustomed to scores and more readily acquiring music aurally, learned the repertory by repeating their parts after the conductor, following his instructions and rehearsing in smaller groups—a practice adopted initially at the Qurmanghazy Orchestra. The slow pace of musical change in western Mongolia during the 1950s and early 1960s contrasted with the situation in Kazakhstan during the same period. There, socialist cultural reforms dating back to the 1930s resulted in a significant transformation of musical life and performance practice. Nevertheless, increasing professionalization of training and performance in western Mongolia brought about a gradual parting of ways between the theater and the broader musical environment.

Musical innovations in Bayan-Ölgii province concerned primarily the dissemination of the *dombyra* repertory from Kazakhstan, first and foremost the western *tökpe* style, which was increasingly featured in theater productions and, beginning in 1965, on the new Bayan-Ölgii Radio. The preeminence of this style echoed changes in Kazakhstan itself, where modernization and the formation of a national musical culture had led to the elevation of *tökpe* in mainstream performance.

The preference for *tökpe* on the part of Soviet cultural ideologists had partly arisen from the contrasting social backgrounds of the two major representatives of the regional traditions. Qurmanghazy Saghyrbaiuly (1818–1889), who composed in the *tökpe* style, was a poor man opposed to and persecuted by Kazakh and czarist authorities, while Tättimbet Qazanghapuly (1817–1862), an adherent of the *shertpe* style, was a hereditary aristocrat and a member of the Kazakh elite. Apart from this, classical *tökpe küi*s, with their dynamic, life-asserting character, were found suitable for getting across the socialist message of progress and were, above all, more adaptable to orchestral arrangements and setting in four-part harmony. Consequently, they became central to the concert programs of folk orchestras, notably the famous Orchestra named after Qurmanghazy. *Küi*s in the contrasting *shertpe* style, on the other hand, whose intimate and lyrical nature did not conform to the ideology and spirit of the times and was unsuitable for the standard orchestration, were sidelined in the shaping of musical culture in Soviet Kazakhstan.

When, in the 1950s and 1960s, a group of musicians from Kazakhstan came to Bayan-Ölgii to work at the theater, *tökpe küi*s, in solo and orchestral renditions, played a prominent role in theater productions, while the repertory of *küi*s from eastern Kazakhstan, despite its stylistic affinity with local tradition, was limited. From that time onward, the *tökpe* style began to influence local performance and creativity. The strumming technique and sectional principle (*buyndyq*) typical of *tökpe* (see chapter 14) came to figure in reinterpreted traditional *küi*s and compositions by contemporary *küi* masters. The transition from the local *qalaqsha dombyra* to the modern instrument with nineteen chromatic frets gave scope to the sectional form, as the small compass of the older instruments did not allow for wide-ranging tonal development. The shift in stylistic and aesthetic notions of local *dombyra* performance was an aspect of wider cultural developments among Mongolian Kazakhs. Though introduced as part of socialist campaigns, the modernized *dombyra* and western Kazakhstan repertory came to epitomize a "national" style of *dombyra* performance, underscoring the diaspora's ties to the homeland.

Since the 1990s, the process of emigration from Mongolia to Kazakhstan has drawn the instrumental tradition of Bayan-Ölgii further into the orbit of *dombyra* performance in Kazakhstan, where the continued prevalence of *tökpe* in the institutional scene is paralleled by an increasing interest in and revival of *shertpe* repertory. Raikhan Mukhambetuly is among a few well-known Mongolian Kazakh *dombyra* players and *küi* masters, now "returnees" (*oralmandar*), who arrived in Kazakhstan in the 1990s, following their relatives, seeking a better livelihood and prospects for their children, or aspiring to join their kinsmen in the historic homeland. After retiring from the theater in 1991, he moved to the Qaraghandy region of central Kazakhstan, where he has taught the *dombyra* at a primary school, the House of Culture, and now privately. Equally adept in *Kerei küi*s and the former theater repertory, and now adding classical *shertpe küi*s from Saryarqa, Raikhan can teach a varied range of styles. Yet when preparing his pupils—and a grandson

Raikhan Mukhambetuly.

who is a *dombyra* student at the Humanities College in Qaraghandy—for concerts and *dombyra* competitions at the regional level, he makes sure that their program includes a number of *tökpe küi*s, first and foremost those by Qurmanghazy, whose mastery is considered essential for a professional *dombyra* player.

Raikhan's creative work includes some *küi*s with features of both *shertpe* and *tökpe,* and others entirely in the *tökpe* style of western Kazakhstan. An example of the latter is "Mereke tolghau" (Celebratory contemplation), composed by Raikhan in 2006 for the celebration of the Bayan-Ölgii Theater's fiftieth anniversary, in which he participated as an honored former theater artist. The *küi* conveys both a festive spirit and an air of nostalgic contemplation prompted by the current decline of the theater and the dispersal of its once-celebrated orchestra. Stylistically, it is a large-scale *tökpe küi* modeled on classical western *küi*s. The *tökpe* style is evident in the dense two-voiced texture and elaborate sectional form, which is composed of a succession of sections (*buyn*) set at increasingly higher pitch levels that alternate with a low-pitched refrain. Other features of "Mereke tolghau" that depart from the instrumental tradition of Mongolian Kazakhs are the tuning of the strings of the *dombyra* to the interval of a fourth, the use of a minor mode with a modulation in the course of the *küi,* and a developed lower voice.

LISTEN

Example 17.5. "Mereke tolghau" (Celebratory contemplation), composed and performed by Raikhan Mukhambetuly. Saryözek, Qaraghandy region, Kazakhstan, 2006.

STUDY QUESTIONS

1. How is this *küi* different from the traditional Mongolian Kazakh *küi*s you listened to earlier?

2. What, in your view, makes it similar to or distinguishes it from the *tökpe küi*s by Qurmanghazy and Qazanghap exemplified in chapter 14?

The life stories of the *dombyra* players from the "*Dombyra* Community" (*Qalaqshanyng auyly*) and the performance histories of their *küi*s demonstrate a stylistic and aesthetic evolution in Mongolian Kazakh *dombyra* performance from the diaspora's formation down to today. Although the community over time has kept a strong awareness of local repertory, the perceived locus of their musical "tradition" has moved along the path of their migration—from eastern Kazakhstan to Chinese Altai and western Mongolia, re-establishing contact with Kazakhstan in the present day. Some of the *dombyra küis*, for example "Zar zaman," that once represented among Mongolian Kazakhs the source of their tradition and a stimulus for creativity in performance, are no longer part of living practice, and are preserved in published notations or stored in the memories of elderly performers. Other *küis*, like "Beibitshilik," have been reinterpreted according to the standards of a later age. Still others, modeled on *dombyra* performance in Kazakhstan, represent an "invented tradition" of recent times. These historical and stylistic shifts in the music of the Mongolian Kazakh community are a testament to the changeable nature of social memories and perceptions of identity, not least in the way they define themselves in relation to broader Kazakh ethnicity and culture.

NOTES

1. Saqai Qarsyuly, *Küi kerueni: Kümbirli küiler kerueni; Küi jäne küishiler khaqyndaghy angyzdar men aqikhattar* [*Küi* caravan: Caravan of resonant *küis*; Legends and truths concerning *küis* and *küishis*], ed. Rysbek Zurghanbaiuly (Ölgii: Bayan-Ölgii aimaq baspakhanasy, 1991), 48–52.

2. Ibid., 50.

3. These included the fall of the Qing dynasty and proclamation of Mongolia's independence in 1911, the 1921 revolution, and the establishment in Mongolia of a Soviet-backed socialist regime in 1924.

4. Qarsyuly, *Küi kerueni,* 55.

5. Ibid., 84.

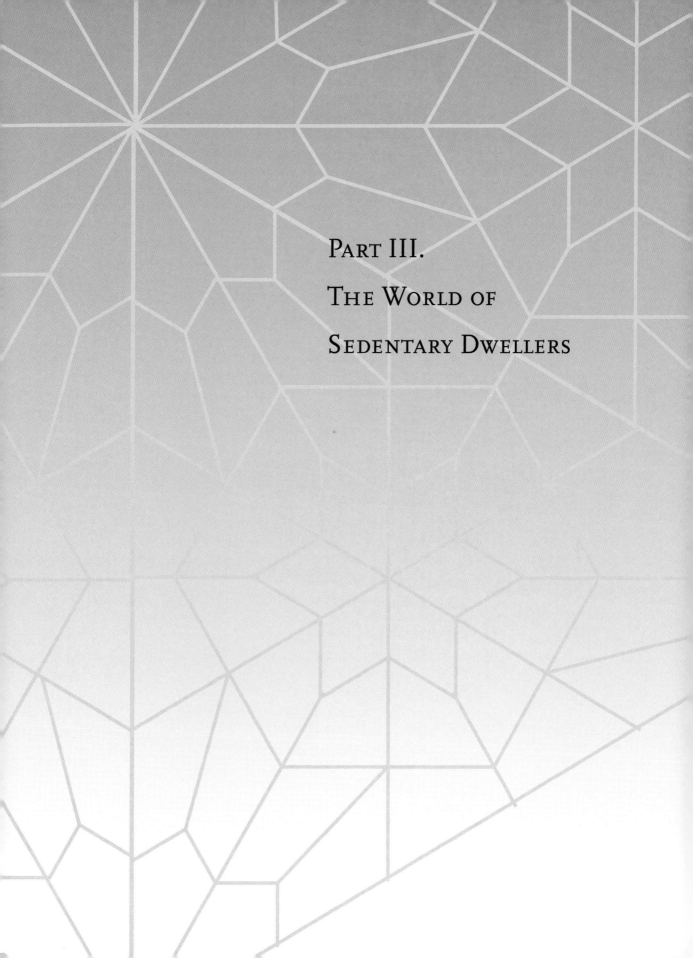

Part III.
The World of
Sedentary Dwellers

PROLOGUE ## Patterns of Culture

SEDENTARY DWELLERS

THEODORE LEVIN

The chapters grouped together in this third section of *The Music of Central Asia* address music, musicians, and musical life in the culture of sedentary dwellers, one of the two major axes of Central Asian civilization discussed in chapter 1. The term "sedentary dwellers" refers to settled residents of cities, towns, and villages, as opposed to mobile pastoralists, or nomads, who make regular seasonal movements or migrations linked to the economy of stockbreeding. These distinctions are not absolute, nor are the boundaries between nomadic and sedentary life impermeable. That is, sedentary dwellers may become nomads, and, as has more frequently been the case, nomads may become sedentary dwellers. Indeed, many sedentary dwellers in contemporary Central Asia can trace their

A bazaar in Dushanbe, the capital of Tajikistan.

lineage to historically nomadic groups. Sedentarization has been ongoing in Central Asia for several centuries. Moreover, in some parts of Central Asia, nomadic and sedentary patterns of culture have merged, creating a hybrid culture with elements of both. A good example of such merging can be found in the culture of the Karakalpaks, a once nomadic people who adopted farming as well as stockbreeding in the delta region of the Amu Darya River (see chapter 6). But merging and social fluidity notwithstanding, certain core patterns of culture characteristic of nomads and sedentary dwellers can be compared and con-

trasted in a generalized form. Such patterns encompass material, spiritual, and expressive culture, and shape musical practices in significant ways.

A town in Tuva created from the forced sedentarization of nomadic herders.

One of these practices concerns the way that musicians use language. The musical expression of nomadic or historically nomadic peoples—as repeatedly demonstrated in the preceding section of the book—reflects the central role of orality, for example, in the oral composition and transmission of epic poetry and other narrative poetic forms by bards who are at once singer-reciters, historians, genealogists, actors, and, in some cases, virtuoso instrumentalists. Though music among sedentary dwellers has also traditionally been transmitted orally, singers often kept small notebooks consisting of poetic verse that they set both to well-known melodies and their own compositions. The works of famous poets who wrote in different dialects of Persian and Turkic languages—Hafez, Rumi, Yassawi, Sa'di, Fuzuli, Navo'i, Bedil—circulated widely in sedentary-dwelling Central Asia, and great singers were expected to be connoisseurs of poetry. By contrast, the authors of the great oral poetic works of nomadic cultures are anonymous and, in all likelihood, multiple. No one knows the names of the long-ago bards who created the epic poems *Manas, Körughly,* or *Alpamys.*

In contrast to the solo performances of bards that have been so highly valued in nomadic cultures, sedentary dwellers have cultivated the art of small ensembles. These ensembles traditionally consisted of a singer and a few musicians, although during the Soviet era, ensembles became much enlarged as part of the campaign to adopt European models—including orchestras, choirs, and consorts—for the performance of Central Asian music. One nearly universal distinction between the music of nomads and sedentary dwellers is that the ensemble music of sedentary dwellers invariably includes a percussion instrument—typically a frame drum—whereas nomadic music is typically performed without percussion (drums used by shamans, and for martial or military purposes, e.g., the Kyrgyz *dobulbas,* are exceptions). Percussion instruments articulate the metrical patterns that frame the setting of poetic texts to music, and keep rhythm for dancing—an all but ubiquitous element of the expressive culture of sedentary dwellers, but one that is rare among nomads. Moreover, in the music of sedentary cultures, meter and rhythm are highly theorized constructs expressed in the form of rhythmic cycles, or regularly recurring metro-rhythmic patterns, called *usul* ("procedure," "principle"). Among musicians in sedentary cultures, *usul* is also a general name for the metro-rhythmic dimension of music, analogous, for example, to the general meaning of *tala* in the classical raga tradition of India. Nomadic musicians, by contrast, do not speak about *usul.* This is not to say that nomadic music lacks rhythm. On the contrary, the many music examples included in the previous section of the book offer ample evidence of the complex rhythms of much nomadic music, in particular, instrumental music.

Another pattern of culture that shapes the music of sedentary dwellers is the defining role of gender in musical performance. While many musical genres in nomadic cultures have

Alim Qasimov, *mugham* singer.

Photo by Sebastian Schutyser. Courtesy of Aga Khan Music Initiative.

been receptive to both male and female performers, and audiences for musical entertainment tend to be mixed, traditional music in sedentary cultures reflects a strict gender divide in musical genres, performers, and audiences: male performers entertain men, and female performers entertain women. Nowadays, these social and musical boundaries are less rigid than in times past, particularly in the realm of professional artists who perform in the public sphere (see chapter 25). But vestiges of strict gender divisions still exist in the musical practices of sedentary dwellers—for example, in the performance of music at the male-only early-morning ritual meal (*osh*) that is an obligatory part of weddings in Uzbekistan and Tajikistan. The abiding practice of gender divisions surely reflects the deep impact of Islam as a spiritual and cultural force in sedentary-dwelling regions of Central Asia, in contrast to its more superficial impact on the culture of nomads. Several of the chapters in this section focus on religious music among both urban and rural sedentary dwellers. Other chapters address forms of *maqom,* the urban musical tradition that is organized in canonical repertories that are often referred to as "classical" music. *Maqom* is rooted in an old cultivated tradition of music theory, mathematics, and philosophy that developed under the patronage of Muslim rulers in great centers of culture and commerce such as Baghdad, Samarkand, Herat, and Bukhara. It draws on a rich legacy of poetry that has been transmitted through the centuries in written form, and it is performed by small musical ensembles whose members have achieved their musical mastery through the institution of *ustod-shogird* ("master-apprentice" or "master-disciple") pedagogy. Yet other musical traditions of sedentary dwellers that developed independently of *maqom*—for example, *falak* and *maddoh*—also reflect the deep impact of Islam, the mystical power of contemplative poetry, and the creative power of consummate composer-performers. The chapters that follow offer an introduction to these and other musical sub-cultures of sedentary dwellers in Central Asia.

Below left: In contrast to the solo performances of bards in nomadic cultures, sedentary dwellers have cultivated the art of small ensembles, like this one in Baku, Azerbaijan. *From left,* Ali Asgar Mammadov, *tar;* Natiq Shirinov, *naghara;* Rauf Islamov, *kamancha;* Rafael Asgarov, *balaban.*
Photo by Sebastian Schutyser. Courtesy of Aga Khan Music Initiative.

Below: Kamoliddin Khamdamov, *tanbur,* and Murod Jumaev, *doira,* students at the Academy of Maqom, in Dushanbe, Tajikistan.
Photo by Sebastian Schutyser. Courtesy of Aga Khan Music Initiative.

CHAPTER 18 *Maqom* Traditions of the Tajiks and Uzbeks

WILL SUMITS AND THEODORE LEVIN

Music scholars in Central Asia have coined the term "professional oral tradition music" to refer to a vast domain of sophisticated art song and instrumental music that has evolved over at least a millennium in a variety of local and regional "dialects" in the Eastern Mediterranean, Iraq, Iran, Azerbaijan, North Africa, and Central Asia. These geographically diverse but musically kindred traditions share broadly cognate features of musical form, melodic and rhythmic structure, aesthetics, affect, and terminology—the latter including their very names: *maqom-maqām-makam-muqam-mugham* (*maqām* in Arabic means "place," "position," "station").

TWO MEANINGS OF *MAQOM*

In music, the word *maqom* has had two principal meanings. One of these can be rendered most closely in Western music theory by the concept of "melodic mode" or "melody type." Melodic modes figured prominently in the music of ancient Greece, and may well have existed in the music of even older civilizations—Pharaonic Egypt, ancient Babylon, Achaemenid Persia. A melodic mode is similar to a musical scale, i.e., a sequence of ascending or descending pitches that can provide the basis for melodic improvisation, extemporization, or composition. Modes are widely perceived by acculturated listeners as having the power to evoke a particular color, emotion, or affect, which arises not only from the sequence of pitches but from a specific set of conventions and constraints that collectively constitute the structure or "syntax" of the mode. For example, a mode may allow certain melodic motifs but prohibit others. It may emphasize certain scale degrees and de-emphasize others.

As the primary building blocks of melody, the *maqom* modes were a central aspect of music theory for many centuries in the Middle East and Central Asia.

Jamshed Ergashev and Kamoliddin Khamdamov from the Academy of Maqom.

Photo by Sebastian Schutyser. Courtesy of Aga Khan Music Initiative.

But at least since the beginning of the nineteenth century, the term *maqom* has acquired a second meaning in Central Asia. This second meaning refers to a suite of musical pieces sequentially organized by melodic mode, metrical pattern (the temporal organization of a succession of rhythmic pulses), and rhythm. Such suites came to be referred to as *maqom*s, and nowadays, when musicians in Central Asia speak about *maqom*s, they typically have in mind one or another of these suites.

The Geography of Central Asian *Maqom*

In Central Asia, *maqom* (as it is commonly transliterated into Latin script in Tajikistan and Uzbekistan) has been primarily the province of urban musicians, and the tradition of *maqom* has particularly strong historical ties to the cities of Bukhara, Khiva, and Qoqand. These cities served as the cultural and political centers, respectively, of the Bukharan Emirate, and the Khanates of Khiva and Qoqand. The power of the three contiguous city-states waxed and waned over a period of four hundred years, from the early sixteenth century until 1920, when the Bukharan Emirate and Khivan Khanate became part of the Union of Soviet Socialist Republics (the Qoqand Khanate was dissolved in 1865, and its territory absorbed into Russian Turkestan). The Bukharan emirs and the khans of Khiva and Qoqand supported retinues of master artisans, craftsmen, and entertainers, among whom musicians played a prominent role under the patronage of certain rulers. As these musical masters transmitted their knowl-

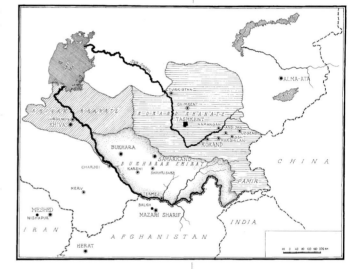

The three khanates of Transoxania around 1850.

edge and skills to talented disciples, the performance of *maqom* in each of the three city-states evolved over time into three distinct musical traditions, each with its own characteristic performance style and local repertoire.

The three, primarily urban, principal traditions of Central Asian *maqom* are as follows:

- Shashmaqom (six *maqom*s): most strongly associated with the city of Bukhara, and also performed by musicians in nearby Samarkand.
- Alti-yarim Maqom (six and a half *maqom*s): associated with the city of Khiva and also performed by musicians in the nearby city of Urgench. Khiva and Urgench are the largest cities in Khorezm, a culturally autonomous region in the northwest of Uzbekistan, and the Alti-yarim maqom is often called the Khorezm or Khorezmian Maqom.

- Chormaqom (four *maqom*s): associated with the territory of the Qoqand Khanate, which included the Ferghana Valley and the city of Tashkent, now the capital of the nation of Uzbekistan. This *maqom* tradition is also widely referred to as the "Ferghana-Tashkent Maqom"—a designation often used nowadays as a synonym for Chormaqom.

Though the three Central Asian *maqom* traditions have their own distinctive features, they share many common characteristics of musical form and overall sound. For example, the form in which songs are composed is very similar, and the same kinds of musical instruments are used. Moreover, the three *maqom* traditions exemplify aesthetic ideals that were widely shared by musical connoisseurs in Bukhara, Khiva, Qoqand, Samarkand, Khujand, and other centers of urban culture, and the persistence of these aesthetic ideals reaffirms the status of *maqom* as "classic" or "classical" music. The individual songs that presently compose the *maqom* suites have arguably been in the repertoire of *maqom* performers for well over a century, and reflect a musical aesthetic that is even older.

The *maqom* traditions are also a part of the classical literary heritage of Central Asia. The poetry of Mavlana Balkhi (better known as Rumi), Hafez, Shams-i Tabrizi, Jami, Hiloli, Sa'di (Saadī), Sayyido, Yusuf Andijani, Bedel (also Bedil or Bīdel), Navo'i (also Navā'ī or Nawā' ī), Fuzuli, Sabri, and many other great poets is set to music in the *maqom* suites. In order to properly match the metrical scheme of texts composed in poetic genres such as *ghazal* and *rubā'ī* with the metrical scheme of the melody to which it is sung, singers must possess a thorough understanding of the complex system of verse meters known as *aruz*. Indeed, many of the musical rhythms that shape melodic form in the *maqom* suites developed alongside

Masters of Persian Mystical Poetry: Rumi and Hafez

Khwaja Shams ad-Din Muhammad Hafez-e Shirazi (c. 1320–1389), known simply as Hafez, was born in Shiraz, a cultural center of medieval Persia (modern Iran). Hafez, a devout Sufi, is thought to have written over 5,000 poems, whose overarching theme is longing for union with the Divine. He is revered in the Persian-speaking world for his sublime lyricism and mystical symbolism as well as for the complex puns that permeate his poetry. Generations of singers have set Hafez's poems to music, and in Central Asia, texts attributed to Hafez appear frequently in the repertoire of traditional singers in Badakhshan as well as in the vocal suites of the Tajik Shashmaqom.

Jalal ad-Din Rumi (1207–1273), known to his followers as Mevlana (Our master), produced a prolific corpus of poems that express the Sufi ideal of mystical union with the Divine. Born in Balkh, in what is now northern Afghanistan, Rumi spent most of his life in the Anatolian city of Konya, where he is buried. Following his death, his disciples created the Mevlevi Sufi order, which cultivated the practice of mystical dance and music as a central element of *zikr*, the Sufi ceremony of remembrance. The appeal of Rumi's poetry has reached across religions and cultures, with translations of his poems appearing in many languages.

the verse meters of *aruz* to accommodate the performance of sung texts. Thus the rhythmic pulse of melody and that of sung poetry are inextricably intertwined in *maqom* performance.

Aruz has been a core element of classical Arabic, Persian, and Turkic-language poetry for more than a millennium, and is still part of a living artistic practice. Poets composing text within the *aruz* system draw from a complex of quantitative meters in which syllables are classified by vowel length (long or short) and linked together into poetic feet characterized by a fixed pattern and specific number of long and short syllables (usually three or four). Poetic feet are in turn sequenced into lines of text according to the conventions of one or another poetic form. Analogues of *aruz* exist in the quantitative verse meters of classical Greek and Latin poetry, such as iambic pentameter and hexameter. (In English-language hexameter or pentameter, rhythm is expressed through the alternation of stressed and unstressed syllables rather than long and short vowel lengths, as in classical verse.)

THE HISTORICAL DEVELOPMENT OF *MAQOM* IN CENTRAL ASIA

Music has a long history of patronage within the courts of the khans and emirs who ruled over the Central Asian city-states. Patronage of urban music and musicians reached its peak during the fifteenth century as a result of socio-economic policies that allowed for tax exemptions, land grants, and pious endowments to be given to artists, musicians, and scholars. Husayn Bayqara (ruled 1469–1506), the last ruler of the Timurid dynasty in Central Asia, whose court was in Herat, provided an ideal model of royal patronage of the arts for later rulers in Central Asia as well as for the royal courts of the Ottoman and Mughal empires. Husayn Bayqara's patronage of the arts was so generous that several of the poets and musicians in his court and ministry themselves became wealthy patrons. The great poet 'Ali Shir Navo'i (1444–1501), for one, was a minister and close advisor to Husayn Bayqara, and Navo'i also became an important patron of the arts and music and contributed significantly to the development of *maqom* practice and theory.

During the Timurid and subsequent Shaybanid era, many theoretical treatises were written about the "science" of music. These theoretical treatises discussed melodic modes, song genres, rhythms, and other aspects of music from both a theoretical and practical perspective. While treatises on music theory played an important role in developing the conceptual basis of melodic mode from the thirteenth

Musical entertainment at a scholar's house. Folio from a late-sixteenth-century manuscript of the Akhlaq-e Nasiri (Ethics of Nasir) by Nasir al-Din Tusi (d. 1274).
From the collection of Prince and Princess Sadruddin Aga Khan. Courtesy of the Aga Khan Trust for Culture.

The *tanbur* is the fundamental accompanying instrument for performances of Shashmaqom.

through the seventeenth centuries, theoretical treatises ceased to be written after the seventeenth century. Adumbrations of this cultural turn were apparent during the sixteenth and seventeenth centuries, when treatises on music began to focus increasingly on musical practice rather than on the "science" of music.

In the seventeenth century, the performance of musical suites consisting of pieces representing different *maqom*s (i.e., *maqom* in the sense of "melodic mode") assumed a position of cultural importance because such suites exemplified in musical practice the intellectual prestige of music theory itself. In the seventeenth century, these modal suites were known as the *chahor shadd* (four suites), each of which consisted of a collection of pieces that progressed through a sequence of several different melodic modes. The *chahor shadd* were widely performed, and it is likely that they eventually led to the formation of the *maqom* suites during the eighteenth century. Despite a paucity of sources from the eighteenth century, one can infer that the performance tradition of the four *shadd* continued to expand and develop during the seventeenth century, and that at some point these suites began to be referred to as *maqom*.

The absence of musical treatises in eighteenth-century Central Asia reflects a decline in the patronage of artists and musicians, which may have been the result of the general political turmoil and instability of the period. It may further reflect the imposition of a more conservative Islamic rule that came to question the permissibility of music as a profession. While music continued to be played and to develop throughout the eighteenth century, it was only in the nineteenth century that it re-emerged more fully from the shadows.

The nineteenth-century musical literature of Bukhara, Samarkand, and Khiva revolves around the practical tradition of *maqom* performance, with scant attention to the erstwhile focus on the "science of music." Many treatises were composed in the form of compendiums of poetry, called *bayāz*, which contain poetic texts that particular performers set to the melodies of the *maqom* suites. Some of these *bayāz* compiled in Bukhara in the early nineteenth century are the first documents that refer to the Bukharan repertoire of six *maqom* suites as Shashmaqom: "six *maqom*s."

Meanwhile, in the city of Khiva, musicians in the service of the khan in the second half of the nineteenth century developed a unique system of written musical tablature specifically designed for the performance of the Alti-yarim Maqom suites on the *tanbur* (long-necked lute). This *tanbur* notation represents the first effort to develop a standardized written notation system for music in Central Asia, and provides the first evidence of actual melodic content in the nineteenth-century *maqom* suites. Yet, despite the availability of music notation, Central Asian *maqom* music continued to be transmitted orally well into the twentieth century. Oral transmission was facilitated by the abiding cultural prestige of the *ustod-shogird* (master-disciple) model of musical pedagogy in which aspiring musicians depended on older masters to initiate them into the subtleties and intricacies of singing and playing instruments.

An example of 19th-century *tanbur* notation for the Alti-yarim Maqom. The notation is read from right to left. Horizontal lines represent the musical scale of the *tanbur*. Dots indicate where to place fingers of the left hand on the neck of the *tanbur*. Vertical lines are provided for ease of reading and don't represent a musical sign. The poetic text corresponding to each line of *tanbur* accompaniment is written above the line.

Photo courtesy of Otanazar Matyakubov, from manuscript compiled in the 1920s in Khiva by the poet, musician, and calligrapher Muhammad Kamil Devani (1887–1938).

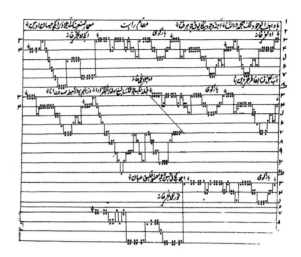

Early Sound Recordings from Central Asia

The history of sound recording in Central Asia dates to the first decade of the twentieth century, when recently founded record companies based in Europe and the United States sent sound engineers to record well-known musicians in Asia, Africa, and Latin America with the aim of building local markets both for records and for the gramophones and cylinder phonographs used to play them. These early recordings—many of which have been preserved in archives and personal collections— offer a remarkable portal to the global sounds of a bygone era. In Central Asia, recordings released by the London-based Gramophone Company and Paris-based Pathé Brothers Company illustrate pre-Soviet performance styles that were later transformed under the influence of Soviet culture policies.

Political turmoil in Central Asia curtailed recording activities in the years surrounding the Russian Revolution of 1917, and recording did not recommence in earnest until the 1930s, by which time the entire Soviet recording industry was managed by a state-controlled monopoly. In the 1930s, however, many master musicians who had come of age in the late nineteenth century were still active, and records from this era preserve their voices with remarkable clarity. One of these musicians was

Domla Halim Ibadov.
Courtesy of Aleksandr Djumaev.

Early Sound Recordings from Central Asia *(CONTINUED)*

Domla Halim Ibadov (1878–1940). Domla Halim, as he was known ("domla" means teacher or master), learned the art of Shashmaqom from his neighbor Sharafkhan, an old singer in the court of Emir Alim Khan, the last emir of Bukhara, and from Ota Jalol Nasirov (1845–1928), who served as head court musician to the last three Bukharan emirs, and who was a key figure in the transmission of Shashmaqom. Domla Halim's 1935 recording of "Navruzi Sabo," a classic piece from the Shashmaqom, is reproduced here. In the recording, Domla Halim sings alone to the spare accompaniment of *tanbur,* played by Shohnazar Sohibov, and frame drum—a notable contrast to the ensemble style of Shashmaqom performance that became standard during the Soviet era.

LISTEN

Example 18.1. "Navruzi Sabo," performed by Domla Halim Ibadov, vocal and *dutar,* and Shohnazar Sohibov, *tanbur,* with unknown *doira* player. The six-minute recording is evenly divided into two sections of three minutes, each corresponding to the length of one side of the record. Musicians in the era of 78 rpm records were accustomed to adapting performances to the constraints of the three-minute side. In this recording, Domla Halim ends the first part of "Navruzi Sabo" precisely at the three-minute mark. The record was produced at the Noginsk record factory in Noginsk, Russia. The number 909 on the label dates the recording to 1935 though the label design is one associated with records pressed by the Noginsk factory in 1939–1940. While the label text notes that Domla Halim both sings and plays the *dutar,* the *dutar* is inaudible. Domla Halim may simply have held the *dutar* during the recording session and intermittently strummed or plucked it lightly to orient himself to the proper pitches.

The *maqom* traditions of the nineteenth century were carried into the twentieth century by a constellation of musicians who are remembered today as patriarchs and consummate masters of *maqom* performance. These musicians witnessed and participated in one of the most far-reaching social and cultural transformations of the modern era: the consolidation of Soviet rule over the vast Eurasian colonial empire pieced together by the Russian czars, and the rapid rise of the Soviet Union as a world power. Unlike other imperial powers, whose rulers exercised their authority indirectly through control of local political proxies while leaving indigenous culture more or less intact, the architects of Soviet cultural policies viewed arts and culture as an obligatory and essential domain of political intervention. Even the most remote villages and settlements of Central Asia were not immune from the efforts of Soviet "culture workers" to reorganize artistic and cultural practices according to priorities mandated by Soviet culture policies. One of the most visible of these priorities was the so-called "struggle against the past," which, by its very definition, challenged the authority of tradition in all domains of cultural life, including music (see chapter 1).

Performer Profile: Barno Ishakova (pronounced Is'hakova)

Barno Ishakova (1927–2001) was one of the leading Shashmaqom singers of the 20th century and remains an enduring model for female performers of Tajik and Uzbek *maqom* repertoires. Ishakova was born into a Bukharan Jewish family in Tashkent, Uzbekistan, and later moved to Tajikistan, where she built her singing career, performing as a member of the Shashmaqom Ensemble created in 1947 under the aegis of Dushanbe's state radio station, and teaching at the Mirzo Tursun-Zade Institute of Arts. In 1992, Ishakova emigrated to Israel. Though Barno Ishakova was not the first female singer to break into the traditionally male cultural space of Shashmaqom performance, she became the most revered. The warm lyricism, broad tonal range, delicate ornamentation, and sheer dynamic power that characterize her vocal style, combined with her refined expression of the poetry she sang made her a musical icon among connoisseurs of Shashmaqom music—widely imitated, but never equaled.

A framed photo of Barno Ishakova wearing medals she was awarded for artistic achievement hangs in the Tajik National Conservatory.

While Soviet cultural policies radically reconfigured popular culture, concert life, music education, and music scholarship, *maqom* masters continued to perform their traditional repertoire in private gatherings of friends and at festive family celebrations. Beginning in the late 1940s, and continuing into the 1950s, the performance of *maqom* began to reemerge into official cultural life with the establishment of a *maqom* ensemble under the aegis of the state-controlled radio stations in Dushanbe, Tajikistan (1947), and Tashkent, Uzbekistan (1958). Meanwhile, musicologists began to transcribe *maqom* music from the performance of the most authoritative master musicians and publish systematic collections of the various *maqom* repertoires in Western staff notation. These publications created canonical versions of *maqom* music that became the basis for the study and performance of *maqom* traditions during the remaining years of the Soviet era as well as in the post-Soviet era.

Since the breakup of the Soviet Union, *maqom* music has become a highly visible symbol of national cultural identity in both Uzbekistan and Tajikistan. In 2008, UNESCO inscribed Shashmaqom music on the Representative List of the Intangible Cultural Heritage of Humanity on behalf of both Uzbekistan and Tajikistan.[1] Musicians and music scholars have prepared new redactions of several *maqom* repertoires (see "Further Reading, Listening, Viewing" section on the companion website), and in Tajikistan, an academy was opened to train a new generation of musical leaders in the performance of *maqom* music.

Title page of Viktor Uspensky's 1924 edition of the Shashmaqom. The title reads "Six Musical Poems (Makom) Transcribed by V. A. Uspensky in Bukhara."
Courtesy of Aleksandr Djumaev.

The Academy of Maqom
ABDUVALI ABDURASHIDOV

These days, no one in Tajikistan needs to be convinced of the extraordinary importance of Shashmaqom—the classical music heritage of the Tajiks and also the Uzbeks. Much of the credit for this should go to the president of Tajikistan, Emomali Rahmon. His understanding, vision, and decisiveness in creating a new approach to the Shashmaqom have energized our society at the beginning of the twenty-first century. At a time when the Shashmaqom seemed to be fading, the president took sensible and timely steps to provide support. He funded new artistic and educational organizations, created a special "Day of Shashmaqom," and mandated the organization of children's studios throughout the country devoted to the study of Shashmaqom.

Like other forms of classical music in the East, Shashmaqom was traditionally taught and learned through a system of "master-disciple" (ustod-shogird) oral pedagogy. The master-disciple system not only facilitated the transmission of knowledge and experience but also provided a framework for musical creativity and evolution. Beginning in the late 1920s, however, Soviet cultural strategists introduced European musical forms and genres into Central Asia—symphony, opera, ballet, oratorio—together with a system of music education in which students learned music from notation, rather than by ear. The Soviet Union's official cultural

The Academy of Maqom models itself on an older ideal of Islamic learning, in which the study of music is inseparable from the study of poetry, prosody, metaphysics, ethics, and aesthetics.

Photo by Sebastian Schutyser. Courtesy of Aga Khan Music Initiative.

establishment viewed this new musical life as a promising substitute for "backward" indigenous music. Now we understand that this model was misguided. Classical music from Asia and Europe both have their own unique qualities, their own self-contained worlds of thought and feeling. And how fortunate are those who have a place in their soul for maqom as well as Mozart!

The erosion of the traditional master-disciple system had an adverse effect on our classical music, and it was the idea of reanimating this system in a contemporary setting that inspired me to found the Academy of Maqom. I observed that in Iran, India,

Azerbaijan, and other Asian nations, many master musicians have their own schools, and students are free to choose whichever school best suits them. I wanted to create a school where students would learn not only to perform maqoms of the past but to master the principles and techniques that would allow them to compose new maqom music. In the academy, I emphasize that the seeds of musical creativity and evolution are contained in the knowledge passed on to us by our musical forebears. A fundamental aspect of the academy's curriculum is the study of maqom as a musical cycle or suite. I learned from my own experience that performing and listening to the *maqom* as an integral cycle can lead to an entirely different understanding and experience of the music—to a kind of self-purification. You cannot get that experience simply by listening to individual pieces extracted from the cycle, which is how *maqom* is mostly performed these days.

In the twenty-first century, much has changed, but traditions more than a thousand years old continue to thrill and delight us. They reflect the variety of the world and enrich our ability to transmit to one another our most beautiful and precious feelings and thoughts, while filling us with optimism

and hope for the future. The art of Shashmaqom has emerged on the world stage and is enjoyed by listeners in many countries of Europe, North America, and Asia. The Academy of Maqom is proud to contribute to the preservation, development, and dissemination of this remarkable art.

THREE PRINCIPAL FORMS OF CENTRAL ASIAN *MAQOM*

The following section describes each of the three principal forms of Central Asian *maqom* and illustrates them with listening examples.

Shashmaqom

Shashmaqom takes its name from the six *maqom* suites that constitute the core of the classical repertoire most closely tied to Bukhara, which is also performed in Samarkand and across northern Tajikistan. The first mention of Shashmaqom occurs in a musical treatise written in Bukhara in the first half of the nineteenth century. Even in this earliest description of Shashmaqom, it appears to be a well-developed tradition that probably dates back at least to the eighteenth century, and resembles the earlier performance tradition of the modally organized *chahor shadd* (described above) that became widespread during the seventeenth century. The poetry set to the melodies of the various pieces that make up the Shashmaqom suites was most frequently drawn from the Tajik-Persian literary heritage, but many Shashmaqom singers have been bilingual in Tajik and Uzbek, and have also sung poetic texts written in Uzbek or Chagatay, a Turkic language that is a precursor of modern Uzbek.

Each of the six Shashmaqom suites consists of some forty individual pieces. Performed in its entirety, each suite can last up to several hours, but opportunities for the performance of an entire *maqom* are rare today. Performers typically perform individual pieces or mini-suites created from the *maqom* repertoire. The six principal suites have also spawned several secondary suites, which are most likely a product of the mid-nineteenth century.

The melodic structure and development of the Shashmaqom suites is closely linked to the *tanbur*, the long-necked plucked lute on which Shashmaqom singers typically accompany themselves. The tuning system of the *tanbur* and the arrangement of frets on the instrument's neck define the melodic contours of the Shashmaqom repertoire, making it likely that the performance of Shashmaqom has been linked to the *tanbur* since the earliest stages of the Shashmaqom's development.

Each Shashmaqom suite includes both instrumental and vocal sections. A *maqom* begins with the instrumental section, which usually consists of six to ten instrumental compositions in distinct rhythmic patterns. Following the instrumental section, the vocal section of the *maqom* begins. The main vocal musical compositions in a *maqom* suite are often joined together by brief songs called *tarona,* which are typically sung in unison by two or more vocalists. Through the course of a *maqom* suite, the melody progresses through several contrasting melodic modes, thus giving each suite its own distinct color and emotional character. The melodic development of a *maqom* suite often follows an ascending pattern in which the musical compositions rise to higher pitches before returning to the pitch in which the *maqom* suite first began. Some suites also integrate compositions that reside in the lower register of the melodic mode. The pattern of gradual ascent and descent, and eventual return is mirrored in the melodic structure of individual compositions within each suite.

LISTEN

Example 18.2. "Talqincha-i sabo," performed by the Academy of Maqom. From *Invisible Face of the Beloved: Classical Music of the Tajiks and Uzbeks,* vol. 2 of *Music of Central Asia* (SFR, 2006), track 15.

"Talqincha-i sabo" is a song from the Shashmaqom suite Maqom-i Rost. In the recording featured in example 18.2, the performers are members of a small ensemble consisting of seven singers accompanied by the *tanbur* (plucked long-necked lute), *dutar* (strummed long-necked lute), *sato* (bowed long-necked lute), and *doira* (frame drum). The word *talqincha* in the song title refers to a reoccurring rhythmic pattern or cycle, called *usul,* while *sabo* refers to a melodic mode. "Talqincha-i sabo" thus means "a song in the rhythmic pattern *talqin* composed in the melodic mode *sabo.*"

Listen to the instrumental introduction at the beginning of "Talqincha-i sabo" (0:00–0:26) and attune your ear to the percussive sound of the *doira* (frame drum), whose player beats out the *usul* pattern. One cycle of *usul* consists of five drum strokes, which are conventionally transcribed according to the scheme shown below. Strokes to the center of the drum, which produces a lower pitch, are placed below the solid line, while strokes to the rim, which produces a higher pitch, are placed above the solid line.

Talqin is an example of an asymmetrical *usul* in which regularly reoccurring groups of beats have uneven length. In the case of *talqin,* the first two drum strokes belong to one group, and the second three drum strokes belong to another group (the two groups are indicated in the time signature as 3/8 + 3/4). Asymmetrical rhythmic patterns occur not only in the Shashmaqom, but in other *maqom* repertoires, notably Uyghur *muqam* and Ottoman *makam,* where combinations of binary and ternary rhythmic groups are classified as *aksak:* "limping" (see chapter 19). So-called "limping" rhythms are also common in various genres of folk music of Turkey, the Balkans, West Asia, and Central Asia, perhaps revealing an old genetic relationship between what are now geographically disparate repertoires.[2]

As for the melodic component of "Talqincha-i sabo," the song is composed in a melodic mode called *sabo,* which is one of several different modes that occur in the "Rost" suite of the Shashmaqom. The basic scale of this mode is illustrated below:

Musicians conceive of *sabo* not as an octave scale, but as the combination of a pentachord and a tetrachord. The lower five pitches create the pentachord, and the upper four pitches create the tetrachord. The highest pitch of the pentachord is the same as the lowest pitch of the tetrachord, thus providing a "hinge" between the pentachord and the tetrachord.

The third scale degree occurs both as B♮ and B♭—in ascending phrases, it is typically sung as B♮ and in descending phrases, it is sung as B♭. The sixth scale degree, E, is also sometimes sung as E♭ in descending phrases. The juxtaposition of natural (♮) and flatted (♭) versions of the third and sixth scale degrees contributes to the distinctive modal character or "color" of *sabo.* (The performance in example 18.2 is pitched approximately a semitone lower than the pitches indicated in the schematic scale above. As long as intervals between successive pitches are maintained, the actual pitch level at which the piece is performed may shift up or down, depending on the preference of performers, which typically depends on the pitch level at which their voices and instruments sound best.)

The poetic text of "Talqincha-i sabo" is attributed to Hafez and speaks of the sublime joys of love, and the pain caused by separation from the beloved. The song's melody is set to eight lines of poetry consisting of four couplets, or two quatrains.

Each quatrain is taken from a different poem. The verse form of both quatrains is *rubā'ī* (plural form: *rubā'īyat*, or *rubaiyat*), a canonical genre of Persian poetry, later adopted by poets writing in other languages, whose most common rhyme scheme is aaba. This is indeed the rhyme scheme of the two *rubā'ī* quatrains that make up the text of Talqincha-i sabo, which is transcribed and translated below (the final word of each line is in boldface to show the rhyme scheme).

Rubā'ī is characterized not only by its end rhyme scheme but by adherence to one of a set of standard *rubā'ī* verse meters that are part of the *aruz* system described earlier. The verse meter for each line is indicated by short (˘) and long (–) marks separated into poetic feet by a diagonal slash (/). The first four lines each have a slightly different verse meter while lines 5–8 all share a single meter. The conventional name of each meter appears to its right (these names are in Arabic, for *aruz* originated as a prosodic system for Arabic poetry).

> – – ˘/˘ – – –/– – – /– (Hazaj musammani axrabi muxannaki abtar)
> (1) Rū-ze, ki fi-roq az tu du-ram so-**zad**,

> – – ˘/˘ – ˘ –/˘ – – – / – (Hazaj musammani axrabi maqbuzi abtar)
> (2) Vaz haj-ri ru-khi tu no-sa-bu-ram so-**zad**,

> – – ˘/˘ – ˘–/˘ – – ˘/˘ – (Hazaj musammani axrabi makfufi majhuf)
> (3) Gar chash-m ba sū-yi di-ga-re bo-z ku-**nam**,

> – – ˘/˘ – – ˘/˘ – – –/– (Hazaj musammani axrabi makfufi abtar)
> (4) Haq-qi na-ma-ki hus-ni tu kū-ram so-**zad**.

> – – ˘/˘ – ˘ – /˘ – – – –/–(Hazaj musammani axrabi maqbuzi abtar)
> (5) Man ban-da-yi on ka-sam, ki shav-qe do-rad,

> (6) Bar gar-da-ni khud zi ish-q, tav-qe do-rad.
> (7) Tu laz-za-ti ish-qu o-shi-qī kay do-**nī**?
> (8) In bo-da ka-si khū-rad, ki zav-qe do-rad.

(1) The day when separation shall cut me off from you,
(2) When absence of your face shall intensify my longing for you,
(3) If I shall open my eyes to behold another,
(4) I would transgress loyalty to you, and for this crime, your beauty shall strike me blind.
(5) I am a slave to the one who is charged by love's longing, and its ache,
(6) The one who wears the token of love's bondage around his neck, as others would a necklace.
(7) What do you know of the lover's joy, happiness, and bliss?
(8) Only one who has refined taste drinks this wine, but the intoxication all others will miss!

As set to music in the song, each line of poetry corresponds to a self-contained melodic segment—or, to use an analogy to language, a complete melodic "sentence." As the song progresses from one line of poetry to the next, some poetic lines are set to a melodic segment that has previously been heard, while other lines of poetry are set to new melodic segments. Following most lines of poetic text, the singers add additional vocables (sounds or words without a conventional meaning), such as "o," or words such as *yoram* ("my friend"), *jona* ("soul"), *nozaninam* ("beautiful one"), *sarvinozam* ("my cypress"—a metaphor for a slender figure)—all of which imply a mystical reference to the Divine. These extra syllables stretch the vocal lines so that they correspond to the length of the melodic segments, which tend to be a little longer. Part of the art of setting a poem to music in the Shashmaqom is to arrange the text so that long and short syllables of text are matched with long and short musical notes.

Table 18.1 shows the relationship between lines of text and melodic segments (columns 2 and 3 in the table). Melodic segments identified by the same number are identical, or almost identical. The terms in column 4 designate sequential structural sections of the song that each play a specific role in the development of the melody: *sarkhat* is the opening section, sung in a low tessitura (vocal range); *dunasr* begins an octave above *sarkhat,* propelling the melody higher, before descending to the initial low register; *awj-i Zebopari* introduces a melody composed in a different mode and marks the melodic and emotional culmination of the song (*awj* means "apogee" or "zenith"); *furovard* ("descent") modulates back to the original melodic mode, *sabo,* and descends to the original low vocal register, bringing the song to a conclusion.

Listen to "Talqincha-i sabo" and try to hear the beginning and end of each melodic segment and each structural section (you can refer to the time code in the left column if these beginning and ending points are unclear). Listen for melodic repetition where it is indicated in the table.

Each of the melodic segments that compose "Talqincha-i sabo" can be described by a contour that represents the rise and fall of successive pitches in the melody. These pitches can move in one of three ways:

1. Ascending

2. Descending

3. Maintaining same pitch level

Now listen to "Talqincha-i sabo" again, focusing on the melodic contour of each segment. Listen for the way the melody ascends and descends, and how it does so. Does it move in a straight line? Or are there zigzags, twists, and turns?

TABLE 18.1. RELATIONSHIP OF TEXT, MELODY, AND MELODIC CONTOUR IN "TALQINCHA-I SABO"

TIME CODE	TEXT LINE	MELODIC SEGMENT	STRUCTURAL SECTION OF SONG	MELODIC CONTOUR
0:00–0:26	Instrumental Introduction	1	Sarkhat	
0:26–0:53	1	1		
0:53–1:21	2	1		
1:21–1:47	3	2	Dunasr	
1:47–2:14	4	3		
2:14–2:53	5	4	Awj-i Zebopari	
2:53–3:33	6	5		
3:33–4:01	7	6	Furovard	
4:01–4:27	8	3		

Just as each melodic segment has a contour that describes its movement through melodic "space," the entire piece also has a contour that represents its overall melodic shape. Like many songs in the Shashmaqom suites, the melodic contour of "Talqincha-i sabo" looks like an arc:

Now listen once more to "Talqincha-i sabo," this time focusing on its overall melodic shape. Note how the initial pitch of some melodic segments is higher than the final pitch of the segment that precedes it.

Analyzing the process by which musicians set poetry to music in the Shash-maqom shows that this process is a highly artistic one rooted in a thorough knowledge of melodic and rhythmic elements of Shashmaqom as well as the *aruz* system of quantitative verse meters. The ability to perform and ultimately to compose new music according to the rules and constraints of *maqom, usul, and aruz* is what was cultivated in the traditional *ustod-shogird* pedagogy of Shashmaqom.

STUDY QUESTIONS

1. After which melodic segment(s) does the subsequent melodic segment begin from a higher initial pitch?

2. In which line of poetic text does the song reach the highest pitch level?

3. Based on your experience of listening to the performance while following the long and short syllable markings of the *aruz* verse meter in the transcription, would you say that the singers consistently align short and long rhythmic values in the music with syllables scanned as short and long in the *aruz* pattern, or are there inconsistencies? If so, to what do you attribute them?

ALTI-YARIM MAQOM OF KHOREZM

The *maqom* suites rooted in the culturally autonomous region of Khorezm, in northwestern Uzbekistan, have been called Alti-yarim Maqom (six and a half *maqom*s) because, in addition to six suites that include both an instrumental and vocal section, the Alti-yarim Maqom has a partial seventh *maqom* with only an instrumental section—the "half" of the six and a half *maqom*s. In Khorezm, the Alti-yarim Maqom occupies a social and musical niche analogous to that of the Shashmaqom in Bukhara as a much-respected tradition at the center of what is commonly glossed as "classical" music. Indeed, the two repertoires appear to be closely related. Written sources and oral tradition both attest that in the early nineteenth century, a well-known musician from Khiva named Niyozjon Khoja brought the Shashmaqom tradition from Bukhara to Khorezm. While studying in Bukhara, Niyozjon Khoja learned the Shashmaqom suites in their entirety, and when he eventually returned to Khiva, he began to pass the tradition on to his students. Some of these students not only performed the repertoire they had learned from Niyozjon Khoja but also created their own original compositions. Among them are the instrumental pieces that constitute the "half" *maqom* in the Alti-yarim Maqom: Panjgoh. Table 18.2 shows the names of the *maqom* suites in the Bukharan Shashmaqom and Khorezm Alti-yarim Maqom, listed in their traditional performance order.

TABLE 18.2. SEQUENCE OF *MAQOM* SUITES IN SHASHMAQOM AND ALTI-YARIM MAQOM

BUKHARAN SHASHMAQOM	KHOREZM ALTI-YARIM MAQOM
Buzruk	Rost
Rost	Buzruk
Navo	Navo
Dugoh	Dugoh
Segoh	Segoh
Iroq	Iroq
	Panjgoh

With the exception of Panjgoh, the names of the suites in the Shashmaqom and Alti-yarim Maqom are identical, however, the specific songs and instrumental pieces that compose the suites are largely different in the two traditions.[3]

The *maqom* tradition continued to develop in Khiva, acquiring its own local color, repertoire of songs and instrumental pieces, and performance techniques. In the eighteenth and much of the nineteenth centuries, the musicians of Khiva sang Persian-Tajik poetic texts to the musical performance of the Shashmaqom suites, but because Khiva was located in the heart of the Turkic-speaking world, *maqom* performers gradually began to sing lyrics drawn from the works of poets who wrote in a variety of Turkic literary languages and dialects, such as Navo'i, Ogohi, Mashrab, and Fuzuli.

While the "six and a half" *maqom* suites of Khorezm include several hundred individual pieces, there are also several smaller groups of suites created for specific solo instruments. One such group of instrumental suites is performed on the *dutar,* and is known as *dutar maqomlari.* Another group is performed on the *surnai,* a loud clarinet best known for its use in festive celebrations. These instrumental pieces are called *surnai maqomlari.* Although the instrument-specific *maqom* repertoires share features of melodic mode and formal structure with the Alti-yarim Maqom, their actual melodies are different, and thus they constitute a distinct *maqom* tradition.

LISTEN

Example 18.3. "Muqaddima-i segoh," performed by Farhod Davletov (vocal and *tar*), accompanied by Shuhrat Razzaqov (*dutar*), Habibulla Kurambaev (*doira*), and Murod Norkuziev (*ghijak*). From *In the Shrine of the Heart: Popular Classics from Bukhara and Beyond,* vol. 7 of *Music of Central Asia* (SFR, 2010), track 7.

"Muqaddima-i segoh" is a well-known song in the Khorezmian Alti-yarim Maqom tradition—specifically, in the suite Segoh (see table 18.2, above). *Muqaddima* means "introduction" or "prologue," and *segoh* is the name of the principal melodic mode in the eponymous suite, Segoh. Thus "Muqaddima-i segoh" means "Introduction to the suite Segoh" or "Introduction to the melodic mode *segoh*." The basic scale of *segoh* is illustrated below:

As in melodic type *sabo*, melodic type *segoh* includes a scale degree (in *segoh*, the sixth) that may be rendered either as a natural or flatted pitch (in this case, B♭ or B♮). Both pitch options are used in ascending as well as descending melodic motifs.

Farhod Davletov, the vocalist whose gripping performance of "Muqaddima" is presented in example 18.3, sings lyrics from a *ghazal* by Feruz Khan, the last ruler of the Khanate of Khiva, who was an avid poet and musician as well as a great supporter of artists and musicians. True to the *ghazal* genre, the theme of the poem revolves around love, beauty, and longing. The *ghazal*'s Uzbek text is transliterated and translated below. Note the end rhyme scheme, which is a defining feature of the *ghazal* genre: aa ba ca da and so on.

Gul yuzing ochib, ei gul, majlisim guliston qil,	Unveiling your face, oh rose, turn my gathering into a garden,
Mehri orazing uzra kokiling parishon qil.	Dishevel your hair like clouds around the sun of your face.
Ilkingga olib soghar, nösh etib mayigulrang,	Taking a cup in your hands and drinking rose-colored wine,
Jonfizo tabassumdin lablaringni khandon qil.	Put a smile on your lips, which torment my soul.
Közinga chekib surma, yuzinga urib ghoza,	Adorning your eyelashes with *surma*, and your face with powder,
Lola birla nargisin ul ikkovga hayron qil.	Make them the envy of the tulip and the narcissus.
Hasrat ötiga kuysin qomating körub shamshod,	Let boxwood burn with jealousy from seeing you,
Qaddi nozparvardin noz ila khiromon qil.	Make your walk as tender as a tree in the wind.

> *Lutf etib agar yoring kelsa*
> *bazmingga, Feruz,*
> *Bu aziz joningni maqdamiga*
> *qurbon qil.*

If your beloved comes to your feast out of politeness, oh Feruz,
Then sacrifice your dear life to her steps.

"Muqaddima-i segoh," like "Talqincha-i sabo," can be divided into structural sections that distinguish successive blocks of melodic activity, as illustrated in table 18.3.

The brief *daromad* is repeated several times throughout the piece and introduces the melodic phrase to which the first line of text is sung. The first two lines of text and their accompanying melody constitute the *sarkhat,* and it is this section that establishes the melodic and poetic themes of the piece. The next section, *miyonkhat,* begins an octave higher than the initial pitch of the *sarkhat* (the *miyonkhat* section was absent in "Talqincha-i sabo"—a rare departure from the typical formal structure of a Central Asian *maqom* song). The *dunasr* section repeats the melody introduced in the *sarkhat* section, but is sung one octave higher. Following *dunasr,* the vocalist stretches to reach the *awj,* the highest point of the melodic line, which serves as the melodic and rhythmic culmination of the entire piece. After the *awj,* the melody gradually descends in the *furovard* toward its initial starting point, where the piece ends.

FERGHANA-TASHKENT MAQOM (CHORMAQOM)

The Ferghana-Tashkent Maqom is most closely tied to the cities of Tashkent and Qoqand, the seat of the former Qoqand Khanate, and is performed throughout the greater Ferghana Valley as well as in northern Tajikistan. While the musical culture of the Ferghana Valley has its own distinct color and flavor that

TABLE 18.3. FORMAL STRUCTURE OF "MUQADDIMA-I SEGOH"

TIME CODE	TEXT LINE	MELODIC SECTION
0:00–0:19	Instrumental Section	*Daromad* (entry, prelude)
0:19–1:08	1 and 2	*Sarkhat* (principal level)
1:08–2:06	3 and 4	*Miyonkhat* (middle level)
2:06–3:06	5 and 6	*Dunasr* (2nd vocal section)
3:06–3:46	7 and 8	*Awj* (apogee)
3:46–4:38	9 and 10	*Furovard* (descent)

reflect local geography, language, and lifestyle, it has also integrated elements of the musical cultures of surrounding regions. Ferghana has long been a cultural crossroads within Central Asia, and the *maqom* traditions of Ferghana reflect an intermingling of musical styles. For example, in the early nineteenth century, one of the best-known music masters in the Ferghana Valley was a man known as Khudoberdi Ustaz. Oral and written histories recount that he was originally from Kashgar, the old city on the eastern side of the Tian Shan Mountains in what is now the Xinjiang Uyghur Autonomous Region of China, and that he spent eighteen years in Khorezm, where he studied music with Niyozjon Khoja, the musician who is believed to have brought the Shashmaqom tradition from Bukhara to Khiva.

The Ferghana-Tashkent Maqom, however, is not simply a transplanted version of the Bukharan or Khorezmian *maqom* suites but a unique repertoire. Musicians call the Ferghana-Tashkent repertoire Chormaqom (four *maqom*s), suggesting that it once consisted of four *maqom* suites. The present-day repertoire, however, is considerably larger. The name Chormaqom is likely a vestige of an earlier time, perhaps the eighteenth century, when the tradition may have indeed centered around four principal *maqom* suites. The current repertoire includes numerous small suites consisting of two to six pieces as well as individual pieces unaffiliated with a suite that performers nonetheless consider a part of the *maqom* tradition.

Compared to the Bukharan Shashmaqom and the Khorezmian Alti-yarim Maqom, the formal structure of the Ferghana-Tashkent Maqom is conceived on a smaller scale. The repertoire as a whole is smaller; each suite includes fewer pieces, and the pieces themselves tend to be shorter and less structurally complex, with fewer modulations to different melodic types. A typical suite includes three to four pieces that follow a progression from slow to fast rhythm and tempo, all in the same melodic mode. The Ferghana-Tashkent Maqom also includes a sizeable repertoire of instrumental music. One of the best known of these instrumental pieces is "Nasr-i segoh," presented in example 18.4.

LISTEN **Example 18.4.** "Nasr-i segoh," arranged and performed by Turgun Alimatov. Tashkent, Uzbekistan, 1993.

"Nasr-i segoh" exemplifies the element of the Ferghana-Tashkent Maqom repertoire described above as "individual pieces unaffiliated with a suite that performers nonetheless consider a part of the *maqom* tradition." "Nasr-i segoh" was composed by one of the great modern masters of *maqom* instrumental music, Turgun Alimatov (1922–2008), and beautifully represents the laconic Tashkent-Ferghana style. These days it is performed by many of Alimatov's former students and acolytes, frequently in the arrangement for *tanbur* and *dutar* presented in example 18.4 (see "Performer Profile: Turgun Alimatov"). Like "Muqadimma-i segoh," presented in example 18.3, Alimatov's "Nasr-i segoh" is composed in melodic type *segoh* and uses the same basic scale, with one small difference: whereas the melody of "Muqadimma-i segoh" includes both a flatted and natural sixth scale degree (B♭ or B♮), "Nasr-i Segoh" uses exclusively B♮ for the sixth scale degree, yielding the modal scale widely known in Western music as "Dorian."

Like the vocal songs discussed earlier in this chapter, instrumental *maqom* music can also be divided into structural sections that describe blocks of melodic activity. The names of these sections, however, are different than those used to describe vocal music.

"Nasr-i segoh" consists of two formal sections called *khona* (house) and *bozgui* (refrain), which alternate throughout the short piece. *Khona* is the dynamic, developmental element in the piece, while *bozgui* provides a stable frame that links together the various *khona* episodes. The formal principle of episodic development linked by a recurring refrain is widespread in the music of both East and West—for example, in the *peshrev* instrumental genre of Ottoman classical music, and in the rondo form of Western classical music, whose formal structure is typically expressed as: a b a c a d a . . . Table 18.4 presents the sequence of *khona* and *bozgui* sections in "Nasr-i segoh."

STUDY QUESTIONS

1. After listening to the three different regional varieties of *maqom*, which one do you find most accessible? Which one do you find the most difficult to listen to and assimilate? What explanation can you offer for each of your responses?

2. The two vocal compositions presented in the listening examples—"Talqincha-i sabo" and "Muqaddima-i segoh"—are performed by different ensembles and represent different approaches to the performance of Central Asian *maqom*. How would you characterize these differences?

3. Differences in performance style notwithstanding, what similarities do you perceive among the three examples of Central Asian *maqom*?

Table 18.4. Formal Structure of "Nasr-i segoh"

Time Code	Section	Description of Melodic Activity
0:00–0:20	*khona*	Introduces principal melodic theme in melodic mode *segoh*
0:20–0:39	*bozgui*	First occurrence of refrain
0:39–1:07	*khona*	2nd *khona* set at higher pitch level
1:07–1:31	*bozgui*	Beginning at 1:17, melody is slightly different than in the first *bozgui*, reflecting the ever-higher pitch level of the piece
1:31–1:59	*khona*	Melody begins an octave above initial pitch of the first *khona*
1:59–2:31	*khona*	Includes brief melodic excursion outside *segoh* melodic mode then returns to *segoh* for melodic culmination (*awj*)
2:31–3:00	*bozgui*	Melody descends to final appearance of refrain

Performer Profile: Turgun Alimatov, an Innovator in Tradition
Theodore Levin

Turgun Alimatov (1922–2008) was a master performer on the *tanbur, dutar,* and *sato* (bowed *tanbur*). He was also a unique musical innovator who created a repertoire of new compositions that are rooted in the melodic modes of the Tashkent-Ferghana *chormaqom* (four *maqom*) tradition, yet speak in a distinctive and immediately recognizable musical language. Alimatov's music has been widely performed, recorded, and imitated by younger musicians, and remains a strong influence among Uzbek and Tajik performers of classical *maqom* music.

Turgun Alimatov was not only a great musician but an original thinker and lively conversationalist. Like a Sufi sheikh, he conveyed his ideas through didactic stories and epigrammatic explanations, and drew on notions such as *saz* (harmony), *ishq* (love), *dard* (passion), *halat* (state), and *kaif* (intense pleasure or delight) to explain his views.

I was fortunate to have many conversations with Turgun Alimatov. Following are some excerpts

Performer Profile: Turgun Alimatov, an Innovator in Tradition (CONTINUED)

(translated from Uzbek and Russian).

Ted Levin (TL): I want to write about how you took *maqom* and, from it, created your own new music.

Turgun Alimatov (TA): I didn't create music. I took what existed, ready-made, and I played it. I listened, I played, listened, played. I didn't compose melodies. Why search for new music when there's so much ready-made music?

TL: But you took *maqom*—and what you play, your style, it's not similar to the Bukharan Shashmaqom. You changed something. You don't consider that you created new music?

TA: No. One person builds a house and leaves that house. I come to that house and remodel it. And that remodeling will be valued for a long time. And then a still better master will come along and do another remodeling. He'll take down certain parts and build them up again in his own way. It will be still better. That's how I understand it. I'm not the one who built the house. I just did the remodeling. I can't say that it's mine. Whoever sees this house says that a workman gave it a good paint job. He doesn't say that the workman built it. If I play *segoh*, it doesn't mean that I wrote it; but people know that I play well. They know when they hear me that Turgun-*aka* is playing. And that's enough.

The way I play *maqom*—that's the spirit in which all *maqom* should be played. Each *maqom* should be taken by a musician and worked up into

something beautiful. You shouldn't just make a copy of what someone else does. If you just make a copy, there won't be any growth, any progress.

TL: Then what is tradition? On the one hand, you say that your tradition was beaten up and broken by the Communists. On the other hand, you say that each person should find his own style of performance. If you find your own style, why do you need tradition?

TA: In every tradition, there are two poles: the individual and the collective; that is, many individuals who, through the centuries, create a direction. Tradition has its laws, its regularities. A person who wants to be in a tradition has to take account of those regularities.

TL: Did you have an *ustaz*—a teacher?

TA: No. I never went to anyone to learn how to play. I just listened to records and to the radio. I listened, and then I figured out how to play the music myself. I began playing the *dutar* in 1929 or 1930 when I was around nine years old. Later, when I was fifteen, I added the *tanbur*. There were a lot of musicians who played the *dutar* and *tanbur*. They played the same way that people played before them. They took something from those who came before them and gave it to those who followed them. That's what a tradition is. But I play not the way that everyone else plays, but the way I myself want to play. I didn't take into account any of these outer conditions, but played the way my soul told me to play—both on the *dutar* and the *tanbur*. People

who watch me play are interested in the way I move my hands, because I don't follow the usual forms and techniques of movement. What I do is completely different.

TL: Do you teach students yourself?

TA: Now I go to the [Tashkent] Conservatory, and the students— they have my records at home—they listen to them, and they come to me and say, "I want to learn to play *chargoh*." I play a little bit, and then I say, "Okay, you play it." He plays it, and then I play it again. He plays it exactly the way I play it, because he wants to learn to play the way I do on my records. So students listen to musicians who play and sing well, and they follow after them. That's also tradition. There are recordings of other *tanbur* players. They don't go to them. They come to me. People always search for the best; if students knew that there were a better *tanbur* player than me, they'd go to him. It's not necessarily that I'm good, but I'm the last. Ideally, there should be a lot of musicians like me. But the tradition has been broken.

TL: Do you think that these students ought to be creating their own music, as you did?

TA: If you plant four kinds of plum trees, one there, one five meters farther, one five meters farther, and so on, they'll live in the same weather, the same sun, the same earth and water; yet when they grow up, they'll be different. Each has its own place. But only one will be high, the others will be low. And musicians are like that.

NOTES

1. Information about the inscription is available on UNESCO's website at: http://www .unesco.org/culture/ich/index.php?lg=en&pg=00011&RL=00089#identification

2. For a detailed analysis of *aksak,* see Simha Arom, "L'aksak: principes et typologie," *Cahiers de musique traditionnelles,* 17 (2004): 11–48.

3. For a more detailed presentation of the suite principle in Central Asian *maqom,* see Theodore Levin and Razia Sultanova, "The Classical Music of Uzbeks and Tajiks," in *The Middle East,* vol. 6 of *The Garland Encyclopedia of World Music* (New York and London: Routledge, 2002), 909–920.

CHAPTER 19 The Uyghur *Muqam*

RACHEL HARRIS

The Uyghur *muqam* consists of a group of distinct but related repertoires of large suites that include sung poetry, stories, dance tunes, and instrumental sections. *Muqam*s are typically performed by a small ensemble of singers led by a *muqamchi* (lead singer) and accompanied by plucked or bowed long-necked lutes (*satar, tämbur,* and *dutar*), sometimes a spike fiddle (*ghijäk*) or violin, and one or more frame drums (*dap*s). *Muqam*s may also be played in purely instrumental form by kettle drum-and-shawm (*naghra-sunay*) bands. Many of the lyrics of the *muqam* are drawn from the classical Central Asian poets, and are strongly flavored with Sufi imagery and ideals.

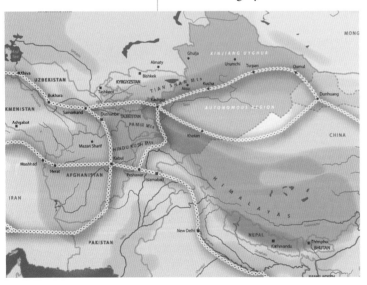

Uyghurs inhabit the northwestern borderlands of China, comprising the Xinjiang Uyghur Autonomous Region. East-West trade routes (the "Silk Road") skirted the edge of the region's Taklamakan Desert.

The performance of *muqam*s is not restricted to an exclusive group of professional musicians; historically, they were performed in folk contexts as well as in the courts of the local nobility, and today they cross the boundaries of rural and urban life, and professional and popular musical domains. Playing *muqam* is sometimes regarded as a spiritual, even physical need. One old folk singer explained it like this: "During the Cultural Revolution I was forbidden to sing the *muqam*, and I could feel it building up inside me with great heat. Finally I got on my donkey and rode into the desert. I rode until I was far away from all people, then I started to sing. I sang all the *muqam* I knew, and then I went back. If I had not done this, I would have become ill." Listening to *muqam* is often said to serve a religious and meditative function, especially in the context of religious festivals, while the lighter pieces towards the end of the suites are commonly used to accompany dancing.

Contemporary scholars identify four distinct but related regional genres: the Twelve Muqam of the Kashgar-Yärkänd region; the Turpan Muqam; the Qumul Muqam; and the Dolan Muqam, which is performed by the Dolan Uyghurs who live in the region northeast of Kashgar. Here I introduce two of these traditions (the Twelve Muqam and the Dolan Muqam) and discuss aspects of their music, performers, and contemporary performance contexts.

THE TWELVE MUQAM

The number twelve has important symbolic meaning to the Uyghurs, as is evident in folk sayings such as "twelve months in a year, Twelve Muqam, twelve strings of my *satar*." This symbolism is sometimes traced back, via the Islamic tradition, to ancient Greek notions of the twelve melodic modes.

The Twelve Muqam (*on ikki muqam*) are the most prestigious of the regional *muqam* traditions, and today are generally regarded as the Uyghur national tradition or canon. Often the roots of the Twelve Muqam are ascribed to the seventh or eighth centuries (the Tang dynasty period of Chinese history), but the evidence for such old roots is tenuous. Uyghurs attribute this tradition somewhat more reliably to the sixteenth century and the court of the Yärkänd Khanate, where one Amanissa Khan, wife of the khan, is said to have been responsible for collecting and ordering the Twelve Muqam in the form we know them today. Each *muqam* in this repertoire has its own characteristic mode, melodic patterns, and modulations, but a *muqam* is basically a suite structure consisting of up to thirty-six vocal and instrumental pieces that begin with a meditative unmetered introduction (*muqäddimä*), move through a series of metered pieces in contrasting rhythms, and culminate in fast dance pieces (*mäshräp*). Such a suite would last around two hours if played from start to finish—which happens rarely.

LISTEN **Example 19.1.** *Nawa muqäddimä*, **performed by Abliz Shakir, 1997.**

This track is sung by Abliz Shakir, one of the region's most celebrated senior *muqam* performers, who appears regularly on television, works with the official state-sponsored Muqam Ensemble, and has released a series of popular and

Cover of Abliz Shakir's
1980s cassette release,
Nawa and Äjäm Muqam.

influential recordings of the Twelve Muqam. Born in 1939 in the town of Ghulja[1] in the northern Ili Valley, he began to learn the Twelve Muqam during the Cultural Revolution in the 1960s, while he was undergoing reform-through-labor—the fate of many prominent musicians at that time. He tells stories of secretly listening to old recordings in order to learn the repertoire when he should have been loading mule carts.

The Uyghur Muqam is today a fixed repertoire, unlike the improvisatory Azeri *mughum,* for example, but if there is any vestige of an improvised tradition in the Twelve Muqam, then it would be these opening, unmetered *muqäddimä* sections, which are structured like an exploration of the melodic mode. They are always sung solo, accompanied by the bowed *satar* or the plucked *tämbur.* They rise in pitch and intensity phrase by phrase toward a climax (*äwäj*), then descend more rapidly toward the original pitch. The melody is highly melismatic, and modally this is the most complex section of the suite. In Nawa Muqam, as in several of the Twelve Muqam, one or more of the important tones of the mode are unstable in two ways: they are always played vibrato, and they change in pitch depending on the direction of the melodic movement. Local musicologists have coined the term "lively notes" to describe them.

STUDY QUESTIONS

1. Listen to example 19.1: Abliz Shakir singing Nawa Muqam *muqäddimä* accompanied by bowed *satar* and plucked *tämbur.* Using the chart and timings below, follow the development of the phrases, noting how they rise in pitch and intensity towards the *äwäj*, then fall back to the original pitch range.

äwäj (climax: 3:53)

kutirilmä (rising: 2:22) qaytish (return: 4:25)

kutirilmä (rising: 1:35) chushirilmä (falling: 4:59)

bashlanma (beginning: 0:50) chushirgisi (end: 5:21)

chalgu (instrumental introduction)

2. Now listen in more detail to the opening couplet of the first sung phrase (*bashlanma:* 0:50). If you read musical notation, look at the transcription on the following page, which shows 0:33–1:12. Abliz Shakir sings: "*bela deshti ara majnun, meningdek, meningdek kormemish devran.*" Listen closely to the first "*-dek*" of "*meningdek*" (0:57–1:03). Note how melismatic this is, i.e., how many notes are sung to the same syllable. Can you hear how the singer moves in a mini arc up to the D and down again? On the way up his vibrato falls on B♭, on the way down it falls on the slightly lower pitch of B♭. These are the "lively notes" that define the mode of Nawa.

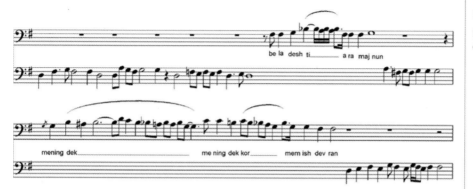

Nawa Muqam *muqäddimä*, performed by Abliz Shakir, 0:33–1:12.

be la desh ti_____ a ra maj nun

mening dek_____ me ning dek kor_____ mem ish dev ran

OUR NATIONAL TREASURE

In the early 1950s, soon after the People's Republic of China (PRC) had established its rule over the Uyghur region and renamed it the Xinjiang Uyghur Autonomous Region, the new authorities set up a project to "rescue" the Twelve Muqam. They chose one musician to provide the raw material for this project: a respected *muqam* performer named Turdi Akhun. His biography tells, in the classic revolutionary style of the time, that the "old society" did not value his art, and he wandered, *satar* on his back, through the cities of Kashgar, Yärkänd, and Khotän for fifty years before the "masses," led by the new Chinese authorities in Xinjiang, accorded him the respect he deserved. He participated in recording sessions in the mid-1950s during which he selflessly handed over all his precious musical knowledge.

Turdi Akhun with his pupils.

Staff transcriptions of the Twelve Muqam, based primarily on these recording sessions, were published in 1960 in impressively bound volumes, with a foreword by the Xinjiang regional chairman Säypidin Äzizi, who wrote: "The 'Twelve Muqam' are a great treasure created through the hardship, struggle and experience of generations of our ancestors, the Uyghur laboring masses. . . . [T]he reason why they are a treasure is that their content is deep and broad, they contain practically all the Uyghur national artistic forms, and they are a full set of twelve suites. . . ." Since that time a succession of transcriptions and recordings—both audio and video—of the Twelve Muqam have been produced. A state-funded Muqam Research Committee and a Muqam Ensemble employing 120 musicians pursue research, reworking, and performance of the Twelve Muqam. In 2005 these efforts were rewarded when the Uyghur Muqam was recognized by UNESCO as one of the Masterpieces of the Oral and Intangible Heritage of Humanity.

An aesthetic gulf has developed between the performance style of the rough-and-ready village bands and the precision and polish of the Muqam Ensemble. The latter professional musicians, formally trained in the conservatories set up under

Muqam Ensemble from the 1980s.
Photo from *Anthology of Chinese Instrumental Music: Xinjiang* volume.

the PRC, now perform the Twelve Muqam from written scores in a large orchestra of instruments newly created or modified since the 1950s, alongside a choir of mixed male and female voices. Women singers and instrumentalists are prominent in the professional ensemble, though not in traditional contexts. In large ensemble performances, a string section of treble bowed instruments (*khushtar* and *ghijäk*), and a bass line (cello or bass *ghijäk*) playing in counterpoint with the main melody, aim to reproduce the sound of the Western orchestra.

Similar changes in performance style can be found throughout the world where folk traditions have been transformed into national treasures. The professional style has dominated Uyghur music at a national level (though not, of course, in the villages) for the last fifty years, but beneath the polished surface it is still easy to find the rich roots of this musical world.

WATCH

Example 19.2. Muqam Ensemble musicians perform a short suite-within-a-suite from Öjal Muqam. Filmed at the Bath International Festival, 2003.

Example 19.2 shows a small group of professional musicians; the instrumental arrangement is simpler than some of the large orchestral renditions, closer to folk renditions, but the musicians' training and professionalism are evident in the polished style of their performance. From left to right, the performers are playing a *tämbur* (plucked long-necked lute), *ghijäk* (spike fiddle), *dap* (frame drum), *qalon* (plucked zither), *diltar* (double-necked plucked and bowed lute—a unique contemporary creation), and *dutar* (strummed long-necked lute). On the far right is a singer. The dancer performs a choreographed version of the traditional "tea bowl" dance.

STUDY QUESTIONS

1. Listen to the rhythm. This clip contains three metered pieces and an unmetered coda: *jula* (0:00–2:22), *sänäm* (2:23–3:45), *chong säliqä* (3:46–5:08), and *chushirgisi* (5:09–5:39). Can you hear the changes in meter between the three pieces? Listen to the five-beat meter in the *chong säliqä*. If you read music, the notation will guide you.

2. Now listen to the melody. Can you hear that the same melody is being stretched in different ways over the three different meters?

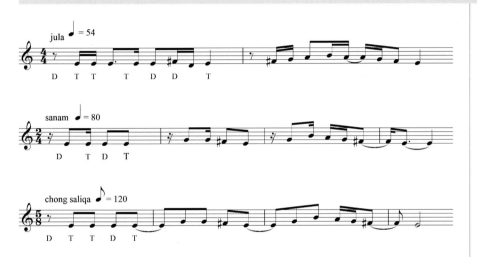

Mäjnun: The Intoxicated Fool

In 2001, I spent several months working with Abdulla Mä-jnun, a brilliant musician and colorful character who was then working in the Muqam Ensemble. You can see Abdulla playing *diltar* in example 19.2.

The word *mäjnun* came to Central Asia from Arabic. It denotes intoxication or infatuation, most famously in the tragic tale of Leila and the lovesick Majnun, which is retold and referred to in countless poems and sung lyrics across the Islamic world. Among the Uyghurs, a *mäjnun* is a type of musician akin to the dervishes or *ashiq*s, the religious mendi-cants who can still be found singing for alms at the festivals held at the holy shrines dedicated to Islamic saints that are scattered across the Taklamakan Desert.

Abdulla Mäjnun playing his *diltar*.
Photo by Feng Li.

Example 19.3. Chahargah Muqam *mäshräp*, performed by Abdulla Mäjnun. From *Borderlands: Wu Man and Master Musicians from the Silk Route,* vol. 10 of *Music of Central Asia* (SFR, 2011), track 14.

Ashiq at a shrine festival in southern Xinjiang.
Photo by Rahile Dawut.

In this fourteen-minute abridged version of Chahargah Muqam, Abdulla Mäjnun sings the opening *muqäddimä* and final *mäshräp* sections, accompanying himself on *tämbur* (he later overdubbed a *dutar* track in the last *mäshräp*), with Yasin Yaqup playing the *dap* (frame drum). Mäjnun sings solo, which is somewhat unusual for *mäshräp* sections. The *mäshräp* ("gathering") concluding section of a *muqam* suite consists of three to five short sung pieces in fast 7/8 and 2/4 rhythms. This section of the *muqam* is for dancing. From a musical perspective, these final *mäshräp* sections of the Twelve Muqam are similar to the *hikmät* (prayers) sung in Sufi rituals and by mendicants (*ashiqs*) when they beg for alms. "This *muqam* is for *ashiqs*," Abdulla said. "Their *mäshräps* are the most lovely and intoxicating. They play like they're going to war, like they are drunk on it, with their wild hair everywhere. When they sing this at the festivals, everybody cries." Indeed, many of the older professional musicians, among them Mäjnun, claim to have learned this part of the repertoire from *ashiqs*. Even Turdi Akhun's son has said this of his father:

> He would go to a *gül[kh]an,* which is a house where they sold meat and tea and smoked *nä[sh]ä* [hashish]. . . . He went with the intention of learning *mä[sh]räp* songs, but they would not let him in if he did not smoke *nä[sh]ä*. All the performers were [a]shiqs.[2]

The lyrics of the third *mäshräp*, beginning at 5:48 on the recording, are transcribed and translated below.

Yarning köyida män diwanä boldum aqibät alla	My love's flames, I have become a beggar, indeed Allah
Khälqi aläm aldida alla biganä boldum aqibät alla	Before the whole world I stand alone, indeed Allah
Bir zaman chäktim japa alla qilargha säbrim qalmidi alla	I have suffered for an age, Allah, my patience is ended, Allah

Ay yuzning shäwqigä alla pärwanä boldum aqibät alla	I have become a moth drawn to the beauty of your face, indeed Allah
Äy yaranlar yaru wäsli alla meni äyläp dil khumar alla	Oh lovers, your desire, Allah, my heart is addicted, Allah
Ishtiyaqing käypidä alla mästanä boldum aqibät alla	I revel in your pleasure, Allah, I have become a drunkard, Allah
Mustisil astanidä alla mäykhanä boldum aqibät alla	In the city, Allah, I have become a wine shop, indeed Allah
Khälqi aläm aldida alla wäyranä boldum aqibät alla	Before the whole world, Allah, I have been ruined, indeed Allah

In the recording, following the unmetered introductory *muqäddimä* section (0:00–5:47), the first *mäshräp* begins (5:48), marked by the entrance of the *dap*. This *mäshräp* is in the striking *aqsaq* (limping) rhythm characteristic of sections of the Twelve Muqam and some Uyghur folk songs. It is usual practice in Uyghur musicology to transcribe *aqsaq* in 7/8 meter, but a "limping" six-beat meter (i.e., with the first two beats played slower) might be a more natural way to conceive it. The following table aligns the basic pulse of the *aqsaq* rhythm—represented in the conventional 7/8 time signature—with the rhythm played on the *dap* in the first *mäshräp*. In the line showing the *dap* rhythm, downward-pointing note beams represent the low-sounding "*dum*" stroke to the center of the drum head while the note beams pointing upward represent the higher "*tak*" stroke near the rim of the drum.

Limping rhythms are believed to help listeners enter a trance state during Sufi rituals. The lyrics of the *mäshräp* sections of the Twelve Muqam are usually attributed to classical poets, and are imbued with the ecstatic religiosity of the Sufi tradition.

STUDY QUESTIONS

1. Listen to the audio clip, and try to beat out the basic "limping" six-beat pulse of the first *mäshräp*.

THE DOLAN MUQAM

Compared to the Twelve Muqam with its courtly roots and contemporary professionalization, the Dolan Muqam has a pure village style—the rough, raw end of

Uyghur music. The Dolan were traditionally the poorest, most despised class of Uyghurs. Under Chinese Imperial rule, they served the Chinese administration as indentured serfs, and they were well known for their enthusiasm for rebellion.

At only eight minutes in length, a Dolan Muqam suite is very different from the weighty Twelve Muqam, but many aspects of these two repertoires are shared, from the general structure and instrumentation to specific melodies and rhythms. The locally handmade Dolan instruments—*qalon* (plucked zither), Dolan *ghijäk* (spike fiddle with a single horsehair playing string and metal sympathetic strings), and Dolan *rawap* (plucked lute with sympathetic strings)—differ from those now used in the Twelve Muqam, which have been modernized and tend to be factory produced. The Dolan Muqam has been dubbed "Central Asian jazz" thanks to its syncopated riffs played on the melodic instruments. These instrumental riffs float over the top and seem to bear no direct relation to the sung melody, which is belted out by singers who also play frame drums (*dap*s). The lyrics are folk love poems, and they are full of the inflamed passion that is typical of Uyghur poetry:

> Can she be mine who is loved by another?
> You have planted a dagger in my soul
> Black eyes laughing
> My love is like sugar . . .

Over the last few years, the Dolan Muqam has become quite a media phenomenon in China, where "authentic performance" is becoming more fashionable, and has even started to enter the global "world music" market. Since the video in example 19.4 was taken in 2000, this village group has performed in Beijing, Japan, and Europe; but the home of this music is still poor and dusty villages in the oasis belt between the Tarim River and the Taklamakan Desert.

WATCH **Example 19.4.** Musicians from Mäkit play Dolan Muqam, 2000.

STUDY QUESTIONS

1. Listen to the changes in rhythm beaten out on the frame drums. Can you identify the drum patterns?

2. Listen to the melodic instruments. What do you think they are doing? Are they playing the same melody as the voices?

3. What do you think of the style of the voices? Compare it to the vocal style in example 19.1.

For the Dolan villagers, as for most Uyghurs, music making revolves around the *mäshräp* (a gathering or party), where people come together for food, music, and dancing. The *mäshräp* lies at the heart of village life. Häkhät Tokhti, who plays the *rawap,* says, "After a week of labor in the fields, the villagers make a *mäshräp,* and the people are as happy as if they have killed two sheep."

A *mäshräp* is also a kind of informal court—an occasion when villagers who have done something wrong are called to account—and it is the musicians who act as court officials and clowns. At the *mäshräp,* they punish lapses in morality by ritual humiliation for the delight of the crowd. A man might be "fined" for flirting, for example, by being "married to two wives": two mincing musicians in women's head scarves lie on each side of him in the middle of the dance arena and take turns smacking his face, hard! In example 19.5, the unfortunate victim of justice is made to act the role of the grinding mill for wheat, while Häkhät Tokhti clowns as the water buffalo who turns the mill.

The *mäshräp* culminates with a remarkable competitive whirling circle dance, accompanied by the musicians playing the Dolan Muqam. They go through various rhythms including different kinds of *aqsak* (limping) rhythms beaten out on the *dap,* which gradually become faster and faster. Dancers gradually drop out, tired or dizzy, until one winner is left in the arena performing high victory leaps.

Dolan musicians at a rural *mäshräp* held in Qizil Awat, southern Xinjiang.
Photo by Rahile Dawut.

WATCH   **Example 19.5.** Mäkit *mäshräp,* clowning, 2000.

NOTES

1. Ghulja is the traditional Uyghur name of the town—now a city with close to half a million inhabitants—whose Chinese name is Yining.

2. Quoted in Nathan Light, *Intimate Heritage: Creating Uyghur Muqam Song in Xinjiang,* vol. 19 of Max Planck Institute for Social Anthropology/Halle Studies in the Anthropology of Eurasia, ed. Chris Hann, Richard Rottenburg, and Burkhard Schnepel (Berlin: Lit Verlag Dr. W. Hopf, 2008), 286.

CHAPTER 20 New Images of Azerbaijani *Mugham* in the Twentieth Century

AIDA HUSEYNOVA

AZERBAIJAN AND CENTRAL ASIA: CULTURAL AND MUSICAL DIMENSIONS

As ought to be clear from many of the examples in this book, Central Asia as a region of shared cultural practices, historical links, and ethnic consanguinities extends well beyond the conventional geographic borders commonly used to define it. The rationale for including Azerbaijan in this imagined greater Central Asia is particularly clear from the perspective of music, for despite Azerbaijan's geographical separation from the core region of Central Asia, Azerbaijani music shares many common elements with the musical traditions of both historically nomadic and sedentary-dwelling peoples in Central Asia proper.

Other aspects of culture and history link Azerbaijan to Central Asia. For example, Azerbaijani is a Turkic language that belongs to the same large language family as Central Asian Turkic languages, e.g., Kazakh, Kyrgyz, Turkmen, Uzbek, and Uyghur. Historically, Azerbaijanis have been followers of the Shi'a branch of Islam, which has many adherents in Central Asia, in particular in the Pamir Mountain region of eastern Tajikistan and northeastern Afghanistan. In the nineteenth and twentieth centuries, Azerbaijan and Central Asia both came under the rule of the Russian Empire and, following the Bolshevik Revolution of 1917, the Soviet Union, with the consequence that Azerbaijanis, like Uzbeks, Tajiks, and other Central Asian peoples, experienced more than a century of colonial rule.

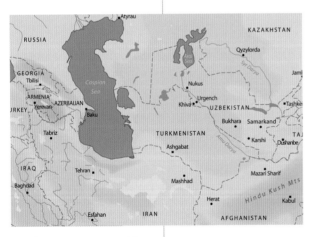

Azerbaijan is separated from Central Asia by the Caspian Sea, yet closely linked to it by language and culture.

Azerbaijan's rich and versatile traditional music and literary heritage shares at least two phenomena with Central Asia. The first is *mugham,* Azerbaijan's variant of the transnational tradition of canonized, modally organized music that, in a variety of local forms, has been cultivated by professional musicians in Central Asia, Turkey, the Middle East, and North Africa (see chapter 18). The second shared phenomenon is the bardic tradition of the *ashig,* which involves singing, playing instruments, and telling epic stories. Azerbaijani *ashig*s, like Kazakh *jyrau*s and Turkmen *bagshy*s, embody the cultural traditions of nomadic pastoralists, which in Azerbaijan no less than in Central Asia have long existed in a symbiotic relationship with the cultural traditions of sedentary dwellers.

Oil derricks in Balakhani, a suburb of Baku, at the beginning of the 20th century.
Courtesy of *Azerbaijan International* magazine, Betty Blair, editor-in-chief.

At the same time that Azerbaijan preserves strong links to Central Asia, it is also distinguished from Central Asia by its strategic location at the crossroads of Europe and Asia. The proximity of Transcaucasia to Europe has provided Azerbaijan with abiding contact with European cultural values and institutions. Particularly after the oil boom of the mid-nineteenth century, when the world's leading oil companies began drilling operations in and around the Caspian Sea, Azerbaijan experienced intense Westernization in all domains of culture and social life.

Music responded to these globalizing processes immediately. Traditional music came into close contact with forms and genres of Western music, and by the first decades of the twentieth century, this fusion had already yielded fruitful results. In 1911, an Opera and Ballet Theater opened in Baku, Azerbaijan's largest and most cosmopolitan city, and alongside Russian and European classics it presented operas and operettas by local composers on themes drawn from Azerbaijani history and contemporary life. Soviet culture and nationalities policy, one of whose aims was to bring Russian and European cultural values to the non-Slavic peoples of the vast Soviet empire, stimulated the processes of East-West fusion in Azerbaijani music. However, a solid foundation for this fusion process as well as several notable artistic achievements that resulted from it pre-dated the Soviet era. The history of Azerbaijani music in the twentieth century provides valuable case studies of cultural fusion and the reimagination of tradition, and offers insight into similar processes that occurred in other parts of the former Soviet Union. This chapter focuses on three very visible genres of East-West fusion that emerged in twentieth-century Azerbaijan: *mugham* opera, symphonic *mugham,* and jazz *mugham.*

Mugham: The Quintessence of Azerbaijani Music

Mugham is an integral part of Azerbaijani culture. The embellishments of *mugham* melodies are often compared to the beautiful metaphors in classical Azerbaijani poetry, the detailed patterns of Azerbaijani carpets, or the architectural design of ancient Azerbaijani dwellings. The power of *mugham* has long been recognized beyond Azerbaijan as well. In the early twentieth century, international record labels, including the Gramophone Company and Sports Records, released recordings of prominent *mugham* performers largely for local markets. In 1977, a short piece of Azerbaijani *mugham* was included on the United States spacecraft Voyager I and Voyager II as they journeyed into interstellar space. The *mugham* excerpt was among twenty-seven pieces of music—Bach, Beethoven, Peruvian panpipes, Navajo night chants—that represented the variety of earthly musical traditions.

Mugham is usually performed by a trio consisting of a singer and two instrumentalists. One of the instrumentalists plays the *tar* (long-necked lute) and the other, the *kamancha* (spike fiddle). Singers typically accompany themselves on a frame drum (*gaval* or *daf*). The composition of *mugham* is based on the alternation of *shoba*—improvised parts where singers demonstrate their creativity and virtuosity—and fixed interludes that are either dance-like (*rang*) or song-like (*tasnif*). These set pieces give both performers and listeners an opportunity to rest before the *mugham* proceeds to the next stage of improvisation, which is usually higher in pitch and more dynamically intense. It takes years to master the art of *mugham.* For centuries, *mugham*s have been performed at small gatherings of music lovers, but since the early twentieth century they have also found their way to the stage of concert halls and theaters—sometimes fused with forms of Western music.

MUGHAM OPERA

Uzeyir Hajibeyli, the founder of the composer tradition in Azerbaijan and the father of *mugham* opera.
Courtesy of the State Museum of Azerbaijani Musical Culture and Dr. Alla Bayramova, Director.

In the early twentieth century, a cohort of young intellectuals emerged in Azerbaijan who considered the fusion of native heritage with forms of Western art and music a desirable objective for the development of national culture. Among these young intellectuals was the composer Uzeyir Hajibeyli (1885–1948), now respected by Azerbaijanis as a national genius who turned a new page of Azerbaijani music history.[1] In 1908, he wrote *Leyli and Majnun,* a musical-dramatic work that pioneered the genre later known as "*mugham* opera."

The textual origins of Hajibeyli's *Leyli and Majnun* (also transliterated into English as *Layla and Majnun*) can be found in a classical Arabic tale about a seventh-century Bedouin named Qays ibn al-Mulawwah who fell in love with Layla, a girl from the same tribe, and began composing love poems dedicated to her. Prevented from marrying by Layla's father, the two lovers parted. Qays subsequently went mad and spent the rest of his short life wandering in the desert, becoming known among locals by the sobriquet *majnun* ("madman," or by extension, "love-crazed"). The story was later appropriated by Persian and Turkic poets, and Hajibeyli based his opera libretto on an epic poem by the sixteenth-century Azerbaijani poet Fuzuli.

The dramaturgical structure of *Leyli and Majnun* draws in obvious ways on opera: it is divided into several acts, solo pieces alternate with small ensembles and choruses, and singing is accompanied by an orchestra. The musical concept, however, is almost totally based on *mugham* in its original non-notated and improvised form. The composer's score indicates only the names of *mugham*s and the lyrics to be performed, and performers are expected to improvise the actual music on stage.

Hajibeyli seamlessly incorporated *mugham*s into the musical structure of the opera and its emotional lexicon. He chose particular *mugham*s based on the emotion or ethos associated with them. For instance, to express the love that seizes Leyli and Majnun, Hajibeyli used *mugham* Segah, which is always associated with romantic feelings. By contrast, *mugham* Chahargah perfectly conveys the tragic essence of the scene in which Majnun's parents try to dissuade him from his dangerous love.

Hajibeyli's knowledge of Western cultural history as well as traditional Azerbaijani music and spiritual culture enriched *mugham* opera with eclectic sources that extend beyond *mugham* itself. For example, *Leyli and Majnun* includes numerous ensembles and choruses that are mostly based on authentic folk melodies and were appropriated and arranged by Hajibeyli. Choruses are of particular interest because they feature four-part vocal writing, which is unknown in traditional Azerbaijani music. The chorus in *mugham* opera often comments on events, like the chorus in ancient Greek tragedy. For example, the opening chorus in *Leyli and Majnun,* called "Shabih-Hijran" (Parting night), predicts the tragic ending of the story by foretelling the lovers' separation before the story even begins. This episode features the strong influence of *shabih* (also called *taziyah*)—a form of traditional liturgical drama that is a part of Shi'a Muslim rituals and is performed during Muharram, the first month of the Islamic calendar and a traditional period of mourning. A performance of "Shabih-Hijran" is reproduced in example 20.1.

LISTEN

Example 20.1. "Shabih-Hijran" (Parting night) from *Leyli and Majnun,* composed by Uzeyir Hajibeyli. Performed by the orchestra and choir of the Azerbaijan State Opera and Ballet Theater, Kazim Aliverdibeyov, conductor. From Uzeyir Hajibeyov, *Leyli and Majnun,* AICD 1301, STATOIL and *Azerbaijan International*, 2001. Courtesy of Betty Blair and *Azerbaijan International.*

STUDY QUESTIONS

1. What features of tempo, rhythm, and melody in this chorus indicate that it is rooted in the traditional mourning ritual of *shabih*?

2. Are all four parts of the vocal texture of this chorus equally important, or does the melody dominate other voices? How does this arrangement of voices compare to the typical texture of traditional music from Azerbaijan?

Azerbaijan Opera and Ballet Theater, the first opera house in Central Asia.

The Silk Road Project's production of "Layla and Majnun."

After *Leyli and Majnun,* Hajibeyli wrote five more *mugham* operas: *Sheykh Senan* (1909), *Rustam and Sohrab* (1910), *Shah Abbas and Khurshud Banu* (1911), *Asli and Karam* (1912), and *Harun and Leyla* (1915). Encouraged by the success of Hajibeyli's productions, other Azerbaijani composers turned to this genre as well. Zulfugar Hajibeyli's *Ashig Garib* (1916) and Muslim Magomayev's *Shah Ismayil* (1919) presented new interpretations of *mugham* opera. Although the number of *mugham* operas composed in Azerbaijan is not large, the genre itself has historical significance as the first manifestation of opera not only in Azerbaijan but in the entire Muslim East.[2]

A remarkable breakthrough in the history of *Leyli and Majnun* occurred in the first decade of the twenty-first century. The Silk Road Project, an educational and cultural initiative under the artistic direction of the American cellist Yo-Yo Ma, and its performing group, the Silk Road Ensemble, prepared a new chamber arrangement of Hajibeyli's opera that became one of the highlights of the Project's repertoire. The Silk Road Ensemble's version of *Leyli and Majnun,* arranged and scored by violinists Jonathan Gandelsman and Colin Jacobsen, condenses Hajibeyli's three-and-half-hour work into a tautly conceived forty-five-minute performance. In contrast to the large cast of Hajibeyli's opera, the Silk Road Ensemble's chamber version focuses entirely on the two protagonists, who were played by Alim Qasimov (b. 1957), an outstanding master of *mugham* often referred to as a "Living National Treasure of Azerbaijan," and Fargana Qasimova (b. 1979), his daughter and student, and a wonderful *mugham* singer in her own right (see "Artist Profile: Alim and Fargana Qasimov").

From a musical perspective, the Silk Road Ensemble's arrangement merges elements of improvised *mugham* and notated music. Episodes of notated music that were originally performed strictly from the score are now quasi-improvised, with each member of the ensemble adding extemporized melodic gestures. Moreover, in the Silk Road Ensemble version, the *mugham* sections are performed by the entire ensemble of ten players, whereas in Hajibeyli's opera they are performed by singers supported by traditional instruments while the orchestral instruments remain silent.

Excerpts from the Silk Road Ensemble's adaptation of Hajibeyli's opera are reproduced in examples 20.2 and 20.3. The Ensemble represents the historical setting of *Leyli and Majnun*—a story told and retold in the lands of the Silk Road—by performing it with its own eclectic consort of Silk Road instruments: European strings, Azerbaijani *tar* and *kamancha,* a variety of Eastern and Western percussion, Chinese *pipa* (plucked lute), and Japanese *shakuhachi* (bamboo flute). The excerpts illustrate the dynamic way in which the characteristic sounds of two different *mugham*s are woven into the texture of the Ensemble's performance. Both excerpts illustrate solo expressions of the protagonists, which in Western music would be operatic arias. In example 20.2, Alim Qasimov sings in *mugham* Shahnaz, representing Majnun's passionate declaration of his troubled love and suffering. In example 20.3, Fargana Qasimova, as Layla, sings sorrowfully in *mugham* Bayati Shiraz before her death.

WATCH **Example 20.2 and 20.3.** Uzeyir Hajibeyli, *Layla and Majnun,* adapted and arranged by Jonathan Gandelsman and Colin Jacobsen for the Silk Road Ensemble and performed by the Silk Road Ensemble, Artistic Director Yo-Yo Ma. Harvard University New College Theater, November 29, 2007. Courtesy of the Silk Road Project.

STUDY QUESTIONS

1. Discuss the combination of Western and non-Western instruments within the Silk Road Ensemble. How are these voices from different cultures smoothly integrated?

2. Name two non-Western instruments that play short solo parts in the introductory section.

3. What musical features of the excerpt depicted in the video reveal that it is derived from an opera? Can you think of any Western operatic aria or song whose literary contents and music could be compared to Majnun's "Shahnaz"?

SYMPHONIC *MUGHAM*

In 1948, Azerbaijani composer Fikrat Amirov (1922–1984) composed two works—"Shur" and "Kurd Ovshari"—that fused *mugham* and symphonic music to create what came to be known as "symphonic *mugham.*" Amirov was well qualified for his fusionist undertaking. His father, Meshadi Jamil Amirov (1875–1928), was an outstanding *mugham* singer and *tar* player, and Fikrat grew up surrounded by the sounds of *mugham.* As an aspiring composer, he recorded and notated *mugham* music at the same time that he studied composition at the Azerbaijan State Conservatory (now Baku Music Academy). Fikrat Amirov was himself an outstanding *tar* player, and throughout his life he maintained close links with great masters of *mugham,* such as the singer Khan Shushinski (1901–1979) and the *tar* player Gurban Pirimov (1880–1965). This precious knowledge became a principal source of inspiration and a solid base for developing the concept of symphonic *mugham.* In 1973, twenty-five years after the appearance of "Shur" and "Kurd Ovshari," Amirov wrote another symphonic *mugham,* "Gulustan Bayati Shiraz."

In "Shur," Amirov followed the formal scheme of his *mugham* model, in which improvised *shoba* episodes alternate with fixed *tasnif* (or *rang*) sections. Amirov fully notated the *shoba* sections of his "Shur," since they were played by a symphony orchestra. At the same time, he retained the spirit of improvisation by writing sections of the piece that were free of strict metric and rhythmic control.

The symphonic *mugham* "Kurd Ovshari" is modeled after the eponymous *mugham* "Kurd Ovshari." "Kurd Ovshari" represents a *mugham* sub-genre called *zarbi-mugham* (rhythmic *mugham*) in which melodic improvisation occurs over a steady rhythmic background. Amirov's "Kurd Ovshari" consists of four sections:

Performer Profile: Alim and Fargana Qasimov
THEODORE LEVIN

Alim Qasimov (b. 1957) and his daughter Fargana (b. 1979) exemplify the explosive artistic energy that results when a powerful musical model ignites the spark of young talent.[3] "To be a musician, there has to be a fire burning in you," explained the elder Qasimov. "It's either there or it isn't. I'm convinced that if young people have this spark—call it inspiration, call it spiritual fire—they can perform any kind of music. It could be pop, folk, or classical, but whatever it is, they'll stand out."

Alim Qasimov's authority on matters of artistic creativity derives from his position as one of Azerbaijan's most beloved musicians. A walk with Qasimov down any street in Baku, Azerbaijan's capital city, confirms his renown. Greeting well-wishers, shaking hands, and making small talk, he is ever polite and humble. It is when Qasimov sings that his own inner fire burns brightest.

Fargana Qasimova's talent gravitated naturally toward the music she heard from her father: Azerbaijani classical music (*mugham*) and the repertory of popular bardic songs sung by *ashigs*—singer-songwriters who accompany themselves on the *saz*, a strummed long-necked lute. "There was never any question about my being given to a teacher," Fargana recalled. "Music was always just a part of everyday life—I sang with my father for fun, and it was only when I was around seventeen years old that I seriously understood that I'd be a musician."

"We never put before ourselves the aim of singing *mugham* in the form of a duet or carrying out any kind of reform," said Alim Qasimov of the sinuous vocal arrangements he performs with Fargana.

"Rather, what we do appeared spontaneously in the process of rehearsing. We liked it, and we started to practice it. Nowadays, *mugham* is always performed by a single vocalist, but there used to be a way of performing where one singer would begin a phrase and another singer

Photo by Sebastian Schutyser. Courtesy of Aga Khan Music Initiative.

would finish it, and they'd alternate like that through a whole piece. We do the same thing: I begin a line, and Fargana continues it, and the effect is as if one person is singing. In places our voices overlap, so there's a kind of polyphony. I can't explain why it turned out that way—perhaps because Fargana is my daughter and we live in the same house. But I think it's that spiritually we're very close. We understand each other in an inner sense, and this is how our understanding is expressed. It all comes from singing together, and it's

Performer Profile: Alim and Fargana Qasimov (CONTINUED)

spontaneous. We can do it one way in a rehearsal, and then in a concert, it will turn out completely differently.

"When I started performing with Fargana, there was no small amount of criticism but now there's less and less. People have started to accept our 'experiment' because they feel that it's sincere, and that it's our spiritual discovery. In fact, it's not an experiment. The way I sing and the way I improvise represents my soul at that moment. It represents my *hal:* the state of my soul."

The term *hal,* an Arabic word that is also commonly used in other Turkic languages and in Persian, has strong associations with Sufism, the mystical dimension of Islam. For Sufis, *hal* is a state of spiritual awakening that creates openness to the mystical presence of the Divine. Qasimov, translating *hal* into the language of art, defines it as "inspiration." "It's not something you can pull out of your pocket," he emphasized. "I can't command myself to get inspired at a particular moment and perform something. Moreover, you have to transform the musicians you're playing with so that they can share that inspiration, and then give it to the audience. When I meet with the musicians in my ensemble, it's almost like a gathering of dervishes. There's an atmosphere that starts to nourish us that comes from beyond our own will, and that's the source of the unpredictability in our music. It's almost a feeling of ecstasy that leads to some kind of meditation. There isn't any point in performing *mugham* without *hal.*"

Photo by Sebastian Schutyser. Courtesy of Aga Khan Music Initiative.

The musicians in Alim Qasimov's ensemble include not only performers on the *tar* and *kamancha,* as in a conventional *mugham* trio, but also on the oboe-like *balaban,* on a variety of hand drums, and, at times, on the oud. The expanded ensemble is also an example of Qasimov's search for the fullest expression of *mugham*'s range of moods and emotions. "If it were up to me, I'd invite not four or five musicians but an entire chamber ensemble, and I'd create wonderful compositions for them that would be performed in the world's most prestigious concert halls," Qasimov said. "I observed that in Turkey and Iran, they have ensembles with violins, cellos, flutes—real orchestras that aren't restricted to just the local instruments. I can only imagine what you could do with our *mugham* if you had those instruments. But since I don't work with musical notation, it's hard for me to do arranging, and performing with a large ensemble has remained only a dream."

"*Mugham* is an elite art," Alim Qasimov concluded. "It's for a select group—for people who have some kind of inner spirituality, who have their own inner world. These days 'elite' refers to something more commercial than spiritual—for example, to the kind of people who can buy a new car every year. But that's not what I have in mind. An elite person is one who knows how to experience, how to endure, how to feel, how to listen to *mugham* and begin to cry. This ability doesn't

Performer Profile: Alim and Fargana Qasimov (CONTINUED)

depend on education or upbringing, nor on one's roots. It's something else. It's an elite of feeling, an elite of inspiration. These kinds of listeners aren't always available. I can't speak about the distant past, but it's clear that *mugham* hasn't developed in a straight line. There were lapses and dips and ascents, and surely it will always be like that. I can't say whether we're in a dip or an ascent—it's not for me to judge— but I think there will always be an attraction to this music until the end of humanity."

WATCH

Example 20.4. Excerpt from documentary film about Alim and Fargana Qasimov by Saodat Ismailova and Carlos Casas in *Alim and Fargana Qasimov: Spiritual Music of Azerbaijan* (DVD), vol. 6 of *Music of Central Asia* (SFR, 2007).

LISTEN

Example 20.5. Mugham Chargah: "Bardasht," performed by Alim and Fargana Qasimov (vocal) on a text by Seyyid Azim Shirvani (1835–1888), with Rafael Asgarov (*balaban*), Rauf Islamov (*kamancha*), Ali Asgar Mammadov (*tar*), and Natiq Shirinov (percussion). From *Alim and Fargana Qasimov: Spiritual Music of Azerbaijan,* vol. 6 of *Music of Central Asia* (SFR, 2007), track 1.

Mugham Chargah (Persian: Chahargah) is one of the seven principal suite forms of Azerbaijani classical music. Each *mugham* suite consists of a conventional sequence of pieces (*shu'be*) that take listeners on a journey through varied musical and emotional terrain. The great Azerbaijani composer Uzeyir Hajibeyli (1885–1948) believed that *chargah* excites the passions and conveys pride, virility, and a martial spirit. Throughout the suite, high dramatic tension contrasts with moments of repose and détente.

Bardasht (from Persian: "summing up") is a generic compositional form that serves as a short overture to a *mugham* suite. This lively *bardasht* begins with a rhythmic instrumental introduction that prepares the dramatic, high-register entrance of the vocalists with the signature melodic interval of *chargah*: an upward leap from *la* to *do* (*la* is slightly flattened). Alim and Fargana Qasimov render the opening verses of Shirvani's *ghazal* antiphonally in free rhythm over an embellished drone provided by the *kamancha, tar*, and *balaban*.

The final four lines of "Bardasht" gradually descend a full octave to the initial pitch of the subsequent piece, "Maye." The text of "Bardasht" begins:

Oh friend, do not drag me to the edge of that desert today,

That moon is not here, so do not take me to this empty spectacle.

I became love-crazed from the fairies' braids,

What excuse can I give to Adam, who brought me into this world?

STUDY QUESTIONS

1. How would you describe the vocal sound of Alim and Fargana Qasimov in "Bardasht"?

2. What connection do you feel between the meaning of the lyrics and the vocal sound?

3. For the instrumentalists, what kind of skill is involved in working with the Qasimovs?

4. What is your own response to the Qasimovs' "experiment" with antiphonal (responsorial) singing?

"Ovshari," "Shahnaz," "Kurdi," and "Maani," just as in its traditional model. Example 20.6 reproduces a brief introduction to the entire piece followed by an excerpt from the first section, "Ovshari." It opens with a clarinet playing a slow and melancholy melody based on an authentic folk tune. The preeminence of the melodic line is maintained throughout this section; however, the composer creates new melodies that emerge in the orchestra and enter into a beautiful dialogue with the principal melody. This sort of polyphonic texture represents a compositional innovation not found in traditional performances.

Fikrat Amirov, the author of the first symphonic *mugham*.

Courtesy of the State Museum of Azerbaijani Musical Culture and Dr. Alla Bayramova, Director.

LISTEN

Example 20.6. "Kurd Ovshari," composed by Fikrat Amirov and performed by the Azerbaijan State Symphony Orchestra, conductor Yalchin Adigozalov. From *Symphonic,* vol. 1 of *Classical Music of Azerbaijan*, *Azerbaijan International* (1997), track 1. Courtesy of *Azerbaijan International* magazine editor-in-chief Betty Blair.

STUDY QUESTIONS ————————————————————————

1. What elements of music in this symphonic *mugham* reveal links with traditional *mugham*?

2. Does Amirov prefer to mix the timbres of different instruments in the symphony orchestra or present them separately? Overall, how is his score influenced by traditional *mugham* performances?

3. Comment on the role that repetition of melodic and rhythmic patterns plays in this music. Are such repetitions typical for the source music, i.e., *mugham* in its original form?

Fikrat Amirov's symphonic *mugham*s have been well received beyond Azerbaijan. In the 1950s, "Shur" was performed by the Houston Symphony Orchestra under Leopold Stokowski, and "Kurd Ovshari" was performed by the Boston Symphony Orchestra under Charles Munch. In 1997, Michelle Kwan, the celebrated American figure skater, included Amirov's symphonic *mugham* "Gulustan Bayati Shiraz" in her program at the World Figure Skating Championships. Symphonic *mugham*s by other Azerbaijani composers have also entered the symphonic repertory: Niyazi's "Rast"; Tofig Bakikhanov's "Humayun," "Nava," and "Rahab"; and Suleyman Alasgarov's "Bayati Shiraz."

JAZZ MUGHAM

Jazz has long been a significant part of the Azerbaijani musical landscape, and in the early 1960s, jazz players in Baku began experimenting with the fusion of *mugham* and jazz.

Though jazz and *mugham* arose in completely different cultural spheres, they share many common features. Both are musical forms based on egalitarian improvisation shaped by an array of structural constraints. Both are typically performed by small ensembles or "combos," in which soloists take turns displaying their virtuosity against the backdrop of the group. In Azerbaijan, both jazz and *mugham* experienced difficult times during the Soviet era because the architects and implementers of Soviet cultural policies viewed them as misaligned with the values and aims of socialist art. At the beginning of the Soviet era, jazz was denounced as the "voice of the capitalist world," while *mugham* was labeled a "relic of the past" and an exemplar of "feudal court music." Both genres were finally admitted to the domain of officially recognized Soviet art and culture; however, they were placed under strict ideological control.

Jazz arrived in Azerbaijan in the early twentieth century, at the time of the oil boom. Westerners enjoyed listening to the European musicians who played jazz in Baku's cafes and restaurants, and in those days, Baku's jazz scene depended heavily on imported talent. This situation changed in the late 1930s with the founding of the Azerbaijan State Jazz Orchestra. Local composers Tofig Guliyev (1917–2000); Rauf Hajiyev (1923–1997); and Niyazi Tagizade-Gajibekov, known professionally simply as Niyazi (1912–1984), contributed works to the orchestra's repertory. Unfortunately, the group didn't exist for long as a jazz orchestra. In 1941, after the Soviet Union entered World War II, it was reconfigured as a military orchestra and its repertory shifted to patriotic songs and military marches. During the so-called Khrushchev Thaw of the early 1960s, when the strict ideological control of the Stalin era was partially relaxed, Azerbaijanis, like other citizens of the Soviet Union, gained access to previously forbidden recordings, musical scores, books, and radio broadcasts. Artists and musicians embraced a spirit of experimentalism, and among these bold experimentalists was the pianist and composer Vagif Mustafazade (1940–1979), who created the first fusion of *mugham* and jazz. Jazz *mugham* has been shaping the creative explorations of Azerbaijani musicians ever since. A recording of Vagif Mustafazade's "Composition-2" is reproduced in example 20.7.

Vagif Mustafazade, founder of jazz *mugham*.

Courtesy of the State Museum of Azerbaijani Musical Culture and Dr. Alla Bayramova, Director.

Example 20.7. "Composition-2," composed by Vagif Mustafazade. From *Vagif Mustafazade* (2-DVD set), *Azerbaijan International* magazine (2007). Sponsored by the Ministry of Communication & Informational Technologies of the Republic of Azerbaijan. Courtesy of *Azerbaijan International* magazine editor-in-chief Betty Blair.

STUDY QUESTIONS

1. What features of the original *mugham* are clearly represented in this excerpt?

2. Can you relate Vagif Mustafazade's performance style to any existing jazz styles that you know (e.g, swing, bebop, "free jazz," etc.)?

In 1978, Vagif Mustafazade was awarded First Prize at the International Competition of Jazz Themes in Monaco—a remarkable accomplishment in the Cold War era. In 1966, Willis Conover, the well-known Voice of America radio broadcaster whose program Jazz Time reached millions of listeners in the Soviet Union, characterized Mustafazade as an "extraordinary pianist." Conover said, "It is impossible to identify his equal. He is the most lyrical pianist I have ever known."[4]

Rafig Babayev (1936–1994), another Azerbaijani pianist and composer, contributed significantly to the development of jazz *mugham,* though with a somewhat different approach than Mustafazade. For Vagif, *mugham* was the main source of inspiration, and the primary source of fusion material. By contrast, Rafig maintained the prevalence of jazz idioms and incorporated elements of *mugham* such as traditional instruments and modes into Western jazz forms.

These two masters paved the way for many performers of jazz *mugham* who are active today. Pianists Salman Gambarov (b. 1959) and Shahin Novrasli (b. 1977) meld the timbres and modal idioms of traditional instruments with the harmonic language of contemporary music from the West and post-bop jazz styles. Pianist Jamil Amirov (b. 1957) is a proponent of jazz-rock fusion with a strong ethnic component. His proclivity for authentic "roots" music is not accidental, for Jamil represents the next generation of the Amirov dynasty, known for their impeccable knowledge and dedication to Azerbaijan's musical heritage. Emil Afrasiyab (b. 1982) is a direct heir of Vagif Mustafazade's fusion experiments. The same is true of Aziza Mustafazade (b. 1969)—Vagif's daughter—whose singing and piano playing fuse jazz with traditional music idioms as well as with music of the European baroque and romantic eras. At the age of eighteen, Aziza won third prize at the Thelonious Monk International Jazz Competition in Washington, D.C. Since

Jazz Center at the Baku Music Academy.

then, she has released recordings with prestigious companies and collaborated with a host of contemporary jazz stars.

Nowadays, both elements of jazz *mugham*—jazz and *mugham*—are enjoying a revival in Azerbaijan. Not coincidentally, this revival is occurring simultaneously with a new oil boom that provides a powerful impetus for the development of art and music. Contemporary Azerbaijani jazz musicians keep current with new trends and developments among their counterparts in the West. In contrast to their predecessors in the Soviet era, they tour internationally and host prominent jazz musicians at home. Azerbaijani jazz musicians have competed successfully in international events, including at the prestigious Montreux Jazz Festival (Switzerland), where pianist-composer Isfar Sarabsky (b. 1989) was a co-winner of the 2009 jazz solo piano competition. Azerbaijan itself has hosted international jazz festivals that have featured luminaries such as Al Jarreau, Herbie Hancock, and Joe Zawinul.

Mugham is also enjoying a revival, and many large-scale projects that involve the performance, recording, study, and promotion of *mugham* have been initiated in Azerbaijan—a number of them under the personal patronage of the President, Ilham Aliyev, and First Lady Mehriban Aliyeva. *Mugham* continues to inspire the creative explorations of Azerbaijani composers and jazz musicians, and in so doing, underscores the abiding vitality of East-West fusion in Azerbaijani music.

NOTES

1. Uzeyir Hajibeyli is also known under the russified forms of his last name, Hajibeyov, Hajibekov, or Gadzhibekov.

2. Opera was presented earlier in the Middle East, for example, in Cairo, Egypt; however, the works presented there were neither written by native composers nor based on indigenous traditional heritage. Hajibeyli's experience was unique in this regard, since the plot and music of *Leyli and Majnun* were entirely derived from the traditional heritage of Azerbaijan.

3. This text was previously published in the booklet notes for *Alim and Fargana Qasimov: Spiritual Music of Azerbaijan,* vol. 6 of *Music of Central Asia,* Smithsonian Folkways Recordings, 2007.

4. Quoted in Vagif Samadoglu, "The Emergence of Jazz in Azerbaijan," *Azerbaijan International* 5 (Winter 1997): 74.

CHAPTER 21

Popular Classics

TRADITIONAL SINGER-SONGWRITERS IN UZBEKISTAN AND TAJIKISTAN

THEODORE LEVIN

"Our songs—they don't grow old!" exclaimed Nodira Pirmatova, the affable young alto from Tashkent, Uzbekistan, whose haunting performances of "Galdir" (Fool of God) and "Ufor-i Iroq" are reproduced below in examples 21.2 and 22.5, respectively. "They're passed along from one generation to the next, and younger singers perform them as if they were new—with a different voice and fresh passion. When you listen to one of these classics, it's always as if you're hearing it for the first time."

The songs Nodira described with such ardor represent an extensive repertoire of popular classic music created by generations of talented singer-songwriters. These songs, performed in the audio examples that follow by some of Uzbekistan's and Tajikistan's finest singers, are the focus of the present chapter.

In the early Soviet era, when Russian and European models of music and musical life were imported into Central Asia with the aim of "improving" local culture, Western musical terms and concepts were also appropriated. Among them was the concept of "composer," translated into Uzbek and Tajik by the neologisms *bastakor* (Uzbek and Tajik) and *ahangsoz,* or *taronasoz* (Tajik). These terms were applied both to artists who wrote music using conventional Western notation and to traditional singer-songwriters who composed orally and memorized their songs. Music produced by *bastakor*s has ranged in compositional form and style from indigenous and traditional to innovative and experimental, the latter typically melding European and local musical instruments and sensibilities to create various kinds of hybrid music. Diverse directions and tendencies in the art of *bastakor*s, called *bastakorlik,* continue to coexist in the music of Uzbekistan and Tajikistan. The music of *bastakor*s is performed in a variety of regional styles and genres, in different languages and dialects, by female and male singers, and with different formations of instrumental accompaniment as well as a cappella. Instrumental versions of songs and short pieces composed specifically for a solo instrument are also part of the *bastakor* tradition.

Unlike contemporary singer-songwriters in the West, who typically write both the music and lyrics of their songs, either alone or with a collaborator, most *bastakor*s compose only melodies. For lyrics, they draw on a vast corpus of classical poetry—*ghazals, rubā'iyāt, mukhammas*—and other forms of verse written in Persian and a variety of Turkic languages and dialects between the tenth and twentieth centuries. (*Ghazals* and *rubā'iyāt* have also been written in Arabic, Urdu, and other languages, including English.) *Bastakor*s aim to move their listeners with the lyrical beauty and imagery of verse written by famous poets. The typical theme is unrequited love and the pain of separation from a beloved. The heartrending passions and anxieties anatomized in such poems can be understood on one level as representing human feelings, but the poems can also be read as mystical allegories in which the figure of the beloved alludes to the invisible presence of the Divine.

By singing the texts of classical poems to newly composed melodies, singer-songwriters render the poems—and their lyrical affirmation of the value of faith, devotion, and humility—instantly contemporary.

One such song is "Dilhiroj" (Tormented heart), composed by a well-known *bastakor* from the city of Khujand, in northern Tajikistan, Sodir

Photo by Sebastian Schutyser. Courtesy of Aga Khan Music Initiative.

I was born in Khujand, in Soghd Region. My father and mother are workers. There were never musicians in our family, but my brother and I

Performer Profile: Nasiba Omonboeva

were interested in music, and we went to music school. After finishing school, I went on to music college and university, where my *ustod* was Jurabek Nabiev, a famous singer. He taught me a lot about Shashmaqom. Later I went to Dushanbe and studied Shahmaqom with Abduvali Abdurashidov at the Academy of Maqom [an intensive four-year program sponsored by the Aga Khan Music Initiative devoted to historically informed Shashmaqom

performance]. I sing Shashmaqom in the Ferghana style, since I'm from there and studied there. In the Ferghana style, you feel more free. The *maqom*s are short, but they express a lot of passion and emotional pain. Bukharan *maqom*s have less feeling but more rules—you shouldn't depart from the mode, you can't break the rhythm, you have to stay within the *aruz* [verse meters], and so on. In the Ferghana style, you're free to break these rules.

Khan Baba Sharifov (d. 1933). Sodir Khan, as he is known, composed "Dilhiroj" ("Dilkharosh" in literary Tajik) on a text of Hafez, the great fourteenth-century Persian poet from Shiraz whose lyrical verse has been set to music through the centuries by myriad composers and singers. In the following example, "Dilhiroj" is passionately performed by Nasiba Omonboeva, who also hails from Khujand and, like many residents of Khujand, is bilingual in Tajik and Uzbek.

LISTEN

Example 21.1. "Dilhiroj" (Tormented heart), composed by Sodir Khan Baba Sharifov on a text of Hafez, performed by Nasiba Omonboeva (vocal), accompanied by Sirojiddin Juraev (*dutar*). From *In the Shrine of the Heart: Popular Classics from Bukhara and Beyond*, vol. 7 of *Music of Central Asia* (SFR, 2010), track 10.

Though more typically performed by male singers, "Dilhiroj" is one of Nasiba Omonboeva's favorite songs.

Dūsh didam, ki maloyik dar-i maykhona zadand,	Last night I saw that angels knocked on the door of a wine shop
Gil-i odam bisirishtand-u ba paymona zadand.	They kneaded Adam's clay and formed a cup.
Sokinon-i haram-u sitr-u afof-i malakut	The purest of the pure heavenly angels
Bo man-i rohnishin boda-yi mastona zadand.	Drank intoxicating wine with me as I sat on the side of the road.
Osmon bor-i amonat natavonist kashid,	The heavens could not sustain the burden of that trust.
Qur'a-i fol ba nom-i man-i devona zadand.	And cast their lots for me, crazy from love.
Nukta-i ishq dil-i gūshanishinon khun kard,	The well of love in the departed one's heart flushed with blood.
Hamchu on khol, ki bar oraz-i jonona zadand.	Like the birthmark that adorns the face of the beloved.
Kas chu Hofiz nakushod az rukh-i andesha niqob,	No one has unveiled the face of thought like Hafez.
To sar-i zulf-i sukhan-ro ba qalam shona zadand.	Others only created fancy hairdos of puns.

1. How would you characterize Nasiba Omonboeva's vocal style in "Dilhiroj"?

2. Compare this vocal style to that of the bardic singers (for example, *aqyn, jyrau*) in historically nomadic cultures. How are they similar and different?

3. Now compare "Dilhiroj" to "Talqincha-i sabo," from example 18.2. How are these two songs similar and different, both in their musical structure and in their performance style?

Not all *bastakor* music features classical lyrics set to new melodies. Old melodies may also be set to newly written lyrics. Traditional folk tunes offer a rich melodic source for poet-lyricists and have been widely appropriated. During the Soviet era, particularly in the 1940s and 1950s, older songs were sanitized by replacing allegorical spiritual texts with poems whose content was unmistakably earthly and, in many cases, overtly patriotic. Some of these texts remain popular, particularly among older listeners.

While Soviet-era song lyrics commonly represented politically mandated bowdlerizations, older forms of lyrical spirituality did not entirely disappear. For example, a leading Uzbek poet of the 1920s and 1930s, Abdulhamid Cho'lpon, wrote somber lines to the melody of "Galdir," a popular folk song. A performance of "Galdir" by singer Nodira Pirmatova is reproduced in example 21.2.

LISTEN

Example 21.2. "Galdir" (Fool of God), composer of music unknown, performed by Nodira Pirmatova (vocal and *dutar*). Lyrics by Abdulhamit Cho'lpon (d. 1938). From *In the Shrine of the Heart: Popular Classics from Bukhara and Beyond*, vol. 7 of *Music of Central Asia* (SFR, 2010), track 1.

Unattributed traditional lyrics for this popular folk song from the Ferghana Valley describe a woman's anxiety about an inattentive suitor. By contrast, Cho'lpon's new lyrics, written in 1923, can be read as representing the voice of its male author or, alternatively, the personified voice of the sad melody itself.

Men dutar birlan tughishgan köhna bir devonaman,	I was born with a *dutar*, I'm an old fool of God.
Ul tughishgonim bilan bir ötda doim yonaman.	Together with my *dutar*, I always burn with fire.

Dillarida gham töla bechoralarga yorman,	I'm a friend of the unfortunate ones whose hearts suffer.
Vakhti khush gham körmaganlardan tamom bezorman.	I get no pleasure from seeing those who are self-satisfied and don't know misfortune.
Pardalarning har biri bergay bölak ghamdan khabar,	Every melody of my instrument pours forth sorrow.
Ghamli öt chiqmas öshal torlarda galdir yighlamay	You won't free yourself from the fire of sorrow until you cry the tears of these strings.
Ahli ghamlar men kabi Majnun sifat galdir bölar,	Sufferers like me are fools of God,
Shul sababdin bandaning nomini galdir qöydilar.	And for that reason they gave me the name "fool of God."

Cho'lpon's literary activities led to his conviction for "nationalism" and his execution, in 1938, as an enemy of the people at the height of the Great Terror launched by Stalin. Beginning in the 1950s, Cho'lpon's reputation was restored, and his text for "Galdir" is often sung in place of the older folk lyrics.

STUDY QUESTIONS

1. How would you compare "Galdir" to singer-songwriter music in your own culture? Think about both lyrics and the music.

2. What does Cho'lpon mean by the expression "fool of God" (*galdir*)?

3. Do you find this song powerful? If so, what is the source of its power?

In the northwest of Uzbekistan, across the desolate sands of the Kara Kum Desert, are the oasis cities of Khiva and Urgench—both principal cultural centers of Khorezm, an administrative region of the Republic of Uzbekistan that is well known for its *bastakor*s. Khorezmians have long been identified with distinctive traditions of language and oral literature (Khorezmi is a dialect of Uzbek), festivity and celebration, music and dance. Perhaps the extremes of the region's continental climate—harsh winters and scorching hot summers—have molded the Khorezmian temperament and, with it, the extroverted and powerfully intense forms of traditional art for which Khiva and Khorezm are renowned among Central Asians.

Performer Profile: Farhod Davletov

My mother's father was a mullah and a musician. When I was a kid, we often went to his place, and I grew up surrounded by music. I think that music should be transmitted through blood. I didn't study music at a university or conservatory, but I was very interested, and went to see some *ustod*s. Then in 1980, I went to Tashkent to study in the Institute of Culture and stayed there five years. In 1985, I took part in the state *maqom* contest and won it. The same year, I won another prestigious competition. It was a turning point for me. I had always liked traditional music, but after winning the awards, I began paying more attention to classics and *maqom*s. And I became a disciple of Ruzimet Jumaniyazov. He was a great *ustod,* and I learned a lot from him. Now I have many disciples myself. They discover me from recordings and come and ask me to teach them.

Among young people in our country, pop music is very popular. I like pop music myself, and listen to it with musical pleasure. There are some good singers in pop, but they shouldn't forget about our own songs. These songs, especially *maqom*s, have an educational value, if you're able to listen attentively. They teach how to respect elders, how to be more concentrated, and not waste time. The poetry of *maqom*s is difficult. It's from high-level, sophisticated poets, but if you just listen, it will nourish your heart and give you peace and confidence. It's not about religion, but about belief. When someone is praying beautifully, you are touched, and it can even bring tears to your eyes. Singing is the same. When it comes from the heart, it will

Photo by Sebastian Schutyser. Courtesy of Aga Khan Music Initiative.

move listeners. And when there are understanding listeners, singers have much more pleasure and inspiration, and the music turns out well.

One of Khorezm's most renowned *bastakor*s was Komiljon Otaniyozov (1917–1975), the composer of dozens of songs that remain popular throughout Uzbekistan today. Ataniyazov's song "Ranoni Gördim" (I saw Rano), set to a text by an unknown lyricist, is reproduced in example 21.3, in a performance by Farhod Davletov. A video clip featuring Farhod Davletov comprises example 21.4.

Listen

Example 21.3. "Ranoni Gördim" (I saw Rano), composed by Komiljon Otaniyozov, performed by Farhod Davletov (vocal and *tar*), accompanied by Shuhrat Razzaqov (*dutar*), Habibulla Kurambaev (*doira*), and Murod Norkuziev (*ghijak*). Author of lyrics unknown. From *In the Shrine of the Heart: Popular Classics from Bukhara and Beyond,* vol. 7 of *Music of Central Asia* (SFR 2010), track 2.

Ta'rif etay bir yor aslin	Let me describe the essence of the beloved one,
Man shu kun Ra'noni gördim	On that day, I saw Rano.
Orzu etib oning vaslin	Dreaming about meeting her,
Man shu kun Ra'noni gördim	On that day, I saw Rano,
Qoshlari qaroni gördim.	With the black eyebrows.
Refrain:	Refrain:
Gördim, gördim nani gördim	I saw her, I saw her, what did I see?
Dodai toghlarda sönani gördim	I saw a deer on the hills and mountains,
Man shu kun Ra'noni gördim.	On that day, I saw Rano.

WATCH

Example 21.4. Profile of Farhod Davletov. Excerpt from documentary film by Saodat Ismailova and Carlos Casas in *In the Shrine of the Heart: Popular Classics from Bukhara and Beyond* (DVD), vol. 7 of *Music of Central Asia* (SFR, 2010).

Uzbek and Tajik "popular classics" also include individual songs from the Shashmaqom—the local Bukharan variant of *maqom*. The Shashmaqom is a suite form, consisting of six long suites of vocal and instrumental pieces that progress gradually "from prayer to dance," i.e., from slow, contemplative pieces to lighter, livelier, and more rhythmic songs. Songs that have entered the repertoire of popular classics tend to be drawn from the lighter end of the Shashmaqom suites. One example of such a song is "Ufor-i Iroq," from the sixth suite of the Shashmaqom, "Iroq." *Iroq* signifies the melodic mode, and *ufor* signifies the rhythm. *Ufor* is a dance genre that is represented in a stylized form in the Shashmaqom. Nodira Pirmatova sings this small jewel of a song in Tajik Persian in the soft and refined style associated with the great Bukharan Jewish singer Barno Is'hakova (1927–2001), whom Pirmatova considers one of her teachers, even though the women never had a formal *ustod-shogird* (master-disciple) relationship (see chapter 18).

LISTEN

Example 21.5. "Ufor-i Iroq," composer of music unknown, performed by Nodira Pirmatova (vocal), accompanied by Mahmudjon Tojibaev (*tar*). Text by Hajji Husaini Kangurti (1880–1916). From *In the Shrine of the Heart: Popular Classics from Bukhara and Beyond*, vol. 7 of *Music of Central Asia* (SFR, 2010), track 14.

Chi sabab ki shukh-i mastam bar-i mo nodida bigzasht?	Why did my mischievous beloved one walk by without glancing at me?
Nanishast-u nola-i mo dame noshunida bigzasht	She didn't sit and didn't listen to a single one of my moans.
Dil-u jon-u din rabuda, rukh-i sharmgin namuda,	Having stolen my heart, soul, and faith, her face blushing with embarrassment,
Gireh-i jabin kushuda ba miyon rasida bigzasht	She walked among the crowd with head high and hid herself.
Chu khilol paykar-i man ba tabozu-i dar-i u,	Having humbly bent my waist, like the crescent of a new moon, I stood at her door,
Ba umed-i jabkhasoī, ba qad-i khamida bigzasht.	I hoped my modesty would make her look at me, but she passed with her head down.
Ba chaman ba subhgohī chu ghizol-i rom omad,	At dawn, like handmade chamois, she came to the meadow,
Zi savdo-i dida-i man chī qadar ramida bigzasht.	But why, seeing the blackness of my eyes, did she flee in fear?
Zi gham-i firoq, Hojī, ba fighon charo nanodam?	How, Hajji, can I not cry and moan like a flute, from the grief of separation,
Ki chu nay zi nayistonam, hama kas burida bigzasht.	If longing for the beloved fells me, like a reed cut down to make a flute?

STUDY QUESTIONS

1. Compare "Ufor-i Iroq" to the other singer-songwriter songs you have listened to thus far ("Dilhiroj" and "Galdir"). How is the vocal style of "Ufor-i Iroq" similar to and different from the vocal style of "Dilhiroj" and "Galdir"?

2. Do you find the melody of "Ufor-i Iroq" easy to remember? Can you sing the melody?

3. In your view, how successful was the unknown composer in creating a melody that was suitable for the text of "Ufor-i Iroq"?

Performer Profile: Nodira Pirmatova

I'm the youngest of seven children—six girls and a boy—and we all have a passion and talent for music. We didn't go to music schools; everything we learned was at home. My father was my first teacher. He didn't study music formally, but he's a good singer, and we always had musical guests and visitors—singers, instrumentalists, and devotees of traditional music. Later I went to a music college in Khujand, and then to the conservatory in Tashkent. For vocal music, my *ustod* was Saodat Qabulova, originally from Margilan, a city in the Ferghana Valley. She taught me about breath control, poetic rhythm, clear speech. Ensemble singing was taught by the great *ustod* from Andijan, Fattahhon Mamadaliev. And I was very lucky to be able to

spend time with Halima Nasyrova. She was one of the greatest female traditional singers. She used to sing in the opera as well. When you say "*ustod*," it doesn't just mean a music teacher. They teach you more than that: how to love music, how to understand and feel it, how to appreciate local culture and its human qualities. I miss my *ustod*s. I am grateful to them for what they gave me, and the best way to show my appreciation is to sing the songs they transmitted to me. First and foremost, they wanted their disciples to be honest people. Our music is a type of music that demands honesty and cleanliness. They used to say that we have to respect the spirits of our *ustod*s when we sing, so we should be clean in our deeds.

Photo by Sebastian Schutyser. Courtesy of Aga Khan Music Initiative.

Example 21.6. Profile of Nodira Pirmatova. Excerpt from documentary film by Saodat Ismailova and Carlos Casas in *In the Shrine of the Heart: Popular Classics from Bukhara and Beyond* (DVD), vol. 7 of *Music of Central Asia* (SFR, 2010).

WATCH

In both Khorezm and the Tashkent-Ferghana Valley region, instrumental music has developed alongside vocal music as a compositional and performance art. Some singers are also outstanding instrumentalists, but instrumental music has attracted its own cadre of virtuosic specialists who arrange and perform instrumental versions of songs, or compose pieces specifically for their instrument. Foremost among such innovators are composer-performers on the Uzbek-Tajik *dutar*, one of many varieties of two-stringed long-necked lutes that exist throughout Central Asia. The *dutar*'s simplicity of construction belies the complexity of its performance techniques. These techniques are amply demonstrated in the following

Performer Profile: Sirojiddin Juraev

Photo by Sebastian Schutyser. Courtesy of Aga Khan Music Initiative.

Both my father and grandfather played the *dutar*, and my first *ustod* was my father. When I was a very little boy, my father sent me to the local music school. Later I studied at the Music College in Khujand and at Khujand University, where my *ustod* was Sultonali Khudaiberdiev, and after that, at the Academy of Maqom, in Dushanbe, where my *ustod* was Abduvali Abdurashidov. I listen a lot to old recordings of the great *ustod*s, for example, Mirzaqurbon Soliev, Komiljon Jaborrov, Turgun Alimatov. When I listen to their records and hear something I really like, I try to learn those tunes. These *ustod*s represented the Ferghana Valley style, so what I play is close to that. I was born there, grew up there, and am a child of that environment. Now I teach *dutar* in the National Conservatory in Dushanbe. When I feel inspired, I also compose my own music on the *dutar*. If you listen a lot to old records that are inspiring, there should be some push to compose. You can't compose from a void. There has to be an inspiration that comes from listening to a master.

four examples by *dutar* master Sirojiddin Juraev, who plays in the tradition of the Ferghana-Tashkent style.

LISTEN

Example 21.7. "Qushtar" (Double strings), composer of music unknown, performed by Sirojiddin Juraev (*dutar*). Performance version of Kuzikhon Madrahimov (1888–1954). From *In the Shrine of the Heart: Popular Classics from Bukhara and Beyond*, vol. 7 of *Music of Central Asia* (SFR, 2010), track 4.

LISTEN

Example 21.8. "Qushtar," composer of music unknown, performed by Sirojiddin Juraev (*dutar*). Performance version of Kuzikhon Madrahimov (1888–1954). Unreleased studio recording, Joel Gordon, sound engineer, 2014.

"Qushtar" is a virtuosic composition for solo *dutar*. It shows off an unusual technique that involves simultaneously fretting and plucking the strings with the left hand while tapping the deck of the instrument lightly with the right hand to make a beat. The two gut strings of the *dutar* are tuned in unison, rather than in the customary fourth or fifth. For aspiring *dutar* players of the Ferghana-Tashkent school, mastery of "Qushtar" is considered obligatory.

STUDY QUESTIONS —————————————————————————————————

1. What differences do you hear between the 2009 and 2014 performances of "Qushtar"? How has Sirojiddin Juraev's performance of the piece changed over time?

2. Comment on the rhythm in "Qushtar." What makes it unusual?

3. In addition to the left-hand simultaneous fretting and plucking technique described above, what other techniques—both right hand and left hand—contribute to the sense of virtuosity?

LISTEN — **Example 21.9.** "Mehri Vatan" (Love of my homeland), composed and performed by Sirojiddin Juraev, *dutar.* Unreleased studio recording, Joel Gordon, sound engineer, 2014.

LISTEN — **Example 21.10.** "Zavq-i Javoni" (Interest of youth), composed and performed by Sirojiddin Juraev, *dutar.* Unreleased studio recording, Joel Gordon, sound engineer, 2014.

"Mehri Vatan" shows Sirojiddin Juraev as not only a master performer but also a composer of what might be called "neotraditional" *dutar* music, which is rooted in traditional styles of melody and rhythm, but develops them in new ways that lie beyond the boundaries of traditional stylistic conventions. "Mehri Vatan" develops from a tuneful theme in the form a b a introduced at the beginning of the piece. (The "a" and "b" parts are each repeated, thus the form could be more accurately notated as |:a:||:b:||:a:|). Following the initial presentation of the theme, it is re-presented in a series of increasingly virtuosic variations that break up the steady rhythm of the opening theme into syncopated bursts of rhythmic energy and rolling flamenco-like strumming patterns. "Zavq-i Javoni" follows much the same theme-and-variations formal development.

STUDY QUESTIONS —————————————————————————————————

1. As you listen to "Mehri Vatan" and "Zavq-i Javoni," can you identify the "a" and "b" sections of the original theme melody?

2. What techniques does Sirojiddin Juraev use to create variations of the opening thematic material?

3. Of all the instruments played by sedentary-dwelling populations in Central Asia, what is it about the *dutar* that has made it such a locus of virtuoso performance technique in instrumental music?

The popular classic songs and instrumental pieces composed by *bastakor*s of the nineteenth and twentieth centuries remain a respected if increasingly marginalized element of musical life in Uzbekistan and Tajikistan in our own time. Even in lighter genres, the classical lyrical style of *bastakor*s cannot compete against the juggernaut of contemporary pop, modeled on Russian, European, and American bands; and singer-songwriters who compose their own melodies and lyrics in standard pop formats and perform them to the accompaniment of amplified instruments liberally processed with digital effects. Yet Nodira Pirmatova's paean to old songs—that they don't "grow old"—and their abiding rejuvenation by younger singers may be reason to hope that the old popular classics will not disappear.

NOTE

The text and textboxes in this chapter were adapted from the booklet notes of *In the Shrine of the Heart: Popular Classics from Bukhara and Beyond,* vol. 7 of *Music of Central Asia* (Smithsonian Folkways Recordings, 2010).

CHAPTER 22 # Religious Music and Chant in the Culture of Sedentary Dwellers

ALEKSANDR DJUMAEV

PATTERNS OF CULTURE IN CENTRAL ASIAN ISLAM

For a millennium, Central Asia has constituted a unified civilization linked by cultural and economic ties, a common political history, and, perhaps most crucially by the cultural and religious predominance of Islam. While adherents of other religions, particularly Orthodox Christianity and Judaism, lived and continue to live in Central Asia, they have all in some measure adapted to the abiding influence of Islamic mores and institutions in the region. Yet, while ubiquitous, Islam in Central Asia is not monolithic. Rather, Islam itself has adapted to the particular patterns of culture in which it exists, ranging from Kazakh and Kyrgyz pastoralism to the sedentary agricultural and urban milieu that has been shaped primarily by Tajiks and Uzbeks.

The principal centers of Islamic culture in Central Asia are in the cities, and among these, Bukhara and Samarkand have played a particularly important role. The central institutions of Islam—mosque, madrasah (religious college), minaret, *khanaqa* (Sufi dwelling), mazar (tomb of a saint)—are concentrated in cities. The madrasahs of Bukhara trained Muslim clerics who served all over Central Asia and Kazakhstan as well as in the Volga-Ural region, the traditional territory of many of Russia's Muslim peoples. Among the inhabitants of oases and cities, the daily observance of religious custom and the practice of religious rituals was obligatory, and thus the influence of Islam on expressive culture was significant. City-dwelling Uzbeks and Tajiks placed particular importance on sacred music and chant, and to this day, the core forms and genres of Islamic religious music in Central Asia are most strongly present in Uzbek and Tajik cultural heritage. By contrast, religious music has never been as important among peoples with a tradition of pastoralism—Kazakhs, Kyrgyz, and in particular the Turkmen, who were Islamized much later than city-dwellers. For example, the southern regions of Kazakhstan came under the influence of Islam in the eleventh and twelfth centuries as a result of contact with the neighboring urban civilization of Tashkent and Bukhara, while in the central Kazakh steppe regions and in Kyrgyzstan, Islam began to take root only at the end of the eighteenth century. Muslims in Central Asia and Kazakhstan overwhelmingly belong to the Sunni branch of Islam. The Shi'a minority has been largely confined to two areas: the cities of Bukhara and Samarkand, and the culturally autonomous region of Badakhshan, in eastern Tajikistan and northeastern Afghanistan, where many if not most inhabitants are Shi'a Ismaili Muslims (see chapter 27).

Broadly speaking, in both the cities and on the steppe, the practice of Islam was divided into two divergent streams: on the one hand, an official, canonical practice; and on the other, various forms of popular Islam that represented a synthesis of Islamic and pre-Islamic cults and beliefs. Non-Islamic influences in popular Islam include Buddhism, shamanism, and cultic practices such as ancestor worship. To a large extent, these influences entered the world of Islam through Sufism, the mystical branch of Islam that flourished in Central Asia as early as the tenth century.

Sufism, which first arose as a form of opposition to official Islam, eventually merged with it in the eighteenth and nineteenth centuries, and subsequently began to replace it in practice. Sufi practices assumed a number of different directions, and Sufism created its own rituals connected to music, dance, and poetry. Popular Sufism relied on numerous holy places of pilgrimage and worship (*kadamjai*, *ziyaratgakh*) that can often be traced to the existence of pre-Islamic cultic practices at the same sites. Before the advent of Soviet rule, such sites could be found across the entire territory of Central Asia and were distinguished according to a hierarchy of religious significance.

THE DEVELOPMENT OF RELIGIOUS MUSIC AND CHANT

When the first proselytizers of Islam reached Central Asia near the end of the seventh century, they found a multitude of diverse religious practices in both cities and steppe. Ancestor cults, Buddhism, Christianity, Judaism, Zoroastrianism, Manichaeism, and a variety of local animist-shamanist practices and beliefs all existed in Central Asia, and all used some form of poetry and music in their ritual practices. This poetry and music itself represented an intermingling of the myriad local traditions that developed within Central Asia's historical geopolitical regions: Bactria, Tokharistan, Sogd, Parthia, Bukhara, Khorezm, and others. Archaeological evidence suggests that in the pre-Islamic era, religious music existed alongside secular court repertories, military music, and music for festive ceremonial occasions. Sacred ceremonies, in particular those of the Buddhists, used a rich collection of musical instruments and a variety of forms of instrumental music whose development was influenced by the civilizations of the ancient East, India, and Greece.

The development of Islamic religious music and chant in Central Asia reflects the variety of ways in which Islam has been assimilated into the region—its diversity of local forms, and its tendency to draw on elements of the region's rich pre-Islamic musical legacy. The Hanifite school of Islamic law that predominated in Transoxania[1] was distinguished by a measured approach to music. From the very beginning of the Arab conquest of Khorasan and Transoxania, Islamic rulers displayed a great interest in local music and musicians. For example, the Umayyad caliphs ordered that lutenists and singers from Khorasan and Transoxania be brought to serve at the Umayyad court in Baghdad. At the same time, however, Islam struggled against the influence of expressive culture linked to other religions—Christianity, Judaism, and in particular "idol-worshipping" religions such as Buddhism, shamanism, and Zoroastrianism. Yet despite early Islam's essentially negative attitude toward music and entertainment, elements of pre-Islamic ritual chant and dance were incorporated into a variety of Islamic practices—above all, Sufism—and in this form have been preserved down to the present day.

Mausoleum of Khoja Ahmad Yassawi (d. 1167) in the city of Turkestan, southern Kazakhstan. Photo from a postcard made in 1916.

From the tenth to thirteenth centuries, Central Asia was overtaken by the Sufi movement. The appearance of communities of Sufis was followed in the twelfth century by the rise of organized brotherhoods: Khojagan, Yassawiyya, Kubrawiyya, and others. At their gatherings (*majlis*) Sufis practiced a special form of sacred music (*sama‘*) and dance (*raqs*) on the basis of which the ritual of *zikr* (Arabic *dhikr*: "remembrance") was born. One of the main figures at these meetings became the Sufi singer (*qawwal*). Sufi treatises of the tenth and eleventh centuries contain numerous polemics regarding the licitness or illicitness of music and dance.

Sufi *khanaqa*s remained the repository of sacred musical traditions during the time of the devastating thirteenth century Mongol invasions, and in the fourteenth and fifteenth centuries, when Central Asia entered a period of relatively stable cultural development under the rule of the Timurids, these traditions flourished. In Timurid Herat and Samarkand, the art of chanting the call to prayer (*adhān*), reciting the Qur'an, and delivering public sermons (*wa‘iz*) reached a high state of development. In the realm of popular Islam, wandering dervishes (*qalandar*) and religious storytellers (*maddoh, qissakhan*) propagated Islamic values through singing and storytelling.

The melding of official and popular forms of Islam, already evident in the fifteenth century, grew stronger between the sixteenth century and the first half of

Above: A *maddoh* in Samarkand and his audience, 1920s.
Photographer unknown.

Above right: Wandering dervishes in Tashkent, early 20th century.
Photo by Viktor Uspensky.

the nineteenth. Sufi *zikr*s began to be conducted in mosques, thus combining the function of mosque and *khanaqa*. At the same time, the classical musical form *maqom* appeared in Sufi rituals, and the ritual practice of *zikr* within the Sufi brotherhoods assumed different forms that were often divorced from the original practices of the brotherhoods.

Largely isolated from non-Islamic influences, the musical traditions of medieval Central Asia continued unbroken until the middle of the nineteenth century, when Central Asia was annexed to the Russian Empire. Russia's conquest of Central Asia set the stage for an essentially new period of history in which Islamic culture came into direct contact with Russian and European civilization and began to absorb its influence. This contact ignited internal conflicts within Islam itself that were reflected in Islam's relationship to music and other arts. In the first two decades of the twentieth century, this relationship was discussed in the local print media, and in books such as *Music and Islam* (*Muzyka ve Islam*), by Hadi Kildebaki (1881–1949), published in Ufa in 1909, which brought to Russian Turkestan new ideas about music education.

The historical period that began with the Socialist Revolution of 1917 and continued through the era of Soviet rule to the breakup of the Soviet Union in 1991 led to fundamental changes in the status of Islam in Central Asia. Communist-style modernization and Europeanization within an ideological framework of secularization and state atheism ruptured traditional culture and created strict limitations on the practice of religious life. In the 1920s, the government instituted a ban on holding large *zikr*s in major religious centers, and the practice of *zikr* was henceforth transformed into a secret, illegal form of worship. Many mosques were closed, religious schools shut down, and spiritual leaders defamed and persecuted. The performance and publication of songs with religious lyrics or associations was discouraged or banned, and such songs, particularly when they enjoyed wide popularity, were transformed through the substitution of secular, often overtly political texts.

By contrast, the post-Soviet period has been characterized by a tendency toward a renaissance of spiritual religious values and traditions, including the practice of Islamic religious music and chant. This revival, however, has focused principally on the canonical practices of Islamic worship. Many old forms of music and ritual have been irrevocably lost, and are known now only through descriptions that predate the Bolshevik Revolution.

Zikr in Tashkent, Uzbekistan, 1958.

Photo by Rakushev.

FORMS OF RELIGIOUS MUSIC AND CHANT

Central Asian religious music and chant of the nineteenth and twentieth centuries can be divided into four distinct categories, which range from relatively autonomous forms to those strictly tied to specific liturgical functions and canonical performance traditions, such as the call to prayer and the reading of the Qur'an. These categories can be characterized as follows:

1. Canonical performance traditions: first and foremost is the recitation of the Qur'an according to the rules and traditions of Qur'anic cantillation (*tajwīd*). A second canonical practice is the chanting of the Call to Prayer (*adhān*, pronounced "*azan*" in Central Asia)—also locally called *bang-i namāz*—literally "call to prayer" in Persian.

2. Music and chant for Muslim holidays: songs connected to the yearly cycle of Muslim holidays, for example "Ya Ramazan," sung during the month of Ramadan. Another example is the mourning ceremony for the Shi'a martyrs Ali, Hasan, and Husein performed during Ashura—the first ten days of the month of Muharram.

3. Sufi ritual music and chant: various forms of *zikr* and spiritual concert (*sama'*) practiced by Central Asian Sufi orders and sects as well as analogous forms used in funerals, healing, and other rituals and ceremonies.

4. Popular religious music and chant: a broad category that includes chant, declamation, and interpretation of spiritual poetry in Persian-Tajik and Turkic languages conceived in a popular, accessible style. It also includes dance, theatricalized presentations on religious themes aimed at popular consumption, and entertainment (*tamasha*) performed during Muslim festivals and religious events, and in various male and female gatherings; also, the propagation of Islamic values and beliefs in a popular form by professional singers and musicians, wandering dervishes (*qalandars*), and storytellers of religious legends and history.

CANONICAL PERFORMANCE TRADITIONS

Recitation of the Qur'an

In pre-Soviet Central Asia, the Qur'an occupied an exceptionally important place in the lives of Muslims, providing guidance for all spheres of human life, from birth to death. Knowledge of the Qur'an was highly valued in society, and every Muslim knew from memory at least several key suras.

The profession of Qur'an reciter (*qari, hafiz*) was considered an occupation pleasing to God, and carried considerable social status. The word *qari* usually became a part of someone's name, e.g., Mahmud qari, indicating the individual's special relationship to the sacred book. The profession of reciter was closely connected to music. Not infrequently, highly ranked professional singers began their path to art with the study of the Qur'an, for example, the outstanding Uzbek singer of Soviet times, Mukhitdin Qari Yakubov (1896–1957).

Reciters of the Qur'an studied in a school (*maktab*) affiliated with a mosque, madrasah, Sufi *khanaqa,* or shrine; or in special institutions (*qarikhana*) that educated and domiciled Qur'anic reciters, and operated on income from donations, bequests, and religious endowments (*waqf*). The boys chosen for training were typically from poor families, orphans, or blind.

Mir-i Arab Madrasah and surrounding city of Bukhara.
Photo by Süha Özkan, ArchNet.

Like other forms of religious music and chant in Central Asia, the recitation of the Qur'an tended toward two contrasting performance styles: on the one hand, an official or "international" style, and on the other, an assortment of popular and more local styles. The first, originating in Cairo and other religious centers of the Arab world, was the purview of professional reciters and Islamic clergy, and is characterized by formal strictness, lyricism, and rhythmic and melodic complexity. Professional reciters typically used six or seven canonical melodic types, which were often borrowed directly from the Arabic tradition of classical *maqom* (see chapter 18). By contrast, local performance styles were practiced in daily life by Muslims who observed popular forms of Islam that arose along the byways and in the hinterlands of Central Asia. These performance styles were characterized by melodic simplicity and accessibility, and typically reflected local folksong styles: Kyrgyz folk melodies among the Kyrgyz, Kazakh melodies among the Kazakh, and so on.

In the twentieth century, the Bukharan style of Qur'anic recitation, considered refined and exemplary, was widely disseminated in Central Asia and in the steppe regions of Kazakhstan. To a large extent, this dissemination stemmed from the centralized training of mullahs, Qur'anic reciters, and imams in Bukhara's religious colleges, in particular the famous late-medieval madrasah Mir-i Arab. As the Soviet policy of state atheism lost its hold on Central Asia, recitation of the Qur'an acquired new prestige. Recordings of Qur'anic recitation were issued by the state-owned record company, Melodiya, and special competitions for recitation of the Qur'an were organized by religious authorities.

Adhān

The *adhān* is traditionally chanted from the top of a minaret by a muezzin, a specially trained singer with a strong and expressive voice. Nowadays, most minarets use loudspeakers, and the muezzin chants into a microphone. In Bukhara at the end of the nineteenth century and the beginning of the twentieth, the muezzin of the emir began the *adhān* that preceded each of the five daily prayers, thus signaling other muezzins in the city to begin their own call to prayer. Ethnographic accounts report that the voice of the emir's muezzin was audible at a distance of close to five miles.

Musicians playing *karnai*s, *surnai*, and drum in front of the Kalyan minaret in Bukhara.
Photo by Shavkat Boltaev.

The term "muezzin" was known among educated people, but in the popular world of Transoxania, muezzins were usually called *azanchi* or *sufi* (*sopi*), terms still in use today. The personnel of a typical mosque included the imam (leader of a Muslim community) and *sufi,* who also served as the mosque's custodian. Typically, a mosque served a neighborhood precinct (*mahalla* or *guzar*), a principal form of spatial and social organization in the late medieval Islamic city. While instructions for the canonical reading of sacred texts existed in Central Asian works on Islamic law (*fiqh*) and in other religious literature, the various cities of Central Asia all had their own local traditions for performing the *adhān*. Musical notation from the late nineteenth and early twentieth century confirms these distinct local traditions. In the twentieth century, the Bukharan style of chanting the *adhān,* which is distinguished by a lyrical melodic quality, enjoyed wide popularity. The performance of the *adhān* reproduced in example 22.1 is by Saifullajan Musaev, who at the time he was recorded, in 1990, was a first-year student at the Mir-i Arab Madrasah in Bukhara. Musaev learned his rendition of the *adhān* from his father, a native of Bukhara. A second example of *adhān,* from a mosque in Dushanbe, Tajikistan, is reproduced in example 22.2.

LISTEN

Example 22.1. Call to Prayer (*Adhān*), performed by Saifullajan Musaev at the Hoja Zainiddin Mosque, Bukhara, Uzbekistan. Recorded by Theodore Levin and Otanazar Matyakubov in Bukhara, 1990. From *Bukhara: Musical Crossroads of Asia* (SFR, 1991), track 7.

WATCH

Example 22.2. Call to Prayer (*Adhān*) in Dushanbe, Tajikistan. Filmed by Saodat Ismailova and Carlos Casas, 2012.

The *adhān* contains seven textual formulas, of which the seventh is a repetition of the first, as follows:

1. *Allah-u akbar* (God is most great) (4x)

2. *Ashhadu an la ilah-a illa 'Ilah* (I testify that there is no god but God) (2x)

3. *Ashhadu anna Muhammadun rasul Allah* (I testify that Muhammad is the apostle of God) (2x)

4. *Hayya'ala 'l-salat* (Come to prayer!) (2x)

5. *Hayya'ala 'l-falah* (Come to salvation!) (2x)

6. *As-salatu khayru min an-nawm* (Prayer is better than sleep) (used only for the Fajr [dawn] prayer) (2x)

7. *Allah-u akbar* (God is most great) (2x)

8. *La ilah-a illa 'llah* (There is no god but God) (1x)

STUDY QUESTIONS

1. What qualities of the *adhān* performance underscore its canonical status as a sacred text?

2. What distinguishes the performance of *adhān* from the performance of other kinds of vocal music or chant with which you are familiar?

3. What do you think is the purpose of the long pauses between lines of chant?

4. How are the performances of *adhān* from Bukhara and Dushanbe similar and different?

MUSIC AND CHANT FOR MUSLIM HOLIDAYS

Ramadan

Music and other forms of entertainment were a central feature of Muslim festivities, especially during the month of Ramadan. In Bukhara, the populace was notified of Ramadan's arrival by rhythmic drum beating and music performed by the emir's orchestra for official state ceremonies (*naqqarakhana*), which was installed at the gates of the emir's residence, called the *ark*. Following the all-day fasting that is obligatory for observant Muslims during Ramadan, the emir's orchestra played after sunset. In Tashkent, during the nights of Ramadan, a percussion orchestra consisting of kettledrums (*naqqara*, or in vernacular pronunciation, *naghora*) and wind instruments performed near the Sheikh Antahur Mosque, setting up on the roof of a house. In other cities, special night bazaars featured performance and pageantry by musicians, singers, and religious storytellers.

City-dwellers had their favorite out-of-town religious sites, usually Sufi *khanaqa*s and shrines set in picturesque gardens, where they gathered at the end of the daily fast. Here, at night, people relaxed and passed the time talking, eating, and taking in various forms of popular entertainment. A popular site for residents of Tashkent was the *khanaqa* and shrine of one of the followers of the Yassawi order, Sheikh Zengi-Ata, situated in a shady garden on the outskirts of Tashkent. People from Bukhara and surroundings—women and men on different days—visited the grave and *khanaqa* of the famous Sufi sheikh Bahauddin Naqshband, located in the suburbs, where well-known singers performed the works of Sufi-inspired poets such as Hafez, Mashrab, and Yassawi.

Ramadan prayers at the Sheikh Antahur Mosque in Tashkent, between 1865–1872.

Courtesy of the Library of Congress, Prints and Photographs Division, reproduction no. LC-DIG-ppmsca-14379.

One of the genres performed during Ramadan was the *na'at*—a chanted song celebrating the life and deeds of the Prophet Muhammad, composed both on the texts of professional poets and on folk texts. The following example of a *na'at* was recorded in Bukhara in 1990 from an eighty-three-year-old singer who called himself a "dervish," though he did not belong to an organized Sufi *tariqa*. The origin of the text, sung in Tajik Persian but containing many Arabic words, is unknown.

LISTEN

Example 22.3. *Na'at,* performed by Dervish Orif Bobo Hamro Ogli. Recorded by Theodore Levin and Otanazar Matyakubov in Bukhara, 1990. From *Bukhara: Musical Crossroads of Asia* (SFR, 1991), track 8.

The text for this example is available on the companion website.

STUDY QUESTIONS

1. How would you describe the performance style of the singer?

2. Within the limited tonal range of the recitation, what expressive techniques does the singer use to focus the attention of his listeners on the meaning of the text?

3. Even if you can't understand the text, is it easy to follow the words?

Another genre sung during Ramadan consists of special greeting songs whose titles all contain the word Ramadan or a cognate form (in Central Asia, "Ramadan" is pronounced "Ramazan"): Uzbeks sang "Iya Ramazan"; Kazakhs had "Jarapazan"; Kyrgyz and Karakalpaks, "Zharamazan"; Turkmen, "Yaremezan"; and so on. Such songs are typically sung by children and teenagers while strolling past the homes of neighbors. Their texts wish happiness and well-being in the family, the birth of a baby, and so on, and singers receive small gifts such as sweets or coins. An Uzbek version of such a song goes as follows:

Ramazan aytib keldik eshigingizga,	Serenading Ramazan, we came to your door
Qochqordai oghil bersin beshigingizga.	Let it give to your cradle a son, strong like a ram.

In Uzbekistan, and in particular in the eastern region of the Ferghana Valley, during Ramadan women commonly perform songs called *rabbimman,* which means "My Lord, God." The following Uzbek example was recorded by musical ethnographer E. E. Romanovskaya in 1931, and illustrates a folk-inspired representation of Islam:

Rabbimman, yo rabbimman, yo ramazon	My Lord, God
Khush muborak, mohi ramazon.	Blessed is the month of Ramadan.
Havoda turli tumanning izi bor,	In the air are traces of fog,
Chor kitobda Mustafoning sözi bor	In the Four Books is the word of the Prophet.[2]
Rabbimman, yo rabbimman, yo ramazon,	My Lord, God,
Muhammad ummatiga mohi ramazon.	The month of Ramadan is for the community of Muhammad.

Celebrating Kurban-Bairam in Tashkent, between 1865–1872.

The breaking of the fast at the end of Ramadan is observed as a major holiday (*Ruza khayit* or *Ruza bayram*; in Arabic: Eid al-Fitr). This holiday lasts three days, during which believers observe the successful completion of the fast. Local neighborhoods organize banquets and give gifts to each other and to the mullahs. In the past, various forms of entertainment (*tamasha*) played an important role in this holiday: musicians, male dancers (*bacha*), clowns (*maskharavoz*), puppet theater, acrobats, and so on. Representatives of various Sufi orders, *qalandar*s, *maddoh*s, and others sang religious songs and performed public *zikr*s.

The most important holiday in Central Asia, the Feast of the Sacrifice (*Kurban bayram* or *Kurban khayit,* or simply *Khayit;* in Arabic: Eid al-Adha), is celebrated in an analogous way. The Feast of the Sacrifice was held seventy days after the end of the Ramadan fast and lasted for three to four days, the conclusion coinciding with the end of the Pilgrimage. The holiday commemorates the test of faith in which Abraham, a prophet in the Muslim faith, prepared to sacrifice his son, Ismail (Isaac, in Judaism), to God, and who at the last moment was instructed by God to replace his son with an animal. To mark the holiday, animals are sacrificed, large amounts of food are prepared and given away as an offering, and friends visit one another, as well as the graves of those who were close to them. Music and other forms of performing arts are also an important part of observing the Feast of the Sacrifice.

Shi'a Ceremonies

Shi'a ceremonies and rituals were widely observed in the cities of Central Asia and were perceived as a part of the common Islamic tradition of both Sunni and Shi'a communities. This tradition included the period of mourning during the first ten days (Ashura) of the month of Muharram, which memorializes the Shi'a martyrs Ali, Hasan, and Husein. In pre-Soviet times, Sunnis sang songs during Ashura such as "Shahadati Imam Hassan, Imam Hussein" (The martyrs Imam Hasan and Imam Husein), and practiced special *zikr*s and dances. Shi'as who lived in some neighborhoods of Bukhara inhabited by Iranians (who were known as "Farsi") observed Ashura in Shi'a prayer houses called *Husayniya-khona*. This tradition was preserved in the Soviet period in the private houses of Bukharan Iranians. Nowadays Bukhara's Shi'a population holds Ashura ceremonies in official *Husayniya-khona*s and in private houses. In place of the *taziyah* religious pageant for Ashura that developed in Iran, the Bukharan Shi'a have their own local form of ceremony, called Ashuro, which includes Qur'an recitation, common prayer, singing of special songs by soloists (*nawakhon*s and *mankabatkhon*s), sermons delivered by *rawzakhon*s, and ritualized physical movements. Older Bukharan elements combine with new Iranian tunes. One of the typical forms of singing during Ashuro is a dialogue between a soloist and a choir of participants. Women and men participate separately, and Sunni Bukharans also visit the yearly mourning gatherings of the Shi'as.

Top: Men celebrate Ashuro in Zerabad village, near Bukhara, 2006.

Above: Women celebrate Ashuro in Tar-Tar village, near Bukhara, 2004.
Photo by Shavkat Boltaev.

SUFI RITUAL MUSIC AND CHANT

Zikr

A number of major Sufi orders existed in Central Asia in the first third of the twentieth century, each with its own traditional territory. In the Khorezm oasis was the Kubrawiyya; in the Bukhara-Samarkand region, the Naqshbandiyya; in Tashkent-Ferghana, the Yassawiyya and Qadiriyya. Almost everywhere were groups of *qalandar*s, or "wandering dervishes." There were also small mystical groups, for example, the Yazdahum, literally "eleventh," who lived in Bukhara and were linked with the name of the famous medieval Sufi *sheikh* Abdulqadir Jilani (also transliterated as Gilani). Their name derives from the fact that they celebrated their *zikr* on the eleventh day of each month in memory of Jilani, who died on the eleventh day of the Islamic month of Rabī ath-Thānī, in 1166 CE.

All Sufi orders practiced a form of *zikr*—the ritualized performance of sacred music, texts, and dance—and each order had its own particular way of conducting

The complex of Bahauddin Naqshband (d. 1389), after whom the Naqshbandi Sufi order is named, combines historic and recent architecture.
Photos by Shavkat Boltaev.

zikr. These ranged from the classical practice in the great *khanaqa*s of the urban Tajik-Uzbek social world to various hybrid forms of prayer and healing rituals linked to shamanism, funerary rituals, and even dance intended as entertainment (among the Turkmen of western Turkmenistan). Among the Kyrgyz, the term *zikr* designated a broader set of activities practiced by itinerant dervishes known as *duwan,* from Persian *diwana:* "mendicant," "holy fool," "possessed."

Two types of *zikr* existed in the ritual practice of the Central Asian orders: *zikr khafi* (or *khufi*)—a silent, hidden *zikr*—and *zikr jahri* (also, *jari, jakhri*), or loud *zikr.* In the silent *zikr,* the name of Allah and the sacred formulas were pronounced silently, and in the loud *zikr,* people sang, recited poetry aloud, and danced. Musical instruments were not used with the exception of the frame drum (*doira*) and, more rarely, the *safail,* a type of rattle. The loud *zikr* was traditionally practiced by the Kubrawiyya order in Khorezm, and by the Yazdahum sect in Bukhara, but in the nineteenth and early twentieth century, this practice was adopted by many Sufi orders and groups throughout Central Asia. *Zikr* was conducted not only in *khanaqa*s, the special buildings constructed for this purpose, but in shrines and mosques, at pilgrimage sites, and in the open air. Major centers for the performance of *zikr* included the Yassawi *khanaqa* in Turkestan, the shrine and *khanaqa* Zengi-Ata near Tashkent (where mass *zikr*s were conducted in the autumn), the *khanaqa* of Bahauddin Naqshband outside of Bukhara, and the Shah-i Zinda complex in Samarkand. Along with male *zikr*s, there were also female *zikr*s, usually led by an *ishan-bibi*—the wife of an *ishan. Ishan*s were religious teachers whose authority came not from a formal religious post but from a reputation for spiritual mastery among a circle of disciples.

The largest and most influential orders in Central Asia were the Naqshbandiyya and Yassawiyya. The Naqshbandiyya drew their membership primarily from the sedentary, urban Tajik-speaking population: artisans, merchants, shopkeepers, and tradesmen. Its center was the *khanaqa* of Bahauddin Naqshband outside of

Bukhara, a site of mass pilgrimage (*ziyaratgah*) where performers of spiritual songs and chant were always on hand to entertain visitors in return for alms. The Naqshbandi practiced both silent and loud forms of *zikr* and used primarily Persian-Tajik mystical poetry.

The Yassawi order (sometimes known as the Jahriyya, after the type of loud *zikr* they practiced) drew its membership primarily from the Turkic nomadic, semi-nomadic, and sedentary world. Its center was the *khanaqa* of Ahmad Yassawi (also spelled Yasawi) (d. 1166) in the city of Turkestan (formerly Yassy, or Yasi) in present-day Kazakhstan. The form of loud *zikr* practiced there was known as *zikr-i arra,* or "saw" *zikr,* from the raspy, antiphonal chanting that resembled the sound of a saw being pulled back and forth. The *zikr* was held once a week in the *khanaqa* and, during the period of mass pilgrimage (in the winter *chilla,* a 40-day period from the end of December to the beginning of February), continued for three days in an underground room (*khilvat*).

Men at a Sufi *zikr* in Dargh, Tajikistan, 1991.
Photo by Theodore Levin.

The *zikr* began with the recitation of the Qur'an and then segued into a form of chanting called *chorzarb,* literally "four strokes," which constituted the basis of the *zikr.* From a musical perspective, *chorzarb* represented one of the names of God chanted in a metro-rhythmic formula (*usul*) consisting of four syllables within one breath. Usually, the *chorzarb* reflected the four-beat rhythmic structure of the chanting of the Islamic creed called *tawhid: La ilah-a illa 'llah* (there is no god but God), which provides the nucleus of the loud *zikr* among the Yassawi and other orders. In chanting, the four rhythmically even accents are applied as follows (capitalized syllables are accented):

LA il-LAH-a IL-la 'l-LAH.

Analogous forms called *sezarb* (three syllables), *duzarb* (two syllables), and *yakzarb* (one syllable), together with the *chorzarb* formed a cycle of four metro-rhythmic formulas. Usually they were chanted by all the participants in the *zikr* at the beginning of the ceremony, between its parts, and in a repetitive, ostinato form during the whole event. Against this background, the soloist (*hafiz*) sang devotional songs called *talqin,* which usually consisted of a strophe drawn from the spiritual poetry of Yassawi (for an example, see chapter 23). The performance of a *talqin* required a high level of artistry, and was transmitted through lineages of musical specialists (*talqinchi*). The Yassawi *zikr* also included a form of sacred dance that suggested the dance-incantation of shamans, and in fact seems to have originated from it.

In the 1920s, after Soviet power was established in Central Asia, restrictions and prohibitions were placed on the practice of *zikr.* However, the practice was preserved through the entire Soviet era in remote settlements and, secretly, in cities such as Tashkent, Namangan, Kokand, and Khujand.

Title page of an edition of the 12th-century *Diwan-i Hikmat* of Khoja Ahmad Yassawi printed in Bukhara between 1908–1912.

WATCH

Example 22.4. Excerpt from a Yassawi *zikr* in the city of Turkestan, southern Kazakhstan. Filmed by Saodat Ismailova, 2004.

This short video was made in 2004 by Uzbek filmmaker Saodat Ismailova at the site of the fourteenth-century Khoja Ahmad Yassawi Mausoleum in the city of Turkestan, in southern Kazakhstan. The participants are young Kazakhs, many of whom studied in Turkey and were initiated into Sufi brotherhoods there. During the Soviet era, *zikr* was not practiced publicly in Kazakhstan, and the ceremony shown in the video represents a recent revival of the tradition. The leader of the *zikr* explained that the group does two different forms of *zikr*—*halqa* (circle) and *arra* (saw)—and that both offer ways to cleanse the soul and bring participants closer to God.

During the *zikr*, a soloist sings a spiritual song whose lyrics are drawn from the poetry of Yassawi. This is not the form of classical *talqin*, described above, but a more popular vocal genre whose melody and performance style suggest that the practice is borrowed from Turkey, and from the repertoire of *ilahis* (spiritual songs) performed by Sufi groups there. A recent development in this practice is the presence of choral harmony, which can be heard toward the end of the *ilahi*. After the singing ceases, the participants continue to chant "*Al(lah)—Hu—Hu—hai*" (*Hu* is one of the names of God), while moving their heads from the right shoulder downward toward the heart. This sound illustrates the onomatopoeic "saw" (*arra*) *zikr*.

STUDY QUESTIONS

1. What is the source of the spiritual power of *zikr*, and how does it act on participants and observers?

2. What kind of initiatic knowledge or understanding (i.e., knowledge or understanding available only to those who have been initiated into the specific ritual practices of a Sufi brotherhood) might be necessary to experience the effect of the *zikr* to the fullest?

Other Forms of Sufi Music

The classical *zikr* influenced many other forms and types of religious chant. One of these was known as *yakkakhoni* (in Tajik) or *yakkakhonlik* (in Uzbek), meaning "individual song." As a constituent part of the *zikr*, *yakkakhonlik* was usually performed during the breaks between the principal parts of the ritual, or upon conclusion of the entire cycle of the *zikr* while the participants rested. In time, *yakkakhonlik* became an independent practice with its own style of singing.

Katta ashula (Great song) is another song genre connected to the chanting style of *zikr*. *Katta ashula* was widely performed in the Ferghana Valley, particularly in the cities of Andijan, Ferghana, Kokand, Namangan, Khujand, and in Tashkent and environs. *Katta ashula* sets spiritual poetry in an unmetered, declamatory style sung loudly yet expressively, in a high tessitura. At the same time that it reflects the influence of the *zikr*, its poetic form reflects the quantitative meters of the classical *aruz* system of prosody, whose origin was in Arabic and Persian poetry. Most *katta ashula* compositions are set to the poetic forms *ghazal*, *masnavi*, or *mukhammas*, and the musical material is "through composed": that is, rather than repeat a short musical structure through many couplets or quatrains of text, as is typical in folk music, the melody of *katta ashula* develops to a point of culmination, called *awj*, as is characteristic in Uzbek-Tajik songs from the classical *maqom* repertory (see chapter 18).

LISTEN

Example 22.5. "Qoilman" *katta ashula*, composed by Hamroqulqori Turaqulov, performed by Mahmudjon Tojibaev. Lyrics by Muqimiy. From *In the Shrine of the Heart: Popular Classics from Bukhara and Beyond*, vol. 7 of *Music of Central Asia* (SFR, 2010), track 9.

Mahmudjon Tojibaev performs "Qoilman" a cappella, as is traditional for *katta ashula*. During the Soviet era, however, *katta ashula* was codified as a strictly artistic practice, and was transformed into a secular genre that included spare instrumental accompaniment—often in the form of sustained drone notes.

Nigoro, ohu yangligh chashmi mastoningga qoyilman,	Oh beloved, I am enchanted by your gazelle-like eyes,
Qizil gulghunchasidek la'li khandoningga qoyilman.	I am enchanted by the ruby color of your lips, red like a flower bud.
Qoronghu kechani ravshan qilur yuzdin niqob olsang,	The dark night brightens when you lift the veil from your face,
Emas kim bölsa mundogh mohito-boningga qoyilman.	I am enchanted by your incredible moon-like face.
Khirom etsang chamanlarda, qad-aming, körsa raftoring	If you appear in the flower garden with your graceful step, then seeing your step
Giribon chok etib ma'yus guliston-ingga qoyilman.	And tearing down the gates from despair, I'll be enchanted by your rose-colored garden.

Muqimiy dam-badam yuz jon nisor
   otingni bilmayidur

       With each breath, Muqimiy sacrifices his
       soul to you a hundred times, but he
       doesn't know your name.

Bölib ohu suman yölingda tobon-
   ingga qoyilman.

       Like a gazelle following your jasmined
       trail, I am enchanted by your radiance.

Another example of *katta ashula* is presented in example 22.6—this one performed in antiphonal style by two older singers from Isfara, a small city in northern Tajikistan where musical traditions of the Ferghana Valley have been well conserved.

WATCH   **Example 22.6. Bobo Raykhon and companion perform *Katta Ashula* in Isfara, Tajikistan. Filmed by Saodat Ismailova and Carlos Casas, 2012.**

STUDY QUESTIONS

1. Compare the performance of Mahmudjon Tojibaev with that of Bobo Raykhon and his companion. How are they similar and different? Which one do you think is closer to the kind of music and chant that took place during *zikrs*?

2. What do you think is the purpose behind singing *katta ashula* in a high vocal tessitura?

3. In what ways is *katta ashula* similar to and different from other genres of religious song and chant?

4. Even if you cannot understand the words, do you find the text easy to follow? Why do you think the singer repeats certain words and phrases?

POPULAR RELIGIOUS MUSIC AND CHANT

Sufi orders were not the only religious organizations in Central Asia. Other religious groups included the community of *qalandar*s or "wandering dervishes," who at times assumed the form of an independent order, the Qalandariyya. Many cities had a *qalandarkhona* (*qalandar* house) where *qalandar*s lived. *Qalandar*s wandered through the neighborhoods and bazaars of the city in search of alms, chanting prayers and spiritual songs that were sometimes accompanied by a noisy rattle (*safail*). *Qalandar*s had their own traditions of vocal performance rooted in an antiphonal alternation of chorus and soloist, and also practiced their own simplified form of *zikr*.

Tellers of religious legends and history called *maddoh* were close in spirit to the *qalandar*s as well as to the Arab folk preachers of the first centuries of Islam, the *kassam* (storytellers). At the same time, they represented a folk version of the professional preachers (*wa'iz*) found throughout the Muslim world, including Central Asia. In the cities, the *maddoh*s usually lived in a separate group or constituted an independent neighborhood. They were in close touch with musicians, *qalandar*s, and other like-minded denizens of the medieval city, and together with them created a kind of bohemian cultural milieu. The principal repertory of the *maddoh*s consisted of *dastan*s—narratives, stories, and legends with historical, religious, and homiletic contents. They were well acquainted with music, knew a variety of spiritual songs and chants, and skillfully employed theatrical methods of religious persuasion. Like the *qalandar*s, the *maddoh*s performed spiritual songs on texts by Sufi poets that used similar means of musical expression. Performances by *maddoh*s became noticeably more active during the major Muslim holidays.

Among Central Asian Sufis, *qalandar*s, and *maddoh*s, the interpretation and singing of Sufi-inspired poetry by authors such as Yassawi, Mashrab, Bedil, and Hafez enjoyed great popularity and constituted an independent type of spiritual art. Cities, towns, and even villages cultivated a tradition of spiritual gatherings devoted to the work of particular poets: a gathering devoted to the Hikmat (collected works)

Mahmudjon Tojibaev.
Photo by Sebastian Schutyser. Courtesy of Aga Khan Music Initiative.

*Qalandar*s in the courtyard of a *qalandarkhane* in Samarkand, between 1904–1915.
Courtesy of Library of Congress, Prints and Photographs Division, Prokudin-Gorskii Collection, reproduction no. LC-DIG-prok-02313.

of Yassawi was known as Yassawikhonlik; if devoted to Hafez, it was called Hafez-khonlik, to Bedil, Bedilkhonlik, and so on.

The following musical example presents a *qalandar* song recorded in Bukhara from a blind singer named Muhammad Aminjon Nasriddinov (b. 1927), who was not himself a *qalandar* but who remembered this song from his childhood, when itinerant *qalandars* often visited his neighborhood.

LISTEN

Example 22.7. *Qalandar* song, performed by Muhammad Aminjon Nasriddinov. Recorded by Theodore Levin and Otanazar Matyakubov in Bukhara, 1990. From *Bukhara: Musical Crossroads of Asia* (SFR, 1991), track 12.

Muhammad Aminjon Nasriddinov.

Photo by Theodore Levin

An English translation of the *qalandar* song is provided below. As the performer sings, he taps his fingers softly on a frame drum.

> God, don't separate us faithful ones from our prophet,
> Don't separate us from Abu Bakr, Omar, Usman, and Haydar.
> Faith is a jewel, don't separate your servants from faith.
> Amen, amen, amen.
> If you want to know my essence, know that it is from the
>   cleanest rays.
> This precious jewel is higher than the very depth of good.
> I am eternally yearning for you, our Lord.
> Don't separate us from you until the Day of Judgment.
> (first four lines repeat)
> When the Day of Judgment approaches, Truth will triumph,
> Everyone will find his prophets.
> Whoever renounces his faith will regret it.

STUDY QUESTIONS

1. How does the *qalandar* song distill religious teachings for popular consumption? What is the principal theme of the text?

2. Would the effect of the text be equally as strong if it were recited instead of sung? What is it about singing a text, even in a simple melodic style like that of the *qalandar* song, that makes it powerful?

Carriers of Religious Tradition among Women

In the social world of Central Asian women, carriers of religious and spiritual traditions typically filled several different roles that all served women's spiritual and cultural life (see chapter 25). In Uzbekistan and Tajikistan, these figures included the *otin-oy* or *otin-bibi*, *khalfa* (wedding entertainer in Khorezm), *sozanda* (wedding entertainer in Bukhara), and *guyanda* (professional mourner). Major functions included reading the Qur'an and saying prayers for women, lamenting and reciting poetry at funerals; performing at women's gatherings that featured spiritual songs and readings of religious poetry, and leading female *zikr*s, which sometimes had the special aim of promoting healing. Folk forms of *zikr* also found an outlet in melodramatic or ecstatic funerary rituals known as *sadr* or *sama'* performed by women.

Female singers (*zakir* and *atin*) distinguished by a high level of vocal mastery performed the technique of "saw *zikr*," which was developed through long years of practice. Women had their own forms of ritual connected to the patrons of female professions and to women's way of life. These patrons included Bibi Fatima, Bibi Seshanba (literally, "Mrs. Tuesday," the day on which women gathered to perform special songs, read prayers and poems, and share food), Bibi Mushkul Kushod ("Mrs. Overcoming Difficulties"), and others. These rituals included special chants dedicated to mythical figures. In religious songs, women typically used poems of Yassawi, Mashrab, Huvaido, and other mystical poets.

Women's folk songs appeared most commonly at women's social evenings and weddings, and in festivals and rituals such as *Lola* (the tulip holiday) and *Nowruz* (New Year's)—in particular, in connection with the preparation of the ritual food *sumalak* (a type of porridge). Among musical instruments, the most popular were *dutar* and *doira*, and in Khorezm, also the harmonium.

The declaration of independence by the new governments of Central Asia following the breakup of the Soviet Union in 1991 set off an intensive process of Islamic revivalism. This revivalism led in turn to a corresponding revival of many forms of religious music that either had been forgotten or were being practiced illegally. For example, during Ramadan, children have once again started visiting houses, and even offices, to ask for money or sweets. At the beginning of the twenty-first century, religious music in the cities, towns, and villages of Central Asia shows signs of reclaiming its former place as a central element in the spiritual culture of the region.

Khalfas Ulibibi (*left*) and Nazira Baijanova in Khiva, Uzbekistan.
Photo by Theodore Levin.

Women playing *doira*s at a wedding in Dargh, Tajikistan.
Photo by Theodore Levin.

RELIGIOUS MUSIC AND CHANT OF SEDENTARY DWELLERS   **397**

NOTES

A proto-version of this chapter was published as "Sacred Music and Chant in Islamic Central Asia" in *The Middle East,* vol. 6 of *The Garland Encyclopedia of World Music,* ed. Virginia Danielson, Scott Marcus, and Dwight Reynolds (Routledge, 2002), 935–947.

1. Transoxania: literally "Beyond the Oxus," from Arabic *mā warā al-nahr:* the territory between the two great rivers, Amu Darya—the River Oxus of antiquity—and Syr Darya).

2. The "Four Books" (*Chor* [or *Chakhor*] *Kitob*) is a popular book and textbook for religious schools in Central Asia. It consists of four works by different authors in Tajik-Persian that spell out the pillars of Islam and the ritual duties of Muslims on the basis of Hanafi doctrine.

CHAPTER 23 Sufism and the
Ceremony of *Zikr*
in Ghulja

MUKADDAS MIJIT

Sufism profoundly affected Uyghur culture in the region of Ghulja, an old city
in the Ili Valley region of northwestern China.[1] Scholars have documented
the genealogy and development of several Sufi brotherhoods in the region—the
Naqshbandi, Yassawi, and Qadiri were the most prominent—and each brotherhood had its own *khanaqa* (prayer house) with its own adherents. The Sufi practice
of *zikr* (remembrance of God), which typically includes singing and music, was
widespread in and around Ghulja. These ceremonies were led by Sufi masters who
had spent many years studying in the madrasahs of great centers of Islamic culture
and spirituality, such as Bukhara and Samarkand, and who acquired their religious
titles from these schools.

Every Wednesday and Thursday, members of the Sufi brotherhoods used to
meet in their *khanaqa*s, where they prepared meals for the poor people of the city
or the village, prayed together, and practiced the ceremony of *zikr*. The Sufi masters, or *khelipe* (cognate with "caliph," from Arabic *khalifah*: "successor," "representative"), were highly respected in their particular quarter of the city, and they were

Views of the old city of
Ghulja.

sometimes considered to be the spiritual fathers of Ghulja. No marriage or funeral took place without the presence and participation of a *khelipe*. Numerous rituals and ceremonies were linked to Sufism, but over the centuries, some of them lost their original meaning, and these days, they are simply considered to be activities that perpetuate Uyghur tradition.

Following China's establishment of the Xinjiang Uyghur Autonomous Region in 1955, and especially during the Cultural Revolution, which affected the whole of China, Sufi brotherhoods suffered a great setback. All religious practices were banned, all *khanaqa*s were closed, Sufi masters were sent to prison, and their books and manuscripts were destroyed. All Sufi activities stopped. Negative official propaganda about Sufism also played an active role in excluding this tradition from Uyghur culture. Fortunately, the government ban and the forced indifference of Uyghurs to Sufi practices did not completely obliterate the cultural memory of the musical and poetic treasures of Sufism.

For the Uyghur Sufis of Ghulja, as for all Sufis, *zikr* is one of the essential forms of praying to God, and for showing the pathway to God. *Zikr* is at once a spiritual practice that involves specific verbal and physical techniques and a form of ceremony that requires a special place, a favorable time, and a clear reason for being held. It also requires the presence of people who are experienced in the practice of *zikr* as well as one or more singers (*hapiz*). Beyond the obligatory participation of these specialists, however, a *zikr* may be open to anyone, regardless of their nationality or religion, and there is no demand for specific knowledge of Sufi practices. Songs, poems, prayers, and other ritual elements such as meals and salutations are important in the *zikr,* and non-initiates can readily participate in many of them.

I have had the opportunity to witness two *zikr* ceremonies: the first, indirectly—from a film made by a friend at my request—and the second, personally. In both cases, the reason for organizing the *zikr* was important. The first *zikr* was held in observance of Mevlut (Arabic: Mawlid)—the birthday of the Prophet Muhammad; the second *zikr* was part of a circumcision ritual conducted in a village on the outskirts of Ghulja. In present-day Ghulja, the yearly ritual of Mevlut takes place in a pre-designated house belonging to one of the members of a Sufi brotherhood. At the end of every Mevlut gathering, someone will ask for general approval to observe Mevlut in his house the following year. To organize such an event is an honor and joy for the host and his family. Praying together with one's Sufi brothers, nourishing them, and lodging them overnight, allows the host to perform a pious act called *oshre zakat* (making an offering). In the past, this kind of ritual was held in the *khanaqa*s with a large number of people. Nowadays, attendance at *zikr*s is reduced to small numbers of Sufi brothers at individual houses. Nonetheless, the door is open to everyone; even children have the right to attend, and they are allowed to imitate all the movements and singing. Women do not participate in the *zikr* of men, but they are welcome to be a part of the event by standing outside of a door or window. This is not considered discriminatory because there is also a *zikr* in which women are the main participants. As in other situations, men and women are separated—men on one side and women on the other, with the division clearly defined.

Following is a short description of the *zikr* ceremony I attended in the village of Rozimetyuz, near Ghulja, which preceded the ritual circumcision of a young boy. Not all circumcision ceremonies are accompanied by a *zikr*. But the boy's family was religious—his grandfather was a Sufi—and the grandfather had asked his Sufi brothers to come to the family compound for the first important event in the life of his grandson.

At 9:00 PM, one of the guests began the call to evening prayer in the courtyard. The guest was the muezzin from the mosque in Rozimetyuz. Then, as the last prayer of the day began with everyone together, there was a brief silence in the courtyard. The Sufi brothers were in one of the rooms, all in line to pray, as in the mosque. After the prayer, there was a light meal (*ash*) after which the men kneeled and formed two concentric circles (*helqe*). The smaller circle in the center of the room consisted of twelve people, while everyone else who could fit joined the larger circle outside it. Those who could not fit in either of the circles remained standing in front of the entrance to the room.

The circle in Sufism is a phenomenon that has been discussed in numerous works as a symbol of the Sufi way. The system of two circles offers those who have never participated in a *zikr* an opportunity to learn the ritual. The man who directed this *zikr*, Nurjan Hapiz, an erudite *hapiz*, born in 1927, explained: "When people first come to the *zikr*, they stay in the second circle and they're somewhat intimidated by the event. But as they watch the *zikr*, they get acclimated and start learning the movements. Little by little, they become assimilated and start doing the *zikr* like everyone else. The magnetism of the *zikr* is stronger than the ego."

For some minutes, nobody spoke or moved. Everyone prayed intensely but silently in the so-called *zikr khupi*, which marks the beginning of the ceremony. The word *khupi* (Arabic/Persian: *khafī*) means "secret," "hidden," "inner," or "silent," and in this case indicates prayer or *zikr* of the heart, or "silent *zikr*." This practice is symbolically linked to Abu Bakr, the first caliph, and was spread by the Naqshbandi brotherhood.

Nurjan Hapiz.

The second part of the evening took place after the *zikr khupi*, and was much longer. This was the *zikr jehri* (Arabic/Persian: *jahrī*)—"*zikr* with loud voice." There are two kinds of *zikr*s with loud voice. One is collective, where everyone rhythmically repeats a short refrain to a single melodic phrase, accompanied by a *hapiz* who sings the lyrics to a spiritual poem above the repeating refrain phrase.

The second kind of "*zikr* with loud voice" is a solo performance: one person sings emotional poems—usually about death and final judgment—to a melismatic melody. These two kinds of *zikr* may be combined in a single ceremony.

The *zikr* I attended began with a recitation of verses from the Qur'an. Following the recitation, Nurjan Hapiz started to sing in his bel canto voice. The Sufi brothers followed, chanting a melody in unison. The melody had no text but rather a few basic words such as "Allah" and "Hu" (names of God), and was sung in a very slow, unmeasured, and melismatic style. Every syllable was carefully articulated, and there were many sustained notes. A short phrase consisting of these few words was repeated for almost three minutes. Just after this came the ceremony's first "*zikr* with loud voice." Nurjan Hapiz began the *zikr,* and all the others in attendance joined their voices with his. Nurjan Hapiz got up and stood behind the first circle. The *zikr* started with quite a slow rhythmic pulse. The kneeling brothers began moving their bodies backward and forward to the pulse while rhythmically repeating *"Hu Hu Allah!"* with heavy breaths that emphasized the rhythm. After several repetitions of this phrase, Nurjan Hapiz abandoned the refrain and began singing over the rhythmic chanting. For five or six minutes, Nurjan Hapiz sang different poems to the same melody while the other participants in the *zikr* continued to chant. Gradually, the rhythm began to accelerate, and the body movements became more agitated. From time to time, Nurjan Hapiz offered words of encouragement to the Sufi brothers: "That's good! Keep it up! There you go!" As the rhythmic pulse quickened, the melody changed as well. With eyes firmly closed, and bodies

Participants in the *zikr* in the village of Rozimetyuz, near Ghulja.

swaying to the rhythm, the Sufi brothers appeared to have submitted completely to the power of the *zikr*. From time to time, I heard sighs of *"uf Allah"* both from the participants in the *zikr* and from the women who were standing outside the windows. After about twenty-five minutes, Nurjan Hapiz paused and gave a signal to stop the *zikr*.

The Sufi brothers seemed exhausted. Twenty-five minutes of moving their bodies to rhythmic breathing had made them sweaty. While they were resting, Nurjan Hapiz began a solo *zikr*. He sang poems of classical Sufi poets such as Qul Khoja Ehmet (Ahmad Yassawi) and Shah Meshrep (Mashrab) to a highly ornamented melody. When, with tears in his eyes, he sang phrases that spoke about the transience of life, a feeling of sadness descended on those in the room. When one of the Sufi brothers, Haji Ekper, started another chant, almost everyone was crying.

The ceremony continued with one *zikr* after another, the atmosphere growing increasingly intense as the brothers swayed their bodies to and fro. After a number of *zikr*s, Nurjan Hapiz and Haji Ekper sang some poems that spoke about death, the final judgment before God, and the exemplary acts of the Prophet Muhammad. Collective *zikr*s continued one after another, alternating with one or more individual *zikr*s. Some people in the circle seemed to be completely in another world. At 2:00 AM Nurjan Hapiz stopped. He asked everyone to get up and greet one another. Maintaining the form of two concentric circles, the men in each circle moved slowly in opposite directions—clockwise and counterclockwise—greeting each other one by one. "This is our tradition," said Nurjan Hapiz. The Sufi brothers were in the process of greeting each other when I heard cries. I craned my neck to see what was happening. Two men were holding one another by the arms, trembling and crying. They were still in the spiritual ecstasy of the *zikr,* and their emotions exploded. Immediately all the Sufi brothers re-formed the circles and reprised the last *zikr* in order not to leave the two Sufi brothers who were still in spiritual ecstasy without the *zikr*. Little by little, the two men began to return to reality, their tears stopped, and then Nurjan Hapiz slowed the *zikr* down in order to come to the end. "There was great energy and a strong warmth emerging from the room," said Nurjan Hapiz afterward. "After a while we lose ourselves and enter the *zikr*."

The Collective *Zikr*: Breath and Rhythm

I have analyzed the different rhythms, and the close relationship between the rhythms and the Sufi brothers' breathing technique. Nurjan Hapiz had repeatedly insisted on breath as the measure of a well-performed *zikr* (in a collective *zikr*). He also showed me a classification of different *zikr*s based upon the number of inhaled breaths in a single phrase. A *zikr* in which all participants collectively perform two inhaled breaths is a two-beat *zikr,* and the name of this *zikr* is *do zerp* (*do:* "two" in

Persian; *zerp*: "beat," from Persian *zarb*). The other *zikr*s are: *se zerp* (three beats); *chahar zerp* (four beats); and *yek zerp* (one beat), which is no longer practiced. What's most important in a *zikr* is to keep a regular, well-accentuated beat by the use of rhythmic breathing. *Do zerp, se zerp,* and *chahar zerp* are illustrated in example 23.1, and the rhythms are transcribed in the figure below. Upward arrows denote an accented inhalation of breath within the rhythm of the chant.

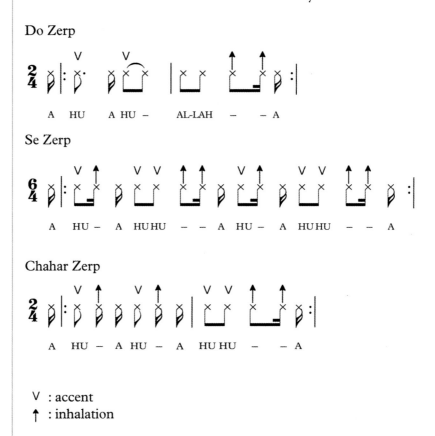

Do Zerp

A HU   A HU –   AL-LAH   –   – A

Se Zerp

A   HU –   A HUHU   – – A HU –   A HUHU   – –   A

Chahar Zerp

A   HU – A HU – A   HUHU   –   – A

V : accent
↑ : inhalation

WATCH **Example 23.1.** Excerpts from the ceremony of *zikr*. Ghulja (Yining), Xinjiang Uyghur Autonomous Region, China, 2007.

This short video shows examples of *do zerp, se zerp,* and *chahar zerp* in the third *zikr* that was done the evening of my visit. The participants chant the syllable *Hu*, one of the names of God, sometimes with phonetic variation of the vowel sound. The physical location of the participants in the *zikr* is linked to the extent of their knowledge of the ceremony: those who know it best are closest to the center.

Time Log

0:00	*Do zerp*
1:00	*Se zerp*
2:24	*Chahar zerp* (while the Sufi brother chant the *chahar zerp,* Nurjan Hapiz sings a *telqin,* a Sufi spiritual poem.)
2:48	This segment picks up 10–15 minutes after the end of the first segment. The tempo of the *chahar zerp* has accelerated slightly. Nurjan Hapiz insists that those who do the *zikr* participate in its rhythmic physical movements in order to coordinate the chanting of the *chahar zerp.*
3:14	*Zikr Kabuter* (*zikr* of pigeons). This segment was filmed in the home of Nurjan Hapiz, who chants an excerpt of a *du zerp.*

These days, those who participate in the Naqshbandi *zikr* in Ghulja have for the most part lost contact with older forms of Naqshbandi spirituality. As the last link to these older traditions, Nurjan Hapiz helped to sustain a cultural memory of the Naqshbandi *zikr* among younger people. Yet the *zikr* cannot exist merely as a social institution. It depends on the spiritual transmission of a leader or teacher (*khalipe*). After the death of Nurjan Hapiz in 2011, the future of the Naqshbandi *zikr* in Ghulja seems uncertain.

NOTE

Ghulja is the traditional Uyghur name of the town—now a city of close to half a million inhabitants whose Chinese name is Yining.

CHAPTER 24 *Dastan* Performance
among the Uyghurs

RAHILE DAWUT AND ELISE ANDERSON

Dastan is a form of oral epic narrative that uses both poetry and prose to tell dramatic stories. Performed throughout Turkic Central Asia as well as by Persian-speaking musicians in Iranian Khorasan and, to a limited extent, in Tajikistan, *dastan* is important and widespread among the Uyghurs, Kyrgyz, Kazakhs, Tajiks, and other non-Han peoples of the Xinjiang Uyghur Autonomous Region (referred to in the remainder of this chapter simply as Xinjiang) of the People's Republic of China, and constitutes the largest category in Uyghur oral literature. With its great length, complex subject matter, and intricate performance style, *dastan* places strenuous demands on the performer, called *dastanchi*. (In southern Xinjiang, performers of *dastan* are typically called *mäddah* rather than *dastanchi*, but for the sake of consistency, the term *dastanchi* will be used throughout this chapter.)[1] Poetic sections of *dastan*s are typically set to music, and most *dastanchi*s accompany their own performance on local instruments.

As a living, performed tradition among the Uyghurs—and, indeed, among other groups in Xinjiang—*dastan* is currently threatened by the fast pace of contemporary life that too often seems incompatible with attendance at multi-hour cultural events and performances. Morever, the number of physical spaces in which *dastanchi*s have traditionally performed are increasingly limited. Compounding the problem is the declining number of *dastanchi*s—a result of an older generation of *dastanchi*s passing from the scene without having trained a younger generation of successors. At the same time, oral epic poetry traditions around the world, such as *dastan,* have achieved regional, national, and international cultural heritage status in some of the places where they are practiced. Scholars and practitioners hope that heritage protection initiatives will help to secure an abiding social space for this art form.

This chapter provides an introduction to the *dastan* tradition of Xinjiang Uyghurs, emphasizing the tradition's repertory, pedagogy, and performance practice. The last section summarizes the most salient characteristics of the tradition, and provides listening and viewing examples for study and analysis. Although our discussion focuses primarily on *dastan* as performed among Xinjiang Uyghurs, we also compare and contrast this performance tradition with the epic poetry traditions of other ethno-linguistic groups in Xinjiang, and more broadly, in Central Asia.

DASTAN REPERTORY

During the last few centuries, the Uyghur *dastan* repertory has circulated and been transmitted both orally and in writing. Manuscripts of *dastan*s from the nineteenth and early twentieth centuries still exist in both private hands and in Xinjiang government archives. State-supported collection, transcription, archiving, and publication of Uyghur folk literature, including epic poetry, in the People's Republic of China began in the 1980s. To date, around a hundred *dastan*s have been collected and published in eight volumes as a result of this work. Besides state-supported collecting, different versions of the same *dastan*s have been collected, analyzed, and published in numerous books and journal articles written by individual local scholars. While publication has led to attempts to standardize and codify the tradition, most *dastan*s continue to exist in multiple versions, both oral and written. Moreover, *dastanchi*s neither learn nor perform *dastan*s in uniform ways, due to the prevalence of local dialects, performance practices, and stylistic idiosyncrasies in the different oasis regions of Xinjiang.

Broadly speaking, two principal traditions of *dastan* have developed among the Turkic-speaking peoples of Central Asia whose names—Oghuz and Kipchak— refer to large tribal confederations and linguistic groupings. Uyghur *dastan* performance belongs to the Oghuz tradition, and differs in a number of ways from the Kipchak *dastan* of the Kyrgyz, Kazakhs, and Tatars. Uyghur and other Oghuz *dastan,* for example, contains sections of prose and sections of poetry that are of more or less equal length, though the amount of prose can sometimes exceed the amount of poetry. Kipchak *dastan,* however, is primarily based on poetry, and typically includes very little prose.

A second difference between Oghuz and Kipchak *dastan* concerns meter and musical accompaniment. Generally, Uyghur and other Oghuz *dastan*s are composed in a variety of meters, and their musical accompaniment is consequently complex and varied. Kipchak *dastan*s, on the other hand, are based on the form of folk *qoshaq*s (short, rhyming verses). Their stanzas are short and relatively simple, and their music favors simpler, more repetitive melodic phrases.

A third difference lies in the topics and contents of narratives in the two traditions. Oghuz narratives incorporate subjects and narratives from the Arab, Persian, and Indian literary traditions, while Kipchak *dastan*s tend to draw more exclusively from local subjects. Uyghur *dastan*s describe the lives of sedentary dwellers in cities and kingdoms, whereas Kipchak *dastan*s narrate events within clan-based nomadic societies. Uyghur *dastan*s are broad in content, taking thematic material not only from the ancient "heroic age" but also from wars, farmer revolts, and other historical episodes of later eras, as well as from classic love stories. Heroic epics occupy a relatively small part of the Oghuz repertory compared with the Kipchak tradition, in which heroic epic dominates.

Uyghur *dastan* can be divided into five main types on the basis of content: heroic, romantic, religious, historical, and didactic.

Heroic *dastan*s tell of the deeds of individual heroes throughout history. *Oghuznamä*, arguably the most famous heroic epic of the Uyghurs, recounts heroic acts in the period of Uyghur ethnic identity formation. This *dastan,* also extant among other Turkic-speaking peoples, is often regarded as a "mother" *dastan.* It describes at great length the Oghuz khan's adolescence and the wars in which he engaged with the enemies of the Turkic peoples; how he brought together surrounding small tribes and built a kingdom; and the ways in which he divided up his land among his children—Ay (moon), Pärizat (born of a fairy), Kün (sun), Yultuz (star), Tagh (mountain), and Déngiz (sea), who were born to his two wives.

Romantic *dastan*s focus on the contradictions, struggles, and tragedies of romance, sharing titles and themes with epics known throughout West Asia and Central Asia while also incorporating local lore and history. One of the best known of these, *Tahir-Zöhrä,* begins with the arranged marriage of the future children of two kings, Aqkhan and Qarakhan. When Aqkhan dies, his son Tahir is orphaned, and Qarakhan helps to raise him. As they grow up, Tahir falls in love with Zöhrä, Qarakhan's daughter. Because Tahir is an orphan, however, Qarakhan does not agree to a marriage, instead drowning Tahir and arranging to give Zöhrä in marriage to a local hero, Qara Batur. Qarakhan is hanged for killing Tahir; Zöhrä then buries Tahir on a mountaintop and takes her own life with a dagger. Qara Batur later takes his own life between Tahir and Zöhrä's resting places.

Religious *dastan*s relate stories of figures such as the Prophet Muhammad and Caliph Ali and his descendants; conflicts like the Karbala War; the origin of various Islamic rules and customs; and various ethical prescriptions for daily life. Although most Uyghurs practice Sunni Islam, most Uyghur religious *dastan*s concern people and events connected to Shi'a Islam, which is likely explained by the presence in southern Xinjiang, where *dastan* is most widely performed, of small communities of Shi'a Muslims actively engaged in the perpetuation of the epic poetry tradition. The *dastan Päyghämbär äläyhissalamning täwällutnamisi* (The account of the prophet's birth) recounts the early life of the Prophet Muhammad, describing how he was raised by his uncle, Abdul Mutallip, after his parents' death. It also tells of how the angels Gabriel and Michael descended from the heavens on the wings of two birds when Muhammad was four years old, how they tore open his stomach, throwing out the jealousy and arrogance they found inside, and replaced them with patience, satisfaction, and care for others.

Historical *dastan*s are based on real people and events, including farmer rebellions and the exploits of famous figures, mostly drawn from the eighteenth century or later. *Abdurakhman Pasha* tells about the life of its eponymous figure. When Abdurakhman Pasha turned seven, he drank *khizir* (a type of "life-giving water" or "fountain of youth," connected to a mythical figure of the same name), which turned him into a learned person. In his teenage years, he gathered and began conducting military exercises with a group of young men in Khotan, secretly training them for an uprising. They battled with Qing soldiers, ultimately killing the leader who had taken Khotan, and set up a new government. Abdurakhman Pasha was eventually killed by Ismayil, a traitor within his own circle.

Didactic *dastan*s are meant to teach life lessons. While all *dastan*s include didactic elements, an explicitly didactic *dastan* is one that tells a morality tale. For example, a famous didactic poem, *Ziwidä qara köz* (Ziwidä the black-eyed), describes how Mämät Kérim taz (Mämät Kérim the bald), a lazy, greedy, poor, and dim-witted man, takes a girl named Ziwidikhan as his wife. Ziwidikhan, who suffers because of her husband's laziness, wants a divorce, and when Mämät Kérim taz does not agree, she runs away to her native village. Mämät Kérim taz eventually regrets his actions and asks forgiveness from his wife, whom he then takes back home. He works hard to improve his life and provide for his household.

The Uyghur *dastan* tradition has been enriched by epic poems that are widely known not only throughout Central Asia but in West Asia, the Middle East, and India, thus reflecting the complex historical, ethnic, cultural, and religious ties that bind the Uyghurs to the peoples and cultures of surrounding regions.

The breadth of the Uyghur *dastan* repertory means that no single performer can perform all of it. Rather, individual performers develop a personal repertory from within the larger *dastan* repertory. Some *dastanchi*s know only one or two *dastan*s. Many more know at least several epics, and some of the most skilled performers might know ten to fifteen different epics. Repertory varies according to a performer's location, master (*ustaz*), interests, and talent.

Learning to Perform *Dastan*

Dastan has traditionally been transmitted to successive generations of performers through *ustaz-shagirt* (master-apprentice) relationships. Would-be performers

TABLE 24.1. SOME POPULAR EPICS IN THE UYGHUR *DASTAN* TRADITION

HEROIC	ROMANTIC	RELIGIOUS	HISTORICAL	DIDACTIC
• *Oghuznamä* • Chin Tömür Batur • Alip Ärtunga • Dädä Qurqut • Gör Oghli • Yüsüp-Ähmäd • Iskändärnamä	• *Hörliqa-Hämrajan* • Qämärshah-Shämsijanan • Sänubär • Pärhad-Sherin • Läyli-Mäjnun • Yüsüp-Ziläykha • Tahir-Zöhrä • Gherip-Sänäm	• *Päyghämbär äläyhissalamning täwällutnamisi* (The account of the prophet's birth) • *Patimämning wapatnamisi* (The death of Fatima) • *Kiyiknamä* (The deer) • *Kärbala*	• Yachibäg • Ömär Batur • Siyit Nochi • Abdurakhman Pasha • Nuzugum • Tömür Khälipä • Ebäydullakhan • Häwzikhan	• *At bilän tögining eytishishi* (A conversation between a horse and a camel) • *Ziwidä qara köz* (Ziwidä the black-eyed)

of epics, usually male, apprentice themselves to an *ustaz,* often early in life. They generally learn the narratives of *dastan*s from manuscripts and books while the transmission of music in their lessons is oral and aural: students learn by repeating melodies and phrases demonstrated by their *ustaz* rather than from notated musical scores. After several years of study, usually a sufficient time for a pupil's skill to grow, a *shagirt* gradually earns the right to begin performing in public.

The length and complexity of Uyghur *dastan*s demands skilled performers. A *dastanchi* is responsible for developing a wide range of skills as he learns a repertory, and the process of learning *dastan* is thus long and complex. The length of *dastan*s alone demands that performers have excellent memorization skills. Moreover, because *dastan*s contain both prose and poetry, performers must be able to perform both: prose sections are recited, while poetic sections are sung to the accompaniment of an instrument played by the *dastanchi*. *Dastanchi*s must also be adept at mimicry: their ability to draw in and hold the attention of a crowd comes through their skill at adjusting melody, language, movement, and expression to convey the voices of different characters within a single epic. Additionally, they should have good interpersonal skills and the ability to read crowds in order to adjust a performance to the mood of a particular audience. *Dastanchi*s regularly lengthen performances at which audience members are listening with rapt attention; conversely, they shorten performances when they realize that the audience is unengaged.

PERFORMANCE AND CULTURAL SPACE

Uyghur *dastan*s are recited in important social gathering places, such as village bazaars; *mäshräp* gatherings, where people come together for food, music, games, and dancing; *mazar* (shrine) festivals; and in front of mosques around the time of Friday prayers. Performers may sometimes recite *dastan*s in more private settings, but in general the performances take place in larger social spaces.

Occasionally, groups of two to three *dastanchi*s—usually "classmates" who learned from the same master, or good friends—form a group and perform together in one setting. Prior to the formal start of the performance, they sing a local folksong, or perform a selection from the *muqam* tradition, signaling that *dastan* will be performed in that space. A crowd gathers, circling around the *dastanchi*s; the performance proceeds within this circular configuration. After listeners gather, one *dastanchi* begins to perform. The remaining *dastanchi*s attempt to draw other listeners into the audience by crying out "*ya dost*" (hey, friend) and "*woy*" (oh) to passersby. After the first performer finishes, he prays for the people around him and then collects money from them. Another *dastanchi* follows, first drawing attention—and potential listeners—to himself, and eventually performing another *dastan.* If the audience is large and attentive, a group performance might continue for as long as four to five hours.

According to many *dastanchi*s, in the past, performances of a single *dastan* could last two to three days. On the first day, upon reaching a particularly enthralling place in the epic, a *dastanchi* would stop, pray, collect money, and then tell his audience that he would continue singing the next day. The *dastanchi* would then depart. The next day, audience members would arrive at the performance space and sit, waiting for the *dastanchi* to return. Once again, when the performer came to a particularly interesting point in the *dastan,* he would stop, tell everyone that he would continue the following day, and leave. Dedicated listeners—usually local to the area where the performance was taking place—would return each day, eager to hear the performance through to the end.

Many present-day *dastanchi*s express anxiety about the disappearance of this traditional style of performance, and cite a variety of causes—mainly a lack of time

Listeners gather around a *dastan* performer at the Imam Asim shrine festival, in Khotan, 2011.

Above: Pilgrims making their way into the Imam Asim shrine in Khotan, 2011.

Above right: A view of the Imam Asim shrine, 2011.

and patience on the part of listeners to sit through long *dastan* performances, and a dearth of dedicated listeners connected to a particular village or bazaar. Several *dastanchi*s point out that nowadays the ease of travel and growth of local tourism allows listeners to come from near and far, and these transient audience members might listen to a performance for only part of one day. *Dastanchi*s have also begun shortening their performance of *dastan*s from three to four hours to one to two hours. On the one hand, the ability to "shorten" a *dastan* based on audience response is a skill expected of *dastanchi*s; on the other hand, consistently shorter performances are a contemporary phenomenon—indeed, one that threatens to change the mode and character of the tradition.

Recitation and storytelling inside the Imam Asim shrine in Khotan, 2011.

*Dastanchi*s also express anxiety over the fact that the cultural space for epic poetry performance seems to be disappearing. Changes in shrine visitation and the celebration of shrine festivals as well as changes in the character and frequency of large public gatherings mean that both physical and conceptual spaces for performance are disappearing rapidly. For example, the May shrine festivals at the Imam Asim *mazar* in the Khotan region were the only shrine festivals and the largest forum for *dastan* performance left in Xinjiang in the early 2000s. By 2013, however, the festival was no longer taking place. Additionally, much of the space at bazaars that used to be reserved for epic poetry performance has been sold or rented out to businesspeople. Moreover, the sounds of business, radios, cars, and other modern devices tend to drown out the sound of poetry performance.

SALIENT CHARACTERISTICS OF UYGHUR *DASTAN*

The final section of this chapter addresses five salient characteristics of Uyghur *dastan*. Video examples offer excerpts from performances of different *dastan*s by a variety of *dastanchi*s.

Performer Profiles: Shamämät Pasar'akhun

Shamämät Pasar'akhun was born in 1912 in Kuya Village, Qaraqash County, Khotan. Shamämät studied *dastan* with his father from the age of twelve until he was twenty-six, at which point he began performing *dastan* on his own. The first *dastan* that he learned and performed was *Abdurakhman Pasha*. His repertory included *Qurbannamä*, *Iptamamä*, *Nikahnamä*, *Imami Hüsäyin*, *Siyit Nochi*, *Yüsüp-Ähmäd*, and others. He trained numerous apprentices. In March 2008, Shamämät was recognized as a representative heir of the *dastan* tradition on the Xinjiang Uyghur Autonomous Region Intangible Culture Protection list, and in June 2009, he was recognized on the People's Republic of China National Intangible Culture Protection list.[2] He died in 2009, at the age of ninety-seven.

Shamämät Pasar'akhun reciting *dastan*, 2009.

Performer Profiles: Ubulhäsän Muhämmät

Ubulhäsän Muhämmät was born in 1955 in Kuya Village, Qaraqash county, Khotan, and is a sixth-generation *dastanchi* who learned the tradition from family members. By the age of eighteen, he was able to perform *dastan* independently, accompanying himself on the *rawap* and *tämbur*. His repertory includes more than ten *dastans*, including *Abdurakhman Pasha*, *Iptarnamä*, *Siyit Nochi*, *Imami Hüsäyin*, *Kiyiknamä*, *Toynamä*, and others. In March 2008, Ubulhäsän was recognized as a representative heir of the *dastan* tradition in the Xinjiang Uyghur Autonomous Region Intangible Culture Protection list and in 2013 on the national list.

Ubulhäsän Muhämmät accompanying himself on *tämbur*, 2011.

1. Epic texts show the reciprocal relationships between oral and written literature.

Live, extemporized performance of *dastan* has had an enormous influence on written *dastans*, as well as on other literary forms. Many writers and poets in Uyghur literary history have been inspired by themes and imagery from popular epics. At the same time, written literature has affected—and continues to affect—oral literature. The relationship between the oral and the written is complex and reciprocal. For example, field research in southern Xinjiang, particularly in Khotan, shows that numerous *dastanchi*s have learned epics such as *Abdurakhman*

Above: Dastan performance at Mädäniyät baghchisi (Culture park) in Yäkän (Yarkänd, Shache), 2011.

Above right: A *dastan* in manuscript version, 2011.

Pasha from written versions and altered their language and content slightly in the course of their own performances. In turn, contemporary oral performances are often committed to writing, as scholars work to record, transcribe, translate, and re-disseminate them.

2. The interweaving of prose and poetry in *dastans* is complex and varied.

The vast majority of Uyghur *dastans* contain both prose and poetry. The most salient way to distinguish the two is that prose is spoken, while poetry is sung. The settings of many epics are described in a mixture of poetry and prose, while the main narrative action, along with the inner feelings of the characters, is almost invariably sung in poetic language. There are *dastans* constructed entirely of poetry or entirely of prose, although these are rare. Some older *dastanchi*s have told us about the existence of separate prose and poetry versions of one and the same *dastan,* though no such parallel versions have been documented by scholars. For example, the introduction to a version of *Abdurakhman Pasha* recorded from Ubulhäsän Muhämmät begins in exclusively rhyming poetic form. Other epics, such as a version of *Yüsüp-Ähmäd,* recorded from Turdimämät Nasir, mix prose and poetry throughout both the introduction and the main narrative.

WATCH

Example 24.1. Introduction to *Abdurakhman Pasha,* performed by Ubulhäsän Muhämmät. Filmed by Rahile Dawut, Aynur Kadir, Nijat Niyaz, and Aysajan Yusup, Khotan, Xinjiang Uyghur Autonomous Region, China, 2009.

Time Log

0:00	Introductory melody
0:08	Begins singing "Äy"
0:18	Change in rhythm and pitch
0:19	"Bu taghlar" (these mountains)
1:12	New melody material
1:40	The melody descends; changes in rhythm and pitch signal new material
2:30	Excerpt ends

The text for this example is available on the companion website.

STUDY QUESTIONS

1. The time log notes two rhythmic changes in the excerpt. Can you write out the different rhythmic patterns, and identify what time signature(s) is (are) being used?

2. This excerpt is dominated by relatively consistent, repetitive melodic patterns; as with rhythm, the time log notes points in the *dastan* where melodic changes occur. First, trace out the contours of these different melodic patterns. Second, devise a form of transcription for drawing these patterns in relation to each other.

WATCH   **Example 24.2.** Introduction to *Yüsüp-Ähmäd*, performed by Turdimämät Nasir. Filmed by Rahile Dawut and Mutallip Iqbal, Khotan, Xinjiang Uyghur Autonomous Region, China, 2010.

This longer excerpt is particularly interesting because the rhythmic and melodic material are more varied than in the previous excerpt from *Abdurakhman Pasha*. Additionally, the excerpt provides excellent examples of vowel elongation and high harmonic frequencies, which sound similar to throat-singing. Vowel elongation and high frequencies occur at several places throughout the excerpt, though they are particularly prominent in the section lasting from 4:11 through 7:56.

Time Log

0:00	Recitation of prose opening begins
0:24	Accompaniment begins
0:38	Poetic section begins

1:15	First instance of vowel elongation at the end of a phrase
2:06	More vowel elongation
2:21	Stops playing and returns to prose
2:35	Straight accompaniment; performer tunes *dutar* as he strums
3:09	Singing begins, this time higher than previous melodic material
3:17	Accompaniment and melody descend
4:09	Meter, rhythm and strumming change; following melody contains new material as well; section contains many instances of vowel elongation at the ends of phrases
7:56	Meter change, accompanied by changes in rhythm in melody
8:09	Prose narration through end of excerpt

The text for this example is available on the companion website.

STUDY QUESTIONS

1. There are two major rhythmic changes in this excerpt—at 4:09 and 7:56, as noted in the time log. Can you identify the time signatures that correspond to them?

2. Attempt to draw the different rhythmic patterns used in this excerpt.

3. Draw the melodic contours, as well.

4. What are the differences in the way that poetry and prose appear on the page?

5. How does the musical accompaniment differ in poetry and prose sections?

6. How do the rhythmic qualities of the two sections differ?

7. Can you hear or see any other differences between *dastan* prose and poetry? Can you guess what other differences there might be?

3. *Dastans* use two types of versification: *barmaq* and *aruz.*

The repertory of Uyghur *dastan*s includes two distinctive types of poetic prosody (*wäzin*): *aruz* and *barmaq. Dastan*s tend to be written in one or the other *wäzin* and performed consistently in that way. Aruz *wäzin*, a quantitative system that classifies syllables as "long" or "short," is an Arabo-Persian versification system whose use in Turkic poetry and oral tradition began sometime around the eleventh century. Famous Central Asian literary works found among the Uyghurs and other Central Asian peoples, such as *Qutadghu Bilik* (The wisdom of royal glory), use *aruz wäzin. Aruz* is often used in Uyghur epics that address themes of religion and love as well as in the texts of the Uyghur *on ikki muqami* (Uyghur twelve *muqam*s). (For an explanation of *aruz*, see chapter 18.)

Barmaq (finger) *wäzin* is a traditional scheme of poetic verse organization in Turkic languages that is based on the number of syllables per line—usually seven, eight or eleven. Among the Uyghurs it was used widely up through the time of the Quju (Qocho; Gaochang) Uyghur kingdom (c. 860–1284), and even appears in some of the poetry found in the *Qutadghu Bilik,* but fell out of wide use during the Chaghatay literary period (c. fourteenth to mid-twentieth centuries), when Arabo-Persian literary forms were more in vogue. *Barmaq wäzin* came back into popular use in Uyghur epic poetry performance around the 1940s—a period in which a revival of traditional Turkic cultural forms began—and is still used today, particularly in historical *dastan*s, as well as in folk *qoshaq*s (short rhyming verses).

The following two examples illustrate the difference between *aruz wäzin* and *barmaq wäzin*. Example 24.3 is a religious *dastan, Patimämning* wapatnamisi (The death of Fatima), which is composed in *aruz wäzin*. Example 24.4 is a historical narrative, *Häwzikhan,* which is composed in *barmaq wäzin*.

ACTIVITY

In each example, count the number of syllables per line of text. For example 24.3, which is composed in *aruz wäzin*, try to jot down the pattern of "long" and "short" syllables in each line of text. Now go back to examples one through four, listen to the recordings and, as you follow the text, try to determine whether it represents an example of *barmaq* or of *aruz*. Do any of the texts include both verse forms? Based on the four examples, can you identify a pattern that links the type of metrical scheme (*barmaq* or *aruz*) with the contents of the *dastan* (historical, religious, romantic)?

Example 24.3. Excerpt from the *dastan Patimämning wapatnamisi* (The death of Fatima), WATCH performed by Mämättokhti Yasin. Filmed by Aynur Kadir, Khotan, Xinjiang Uyghur Autonomous Region, China, 2010.

Bü–wi Pa–ti–mäm bir kün–i–si uy–qi–lap är–di,	One day when Fatima was sleeping,
A–shul za–man Rä–su–lil–la chüsh–i–gä kir–di.	The Prophet appeared in her dream.
Äh–ding–gä tur–ghin jan–im qiz–im, däp är–di,	"Hold to your promise, my dear daughter," he said,

Yul–ing–iz–gha mun–tiz–ir–män dé–di dost–lär.	"I expect you to come," he said,
Bu chüsh–lär–ni kör–gän za–man oy–ghan–di–lär,	She woke up at the time when she had this dream,
Där–hal qop–up khé–mir qil–ip, nan yaq–ti–lär.	She immediately got up, made dough, and baked bread.

—TRANSLATION BY ELISE ANDERSON AND MUTALLIP IQBAL

WATCH

Example 24.4. Excerpt from the *dastan Häwzikhan,* performed by Mämättokhti Tokhti Daka. Filmed by Mutallip Iqbal, Kashgar, Xinjiang Uyghur Autonomous Region, China, 2010.

Bagh–e–riq di–gän yär–dä,	In the place called Bagheriq,
Yü–süp Mi–rap Bi–gim bar i–di	There was Yüsüp Mirap Bigim,
A–ri–ghol di–gän kän–ti–dä,	In the village called Arighol,
Ba–ha–wu–dun Yüz Besh–i bar idi	There was Bahawudun Yüz Beshi.
Bu ikk-äy-län a-ghi-nä idi	The two of them were close friends.

—TRANSLATION BY ELISE ANDERSON

4. Dastan melodies may be either simple or complex.

Scholars in Xinjiang divide the melodies that accompany poetic sections of a *dastan* into two categories: complex (*muräkkäp ahang*) and simple (*addiy ahang*). For example, based on melodic range and content, *Yachibäg,* a Qomul (Hami) *dastan,* is classified as a "melodically complex *dastan*" (*muräkkäp ahangliq dastan*). Meanwhile, popular Khotan *dastan*s, such as *Siyit Nochi* and *Abdurakhman Pasha,* which are performed to repetitive melodic patterns, are referred to as "melodically simple *dastan*s" (*addiy ahangliq dastan*). The distinction between simple and complex melodies tends to correspond to region, such that most Qomul melodies are glossed as "complex" and most Khotan melodies as "simple." For sake of comparison, an excerpt from the Qomul *dastan Yachibäg* is provided in example 24.5 (compare with *Abdurakhman Pasha,* a *dastan* from Khotan, excerpted in example 24.1).

LISTEN

Example 24.5. Excerpt from the *dastan Yachibäg,* performed by Ibrahim Yaqup (vocals, *ghijäk*) and Säydul Nursha (*rawap*). Recorded by Rahile Dawut, Qomul, Xinjiang Uyghur Autonomous Region, China, 2009.

5. *Dastanchis* often incorporate multiple voices into a single epic poem.

The language of *dastan* is rich in lively and expressive forms. The heightened poetic and aesthetically pleasing language of epic poetry sets it apart from the language of everyday life. While a *dastan* may be performed in the first person or sometimes in a mixture of first and third person perspectives (for example, *Siyit Nochi* and *Nuzugum*), most *dastan*s are performed in the third person, with the *dastanchi* acting as an omniscient narrator who possesses the power to tell stories from multiple viewpoints. A *dastanchi* must be skilled at conveying different voices and personalities within a single *dastan*. To do so *dastanchi*s may change the tone and pitch of their voice and use distinctive gestures, body movements, and facial expressions. Representations of voices and personalities are often quite subtle, and are sometimes signaled only through the narrative itself, for example, in linguistic cues such as "he said" at the end of a block of quoted text. Consequently, it can be difficult to discern where characters change.

WATCH

Example 24.6. Excerpt from the *dastan Siyit Nochi,* performed by Mämättokhti Yasin. Filmed by Rahile Dawut and Aynur Kadir, Khotan, Xinjiang Uyghur Autonomous Region, China, 2009. Subtitles translated by Joshua L. Freeman and Zulpiye Zumretshah.

Time Log

0:01	Introductory music
0:13	Text begins with "Hey"
1:34	A leader named Khan Dotey speaks
1:49	Khan Dotey's speaking ends
1:52	Siyit Nochi speaks
2:00	Siyit Nochi's speaking ends
2:03	Group of people speak to Siyit Nochi
2:25	Group speech ends
2:29	Siyit Nochi speaks again
2:32	Siyit Nochi's speech ends
2:32	Narrative description begins
2:52	Leader jokes with Siyit Nochi
3:05	Clip ends

STUDY QUESTIONS

1. Can you hear changes in the performer's voice?

2. Can you see changes in the performer's body or face?

3. Would you have been able to identify any changes in character without being provided with a log?

NOTES

1. In the past, *mäddah* denoted a performer who recites poems without instrumental accompaniment, while *dastanchi* referred to performers who accompany their epic poetry on instruments. This distinction is no longer common. Today, scholars in Xinjiang tend to refer to all epic poetry reciters as *dastanchi*.

2. National- and regional-level intangible cultural heritage lists in China, which date to 2006 and 2007, are separate from but modeled clearly on those created by UNESCO. Regional-level cultural heritage (for example, that of Xinjiang or another autonomous region/province) is determined and administered by the *Wenhua ting* (the regional-level culture bureau), while national-level cultural heritage is the sole province of the *Wenhua bu* (the highest national-level bureau of culture in China).

CHAPTER 25 # Female Musicians in Uzbekistan

OTIN-OY, DUTARCHI, AND MAQOMCHI

RAZIA SULTANOVA

These days, the most famous Uzbek musicians beyond the borders of Uzbekistan are women. Yulduz Usmanova and Sevara Nazarkhan are admired worldwide by pop music audiences, and represent Uzbek music to global youth culture. Munojat Yulchieva is the classical music diva who first introduced the beauty of Uzbek classical music to the West, performing for the last twenty years at the world's best festivals. Nodira Pirmatova's recordings of classic Uzbek popular songs, released by US-based Smithsonian Folkways Recordings, have launched the singer into an active international touring schedule. By contrast, in Uzbekistan itself, the biggest music stars are male. What accounts for this discrepancy? To seek answers, we must look at the social role of female musicians in Uzbekistan, both historically and in the present. We also need to clarify what we mean by "women's music." Is it music performed *by* women *for* women, or does it include music performed by women for mixed audiences? How did the radical social changes that engulfed Central Asia beginning in the 1920s with the rise of Soviet power in the region affect women's role in musical life? And how did the role of female musicians evolve after the breakup of the Soviet Union, when Uzbekistan became an independent country?

Nodira Pirmatova.
Photo by Sebastian Schutyser. Courtesy of Aga Khan Music Initiative.

As a preface to answering these questions, we must keep in mind that for centuries women in sedentary regions of Central Asia, which includes much of the territory that comprises the modern nation of Uzbekistan, were largely segregated from men. Islamic law and local interpretations of Islamic custom dictated that most women were traditionally subordinated to male power and authority, although female members of royal and aristocratic families were frequently active in literature and the arts, including the performing arts. In cities, towns, and even villages, dwellings were typically divided into a male area and a female area. The female area, called *ichkari* (interior), was accessed through a corner of the courtyard, away from the entrance used by men. When community gatherings or festivities were held in a family dwelling, men and women gathered in their own respective parts of the household. Female musicians and dancers shared their talent with other women while remaining unseen—if not entirely unheard—by men.

In remote parts of Uzbekistan there are still women who have spent most of their life in the *ichkari,* with limited access to the male part or guest area of their household. There, they raised children behind the high clay walls of their familial dwelling, and only rarely traveled away from their home. Usually the *ichkari* of one household is interconnected with the *ichkari* of neighboring households through openings in the walls that make it possible for women to move from their own house through an entire village while remaining hidden from the gaze of men. The lives of rural women developed in this enclosed environment, which was subject to few outside influences.

In rural areas today, women often perform music at home. They sing lullabies to infants, teach songs to children, and improvise singing-dialogue joke-songs that use different sayings and proverbs. Since women are typically in charge of child-care, they are also typically responsible for a child's first steps in music. Some forms of music-making that publicly belong to the world of male musicians may initially be taught by women. For example, one well-known Uzbek male musician confided to an interviewer, "Don't tell anyone, but my first music lessons on the *ghijak* [spike fiddle] were given to me by my grandmother!"

Women's music-making in contemporary Uzbekistan includes domestic music performed inside the household—as a rule by the women of the household themselves—for family celebrations, gatherings of female friends, or healing purposes, as well as various kinds of professional musical genres performed for a larger public or audience, often at festivals or competitions held in cities. Examples of the latter include Western classical music performance and composition, and various forms of pop music (see chapter 33). This chapter discusses both domestic and professional music-making by women, with special attention to domestic music, which has rarely been a focus of scholarly research or documentation.

DOMESTIC MUSIC: *OTIN-OY*

Otin-oy is the word used to designate women who are spiritual leaders within communities of women—usually in rural areas. Although uneducated in the conventional sense, they are widely viewed as bearers of spiritual and religious knowledge accessible only to select individuals. The "profession" of *otin-oy* may be learned both through informal apprenticeship within a family lineage and through professional training, which culminates in a formal rite of initiation.

Suppressed by the ideologically ordained "struggle against the past" that was a cornerstone of Communist cultural politics, *otin-oy*s remained underground during the seven decades of Soviet power in Central Asia. Yet while rejected by the Soviet authorities, *otin-oy*s were held in great esteem by the local population. *Otin-oy*s were less vulnerable than male clerics such as mullahs or imams to Soviet efforts to minimize the influence of organized religion, and were able to sustain the religious traditions of their families, passing along sacred knowledge to their children. In this process of transmission, music played an important role in maintaining religious rituals and traditions.

The ritual of Beshik-toy, in which a 40-day-old baby is first put in the cradle. Boisun, Qashqadarya Region, Uzbekistan.

*Otin-oy*s are typically middle-aged or older women of irreproachable reputation who are devoted mothers and wives. In rural areas, *otin-oy*s participate in all significant events in the life of their family and in village life as a whole. However, their activity is strictly limited to the women's social sphere, and as a rule, they are invited only into the *ichkari*—the women's half of the house. Each phase of life can be signified by the performance of an *otin-oy*: the birth of a child; different stages of child-rearing (appearance of the first tooth, first haircut, a child's first time sitting and walking, first day of school); the ritual of circumcision for boys (*Sunnat toy*); meeting classmates after graduating; applying for, obtaining, or leaving a job; betrothal, wedding, divorce; hospitalization or discharge from a hospital; death and mourning rituals; and days of remembrance or commemoration.

For the past twenty years I have been conducting research on *otin-oy* rituals in different areas of Uzbekistan—Andijan, Ferghana, Namangan, Kokand, Samarkand, Bukhara, Tashkent, Boisun, Termez, Denau, Khorezm—as well as beyond Uzbekistan, in Tatarstan (where women who fill an analogous role are called *abystai*), Azerbaijan, Afghanistan, Turkey, and Cyprus (where analogues of *otin-oy* are called *marsiya*). As experience has shown, the advantage of being a female researcher is that I have been able to study hidden and unknown aspects of musical phenomena related to gender, and been able to clarify distinctions between female and male repertories and performance cultures in traditional Muslim societies.

Otin-oy Mukkaram Halilova.

Female gathering in Denau.

Otin-oy Malika in daily life.

Today many young Uzbek girls are eager to learn the professional skills of an *otin-oy*. Recently, while visiting the tiny city of Denau in southeastern Uzbekistan, I was introduced to the local *otin-oy*, Mukkaram Halilova. She had a stunningly beautiful appearance and looked so young that at first I doubted whether she could have had any appropriate training. However, it turned out that her training had been traditional and intensive. She learned her skills from a famous local *otin-oy*. The pure voice and confident demeanor with which she performed rituals was impressive. But four children, a husband, and a variety of family duties kept her busy, and her only excuse for leaving the house was to fulfill her obligations as an *otin-oy*. The house where I was invited to observe her rituals was one of the richest in Denau: spacious rooms traditionally decorated with local ornaments, massive, lavish furniture, rare carpets on the floor, an elegant set of cups and dishes, delicious food—all obligatory trappings of wealth. Otin-oy Mukkaram had been summoned to mark the man of the house's recent promotion in his workplace: he had become the head of the local train station. Otin-oy Mukkaram was surrounded by a circle of friends and neighbors. She performed for a couple of hours, singing and chanting a large range of *ghazal*s and Qur'anic *sura*s. She performed these according to her own preference and choice, with rare taste and confidence. Repetition of rhythmic patterns, a wave-like rise and fall in the dynamics of loudness and softness, and clear tone development were typical features of her style. Otin-oy Mukkaram's unique voice, strong spirit of devotion, and bright personality confirmed that the tradition of the *otin-oy* had indeed been transmitted to a new generation of talented practitioners. And though this transmission continues to take place outside of institutionalized religious education, girls now have the opportunity to study in an official religious school, or madrasah.

In 2006, I visited Jubari Kalon, the only madrasah for girls in Bukhara. The madrasah was an impressive building with a number of rooms where girls receive a high standard of education, not only in reading the Qur'an but also in sewing and computer skills—a new trend in traditional religious education. The girls were well behaved and friendly, and they were fortunate to have the chance to receive a diploma from a prestigious academy. Most of them do not plan to take up Qur'an reading as a future profession, but they want to enjoy their years of study before getting married later. None of the girls studying at Jubari Kalon knew the *otin-oy* repertoire of sacred texts and devotional songs. However, these first steps in opening Muslim education to girls within the framework of Uzbekistan's secular ideology seem to be very successful.

Example 25.1. Excerpt from the "Diwan-i Hikmat" of Hoja Ahmad Yassawi (d. 1166), performed by *otin-oy* Malika Asqarova (b. 1955).

Example 25.1 presents an excerpt from the "Diwan-i Hikmat" of the twelfth-century Sufi poet Hoja Ahmad Yassawi, performed by *otin-oy* Malika Asqarova, who began acquiring the skills and repertoire of an *otin-oy* as a schoolgirl growing up in a village in the Ferghana Valley region of eastern Uzbekistan. The somber, melancholy sound of her voice brings to mind a song of mourning. The poetic text is framed by the Qur'anic phrase *b-ismi-ilāhi r-rahmāni r-rahīmi*—often transliterated as "*Bismillāh al Rahmān al Rahīm*" (In the name of God, the Merciful, the Compassionate)—thus emphasizing the link between spiritual and musical dimensions from the very beginning. This link encourages the listeners' movement from the reality of daily chores to the spiritual world. *Otin-oy* Malika sings each line in a slow and lament-like repetitive manner, calling to mind the Sufi ritual of *zikr*, in which the participants all join together to sing and chant in unison.

Bismillohi rahmoni rahim!

Endi adashdim döstlar, kelgan yölim-dan. (2x)	Now I have lost my way, oh friends!
	Now I have truly lost my way, my friends!
Turgan davlatlarim ketdi qölimdan,	All my wealth and riches have slipped through my fingers,
Ayrildim döstlar yolghiz gulimdan,	I have parted, my friends, with the one and only flower—my Rose,
Hechkim qutilmas faryod ölimdan,	No one can save themselves from their death,
Hechkim qutilmas döstlar jallod Ölimdan.	No one, my friends, can save themselves from their death.
Dunyoni harqiz poyoni yöqdur,	This world has no borders,
Ishqsiz kishilarni iymoni yöqdur.	No faith in passionless people.
Iymonli qullar ölgani yöqdur,	Believers do not perish,
Hechkim qutilmas ushbu ölimdan,	No one can save themselves from their death,
Hechkim qutilmas döstlar faryod ölimdan.	No one, my friends, can save themselves from their death.
Bir kun tiriklik aylar ghanimat, (2x)	Realize that every day of your life is fleeting,
Dunyo sarosar andoq mehnat.	Because in the world there is so much suffering.

Qöymadi hargiz Odam atoni,	Death has not spared even Adam,
Barcha payghambarlar shohu-gadoni.	Nor all prophets, kings, and paupers.
Hechkim qutilmas ushbu ölimdan,	No one can save themselves from their death,
Hechkim qutilmas dod faryod ölimdan.	No one can save themselves from their death.

STUDY QUESTIONS

1. How does *otin*-oy Malika's performance create an aura of spirituality?

2. What do you think the women who listen to the performance of this text take away from it as a kind of spiritual teaching or wisdom?

DUTAR PLAYERS (DUTARCHI)

The chronicles of Uzbek history have been written by men, and in musical treatises many men have been identified as great masters of the *dutar,* the two-stringed, long-necked lute that is one of the principal instruments played in Uzbekistan. The role of female *dutar* players, however, has been largely undocumented. Nevertheless, drawing on a variety of sources, including literature, painting, and oral tradition, we can trace evidence of women's historical involvement with the *dutar.*

Long-necked lutes similar to the *dutar* are depicted in fifteenth- and sixteenth-century miniature paintings that show musical entertainment inside palaces. Iconographic evidence suggests that during that period women played a variety of instruments, including long-necked lutes, in indoor court music. In keeping with local mores, these women performed only for female members of the royal family, and served as professional entertainers.

Late nineteenth-century photographers captured images of young women holding *dutar*s. One such photograph was taken not later than 1896 by the Russian traveler Volyinski, in Khiva, the capital city of Khorezm.[1] Sitting in an opulent setting, a group of five elaborately dressed young girls pose holding a *dutar,* a frame drum (*doira*), a book for singing poetry, and flowers. From their clothing and demeanor, I conclude that these were professional entertainers. It is very likely that they played the *dutar* in association with marriage ceremonies or female Sufi events.

Descriptions of amateur female *dutar* playing also exist in early twentieth-century novels. The novel *O'tkan kunlar* (Days gone by) by the eminent author Abdulla Qadiry (1893–1938) has a scene set in nineteenth-century Margilan, in the

Young entertainers with *dutar* and *doira* in Khiva, late 19th century.
Photo by Volyinski.

Ferghana Valley, that depicts the beginning of a wedding with a female party in the *ichkari*, the women's area of the house. In an amateur capacity, and in the context of celebration, Qadiry's female characters play songs and dances while accompanying themselves on the *dutar*.[2] Another description occurs in a novel by the eminent Uzbek writer Abdulhamid Cho'lpon (1895–1938), *Kecha va kunduz* (Night and day). Cho'lpon's heroine Zebihon and her female companions make music to enliven a journey to another village, playing the *dutar* and singing songs as they travel in a private, enclosed, ox-drawn carriage.[3]

The *dutar* has remained especially prominent in the traditions of Ferghana's female professional musicians. The British National Sound Archive houses recordings by Tajiniso, a famous female Sufi performer, whose semi-classical and folk pieces on the *dutar* were recorded in 1906 by the Latvian company Gramophone. For some time female actresses played the *dutar* onstage at the Theatre of Musical Drama, established in 1920 in Andijan, the Ferghana Valley's largest city. By 1997 the theatre had become moribund, but Sharopat Ahmedova, a retired actress born in 1907, maintained her skill as a *dutar* player into old age. During my research on female *dutar* players in 1996 she told me that all actresses were required to be *dutar* players. The dramatic productions were heavily interspersed with musical interludes in which actresses sang and played the *dutar* on stage. Various female professional performers from Ferghana became prominent. Muhtaram Azizova and Kimsanhan Ahmedova (1942–2004) sang in the demanding improvisational style of *katta ashula* or *juranavoz*, a song genre from the Ferghana Valley that draws on texts in classical poetic forms (see chapter 22).

Uzbek girl playing the *dutar*.
Photo by S. Dudin, circa 1885–1892.

Kimsanhan Ahmedova.

Malika Ziyoyeva Dutar Group.

In the decades that followed the establishment of Soviet rule in Central Asia, in the 1920s, one positive outcome for women was that female professional musicians were encouraged to perform lyrics by contemporary women poets. In Ferghana several women musicians—Lutfihonim Sarymsakova, Mehro Abdullaeva, and Bashorat Hojaeva—sang the poetry of Aminkhudja Mukimy, accompanying themselves on their *dutar*s. In the 1950s and 1960s, another musician, Mavluda Agzamova, sang pieces by the female poets Nodira-begim and Jahonotin Uvaysiy.[4] Mavluda maintained the Sufi tradition of playing *dutar* and singing Sufi songs throughout the entire Soviet period. Archives of the Uzbek State Radio house her recordings of Sufi songs, such as "Topmadim" (I couldn't find him/her/it), "Munojot" (Ascent to God), and many others.

At the same time that the cultural policies of the nascent Soviet Union provided opportunities for women to become professional musicians, they also placed music and musicians baldly in the service of its broad cultural agenda to transform Central Asian traditions through the imposition of European cultural models. This was often done crudely and awkwardly, as chronicled by the conductor of one of Uzbekistan's first new folk orchestras: "We had to overcome the folk musicians' solo traditions, to tune all the instruments to a single orchestra pitch, and to get all its members, used to creative improvisation, to play in a similar manner. Each had to be taught anew even those pieces they had known before."[5] Commenting on the first Uzbek women's *dutar* ensemble, formed in 1939, Uzbek musicologist Ilyas Akbarov remarked: "Most of the girls had only a very vague idea of their instrumental technique."[6] In fact the technique was that of the balalaika, not the *dutar*, Suddenly the *dutar* was expected to be loud and artificially lively, like the balalaika, and its soft and lyrical nature was completely destroyed.

Across the Soviet Union similar innovations were occurring with the development of massed instrumental ensembles and the recruitment of female performers to create an image of emancipation. One student from the Ferghana area, Malika Ziyoyeva (b. 1955), became a celebrated performer, teacher, and innovator of *dutar* traditions in her own right. Malika Ziyoyeva has made many recordings as a soloist, both with the State Radio of Uzbekistan and the Moscow-based recording company, Melodiya, which awarded her a Golden Record disk. Another example of virtuoso *dutar* performance is that of Dutarchi Kizlar (*Dutar* Girls), a female group that displays its astonishing performing skills at home and internationally. This ensemble, created in 1939 by the Uzbek Television and Radio Company under the baton of Ganijon Toshmatov, recently celebrated its seventieth anniversary. During its long life the ensemble has undergone a number of transformations in performance

Example 25.2. "Nolish" (Groan, lament) from the repertoire of Kamiljon Jabarov, performed by Malika Ziyoyeva and her *dutar* ensemble: Dilfuza Yulchieva, Dilorom Turgunova, and Malika Zufarova. From *Uzbekistan: Instrumental Art Music,* VDE CD 974 (Geneva, Switzerland: VDE-Gallo, 1998).

style and the configuration of musicians, but its rich and wide repertoire of classical and folk tunes and songs is still popular with audiences in Uzbekistan.

"Nolish" is drawn from the repertoire of female *dutar* players. The name of the song refers to a particular technique of strumming the *dutar* whose sound brings to mind a groan or lament. The four *dutar* players play the song's irregular rhythms, tremolo strumming patterns, and specially embellished notes in a well-coordinated unison.

STUDY QUESTIONS

As you listen to "Nolish," use letters (A, B, C . . .) to create a diagram that represents the formal structure of the piece. Use A¹, B¹, etc. to indicate variations of "A" and "B." Each letter should represent an identifiable segment of melody that typically is repeated, sometimes with small variations, later in the piece. New melodic material should be indicated by a different letter. Once you have created your diagram, respond to the following questions:

1. How long is the core piece?
2. How many melodic patterns are repeated?
3. What are the main features of the tune?
4. Is "Nolish" a dance or a song? Why?
5. What is the main repetitive rhythmic pattern?

PROFESSIONAL MUSIC: *MAQOM SINGERS (MAQOMCHI)*

Part of the Soviet Union's "struggle against the past" was a broad campaign to combat local traditions in Central Asia that divided men and women into parallel but separate social worlds. One of the campaign's strategies was to create a place for women in previously all-male performing arts traditions. The public concert life that developed rapidly under the aegis of Soviet culture policies mandated not only that opportunities to perform be made available to women but that concert venues be open to mixed male-female audiences. It was in this way that women musicians began to publicly perform the classical urban style of music called *maqom,*

Berta Davydova.

which in pre-Soviet times had been exclusively the province of male performers and male audiences. During the Soviet era, a stellar group of women *maqom* singers burst into public view. Among them, the most famous were Berta Davydova and Kommuna Ismailova.

Berta Davydova (1927–2008) was born into a wealthy Bukharan Jewish family in Margelan, a city in the Ferghana Valley in eastern Uzbekistan. From early childhood, she pursued her love of singing, but for a career, she chose not music but nursing. Berta sometimes sang at evening concerts for the local hospital, and once, during World War II, some well-known Uzbek musicians visited the hospital to perform for wounded soldiers who were recuperating there. A young soldier on crutches suddenly shouted in the middle of the concert, "We also have a singer here!" The audience encouraged Berta to go on stage, and, feeling embarrassed because she was in her white nurse's uniform, she sang only a few songs. Many years later, she told me, "After the concert, one of the musicians, Imamjon Ikramov, who had the title of 'People's Artist,' came to the director of the hospital and told him that I had a unique voice and that he would like to invite me to work at the radio. The hospital director replied that as soon as I turned eighteen I'd have to go to the front lines to fight the Germans, and that it would be better if they took me to sing." And so it was that as a seventeen-year-old girl, Berta Davydova started to sing *maqom*. In her long career as a vocalist, she also taught many other talented female singers the art of *maqom*.

Another outstanding *maqom* performer in Uzbekistan was Kommuna Ismailova.[7] In an interview, she told me the story of how she became a singer and, in particular, a *maqom* singer. Born in the city of Khiva in 1927, Kommuna Ismailova sang from early childhood. She recalled, "In 1934, the great singer and dancer Tamara Khanum blessed me, and advised me to carry on singing. In the spring of 1943, I was invited as a sixteen-year-old to perform for Uzbek soldiers who were being sent to the front lines of the war. Later, I was invited to work at Uzbek Radio, where I stayed for thirty years. I was involved in 468 recordings, performing songs in Uzbek, Russian, Kyrgyz, Tajik, and other languages. With Berta Davydova I sang Shashmaqom, and that was a great opportunity for us. Together we sang all six *maqom*s!"

Among female *maqom* performers in the generation that followed Berta Davydova and Kommuna Ismailova, the brightest star is Munojat Yulchieva (b. 1960), whose name, Munojat, means "prayer" or "spiritual ascent to God." One of the core traditions of Sufism is the continuity of a spiritual chain (*silsila*). In a musical analogy of *silsila*, Munojat has inherited the musical knowledge of her spiritual and musical *murshid* (teacher, master), Shavkat Mirzaev, who in his turn

Munojat Yulchieva.

inherited this knowledge from his father, Muhammadjon Mirzaev, to whom the knowledge was passed by two well-known musicians active in the first decades of the twentieth century, Fahriddin Sadykov and Jurahon Sultanov. From Sadykov and Sultanov, the chain recedes into the nineteenth century, where it slips away into a lineage of musicians whose identity has been lost in our time.

Born in a village near the city of Andijan in the Ferghana Valley, Munojat studied music at Tashkent State Conservatory from 1978 to 1985 under the guidance of Shavkat Mirzaev, focusing on Uzbek classical music. To develop Munojat's voice, Professor Mirzaev invented a completely new vocal style that incorporated elements of both Eastern and Western vocal techniques. These included the local style of *maqom* singing as well as Italian bel canto. To learn the latter, Professor Mirzaev went to Moscow State Conservatory to consult with experts on vocal training. The resultant sound combined nose, head, throat, and chest voices mixed with contemporary elements of vocal production borrowed from pop music. The exceptional two-and-a-half-octave range of Munojat's mezzo-soprano voice made it possible for her to sing a wide variety of songs—both those typically sung by women as well as many songs normally performed by men. Munojat's repertoire includes many songs set to poems by Ali Shir Navo'i (d. 1501), Fuzuli (d. 1556), and Mashrab (d. 1711), whose content is infused with symbols and images drawn from Sufism. Performing such texts was courageous in Soviet Uzbekistan at a time when Sufi-inspired music and poetry were in official disfavor.

As Munojat's career began to develop, she eschewed performing at weddings, which would have compensated her handsomely, in order to present her art in the best possible concert conditions. One remarkable televised concert in 1978 made her an overnight success, and she joined the *maqom* ensemble of Uzbek State Radio. Since 1982, she has worked with the Uzbek State Philharmonic Ensemble. She has been awarded the titles "Merited Artist of Uzbekistan" (1991) and "People's Artist of Uzbekistan" (1994), and decorated with the order "Respect and Order of the People" (1998).

The following audio example presents "Kelmadi," a well-known classical song performed by Munojat Yulchieva. The text is in the poetic form of a *ghazal*—a poem composed according to a metrical scheme of long and short syllables whose form consists of rhymed couplets that share a refrain. The melodic development of "Kelmadi" progresses through a series of structural divisions distinguished by tessitura: an introductory section, *daromad,* set in a low tessitura leads to a section called *miyonkhona,* typically set at the interval of a fifth above the introduction. *Miyonkhona* leads to *dunasr,* set an octave above the *daromad. Awj* ("zenith"), the high-tessitura musical and dramatic culmination of the song, follows *dunasr,* after which the piece gradually descends to the original tessitura in a concluding section

TABLE 25.1. TEXTUAL AND MELODIC FORM IN "KELMADI"

TIME CODE	TEXT	MELODIC DEVELOPMENT
0:00–1:05	Instrumental introduction	Melodic Introduction
1:06–2:32	1st couplet (*bayat*)	*Daromad*
2:33–3:44	2nd couplet	*Miyonkhona*
3:45–4:34	3rd couplet	*Miyonkhona*
4:35–5:28	4th couplet	*Dunasr*
5:29–7:47	5th couplet	*Awj* (5:29–7:20)
7:48–8:45	Repetition of 5th couplet	*Furovard*

called *furovard*. This melodic form is standard for Uzbek and Tajik classical songs (see chapter 18). A listening guide to "Kelmadi" appears in Table 25.1.

LISTEN

Example 25.3. "Kelmadi" (He didn't come), performed by Munojat Yulchieva on a text by Alisher Navo'i (1441–1501). From *Uzbekistan: Munodjat Yulchieva & Ensemble Shavkat Mirzaev* (Frankfurt: WDR and World Network, 1997).

1. *Kecha kelgumdur debon ul sarvi gulrö kelmadi,*

   Közlarimga kecha tong otquncha uyqu kelmadi.

2. *Lahza-lahza chiqdimu, chekdim yölida intizor,*
   Keldi jon oghzimghavu ul shökhi badhö kelmadi.

3. *Ul purivash hajridinkim yighladim devonavor,*
   Kimsa bormukim anga körganda kulgu kelmadi.

My beloved, with a face like a rose and a figure like a cypress tree, was supposed to come tonight, but he didn't come.
During the whole night until dawn, sleep didn't come.

Full of hope, I would take a few steps on the road toward him.
My soul was taking flight, but this fickle betrayer didn't come.

Bereft of his angel-face, I wept and wept like a madwoman.
Whoever saw me must have thought that I was a fool.

4. *Tolibi sodiq topilmas yöqsakim qöydi qadam*
    Yölghakim avval qadam ma'shuqqa ötru kelmadi.

    Is there such a thing as a faithful suitor?
    If there is one, why does not every step lead him to his beloved?

5. *Ey Navo'i, boda birla hurram et köngul uyin,*
    Ne uchunkim boda kelgan uyga qayghu kelmadi.

    Navo'i, rejoice in the house of your heart,
    For sadness never floods a house where wine flows.

Navo'i's poem, like other Sufi-inspired *ghazal*s, can be read as a spiritual allegory in which the figure of the beloved is described in human form at the same time that it alludes metaphorically and mystically to the invisible presence of the Divine. In Munojat's performance, the expressive culmination (*awj*) that coincides with the fifth couplet is sung with a powerful chest voice that emphasizes the spiritual ecstasy and catharsis described in the text. At this point, the melodic direction shifts from ascent to descent. When unity and proportion are attained, a final structural phase—the sudden, short return to the initial pitch (7:48)—brings the music toward a close.

Preparing the ritual meal of *sumalak* for the celebration of *Nowruz* (New Year's). Surhandarya region, Uzbekistan.

STUDY QUESTIONS

1. What adjectives would you use to describe the quality of Munojat's voice?

2. Can you identify which particular elements of vocal style and technique Munojat took from local music, and which ones she adapted from Western approaches to vocal training?

3. How is rhythm expressed in the vocal line? To what extent does Munojat's vocal line correspond to the metrical pattern (*usul*) provided by the frame drum?

4. Can you think of an analogy in your own culture to the kind of powerful spiritual song represented by "Kelmadi"?

NOTES

1. Volyinski's photo appears in Ergun Cagatay, *Once upon a Time in Central Asia* (Istanbul: Tetragon, 1996), 52–53.

2. Abdulla Qadiry, *O'tkan kunlar* (Ghafur Ghulom: Tashkent, 1974).

3. Abdulhamid Cho'lpon, *Kecha va Kunduz* (Ghafur Ghulom: Tashkent, 1991).

4. Compositions set to poetry include the following: Lutfihonim Sarymsakova: *Uzgancha, Tanovar,* and *Ferghanacha Jonom* by Mukimy. Mehro Abdullaeva: *Ruzi tanovar* and *Tanovar* by Mukimy. Bashorat Hojaeva: *Isma-Hush* and *Kalandar-5* by Mukimy. Mavluda Agzamova: *Chully Irok* and *Yghitlar* by Toshmapulat, and *Korashidur* by Furkat.

5. "Muzikal'naya kul'tura Kazakhstana," *Narodnoe iskusstvo* 12 (1938): 36.

6. Interview with Ilyas Akbarov, 1989, Tashkent.

7. First names such as Kommuna (Commune), Brigad (Brigade), and even Traktor (Tractor) were given to children in the early years of the Soviet era as a reflection of their parents' zeal for building socialism.

CHAPTER 26 **Music in the City of Bukhara**

THEODORE LEVIN AND ALEKSANDR DJUMAEV

Bukhara is one of Central Asia's oldest and most celebrated cities. Continuously inhabited for at least twenty-five hundred years, Bukhara was already an established oasis settlement when Alexander the Great passed through on his way to India in 330–329 BCE. Like Babylon and Byzantium, Bukhara was antiquity's version of a multicultural metropolis. The different peoples who inhabited the city maintained distinctive traditions of expressive, material, and spiritual culture at the same time that they blended these traditions together to create a cosmopolitan cultural amalgam that was uniquely Bukharan.

Music in Bukhara reflects the close and abiding contact that has developed over centuries among the city's various ethnic and religious groups. Muslims have long considered Bukhara a holy city, and in the past it was known throughout Central Asia as *Bukhara, Qubbat ul-Islam:* "Bukhara, the cupola of Islam." At the beginning of the twentieth century, Bukhara had over two hundred mosques and

Below left: Old Bukhara.

Below: Bukhara rises amid the steppe near the banks of the Zarafshan River, some hundred miles east of the Amu Darya—the River Oxus of antiquity—in the Republic of Uzbekistan.

Old Bukhara at the beginning of the 21st century.

Photo by Shavkat Boltaev

almost two hundred madrasahs. The city supported a learned Muslim religious establishment that included Sunnis, Shi'as, and various Sufi brotherhoods. Yet while Islam has been the dominant spiritual force in Bukhara, Jews who trace their ancestry to ancient Persian and Babylonian Jewish communities have lived there since at least the twelfth century, and probably longer. Other groups whose practices and beliefs have been prominently represented in Bukhara's cultural amalgam include the city's Shi'a minority—descendants of Iranians brought to Bukhara as slaves or displaced from the city of Merv, in Khorasan—and the Jugi, as Central Asian Roma (Gypsies) are known.

One local resident who had studied the history of Bukhara painted a vivid picture of the great variety of expressive culture available to its inhabitants:

> There were *maddoh*s who performed *ghazal*s and *madhiya*s [odes to God]. They had their own quarter of the city and their own leader. Before the *maddoh*, a *maskharavoz* ("clown-comedian") would go to the square to gather people. When enough people had gathered, the *maddoh* would appear and begin his sermonizing. They were like religious agitation-propaganda workers [a reference to the political agitprop workers who disseminated Communist ideology in the early Soviet period]. *Qalandar*s also performed in large squares where a lot of people had gathered—they sang *qalandar* songs, and people gave them money for that. In every mosque and in the madrasahs there was a *mathnawikhon* who chanted a *mathnawi* [a Persian poetic form in rhyming couplets] and then provided an interpretation of it. (See chapter 22.)

At the same time that Bukhara served as a center of fervent faith and religious practice, it nourished a strong cult of festivity and celebration. The idea that these different facets of life should each have their place in human experience is summed up in a well-known Bukharan aphorism: "Now for God and the Prophet, now for festivity and dancing" (*Goh Hudoyu Rasul, goh naghmayu usul*). This aphorism neatly summarizes the musical metaphysics that underlie traditional Bukharan culture—that humankind yearns for both a music of the spirit and a music of the flesh, and that it can, and should, have both.

In the sixteenth century, Bukhara emerged as a great musical center, inheriting the sophisticated tradition of music theory and practice that had developed a century earlier in Herat under the patronage of the Timurids, and, in particular, Sultan Husayn Bayqara (ruled 1469–1506) and his cultural adviser, the renowned literary figure Mir Ali Shir Navo'i (1441–1501). It was this tradition that led to the formation of a Bukharan school of *maqom* by Mavlana Nadjm al-Din Kawkabi Bukhari

Comedians (*maskharavoz*) perform with false beards and painted faces between 1865 and 1872.

Courtesy of Library of Congress, Prints and Photographs Division, reproduction no. LC-DIG-ppmsca-09953-00033.

(d. 1531), a distinguished musician, poet, and scholar. Bukhara's importance as a center of *maqom* music continued from Kawkabi's time until the 1930s, when the rise of Tashkent as the Soviet administrative and cultural center of Central Asia eclipsed the importance of Bukhara.

The enthusiasm of Bukhara's citizenry for music and entertainment contributed to a great influx of professional musicians, music lovers, and performers from other artistic domains who contributed to musical life. Among the latter were comedians, storytellers, professional preachers and orators, and street entertainers. In their spare time, many craftsmen became part-time musicians, taking part in a variety of festivities, rituals, and ceremonies. The existence of a whole city block where most of the residents were occupied with the processing of sheep entrails for making *dutar* strings points to the number of musicians in the city and the wide audience for music. The many domed buildings and dwellings in Bukhara offered felicitous acoustics for the Bukharan vocal technique called *ovozi khonaqoi* ("dome voice")—a deep and powerful chest voice that becomes even deeper and more powerful when performed in an acoustically reverberant space. The palaces of the emirs and nobility and numerous drawing rooms (*mehmonkhona*) of Bukhara's intellectual elite and artisans became recital halls where music was frequently performed and listened to.

Musicians and an acrobat, a popular form of entertainment in Bukhara, between 1865 and 1872.

Courtesy of Library of Congress, Prints and Photographs Division, reproduction no. LC-DIG-ppmsca-09953-00016.

When the number of musicians grew too great, rulers who adhered to strict codes of Islamic conduct took certain repressive measures against them, as well as against members of other artistic professions. It was not until the reign of Emir Muzaffar-khan (1860–1885) that a stable social and economic niche was established for musicians. Muzaffar instituted measures to regulate the activities of musicians, circus actors, and other performing artists in Bukhara. He introduced obligatory registration of artists and imposed a "performance tax" that artists were required to pay in order to receive permission to perform in public. To manage the process of registration and permissions, he created a special department known as the *gholibkhona*.

FESTIVITY AND CELEBRATION IN BUKHARA

The special passion of Bukhara's population for musical entertainment stimulated the creation of folkloric songs and dances known as *bukharcha*. The text of a *bukharcha* song typically consisted of popular poetry, sometimes performed in dialogue format and often infused with elements of exquisite sensuality and humor.

*Bukharcha*s were performed at festive occasions generically known as *toy*. Virtually any event could provide the excuse for a *toy*. The most important of these—a birth, a circumcision, or a marriage—could call forth an enormous gathering of relatives and friends. Lesser occasions—a child's first day at school, a boy's first haircut, or, in former times, the first veiling of a girl—were observed in smaller family gatherings. Whatever the size of the *toy*, two elements have traditionally been obligatory: an offering of food, called *dastarkhon* ("tablecloth"), and live music to entertain the guests.

Soviet culture was hostile to public spectacle linked to religious or spiritual practices, and the Bukharan traditions of *qalandar, maddoh,* and *mathnawikhon* withered away as a result of the state-mandated "struggle against the past." The practice of *toy*, however, while holding an important place in both Muslim and Jewish custom and tradition, was not overtly religious and continued in a robust form through the entire Soviet era.

The Bukharan *toy* exemplified the traditional separation of men and women in the social life of sedentary dwellers. At *toy*s, men and women celebrated separately, with women entertained by female performers and men entertained by male performers. Men's celebrations and women's celebrations were often held on different days. Nowadays, men and women tend to occupy shared social space, and many wedding entertainers perform in mixed groups of women and men. But the tradition of professional female singer-dancers who serve religious and secular rituals, ceremonies, family festivities, holidays, and musical gatherings related to the life of women still persists—both as functional music and as "folklore" presented by professional musicians. The local name for such female singer-dancers is *sozanda* (in Uzbek and Tajik, "*sozanda*" means "musician" in a broad sense, but in Bukhara it is typically used in a restricted sense to mean traditional female entertainers).

Female entertainers like the Bukharan *sozanda* are an integral part of Central Asian cultures. Khorezm, northwest of Bukhara, has its *khalfa* (or *khalpa*); in the Ferghana Valley, east of Tashkent, there are *yallachi*—groups of women who perform a folk song genre called *yalla*. Herat, to the south, has—or had—women's minstrel bands.[1] These performers have old roots in the erstwhile tradition of the *mutrib* (or in Persian, *motreb*), and in an even earlier antecedent, the *qiyan*—singing slaves, courtesans, and cupbearers—of pre-Islamic Arab and Persian lands. Women in urban Central Asia who took up what, by local standards, was the morally ambiguous role of wedding entertainer have most frequently been drawn from the ranks of socially marginalized groups. In Bukhara, *sozanda*s were overwhelmingly Jewish from at least the beginning of the twentieth century.

Persian-speaking Jewish communities existed in Bukhara, Samarkand, Balkh (now in Afghanistan), and Merv (now Mary, Turkmenistan) before the

Far left: A street in the Jewish quarter of Bukhara, 1990.

Left: A worshipper in a Bukharan synagogue, 1990.

thirteenth-century Mongol conquest of Central Asia. Documentation of the origins and early history of these communities is sparse, but legends suggest that Timur (d. 1405), the founder of the Timurid dynasty, brought Jewish silk weavers from Iran to Central Asia, where they became integrated into older Jewish communities.[2] Following the sixteenth-century rise of the Safavid monarchy in Iran and the ensuing cultural separation of Shi'a Iran from Sunni Transoxania (the land "beyond the Oxus," the ancient Greek name for the Amu Darya River), Central Asian Jews became isolated from other Persian-speaking communities to the south and west and to a large extent assumed the cultural identity of their Transoxanian Muslim neighbors. Central Asian Jews have traditionally spoken Tajik as a first language, often in a slightly dialectical form that they call Bukhari, which is distinguishable to a native speaker by certain linguistic shibboleths. Many also speak Uzbek, and these days most of them also speak Russian. Since the nineteenth century, Central Asian Jews have been known, and have self-identified, as Bukharan (or Bukharian) Jews, whether or not they lived in Bukhara itself.

Within the Bukharan Emirate, Jews lived under a variety of social constraints. In the city of Bukhara, for example, Jewish settlement under the emirs was limited to particular *mahalla*s (neighborhoods), which, as the Jewish population increased, became the most densely settled areas in a densely settled city. Jews were required to wear a distinctive sash to distinguish them from Muslims. They were forbidden to ride horses within the city, although they could ride donkeys, so as not to appear higher than a Muslim. Certain occupations were forbidden for Jews, while others—cobbler, barber, indigo dyer,

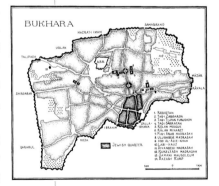

Map showing the Jewish quarter of Bukhara (shaded area at the bottom).

From Theodore Levin, *The Hundred Thousand Fools of God: Musical Travels in Central Asia (and Queens, New York).*

money changer, all of which involved dirtying one's hands—were dominated by them. Another group of occupations involved activities in a morally ambiguous zone between what, for Muslims, was licit (*halal*) and illicit (*haram*). Foremost among these was the public performance of music and dance.

Transoxania's Bukharan Jewish population was never more than a tiny community compared to the Muslim population—in 1900, there were an estimated 20,000 Jews in the Bukharan Emirate and Russian Turkestan (with 4,000–5,000 living in the city of Bukhara itself), while the 1989 Soviet census recorded fewer than 40,000 "Central Asian" Jews in Uzbekistan and Tajikistan among some 20 million Muslims. Given these modest numbers, the prominence of Bukharan Jews in Bukhara's musical professions, which included not only the female *sozanda* but male performers of the classical *Shashmaqom* repertory, is all the more noteworthy. Beginning in the 1970s, many Bukharan Jews emigrated to the United States and Israel. It is estimated that around 50,000 Bukharan Jews now live in New York City—most of them in the borough of Queens—and around the same number live in Israel—mostly in Tel Aviv (those that left Central Asia prior to the 1989 census wouldn't have been included in the census figures). Only a small number of Bukharan Jewish families remain in Bukhara.

Tohfakhon Pinkhasova with troupe of *sozanda*s, 1957.
Courtesy of Tohfakhon Pinkhasova.

PROFILE OF A BUKHARAN *SOZANDA*

The best-known Bukharan female entertainer (*sozanda*) of the late twentieth century was Tohfakhon Pinkhasova (1928–2010). In an interview in 1993, Tohfakhon described how she had become a *sozanda*:

> From childhood, I loved art. My mother's sister was a *sozanda,* and I went with her to weddings. When I was six, I started to dance in school groups. We had concerts all over the place—for the cotton workers and silk workers, in theaters and teahouses, and in private homes. But my father didn't want me to be a *sozanda*, an artist. My father had a higher education, as did my mother. They were teachers. Before the Revolution, my father had been a coach driver. After the Revolution, he became a policeman, and then he went to an evening teacher's college. He worked for two years and then became the principal of a school. I wanted to follow in

my father's footsteps, but the war got in the way. I quit teacher's college after the second year. I had *sozanda* in my blood.

Older *sozanda*s took me on as a pupil. They'd be going to a wedding and they'd say, "Come with us." And I went. They didn't teach me. I just watched them dance and absorbed what they did. One of them was named Karkigi. She had danced for the mother of the emir. If the emir's mother gave her permission, she performed for *toys* outside the *ark* [the residence of the emir]. But if the emir's mother didn't give her permission, she didn't go. The mother of the emir loved to watch dancing, and most of the dancers were Jews.

Three generations of *sozandas:* Tohfakhon with her daughter and granddaughter, 1990.

Karkigi was very beautiful. The emir's mother gave her thin silk dresses to wear all the time, so that her figure would always be apparent. She had very white skin. When she was young, she didn't go out without her mother, and she wore a veil. My mother also wore a veil. All Jewish women wore veils before the Revolution, and they wore veils for two, three, four years after the Revolution. I remember that when I was a girl, women still wore the veil in Tashkent, in Samarkand, in Bukhara. Even in the late 1940s, there were still women who wore the veil in Tashkent.

Until the 1950s and 1960s, there were very few Uzbek and Tajik *sozanda*s. Ninety percent were Bukharan Jews, and maybe 10 percent were Uzbeks and Tajiks. Their husbands didn't allow them to do that kind of work. Now it's the opposite, because Jews are leaving and Uzbeks and Tajiks are permitted to dance.

Sozandas danced without music [i.e., melody instruments], and they didn't work with men—*maqom* players or singers. That's the way it was until the 1960s. It's a tradition that men shouldn't be among women and women shouldn't be among men. Women's wedding celebrations were separate and men's wedding celebrations were separate. They used to hold them on different days. In other parts of Uzbekistan and Tajikistan, maybe 50 or 60 percent of the weddings have men and women sitting together in the evening *bazm* (feast). But in Bukhara, the old tradition still holds. In the 1960s, I quietly took a *rubab* player—a thirteen-year-old boy— to play among the women. I was the first one to take male musicians among women. To this day, I don't sing or dance among men. I don't receive men. I have that rule. I've always been among women. Usually they phone me now. They ask, "Are you free on such and such a day? Then put me down," they say. There's no discussion about money. When we go to their place, they give a bowl of tea, and underneath the tea bowl there's some money. Guests also give us money.

Entrance to the Emir's palace, called the *ark*.

Courtesy of Library of Congress, Prints and Photographs Division, Prokudin-Gorskii Collection, reproduction no. LC-DIG-prok-21871.

In the following video clip, filmed in 1990 in an agricultural village near Bukhara, Tohfakhon performs at a wedding *toy* with members of her ensemble, which by this time included several male musicians.

WATCH **Example 26.1.** Tohfakhon Pinkhasova and members of her ensemble entertain at a *toy* in the outskirts of Bukhara, 1990.

Bukharan Jewish "bachelorette" party, between 1865 and 1872.

Courtesy of Library of Congress, Prints and Photographs Division, reproduction no. LC-DIG-ppmsca-09951-00261.

At the beginning of the video excerpt, Tohfakhon sings the traditional wedding song "Yor-Yor" as the bride, a white cloth held over her head, is led from her parents' house to the women's side of the *toy*. The bride bows low to the female relatives of her new husband. This part of the wedding ceremony, called *challary,* marks the bride's return to the home of her parents accompanied by her new relatives two to three days after the principal wedding festivity. It serves as a reconfirmation of the union of bride and groom, and is observed with a festive meal, dancing, and the giving of gifts. At this particular *challary,* the boundary between the women's space and the men's space is less physical than imagined. Women sit on the ground on a section of street that has been covered with carpets and cushions and is protected by a large awning. Tohfakhon and her ensemble set up their microphones and equipment at one end of the awning, while beyond them, exposed to the sun, men are seated at long tables. After Tohfakhon has entertained the women, a *maskharavoz* (comedian) enters the men's areas outfitted as a hobbyhorse.

As Tohfakhon sings and dances for and with the women, groups of men stand on the margins of the women's area, watching the entertainment. At moments when no women are dancing, a few intrepid men move into the center of the women's area and dance with one another. Later, both women and men line up separately in front of Tohfakhon to receive a *mukhammas*—a poetic blandishment traditionally bestowed upon women only. Tohfakhon was a master of the *mukhammas*. She would glance at the person standing before her and judge instantly what sort of *mukhammas* to recite and in what language (Uzbek or Tajik). For example, for a child, she might say:

> Let your face be in my soul
> So that when you smile, you open flowers.
> Let the dream of your mother who bore you be fulfilled.
> Be so sweet that I die from your sweetness.

For another woman, she could say:

> Won't you please give me a kiss with your sweet lips,
> Give me a kiss.
> Why only one; give two, three, four,
> Five, seven, nine. Give me an even number: ten.

"I'm a woman, and I have a right to say this to another woman," Tohfakhon explained after the *toy*. "We're accustomed to working among women, and that way, we feel free." Despite her claim that she didn't perform for men, Tohfakhon graciously bestowed a *mukhammas* on each man who stepped in front of her (she knew that particular group of men, and that was why she had not felt uncomfortable with them). The quatrains for men, however, were less physically explicit:

Bringing a Jewish bride (*far left*) to the home of the groom, between 1865 and 1872.

Courtesy of Library of Congress, Prints and Photographs Division, reproduction no. LC-DIG-ppmsca-09951-00257.

> May there be life and may you live,
> May you be alive and healthy.
> In such good times,
> Always be happy and dance.

Or:

> May God allow your height not to become stooped,
> May the joy of your heart not see any grief.
> May God give you happiness day and night
> May your shadow always be on my head.

Study Questions

1. Watching Tohfakhon perform at the wedding, what would you guess was the secret of her great popularity? What specific skills and talents made her a successful *sozanda*?

2. To what extent does the bride look as if she is following a scripted code of behavior, as opposed to acting spontaneously, according to her emotions?

3. Does it seem as if the women and the men are having more or less the same kind of social experience at the *toy*, or are the men's and women's celebrations gender-specific? In what ways are they similar and different?

Musical Repertory of *Sozandas*

The *sozanda*'s repertory is designed to provide extended periods of entertainment. Performances may last as long as eight hours, with only occasional breaks. Part of the *sozanda*'s skill is in assembling lengthy blocks, or suites, of dance-songs—the *bukharcha* described earlier. Suites of *bukharcha* are built on the principle of acceleration from slow tempo to fast, and they combine various rhythms and meters played on the *doira*. Antiphonal call-and-response between leader and chorus is an integral part of the *sozanda* style. The artistry of performing such suites is in linking the *bukharcha*s together in such a way that the progression of changing rhythms, meters, and tempos keeps listeners constantly engaged, energized, and, from time to time, surprised.

An excerpt from Tohfakhon's performance of a suite of *bukharcha*s is reproduced in example 26.2.

Example 26.2. "Bukharcha," performed by Tohfakhon Pinkhasova and Nozanin. Recorded by Theodore Levin and Otanazar Matyakubov. From *Bukhara: Musical Crossroads of Asia* (SFR, 1991), track 3.

The text of the *bukharcha* begins:

Solo:
Dar miyon-i chor daryo taxtabandī kardaī
Between four seas you put your platform (of boards)

Boz meguyam doman tar nakun, hushyor bosh
I repeat once again, don't get your hem wet, be vigilant

Taralilalalai, taralilalalai, taralilalalai, yor eh
Taralilalalai, taralilalalai, taralilalalai, my dear.

Chorus:
Taralilalalai, taralilalalai, taralilalai, yor eh

Solo:
Du chashm-i jodu dorī, taralilalalai, yor eh.
Your two eyes are bewitching, *taralilalalai, yor eh.*

Chorus:
(repeats the same refrain after each solo verse)

Solo:
O, az man khabar nadorī-eh, taralilalalai, yor eh.
Why don't you ask after me, *taralilalalai, yor eh?*

O, chashm-i siyoh-i doghat-eh, taralilalalai, yor eh
Your burning black eyes . . .

O, modar nabinad doghat-eh, taralilalalai, yor eh
May your mother never grieve for you . . .

O, padar nabinad doghat-eh, taralilalalai, or eh
May your father never grieve for you . . .

O, modar bubinad tūyat-eh, taralilalalai, yor eh
May your mother live to see your wedding . . .

O, hama bubinand tūyat-eh, taralilalalai, yor eh
May everyone live to see your wedding . . .

MAVRIGIKHON: THE MALE ANALOGUE OF THE BUKHARAN *SOZANDA*

Mavrigi is a form of vocal suite performed at men's festivities that is broadly analogous to the suites performed by *sozanda*s at women's festivities (*mavrigi* is discussed in the context of contemporary cultural innovation and revitalization in chapter 34). *Mavrigi* means literally "from Merv," the oasis city (now called Mary) in present-day Turkmenistan that was once a principal cultural center of Khorasan. Performers who lead a *mavrigi* are called *mavrigikhon*. The typical *mavrigikhon* has been a descendant of the Bukharan Irani or Farsi, who trace their ancestry to slaves captured in Iran by Turkmen tribesmen and brought via Merv to Bukhara. The Bukharan Irani have preserved their Shi'a heritage and, relative to the city's Sunni majority, are a marginalized social group. The Shi'a *mavrigikhon*s, like Jewish *sozanda*s, have performed work traditionally considered unsuitable for Sunni Bukharans.

Mahdi Ibadov performs *mavrigi*. Bukhara, 1990.

In the 1990s, the best-known *mavrigikhon* in Bukhara was a man named Mahdi Ibadov (1932–2006). Unlike Tohfakhon, Mahdi did not work full-time as a musician, and he hadn't come to music in early childhood. His grandfather was a tax collector for the emir. His father went to the front during the Second World War and never returned. Mahdi's mother, grandmother, and brother had all died soon after the war began, and Mahdi was put in an orphanage. He had finished the sixth grade and worked his entire life as a truck driver. Performing *mavrigi* was an avocation. Mahdi started performing a little at weddings of friends and relatives and had been encouraged.

Mahdi explained the routine of the *mavrigikhon* as follows:

> We'd come to a *toy* with five or six people, and we all had *doira*s. We served the weddings of both Shi'as and Sunnis. There's no difference in the way they're conducted in Bukhara. Shi'as invite Sunnis, and Sunnis invite Shi'as. We'd sit near the door, which was the least-honored position. They'd put a mat [*korpacha*] down, and we'd sit down on our haunches. That means that you're serving; that's the way you play. You don't sit with your legs crossed—that's for relaxing. In the center of the room there would be a container for coal to heat the *doira*s [in order to keep the skin taut]. They'd pass around *mai* [a kind of sweet wine] and *musallas* [a strong, thick red wine made by boiling grapes for a long time, often used as a medicament].

> The first thing we'd sing was the *shahd* [Tajik: "honey"]. Whoever could perform, performed. We'd sing in turns. If there were six people, each would sing a couplet or two. After the *shahd* there would be *gardon, sarkhon, chor zarb*, which can have five or six parts. These would make up a *pait* [performance] that would last about an hour, and then people would eat and drink, and there would be a second *pait,* and a third *pait*.

Example 26.3 presents an abbreviated version of the opening two sections of a *mavrigi: shahd* and *shahd-i gardon*. The vocal style, with its nasalized tone set in a high vocal tessitura and concentrated within a narrow ambitus (pitch range), is reminiscent of singing from Azerbaijan or Iran, as if it represented a musical vestige of the *mavrigi*'s cultural origins that had persisted in the Shi'a community of Bukhara.

LISTEN

Example 26.3. "Mavrigi," performed by Mahdi Ibadov. Recorded by Theodore Levin and Otanazar Matyakubov. From *Bukhara: Musical Crossroads of Asia* (SFR, 1991), track 2.

The text of the opening two sections of the *mavrigi* is transliterated and translated below.

Shahd

Yor, amon, amon, amon, amon.	Dear one, *amon, amon, amon, amon.* (grant me safety)
Bo gul bishinam, gul zi man khor gardad	When I turn to blossoms, the blossom turns into thorns.
Bo ghuncha bishinam, girebon chok gardad.	When I turn to the bud, the bud bursts open.

Yor, omon, omon, omon, omon.
Man ba bozor-i tole', tole'i khud imti-
    hon kardam.
Bo harkas khok zar gardad, ba man zar
    khok megardad.
Yor, amon, amon, amon, amon.
Ajab tole'i, ki man doram, shiram
    jughrot megardad.
Ba dastam qarchigae oyad, vayam
    kalkhot megardad.
Yor, amon, amon, amon, amon, amon.

Ai khudo-yi man,
Ai, habib-i man,
Hamin damro ghanimat bidon.

Shahd-i gardon

Dar biyabon nay navokhtam,
Khirman-i gul dar girift.

Haif, ki ruy-i beghuborash,
Chang-u khokistar girift.
Ustukhonam sukhta shudu,
Maghz-i jonam dar girift.
Az baroi rūh-i jonon,
Shishta jonam dar girift berahmoi.
Halqa ba dar mezadam,
To nisf-i shab dar voz nashud.
Nisf-i shab az shab guzashtu,
Yar-i man paido nashud.
Podsho-i shahr baromad,
Band-i dastamro girift.
Hech kase ba misl-i man,
Dar roh-i ishq rasvo nashud berahmoi.

(Text changes to Uzbek)
Köchadan ötib borobman, közlarim
    senga mudom.
Qayirilib bir qaramaisan, muncha
    peshonam yamon.
Ya, saning köngling qolibdi, Ya, mani
    özim yamon.

Dear one, amon, amon, amon, amon.
I experienced my fate at the bazaar of
    fate,
If for others, hard stones turn to gold,
    then for me, gold turns to dust.
Dear one, amon, amon, amon, amon.
I have a surprising fate: in my hands,
    milk turns to yogurt,
But if a hawk fell into my hands, it
    would be turned into an eagle.
Dear one, amon, amon, amon, amon,
    amon.

Oh my God,
Oh my beloved
Consider this moment precious!

In the steppe, I played on the nay,
And from that, flowers began
    to burn.
What a pity that his/her pure face
Became covered with dust and ash,
My bones finished burning,
My soul began to burn,
From the soul of my beloved,
My heart began to burn, pitilessly.
I knock at the door
Until midnight, no one opens it.
Midnight passes,
My beloved didn't appear.
The king of the city came out
And took me by the hand.
No one like me
Has made a fool of himself in love,
    pitilessly.

I walk along the street, and my eyes
    always see you.
How unfortunate am I that you don't
    look at me.
Either you stopped loving me,
    or I am bad.

Oraga dushman kiribdi, endi körgonim gumon	An enemy has come between us, and it's unlikely that we'll see each other.
(Macaronic Uzbek and Tajik).	
Voi, khol dorad halili (refrain)	Halili has a birthmark (refrain)
Khumor dorad halili	Halili has a wish
Qoshingni qarosiga-ye, (refrain)	That I would be a birthmark
Khol bolai arosiga-ye. (refrain)	In the middle of your black eyebrows.

An interesting feature of Mahdi's text is the macaronic juxtaposition of Uzbek and Tajik toward the end of the *shahd-i gardon*. Known colloquially as *shiru shakar,* "milk and sugar," macaronic texts are commonly found in the songs of the *mavrigikhon* and *sozanda*. The metaphor comes from the idea that, like milk and sugar, each of the two languages enhances the taste and effect of the other. Such macaronic texts seem only natural in the repertory of entertainers who so unself-consciously move back and forth across boundaries of language and ethnicity in Bukhara.

While *mavrigikhon*s and *sozanda*s fulfilled analogous social functions for men and women, Mahdi stressed that both kinds of entertainers had their own repertories and melodies built around one and the same aesthetic performance: progression from serious to light, from slow to fast, from meditation to dance. In effect, both types of performer and both types of music served as a mediating link between the two essential poles of Bukharan life—prayer and festivity.

STUDY QUESTIONS

1. What are some similarities and differences between the *mavrigi* repertory performed by Mahdi Ibadov and the *sozanda* repertory performed by Tohfakhon?

2. What accounted for the popularity of *mavrigi* as a traditional form of entertainment? What do you think caused audiences to turn away from it toward more contemporary forms of entertainment?

BUKHARAN JEWISH MUSICAL TRADITIONS: FROM BUKHARA TO QUEENS, NEW YORK

Living for centuries in a city dominated by Muslims and by cultural expressions of Islam, Bukharan Jews assimilated a range of local Muslim practices into their own religious traditions. In the realm of liturgical music and chant, different genres show varying degrees of assimilation. The least assimilation occurred in the chanting of the Torah—the first five books of the Hebrew Bible. Like the recitation of the Qur'an, Torah recitation is governed by canons and traditions that assure a measure of conformity in the way different reciters render a sacred text. In the case of the Torah, written markings (Hebrew: *te'amim*) provide a guide to the grouping and accentuation of words and the contour of melody.

Yakub Meer Ochildiev, Tashkent Uzbekistan, 1990.

The following audio example reproduces a recitation of the Torah recorded in 1990 from a Bukharan Jewish religious singer (*hazzan*) who at the time was eighty-three years old. The singer, Yakub Meer Ochildiev (b. 1907), studied Hebrew from early childhood in Margilan, an ancient city in the Ferghana Valley, which had its own community of Bukharan Jews. At the time of the recording, Ochildiev lived in Tashkent, where he performed the duties of the *hazzan* in one of Tashkent's two functioning Bukharan Jewish synagogues.

LISTEN

Example 26.4. Reading from the Torah by Yakub Meer Ochildiev. Recorded by Theodore Levin and Otanazar Matyakubov. From *Bukhara: Musical Crossroads of Asia* (SFR, 1991), track 10.

The Torah reading is from the book of Genesis, chapter 41: 11–21. The text recounts how Joseph interpreted the dreams of Pharaoh's chief cupbearer and chief baker, and then the dream of Pharaoh himself:

> We had dreams the same night, he and I, each of us a dream with a meaning of its own. A Hebrew youth was there with us, a servant of the chief steward; and when we told him our dreams, he interpreted them for us, telling each the meaning of his dream. And as he interpreted for us, so it came to pass: I was restored to my post, and the other was impaled.
>
> Thereupon Pharaoh sent for Joseph, and he was rushed from the dungeon. He had his hair cut and changed his clothes, and he appeared before Pharaoh. And Pharaoh said to Joseph, "I have had a dream, but no one can interpret it. Now I have heard it said of you that for you to hear a dream is to tell its meaning." Joseph answered Pharaoh, saying, "Not I! God will see to Pharaoh's welfare."
>
> Then Pharaoh said to Joseph, "In my dream, I was standing on the bank of the Nile, when out of the Nile came up seven sturdy and well-formed

cows and grazed in the reed grass. Presently there followed them seven other cows, scrawny, ill-formed, and emaciated—never had I seen their likes for ugliness in all the land of Egypt! And the seven lean and ugly cows ate up the first seven cows, the sturdy ones; but when they had consumed them, one could not tell that they had consumed them, for they looked just as bad as before. And I awoke.

STUDY QUESTIONS

1. In what ways is the melody that Yakub Meer Ochuldiev uses to chant verses from the Torah similar to and different from other music from Central Asia that you have heard?

2. In Ochuldiev's rendition, does the story of Pharaoh's dream come alive for you?

Beyond the canonical chanting of the Torah, Bukharan Jewish religious singing shows a greater assimilation of local music—in particular, the Bukharan tradition of *maqom,* called *Shashmaqom* (see chapter 18). Such assimilation was undoubtedly facilitated by the prominent role of Bukharan Jewish singers and instrumentalists as performers of Shashmaqom, both in Bukhara and in other Central Asian cities. Several Jewish family lineages dominated the performance of Shashmaqom from the late nineteenth century to the last quarter of the twentieth century. Mullakand, Tolmas, Babakhan—Russified as Mullakandov, Tolmasov, Babakhanov—were household names for the musical connoisseurs of Bukhara, Samarkand, and Shahrisabz (see "Performer Profile: Ari Babakhanov"). Other well-known musicians, including Ata Jalol (1845–1928), credited with being the "founder" of the Shashmaqom, were *chalas*—Jews who converted under coercion to Islam but privately preserved elements of Jewish belief or practice.

Bukharan Jewish musicians who performed Shashmaqom appropriated the melodies of particular songs within the Shashmaqom repertory to provide the music for liturgical poems (*piyyut*) sung in Jewish homes after the Sabbath meal. This kind of substitution, in which one text is replaced by another without substantial change to the music, is called a "contrafactum." One well-known Sabbath song set to a melody from the Shashmaqom is "Dror Yikra" (Proclaim Freedom). The text of "Dror Yikra" is a poem written by the tenth-century poet Dunash ha-Levi ben Labrat, who was born in the city of Fez, Morocco. The power of the text has made it popular in Jewish communities around the world, who have set it to myriad local melodies. A recording of "Dror Yikra," sung in Hebrew by Bukharan Jewish singers Ezra Malakov and Roshel Rubinov to the melody of "Chapandoz-i guliyor," a song from the "Rost" suite of the Shashmaqom, is reproduced in example 26.5 ("Dror Yikra" is not set exclusively to the melody of "Chapandoz-i guliyor." Other popular contrafacta settings are to "Saqiname-i iraq" and "Navruz-i sabo"—both part of the Shashmaqom).

LISTEN

Example 26.5. "Dror Yikra" (Proclaim freedom) performed by Ezra Malakov and Roshel Rubinov. From Ezra Malakov, *Musical Treasure of the Bukharian Jewish Community* (Tel-Aviv: World Bukharian Jewish Congress, 2007), disc 1, track 7.

D'ror Yikra leven im bat	He will proclaim liberty to all His children
veyintzorchem kemo vavat	And cherish you as the apple of His eye.
Na'im shimchem velo yushbat	Your name is sweet and will never cease.
shevu nuchu beyom Shabbat	Find repose on the Sabbath day.
Drosh navi ve'ulami	Seek out my dwelling-place and my sanctuary
ve'ot yesha aseh imi	And grant me a sign of deliverance.
Neta sorek betoch karmi	Plant a vine in my vineyard
she'eh shavat benei ami	Look to my people's cries.
D'roch poora betoch Batzra	Crush the wine-press in Bozrah
vegam Bavel asher gavra	and Babylon that overwhelmed us.
Netotz tzarai be'af evra	Uproot my foes in anger and fury.
shema koli beyom ekra	Hear my voice on the day I call out.
Elohim ten bamidbar har	Oh God, plant a mountain in the wilderness,
hadas shita berosh tidhar	Myrtle and acacia, cypress and elm.
Velamazhir velanizhar	And grant those who teach and those who obey
shelomim ten kemei nahar	A peace that flows forever.
Hadoch kamai El kana	Repel my enemies, oh zealous God,
bemog levav u'vimgina	With trepidation and despair.
Venarchiv peh u'nemallena	Then we shall open our mouths and imbibe Your goodness
leshonenu lecha rina	and with full throat sing Your praise.
De'eh chochma lenafshecha	Acquire wisdom for your spirit,
vehi keter leroshecha	Like a crown to your head.
Netzor mitzvat kedoshecha	Safeguard the commandments of your Holy God,
shemor Shabbat kodshecha	Keep the holy Sabbath.

—TRANSLATION COURTESY OF LEWIS GLINERT

1. Compare Ezro Malakov and Roshel Rubinov's performance of "Dror Yikra" sung to the melody of "Chapandoz-i guliyor" with the performance of "Talqincha-i sabo," example 18.2 in chapter 18. What similarities and differences do you notice in (a) the vocal style of the singers, and (b) the musical form of the piece?

2. Can you think of examples of contrafacta from music in your own culture?

Ezra Malakov and Roshel Rubinov, the singers whose performance of "Dror Yikra" is reproduced in example 26.5, are both Bukharan Jews who emigrated from Central Asia in the 1990s and now live in the thriving Bukharan Jewish community of Queens, New York. Malakov was born in 1938 in Shahrisabz, Uzbekistan, and learned religious music from his mother, Yashua Borukhova (1911–1986), whose own family lineage included several distinguished rabbis. In Tashkent, Malakov worked as a soloist in the Shashmaqom Ensemble of the state-run television and radio station, but at the same time he continued to serve the Jewish community as a cantor, or religious singer. Aware that the tradition of Bukharan Jewish religious singing was endangered, and that his own memory offered a reliable source for documenting it, Malakov set about compiling a personal anthology of Bukharan Jewish religious song and chant that included texts, musical transcriptions, and newly made recordings of his own performances, both as a soloist and in various ensemble configurations. Malakov's anthology was published in 2007 as *Musical Treasures of the Bukharian Jewish Community;* it offers an exceptional window on the history of a religious and cultural tradition that has now all but disappeared in Central Asia itself and that is subject to pressures of assimilation in New York and Tel Aviv, the new centers of Bukharan Jewish settlement.

Right: Ezra Malakov in Queens, New York.

Far right: Ezra Malakov (middle row, 2nd from left) and the Bukharan Jewish ensemble Shashmaqom.

In the following short video, Ezra Malakov and fellow Queens-based Bukharan Jewish musician Avrom Tolmasov reflect on the crucial role of Bukharan Jews in preserving, performing, and transmitting Bukharan musical traditions. The film shows a glimpse of the new style of Bukharan Jewish pop music that has replaced the music of *sozanda*s and *mavrigikhon*s at weddings. In the last section of the film, Ezra Malakov chants a *haqqoni,* discussed in the following section.

WATCH | **Example 26.6.** *The Bukharan Jews of Queens, New York: Ezra Malakov, Avrom Tolmasov.* **Filmed by Saodat Ismailova and Carlos Casas in Queens, New York, 2011.**

Among the diverse genres of religious singing in Ezra Malakov's repertory is *haqqoni,* from Arabic: *haqq:* "absolute truth," one of the names of God frequently invoked in Iranian Sufism. The purpose of *haqqoni* is to facilitate inner purification: a renunciation of the physical world and an immersion in the inner world. In both its musical style and its texts, *haqqoni* exemplifies the strong influence of Sufi ideals, and among Muslims, *haqqoni* was indeed performed in the Bukharan *khanaqa*s—Sufi meeting places where members of a Sufi confraternity performed the ritual of *zikr.* But both Muslim and Jewish women performed *haqqoni* in the home of a deceased person while the body was being washed and prepared for removal to the cemetery. Nowadays, the Muslim practice of *haqqoni* in Bukhara is moribund, but it is actively performed by Bukharan Jews—typically in the context of memorial celebrations for a deceased person that take place seven days and one year after the person's death.

The vocal style of *haqqoni,* with its tensed, high-tessitura vocal lines sung rubato, without regular meter, has a close analogue in another genre linked to the practice of Sufi *zikr,* called *katta ashula. Katta ashula* was traditionally associated with the musical culture of the Ferghana Valley. During the Soviet era, *katta ashula* was transformed into a secular genre and became widely popular in Uzbekistan (see chapter 22). In the following video examples, Bukharan Jewish singer Ezra Malakov performs an abridged version of a *katta ashula* followed by an abridged version of a *haqqoni.* Both are sung in Tajik Persian. The performances were filmed at Malakov's home in Queens, New York. In the *katta ashula,* he is accompanied by fellow musicians from the Bukharan Jewish community, and trades verse couplets with singer Abukhai Aminov. In the *haqqoni,* Aminov and Malakov sing a cappella, again trading verse couplets. Note the use in both *katta ashula* and *haqqoni* of a distinctive feature of these genres: the singers hold small plates to the side of their mouth, providing additional resonance for the powerful vocal sound (these days the plates seem to serve more of a symbolic function than an acoustical one).

Women at a Jewish burial between 1865 and 1872.
Courtesy of Library of Congress, Prints and Photographs Division, reproduction no. LC-DIG-ppmsca-09951-00235.

WATCH

Example 26.7. "Katta ashula," performed by Ezra Malakov and Abukhai Aminov (vocal), Matat Barayev (*doira*), David Davidov (*tar),* and Ochil Ibragimov (violin). Queens, New York, 2011.

WATCH

Example 26.8. "Haqqoni," performed by Ezra Malakov and Abukhai Aminov. Queens, New York, 2011.

STUDY QUESTIONS

1. How would you characterize both the similarities and differences between *katta ashula* and *haqqoni* based on the performances in the video?

2. Describe the musical accompaniment that the three instrumentalists provide to the singing.

3. Does the *haqqoni* seem to you like music that would be appropriate for a memorial service?

Performer Profile: Ari Babakhanov: A Contemporary Traditional Musician
ALEKSANDR DJUMAEV

In the very heart of old Bukhara, near the Lyabi Hauz—the early seventeenth-century cistern that is one of the city's best-known landmarks—a densely settled residential neighborhood spreads out along a warren of narrow alleys set between high adobe walls. Once part of a traditional Bukharan Jewish quarter, or *guzar,* these alleys include Levi Babakhanov Street, recently renamed after the legendary Bukharan Jewish singer popularly known as Levicha (1873–1926) who, in the twilight years of the Bukharan Emirate, served as "soloist to His Majesty, the Emir of Bukhara," as he was described by local writers of that time.

Levicha with his *tanbur.*
Courtesy of Ari Babakhanov.

Continuing along Levi Babakhanov Street, the old city leads to a Soviet-era housing development of rectangular four-story apartment buildings. It was one of these buildings that served as the home of Ari Babakhanov (b. 1934), grandson of Levicha, in the decades before Ari and his family emigrated to Germany, in 2002. Ari aka is a virtuoso performer on the Kashgar *rubab* and a third-generation musician.[3] In the generation between Levicha and Ari was Moshe Babakhanov (1910–1983), a well-known Bukharan singer whose life spanned almost the entire Soviet era.

Ari is the last in the musical dynasty of Babakhanovs, a family

Performer Profile: Ari Babakhanov (CONTINUED)

Moshe Babakhanov.
Courtesy of Ari Babakhanov.

that for more than a century has contributed richly to the preservation and development of indigenous classical music in Bukhara, in particular the Bukharan Shashmaqom. (For a detailed explanation of Shashmaqom, see chapter 18)

Despite the Shashmaqom's cultural prestige, by the end of the twentieth century it was on the verge of disappearing in its historical birthplace. One by one, the old masters of *maqom* died, while others, along with younger performers, left Bukhara for Samarkand, or for Tashkent and Dushanbe—the capital cities of Uzbekistan and Tajikistan. During the Soviet era, these capitals became the new cultural centers of *maqom*, and it was in these centers that *maqom* developed in new artistic directions. In Bukhara itself, interest in the Shashmaqom weakened, both on the part of government cultural organizations and academic institutions. The art of *maqom* continued to be preserved and transmitted mainly within large families of classical music performers and connoisseurs (*shinavanda*)— among them, the Babakhanovs.

Ari Babakhanov recalls that in his childhood, well-known musicians frequently gathered in his house for live music and conversation. Some of them—in particular, students of his grandfather Levicha, who lived in Samarkand—came from other cities. The Babakhanovs had a gramophone and a collection of 78-rpm recordings of traditional music, and as a child, Ari loved to play these records and listen to music. From early childhood he was strongly influenced by the music of his father Moshe and his grandfather Levi, absorbing their music naturally, in the ambiance of family life.

Later, Ari attended the local music school and a specialized music high school (*uchilishche*) in Bukhara, following which he enrolled in the Tashkent State Conservatory. In these years—the end of the 1940s and beginning of the 1950s— music schools in Uzbekistan were still using the traditional method of teaching music by ear. At the same time, the use of European notation was becoming popular. Young Ari mastered both methods of learning music—notation and oral transmission—and in both he achieved outstanding results. His teachers in the traditional performance style of Kashgar *rubab* and *tar* were the Bukharan musicians Najmiddin Nasriddinov (1902–1966) and Maarufjon Tashpulatov (1897–1982). Alongside his studies of traditional repertory, Ari learned European and Russian music, winning several prestigious competitions for young musicians.

The worlds of Bukharan tradition and European and Russian music

Ari Babakhanov as a young man.
Courtesy of Ari Babakhanov.

were not mutually exclusive in Ari's mind but, rather, overlapping and intertwined. In this sense, Ari became a prototype for a new kind of contemporary traditional musician: a highly creative individual, steeped in tradition, with an open mind and innovative artistic ideas. Active concern for the revival of forgotten traditions and a creative attitude toward them have been abiding attributes of Ari's musical thought.

One example of this creativity is apparent in his activities as a music arranger—in particular, as an arranger of pieces traditionally performed on one particular instrument that he chose to perform on a different instrument. "Surnai navosi" (*Surnai* Melody) is an example of such a piece— an instrumental melody typically played on the *surnai*, a loud clarinet associated with outdoor festivities and celebrations, whose skirling melodic ornaments Ari arranged for the more intimate sound of the

Performer Profile: Ari Babakhanov (CONTINUED)

Kashgar *rubab*. In the process, he added a rhythmically free opening section that Bukharan musicians call *shahd*. "Surnai navosi" was well received by listeners and has remained in Ari's repertory.

In the 1970s and 1980s, Ari Babakhanov realized that the tradition of Bukharan Shashmaqom was in decline and nearing the point of disappearance in Bukhara. The great vocalists of the past were gone, many of the performance traditions had been forgotten or lost, and the celebrated Bukharan school of *maqom* vocal technique was moribund.

Ari Babakhanov with his *tanbur.*
Courtesy of Ari Babakhanov.

No students were studying *maqom* in the local music high school, nor did the school have any materials or methodologies for teaching Shashmaqom. Ari came to understand that one cause of this decline was the absence of a system of musical notation analogous to European notation that could preserve the music. "In the past, they didn't have any notation; you kept music in your head," Ari explained. "You had to remember it, and this is hard. You get old, and you forget. And as for students, sometimes there are good students, and sometimes there aren't any students at all." The process of oral transmission presumes an unbroken chain of human transmitters. Yet if this chain is broken, the transmission can become distorted or cease altogether. Gradually, Ari realized that his principal creative mission was to reconstruct the forgotten vocal and instrumental sections of the Bukharan Shashmaqom, transcribe the entire Shashmaqom cycle in European notation, and reintroduce the reconstructed Shashmaqom into the performance practice of contemporary Bukharan *maqom* performers. Ari began this work in the early 1990s. As his model for the Shashmaqom cycle, he took the version performed in his own family tradition by his father and grandfather, and before that, by

his grandfather's teacher, the great Bukharan singer Ata Jalol (1845–1928).

Ari frequently underscored his special relationship to Ata Jalol, the founder of the nineteenth-century Bukharan *maqom* school. "He was for me the most authoritative person—an outstanding singer and tradition-bearer of Shashmaqom. I bow down before him—and him alone," said Ari.

Ari completed his restoration and notation of the Bukharan Shashmaqom in Germany, where, in 2010, with the support and assistance of musicologist and Shashmaqom specialist Angelika Jung, it was published in a facsimile edition.[4] The publication presents, for the first time, a performance-based reconstruction of the Bukharan Shashmaqom that is close to the old Bukharan tradition, to the family tradition of the Babakhanovs, and to the version of Ata Jalol, to whom the publication is dedicated.

Ari also assumed the direction of the Shashmaqom ensemble in the Bukharan State Philharmonia, which he led from 1991 to 2002. Working with the ensemble, he realized his long-held dream: the revitalization of the Bukharan Shashmaqom performance tradition. By the late 1990s, the ensemble was performing a large repertory of pieces from the Shashmaqom, and presenting concerts internationally.

LISTEN   **Example 26.9.** "Surnai navosi," performed by Ari Babakhanov on the Kashgar *rubab,* 2002.

Performer Profile: Ari Babakhanov (CONTINUED)

Performer on the Kashgar *Rubab*

As a performer, Ari Babakhanov is first and foremost a soloist. He performs well on a variety of Central Asian instruments—*tanbur, tar, dutar*—but his basic instrument is the Kashgar *rubab*. The Kashgar *rubab* would not be an obvious choice for performing Bukharan Shashmaqom—in the classical tradition of Shashmaqom performance, the typical instrument is the *tanbur*. The Kashgar *rubab* is associated with Eastern Turkestan—with Uyghur musical traditions, and, in the past, with the music of Sufi brotherhoods.

The Kashgar *rubab* came into use among *maqom* musicians after the Bolshevik Revolution, in the early 1920s, when the performance of *maqom* began to expand beyond the closed quarters of the emir and elite gatherings of Bukharan connoisseurs and intellectuals to embrace more diverse audiences. In these performance situations, *maqom* ensembles themselves became more diverse. As Ari recalls, the Kashgar *rubab*'s broad dissemination throughout Uzbekistan came about thanks to Muhammadjon Mirzaev (1913–1999), a popular musician and composer of the Soviet era.

The contemporary Kashgar *rubab* Ari uses is an instrument with equally tempered scales and fixed metal frets. Such an instrument seems maladapted to perform Shashmaqom, with its carefully developed system of melismas and pitch-bending. In Ari's hands, however, the Kashgar *rubab* displays all of the tonal nuance, rich timbral colors, and sophisticated technique that are part of a cultivated classical tradition. The introduction of Kashgar *rubab* to the performance tradition of the Bukharan Shashmaqom was the direct result of Ari Babakhanov's work.

Ari's playing style is distinguished by exceptional clarity and rigor and is devoid of any frills or pretentiousness. His sound is crisp and clear, with a filigree-like texture. His firm technical mastery of the *rubab* frees him to focus on revealing the inner meaning and hidden contents of the music he is performing. As an example, listen to Ari's recording of the miniature instrumental piece "Gardun-i Dugoh," from Maqom Dugoh. The performance is distinguished by external simplicity coupled with extraordinary depth in its revelation of the philosophical content of the music, with its lyrical aura of "light sorrow."

Ari Babakhanov as *Bastakor*

Ari Babakhanov denies that he is a *bastakor*—a composer of

Shashmaqom ensemble in Bukhara. Ari Babakhanov is in the first row, far right.

Photo by Shavkat Boltaev.

LISTEN **Example 26.10.** "Gardun-i Dugoh," performed by Ari Babakhanov on the Kashgar *rubab*.

popular classic songs. "I don't consider myself a composer," he said. "Or perhaps I'm a frustrated composer. I've played a lot of music. I'm always playing, day and night, to ensure that I'm in top form." Ari explains that his ventures into music composition came about simply from a desire to create his own performance repertory. "No one writes music for me," Ari said. "And I don't play anyone else's compositions, not even Muhammadjon Mirzaev's. I create my own pieces and I play them. What's important for me is that every time I play, the repertory should feel fresh and new. That's why I don't play existing compositions. I play what I compose myself."

Ari figures that he has composed around eighty songs and instrumental pieces. The first of these, "Tinchlik diyori" (Country of peace), dates back to 1948, and became well known in Uzbekistan through its performance by the popular singer Kommuna Ismailova (b. 1927). Another of Babakhanov's compositions, "Tarje-i Navo," provided the musical setting for a contemporary dance by choreographer Kizlarkhon Dostmukhamedova. These days, instrumental melodies composed by Babakhanov—for example,

Ari Babakhanov with Kashgar *rubab*.
Photo by Shavkat Boltaev.

"Khurram," "Orom," and "Dilrabo"— have achieved wide popularity. "Khurram," composed in 1957, illuminates the expressive potential of the Kashgar *rubab* with particular clarity, and brought Ari to the attention of a wide circle of musicians in Uzbekistan and Tajikistan. The piece has been covered by a number of contemporary performers— something that traditional musicians call *nazira* ("imitation," "replica") and contemporary performers call "remix."

Despite Ari's modest self-evaluation of his talent as a composer, his compositions

unquestionably represent a clear and original voice in the musical culture of Uzbekistan and Tajikistan. His substantial compositional oeuvre still awaits a specialized scholarly study and systematic archiving.

Composition in the *Maqom* Tradition

As an active revitalizer of a neglected art form, Ari Babakhanov is categorically against preserving the Shashmaqom as if it were an untouchable museum object. On the contrary, with his deep knowledge of the aesthetic principles of *maqom* Ari has long been able to create new music in the style and spirit of the *maqom* tradition.

As a living art form, *maqom* composition has to a large extent been lost. Awareness of this loss has spurred a number of composers in Uzbekistan and Tajikistan to attempt to revive the tradition of composing in the *maqom* style. In different ways, all of these composers are searching for a means to revitalize tradition and traditional musical thought in the conditions of contemporary culture. Ari's experience in this regard offers a useful model.

Ari has used a variety of approaches in his work as a *maqom* composer. One of them is to compose new versions of traditional pieces that already exist

LISTEN Example 26.11. "Khurram," performed by Ari Babakhanov on the Kashgar *rubab*.

Performer Profile: Ari Babakhanov (CONTINUED)

in the Shashmaqom. In this way, Ari produced a series of his own versions of well-known pieces, in the style of a *nazira*. An example is his piece "Tarje-i Navo," where, as an add-on to the canonical melody, Ari composed an additional fast section (*ufor*) that provides contrast and variety through shifts in rhythm and tempo.

Ari has also made new versions of older pieces by separating a melody from its underlying rhythmic pattern (*usul*) and superimposing it on a different rhythmic pattern. The resulting piece can then be joined to its original model to yield a rhythmically contrasting sequence of pieces that are linked by their use of an identical melody. The operation of melodic superimposition on different rhythmic patterns can be repeated multiple times, thus extending the sequence of rhythmically contrasting pieces to build a suite. This technique is at the very core

of the Shashmaqom, whose six modally organized cycles consist of series of metro-rhythmic variations on one tune. Ari Babakhanov revived this technique, which is exemplified in his piece "Talqincha-i Mashq-i Chorgoh." To compose this piece, Ari took a popular instrumental melody, "Mashq-i Chorgoh," and superimposed it on the rhythmic pattern *talqincha*. To this piece, Ari added a second piece with a contrasting rhythm commonly played on the set of small kettledrums called *nagora*. This piece he titled "Nagora Chorgoh." Joining them together, Ari created a "micro-cycle" that was like a miniature model of the entire Shashmaqom. Ari often added a third piece to such micro-cycles that reflected yet another rhythm and tempo—the dance-like *ufor*—thus making a direct analogy to the dramatic shaping of the Shashmaqom and its affective progression from a state of

contemplation to a mood of festivity and celebration.

Ari Babakhanov has produced a remarkable creative synthesis by fusing the artistic and aesthetic consciousness of different cultural worlds: the historical memory and legacy of Bukharan tradition; the paradoxical cultural politics of the Soviet Union that supported elements of traditional musical culture at the same time that it strove to suppress others; and the post-Soviet era of cultural globalization. Ari has combined a host of seemingly contradictory and incompatible domains: tradition and contemporaneity, Europe and Central Asia, the culture of Muslims and Bukharan Jews. But these domains aren't locked in confrontation. Rather, they complement and harmonize with one another, forming the complex, multi-sided identity of this remarkable contemporary traditional musician.

LISTEN **Example 26.12.** "Tarje-i Navo," performed by Ari Babakhanov on the Kashgar *rubab*, accompanied by Tolib Temirov (*doira*).

LISTEN **Example 26.13.** "Talqincha-i Mashq-i Chorgoh" and "Nagora Chorgoh," performed by Ari Babakhanov on the Kashgar *rubab*, accompanied by Tolib Temirov (*doira*).

1. After listening to the five musical examples performed by Ari Babakhanov, describe how tradition and modernity are both expressed in his music. Can you find analogues in your own culture to the kind of "contemporary traditional musician" that Ari exemplifies?

2. Is it appropriate for contemporary musicians to create new compositions based on traditional models? If so, what if any constraints should apply to working with traditional musical materials?

3. How do the physical characteristics of a musical instrument shape the kind of music that can be performed on it? Can any kind of contemporary music be performed on traditional instruments? If not, what are the limiting factors?

4. Do you consider it possible to revive and revitalize neglected forms of traditional music to the point where they can once again become a part of an active performance practice? If so, how must they be adapted in order to have an impact on contemporary listeners, and in particular, on young audiences?

NOTES

1. See Veronica Doubleday, *Three Women of Herat: A Memoir of Life, Love and Friendship in Afghanistan* (London: Tauris Parke Paperbacks, 2006).

2. Michael Zand, "Bukhara vii. Bukharan Jews," in *Encyclopaedia Iranica* online, http://www.iranicaonline.org/articles/bukhara-vii, accessed December 1, 2014.

3. "Ari aka" is an honorific title that means literally "big brother Ari"; in Bukharan-Tajik dialect, the word order is reversed: aka Ari.

4. Angelika Jung, ed., *Der Shashmaqam aus Bukhara uberliefert von den alten Meistern notiert von Ari Babakhanov* [The Shashmaqam of Bukhara, notated by Ari Babakhanov in the tradition of the old masters] (Berlin: Verlag Hans Schiler, 2010).

CHAPTER 27 Music and Culture in Badakhshan

THEODORE LEVIN

Badakhshan is the mountainous region—poetically known in Persian as Bam-i Jahan, the "Roof of the World"—that comprises the sparsely populated eastern half of Tajikistan and northeast Afghanistan, and extends into the borderlands region of China's Xinjiang Uyghur Autonomous Region. Music and other aspects of culture in this tri-national region of what might be called Greater Badakhshan share many common features; however, the authors who discuss music in Badakhshan in this book have all conducted their research in Tajik Badakhshan. There, nestled in a series of riverine valleys that descend from the Pamir Mountains to the Panj River—the boundary line between Tajikistan and Afghanistan—are scores of small settlements whose inhabitants have cultivated a vibrant tradition of devotional song, dance, and contemplative instrumental music.

Photo by Sebastian Schutyser. Courtesy of Aga Khan Music Initiative.

Badakhshani music and dance represent a distinct cultural practice within Central Asia that has been shaped by the combined forces of geography, history, language, and religion. In Tajik Badakhshan, where the majestic Pamirs reach heights only slightly lower than those of the Himalayas, rugged terrain has impeded contact between Pamiri peoples and inhabitants of other regions of Central Asia. One consequence of cultural isolation has been the preservation of so-called Pamiri languages, which belong to the Eastern Iranian family of languages but are distinct from Persian and are not used in a literary form. Orally composed folk song texts in Pamiri languages such as Shughni and Rushani are common in Badakhshan, but the literary texts typically set to music in spiritual songs are drawn from classical Persian or modern Tajik, an eastern dialect of Persian. Oral and literary poetry have merged to a certain extent, and poems by classical poets such as Rumi, Hafez, and Hilali are often transmitted orally in forms that diverge from written sources, if, indeed, written sources exist. Many poems attributed to the great poets, in particular Rumi, are almost certainly apocrypha.

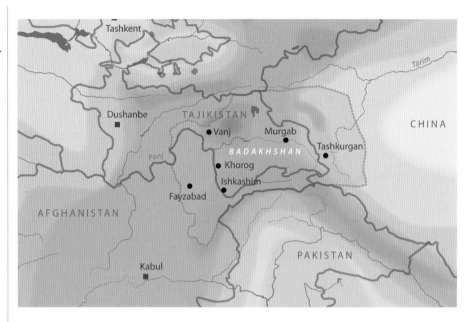

The region of what might be called Greater Badakhshan comprises the eastern half of Tajikistan and northeast Afghanistan, and extends into the borderlands region of China's Xinjiang-Uyghur Autonomous Region.

A portrait of His Highness the Aga Khan hangs in an Ismaili home.

Music in Badakhshan encompasses a number of different styles and genres. Among the most widespread are devotional songs performed at a variety of ritualized events. These include all-night gatherings following the death of a community member, weekly Thursday evening and Friday prayer meetings, and celebrations linked to *Nowruz* (traditional New Year) and Ramadan. Many if not most Badakhshanis are Shiʻa Ismaili Muslims, and the Ismaili spiritual and devotional tradition has had a strong and abiding influence on Pamiri expressive culture. Ismaili communities have existed in the Pamir Mountains for close to a millennium. Badakhshani Ismailis attribute the founding of these communities to Nasir Khusraw (b. 1004), a Persian theologian, philosopher, traveler, and poet who brought Ismaili teachings to Central Asia from Fatimid Egypt in the middle of the eleventh century.

Ismaili religious thought emphasizes a balance between the exterior, literal meaning of sacred scriptures and religious commandments (*zohir*) and their esoteric or inner meaning (*botin*), which illuminates eternal spiritual truths (*haqā'iq*). Such a vision of Islam, common to other esoteric traditions such as Sufism, finds expression in broader cultural forms that are often located in the vernacular and draw on local musical genres and styles. Among the Badakhshani Ismailis, spiritual concerts featuring sung poetry austerely accompanied on stringed instruments and frame drum (*daf*) serve as one route toward the inner—toward the soul—and the illumination of spiritual truths. This performance genre is called *maddoh*—literally, "praise." A *maddoh* typically offers praise to the "Family of the Prophet" (Ahl al Bayt), and in particular to Ali, the first Shiʻa Imam, and to the current Imam, or hereditary spiritual leader, of the Ismailis, His Highness the Aga Khan. *Maddoh* provides a vessel for the spiritual power known as *baraka,* and *maddoh* singers, called *maddohkhon*s, are highly esteemed in Badakhshan (see chapter 28). In the Wakhan Valley region of Badakhshan, a closely related form of religious music performance is known as *qasoid-khonī* (see chapter 29).

Among the younger generation of *maddohkhon*s in and around Khorog, the capital and largest city of Tajik Badakhshan (population around fifty thousand), one of the most sought after is Aqnazar Alovatov (b. 1970). Aqnazar is frequently called upon to sing at memorial gatherings and at Thursday evening prayers. "It's normal to sing for two or three hours at these events," Aqnazar explained. "There's usually more than one *maddohkhon*—sometimes a lot of them show up, and they take turns singing. The skill of *maddoh* performance is in putting together texts that create a particular mood or feeling. I change the text from one performance to the next, and I try not to use texts that are used by other musicians." Rich in mystical allegory and allusion, the metaphysical poems that singers sequence together in *maddoh* purify the soul of the deceased, offer succor to the bereaved, and provide ethical and spiritual guidance to the community.

*Maddohkhon*s are always men, but women have their own ritual music for memorial gatherings, called *lalaik.* Example 27.1 shows an excerpt from a performance of *lalaik* at a memorial ceremony in Khichigh, a village in the Pamir Mountains. The lead singer, a woman named Azatmo Munchoeva, is from the neighboring village of Suniv, in the Roshkala subregion of Badakhshan. She explained that *lalaik* is sung only in Pamiri languages—typically Shughni—as opposed to Tajik Persian. Azatmo visits neighboring villages, performing *lalaik* for women at memorial ceremonies.

WATCH
Example 27.1. "Lalaik," performed by Azatmo Munchoeva and companions. Filmed by Saodat Ismailova and Carlos Casas in the village of Khichigh, 2009.

Another musical genre that figures prominently in Badakhshan is *falak*—sober, lament-like songs that many Badakhshanis believe to possess healing qualities, and whose texts typically address philosophical themes (see chapter 30). One of the meanings that *falak* conveys is "fate," and the poems set to music in *falak* often speak of the vicissitudes of fate and the limitations of human agency. *Falak* is sung both by men and women, and may be performed a cappella, in free rhythm, or with instrumental accompaniment and in a regular meter.

Badakhshani music also includes a rich variety of instrumental genres that, like Badakhshani vocal genres, have a strong regional identity. Archaic dance tunes blend the nasal, metallic timbre of the *ghijak*—a spike fiddle whose resonating chamber Badakhshanis often make from a tin can—with the blunt plucking sounds of the Pamiri *tanbur,* a gut-stringed variant of the more common metal-stringed instruments found in other parts of Central Asia, and the resonant thump of a *daf*—a large frame drum. Badakhshani dance focuses on graceful movements of the arms and hands that are believed to symbolize the flight of birds—an atavistic reference to Badakhshan's animistic, pre-Islamic past. One such dance is "Rapo," illustrated in the following audio and video examples.

LISTEN

Example 27.2. "Rapo," performed by Jonboz Dushanbiev (*ghijak*), Ghulomsho Safarov (Pamiri *tanbur*), and Shodi Mabatqulov (*daf*). From *The Badakhshan Ensemble: Song and Dance from the Pamir Mountains,* vol. 5 of *Music of Central Asia* (SFR, 2007), track 7.

WATCH

Example 27.3. Excerpt from "Rapo" Dance, performed by Ghulomsho Safarov and members of his family with Jonboz Dushanbiev, *ghijak* and vocal. Filmed by Saodat Ismailova and Carlos Casas, 2005.

"*Rapo* is an old dance," explains Jonboz Dushanbiev. "The name comes from two Tajik words: *rah* (road) and *po* (foot), thus 'foot on the road.' It's normally played on the *ghijak*—you can add other instruments, but the *ghijak* has to be there. Men and women both dance it, and the dancing can take different forms.

Right: Jonboz Dushanbiev holding a tin can *ghijak.*

Far right: Mukhtor Muborakqadamov plays the *setar,* accompanied by Shodi Mabatqulov on *daf.*

Photos by Sebastian Schutyser. Courtesy of Aga Khan Music Initiative.

The arms make swimming movements, while the legs work more quickly. These days people dance *rapo* at weddings. It starts slow, gradually speeds up, and in the end, it's really fast."

Some instrumental music consists of instrumental versions of texted songs. One such piece is the following arrangement of "Kholatro Banda" (I'm a slave of your mole), performed on the *setar,* a fretted, long-necked lute whose multiple sympathetic strings provide a gentle drone background to the plucked melody line, creating a contemplative sound reminiscent of the Indian *sitar,* of which the *setar* is most likely a distant ancestor (the name of the song refers to the culturally normative regard for facial moles or birthmarks as a seductive sign of beauty—a common image in poetry and songs).

LISTEN

Example 27.4. "Kholatro Banda" (I'm a slave of your mole), performed by Mukhtor Muborakqadamov (*setar*) and Shodi Mabatqulov (*daf*). *The Badakhshan Ensemble: Song and Dance from the Pamir Mountains,* vol. 5 of *Music of Central Asia* (SFR, 2007), track 8.

Mukhtor Muborakqadamov explained how he came to perform "Kholatro Banda": "I heard this song performed by Qimmatshah Parpishoev, a *ghijak* player now in his seventies, and adapted it to the *setar.* I use two strings to play the melody, and the other strings—there are 12 in all—are resonating strings. When it's sung, the song has a strongly meditative feel. I like Indian music and frequently listen to it, so probably that's why my style sounds Indian."

The distinctive rhythms that underlie Badakhshani music are expressed not only as accompaniment for stringed instruments but in ritualized drumming

Women play frame drums for a wedding in a village near Khorog, Badakhshan.

Badakhshani *setar.*

performed by groups of drummers, both male and female, during weddings, funerals, and other festivities. In example 27.5, frame drummer Shodi Mabatqulov demonstrates basic drum rhythms on the *daf*. The film then cuts to a group of women playing frame drums to accompany a wedding procession, and then to Shodi and other men playing frame drums at the same wedding.

WATCH **Example 27.5.** Shodi Mabatqulov demonstrates frame drum (*daf*) rhythms. Filmed by Saodat Ismailova and Carlos Casas near Khorog, Badakhshan, 2006.

The Badakhshani frame drum *daf* is featured in a form of ritualized competition called *dafsoz*, from *daf* (tambourine) + *soz* (song). In *dafsoz*, two groups of singers, each consisting of four to five singers headed by a lead singer (*sarbaytkhon*), sing strophic songs, accompanying themselves on the *daf*. The *dafsoz* begins at a slow tempo and gradually speeds up as the singers cycle through different song texts. A brief excerpt from a *dafsoz* is presented in the following video example.

WATCH **Example 27.6.** "Dafsoz" performed in Suchon by Abdulakim Abdurakhimov (*sarbaytkhon*), Aliyar Bakhtiyarov, Shanbe Oshurmamadov, Sultonsaid Dodmamadov, Asadbek Shodmonbekov, and Shirinjon Olamov. Video courtesy of Haydar Tawakkalov.

The Badakhshan Ensemble.
Photo by Sebastian Schutyser. Courtesy of Aga Khan Music Initiative.

Nowadays, the performance of *dafsoz* is less common than in earlier times, but as older traditions recede, young Badakhshani musicians, often banding together to form a fixed ensemble, are creating new tradition-based music in styles that range from classical to pop and avant-garde. One such group is the Badakhshan Ensemble, which has performed widely in Europe and North America.

The Badakhshan Ensemble was the brainchild of Soheba Davlatshoeva (b. 1970), a vivacious singer and dancer who grew up in a small village on the Ghund River, fifty miles from Khorog. "We created the ensemble ourselves," Soheba recounted proudly. "It's not a state-sponsored group. We were students in the Institute of Arts in Dushanbe [Tajikistan's capital] at the end of the 1980s. We finished one semester there, and then in the winter of 1990, the Institute closed because of the conflict that grew into Tajikistan's Civil War. We had to leave Dushanbe and return to Badakhshan.

Half the city of Dushanbe left." Eventually, Soheba and other ensemble members regrouped under the umbrella of the regional drama theater in Khorog, where they played music for theatrical productions and gave concerts. Their music-making extended beyond the theater, and at many events they were joined by Jonboz Dushanbiev, a charismatic *ghijak* player a generation older than Soheba and her cohort with a broad knowledge of Badakhshani music, poetry, and musical instrument-building. When not touring abroad or performing in Dushanbe, the Badakhshan Ensemble often provides music for wedding festivities. "We don't perform folklore at weddings," Soheba said matter-of-factly. "If we did, no one would hire us. What people want to listen and dance to is pop music." The pop music Soheba had in mind is a local variety that combines the unmistakable melodic intervals, piercing vocal timbres, and loping rhythms of Badakhshani songs with the accompaniment of synthesizer, bass guitar, and electrified Pamiri instruments. Such hybrid pop music exists in myriad local forms throughout the former USSR and is rooted in older styles of tradition-based popular song that developed during the Soviet era (see chapter 35). An example of the Badakhshan Ensemble performing at a local teenager's birthday party is reproduced in example 27.7.

WATCH **Example 27.7.** Badakhshan Ensemble performing at a teenager's birthday party. Filmed by Saodat Ismailova and Carlos Casas, Badakhshan, 2006.

Members of the Badakhshan Ensemble are active not only as performers but as composers and arrangers. *Setar* player Mukhtor Muborakqadamov, who arranged the contemplative instrumental piece in example 27.4, also sets poetic texts to his own newly composed melodies. Example 27.8 reproduces one such piece, called "Zohidi Pokizasirisht" (The virtuous puritan), whose text is a poem of Hafez. "It's popular among both old and young people in Khorog," said Mukhtor. "Young people here read Hafez. They study his poetry in school, and also read him on their own. Older people know the text by heart. We perform the song a lot in our concerts and at weddings. You can accompany it with a synthesizer, but it's better in a folk style."

A teenager's birthday party in a village near Khorog.

LISTEN **Example 27.8.** "Zohidi Pokizasirisht" (The virtuous puritan), composed by Mukhtor Muborakqadamov (2000) on a text by Hafez, performed by the Badakhshan Ensemble. Vocal solo by Aqnazar Alovatov. *The Badakhshan Ensemble: Song and Dance from the Pamir Mountains,* vol. 5 of *Music of Central Asia* (SFR, 2007), track 3.

'Aibi rindon makun, ay zohid-i pokizasirisht,
Ki gunoh-i digaron bar tu naxohand navisht.

Man agar nekam, agar bad, tu birav, khudro bosh,
Har kase z-on daravad oqibat-i kor, kī kisht.

Hama kas tolib-i yor ast, chī hushyor-u chī mast,
Hama jo xona-yi 'ishq ast, chī masjid, chī kunisht.

Noumedam makun az sobiqa-yi lutf-i azal,
Tu pas-i parda chī donī, ki kī khub ast-u kī zisht?

Bar amal takya makun, khoja, ki az rūz-i azal,
Tu chī donī qalam-i sun' ba nomat chī navisht?

Bogh-i firdavs latif ast, valekin zinhor,
Tu ghanimat shumorī soya-yi bed-u lab-i kisht.

Hofezo, rūz-i ajal gar ba kaf orī jome,
Yaksar az kūh-yi kharobot barandat ba bihisht.

O you virtuous puritan,
    pure-hearted, sober and chaste!

Would you please stop finding faults
    with us drunken vagabonds,
        lowly and base.

Rest assured you won't have to pay the price
    for someone else's sin and vice.

Let me be
    —good or bad—
        as I please!

Why don't you worry about your own deeds?
After all, it is whatever one sows
    That at the end one reaps.

Everyone seeks the Beloved,
    be they sober or drunk.
All places are good enough for acts of devotion and love,
    Be they a mosque, a temple or a synagogue.

Don't let me lose faith
    in the eminence of divine grace.
How can you tell,
    if the face masked by a veil
        is beautiful or hideous?

O superior lord,
       don't rely on your good deeds alone,
       because you can't know
what the strokes of creation's pen
wrote on your behalf
on that first day,
at the primordial dawn.

    The garden of paradise is beautiful, with radiant grace,
    But don't let that blind you!
    Don't miss out on
    the shadow of the willow,
    the grandeur of the meadow's edge.

    O Hafez, on your final day, right before your death
        at the moment you draw your last breath,
    if you happen to stumble on
        a cup of wine,
            you'll be delivered,
                without hindrance or delay,
                    to your eternal abode, the paradise divine!

Badakhshani *daf*.

STUDY QUESTIONS

1. Can you think of an analogue in your own cultural tradition to the poetry of Hafez, which, though written more than six centuries ago, remains vitally alive in popular tradition? What accounts for its lasting power and popularity?

2. How do you understand the meaning and message of Hafez's poem?

3. In your estimation, how successful is Mukhtor Muborakqadamov in providing an appropriate musical setting for Hafez's poem?

NOTE

This chapter represents an edited version of booklet notes to the CD-DVD *The Badakhshan Ensemble: Song and Dance from the Pamir Mountains,* vol. 5 of *Music of Central Asia* (Smithsonian Folkways Recordings, 2007).

CHAPTER 28 The *Maddoh* Tradition
of Badakhshan

BENJAMIN D. KOEN

Maddoh is a term imbued with mystical, historical, and didactic meaning. *Maddoh* means "praise" and generally refers to a genre of sung panegyric poetry that existed historically in Persian-, Arabic-, and Turkic-speaking cultures. The genres that are referred to as *maddoh* in this vast cultural region display similarities in poetic content and in the family of musical instruments used for performance. However, the musical element of *maddoh* and the vocal style in which it is performed vary considerably from one *maddoh* genre to another. This variety is particularly evident in the *maddoh* tradition of Badakhshan, where the Pamir Mountain range that largely isolates Badakhshan from neighboring parts of Central Asia has mitigated the influence of other cultures, leaving Pamiri culture to develop with considerable independence.

Throughout the Middle East and Central Asia, depending on local language conventions, the term *maddoh* and its variants (*madā, maddāh, meddah, madh, maddai, madih*) can have multiple meanings that refer to one or more aspects of performance. These can include the music itself, the poetic text, a section of the performance, the genre as a whole, the master musician-panegyrist, or the regular, often weekly ceremony in which *maddoh* is performed. In Tajikistan, *maddoh* typically refers to the foremost genre of religious music among the Ismailis of Badakhshan; *maddoh-khonī* specifically refers to the ceremony or devotional gathering where *maddoh* is performed; and *maddohkhon* refers to the master singer performer of *maddoh*. All of the *maddohkhon*s with whom I worked were men, which is typical of this genre.

The meaning ascribed to *maddoh* poetry and prayer is central to its purpose and function in Pamiri culture. The sung prayer-poetry of *maddoh* is predominantly from the "classic" period of Persian mystical poetry, roughly from the tenth to the late fifteenth centuries. *Maddoh* draws from the works of such poets as

Shams-i Tabrizi, Sanai, Nasir Khusraw, Sa'di, Rudaki, Hafez, Jami, Hiloli, and others. The vast majority, however, is from Jalal ad-Din Rumi.

Maddoh performance consists of multiple, often overlapping poetic forms, including *ghazal, rubā'ī, qasida, masnavi,* and *mukhammas,* as well as the prayer forms of *munojot* and *du'o.* Passages from the Qur'an and Hadith are also employed in *maddoh* performance, as are spontaneous, inspired poems, prayers, and vocalizations offered by the *maddohkhon,* accompanying musicians, and other community members who attend a *maddoh* ceremony. In addition, the related genre of music-lament known as *falak,* which draws its textual base primarily from the oral tradition of folk poetry, and secondarily from classic Persian mystical poetry, can function as a kind of interlude within the context of *maddoh* performance. All of these forms and expressions are interwoven and linked together in flexible ways, allowing for the inspiration of the moment to guide performance.

Although Badakhshani *maddoh* shares some ceremonial aspects with *samo, zikr, qawwali,* and other religious and devotional music of the region that may be viewed as facilitating healing in varying degrees of intensity and specificity, *maddoh* is unique in its musical forms, as well as its cultural, religious, and medical functions. Musically, the rhythm, melody, and form of *maddoh* bear no resemblance to *samo, zikr,* and *qawwali* in their diverse expressions throughout the Middle East, North Africa, and South Asia. Poetically, *maddoh* is also distinct. For instance, although a subsection of *maddoh* might include a *ghazal* of Hafez that could also be found in a South Asian *qawwali* or classical Persian *radif* performance, the rhythmic, melodic, and formal treatment of the *ghazal* in *maddoh* would be different than in these other musical genres.

During the Soviet era, which lasted until 1991, the traditional practice of *maddoh* was forced underground. Since then, it has emerged as a symbol of cultural and religious identity as well as a means of individual and community healing. Recently, it has been employed as an adjunctive medical treatment and supplement to anesthesia during surgery in the Khorog hospital. *Maddoh* is regularly performed on Thursday or Friday evenings, and can last up to several hours—at times extending to dawn of the following day.

In Pamiri culture, *maddoh* serves multiple functions. It is performed in the context of devotion, worship, and education; at funerals, memorials, and rituals of mourning; on certain religious occasions or commemorations; and as a healing ceremony. These functions are not mutually exclusive, and at any particular *maddoh* ceremony, one or more of these functions might provide an individual's specific reason for choosing to participate.

For a traditional funeral ceremony, *maddoh* and *falak* can be performed in an interwoven and continuous manner for up to three days and nights—men performing *maddoh,* and both women and men performing *falak.* The duration and intensity of a performance depends on the social status of the deceased: the more important the social position, the more elaborate the ceremony. Elaborateness can be expressed by lengthening the duration of a *maddoh* or *falak* performance, expanding the number of musicians and singers, and intensifying the expression of spiritual power, or *baraka,* that lies at the heart of *maddoh.*

Baraka, a central aspect of local belief, is a spiritual power or energy that can heal, bless, protect, guide, edify, enlighten, and transform people, as well as effect change in the physical and spiritual worlds. *Baraka* emanates from God and is manifest throughout all of creation. Most often, *baraka* is associated with the founders of major religions, prophets, holy people, saints, religious leaders, and mystical figures. In addition, personal items and places associated with holy figures, as well as other special places in the natural and built environment, are believed to possess an especially high degree of *baraka*. In the context of a *maddoh* ceremony, *baraka* from different sources comes together to create potential healing energy. For instance, the Pamir Mountains, which are viewed locally as a majestic creation of God and as a region are associated with various holy figures—most importantly with the mystic Nasir Khusraw—are believed to contain and emit *baraka*. The *maddohkhon* himself is believed to embody *baraka* and have the power to facilitate its flow through the performance of *maddoh*. The words of the poems and prayers of *maddoh* are also believed to possess *baraka,* and close association with these empowered words can bring about transformation of the self and healing.

Maddoh is typically performed in the largest room of a Pamiri home. The room is considered sacred and is accorded a special degree of reverence. The main floor is typically raised, providing a sub-floor section that can be heated with coals or embers during the dangerously cold winter months. During *maddoh* performance, the room is transformed into the sacred, ceremonial space known as the *maddohkhona* (*khona:* house, home, room), which means "praise house" or "praise room." The *maddohkhona* is believed to contain a special degree of *baraka*. During the

Right: Exterior view of a Pamiri house.
Far right: The interior of a *maddohkhona.*
Photo by Theodore Levin.

Soviet period, when local beliefs, practices, and expressions of Pamiri and Islamic culture were forbidden and systematically repressed, the *maddohkhona*—which, to the uninitiated, appears to be just a large room—enabled the Pamiri home to function secretly as a family or local mosque. Thus, within the physical structure of the Pamiri home, two central institutions of local belief—the *maddohkhona* and the mosque—were quietly kept alive during much of the twentieth century. This dual function makes the physical room that comprises the sacred place of the *maddohkhona* perhaps the most important built structure in Badakhshan.

HEALING THROUGH *MADDOH*

As a healing ceremony, *maddoh* exists within a web of diverse healing practices, including multiple forms of music and prayer, as well as traditional, herbal, and biomedical treatments. While an underlying aspect of *maddoh* performance relates to overall health and general well-being, the performance also contains the potential for a specific healing effect to occur, or for the *maddoh* to cure a specific illness or disease. With respect to a curative effect, much is attributed to and depends upon an individual's intention and attention. That is, in order for the healing of a patient to take place, that patient must have an intention to become healed. The patient also must pay attention to words, symbols, metaphors, and musical-poetic structures that facilitate the experience of inner spiritual realities (*botin*). Essential as well is the healing energy of *baraka* that emanates from God and imbues the ceremony with transformational potential. In discussions about healing experiences, participants in *maddoh* ceremonies always mentioned that they hoped, wanted, or intended for healing to occur, and that their thoughts were focused on God, a spiritual dimension, or a kind of nothingness—allowing music and words to penetrate deeply into their minds and creating a healing effect.

Elaborating on this theme, one traditional healer and religious leader, who primarily communicated through his apprentice and whose specialty was the application of specific prayers to heal specific ailments, explained that "*maddoh* has a special power to heal the mind and spirit because of the *power of sound* [both of the voice and instruments] to make the spiritual power greater." He added, "If patients are not ready for the power of sound, they might be harmed psychologically."

In the context of *maddoh,* stillness is key to moving the mind across the bridge of transformative consciousness. Participants begin by making their bodies generally still, usually sitting cross-legged in a loosely constructed circle formation in the *maddohkhona*. Some individuals face the musicians; others lean against a wall, another person, or one of the five structural and symbolic pillars that frame the sacred performance space; others might even lie down with their gaze directed upward toward the heavens. Participants direct their attention to an individualized, mystical, indefinable dimension, preparing themselves for the ritual performance. As sacred thoughts and prayers emerge in the consciousness of the individual, they might be whispered or mumbled to oneself, or the individual might remain in a state of silent, introspective communion. Often, the master musician, the *maddohkhon,* quietly utters a prayer to help gather his thoughts and focus his attention before the first note is plucked on the *rubab* (long-necked lute), formally announcing the beginning of the performance. Then, musical prayers begin, sung and chanted in flowing melodies, at times in a gentle, soft voice, at times in a rough, dry, and raspy voice, but always in a sincere voice. The act of performance and mystical conversation between the *maddohkhon* and the *rubab* serves as a metaphor for communication between the Divine and the world of creation. Lines of poetry and prayer build from verse to verse, section to section, until they are wailed out from the depths of the *maddohkhon*'s heart in a booming voice that further draws the attention of participants into a meditative, mystical vortex of music and prayer from which healing can emerge.

THE PAMIRI *RUBAB* AS SYMBOL AND METAPHOR

Pamiri *rubab.*

The principal instrument used in the performance of *maddoh* is the Pamiri *rubab,* a long-necked lute. The *tanbur*—also a long-necked lute—occasionally replaces the *rubab,* but most often accompanies it during a performance. Other accompanying instruments include the *daf* (frame drum), and at times the *ghijak* or *kamancha* (spike fiddle). A *maddoh* performance can include multiple players of any of the above-mentioned instruments; however, *maddoh* can also be performed solo by the *maddohkhon,* who both sings and plays the *rubab.* A typical performance includes one or two *rubab*s (or one *rubab* and one *tanbur*), and one or two *daf*s.

The *rubab* is a local symbol and metaphor for a human being and is believed to have a spiritual essence. In a well-known Pamiri legend, the *rubab* descends from heaven as a gift from God, is modeled after the human form, and the skin and gut of a sacrificial lamb is used for the face and strings of the instrument. The instrument is played by angels and is meant to be used for singing praises to God. This metaphor shows the *rubab* as a reflection of the higher

Rubab with prayer carved in the wooden deck of the instrument.

self within a human being. Both the *rubab* and human beings are instruments of God through which spiritual energy (*baraka*) can flow. The *rubab* often has prayers carved into the middle section of the instrument or written on the skin that covers the body or resonance chamber. Thus the *rubab* is viewed as being in a perpetual state of prayer in which it sings praises to God.

> **Example 28.1.** "Maddoh" (Praise), arranged by Aqnazar Alovatov, performed by Aqnazar Alovatov (vocal), Shodi Mabatqulov (*daf* and vocal), Olucha Mualibshoev (vocal), Mukhtor Muborakqadamov (*setar*), and Ghulomsho Safarov (Pamiri *rubab*, Pamiri *tanbur*, vocal). From *The Badakhshan Ensemble: Song and Dance from the Pamir Mountains*, vol. 5 of *Music of Central Asia* (SFR, 2007), track 6. English translations by Saghi Ghazerani.

This sixteen-minute *maddoh* is an abridged version, created specially for inclusion on a CD, of what would typically be a much longer performance. Poetic texts are fully transliterated and translated below. The English translation, by Iranian literary scholar Saghi Gazerani, is in free verse that strives to convey the spirit and vigor of the original language and imagery.

In performing a *maddoh*, the *maddohkhon* is free to choose the individual poems—or, more commonly, excerpts of poems—whose texts he will sing (*maddoh* is virtually always performed by men), but the performance itself follows standard formal conventions. This *maddoh* begins with an excerpt from an unattributed *ghazal* sung softly in free rhythm to the spare accompaniment of a Pamiri *rubab*. The introduction sets a contemplative mood and draws listeners into the text:

Assalom, ey qimmatitar gavhar-i daryo-yi jud,
Assalom, ey tozatar gulbarg-i sahro-yi vujud.
Assalom, ey on, ki to az jabha-yi odam natoft,
Nur-i pokat kas naburd az qudsiyon ūro sujud.
Sad salomat mefiristam har dam, ay fakhr-i kirom,
Bū, ki oyad yak alaykam dar javob-i sad salom.

Greetings to you,
  The precious pearl of generosity's ocean!
Greetings to you,
  The delicate rose petal of soul's desert!

Greetings to you,
  the only human,
    to whose brilliant light,
      even the angels prostrated.

With each breath,
   I send a hundred greetings to you,
      O pride of the most magnanimous!
So that there may be a single response,
   to one out of a hundred of my greetings.

Next (1:32) comes a *mukhammas* attributed to Hafez, but surely apocryphal, also set in free rhythm and accompanied only by *rubab:*

Ay, shuda, hamd-u sanogū-yi tu murgh-u mohī,
Hamaro dodayī az rahmat-i khud ogohī.
Osiyonro tu burun az khatar-i gumrohī,
Ay, gadoyon-i turo orif-u shohanshohī,
Hama kasro tu dihī davlat-u mansabjoyī.

To ki kardī ba yad-i qudrat-i khud odamī hast,
Mū'min-u kofir-u tarso hamaro rū ba tu hast.
On yake savmiya dorad, digarash bodaparast,
Hama dar masjid-u maykhona chī hushyor-u chī mast,
Hama khonand turo, to tu kiro mekhonī.

Yusuf az choh barovarda dihī davlat-u bakht,
Ba Sulaimon tu dihī mamlakat-u hotam-u takht,
Ba sū-yi takhta-yi tobut kashidand hama rakht,
Be rizo-yi tu yake barg narezad zi darakht,
Kī tavonad, ki ba mulki tu kunad berohī.

Chand khok-i darat, ey dūst ba mijgon ruftan?
Chand shab to ba sahar dar gham-i tu oshuftan?
Chand dar khok-i mazilat zi firoqī khuftan?
Ba tu hojat nabuvad sharh-i gham-i khud guftan,
Chunki az hol-i zamir-i hama kas ogohī.

Hijr-i khok-i rah-i mardon ba mijgon bardor,
Sidq-i ikhlos ba pesh or tu dar okhir-i kor,
To shavad surkh rukhat sol-u mah-u layl-u nahor,
Hofiz az khizmat-i mardon-i khudo or mador,
Z-on, ki tu banda-yi derina-yi in dargohī.

Even the birds sing your praise
The fish swim in the ocean of your grace.

Upon everyone you have bestowed,
   the awareness of your mercy, compassion and grace.

The transgressors,
    you saved from the anger of becoming forlorn.

Those who are your beggars,
    are worthy of throne and crown.
You have blessed everyone with
        fortune and renown.

You fashioned the human by your creative craft
    and bestowed life to everyone,
            by the blessing of your breath.
No wonder then, that everyone
    —be they Muslims, Christians, or unbelievers—
        all move towards you.

One may be in charge
    of a monastery,
    the other might be a drunkard,
but it matters not.
    Whether at a mosque engrossed in prayer
        or at a tavern seeking pleasure
Drunk or sober, everyone is appealing to you, calling you
But the question is,
    whom do you call unto yourself?

You made
    Joseph emerge from the well,
        granted him fortune and auspicious fate.
You made Solomon a king!
Sat him on the throne and gave him his famous ring.

Though everyone's fate is sealed
    and we all end up in a coffin,
Without your consent,
    nothing moves,
        nothing happens,
            not even something as insignificant as
                a single leaf dropping.
Who can, then,
    dare build a false path in the midst of your kingdom?

How many times,
    using my very eyelash,
        have I swept your threshold clean,
            of dust and ash?

How many nights,
  all night long up until daybreak,
    I have stirred in longing,
      all for your sake?

How long,
    have I been sleeping,
      upon this indignity's heap of dirt,
      separated from you.

Yet,
   I speak all this in vain,
     for you know of my sorrow, my pain
After all,
     of all creatures' innermost being, you are aware.

O You, remove the path's obstacles,
     with your eyelashes,
Rise up to the occasion and do this,
      sincerely,
        truthfully.
Do this so that your face becomes glowing
     with radiant light,
        all the time, be it this year, next month,
        today or tomorrow night.

  Hafez, do not be ashamed to serve men of God;
  You are the eternal servant of this court, after all!

At 6:06, a *ghazal* attributed to Nasir Khusraw, the great *pir,* or saint, of the Badakhshani Ismailis, marks a transition to a metrical rhythm articulated by the *daf* in a slow 4/4 meter (*zarb*). The solo *rubab* is joined by a second *rubab* and a *setar,* creating a thicker texture in the instrumental accompaniment.

Onro, ki nadonī nasab-u nisbat-i holash,
Ogah nabuvad hej kas az roz-i fa'olash.

Filjumla darakhtest nadonī samarash chist,
Borash khabar orad, ki chī budast niholash.

Onro, ki pisandida buvad khislat-u fe'lash,
Zinhor mapurs az padar-u az amu kholash.

Shohzoda-yi nodon, ki dar ū ilm-u adab nest,
Beqadr shavad, chunki namonad zar-u molash.

Darvesh, ki ū martaba-yi ilm-u adab yoft,
Khud saltanate yoft, varo nest zavolash.

Az mardum-i nohal ba sad marhila bigrez,
To dar dahan-i sher naaftī zi khisolash.

Andar talabash na'razanon Nosir-i Khusraw,
Kay oyad hamon rūz rasam man ba visolash?

If you don't know someone's pedigree,
    It is best to judge him by his actions.

Once a tree bears fruit,
You know what sapling you had planted.

One who behaves properly, and is well-liked
Is in no need to reveal his pedigree to you,
  You need not know who his uncle was,
          Or where his father was from.

An unwise prince, who hasn't acquired the right knowledge,
Will become dispensable once he spends all his wealth.

Yet a beggar who learns to behave appropriately, and achieves knowledge,
Will become endowed with great, everlasting fortune.

Distance yourself,
    As far as you can
          From ill-mannered people,
lest you fall into the trap,
          laid with their evil deeds.
Seeking him,
    Nasir Khusraw has been screaming like a madman
When will the day of my union with him finally arrive?

Another *ghazal* begins at 9:16, this one by Ghiyosi (d. 1767–68), a Badakhshani poet whose verse is still popular among local performers and listeners. The poetic transition is marked by a change in the vocal texture: Aqnazar's solo vocal is replaced by responsorial singing in which he alternates verses with Ghulamsho and Olucha. A version of this text, with additional couplets and variant wording, is transcribed by Gabrielle van den Berg in *Minstrel Poetry from the Pamir Mountains* (460).[1] Van den Berg mentions that "the name of Ghiyāsī does not seem to be connected with Ismā'īlism, but rather with the Naqshbandiyya Sufi order. This shows once more the variety of material used in the poetical tradition of Badakhshan nowadays" (136).

Dil saro-yi tu, yo Rasūl Allah,	My heart is your abode, o messenger of God,
Sīna jo-yi tu, yo Rasūl Allah,	My chest is your dwelling place, o messenger of God,
Karda paydo sarodiqi Kavnayn, *Haq baro-yi tu, yo Rasūl Allah.*	God created just for you, this world and the next, o messenger of God.
Chun kabūtar shudam zi bolafshon,	We are all but doves, flapping our wings,
Dar fazo-yi tu, yo Rasūl Allah, *Qaysar-i Rumī bo chunin hashamat,*	in your space, o messenger of God. Even the emperor of Rome, with all his glory,
Shud gado-yi tu yo Rasūl Allah.	is a beggar compared to you, o messenger of God.
Jam'i payghambaron-i peshinro, *Iltijo-yi tu, yo Rasūl Allah,*	All the prophets of the past, Take refuge in you, o messenger of God,
Osiyon-ro zi gharq dodī amon, *Nokhudo-yi tu yo Rasūl Allah.*	You saved the sinners from drowning, You are the captain, o messenger of God.
Ahd kardam, ki bokhabar bosham,	I promised that I shall remain steadfast,
Dar vafo-yi tu, yo Rasūl Allah,	in faithfulness to you, o messenger of God.
Loh-i Alhamdi shud Ghiyosiddin, *Benavo-yi tu yo Rasūl Allah.*	Ghiyosiddin became God's canvas, I am your helpless one, o messenger of God.

Maddohkhon Aqnazar Alovatov.

Photo by Sebastian Schutyser. Courtesy of Aga Khan Music Initiative.

At 10:50, the beginning of the next *ghazal*, attributed to Rumi, launches an acceleration in tempo as the responsorial singing builds in intensity.

On yor harif-i most imshab,
Bo mo nazar-i khudost imshab,

In ishrat-u khurrame, ki morost,
V-az rū-yi zamin kirost imshab.

Imshab shab-i qadr-i oshiqon ast,
Kom-i hama kas ravost imshab,

Bar sarfa-yi ishq-i oshiqonro,
Gulbong-i Alī sadost imshab.

Moro ba du'oy-i khayr yod or,
Ya'ne ki shab-i du'ost imshab,

Onro, ki gadoyash khonda budī,
Daryob, ki podshost imshab,

Qadrash zi jamo-li Shamsiddin purs,
Qadre beh az in kirost imshab.

That friend,
    is our drinking companion,
      tonight!

It's evident!
    God's grace is with us,
      tonight!

No one on the face of the earth,
    is as lucky,
    immersed in joy's delight as we are,
      tonight.

The night of *qadr*,[2] for lovers,
      is tonight.
Everything is permissible,
    everyone's wishes are fulfilled,
       tonight.

In the sphere of God's lovers,
The beautiful sound of Ali's name resonates everywhere, tonight.

Pray for me,
    on my behalf tonight,

For the night of prayers is tonight.

The one you had dismissed as a beggar,
    turn to him,
      for he is no less than a king tonight.

Confirm with Shamsiddin his lofty station
Is there anyone surpassing him tonight?

The sixth poem, which begins at 12:06, is not a *ghazal* but a *rubāʾī* attributed to Hafez, sung in the melodic style of a *falak,* in free rhythm. It is typical for a *falak* to be sung somewhere in the middle of a *maddoh* (see chapter 30).

Mardī zi kananda-yi dar-i Khaybar purs,	Seek prowess from the one who tore down Khaybar's gates,[3]
Asror-i karam zi khoja-yi Qambar purs,	Seek generosity's secret from Qambar's master.[4]
Gar tolib-i fayz-i haq ba sidq-i Hafiz,	Hafez! If you truly are after abundance of grace,
Sarchashma-yi ū zi soqi-i Kavsar purs.	About its source, ask the cupbearer of Kowsar.[5]

The concluding *ghazal*, by Nasir Khusraw, begins at 13:07. Here the metrical articulation of the *daf* returns, and the *maddoh* reaches a culmination. A variant of the same text appears in van den Berg's *Minstrel Poetry from the Pamir Mountains* (447).

Dast bar sūrokh barī, az zahr-i mor andesha kun,	When you stick your hand in a burrow, be wary of the snake's venom.
Poy dar gil menihī, az nesh-i khor andesha kun.	When you put your foot in the mud, be wary of the sting of the thorn.
Gar shinovar nestī, po bar lab-i daryo namon,	If you are not a swimmer, do not set foot by the sea,
Dar miyonash gharq gardī, az kanor andesha kun.	Surely you will drown in its core, but be wary even of its shore.
Gar sipohī nestī, tir-u kamon bo dast magir,	If you are not even a foot soldier, do not walk around carrying bows and arrows,
Dar miyon-i dasht raftī az savor andesha kun.	If you find yourself in the middle of the battlefield, be wary of the cavalier.

Dushmanat gar pashsha boshad, kamtar az filash madon.	If your enemy happens to be a mosquito, don't think him less harmful than an elephant, keep my advice in mind, and be wary.
In nasihat gir ba gūsh-u zinhor andesha kun.	
Pashsha-yi shabzindador khun-i mardum mekhūrad, Zinhor az mardum-i shabzindador andesha kun.	The nocturnal mosquito feasts on people's blood, Be wary of idle people who are up all night.
Sirr-i dil bo yori khud harchand bitvonī magū, Yor agar yore buvad az yor-i yor andesha kun.	As much as you can, do not reveal the secret of your heart to your friend, Even if your friend is true, Be wary of the friend's friend.
Nosir-i Khusraw agar may mekhūrī, mastona bosh, Jomro darkash, valekin az khumor andesha kun.	Nasir Khusraw, if you are drinking wine, then dare becoming drunk! Drink to the bottom, but be wary of the hangover that is to follow.

Members of the Badakhshan Ensemble.
Photo by Sebastian Schutyser. Courtesy of Aga Khan Music Initiative.

STUDY QUESTIONS

1. Though abridged (as noted above), this performance of *maddoh* by Aqnazar Alovatov and fellow members of the Badakhshan Ensemble illustrates the principal stylistic features of *maddoh*. What are these features?

2. How do the texts selected by the *maddohkhon* convey moral advice and spiritual images?

3. What is the role of rhythm in the *maddoh*? What is the difference in the feeling or mood created by the sections of text performed in free rhythm and those performed in a metrical rhythm?

4. Based on your own listening, what musical qualities of *maddoh* contribute to its power to promote healing of the sort described in this chapter?

NOTES

The first part of this chapter (up to example 28.1) is adapted from Benjamin D. Koen, *Beyond the Roof of the World: Music, Prayer, and Healing in the Pamir Mountains* (Oxford University Press, 2009), 44–51, 78–81, and is reproduced by permission of Oxford University Press (http://global.oup.com).

1. Gabrielle Rachel Van Den Berg, *Minstrel Poetry from the Pamir Mountains: A Study on the Songs and Poems of the Ismailis of Tajik Badakhshan* (Wiesbaden: Reichert, 2004).

2. *Laylat al-Qadr* is the night near the end of the month of Ramadan when Muslims believe the Qur'an was revealed to Muhammad. At this time, angels and other celestial beings are believed to descend to earth following God's command, sins are forgiven, and special prayers are offered.

3. The name of a legendary fortress whose gate was torn down by Ali, the first Shi'a Imam.

4. Qambar was Ali's servant, thus the master of Qambar is Ali.

5. Kowsar: spring of paradise; all the attributes refer to Ali, who is known in popular culture to be the distributor of the water of this precious spring.

CHAPTER 29   *Qasoid-khonī* in the Wakhan Valley of Badakhshan

CHORSHANBE GOIBNAZAROV

The tradition of religious music performance among Pamiri Ismailis discussed in the preceding chapters (see chapters 27 and 28) has distinct forms and names in particular districts of Badakhshan. Referred to as *maddo* or *maddo-khonī* in the Shughnan and Rushan districts (in Pamiri languages, *maddoh* is written without an "h"), it is known as *qasoid-khonī* in the Wakhan valley of Badakhshan (*qasoid* is pronounced "qa-sa-eed," with the accent on the last syllable).[1] *Maddoh* and *qasoid-khonī* are closely related from the perspective of performance context and religious significance, but differ in musical details such as the rendering of strumming patterns on accompanying instruments, the means of transitioning from one formal section of a piece to the next, and the way in which singers interact with each other during a performance. Another difference concerns the type of song form performed—in Wakhan, narrative songs are more common than the short *ghazal*s typical of *maddoh*. This chapter focuses on *qasoid-khonī* in the Wakhan region of Tajik Badakhshan and explores its religious meanings.

WAKHAN

The Wakhan Valley stretches between two magnificent mountain ranges: the Pamirs to the north and the Hindu Kush to the south. The valley is divided into Tajik Wakhan and Afghan Wakhan by the Panj River, the main source of the Amu Darya. Tajik Wakhan has twenty-three villages with a total population of more than 20,000 inhabitants, and is part of the Ishkashim district of Tajikistan's Gorno-Badakhshan Autonomous Region.

The indigenous inhabitants of Wakhan are known as Wakhi, but refer to themselves as Wakhik, or Khik. Their language, which belongs to the eastern Iranian

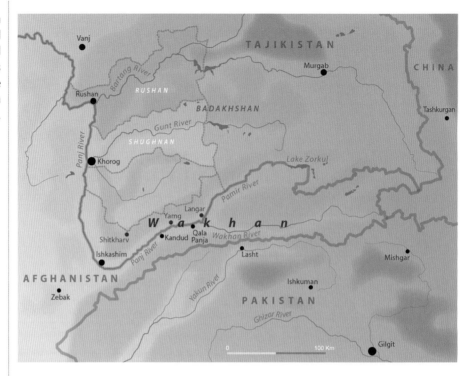

The Wakhan region lies to the south and southeast of Rushan and Shughnan districts. Villages highlighted in red are home to musicians discussed in the text.

group of Pamiri languages, is also called Wakhi, and is referred to by local speakers as Khikwor. Wakhi is spoken in both Tajik and Afghan Wakhan as well as among small Wakhi populations in northern Pakistan and the Xinjiang Uyghur Autonomous Region of China.

Historically, Wakhan served as a corridor for trade routes that were part of the trans-Eurasian network collectively known as the Silk Road. The Wakhan Corridor provided a short and safe passageway for Chinese and Central Asian merchants travelling between China and Badakhshan, and onward to other parts of Central Asia. The region is known for its pre-Islamic fortresses as well as Islamic shrines and places of worship, some of which have been transformed into museums and serve as cultural sites that preserve their sacred significance.

The musical culture of Wakhan is rich and diverse. Musical performances mark various moments of everyday life and play an important role in social events such as weddings, funerals, and religious festivities. Yet many forms of musical practice have disappeared or are on the verge of disappearance as a result of the social and cultural transformations of the twentieth and twenty-first centuries. For instance, *dafsoz*, a form of male singing to the accompaniment of the Badakhshani frame drum (*daf*), and the theatrical genre *maghulbozī*, which used to be performed on the first day of wedding ceremonies, are rarely practiced. On the other hand, musical practices that have a religious dimension have survived despite the pressures and persecution of Soviet cultural and ideological policies. One such practice is *qasoid-khonī*.

WHAT IS *QASOID-KHONĪ*?

Qasoid-khonī is a vernacular term that incorporates two words: *qaśā'id*, the plural form of the Arabic-derived word *qaśīda*, and *khān*, the Persian word for "recite" or "sing," and thus literally means a "recitation" or "singing" of *qaśīdas*. The reason that this practice is called *qasoid-khonī* in Wakhan, but *maddo-khonī* in the Shughnan and Rushan districts of Badakhshan, is explained by the historical development of the literary genre *qaśīda*.

Originating in pre-Islamic Arabia, *qaśīda* became a classical genre of Islamic Arabic poetry and, beginning in the tenth century, extended its influence to other languages of the Muslim world.[2] Persian poets developed new forms of *qaśīda*, such as spring (*bahoriya*), wine (*khamriya*), hunting (*tardiyya*), and praise (*madhiya*) poetry. These forms, in particular the panegyric, *madh* (*madh* is the etymological root of *maddoh*), were brought to Central Asia as part of the Sufi and Ismaili spiritual traditions. Thus, the eleventh-century Persian mystic poet Nasir Khusraw, believed to be the founder of the Ismaili community in Badakhshan, is credited with the introduction of *qaśīda* into local religious and music practice (see chapters 27 and 28). Azizkhon Karimov, a performer of *qasoid-khonī* from Wakhan, recounted that "During his time in Yumgon, Nasir Khusraw asked people who were talented in singing and playing musical instruments to participate in his missionary activities. It is from that time that *qasoid-khonī* became a very important part of our culture." A similar story was related by a retired teacher, Ismoilbek Ismoilbekov: "When Pir Nasir came to Badakhshan, his first contacts were with *mutrīb*s (musicians). In one of the villages in Badakhshan he chose a man who was a *rubab* player to play and sing at his *majlīs* (gathering)."

While the authenticity of such stories can be questioned, they are important in attesting to the historical travels of pre-Islamic Arabic poetic genres to Persia and on to Central Asia, where they acquired new forms and styles. *Qasoid-khonī* can thus be seen as an example of how Islamic traditions associated with Persian literature assumed a vernacular form in Badakhshan. Indeed, the Badakhshani *qaśīda* bears little resemblance to the *qaśīda* of Arabic or Persian literature. In the cultural milieu of the Pamir Mountains, the *qaśīda* was adapted to local social customs and ritual practices, and transformed into a musical genre that employs a range of indigenous terms, religious symbols, metaphors, musical styles, and instruments. In Badakhshan today, the performance of *qaśīda*s is commonly regarded as spiritual music (*musiqi-yi irfonī/rūhonī*), and represents the principal form of spiritual musical practice by and for people who consider themselves religious (*dindor*).

Pamiri House

The Pamiri house has a unique architecture that is rich in sacred and religious meanings. Its interior embodies elements of Zoroastrianism assimilated into and given new meanings in Pamiri Ismailism. The central room of the house, which serves both as a living space and a place for worship, is divided into several interconnected areas marked out by five wooden pillars. According to pre-Islamic beliefs, the pillars represent five divine beings or angels (*Yazatas*), known locally as Surush, Mehr, Anahita, Zamyod, and Oraz.[3] Subsequently the pillars' meaning was reinterpreted according to the Shi'i Ismaili concept of "five pure bodies" (*panj tani pok*), referring to the sacred figures of the Prophet Muhammad, Ali, Fatima, Hasan, and Husein.

The pillar located in the right corner across the room from the entrance is known locally as *shah-istin*. It represents Surush, the

Interior of a Pamiri house.

guardian of conscience and wisdom, and the Prophet Muhammad. The pillar located in the left corner diagonally across the room from the entrance, *razhsar-istin,* symbolizes Mehr, the guardian of the light of honesty, friendship and kindness, and Ali, the first Imam of the Ismailis. The column to the far left of the

entrance, known as *dildung-istin,* stands for Anahita, the guardian of waters and the spirit of nurturing, and Fatima, daughter of the Prophet Muhammad and the wife of Ali. The other two columns to the immediate right and left of the entrance, known as *barkenj-istin* and *putrazh-istin,* symbolize Zamyod, the guardian

TABLE 29.1. MEANINGS OF THE PILLARS IN THE PAMIRI HOUSE

NAMES OF PILLARS		SOLAR SYSTEM	INDO-IRANIAN COSMOLOGICAL (ZOROASTRIAN) FIGURES	ISLAMIC HOLY FIGURES
WAKHI LANGUAGE	SHUGHNI LANGUAGE			
Shah-istin	*Kha-sitan*	Sun	Surush	Muhammad
Razhsar-istin	*Vogznekh-sitan*	Moon	Mehr	Ali
Dildung-istin	*Kampir/kisor-sitan*	Venus	Anahita	Fatima
Barkenj-istin	*Poiga-sitan*	Mercury	Zamyod	Hasan
Putrazh-istin	*Barnekh-sitan*	Jupiter	Oraz	Husein

Source: The table is adapted from Parpisho Qimatshoev, *Sozvezdie strun* [Constellation of strings] (Khorog: Logos, 2007), 5.

of earth and spirit of productivity, and Oraz, the guardian of fire and spirit of truthfulness and goodness, as well as Hasan and Husein, the sons of Ali and Fatima. They are joined with a crossbeam to signify the close relationship between the spirits of productivity and goodness, and between the two Islamic martyr brothers worshipped in Ismailism.[4]

The sacred meanings given to the physical structure of the Pamiri house have a bearing on the spatial placement of participants in various ceremonial and ritual practices. For example, during performances of *qasoid-khonī*, sung in praise of the five holy figures (*panj tani pok*) and Imams, performers, usually men, sit in front of the pillar representing Mehr and Imam Ali, in an area reserved for respected male members of the household and guests. During funeral ceremonies women sit and perform *falak* (discussed in chapter 30) by the pillar associated with Anahita and Fatima, in what is regarded as the female area of the room. At weddings, the first course of the wedding meal is passed around the pillar representing Surush and the Prophet Muhammad three times before being served to the bride and groom and their guests. Through this ritual act, the newly married couple receives blessings for their well-being, happiness, and long life.

MUSICAL GENRE AND RELIGIOUS CEREMONY

As its name suggests, *qasoid-khonī* is a performance of sung poetry (*qaśīdas*) accompanied by musical instruments. Apart from that, and like the *maddoh* tradition elsewhere, it is a spiritual and devotional ceremony that takes place in sessions of many hours on a variety of social and religious occasions, in particular, when a member of the community dies. Participation in the performance depends on the circumstances: in the case of funerals, only adults customarily participate; in the case of religious festivals, all comers are welcome; and in the case of private gatherings, participants are limited to those specially invited. The ceremony is held in the central room of the Pamiri house.

Singers of *qasoid*, called *qasoid-khon*s, are male performers who sing, play musical instruments, and in some cases, mainly during funeral ceremonies, interpret or explain the meaning of the poems they have sung. They are amateur musicians who perform under the guidance of a local master *qasoid-khon*.

Qasoid-khonī normally begins with an instrumental prelude on the *rubab*, followed by an introductory verse, *munojot*, sung by the master singer, leading into the main section performed by a group of *qasoid-khon*s.

The songs performed by *qasoid-khon*s can be divided into several categories, including:

1. Songs associated with funeral ceremonies, such as ritual songs and stories in poetic forms. These constitute the essential part of the *qasoid-khonī* tradition.

2. Songs based on poems by classical Sufi poets, especially Shams-i Tabrizi and Rumi.

3. Songs related to Ismailism and its religious festivities, mostly composed by local poets.

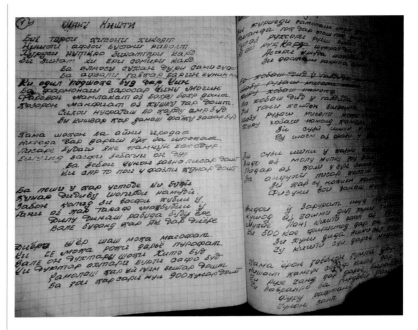

Bayāz of "Panj Kishti" (Five Ships).

Balandzikom.

The themes of the songs are varied and can be narrative or non-narrative. Narrative songs include those with historical, religious, and allegorical content; non-narrative songs develop themes of religious advice, didacticism, devotion, and mystical love. Formerly transmitted orally, the song texts were subsequently preserved in the form of handwritten collections (*bayāz*) in either Persian or Cyrillic scripts that were assembled by *qasoid-khon*s from books or from their predecessors' collections. Today performances of songs from the *qasoid-khonī* tradition are also disseminated on cassette tapes and compact discs. Tunes and melodies are not specific either to a particular song text or to a particular occasion. Rather, each *qasoid-khon* has a personal repertory of tunes that are set to a variety of songs and performed for a variety of occasions. These songs are overwhelmingly sung in Tajiki Persian, which is considered a religious language, rather than in Wakhi, the vernacular language of Wakhan. One currently popular Wakhi poet and singer, Qurbonsho, has written Wakhi-language poems and songs in a variety of genres, including *qasoid,* but it remains to be seen whether this nascent Wakhi-language *qasoid* tradition will thrive and attract contributions from other poets.

MUSICAL INSTRUMENTS OF *QASOID-KHONĪ* AND THEIR SYMBOLIC MEANING

The musical instruments used in the performance of *qasoid-khonī,* as in *maddoh,* include the *rubab, balandzikom* (the local variant of the *tanbur*) and the frame drum, *daf.* The use of the *daf* in *qasoid-khonī,* compared to its use in *maddoh,*

Construction of the *Rubab*

Making a *rubab* is a long and painstaking process that demands considerable knowledge and skill from the maker. Abdulmamad Yormamadov, a *rubab*-maker from Wakhan, locally known as *usto* (master), recounted that in the past, making a *rubab* was a ritual in itself.

Before proceeding with his work, the master performed ablution and prayer (*namāz*), sacrificed a sheep, and prepared a meal locally known as *khudoyī* (God's meal) from the sacrificed animal, which was shared with other people. The gut of the sheep was reserved to prepare strings for the future instrument. After the *khudoyī*, the skin for the head of the *rubab* was soaked in water for 5–10 days to facilitate removing the fleece before the skin was stretched over the instrument's soundboard. A tree was felled, and a part of it suitable for the future instrument was cut and soaked in water for 10–15 days to prevent the

wood from cracking. *Rubab*-makers used hardwoods, such as apricot and mulberry, to make the instrument last longer. One can still find intact *rubab*s in Pamiri houses that are more than a hundred years old.

Today the process of making the *rubab* is not followed fully, and construction methods have changed from earlier times. The ritual before making the *rubab* is no longer performed, gut strings have been replaced with nylon strings, and the classification of stringed instruments into "instruments of hell" (metal-stringed instruments) and "instruments of paradise" (gut-stringed instruments) no longer applies.[5] These changes, however, do not undermine the instrument's cultural value. The nylon strings that replaced gut sound reasonably good. They are readily available and more practical, and are faster to prepare

Rubab maker Abdulmamad Yormamadov.
Photo by Munavvar Bahriev.

than gut strings. As Abdulmamad remarked: "Some of our work has become easier but that does not affect the nature of the *rubab* as a sacred (*muqaddas*) instrument."

---

is limited. In Wakhan the *daf* is associated with joyful occasions and is played at religious festivals only. According to *qasoid-khon*s, because the *daf* symbolizes joy and festivity, if somebody dies in a village where a wedding is about to take place, a member of the family who wishes to celebrate the wedding, together with the village leader, visits the bereaved family to ask their permission to proceed with the celebration and play music at the wedding. During the meeting they invite relatives of the deceased to play the *daf*. This custom of seeking permission has a dual role: it shows the visitors' respect for the family's grief, while at the same time helping them to break their mourning. The family's acceptance of the invitation to play the *daf* accordingly signifies their consent to the wedding arrangements and performance of music.

Pamiri *rubab*.

The original *balandmaqom*, created by Muborak Wakhoni.

The main instrument of *qasoid-khonī*, as in *maddoh*, is the *rubab*, a long-necked lute with six gut or nylon strings. The instrument is approximately two and a half feet long and is made from the wood of an apricot, mulberry, or walnut tree. Its circular soundboard, called the "head," is covered with thick leather fastened with iron nails. Several ornamental holes are drilled in the sound chamber to facilitate sound production. The *rubab* is played with a wedge-shaped wooden plectrum (*zakhmak*) tied to the instrument with a string. A piece of wood located on the instrument's head, called *kharak* (little donkey), acts as a bridge and, along with six pegs (*gushak*), is used for tuning the instrument. The sixth peg is placed in the middle of the instrument's neck.

A distinctive type of *rubab* is the *balandmaqom* (literally, "high stage"), a nineteen-stringed lute that was devised by a Sufi poet, astronomer, and musician from Wakhan, Muborak Wakhonī (d. 1903). The nineteen strings of the *balandmaqom* denote the Arabic letters in the phrase "*Bismillāh-i Rahmān-i Rahīm*" (In the name of God, the Merciful, the Compassionate). The original *balandmaqom* is still preserved in the house of Muborak's great-grandson, Lutfulloh Zaraboev, in the village of Yamg, in Wakhan.

The text for this example is available on the companion website.

WATCH

Example 29.1. Fragments from the *qaṣīda* "Risola-yi Chihil Dunyo" (Treatise of the forty worlds) and a *qaṣīda* known as "Naqsh-i dolon" (Corridor decoration), by Muborak Wakhoni, performed by Khalifa Mamadbek on the *balandmaqom*. Wakhan, November 2011.

STUDY QUESTIONS

1. What features of the *balandmaqom*'s sound make it an appropriate instrument for the performance of *qasoid-khonī*?

2. How do the musical settings of the poetic fragments contrast with one another?

3. On a continuum that ranges from intoned speech or chant at one extreme to song at the other extreme, where would you place Khalifa Mamadbek's performance?

4. What elements of the performance convey a sense of the spiritual content of the text?

Khalifa Mamadbek playing the *balandmaqom*.

THE RUBAB IN THE PAMIRI ISMAILI COMMUNITY

As discussed in chapter 28, the *rubab* holds special significance for Pamiri Ismailis. Each part of the instrument is ascribed a sacred meaning and metaphorically assigned to the physical and spiritual worlds. While the shape of the instrument is associated with a human body, its six strings are thought to represent six prophets: Adam, Noah, Abraham, Moses, Jesus, and Muhammad. The sixth string, representing the Prophet Muhammad, ends midway along the instrument's neck, or fingerboard, signifying the end of the prophethood and the beginning of the Imamate in Ismaili Islam. Inscriptions in Arabic or Cyrillic carved or written on the instrument, such as *Bismillāh-i Rahmān-i Rahīm, Ya Ali* (Oh, Ali), *Ya Ali Madad* (Oh, Ali, help), are also a sign of the instrument's relation to worship.

As a sacred instrument, the *rubab* is always kept at a height in the Pamiri house and never put on the ground. People talk about the *rubab* with reverence and consider it an instrument that has preserved their faith for a millennium. The symbolism of the *rubab* is reflected in verses that perpetuate oral tradition about the instrument and are often quoted by *qasoid-khon*s.

Donī, ki rubab-i mo chiho megūyad?	Do you know what our *rubab* talks about?
Az zot-i pok-i Murtazo megūyad.	It tells us about the pure progeny of Murtaza.[6]
In pora-yi chūb-i qoq az qudrat-i ūst,	This piece of dry wood exists thanks to His power;
Ba kom-i zabonash yo Khudo megūyad.	[So] "Oh God" comes from its mouth.

Donī, ki rubab-i 'ishq-ro tor kī bud?	Do you know who the string of love on the *rubab* was?
Sarpanja-yi on rubab ūstod kī bud?	Do you know who the master of the *rubab* was?
Ustod-i tamom-i anbiyo Jabrail ast, *Donī, ki ba Jabrail ūstod kī bud?*	The master of all prophets is Gabriel, [But] Do you know who Gabriel's master was?

The importance of the *rubab* for the Pamiri Ismaili community can be observed in its continued use within funeral ceremonies. During times of grief and sorrow the sound of the *rubab* is perceived as having a consoling effect on the bereaved. Lutfiya, a woman in her twenties who lost her brother at a young age, told me that during the funeral the only thing that soothed her pain was the sound of the *rubab:* "It somehow penetrates your soul and makes you feel calm and relaxed."

SPIRITUAL AND STRUCTURAL ASPECTS OF *QASOID-KHONĪ*

The main purpose of *qasoid-khonī* is to convey the religious teachings of Ismailism; relate events of Islamic history; and offer praise to God, the Prophet, and the Imams. A central theme of *qasoid* is the spiritual role of the Imams in leading the community on the right path. The Ismailis believe in the guidance and beneficence of divinely inspired Imams, from Ali, son-in-law of the Prophet Muhammad, to Shah Karim al-Huseini, the current Aga Khan.

An important concept of Ismaili spiritual tradition is *didor* (vision), which manifests itself at the moment when Ismailis find themselves in the presence of the Imam of the Time (a present and living Imam) and are able to receive his blessings. There are two possible means of attaining *didor*: physical (*zohirī didor*) and spiritual (*botinī didor*). One implies an actual live encounter with the Imam, and the other the attainment of enlightenment and spiritual empowerment through religious and devotional practice.

Participation in a *qasoid-khonī* performance offers a means of achieving spiritual *didor*. Through the act of listening to *qasoid*, participants seek to approach God and their living spiritual leader and thereby achieve an understanding of spiritual truths (*haqā'iq*). As Azizkhon Karimov pointed out, "during *qasoid-khonī* one receives spiritual beneficence (*baraka*). This is a sign of a constant connection with the Imam." The poetic texts carry a potent religious message that urges listeners to transcend the physical world and brings them closer to the realm of spiritual realities. The music serves to ignite emotions and intensify participants' longing for *didor*. As they listen to *qasoid*, participants quiver,

Celebration of Imamat Day, when Ismailis mark the anniversary of their present Imam's succession of his predecessor to become the Imam of the Time, village of Zong, July 11, 2011.
Photo by Vatani Alidodov.

weep, sway heads, clap, and dance, achieving a state similar to that of trance and ecstasy. This is what makes *qasoid-khonī* so powerful and significant for a Pamiri audience.

One of the stories popular in the repertory of *qasoid-khon*s in Wakhan is "Five Ships" (*Panj Kishti*). The story recounts a miracle performed by the first Shiʻa Imam,

Performer Profile: Zaimkhon Muborakqadamov

Zaimkhon Muborakqadamov is a well-known *qasoid-khon* in Wakhan. A retired man in his sixties, he lives in the village of Shitkharv. Zaimkhon began to sing and play *qasoid* when he was twelve, later developing his knowledge of how to sing *qasoid-khonī* and play the *rubab* under the guidance of a master, Mulloshamsher, a local poet and *qasoid-khon*. He now plays this music daily in his house and during religious occasions and funeral ceremonies in his village and neighboring villages.

While he is recognized as a master *qasoid-khon,* he does not make a living from his performances of *qasoid-khonī*. He goes to funeral ceremonies voluntarily without needing to be invited and considers it his responsibility to play music without financial reward. He lives on his small pension and what he earns by working on his land. Having practiced *qasoid-khonī* for many years, he has many followers, including his sons and close relatives.

Photo by Manuchehr Muborakqadamov.

Ali. As the story goes, the son of a king, in his dream, falls in love with a daughter of the king of China and decides to seek the hand of this princess. He builds five ships and prepares for the voyage. Once he has embarked on the sea, a storm wrecks all the ships, and the passengers drown. The king is devastated on hearing about the accident. His vizier consoles him, saying that the King of Men (*Shoh-yi Mardon*) in Mecca (that is, Ali) can help. Then the story tells how Imam Ali saves the ships and brings the passengers back to life. In the following video example, a *qasoid-khon* from Wakhan, Zaimkhon Muborakqadamov, and his son, Aslamkhon, perform the story of "Five Ships" in the poetic rendition of Forighī, a Badakhshani poet from the sixteenth and seventeenth centuries. They sing the *qasoid* within a section of *qasoid-khonī* called *haidarī*, which will be explained later in the chapter.

WATCH

Example 29.2. "Panj Kishti" (Five ships), a *qaṣīda* by Forighi, performed by Zaimkhon Muborakqadamov (*rubab*) and Aslamkhon Muborakqadamov (*tablak*). Village of Shitkharv, Wakhan, November 2011.

FIRST SECTION (0:05–2:04)

Rasidand to bad on daryo-yi khunkhor,	They reached that cruel sea,
Shah-yi Chin bo shah-yi Kawnain-i Abror,	The king of China with the pious King of the two worlds.
Ba Qambar Shah-yi Mardon amr farmud,	The King of Men asked Qambar,
Ki bitlab mohiyon-ro nazd-i man zud.	"Invite all the fish to come at once."
Ba amr-i Shoh Qambar dod ovoz.	Qambar called out to all the fish as he was asked,
Zi har sū mohiyon kardand parvoz.	[And] they swam from everywhere at once . . .
Buzurg-u khurd yak jo jam gashtand,	Elders and youngsters all gathered,
Biguft sar ba podshoh (chu sham) kham gashtand.	[And] bowed to the King.
Jamol-i Shoh-yi Mardon-ro bididand.	Soon they saw the face of the King of Men.
(Chunin) Ba misl-i murgh-i bismīl bitapidand.	They were shivering like half-alive birds . . .

SECOND SECTION (2:07–4:55)

Ba pesh-i man biyored ustukhonash,	"Bring me a piece of his bone,
Ki khoham az sar-i nav doda jonash.	[So] I can bring him back to life."
Shunidand 'amr-ro az Shoh-yi Mardon,	Having heard the order from the King of Men,
Ba sū-yi bahr raftand jumla jūyon.	All ran towards the sea to look.
Sarosar onchunon daryo davidand,	They searched all around,

Nishon az ustukhon-i ū nadidand.	[But] there was no sign of any bones.
Biguftand shoh, sarosar joro gashtem,	They returned to the King,
E nishon az ustukhon-i ū nayoftem.	[And] said there is no sign of him.
Ki kishtī gharqgashta panj sol ast,	"Five years has passed from the drowning,
E ba daryo rūhashon yoftan mahol ast.	It is not possible to find him."
Shah-yi din guft dar in manī shake nest,	The King of Religion said, "There is no doubt about it,
Vale angusht-i ū yak band boqist,	Something must have remained there . . .
Ki injo nazm kardand nazm-i yoron	Here the companions were praised,
Guzashta hamchu Forigh sad hazoron.	As hundreds of them have passed from Forigh.[7]

"Five Ships" and similar stories that refer to Ali, such as "Empty Head" (*Kallai pūsidasar*) and "Barbar City" (*Shahri Barbar*), are prominent in the *qasoid-khonī* tradition, and they are important for the Ismailis from a doctrinal point of view. By referring to Ali, his generosity, and his heroic and charismatic deeds, the Pamiri Ismailis assert the centrality of the figure of the Imam in their belief system and validate the legitimacy of his authority.

Such *qasoid* are commonly sung during funeral ceremonies, especially on the first night after a person's death. This night is called a "wakeful night" (*shab-i na-khusp*) in Wakhan, as people present in the house are not supposed to sleep. Zaimkhon explained that when a person dies, the soul does not leave the house on the first day because it is not purified. *Qasoid-khonī* is performed during this time in order to purify the soul of the deceased. This serves as both an expression of religious devotion and an aid for the deceased to attain salvation in the hereafter. Through his performance the *qasoid-khon* calls on listeners to forget sorrow, overcome love, and release the beloved. He turns to the Imams as an ultimate source of guidance for comfort and consolation.

STUDY QUESTIONS

1. What is the religious and ritual significance of a performance of the *qasoid* "Five Ships," and how is it communicated through music?

2. Analyze the musical structure of a verse from example 29.2. At which points in the performance is Zaimkhon joined by his son? How would you characterize their singing style? How is the strong percussive effect of the performance achieved?

3. In your view, how successful is Zaimkhon at making the story of "Five Ships" come alive for his listeners, and how does he do this?

Zaimkhon maintains that participation in *qasoid-khonī* demands concentration on the hidden meaning of poetry, music, and musical instruments in such a way that one listens with the "ear of the heart." He describes the music of *qasoid-khonī* as "food for the soul" that strengthens the heart and the inner nature, and induces the descent of spiritual light and life from the unseen world. In his interpretation, the structure of *qasoid-khonī* consists of five sections, each with a distinctive meaning in accordance with the Ismaili belief system.

The introductory section, called *bam,* is slow in tempo. The poetic text is sung at one pitch level in a rhythmically free, declamatory manner. Zaimkhon interprets this section as symbolizing the beginning of a human life when the soul is entering the body:

> You know, during this section only the *rubab* is played because the *rubab* has come from paradise. God (*Khudo*) ordered [the angel] Gabriel to make a human being from sand (*khok*). When the body (*jism*) was ready, God ordered the soul (*rūh*) to enter it. When the soul refused, God asked it to enter the body temporarily. That is why we human beings are temporarily in this world. We come and we go. The angels were asked to play music. The soul became drunk (*mast*) with the sound of the *rubab* and entered the body. Once inside the body, the soul liked it there and decided to remain. As it had promised God to stay there temporarily, it had to come out. The angels were asked to play again and the soul came out of the body. That is why we play when someone dies. So this first tune (*nazm*) is the beginning of the life of the soul in this world. That is why it is monotonic (*yaknavokht*). Our soul is still pure. It just came to the world and has not seen worldly matters yet.

The second section, *bam-u zer* ("up and down"), consists of alternating phrases at higher and lower pitch levels. In Zaimkhon's interpretation, it signifies the vicissitudes of the soul's life in this world:

> Life is a sequence of rises and falls. Here, it says that when the soul comes to this world, it encounters many things. Sometimes it makes mistakes and sometimes it does right things. We have to find and understand what is right for us and what is wrong. Life's path is not smooth, and you cannot just go straight ahead and reach your wishes. In order to achieve success or fulfill your wishes you need to go through all these vicissitudes in life.

The third section, *haidarī,* can progress from a slow to a fast tempo or be sustained at the same tempo. It represents the guidance that comes from the Imams, which helps Ismaili Muslims attain a level of spiritual awareness (*ma'rifat*).

Zaimkhon explained that "This music does not have low and high [phrases], because we overcome the challenges we face in life thanks to the guidance we receive from our spiritual father, the Imam of the Time. Our soul is nourished through his guidance."

An instrumental prelude on the *rubab* and a song that usually follows *haidarī* are called *falak*. They are performed in a high register and are thought to symbolize the stage at which communication is established with angels. As Zaimkhon observed, "Here we sing in a high voice and play music similar to the first section in order to reach out to the angels. Our voice should reach the universe (*falak*). When the soul recognizes the 'truth,' it needs to reach its end. This is why we sing in a high voice."

The last section of *qasoid-khonī*, *sitoyish*, is sung in a low register. This section is believed to help the soul reach its final destination, that is, to reunite with God, as Zaimkhon explained: "Here, with this music, we praise God, our beloved Prophet and confess our love for our Imam. Our soul is now pure of sins and ready to be united with God. I lose myself when I play this music. I feel as if my body does not exist anymore."

Zaimkhon's explanation of the meanings embedded in the musical structure of *qasoid-khonī* demonstrates how the performance of *qasoid-khonī* embodies Ismaili religious beliefs. The purpose of the music is to bring about emotional and spiritual arousal among the listeners, and this is achieved by a combination of means: shifting patterns of rhythm and meter; a gradual increase in the dynamic level of the singing; and alternation between solo and group performance.

Not every *qasoid-khonī* performance includes all of the five sections described above. The entire sequence of five sections is performed only on the first night after a funeral—the "wakeful night." In other contexts the duration of performance is shorter, with a *qasoid-khon* choosing music sections based on the setting and context of a performance.

Example 29.3 consists of a *qasoid-khonī* performed by Zaimkhon and his son, Aslamkhon, in their house after their evening prayer on a Friday night in November 2011. This private performance did not include all the sections described above. It starts with *bam-u zer* and then proceeds to *falak* followed by *sitoyish* then *haidarī* and ends with *falak*.

LISTEN

Example 29.3. "Qasoid-khonī," performed by Zaimkhon Muborakqadamov (*rubab*) and Aslamkhon Muborakqadamov (*tablak*), on texts by Shams-i Tabrizi (1185–1248), Farid ud-Din Attar (1145–1221), and anonymous poets. Village of Shitkharv, Wakhan, November 2011.

BAM-U ZER (0:01)

Ai gul shukufta dar jihon, andar jihon gulzor shud,

Ei sabza bar ob-i rawon, ob-i rawon khush omadī.
Ai murdaye-ro sar buridand, sar burida oshiqon,
Ai tegh-i mo burro-yi mo, burro-yi mo khush omadī.
Ai Shams-i Tabrez ul-ayon, e wo ul-ayon az ishqe
*   guft,*
Ei Mahdi-yi okhirzamon, e oi okhirzamon khush
*   omadi.*

Ai dil dar in dunyo maband, dunyo-yi fonī bigzarad,
Nawbat-i pirī daroyad, navjawonī bigzarad.
Ai tu ki dorī zūr-u noz-u komronī dar jihon.
Arz-u nozat bar sar oyad, komronī bigzarad.
Ai tu ki dorī zūr-u bozu pahlavonī dar jihon,
Zūr-u bozuyat namonad, pahlavonī bigzarad.
Ai tu ki dorī bogh-u būston, khush saropoh
*   mamlakat,*
Bogh-i tu vairona gardad, boghbonī bigzarad.

Rohat-i dunyo turo, mehnat-i dunyo maro

Bar sar-i farzand-i odam har chī oyad bizrad.

Ai in jihon chun pul ast, jon-i moyon korwon,
Ai oqibat bigzar az in, to korwonī bigzarad.

Ai Shams-i Tabrez, hunarma(r)ndon biraftand
*   zer-i khok,*
In hama kore ki dorī korzorī bigzarad.

The flower bloomed in the world, the world
    blossomed,
Grass floats on the water, O flowing water, welcome!
The dead are beheaded, beheaded lovers,
Our blade, our sharp, sharp blade, welcome!
Shams-i Tabrizi openly, openly talked about love,

Mahdi of the End of Time, O End of Time, welcome!

Do not grow attached to this world; it is transient,
Once you grow older, your prime is gone.
Oh, you who have power, allure and pleasure!
All these will end, and your joys will pass.
Oh, you who have strength and bravery!
All that will vanish, and your bravery will end.
Oh, you who have a garden and own beautiful land!

Your garden may one day wither, and your gardening
    days will pass.
All the peace in the world is for you, all the burdens
    of the world are for me.
All that happens to the progeny of man shall also
    pass.
This world is like a bridge, our soul is like a caravan.
Eventually you pass over it, and so too the caravan
    will pass.
Oh, Shams-i Tabrizi! All the men of virtue are lying in
    their graves,
All that which you do, too shall pass.

FALAK (7:13)

Moro ki dar du jahon nest darkor sim-u zar,
Juz yake khudo-vu duvum Muhammad-u seyum Hai-
*   dar.*
Khudov-u Ahmad-u Haidar bikhoham, ki daryobī,
Yake buvad ba nasim jannat, sayum Kausar.

We do not need wealth in the two worlds,
Only God, [the Prophet] Muhammad, and Haidar.[8]
I prefer God, Ahmad,[9] and Haidar,
One is the breeze of paradise and the other is its
    river Kausar (of paradise).

Sitoyish (7:48)

(Ai pisar khez-u vird) kun sahari,	O my son, arise and pray in the morning,
To biyobi (ba) zi sū-yi haq nazari.	So that you are bathed in the glory of God
Ai dilo az dard-i ishqu bekhabari,	Oh, heart! You do not know the pain of love,
Rūz-u shab dar hawoy-i sim-u zari.	Night and day you think of wealth.
Sag ba atlas malak nakhohad shud,	Though you may adorn a dog in satin, it will not be a king.
In sukhan gūsh kun agar bashari.	Hear these words, if you have humanity.
In jihon chu rubot [tu] bar sar-i pul,	This world is like a border-post on the bridge,
Tu dar in jo misol-i rahguzari.	And you are here as if you were a passerby.
Har ki omad dar in jihon biguzasht,	All those who came to this world have passed,
Chande rūz-i digar tu ham guzari.	Some day you too shall pass.
Moh(wu)ruyon ki khuftayand-u ba khok	All the beauties repose beneath the earth [in the grave],
Khok-u gashta rukhash chu moh-wu pari.	Their faces turned to dust, like the Moon and the fairy.
Lahad-i tang-u khona-i torik,	A narrow grave and a dark house,
Shash jihat on ba rawza-i qamari.	Six sites (directions) are in the lunar world.
Padarat bud-u tu pisar budi	Once there was your father, you were a son.
Pisarat ast tu in zamon padari.	Now, you have a son, and you are a father.
Chand-u rūze digar pisar padar ast,	After some time the son becomes a father.
Inchunin ast–u dawr-u charkhigari.	Thus rotates the universe.
Shams-i Tabrez durr-i maknun ast,	Shams-i Tabrizi, is the hidden treasure.
Tu zi kholiq shunaw na dew-u pari.	Hear it from the Creator not from demon and fairy.

Haidari (11:31)

Shunidastam ki Muso dar minojot,	One night I heard Moses in prayer,
Shabe az Haq hamekhost-u hojot.	He asked a wish of God.
Ei ki ya Rab khoham az faiz-i ilohi,	He asked you, oh, my Lord,
Ei ba khoson-i darat r(o)ahm namoi.	To have mercy on your followers.
Manam Muso-i payumbar ki hastam,	I am Moses, the prophet,
Khudoro az dil-u jon meparastam.	I worship God with my heart and my soul.
Nido omad, ki ai Muso-ye safar kun,	A call came, beckoning Moses to journey.
Biraw andar falon wodi guzar kun.	Go, seek out a certain valley.
Chu Muso fahmd-u kard on amr-i Mutlaq,	As Moses grasped that order of the Absolute,
Dar on wodi, ki farmon budash az Haq,	In that valley, where the order was of the Truth (Haq)
Bidid on jo yake mard-i barahna,	He saw there a naked man,
Ki ūro aql-u moro hej b(e)ahra na.	Who had an intellect of which we knew nothing.
Ba mūy-i sar bipechida-ye tanashro,	He covered his body with hair,
Ba hasrat dukhta pairohanashro.	Wistfully, he contemplated his shirt, and
Du chashmonash misol-i vahshi ohu,	Both his eyes, like those of a wild gazelle.
Az ū owoz meomad, ki Yo Hu.	The only sound which comes from him: "Ya Hu." [Oh Lord]
Salomash kard Muso-i sarafroz,	Honorably, Moses greeted him,

Ba juz Yo Hu nayomad hej-e owoz.	Although no sound emanated from him, but "Ya Hu."
Agar mutlab ba didor ast-u bargūy.	If your quest is for vision, then say so.
Agar bo Haq turo kor ast bargūy.	If you are searching for the Truth, then say so.
Chun nom-i Haq shunid on mast-i hayron,	As soon as the drunken wonder heard the name of the Truth,
Bizad Yo Hu bidod bo yod-i Haq jon.	He exclaimed Ya Hu and then perished in the name of the Truth.
Dil-i Muso ba jūsh omad-e ba yakbor,	The heart of Moses erupted,
(Chu) Ki daryo dar khurūsh omad ba yakbor.	Like a river roaring suddenly.
Nido omad, ki ai Muso chī didī?	A voice came: O Moses what did you see?
Magar bar mast-u hairon ham-e rasidī	Did you not reach the drunken wonder?
Maro chandin hazoron oshuqon hast,	I have a thousand such lovers.
(Maro z-in oshiqon chandin hazorand)[10]	
(Chu) Ki nomam bishnavand jon mesuporand.	As soon as they hear my name, they surrender their souls.
Agar tu oshiq-i ishq-i chunin bosh,	If you are also a lover, you should play your role as such.
(Tu gar ham oshig-i naqsh-e chunin boz)	
Ki har kas nest oshuq nest nejonboz.	He who does not love does not bear the scars of battle.
(Har on ki nest oshiq nest jonboz)	
Biyo Attor, ki khushguftor boshī,	Come Attar, speak sweetly,
Az in guftor barkhūrdor tu boshī.	And profit from such sayings.
Khudovand-i jahon Sulton-e Karim ast,	The master of the world is Sultan Karim.[11]
Nigahbon-i zamon Sulton-e Karim ast	The custodian of the age is Sultan Karim.
Buvad behtar zi gawhar khok-i poyash	His footprints are more lustrous than gems.
Ba gawhar khonumon Sulton Karim ast.	For gems the treasury is Sultan Karim.
Shudast mashhur Oghokhon-i chorum	Aga Khan IV became renowned.
Ki jon-i in jahon Sulton Karim ast	The soul of this world is Sultan Karim.
Zi ahl-i khonadon-i Mustafo ast,	He hails from the family of Mustafa,
Hayot-i jovid az Sulton Karim ast.	Everlasting life springs from Sultan Karim.
Ba chashm-i sirr nazar kun hei barodar,	See with your hidden eye (of the mind), O brother!
Ba mo rakhshanda Sulton Karim ast.	A brilliant light for us is Sultan Karim.

FALAK (19:43)

Seb e ki darun-i bogh andar lab-i jūst,	The apple [tree] is in the garden on the river bank,
Būy-i Hasan-u Huseynast meva-yi ūst.	The scent of Hasan and Husein wafts from the fruit.
Ai ki dod-u shokh sar ba sar dar jannat, ai Mawlo,	With your power the boughs of the tree spread in paradise, oh, Mawlā![12]
On chahar shahid-i Karbalo dar tah-yi ūst.	The martyrs of Karbala lie under its shade.

1. Describe the musical structure of this performance and its components (melodic and rhythmic arrangement of poetry, the style of singing, and instrumental accompaniment).

2. How does this structure serve to convey the religious and philosophical meanings of the poems sung?

3. In your opinion, is there a correspondence between the meaning of particular sections of *qasoid-khonī*, as interpreted by Zaimkhon Muborakqadamov, and their melodic pattern and the varying pitch level at which they are sung?

4. *Qasoid-khonī* can be performed both at funerals and on festive occasions. What, do you think, are the effects of its performance in these two different situations?

5. Based on your listening in this and the two preceding chapters, compare the structural and stylistic features of *maddoh-khonī* and *qasoid-khonī*. In what ways are they similar and different?

NOTES

1. In addition to phonetic variations of *maddoh* and *qasoid,* other local terms for this practice are used in Badakhshan, for example, *haidarī* among Ismailis in the Darwaz district.

2. See Stefan Sperl and Christopher Shackle, eds., *Qasida Poetry in Islamic Asia and Africa: Classical Traditions and Modern Meanings* (Leiden, New York: E. J. Brill, 1996), vol. 1.

3. See Mary Boyce, *Zoroastrians: Their Religious Beliefs and Practices* (London and New York: Routledge, 2001).

4. The arrangement of pillars may be a mirror image of that described.

5. On this classification, see Faizulla Karomatov and Nizam Nurdjanov, *Muzykal'noe Iskusstvo Pamira* [Musical arts of the Pamirs] (Moscow: Nauka, 1985), vol. 1: 12–13.

6. The Chosen, nickname of Ali.

7. Pen name of Forighī.

8. The Lion, nickname of Ali.

9. The Highly Praised, a name of Muhammad.

10. The correct version is shown in parentheses.

11. Sultan Karim is a reference to the current Nizari Ismaili Imam, Shah Karim al-Huseini (b. 1936), the fourth Nizari Ismaili Imam to hold the princely title Aga Khan.

12. The Protector, a name of God.

CHAPTER 30 *Falak*

SPIRITUAL SONGS OF THE MOUNTAIN TAJIKS

FAROGHAT AZIZI

*F*alak is a musical genre whose strongest cultural associations are with the mountain-dwelling populations of southeastern and southwestern Tajikistan. The two best-known styles of *falak* take their names from these regions: *falak-i kulob,* a reference to the area surrounding Kulob (also Kulyob) in the southwest, and *falak-i pamiri,* which refers to the Pamir Mountains of Badakhshan, the culturally autonomous region of southeastern Tajikistan and northeastern Afghanistan, where *falak* also has old roots.

Falak means "heaven," "fortune," "fate," or "universe." A musical genre that takes its name from these metaphysically laden words might be expected to express spiritual sentiments or ideas, and this is indeed the case. In music, *falak* describes sober, lament-like songs that many singers and listeners believe to possess healing qualities, and whose texts typically address philosophical themes. The poems set to music in *falak* often speak of the vicissitudes of fate and the limitations of human agency. More broadly, the lyrics of a *falak* can evoke the full range of human emotional and spiritual experience: love, pain, separation, suffering, and hope. *Falak* is sung both by men and women, and may be performed with instrumental accompaniment or a cappella, in free rhythm without clear beat, or in a regular meter. The social and musical context of *falak* performance also varies, ranging from traditional ritual contexts to contemporary pop music. Typical contexts include:

1. Funeral rites (*falak-i motami:* mourning *falak*): In this context, *falak* functions like a lament. It is sung during funeral processions—typically by women from the family of a deceased person—as the body of the deceased is carried by male relatives to the burial site. In the funerary practices of certain parts of Badakhshan, notably Bartang and Rushan, *falak-i motami* is performed to a funeral dance accompanied by frame drums (*daf*) that play an irregular or "broken" rhythm (*zarb-i shikasta*). The traditional dance movements are understood to represent "broken" parts of the body—as if the dance is a literal illustration of the Tajik expression often recited by people who are grieving or mourning. "Fate, you have broken me" (*Falak miyonama shikasti*).

2. Festivities such as weddings or other family gatherings: *Falak* is performed at social gatherings either by a soloist or by several singers. Solo *falak* singing is sometimes called *beparvo falak*—"unconstrained" or "carefree" *falak,* which conveys the idea that the performer is free to improvise outside of a regular rhythmic and metrical pattern. The term *beparvo falak* is also used to characterize a vocal style in which the singer places the melody in a high *tessitura* (vocal register), as well as to characterize a certain type of poetic text whose focus is an emotionally wrought appeal to fate or to the Divine in which the singer asks, "Why are you treating me so indifferently?" Solo *falak* can also be performed on a musical instrument—flutes such as the Badakhshani *ney* or *tutik;* lutes such as the Pamiri *rubab, tanbur, dutar, or setar;* and the *ghijak* (spike fiddle). In instrumental *falak* the "voice" of the instrument becomes the vehicle for expressing prayer or supplication.

3. The *maddoh* religious ceremony regularly performed by Badakhshani Ismailis: In this context, *falak* functions as a spiritual song or praise song within a cycle of sung and chanted texts performed to musical accompaniment (see chapters 28 and 29). Performers sometimes join together a *falak* with a few other songs drawn from a *maddoh* to create a self-standing song cycle.

4. Popular song and dance arrangements: Beginning in the Soviet era, *falak* melodies were arranged in the form of lyrical songs with instrumental accompaniment. Contemporary arrangements of *falak,* which typically feature amplified acoustic instruments or synthesizers, are frequently performed at concerts and in discotheques, where, played at a fast tempo with prominent percussion, they have become popular for dancing. The audio examples that follow illustrate these various kinds of *falak.* The performance styles of the examples, however, are quite different, and reflect some of the various ways in which the underlying concept of *falak* is expressed in contemporary Tajikistan.

Falak singer Soheba Davlatshoeva.

Photo by Sebastian Schutyser. Courtesy of Aga Khan Music Initiative.

Example 30.1 presents a solo *falak* performed a cappella by one of Tajikistan's best known *falak* singers, Soheba Davlatshoeva. Like many *falaks*, this one is the work of an unknown poet whose identity was lost as the song lyrics passed from one singer to another through oral tradition. Likewise the composer of the melody is unknown. The *falak* has no title, and thus for purposes of recording it, Soheba created one: "Falak-i Badakhshani" (Badakhshani *falak*). "I listened to a lot of our old singers, and they always sang this at funerals," said Soheba. "I learned it by ear, and started to sing it myself. You could sing the text at weddings if you used a different melody."

The poetic form of a *falak* text is invariably *rubā'ī* (plural form: *rubā'iyāt*), with the end rhyme scheme aaba, ccdc, eefe, and so on. Singers, however, conceive the poetic form as a sequence of two-line couplets (*bayt*): aa, ba, cc, dc, ee, fe. Singers typically know many couplets by memory and can add, eliminate, or substitute couplets in order to make a *falak* longer of shorter, or adapt it to the mood of a particular performance situation. Performers may also alter the words that comprise a couplet, resulting in variant forms of well-known couplets. In Badakhshan, spiritual poetry circulates widely in oral tradition, forming a large corpus of texts from which singers construct their own version of *falak*.

Listen now to Soheba Davlatshoeva's performance of "Falak-i Badakhshani" while following the transliteration of the Tajik text and its English translation. Then, respond to the questions that follow the song text (as in the previous chapter on "Maddoh," the English translations of *falak* that follow below play with elements of visual form).

LISTEN

Example 30.1. "Falak-i Badakhshani," performed by Soheba Davlatshoeva. From *Badakhshan Ensemble: Song and Dance from the Pamir Mountains*, vol. 5 of *Music of Central Asia* (SFR, 2007), track 1.

> *Dunyo ba misol yak ruboti du dar ast,*
> *Oy, har rūz dar in rubot khalq-i digar ast.*
>
> *Guftam biravam sayr-i tamosho-yi jahon,*
> *Oy, didam, ki tamosho-yi jahon dar guzar ast.*
>
> *Dunyora ba khud vafo nadidem-u guzasht,*
> *Oy, angusht-i pushaymonī gazidem-u guzasht.*

Dunyo bogh ast-u mo chu bod-i sahari,
Oγ, yak subhidame dar on vazidem-u guzasht.

Dunyo guzoro az tu chiho memonad?
Oγ, yak nom-i khush-i mov-u shumo memonad,

Tukhm-i abadī agar bikorem ba zamin,
Oγ, neki-vu badī judo-judo memonad.

The world is like a caravanserai with two doors;
Through these doors,
    different people pass all the time.

I thought to myself, I should see this world's sights
    What I saw was impermanence: fleeting and flight.

The world passed me by like a treacherous lover
I passed my life,
    in pangs of regret that I can't cover.

The world: a garden
I: the dawn breeze
One morning I swept through it
and that too passed.

What shall this passing world leave behind?
Good name is all that remains from you and me

For it is as though we have planted,
    eternal seeds:
        the good ones and bad ones yield crops accordingly.

STUDY QUESTIONS

1. How would you describe the timbre (color or quality) of Soheba's voice?

2. How does Soheba set the text of the *falak* to the melody? Does she sing each line straight through from beginning to end, or are some words repeated? Is the pattern of repetition the same in each verse?

3. As you follow the text, you will notice that Soheba inserts syllables such as "eh," "ah," or "wah-yeh" that aren't part of the actual text. What is the purpose of these syllables?

4. Give a few examples of syllables in the text that Soheba sings with extensive melodic ornamentation. What is your guess about the role of melodic ornamentation in the performance of *falak*?

5. How would you describe the range of the melody? That is, does the melodic line that Soheba sings ascend and descend through a large number of pitches, or is it contained within a small range? (If you have some musical training, can you identify the interval between the lowest and highest pitches?)

6. How many separate pitches does the melody contain? Using solfège syllables (*do, re, mi*), what are these pitches?

7. What is the role of repetition in the melody of the *falak*? What part of the melody is repeated?

8. Is there a steady rhythmic pattern in this *falak*, or is it rhythmically irregular?

9. At the end of each verse couplet, and at the end of the entire *falak*, does the melody leave you with a sense of resolution and finality, or are these melodic end points in some sense like a question mark?

ANSWERS TO QUESTIONS

Soheba's powerful a cappella performance illustrates the drawn-out, forcefully delivered, intricately ornamented melodic style typical of the *falak* genre. The melody itself unfolds entirely within the interval of a whole tone (for example, *do-re*) and consists of three pitches that form two adjacent semitones, for example *do-do♯-re* (approximately G-G♯-A in absolute pitch). The melody to which each verse line is set is identical. This melody is repeated six times—once for each line of verse. The *falak* is sung in free rhythm, without a regular meter, thus illustrating the principle of *beparvo falak*—"unconstrained" or "free" *falak*. At the end of each couplet, and at the end of the song, the melody leads not to a firm sense of finality and closure, but rather to what might be considered an open-ended question. On a metaphysical level, this absence of finality could be understood as representing the defining feature of the *falak* genre: an entreaty to fate, or to God, that asks, "Why have you treated me so indifferently"?

Example 30.2 presents another kind of *falak* performance: vocal music with instrumental accompaniment in fixed meter performed as a concert piece—in this case, by the Badakhshan Ensemble, the group founded and directed by Soheba Davlatshoeva. This particular cycle consists of three songs. The first can be described on the basis of its consistently high tessitura and sad melody as an example of *beparvo falak*. The text, however, is a modern one, which addresses not spiritual suffering, but the homeland of Tajikistan. Such substituted texts, which were common in the Soviet era, have become an enduring element of many singers' repertoires. The opening *falak* segues into two songs from the repertoire of *maddoh* singers. Though these two songs are not, strictly speaking, *falak*s, the entire three-song cycle was described by one of the performers in the Badakhshan Ensemble, Jonboz Dushanbiev, a traditional master musician with a deep knowledge of Badakhshani poetry and music, as *falak-i sūzi*—a *falak* of spiritual suffering. Other musicians have not attested this term, suggesting that it may be particular to the Bartang region of Badakhshan, where Jonboz resides, or indeed, to Jonboz himself.

Local variation in the use of names and terms to describe musical styles and genres is common in Badakhshan and Kulob. One term may be used to describe different styles, or conversely, one style may be referred to by different names.

The second text in the cycle is excerpted from a classical *ghazal*. This *ghazal* is attributed to the great Persian mystical poet Jalal ad-Din Rumi (1207–1273), and describes an experience of mystical ecstasy in which the poet loses awareness of his own being. The third text is also an excerpt from a mystical *ghazal*, and is attributed to the Persian poet Hafez (1325–1389), whose poetry remains extremely popular in Tajikistan more than six centuries after his death. As you listen to the recorded music example, follow the transliteration and translation of the text.

LISTEN **Example 30.2.** "Falak-i sūzi," performed by Olucha Mualibshoev and the Badakhshan Ensemble. From *Badakhshan Ensemble: Song and Dance from the Pamir Mountains* vol. 5 of *Music of Central Asia* (SFR, 2007), track 5.

Bakht-i ajabe maro vatan dodayī tu,
Gulho-yi umed az chaman dodayī tu,
Bovar binamo ba sad jahon nafrūsham,
Ishq-i vatane ajab maro dodayī tu.

What fortune,
      for you gave me a home!
From your garden,
      you showered me with
         hope's blossoms!
Gave me faith and made me safe
      —now I won't exchange this,
      for all the world's riches—
for you settled me,
      with a love for my home.

GHAZAL (ATTRIBUTED TO RUMI)
Khoja, bigū, ki man manam, man na manam, na man manam,
Jon-i man ūst dar tanam, man na manam, na man manam.
Otash-i ishq barfurūz, aql-i majoyil-ro bisūz,
Zulmat-i shab chu gashta rūz man na manam, na ma manam.

Boz-i safed-i ū manam, soya-yi bed-i ū manam,
Rū ba umed-i ū manam, man na manam, na man manam.
Shams daromada zi dar, karda maro zi khud khabar,
Guft: bigū zi khayr-u shar man na manam, na man manam. (repeats)

O superior lord!
Tell me who is me,
For myself I am not,
my self is not me.
This body,
is animated by him.
For myself I am not,
my self is not me.
Ignite love's fire,
Burn down the mind's desires
For myself I am not,
my self is not me.
Now that night's darkness
is turning into day's brightness
Myself I am not,
My self is not me.

I am his falcon, auspicious and white
I am his willow,
I spread my shade for others' delight
My goal is to reach him, and this hope is my light
For myself I am not,
my self is not me.

Shams[1] walked through the door,
—the sun's rays pour through the door—
and makes me aware of myself,
Then he said,
"Now speak of good and evil!"
But, myself I am not,
my self is not me.

GHAZAL (ATTRIBUTED TO HAFEZ)

Yoram chu qadah ba dast girad, bozor-i buton shikast girad.
Dar bahr fitodaam chu mohī, to yor maro ba shast girad.
Dar p-osh fitodaam ba zorī, oyo buvad ū, ki dast girad?
Har kas, ki bidid chashm-i ū, guft: ku muhtasibe, ki mast girad?
Khurram dil-i on, ki hamchu Hofez, jome zi may-i alast girad.

The magnificence of my beloved, when holding a goblet
bankrupts the bazaar, where idols are traded.
I have been thrown into the ocean like a fish,
so that I may fall into his net.

Desolate,
downcast,
dejected
      I have fallen at his feet,
           Will he help me get up by lending me his hand?

Whoever sees my beloved's eyes says:
Let these drunkards be arrested at once!

Blissful is indeed that soul,
      who like Hafez,
           was given a goblet of wine at creation's dawn.

STUDY QUESTIONS

1. How would you compare the timbre of Olucha Mualibshoev's voice to that of Soheba Davlatshoeva, the performer of the *falak* in Example 30.1? How would you compare Olucha's and Soheba's treatment of melodic ornamentation? Based on the two examples you have heard, how would you characterize the distinctive features of *falak* vocal style?

2. In the opening *rubā'ī*, what is the metrical pattern of the frame drum (*daf*)? How many beats are in one metrical unit (i.e., the number of beats before the drum pattern repeats?)

3. What is the role of the other instruments? Do they play harmony (chords) or only melody?

4. How is the melody of the first *rubā'ī* constructed? Is it based on the same principle as the melody in the *falak* sung by Soheba Davlatshoeva, i.e., repetition of one and the same melody for each line of text?

5. At 2:45, where the second poem begins (the *ghazal* attributed to Rumi), what happens to the drum pattern? Using a schematic chart like the one illustrated below, try to represent one complete unit of the drum pattern you hear. Place an *x* below the solid line to represent low-pitched drum strokes, and place an *x* above the solid line to represent higher-pitched beats. Leave spaces between your *x*'s to represent the relative amount of time between beats.

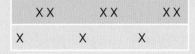

6. Can you hear the asymmetrical "limping" rhythm in the drumming? What effect does it have on you as you listen to it?

7. Based on this example, can you suggest why local performers and listeners consider *falak* to have healing qualities?

2. The correct answer is 3.

5. A complete unit of the drum pattern would look as follows:

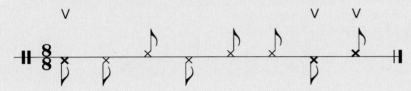

The third example presents a *falak-i dashti,* which is one of the two major *falak* styles of the Kulob region of southwestern Tajikistan (the other major Kulob style is called *falak-i rogi,* and represents the development of *falak* among town-dwellers, as opposed to mountain-dwellers). The word *dasht* means "steppe," but *falak-i dashti* should not be understood literally as "steppe *falak.*" Rather, it should be understood in a metaphorical sense as a *falak* that expresses life's hardships and asks God for mercy. Indeed, *falak-i dashti* is ideally suited to prayer, and it is always performed as a solo, whether by a vocalist or an instrumentalist (typically on the *dombra;* occasionally on the *ghijak* or *tutik* [flute]).

WATCH

Example 30.3. "Falak-i dashti," performed by Gulchehra Sodiqova. Filmed by Kirill Kuzmin, Kulob, 2014.

Jon! Shinam shiname az tu shirin, yod oyade,	Oh my soul! I sit and sweet memories of you come,
Jon! Ohe mekasham, ki az falak dod oyade,	Oh my soul! I sigh, a wail comes from the heavens.
Rozi dilama ey, agar ba sangho gūyame,	If I tell my cherished desire to stones,
Jon! Sang az tag-i daryo ba faryod oyade.	Oh my soul! From the depths of the river, the stones will weep.
Jon! Yo Rab! Tu maro sarkash-u mas-tam nakunie,	Oh my soul! Oh God! Don't make me stubborn and drunk,
Jon! Dar kor-i khudat kūtahdastam nakunie,	Oh my soul! In your deeds, do not make me unfit.

Sabr-u toqatam bideh ba rūz-i sakhtie,	Give me endurance and patience for a hard day,
Jon! Mūhtoj ba mardumon-i pastam nakunī.	Oh my soul! Do not make me depend on lowly people.
Faryod, ki kor-i mo dar in roh nashide,	I weep because on this path nothing has worked out for us,
Jon! Shondem darakht dar zamin bogh nashide,	Oh my soul! We planted a tree, but no earthly garden arose from it.
Shondem darakht parvaridem bo umede	We planted a tree and cared for it with hope,
Jon! In fikr-u khayole, ki mo kardem, nashide.	Oh my soul! What we thought, and hoped for, didn't come to pass.

Falak-i dashti is sung or played in a mid-range or high tessitura—that is, in the middle or high part of the performer's vocal or instrumental range. The melody unfolds in free rhythm and is characterized by extensive embellishment. In contrast to Soheba Davlatshoeva's performance of "Falak-i Badakhshani" in example 30.1, in which the melody remains within the narrow range of a whole tone, the melodic range of the typical *falak-i dashti* is a little broader, encompassing four pitches that comprise the interval of a perfect fourth.

STUDY QUESTIONS

1. Based on the recordings you've heard, how would you characterize both the similarities and differences between the Pamiri and Kulobi styles of *falak*?

2. What musical qualities distinguish the *falak* genre?

The plaintive sound of *falak* is not confined to traditional performance styles but permeates a great deal of Tajik popular music, both new and old. In its popular music guise, *falak* takes on a more lyrical character, and melodies become more individualized by expanding beyond the narrow pitch compass characteristic of traditional styles. One of the most popular and beloved songs to emerge in the genre of what might be called popular *falak* is "Ay pari" (Oh fairy), composed in the early twentieth century by a musician whose identity has been lost. According to Soheba Davlatshoeva, "Ay pari" first came to prominence in the 1950s in an arrangement by the Pamir Ethnographic Ensemble, a Dushanbe-based state-sponsored group that composed, arranged, and performed many songs that remain popular in Badakhshan today. "Everyone sings 'Ay pari,'" said Soheba. "It's performed in concerts, at weddings, and in theater productions. A well-known Tajik musician, Daler Nazar, turned it into a pop tune. The poet whose *ghazal* is used for the lyrics was a Badakhshani from Afghanistan, but none of us in the Badakhshan Ensemble know when he lived."

Example 30.4. "Ay pari," performed by the Badakhshan Ensemble. From *Badakhshan Ensemble: Song and Dance from the Pamir Mountains,* vol. 5 of *Music of Central Asia* (SFR, 2007), track 2.

In this arrangement performed by the Badakhshan Ensemble, as well as by other ensembles in contemporary Tajikistan, "Ay pari" is joined to a second song in a different rhythm and tempo to create a mini-cycle.

Ey, parī, shūkh-i sitamgar, to ba kay sūzī maro, sūzī maro yorume,
Mondaam be bol-u be par, to ba kay sūzī maro, sūzī maro yorume.

Az jafoho-yi ghamat hijron-i khubon nozanin
Karda-yī moro qalandar, to ba kay sūzī maro sūzī maro yorume.

Qodir az ishq-i tu nolad hamchu bulbul dar chaman
Kardaam in qissaro sar, to ba kay sūzī maro, sūzī maro yorume.

Beautiful as a fairy,
    O my beloved!
        You! The flirtatious tyrant!
           How much longer,
               will you burn me, my love?

My feathers are plucked,
    my wings clipped;
        I remain at your mercy,
           yet you keep burning me.
           How much longer,
              will you burn me, my love?

Abandoned am I:
        The beautiful, one possessed of grace,
           left me.
This injustice, my heart could not brace!
Now I am but a lowly vagabond,

514   FAROGHAT AZIZI

yet you keep burning me.
How much longer,
will you burn me, my love?

Your love will even make
Qadir [who once thought himself to be strong, dignified and full of power]
Shed tears of longing,
as the love-stricken nightingale does
when it sees the garden empty of
his beloved, the rose flower.

I have been through it all,
yet you keep burning me.
How much longer,
will you burn me, my love?

SECOND TEXT: IN THE STYLE OF TAHEREH QORET-AL EYN
(QAJAR PERIOD)
ATTRIBUTED BY BADAKHSHANIS TO HAFEZ, BUT NOT BY HIM

Mutrib-i hushnavo bigū toza ba toza nav ba nav,
Boda-yi dilkusho bijū toza ba toza nav ba nav.

Soqi-yi simsoq-i man mastī mayam, biyo ba pesh,
Zud, ki pur kunam zebar toza ba toza nav ba nav.

Shohid-i dilrabo-yi man mekunad az baroyi man,
Naqsh-u nigor-u rang-u būy-i toza ba toza nav ba nav.

Bod-i sabo chu bigzarī, bar sar-i kuy-i on parī,
Qissa-yi Hofizash bigū, toza ba toza nav ba nav.

Let those sweet sounds of yours resonate,
O masterful musician!
With each stroke,
Create them afresh, anew!

Seek that delight-bearing wine,
Seek it each time as if it's the first time, afresh, anew!

My beautiful-bodied cup-bearer!
Come, quickly, at once,
So that I may fill my cup at once!
And then do the same thing afresh, anew!

That boy, my beloved,
  the heart-stealing youth,
adorns himself with new looks, new scents,
  and he does that time and again,
    afresh, anew!

Oh, Dawn breeze!
  if you happen to pass,
    that beautiful fairy's abode,
Tell her Hafez's story,
  each time, afresh, anew!

Falak singer Gulchehra
Sodiqova.

In recent years, musicians in Tajikistan have created arrangements of *falak* in a variety of pop music styles. An example of such an arrangement, "Navo-i kuhiston" (Melody from the Mountains), performed by Muhammadvali Orzuyev and composed by his father, Dosti Orzuyev, is reproduced in example 30.5. Another example of a pop arrangement of *falak* is the song "Zi durī," by Tajik *falak* singer Gulchehra Sodiqova, which is presented as an audio example in chapter 35 (example 35.1). Many analogous examples of contemporary *falak* can be found on YouTube. These arrangements show some of the diverse ways in which pop musicians are drawing on the resources of traditional styles and genres to expand the language of popular music—a process that is very much alive in Tajikistan.

LISTEN

Example 30.5. "Navo-i kuhiston" (Melody from the mountains), composed by Dosti Orzuyev, performed by Muhammadvali Orzuyev. Recording courtesy of Muhammadvali Orzuyev.

STUDY QUESTIONS

1. At what point in the song does the *falak* melodic style enter?

2. How successfully does the composer integrate the *falak* style into a pop musical idiom?

3. Which elements of the *falak* sound are updated, and which ones remain traditional?

As the five examples in this chapter make clear, *falak* includes a considerable variety of musical styles that resist easy generalization or definition. Indeed, performers themselves do not agree on a precise definition of *falak* and its various sub-categories. While the poetic genre *rubā'ī,* with its four-line, aaba rhyme scheme provides a formal template for *falak,* this form is expressed through music in diverse ways, and performed in a variety of social contexts: improvised or memorized; in free rhythm or fixed meter; as part of a ritual or as freestanding song; a cappella or with instrumental accompaniment. The single musical attribute that seems applicable to all examples of *falak* is that their melodies, typically performed loudly in a high tessitura, display strong and sober emotion. The visceral power of *falak* has transcended not only stylistic boundaries, but cultural boundaries, as recordings of *falak* find their way to an increasingly international and cosmopolitan audience.

NOTE

For his pen name (*takhallus*), Rumi used the name of his spiritual mentor, Shams-i Tabrizi.

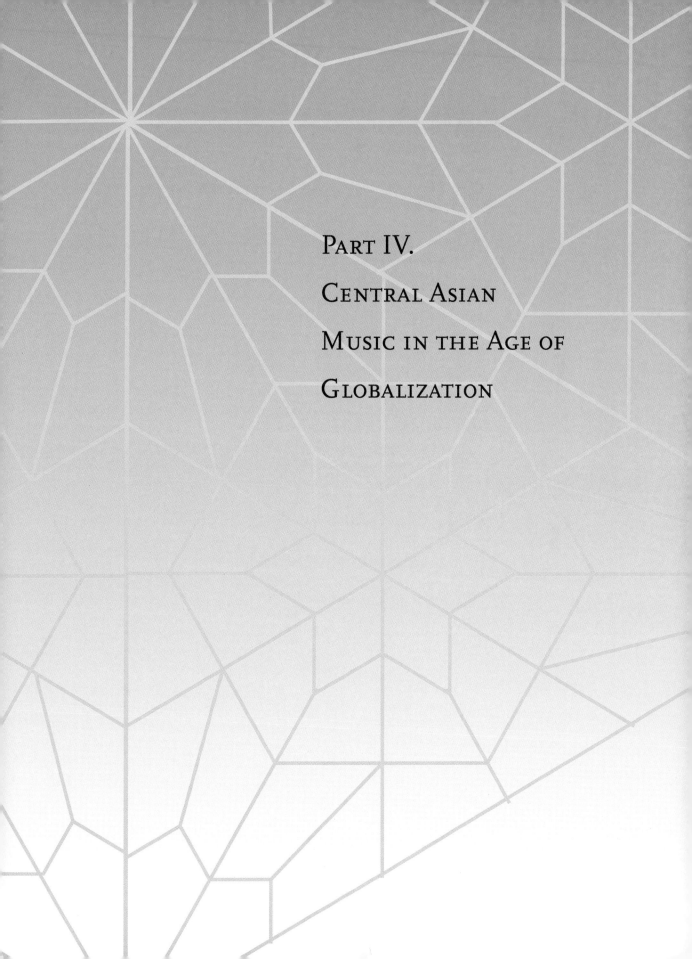

PART IV.

CENTRAL ASIAN

MUSIC IN THE AGE OF

GLOBALIZATION

CHAPTER 31

Revitalizing Musical Traditions

THE AGA KHAN MUSIC INITIATIVE

THEODORE LEVIN

The past reaches out to you, yearning to be reborn. Will you embrace it compliantly for what it was, once and always: 'influence,' 'tradition,' 'convention,' 'custom'? Or will you struggle passionately with the past, as you do with a lost lover or a half-remembered memory, knowing that things can never be the same again . . . not today. Not ever.

—HOMI BHABHA, "ANOTHER COUNTRY"

Photo by Katherine Vincent. Courtesy of Aga Khan Music Initiative.

In the second decade of the twenty-first century, economic and cultural globalization touches the daily lives of an ever-growing percentage of the world's population. The place where we live, the kind of work we do, the language or languages we use to perform this work, the food we eat and clothes we wear, the movies we watch and music we listen to—all are affected by global flows of trade, technological innovation, and cultural trends. The rapid pace of change that propels us inexorably toward new ways of life also leads to a sense of increasing distance from the past—and sometimes to nostalgia for the security and comfort of familiar traditions and customs. It is hardly surprising that the role of tradition, and concerns about the "future of the past," have become such a critically important and contentious cultural issue in our era of globalization.

Throughout the world, strong voices advocate for strict adherence to tradition—social, cultural, legal, or religious—at the same time that other strong voices seek to adapt elements of tradition to the needs and values of the present. In many parts of the world where cultural traditions have been ruptured or are endangered, concerned individuals and organizations have come forward with the aim of restoring or revitalizing them. Yet in whatever way one defines tradition—and many definitions have been proposed—the revival, reanimation, or revitalization of tradition never produces simply a replica of the past. Rather, such initiatives selectively interpret the past through the prism of our own time, place, and culture. The way that we frame notions of "tradition" and the motives that lead us to invoke its authority reveal as much about our own views and values as they do about history itself.

Present-day political leaders routinely appeal to a sense of social or political tradition to stoke feelings of patriotism and celebrate national identity. Tradition in the form of cultural heritage—the legacy of art, architecture, literature, music, and other manifestations of culture from the past—also frequently serves as a means to burnish the cultural prestige and bolster the identity of present-day communities or nations. Calls for a "return to tradition" have at times been used to justify radical social change or even revolution. And nostalgia for tradition routinely asserts itself in times of economic uncertainty and social discord. Yet if "things can never be the same again," as literary theorist and critic Homi Bhabha asserts in the quotation that begins this chapter (excerpted from an essay that addresses the challenge facing contemporary artists whose work references traditional artistic forms), what does it mean to "revitalize" artistic traditions, and what is the aim of such efforts at revitalization?

These questions are particularly pertinent to the artistic traditions of Central Asia, which, during the Soviet era, underwent radical social transformations that ruptured many aspects of traditional culture. Soviet culture policy had a well-developed—and well-funded—strategy to transform traditional culture throughout the entire vast territory of the USSR (discussed in chapter 1). Following the breakup of the Soviet Union in 1991, musicians throughout Central Asia began to find their way back to older traditions. Working at times almost like archaeologists, they reconstructed musical instruments that were no longer made, and learned to play them by listening to old recordings or by studying with elderly tradition-bearers. Other musicians worked to reconstruct older musical styles and repertoires that had been suppressed, censored, or Europeanized by Soviet cultural policies. By looking backward toward older, and, in some cases, truly archaic musical forms, adventurous musicians in Central Asia discovered one of the universal axioms of artistic avant-gardes: that tradition can serve as an invaluable compass for exploring new forms of artistic consciousness and creativity inspired, but not constrained, by the past. The recasting and reimagination of traditional art has played a central role in the work of many innovative artists, fashion designers, musicians, architects, theater directors, and writers—sometimes attached to sobriquets such as neo-traditionalism, neo-classicism, or neo-primitivism.

Despite the salient heuristic role of tradition in their work, musical "revitalizers" in Central Asia have not always been embraced by governmental cultural

An amateur music ensemble in Tuva, an autonomous republic within the Russian Federation situated in the Altai region of south Siberia, performs in a local house of culture, 1987.
Photo by Karen Sherlock.

organizations whose mandate is to promote national forms of "intangible cultural heritage"—the term coined by UNESCO to describe "oral traditions, performing arts, social practices, rituals, festive events, knowledge and practices concerning nature and the universe or the knowledge and skills to produce traditional crafts."[1] On the contrary, as they strive to liberate the innovating power of tradition from official constructions of intangible cultural heritage, some musical revitalizers have found themselves at odds with the policies and priorities of state cultural organizations such as the Ministry of Culture, National Conservatory, or Union of Composers. But in contrast to the cultural politics of the Soviet Union, in which state cultural organizations held a monopoly on artistic patronage, non-governmental organizations have come to play a significant role as patrons of arts and culture in post-Soviet Central Asia. The balance of cultural authority between state-controlled cultural institutions and autonomous non-governmental organizations varies from one Central Asian nation to the next. At one extreme are Turkmenistan and Uzbekistan, where arts, media, and culture are not only dominated by the state but also, to a large extent, under the direct control of the president, his family, and his apparat. The autonomous cultural sector is stronger in Tajikistan, and strongest in Kazakhstan and Kyrgyzstan.

One of the largest and most active non-governmental organizations to respond to calls for support from Central Asian musical revitalizers is the Aga Khan Development Network (AKDN). The AKDN, founded and guided by His Highness the Aga Khan, the spiritual leader of Shi'a Imami Ismaili Muslims, is a contemporary endeavor of the Ismaili Imamat to "realize the social conscience of Islam through institutional action," as the AKDN describes its mandate. The development agencies that comprise the AKDN work in the domains of health, education, architecture, culture, microfinance, rural development, disaster reduction, promotion of private-sector enterprise, and revitalization of historic cities. AKDN agencies

Official Uzbek celebration of 2500 Years since the Founding of Bukhara, 2008.
Courtesy of Kerstin Klenke.

work in over thirty countries in some of the most impoverished and underserved regions of Africa and Asia and conduct their programs without regard to the faith, origin, or gender of the people served. Through a central management structure, the AKDN strives to coordinate the projects of its many agencies to achieve programmatic and organizational synergies. The crucial idea behind the Aga Khan Development Network is that the social impact of development is maximized when social, economic, and cultural initiatives are interconnected and carried out cooperatively, in accordance with a comprehensive and long-range strategic plan.

Organizational structure of the Aga Khan Development Network. The Music Initiative is in the lower right, under the Aga Khan Trust for Culture.

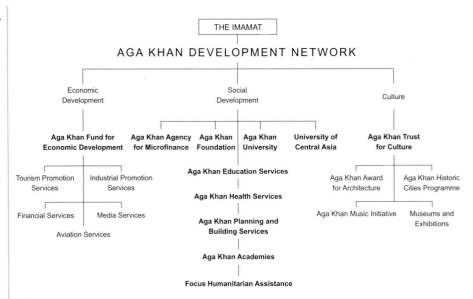

```
                              ┌─────────────────┐
                              │   THE IMAMAT    │
                              └─────────────────┘

              AGA KHAN DEVELOPMENT NETWORK

       Economic              Social                      Culture
      Development          Development

  Aga Khan Fund for    Aga Khan Agency   Aga Khan    Aga Khan    University of    Aga Khan Trust
 Economic Development   for Microfinance  Foundation  University   Central Asia     for Culture

Tourism Promotion    Industrial Promotion    Aga Khan Education Services    Aga Khan Award      Aga Khan Historic
    Services              Services                                          for Architecture    Cities Programme

Financial Services    Media Services          Aga Khan Health Services         Aga Khan Music Initiative    Museums and
                                                                                                            Exhibitions
        Aviation Services                  Aga Khan Planning and
                                             Building Services

                                             Aga Khan Academies

                                        Focus Humanitarian Assistance
```

Music may seem an unlikely domain for an international development organization, but the rich musical heritage of Central Asia, where the impact of Islam as a spiritual and cultural force has been sustained over thirteen centuries of dramatic political, social, and demographic change, indeed offers fertile ground for institutional action through cultural advocacy and development work. To implement and coordinate its support for revitalizing musical traditions in Central Asia, the AKDN, through its Trust for Culture, launched a new program, the Aga Khan Music Initiative in Central Asia (later, as its region of activity expanded to include countries in the Middle East and North Africa, West Africa, and South Asia, the program became known simply as the Aga Khan Music Initiative). Following the collapse of the centralized system of cultural patronage constructed by the Soviet Union, the Music Initiative's initial task was to assess the needs of musicians and audiences, music students and teachers, and musical institutions in post-Soviet Central Asia and, with those needs in mind, to devise a long-term strategy to help revitalize musical culture and creativity in the region. The present book is one of many projects that grew out of the needs assessment and resulting strategic plan.

The book was envisaged first and foremost as a way to introduce students in Central Asia to their own regional musical heritage (translation into local languages is planned for the future) on the theory that when people feel secure in their own historical and cultural identity, they create a strong base for the development of a pluralist worldview that embraces the coexistence of other, different identities.

The Music Initiative's portfolio includes numerous projects in music education and, through a network of master teachers and performers, these projects have been linked to music creation and performance activities that in various ways "translate" traditional artistic languages into contemporary forms of expressive culture. Some of these projects and activities are described in greater detail below.[2]

THE AGA KHAN MUSIC INITIATIVE

When the Music Initiative was launched, in 2000, nearly a decade after the breakup of the Soviet Union, the momentum of Soviet culture policy in Central Asia was still strong. In the formative years of the Soviet Union, the incompatibility of tradition and modernity was taken as axiomatic by political and cultural leaders, and expressed in the form of a national cultural development strategy that mandated a "battle against the past" as a necessary precondition for establishing Socialist culture. In this cultural milieu, traditional music and dance were performed as choreographed, arranged, and theatricalized "folklore" rather than cultivated within local communities as living and continually evolving traditions.

After conducting a needs assessment that included discussions with a range of local stakeholders—musicians, music scholars and teachers, arts administrators, cultural entrepreneurs—the Music Initiative's leadership concluded that development and innovation in the sphere of tradition-based music and expressive culture was impeded not only by a dearth of financial resources but by the absence of a compelling alternative to the legacy of Soviet culture policy and its ideological polarization of tradition and modernity. Based on stakeholders' own ideas and proposals, the Music Initiative formulated an ambitious objective: to help musicians further develop indigenous artistic traditions that validate local identities and cultural heritage while, at the same time, forging an internationally recognized Central Asian artistic modernity that promotes the values of cultural pluralism and cosmopolitanism. To this end, the Music Initiative began to work in three interlinked spheres of activity: music education and mentoring; international performance and outreach; and artistic production and dissemination.

Azerbaijani musician Alim Qasimov leads a workshop with students at Dartmouth College in Hanover, New Hampshire.

In the first area, the principal project was the organization of a network of music schools and centers where outstanding tradition-bearers taught and mentored talented young musicians and developed new methodologies and curricula for general education schools that promoted appreciation of traditional music through group music making. An intended byproduct of these efforts was to raise the prestige of traditional music and performers of traditional music in their own communities. In the second area—international performance and outreach—the

Music Initiative established a global network of partnerships with arts presenters, festivals, and educational institutions that provided a platform for curated concert tours and artist-in-residence programs featuring the tradition-bearers with whom the Music Initiative worked. In the third area—artistic production and dissemination—the Music Initiative cultivated new approaches to music performance and innovative collaborations that revived historical connections among musicians from Central Asia and beyond the region while expanding traditional artistic languages. At the same time, it produced, together with Smithsonian Folkways Recordings, a ten-volume CD-DVD anthology, *Music of Central Asia,* consisting of original recordings and documentary films of the tradition-bearers with whom it worked (see "Further Reading, Listening, and Viewing" on the companion website for full discography).

Music centers and schools supported by the Music Initiative have included the Academy of Maqom, in Dushanbe, Tajikistan, whose focus is on revitalizing the classical Shashmaqom repertoire (see chapter 18 textbox, "The Academy of Maqom"); Khunar Centre, which operates a network of music schools and master-apprentice training programs across northern Tajikistan; Kökil College, in Almaty, Kazakhstan, whose innovative approach to oral tradition–based secondary school music education has been adopted nationally by Kazakhstan's Ministry of Education; master-apprentice training programs in Kabul and Herat, Afghanistan, which are revitalizing musical repertoires suppressed during the years of Taliban rule; and Centre Ustatshakirt, based in Bishkek, Kyrgyzstan, with satellite centers in other cities throughout the country. The activities of Centre Ustatshakirt show

Below: Bardic Divas, a group created by the Aga Khan Music Initiative, poses for a photo following a concert at Théâtre de la Ville, Paris, 2009.

Below right: Poster for a concert at Théâtre de la Ville, Paris, in collaboration with the Aga Khan Music Initiative.

particularly clearly how traditional models of musical practice and pedagogy can inspire contemporary musicians to develop tradition-based music in innovative directions.

"Ustatshakirt" is a Kyrgyz rendering of the Persian expression *ustod-shogird* (master-apprentice), which, throughout the broad geographic sphere of Persian cultural influence, is used to describe the method by which music has traditionally been orally transmitted from one generation to the next. Under the energetic direction of Raziya Syrdybaeva, a Kyrgyz musicologist and cultural entrepreneur, and a contributor to this book (see chapter 32), Centre Ustatshakirt developed a modified form of "master-apprentice" music education in which students met with master teachers in small groups. As an alternative to vestigial Soviet-style music schools, which teach indigenous music through the medium of European music theory and notation, often using Europeanized forms of local instruments, Centre Ustatshakirt's "master-apprentice" methodology won a strong following among music educators and students. The evidence of its effectiveness is in the strong musical skills displayed by its graduates, the most accomplished of whom have become highly visible in Kyrgyzstan's bustling music scene.

For Centre Ustatshakirt, revitalizing and transmitting onward traditional Kyrgyz musical repertoires has been closely integrated with the cultivation of new approaches to music performance and the expansion of traditional artistic languages. This work has been carried out within the framework of an experimental music "laboratory" in which young musicians explore a variety of collaborative forms of music-making that involve both Kyrgyz and European instruments. What distinguishes Centre Ustatshakirt's laboratory from Soviet-era fusions of European and indigenous musical styles and instruments—for example, the much-touted "folk orchestras"—is that, in the Ustatshakirt version, "East" meets "West" on a level playing field. Kyrgyz musicians are left free to apprehend and appropriate European music, or other forms of world music, through the prism of their own aesthetic sensibility. Decisions about style, content, and form are theirs, and the aesthetic parameters of appropriation are under their control.

Like musicians everywhere, musicians in Kyrgyzstan want to be globally connected and networked. Though connectivity in and of itself is no guarantee of artistic quality, musical globalization, on balance, has had a salutary effect on traditional arts by stimulating creativity and innovation. For cultural advocates, activists, and impresarios, the challenge of cultural globalization is to develop organizational mechanisms that

Children in a public school in Bishkek, Kyrgyzstan, learn to play the *komuz* in an innovative program created by Centre Ustatshakirt.
Photo by Adilet Moldobekov.

The New York-based Ari Roland Jazz Quartet performs with students from Centre Ustatshakirt's experimental music laboratory at the Jazz Bishkek Autumn Festival, 2012. Logos of the festival's sponsors, which include the United States Embassy, appear on the right side of the banner.

bring together musicians from East and West, North and South, or, for that matter, East and East, as equal partners in a creative endeavor where music rooted in tradition can meet contemporary musical idioms on equal terms. This was the challenge accepted by the Aga Khan Music Initiative in launching an artistic collaboration with the San Francisco–based Kronos Quartet, whose longstanding commitment to expanding the range and context of the string quartet through cross-cultural musical collaborations and new works commissioning from composers around the world is without peer.

The Kronos Quartet is prominently featured on the Music Initiative's CD-DVD anthology, *Music of Central Asia*. For volume 8 of the anthology, the Music Initiative invited the Kronos Quartet to perform newly commissioned works with performers in the Music Initiative's artist roster. This release became *Rainbow: Kronos Quartet with Alim & Fargana Qasimov and Homayun Sakhi*. The CD features a twenty-nine-minute work, "Rangin Kaman" (Persian for "Rainbow"), composed by Sakhi for string quartet, Afghan *rubab*, and percussion. Sakhi, the leading Afghan *rubab* player of his generation, left Afghanistan in the 1990s, and presently lives in the large Afghan émigré community centered in Fremont, California. Also featured on *Rainbow* is a set of Azerbaijani *ashiq* (troubadour) songs performed by Kronos Quartet and Azerbaijani vocalists Alim and Fargana Qasimov, together with their four-man ensemble playing traditional Azerbaijani instruments (see chapter 20).

Explorations of artistic hybridity like the performances on *Rainbow* represent one good way to create contemporary work rooted in, but not constrained by, traditional models—that is, work that one might call tradition-based, rather than traditional. Hybrid work that mixes up cultural categories and artistic genres challenges the linearity and canonicity often promulgated by constructions of national cultural heritage.

Like Centre Ustatshakirt's experimental music laboratory, the East-West collaboration represented by *Rainbow* may appear on the surface like a re-take of the Soviet-era Europeanization of indigenous music from vast swaths of Eurasia. But, like the music laboratory, *Rainbow* is a collaboration conceived and conducted on a level playing field, where the players meet one another halfway. For producers and presenters of such collaborations, the question is whether traditions such as Azerbaijani *ashiq* songs and Afghan *rubab* music can play a role in facilitating international cross-cultural connectivity—that is, whether they can become cosmopolitan without losing the essential quality of connection to a local spiritual source that makes them powerful.

In his book, *Cosmopolitanism: Ethics in a World of Strangers,* published in 2006, the philosopher Kwame Anthony Appiah underscores the seemingly paradoxical effect of artistic cosmopolitanism in strengthening the appreciation of cultural heritage. Appiah writes: "The connection people feel to cultural objects that are symbolically theirs, because they were produced from within a world of meaning created by their ancestors—the connection to art through identity—is powerful. It should be acknowledged. The cosmopolitan, though, wants to remind us of other connections. One connection—the one neglected in talk of cultural patrimony—is the connection not *through* identity but *despite* difference. We can respond to art that is not ours; indeed, we can fully respond to 'our' art only if we move beyond thinking of it as ours and start to respond to it as art."[3]

The Aga Khan Music Initiative continues to work actively with musicians in Central Asia, as well as in the Middle East and North Africa, West Africa, and South Asia to expand the role of cosmopolitanism and cultural pluralism in the region's musical life. Its work supports the premise that culture evolves through a combination of continuity and innovation, and that traditional arts can not only thrive in pluralist, post-traditional societies but make important contributions to their development. The defining feature of tradition in the context of pluralist modernity is that an individual's embrace of transmitted practices or beliefs ought to represent a choice, not a necessity beholden to lineage, caste, religion, ethnicity, or other inherited social markers. More specifically, in the domain of art, tradition as a system of transmitted formal and stylistic constraints ought to become simply one among many possible sources for creativity and imagination in today's globalized world.

Students in Centre Ustatshakirt's secondary school music education project perform at an education fair that showcases innovative programs and curricula, Bishkek, Kyrgyzstan, 2013.

Nurturing Local Talent, Creating Global Connections
Fairouz Nishanova

Just like pluralism, our work is a process and not a product. It is a mentality, a way of looking at a diverse and changing world. A pluralistic environment is a kaleidoscope that history shakes every day. Responding to pluralism is an exercise in constant re-adaptation. Identities are not fixed in stone. What we imagine our communities to be must also evolve with the tides of history. —His Highness the Aga Khan

Our musical memory is the ultimate iPod—an instantaneously accessible compendium of all the musical sounds we have ever heard, whether in reality or in our imagination. Wherever we are, we go about our daily business carrying a collection of rhythms, melodies, song lyrics, and sonic colors that are available to us at any moment, forming a pool of memory that we can dip into for inspiration, encouragement, or solace. Musical memory is essential to our stability, and often to our sense of heritage and belonging, yet few will ever stop to think about the bricks that form the foundation of this memory pool, laid together in careful mosaics during our childhood and solidified by the musical practices of generations past—practices carried out by our ancestors in their homes and places of worship, during festivals and celebrations, and in rituals of mourning and commemoration.

Preserving and nourishing musical memory is particularly important in societies where the role of music was historically more than that of mere entertainment or a vehicle for self-expression. In such societies, the practice of music and the training of young musicians were trusted means of attaining spiritual union, preserving and transmitting beliefs, customs, and moral values that contributed to

Participants in the Music Initiative's interregional Remix program acknowledge applause following a concert in Cairo, 2009.

the construction of social identities, and, in so doing, reaffirming links between past and present.

But what happens if the musical memory of an entire generation in a vast and culturally diverse region becomes the subject of an experiment with an ulterior political motive? What happens when an experiment that includes suppression, modification, or outright rupture of traditional musical culture imposes foreign musical models that, while promoted as "progressive," often result in soulless cultural uniformity? What if the pool of musical memory is progressively drained of traditional tunes and rhythms, rendering them obsolete and relegating them to dark corners of the past? What if generations are brought up without much exposure to the music and instruments that formed an integral part of their ancestral landscape?

These thoughts flitted through my mind one Sunday afternoon in late November 2011 while observing a lively scene unfolding around me in a coffeehouse in central Beirut, Lebanon. Surveying my unsuspecting fellow caffeine-worshippers, I realized they constituted living proof of how a preserved and cultivated sense of cultural belonging cohabitates comfortably with modernity in today's pluralistic world. The people around me were in their thirties, forties, and even sixties; some were dressed in jeans, others in traditional attire, and still others in the best of Sunday casual. Men and women (in and out of veils) chatted, read, and laughed through cigarette smoke while tapping away on their laptops or smartphones. One thing united them: everyone in the café, whether deep in thought or in the middle of a conversation, unconsciously mimed the words or drummed out the rhythms of a succession of old songs playing through speakers mounted on the walls. The singer was Fairouz, the pan-Arab icon whose unmistakable and powerful voice told the story of her Lebanese homeland. The song's rhythms were traditional yet instantly recognizable as integral to national identity and pride.

This scene, so typical in Beirut and so similar to many of my childhood afternoons in Amman, Jordan, is all but unthinkable in my ethnic homeland

Nurturing Local Talent, Creating Global Connections *(CONTINUED)*

of Central Asia. There, loudspeakers in cafes and restaurants all over the region blare out second-rate pop imports from the West, or Central Asia's own locally produced imitations. The rare young person who sought a way to study traditional music outside of a state-run conservatory would have difficulty finding an alternative training, since the time-honored system of master-apprentice training and oral transmission, known in Central Asia as *ustod-shogird,* had been superseded during the Soviet era by Western-style conservatories and music schools. As the result of a large-scale movement to modernize indigenous musical traditions in Central Asia according to the conventions of European classical music, traditional musical art at the very center of the ancient Silk Route became subject to strict state control. Its historical, religious, and spiritual roots were modified to suit the new ideology, and its transmission and performance tightly regulated by the authorities. Orally transmitted classic repertories that had flourished for centuries under the patronage of the Central Asian nobility suffered particularly strong condemnation due to their association with the cultural elite and with Islamic spirituality. Large folk orchestras replaced small ensembles, and, as traditional instrument- and music-making techniques began to disappear, they carried away with them the foundation stones of a vast and deep pool of musical memory.

The result of these policies—a depleted pool of musical memory

and consequent loss of cultural identity—became apparent after the breakup of the Soviet Union and the end of the state-controlled monopoly on "patronage" of the arts. Music enthusiasts and revitalizers who set out to restore and reimagine their own cultural heritage found themselves having to do so without any means of structural or financial support. Many in the world of music, demoralized by economic hardship, governmental neglect, and lack of interest and respect from the public, abandoned music-related professions. An aphorism from Mali aptly summarized the situation in Central Asia: "When an old master dies, it is as if a library has burned down."

It was at this critical moment for Central Asian music that the Aga Khan Music Initiative (AKMI) was launched. The Music Initiative is one of the youngest programs of the Aga Khan Trust for Culture, a cultural agency of the Aga Khan Development Network (AKDN). The AKDN is well known and respected for its work in the physical, social, cultural, and economic revitalization of communities in the Muslim world (see: http://www.akdn.org). As a new stakeholder in a multi-domain action implemented by the AKDN in Central Asia, the Music Initiative responded to calls for support from artists, music educators, and music enthusiasts. Its initial mission was to assure the transmission of musical traditions that link people in Afghanistan, Kazakhstan, Kyrgyzstan, Tajikistan, and Uzbekistan to their history and cultural

heritage. This mission was later expanded to include the development of indigenous music traditions in contemporary forms that validate local identities and cultural heritage while building cultural pluralism.

We quickly discovered that no single development strategy suited all the countries in which AKMI was invited to work. Each country called for a specially tailored approach that blended the core activities of music education, music presentation, and music production. The Music Initiative devised a set of distinct but complementary strategies designed to revitalize indigenous musical traditions and simultaneously reaffirm its own long-term objectives:

• Preserve key repertories and assure their transmission to the next generation of artists and audiences

• Help create a mechanism to provide training for a new generation of young artists

• Contribute to the revival of regional festivals, performances, and outreach activities

• Professionalize the presentation of Central Asian music and bring this music to audiences worldwide

• Connect musicians and arts educators in Central Asia with a global network of artists, arts presenters, producers, and media

In practice, carrying out these strategies resulted in the development of new curricula, teaching methodologies, and models for music education,

Nurturing Local Talent, Creating Global Connections *(CONTINUED)*

Poster for the Music Initiative's Spiritual Sounds of Central Asia concert tour, 2007.
Photo by Theodore Levin.

as well as CD-DVD recording projects and the creation of innovative performance programs at regional and international levels.

A decade later, the Music Initiative has been instrumental in creating a comprehensive alternative method for traditional music education,

analogous to those in South Asia and the Middle East, which is available through AKMI schools and partner institutions to students who want to study traditional music in Kazakhstan, Kyrgyzstan, Afghanistan, and Tajikistan. To date, more than ten thousand students and master musicians have directly benefited from AKMI schools, centers, and teacher-training seminars. Numerous musicians and arts educators in Central Asia are connected with global networks of artists, arts presenters, producers, and media. Contemporary, tradition-inspired music has been presented in numerous AKMI concert productions and artistic residencies in Europe, North America, Asia, and Africa. More than two million audience members have benefited from concert

and festival presentations and artist-in-residence programs previously unavailable to those outside the realm of "world music," thus combating international ignorance about music from Central Asia—ignorance that often translated into indifference.

Measuring the results of this work presents a challenge, since such results cannot be measured with the tools of an economist. However, the growth of awareness and appreciation of Central Asian culture—previously all but unknown to international audiences—and the sheer freedom with which a young person who benefited from a comprehensive arts education communicates with the outside world, speak for themselves.

Among our biggest achievements to date is the fact that in many corners of Central Asia, the unthinkable is happening: carrying a *dombyra*—or a *dutar, tanbur, komuz, rubab*—has become cool. Perhaps, very soon, so

Musical performance organized by the Music Initiative for the Aga Khan Award for Architecture prize ceremony at the Red Fort, Agra, India, 2004.
Photo by Kamran Adle.

Young Tajik musicians at an interregional summer camp organized by the Music Initiative at Lake Issyk-Kul, Kyrgyzstan, 2008.
Photo by Sabine Chatel.

Sanubar Tursun (*left*) and Wu Man rehearse in Beijing before recording *Borderlands: Wu Man and Master Musicians from the Silk Road.*
Photo by Feng Li.

shall the drumming of old rhythms in a swanky coffeehouse, along with the use of those very rhythms as an inspiration for, not an impediment to, the creation of new music.

AKMI's investment in educating cosmopolitan individuals, who are knowledgeable about their own traditional art and culture, respectful and appreciative of art from other parts of the world, and curious about what dialogue between the two might yield, has already begun to produce encouraging returns. From its modest beginnings in Central Asia, the Music Initiative has grown into an interregional music and arts education program with worldwide performance, outreach, mentoring, and artistic production activities and direct links with musicians, music educators, and artistic communities in the Middle East, North Africa, South Asia, and West Africa. The Initiative's new activities include the creation of a mechanism for education in grants management and operational support in the countries it invests in, as well as the creation of an integrated model

for tangible and intangible cultural heritage revitalization—the latter in close collaboration with the Aga Khan Historic Cities program. Now that preservation efforts it helped support have firmly taken root, AKMI recognizes that preservation only carries musical creativity so far; to remain fresh, it needs contact with other traditions, other ways of hearing and experiencing the world. Through its collaboration with the Aga Khan Trust for Culture's Historic Cities Program and other international partners, AKMI is working on developing a new set of tools and activities to reignite interregional creative collaboration and lively artistic exchanges along the legendary silk and spice routes by facilitating the creation, performance, and dissemination of new musical works inspired, but not constrained by, traditional musical practices. Regional and international composition and commissioning programs that are currently being designed in Egypt, Syria, Pakistan, India, and Mali construe music, arts education, and performance activities as an integral part of cultural development strategies. Three key principles for the future development of the program are:

•Increasing the independence of beneficiaries

•Involving local communities

• Securing the support of public and private partners

Master and disciple tabla players in a class at the Music Initiative–sponsored Ustod-Shogird Centre in Kabul, Afghanistan, 2005.
Photo by Gary Otte.

As it makes its presence known in the countries where it is beginning new programs, AKMI will continue to underscore its most important goal: to cultivate promising new voices that contribute to the rediscovery and worldwide circulation of tradition-based contemporary music and art, thus reaffirming that in the hands of exceptional talent, the resources of tradition are inexhaustible.

Uzbek *karnai* players in a performance sponsored by the Music Initiative at the Festival d'Île de France, 2006.
Photo by Sabine Chatel.

WATCH

Example 31.1. One example of an activity designed to reignite interregional creative collaboration is Remix, a workshop that brings together young musicians from historically related artistic communities in the Middle East and North Africa, West Asia, Central Asia, and South Asia. In this excerpt from a concert performance that took place at the conclusion of an intensive 10-day-long Remix workshop in Aswan and Cairo, Egypt, Tajik *dutar* player Sirojddin Juraev improvises an arrangement of "Qushtar," a virtuoso piece for *dutar* solo, with vocalists Rebal Alkhodri (Syria) and Badiaa Bou Hreizi (Tunisia). The performance took place in 2011 at Al Genaina Theater, Al Azhar Park, Cairo, and was a co-production of the non-governmental organization Al Mawred Al Thaqafy (Cultural Resource) and the Aga Khan Music Initiative. Filmed by Ahmed Zeidan.

WATCH

Example 31.2. Like the previous example, this excerpt, which features Afghan *rubab* player Homayun Sakhi leading a multi-instrumental and vocal arrangement of the Indian raga *madhuvanti,* is from a concert that took place at the conclusion of the 2011 Remix workshop at Al Genaina Theater, Al Azhar Park, Cairo, co-produced by Al Mawred al Thaqafy and the Aga Khan Music Initiative. Filmed by Ahmed Zeidan.

The Genesis of *Rainbow*
THEODORE LEVIN

Rainbow emerged from an ambitious process of collaborative creativity that reached across continents and cultures, and across musical categories and conventions.[4] Cross-cultural artistic collaboration has arguably never been easier than in our era of social networking, jet travel, and instant access to a seemingly infinite digital storehouse of music from around the world. Yet the ready availability of so many musical "elsewheres" makes the prospect of artistic collaboration at once alluring and daunting, full of promise as well as potential pitfalls: where in the world to begin? How to move beyond superficial grooves toward deeper levels of music connection? What standard to use as a measure of artistic success?

To the first of these questions, David Harrington, first violinist

Alim Qasimov and David Harrington in a recording studio in London.

The Genesis of *Rainbow* (CONTINUED)

and founder of the Kronos Quartet, offered a straightforward answer: "I follow my ears," he said. Harrington's relentless musical curiosity has been the engine behind Kronos's adventurous musical travels. "I started playing string quartet music when I was twelve," Harrington related, "and I remember one day, as a young teenager, looking at a map of the world and realizing that the only string quartet music I'd ever played was written by men who lived in the same city: Vienna, Austria. That just struck me. And so at that age, it became a part of my thinking to try to learn more about other parts of the world through music." Harrington has devoted his career to doing just that—in the process, forging, under the aegis of Kronos, a living legacy of pioneering and wide-ranging collaborations with musical creators from many cultures.

David Harrington's global musical explorations led him to recordings of Alim Qasimov and, later, Homayun Sakhi. Harrington recounted his first impressions of listening to Qasimov: "I realized immediately that there was a quality I had never heard before from a singer. The way he inhabits the notes he makes is profoundly beautiful. It's like he's molding and shaping these notes in a way that we can only try to do with our bows. I hoped that one day we might be able to meet and find a way of making music together."

That musical meeting happened in 2008, as the first project in an ongoing collaboration between Kronos Quartet and the Aga Khan Music Initiative. In

its mission to revitalize and assure the onward transmission of musical traditions in regions where they are endangered, the Music Initiative came to understand that cultivating creative processes which lead to artistic innovation and evolution is as important as conserving links to the past. Kronos's long experience in creating new music—oftentimes with artists from other cultures who didn't share a common musical lexicon of terms and concepts—offered a successful model of how to do such work.

To launch the Kronos-Qasimov collaboration, Alim Qasimov and two members of his ensemble, *kamancha* player Rauf Islamov and *tar* player Ali Asgar Mammadov, traveled to San Francisco to rehearse with Kronos a set of Azerbaijani songs drawn from Qasimov's repertory. The challenge of the weeklong rehearsal period was to create a seamless interface between the note-reading Kronos players and the Qasimov Ensemble, whose performances typically feature an ever-shifting blend of memorized and extemporized musical gestures.

The details of working out the Kronos-Qasimov interface fell to Jacob Garchik, a multi-talented performer-composer-arranger

from New York who had collaborated with Kronos on previous projects. "It was difficult," said Garchik of the arranging work. "You have highly skilled, virtuosic musicians, but they have very different ways of learning and teaching music. Alim Qasimov's music is more improvised and unpredictable, but at the same time, it's based on arrangements. Someone in Azerbaijan had already composed and arranged these songs, and then, in the process of recollecting them, Alim turned them into quasi-improvisations. Now his improvisations are being turned back into arrangements again."

Just as Kronos and Jacob Garchik were challenged by the Azerbaijani musicians' "unpredictable" improvisations, Alim Qasimov found it challenging to work with note-reading musicians. "Our traditional

The Kronos Quartet performing with Alim and Fargana Qasimov and their ensemble.

Photo by Sebastian Schutyser. Courtesy of Aga Khan Music Initiative.

The Genesis of *Rainbow* (CONTINUED)

musicians don't learn folk songs or classical *mugham* from notes," said Qasimov. "When I perform with my ensemble, I'm usually free, but here, everything depends on notation. If something is written two times, I have to sing it two times. To absorb this music deeply and get close to its inner sentiment, you have to put the notes aside and learn how to improvise."

"I remember the first time we tried to do that," said David Harrington of Kronos's efforts to "move away from the page," as he characterized the process of improvisation. "It's something that we've become more and more comfortable with as time has gone on. From Kronos's perspective, there's a lot of improvisation going on in the Azerbaijani songs, but hopefully, the listener won't even know when those moments are."

Example 31.3 offers a glimpse of the five-day rehearsal period during

which the members of Kronos worked with Alim Qasimov and two members of his ensemble to put together the six Azerbaijani songs.

The enthusiastically received world premiere performance of the Azerbaijani songs took place at London's Barbican Centre during "Ramadan Nights," the Barbican's eclectic survey of music from the world of Islam. For the concert, Kronos and Alim Qasimov were joined by Alim's daughter and musical protégée, Fargana, and his full ensemble of four instrumentalists. The songs were recorded for the *Rainbow* CD the day after the concert. Alim Qasimov succinctly summed up the artistic results: "I think we have planted a tree, and now we have to work to make it grow and bear fruit. God willing, it will happen."

Example 31.4 reproduces one of the collaborative songs from *Rainbow*, "Mehriban Olaq" (Let's be kind).

This vibrant performance of "Mehriban Olaq" fuses multiple layers—both old and new—of composition, arrangement, and improvisation. The oldest layer is the strophic song composed by Shafiqa Akhundova in the mid-twentieth century, when Azerbaijan, like other Soviet republics, cultivated an active tradition of popular songwriting that blended local and European musical instruments and styles. As was the case with other Azerbaijani popular songs, "Mehriban Olaq" became a part of oral musical tradition, with the result that performers came up with their own arrangements. Alim and Fargana Qasimov are among the performers who have arranged "Mehriban Olaq," and it was their arrangement that was given to the Kronos Quartet's arranger, Jacob Garchik, to re-arrange for the Alim Qasimov Ensemble and Kronos

WATCH

Example 31.3. Kronos Quartet and Alim Qasimov. Excerpt from documentary film by Saodat Ismailova and Carlos Casas in *Rainbow: Kronos Quartet with Alim & Fargana Qasimov and Homayun Sakhi* (DVD), vol. 8 of *Music of Central Asia* (SFR, 2010).

LISTEN

Example 31.4. "Mehriban Olaq" (Let's be kind). Music and lyrics by Shafiqa Akhundova. String quartet parts arranged for Kronos by Jacob Garchik. Performed by the Kronos Quartet (David Harrington, violin; John Sherba, violin; Hank Dutt, viola; and Jeffrey Zeigler, cello) and the Alim Qasimov Ensemble (Alim Qasimov, vocal; Fargana Qasimova, vocal and *daf*; Rafael Asgarov, *balaban*; Rauf Islamov, *kamancha*; Ali Asgar Mammadov, *tar*; and Vugar Sharifzadeh, *naghara*). From *Rainbow: Kronos Quartet with Alim & Fargana Qasimov and Homayun Sakhi*, vol. 8 of *Music of Central Asia* (SFR, 2010), track 3.

The Genesis of *Rainbow* (CONTINUED)

Quartet. Garchik's score not only skillfully melds the four Western and four Azerbaijani instruments into an integral octet that accompanies the singers, but it departs from the core song melody to create original quartet music for Kronos.

Translation of "Mehriban Olaq"

I am going to voice my feelings again.
Hey people, please, listen to me!
Let thousands of hearts beat together,
Let's be more friendly to each other,

Let's be kind and caring,
Let's be kind.
Let's treasure a pure and sincere love.
Let's talk and laugh, and get far from sorrow.

STUDY QUESTIONS

1. How successful was arranger Jacob Garchik in integrating the Western strings of the Kronos Quartet with the Azerbaijani instruments and vocal style of the Alim Qasimov Ensemble?

2. From a musical perspective, does the cross-cultural fusion "work"?

3. Are the two groups evenly matched in their musical contribution to the collaborative piece, and does the overall scheme of the collaboration bring them together as equals?

Rainbow, Part II: Kronos Quartet and Homayun Sakhi

For Homayun Sakhi, the process of creative collaboration with Kronos unfolded differently. Whereas the starting point for Alim Qasimov's work with Kronos was a set of popular songs performed by Qasimov but composed by an older generation of Azerbaijani songwriters, Homayun Sakhi delivered to Kronos a musical work that he composed himself. The work was "Rangin Kaman"— "rainbow" in Persian—for Afghan *rubab*, string quartet, and percussion. The percussion instruments include Indian tabla and Central Asian frame drum (*doira*) and clappers (*qairaq*). Like many contemporary composers who do not notate their compositions

Kronos Quartet with Homayun Sakhi, Salar Nader, and Abbos Kosimov.

but simply record them directly from instruments or computers to hard drives or digital recording devices, Homayun Sakhi composed and recorded the Afghan *rubab* part on

The Genesis of *Rainbow* (CONTINUED)

his own instrument and realized the string quartet sounds on a Casio synthesizer. The percussion was added during rehearsals, with the musicians improvising in traditional rhythmic cycles and patterns.

Sakhi's Casio and Afghan *rubab* recordings were given to Stephen Prutsman, an award-winning concert pianist, composer, arranger, and music festival founder whose long collaboration with Kronos has resulted in over forty arrangements for the quartet. Prutsman transcribed the entire piece and wrote it out in Western musical notation. In the sections of the piece where *rubab* and quartet play together, Prutsman created the quartet parts from the implied harmony suggested by the modal melodic lines of the *rubab*.

In sections where the quartet plays alone, Prutsman assigned each of the pitches he heard on the Casio to a particular instrument—what composers and arrangers call "voicing." "I voiced it according to what I thought would be most natural for the quartet," said Prutsman. "I also marked articulation, dynamics, slurs, and phrases. Most of the time, people don't do that, but I've found that it's always helpful as a guidepost to Kronos." During rehearsals, Kronos rearranged of some of Prutsman's markings based on their experience of working with the *rubab* and percussion. Traditional Afghan meters and rhythms in the piece presented another challenge for Prutsman and Kronos. Prutsman explained, "There are lots of groupings of seven, but where are the strong beats in those

groupings? Oftentimes, strong accents don't correspond with downbeats. We spent a lot of time getting comfortable with the rhythmic units."

Homayun Sakhi composed "Rangin Kaman" as a way to represent "all the peoples and regions of Afghanistan and connect them to other parts of the world." Sakhi elaborated, "There are influences from both classical and folk music. The folk music comes from Herat, Mazar-i Sharif, Kandahar, and other places; it's music that's performed by Hazaras, Pashtuns, Uzbeks—I tried to bring together a little bit from each region and people of Afghanistan."

"Homayun is a great bandleader," said David Harrington. "He knew exactly what he wanted from us; he knew every rhythm that he wanted the tabla to play, and basically he taught everybody. He has the whole score completely imprinted in his mind, so in one sense, there's nothing left to chance. But Homayun is very open to changes that arise from the experience of working together. For example, in one place I suggested using a practice mute to achieve a different timbre on the violin. He loved the sound when he heard it, and it got worked into the piece. As Homayun got to know us better, he refined the writing through a lot of little changes like that. In the end, 'Rangin Kaman' was literally tailor-made for Kronos."

Homayun Sakhi added his own assessment of the artistic collaboration. "Working with Kronos, I realized that through

Violin part and Afghan *rubab* notation for "Rangin Kaman."

music you can cross not only boundaries between different regions of Afghanistan but even bigger boundaries, such as between East and West. When we play together, the music really connects well, and we all get a lot of pleasure from it." In this impromptu critique, Homayun Sakhi may have inadvertently provided as good an answer as any to the question of how to measure the artistic success of collaborative music-making. If a piece "connects well," as Sakhi put it, and if performers with the keen musical sensitivity of Kronos Quartet and Homayun Sakhi enjoy performing it, there's a good chance that it has something to say.

David Harrington echoed Sakhi's critique. "If we're involved in a piece of music and I get a recording of a performance and can't stop listening to it and, when I wake up in the morning, the music is part of my consciousness, then I know it's something I'm really happy with." The riveting performance of "Rangin Kaman" on *Rainbow* makes a strong case for this piece, and for the prodigious talent of its young Afghan-American composer, Homayun Sakhi.

The Genesis of *Rainbow* (CONTINUED)

Homayun Sakhi (*center*), tabla player Salar Nader (*left*), and frame drummer Abbos Kosimov (*right*) perform "Rangin Kaman" with the Kronos Quartet.

Photo by Rachel Bleckman.

"I love color," said Homayun Sakhi, "and in 'Rangin Kaman,' I piece together different colors as a way of expressing hope for peace and harmony among different peoples and nations." In Sakhi's composition, these colors are represented both by the different styles of Afghan music played on *rubab,* tabla, and *doira,* and by broader contrasts between Eastern and Western instruments. The piece begins with an elegiac prelude for solo string quartet. The dramatic entrance of the *rubab,* with a gliding sweep of the instrument's sympathetic strings, introduces a contrasting musical style and establishes an antiphonal relationship between *rubab* and quartet: East is East, and West is West. In the meditative section that follows, the plucked *rubab* and bowed stringed instruments of the quartet coalesce in a tonal and textural equipoise as they take turns improvising solos above a steady drone pitch. In the jaunty second half of the piece, *rubab* and quartet become increasingly entwined, framed by subtle rhythmic patterns marked out on the tabla and *doira.* Gathering momentum, the drums emerge from their accompanying role in a brief but brilliant percussion break. A cadenza-like section for string quartet leads to a reprise of the austere solo entrance of the *rubab.* In the fiery finale, *rubab* and quartet converge into a sinuous composite voice—a sonic rapprochement of East and West that resolves the structural tension of the opening, and, in so doing, perhaps serves as a musical metaphor of hope.

LISTEN

Example 31.5. Excerpt from "Rangin Kaman" (Rainbow). Composed by Homayun Sakhi (2008). Arranged by Stephen Prutsman. Performed by Kronos Quartet (David Harrington, violin; John Sherba, violin; Hank Dutt, viola; and Jeffrey Zeigler, cello) and Homayun Sakhi, (Afghan *rubab*), Salar Nader (tabla), and Abbos Kosimov (*doira* and *qairaq*). From *Rainbow: Kronos Quartet with Alim & Fargana Qasimov and Homayun Sakhi,* vol. 8 of *Music of Central Asia* (SFR, 2010), track 1.

1. How successful was arranger Stephen Prutsman in integrating the Western strings of the Kronos Quartet with the sounds of the Afghan *rubab,* tabla, frame drum (*doira*) and clackers (*qairaq*)?

2. From a musical perspective, does the cross-cultural fusion "work"?

3. Are the musicians evenly matched in their musical contribution to the collaborative piece, and does the overall scheme of the collaboration bring them together as equals?

NOTES

Epigraph source: Homi Bhabha, "Another Country," in *Without Boundary: Seventeen Ways of Looking,* ed. Fereshteh Daftari (New York: Museum of Modern Art, 2006).

1. http://www.unesco.org/culture/ich/index.php?lg=en&pg=00002, accessed December 20, 2015.

2. Analogous strategies in the domain of architecture and the built environment have played a prominent role in the work of other programs of the Aga Khan Trust for Culture, principally its Historic Cities Preservation program. See: http://www.akdn.org/aktc.asp.

3. Kwame Anthony Appiah, *Cosmopolitanism: Ethics in a World of Strangers* (New York: W. W. Norton, 2006), 134–135.

4. This text was previously published in the booklet notes of the CD-DVD *Rainbow,* vol. 8 of *Music of Central Asia* (Smithsonian Folkways Recordings, 2010).

CHAPTER 32 Cultural Renewal in Kyrgyzstan

NEO-TRADITIONALISM AND THE NEW ERA IN KYRGYZ MUSIC

RAZIYA SYRDYBAEVA

Since the breakup of the Soviet Union, in 1991, all the newly independent states of Central Asia have experienced a dynamic process of cultural revival and national awakening. In this process, each nation pursued its own path, yet all of the Central Asian nations have shared a strong focus on the role of arts and culture in constructing and exemplifying their national identity. This chapter addresses the case of Kyrgyzstan, and traces the development of Kyrgyz national culture in the first three decades following the establishment of the independent Kyrgyz Republic.

In Kyrgyzstan, the national awakening began in the twilight years of the Soviet Union, during the Perestroika period of the mid-to-late 1980s, when Kyrgyzstan was still the Soviet republic of Kirghizia. During this period of nascent identity formation, the rigid ideology-driven politics of the Soviet era were in retreat, and new social priorities began to emerge in the resulting political vacuum. Foremost among these was the search for a new form of national consciousness and self-identity—both among individuals and at the level of the entire nation. Professional arts unions as well as individual artists redirected their work towards these new priorities, which represented an abrupt shift toward the embrace of indigenous culture and almost forgotten traditions. This process was rapid and intense, and involved all the eighty-odd ethnic groups represented in present-day Kyrgyzstan.

The first period of cultural change occurred in the decade immediately following the breakup of the Soviet Union, from 1991 to 2001, and could be characterized as a time of "foreseeing freedom." Many citizens

of Kyrgyzstan reconnected with older cultural traditions and values, and gained a deeper understanding of the challenge of cultural renewal that Kyrgyz society faced as an independent nation. Initial feelings of euphoria were followed by a logical search for new strategies of cultural development. Kyrgyz literature, cinema, visual arts, and theater reflected this process in the most obvious way. Several remarkable figures whose work became visible during this period are regarded as leading luminaries in the cultural history not only of Kyrgyzstan but of Central Asia as a whole. They were all bold innovators, and their works depicted Kyrgyzstan both to its own citizens and outside the country from a completely new perspective. Among the works and performances that signified important breakthroughs are the following:

- The film trilogy *Selkinchek* (1993), *Beshkempir* (1998), and *Maymyl* (2001), by director Aktan Abdykalykov (AKA Aktan Arym Kubat)
- Paintings by Yuristanbek Shygaev that use a minimalist technique and present symbolic images
- Performances by the folk ensemble Kambarkan under the artistic direction of Chalagyz Isabaev
- Theatrical productions by Vladimir Pazi at the Russian Drama Theater
- Performances and concerts at the Bishkek City Drama Theater founded and directed by Arsen Umuraliev; these also included groups operating under the aegis of the theater, such as the folk ensemble Saamal (artistic director Nurlanbek Nyshanov) and the folk jazz group Aura (artistic director Taalay Beysheev)

A second period of cultural change, which began in 2001 and continued through 2010, was characterized by an embrace of stylistic pluralism. In fact, openness to stylistic diversity was typical of the previous decade as well. The more recent period, however, turned out to be much less productive than the previous one, and for this reason should be considered as the end point of a twenty-five-year era of postcolonial cultural development that began with the advent of glasnost in the Soviet Union (1985–2010). It is difficult to judge whether any new historical period is on its way. More time is needed to clarify whether the political and social turmoil that shook Kyrgyzstan in 2010 has opened a new era in the nation's history and culture, and, if so, whether it is going to be a new dawn or a period of decline.

During the first decade of post-Soviet Kyrgyzstan, the absence of censorship and of numerous restrictions and prohibitions posed by the Soviet government and the Communist Party created favorable conditions for processes of liberalization in the domain of arts and culture. Numerous non-governmental cultural, educational, and artistic organizations (NGOs) were founded that put forward innovative and challenging projects. As its geographic, political, and ideological boundaries became increasingly porous, Kyrgyzstan discovered new creative opportunities to represent its indigenous culture both to its own citizens and to the rest of the world. International institutions, donor organizations, and local companies that were operating in the country funded and implemented many cultural initiatives. With the government unable to manage cultural activities effectively, NGOs assumed many of the erstwhile responsibilities of state ministries and other governmental units, as well as of the state-sponsored artistic unions. For artists, keeping a distance from governmental institutions and the ideological clichés associated with them was considered desirable, if not obligatory. Theatrical plays by Sultan Raev, jewelry by Victor Syrnev, and films produced by Kyrgyz cinematographers were all significant accomplishments of that period. Artistic production was characterized by stylistic eclecticism, as might have been expected in a multiethnic country and region.

A production photo from the Sakhna Theater, founded by Nurlan Asanbekov.
Courtesy of Sakhna Theater.

The rich historical legacy of Kyrgyz oral tradition—in particular, epic—became a central focus of artistic creativity. Epic was presented both in an authentic form and through reflections in contemporary literature, music, theater, cinema, and visual arts, for example, in the work of theater director Nurlan Asanbekov's nomadic Sakhna Theater.

Masters of Kyrgyz art and culture sought appropriate and effective strategies for preserving cultural and historical heritage, and comprehending its role in the modern era. So-called neo-traditionalism, in which tradition is reproduced in a new format that reflects contemporary realities, is one way in which cultural heritage has been preserved and further developed. In neo-traditionalist music, for example, traditional musical material is conveyed in a contemporary idiom that modifies its original essence and contents to the extent that the music becomes a part of the contemporary cultural landscape—as if an old story is being told in a modern language, and as such becomes clearer, closer, and more attractive to contemporary audiences.

Kyrgyz culture offers many examples of neo-traditionalism in a variety of artistic domains: music, theater, crafts and applied arts, and fashion, among others. In music, the ensemble Kambarkan, founded in 1988 by Chalagyz Isabaev, was the first group to introduce a neo-traditionalist approach to representing Kyrgyz musical heritage. Its members included talented musicians from provincial regions of Kyrgyzstan such as Samarbubu Toktakhunova, Nurak Abdyrakhmanov, Nurlanbek Nyshanov, Bakyt Shatenov, and Salamat Sadykova. Kambarkan became popular not only in Kyrgyzstan but beyond its borders by reintroducing traditional instruments in their authentic, pre-Soviet form. Under Soviet cultural policies, traditional instruments had been reconstructed *en masse* to make their sound compatible with the sound of European instruments (see chapter 1). These reconstructed instruments looked the same as their original counterparts, however, they lost many of their indigenous features—first and foremost, their unique, authentic sound. Instruments that were not selected for reconstruction simply fell into obscurity. For

Kyrgyz neo-traditional
fashion created by designer
Tatyana Vorotnikova.

Courtesy of Tatyana Vorotnikova.

example, the *kyl-kiyak,* which was widely played in the 1920s and 1930s, had disappeared from performance practice by the end of the 1980s. Many woodwind instruments had been forgotten by the mid-twentieth century and were completely lost after the death of their best-known performer and advocate, Asanbay Karimov, in the 1980s.

Beginning in the late 1980s, a group of Kyrgyz instrument makers led by Suragan Aidyraliev began to restore and reconstruct instruments in their older, pre-Soviet forms, and it was these "new" traditional instruments that became popular among Kyrgyz audiences. Not only the instruments, but the performance traditions built on them needed to be reconstructed and revitalized. This process of neo-traditional reconstruction and revitalization was spearheaded by a group of musician-instrument makers that included Nurlanbek Nyshanov, Maratbek Berikbaev, Turatbek Akunov, Shaken Jorobekova, and Bakyt Chytyrbaev. Their efforts focused on the *choor* (reed flute), *chopo choor* (ocarina), *temir ooz komuz* (metal jaw harp), *jygach ooz komuz* (wooden jaw harp), and *kyl-kiyak* (bowl fiddle). One traditional instrument that did not need the attention of these musical restorers and revitalizers was the *komuz*—the three-stringed lute that might be regarded as the emblematic musical instrument of the Kyrgyz. Thanks to its wide popularity and availability, many of its original features as well as its repertory were preserved through the Soviet era.

Kyrgyz instruments newly made by luthiers associated with Centre Ustatshakirt.

Apprentice luthier Ulukbek Berikbaev demonstrates how to build a *komuz* at an education fair in Bishkek, 2013.

Photo courtesy of Adilet Moldobekov.

The New Era in Kyrgyz Music: Neotraditionalists and Post-Neotraditionalists

The reconstruction of traditional instruments and revitalization of their musical repertoires set the stage for a new era of creativity in Kyrgyz music dominated by neotraditionalist approaches to composing and arranging. Among the leading voices of neo-traditionalism were Nurlanbek Nyshanov (b. 1966) and Ruslan Jumabaev (b. 1973). Nyshanov, in addition to his contributions to the revival and reconstruction of musical instruments described earlier, is a performer on multiple instruments, a charismatic teacher, and a composer, arranger, and ensemble leader. He serves as artistic director of the Ordo-Sakhna folk-ethnographic ensemble and was the founder and artistic director of Ensemble Tengir-Too, which existed from 2003 to 2009. Nyshanov is the author of dozens of compositions for instrumental ensembles, theatrical productions, and film soundtracks. Among the latter are soundtracks for the documentary film *Choorchu* (*Choor* Player), directed by Shaiymbek Apylov, as well as for the feature films *Beshkempir* by Aktan Arym Kubat and *Where the Sky Meets the Land* by Frank Muller.[1] The latter won Nyshanov an IDA Documentary Award in 1999 and the Golden Spire Award of the San Francisco Film Society in 2000. Ruslan Jumabaev is a virtuoso *komuz* player who performs widely as a soloist. As a composer and arranger of traditional material, he has created new works for solo *komuz, komuz* duos and trios, and for *komuz* and orchestra. In 2012, he founded the ensemble Khan-Tengiri, named after a peak in the Tian Shan Mountains, to perform his own work, and the work of other neo-traditionalist composers and arrangers.

Given Nyshanov's and Jumabaev's strong commitment to the revitalization of Kyrgyz cultural traditions, their choice to compose music with an obvious ethnic component is natural. Yet their compositions and arrangements invariably present traditional source material in new forms, textures, and instrumentation. Three such neo-traditionalist pieces are presented in the audio examples below: Nyshanov's "Ordo" (Yurt camp) and "Ak Kepter" (White doves), and Jumabaev's "Erke Sary" (Darling redhead younger brother).

Nyshanov composes and arranges for a small instrumental ensemble—a practice that contrasts sharply with the traditional performance style, which is dominated by soloists. Similarly, Jumabaev's "Erke Sary" expands the traditional solo instrumental genre *küü* (see chapter 14) to embrace two or three instruments—in this case, *komuzes*. Both composers cited the demands of their audiences' changing listening habits as a motivation for their neo-traditionalist innovations: a preference for ensembles over soloists, and for multi-part musical textures over linear melodies.

Top: Nurlanbek Nyshanov.
Photo by Katherine Vincent. Courtesy of Aga Khan Music Initiative.

Above: Ruslan Jumabaev.
Photo by Katherine Vincent. Courtesy of Aga Khan Music Initiative.

Below: Ensemble Tengir-Too, 2004.
Photo by Katherine Vincent. Courtesy of Aga Khan Music Initiative.

Example 32.1. "Ak Kepter" (White doves) arranged by Nurlanbek Nyshanov, performed by Ordo-Sakhna Ensemble with Damyra Niyazbekova. Recording courtesy of Orda-Sakhna.

"Ak Kepter" (White doves) is a popular Kyrgyz song traditionally performed by women. Nurlanbek Nyshanov arranged the song for the Bishkek-based ensemble Ordo-Sakhna and female vocalist Damyra Niyazbekova, and in so doing, he added a substantial amount of newly composed material. In Nyshanov's arrangement, the darkly lyrical melody is harmonized in a way that suggests the sound of seventeenth-century European music, with the Kyrgyz *chopo choor,* a clay ocarina (see the musical instrument glossary), simulating the reedy sound of a baroque recorder.

Nyshanov's arrangement of "Ak Kepter" has an a b a form in which the "a" section represents the core melodic theme and the "b" section represents a contrasting area of melodic development. The music in the "b" section, which begins at 2:41, is Nyshanov's original composition. The first minute of this short composition sounds like a variation on the "Ak Kepter" melodic theme, but starting around 3:41, the music transitions to new melodic material unrelated to the song theme. The instrument that sounds like a cello, which briefly solos from 2:41 to 2:49, is actually a bass *kiyak*—a larger version of the traditional *kyl-kiyak* that was developed during the Soviet era as part of the folk orchestra movement. At 5:30, the "a" music returns as an instrumental prelude, and finally, at 5:55, the "Ak Kepter" vocal melody is reprised to end the piece.

In Nyshanov's arrangement-composition, "Ak Kepter" loses its indigenous Kyrgyz identity. Indeed, aside from the language of the song lyrics, Nyshanov's "Ak Kepter" offers few clues to its Kyrgyz folk origins. Like many examples of neo-traditional music, Nyshanov's arrangements and compositions incorporate elements of contemporary musical styles, traditions, and idioms that give his music what might be called a cosmopolitan sound.

STUDY QUESTIONS

1. How would you critique Nurlanbek Nyshanov's neo-traditional arrangement of "Ak Kepter"? To what extent does Nyshanov succeed in framing the song in a contemporary and cosmopolitan musical language while preserving elements of its traditional roots?

2. What elements of Nyshanov's arrangements help make it accessible to listeners who may not be familiar with Kyrgyz musical traditions?

3. How does the use of traditional instruments affect the character and atmosphere of the song?

Example 32.2. "Ordo," (Nomadic campsite) composed by Nurlanbek Nyshanov, performed by Ordo-Sakhna Ensemble. Recording courtesy of Ordo-Sakhna.

Unlike "Ak Kepter," which is an arrangement of a traditional song, albeit with newly composed material, "Ordo" is a completely new composition that uses traditional Kyrgyz instruments. "Ordo" has a narrative form that represents a specific "program"—in this case, an image of a landscape in the high alpine pasturelands of Kyrgyzstan known in Kyrgyz as *jayloo*. In summertime, Kyrgyz herders bring their flocks of sheep, horses, and cows to the *jayloo* to graze on nutrient-rich mountain grasses. While they are in the *jayloo,* herders live in yurts—circular felt tents that can be set up and taken down quickly, and transported from one pasturage to the next on the backs of animals. The name of Nyshanov's composition, "Ordo," refers to a camp consisting of several large yurts, which are often inhabited by members of an extended family or clan. The narrative program of Nyshanov's composition represents the passage of a day in traditional nomadic life. The piece begins in the still period before dawn. As the piece progresses, the sun rises, and the *ordo* wakes up. Children run about the camp while foals and lambs prance in the pasturage. Meanwhile, adults are busy with their routine daily responsibilities. As evening approaches, the skies become hazy, as often happens in the *jayloo,* surrounded by white mountains and old pine trees at an altitude of several thousand meters above sea level. The entrance of female voices signifies nightfall. Traditionally, men looked after a family's herd animals during the day, and women took over at dusk. In order not to fall asleep, women talked to one another, often singing songs or vocalizing simple melodies.

STUDY QUESTIONS

1. How effective is the narrative program of "Ordo" in conveying the imagery that the composer strives to evoke? Can you identify the moments in the piece that denote sunrise and sunset? How does the music mark these moments?

2. Which elements of "Ordo" are neo-traditional, and which elements are traditional?

3. How is the musical style of "Ordo" different from that of "Ak Kepter"? How is it similar?

Example 32.3. "Erke Sary" (Darling redhead younger brother), composed by Ruslan Jumabaev, performed by Ordo-Sakhna Ensemble.

"Erke Sary" has become well known in Kyrgyzstan among aficionados of *komuz* music. The musical content of the piece is new, but Jumabaev composed it in a traditional "variation form" that is typical for Kyrgyz instrumental music. In this structure, a composition has one or more short themes that are continually repeated with slight changes. Each new occurrence of the theme is a variant or variation. Using the variation form, Ruslan Jumabaev changes the rhythmic and melodic content of the song from one variation to the next. Jumabaev first composed "Erke Sary" as a virtuosic duet for two *komuze*s and later rearranged the piece, adding a third *komuz* to make a trio. In Ordo-Sakhna's arrangement, the *komuz* parts are joined by other instruments to create a lush ensemble sound.

STUDY QUESTIONS

1. What qualities of "Erke Sary" reveal it to be a neo-traditional composition, as opposed to a traditional *küü*?

2. What elements of "Erke Sary" make it more accessible to contemporary audiences than a traditional solo *küü*? What factors contribute to changes in the taste and sensibility of listeners over time and across cultures?

Both "Erke Sary" and "Ordo" have become popular examples of "national" music among audiences in Kyrgyzstan, but their popularity was not immediate. At first, both compositions jolted some listeners, and their composers were reproached for breaking centuries-old rules and showing disrespect toward tradition. Nowadays, no one denies the Kyrgyz roots of these pieces, and they are considered an organic part of Kyrgyz music and culture.

In interviews, Nurlanbek Nyshanov has mentioned that his decision to compose music in the neo-traditional style was spontaneous and intuitive—that he was driven by an intention to capture the attention of his contemporaries by "rediscovering the old via the new," or, in other words, conveying forgotten musical forms through a new language that would be familiar and easily understood today.

The ensembles Ordo-Sakhna (beginning in 1999) and Tengir-Too (2003–2009) both made important contributions to Kyrgyz neo-traditionalism, yet in somewhat different ways. Ordo-Sakhna's populist fusion of music, theater, dance, and fashion has brought it success among mass audiences. By contrast, Tengir-Too, under Nurlanbek Nyshanov's direction, worked within the boundaries of conventional Kyrgyz musical forms and genres at the same time that it explored innovative approaches to rhythm, melody, timbre, and tuning systems. Nyshanov sees the challenge facing the neo-traditionalist as one of maintaining an appropriate balance between the old and the new—a balance that he is continually fine-tuning

Above: Nurlanbek Nyshanov leads students in a rehearsal of one of his own compositions in a room at the Kyrgyz National Conservatory.
Photo by Theodore Levin.

Above right: Students at Centre Ustatshakirt, 2012.
Photo by Theodore Levin.

in his work. Nyshanov also understands that transmitting traditional knowledge to younger generations is a necessary condition for maintaining the vitality of cultural heritage. To this end, he has pursued an active teaching career in which his concept of musical neo-traditionalism has expanded to embrace musical pedagogy, and arts education more broadly. From 2004–2012, Nyshanov's activities as an educator were integrated into the work of Bishkek-based Centre Ustatshakirt, which has assumed a leading role in developing new methodologies and materials for arts education in Kyrgyzstan (see insert, "Centre Ustatshakirt and the New Era in Kyrgyz Music"). Since 2012, he has directed his own music performance program, called Ustatshakirt Plus. Nyshanov's classes in ensemble playing, composition in traditional and neo-traditional styles, music transcription and arranging, and digital recording and sound technologies have inspired a rising generation of Kyrgyz performer-composer-arrangers. While Nyshanov's own compositions form the core of the repertory he teaches to students, he encourages young composers to follow their own muse, resulting in a profusion of new music that explores an eclectic range of musical styles and languages. Two of the most talented composers of this new generation are Kambar Kalendarov (b. 1988) and Askat Jetigen uulu (b. 1993). Examples of their work are presented below.

POST-NEO-TRADITIONALISTS: KAMBAR KALENDAROV AND ASKAT JETIGEN UULU

WATCH

Example 32.4. "Echo of Time" (*Mezgil jangyrygy*), composed and arranged by Kambar Kalendarov, performed by Ensemble Ustatshakirt Plus. Filmed by television station Pyatyi kanal, program "Kvartira No. 5," Bishkek, 2014.

Kambar Kalendarov composed "Echo of Time" in 2009 soon after returning from a visit to the United States, where he participated in a summer workshop and festival organized by the New York-based performing arts organization and contemporary music group Bang on a Can. This short but ingenious composition features the distinctive timbre, or sound color, of the metal jaw harp (*temir komuz*), an instrument that traditionally was widely played by Kyrgyz herders. The piece begins with two jaw harps and later adds other layers of sound provided by a *choor* (end-blown flute) and *dobulba*s (tuned goblet drums). To create the musical form of "Echo of Time," Kalendarov used the traditional compositional principle of slowly shifting variations on a melodic theme—the same principle used by Ruslan Jumabaev in "Erke Sary," described above. In "Echo of Time," however, the melodic theme is reduced to short, rhythmically syncopated motifs of five to seven notes. These motifs are repeated in succession with barely perceptible changes in melody, rhythm, and timbre from one repetition to the next. The slowly shifting variation of melodic motifs within a repeating rhythmic pattern calls to mind the musical style known as minimalism, which emerged in the 1960s in the work of American composers La Monte Young, Terry Riley, Philip Glass, and Steve Reich. Indeed, Kalendarov acknowledges the strong influence of Reich's music, which he first encountered during his 2009 visit to the United States. Kalendarov, however, has not simply imitated the American minimalists but developed his own style of minimalism by pursuing the implications of the variation principle intrinsic to Kyrgyz instrumental music. "Echo of Time" reflects the intense pace of contemporary life, yet the voice of Kalendarov's nomadic ancestors still resounds strongly in the mesmerizing timbre of the jaw harp.

Kambar Kalendarov.
Courtesy of Kambar Kalendarov.

Kambar Kalendarov's compositional achievement has been recognized by Bang on a Can, which in 2011 released a CD of music by Kalendarov and fellow Kyrgyz jaw harp performer-composer Kutmanaaly Sultanbekov on its CD label, Cantaloupe Music. The CD is titled *Jaw.*

STUDY QUESTIONS

1. What compositional devices does Kambar Kalendarov use to keep a listener's interest throughout the four-minute duration of "Echoes of Time"?

2. At several moments during the piece, the sound undergoes a notable change in instrumental texture (e.g., 0:58, 2:03, 2:42, 3:31). What happens at these moments to cause the change?

3. Do you know other music that uses the compositional principle of minimalism?

In contrast to Kambar Kalendarov, who took piano lessons as a youngster, Askat Jetigen uulu began his musical studies with the *komuz* as a *shakirt,* or disciple, of master musician Zainidin Imanaliev (b. 1947). Later, Jetigen uulu worked with Nurlanbek Nyshanov, learning how to arrange Kyrgyz instrumental music for small ensembles and to compose his own neo-traditional music. Jetigen uulu, however, soon went beyond the templates of neo-traditionalism in search of his own compositional voice. He found it in composing original works for chamber ensemble that merge Kyrgyz and European instruments, thus enlarging the palette of musical colors and textures available to the composer. Two examples of Jetigen uulu's work are presented below.

WATCH

Example 32.5. "Vocalese," by Askat Jetigen uulu, performed by Ensemble Ustatshakirt Plus and the Manas Presidential Chamber Orchestra. Filmed by television station Pyatyi kanal, program "Kvartira No. 5," Bishkek, 2014.

According to the composer, "Vocalese" was inspired by the experience of becoming lost in Moscow's Sheremetovo Airport on the way home from a music tour in the United States.

Like Kambar Kalendarov, Jetigen uulu drew inspiration from American minimalism, expressed in "Vocalese" through its pulsing rhythmic energy, abrupt harmonic shifts, and burnished sonorities. Yet Jetigen uulu's sound is very much his

Centre Ustatshakirt and the New Era in Kyrgyz Music

Centre Ustatshakirt was founded in 2005 as a non-governmental organization (NGO), with support from the Aga Khan Trust for Culture and its Music Initiative. Ustatshakirt is the Kyrgyz rendition of *ustod-shogird,* a Persian expression that means "master-apprentice" or "master-disciple," and refers to the method through which art, music, and many other skills and professions have been traditionally transmitted in Central Asia. Centre Ustatshakirt's initial mission was indeed the revival and revitalization of the traditional Kyrgyz master-apprentice (*ustat-shakirt*) system of music pedagogy, which languished during the Soviet era. Around a half-dozen outstanding master performers were invited to teach small groups of students in different locations in Kyrgyzstan. The masters were given complete freedom to use their own original teaching methodology to transmit knowledge of traditional repertoires and performance techniques. The most accomplished students to emerge from this program auditioned for places in an experimental performance laboratory, where they learned to compose and arrange music in hybrid musical genres, experimented with different combinations of instruments, and developed competence in computer music applications and digital sound technology. They also studied English—an essential tool for a cosmopolitan artist. More recently, Centre Ustatshakirt has focused on developing new teaching methodologies and curricula for music classes in primary and secondary schools and launching music criticism and journalism training

A student *komuz* ensemble organized by Centre Ustatshakirt.
Photo by Adilet Moldobekov.

for university students. The aim is to scale up these programs to a national level in Kyrgyzstan. In all of its work, Centre Ustatshakirt strives to secure a place in the cultural life of contemporary multi-ethnic Kyrgyzstan for music and other forms of artistic expression that are at once rooted in but not constrained by tradition.

Centre Ustatshakirt's Kutmanaaly Sultanbekov teaches students to play the *chopo-choor,* a Kyrgyz ocarina.
Photo by Adilet Moldobekov.

Student *komuz* players participating in Centre Ustatshakirt's Umtul music education program at School no. 162 in Bishkek.
Photo by Adilet Moldobekov.

own. Indeed, Askat Jetigen uulu and Kambar Kalendarov are very possibly the harbinger of a new generation of what one might call "post-neo-traditionalist" Kyrgyz composers. These composers not only eschew the conventions that tethered Kyrgyz composers of the Soviet and immediate post-Soviet era to Russian musical models, but are venturing beyond the models of their own neo-traditionalist mentors.

Study Questions

1. How would you characterize the balance between Western and Kyrgyz instruments in "Vocalese"? What is the function of each group of instruments? How are their sounds integrated (or not integrated)?
2. Can you detect any quality of the sound of "Vocalese" that would identify it as specifically Kyrgyz?

The second example of Jetigen uulu's work is "Emotional Tango," which its composer describes as a "passionate dance with a Kyrgyz accent." Like "Vocalese," it was composed for a mixed ensemble of Western strings and traditional Kyrgyz instruments. While the melody is clearly tango-like, the syncopated rhythmic gestures that pervade the piece express the composer's perception of musical common ground that bridges tango and nomadic music.

WATCH **Example 32.6.** "Emotional Tango," composed by Askat Jetigen uulu, performed by Ensemble Ustatshakirt Plus and Manas Presidential Chamber Orchestra. Filmed by television station Pyatyi canal, program "Kvartira No. 5," Bishkek, 2014.

Askat Jetigen uulu's appropriation of tango in some sense illustrates the reverse process of Western appropriations of "world music" like those of the Kronos Quartet, described in the previous chapter. Created by a precocious nineteen-year-old, "Emotional Tango" represents the exuberant incorporation of globalized and cosmopolitan cultural influences that are shaping the work of a new generation of Kyrgyz composers.

Study Questions

1. How does the composer of "Emotional Tango" express the element of "nomadic rhythm"? To your ear, is it persuasive?
2. In the musical texture of "Emotional Tango," which element is syncopated, rhythm or melody?
3. How would you assess the success of Askat Jetigen uulu's attempt at musical hybridity?

NOTE

1. The soundtrack of this movie is available at www.cinedok.de.

CHAPTER 33　Popular Music in
Uzbekistan

KERSTIN KLENKE

TASHKENT, CAPITAL OF UZBEKISTAN, AUGUST 2008

6:00 PM: Azamat and Kirill are about to close the record store where they
work in the city center. Their last customers are a man who searches for a
rare album of 1980s British rock and a girl who buys a collection of songs
from Indian movies. Not far from their shop, at the conservatory, Irina
and Shahlo, two students in the *estrada* singing department, are rehearsing "Geri Dön" (Come back) by Turkish pop diva Sezen Aksu, "Let's Get
Loud" by US singer Jennifer Lopez, and "Byla lyubov" (There was love)
by Russian pop star Valeriya. In the classroom next to theirs, someone
practices jazz standards on the piano.

A record store in Tashkent
with a great variety of
music, videos, and films
mainly from Uzbekistan and
Russia, but also from other
Asian countries, Western
Europe, and the US.
Photo by Theodore Levin.

8:00 PM: Kirill and Azamat sit in a nearby café and talk about a demo CD they
received today: a mixture of classical Uzbek music and electronics. They agree that
this is something quite unusual for Uzbekistan and think that Chaykhana lounge
(Teahouse lounge) would be a good name to describe the style. Irina and Shahlo
have dinner in a Khorezmian restaurant. They like to come here not only for the
food but also for the music—Khorezmian-style *estrada,* sung live to an instrumental playback on minidisk. The music is too loud for talking, but just right for
dancing—before, during, and after eating.

10:00 PM: Kirill and Azamat have met with friends at their favorite club, Vertikal'ni
Mir (Vertical world), for a tribute night to Viktor Zoy, the late frontman of the
famous Soviet Russian rock band Kino. Irina and Shahlo are on their way home.
They pass the open-air stage, where a few weeks later the big state celebration for
Independence Day will take place. Rehearsals have already been going on every
night for weeks. Irina and Shahlo manage to catch a glimpse of one of the Uzbek

estrada stars, Ziyoda, who always close these events: she is leaving to perform one of the usual three-song acts at a wedding. It is high season for marriages, as Ramadan will start soon.

12:00 AM: Kirill and Azamat are at the house of their friend Firdavs. It is Firdavs's birthday, and as he is a big fan of retro, that is, music at least as old as the 1980s, they give him two LPs that they managed to find at the flea market—one by Uzbek singer Botyr Zakirov and one by Rashid Behbudov from Azerbaijan. Irina and Shahlo relax a bit at home and watch some rap video clips on television before getting ready to go dancing at their favorite nightclub, where the DJs usually present a mix of US hits and electronic music.

2:00 AM: Azamat and Kirill get into Azamat's car and pick up their sisters Irina and Shahlo. They turn on the radio and tune in to one of the Uzbek stations with a focus on Eastern music. The car is vibrating with Iranian pop, but somehow, they can't take in any more music. They switch off the radio, and as the four of them drive home, for the first time that night they are surrounded by silence.

Tapes for sale at a small street stall in Tashkent.
Photo by Theodore Levin.

STUDY QUESTIONS

1. Describe a "music night" in the place where you live, or in a place where you used to live. What styles of popular music can be found? Where do they come from? Where and how are they produced? What kinds of places and events are available to people who want to listen to music? Are there different kinds of music scenes that you can differentiate?

TRICKY TERMINOLOGY

As this short sketch of Tashkent night life makes clear, popular music in contemporary Uzbekistan is very diverse. This diversity is expressed through the styles of the music and its origins, the places where popular music is played and listened to, and the ways that this is done—live or recorded, at concerts or weddings, on television or radio, in clubs or restaurants.

Some people love Russian rock, some prefer American rap, others only like Uzbek *estrada,* still others are fans of almost anything Asian, and most have some sort of mixed taste. This diversity makes it difficult even to generalize about what constitutes "popular music" in Uzbekistan—a task that is even harder because the term is not part of the musical vocabulary in the country. Classifying such a wide array of styles under the banner of popular music is a Western idea. In Uzbekistan, other concepts are used to denote and organize these different musics. As in most

Estrada

The Russian word *estrada* has its origin in the Romance languages French and Spanish, where *estrade/estrado* means "stage" or "platform." The term *estrada* was already in use in late czarist Russia to denote various kinds of popular stage entertainment, but it became a more structured concept of scenic performances after the Bolshevik Revolution of 1917, when officials placed it within the socialist framework of Soviet artistic production. Often referred to in Russian as the "small stage," in contrast to the "large stage" of opera and drama, *estrada* included a wide range of popular arts such as comedy and satire, folk and popular song, recitation of poems, dance, and circus acts. In content, *estrada* thus resembled the English music hall or French *varieté,* but socially and politically, *estrada* was located within a different ideological sphere. During the Soviet era, not only did *estrada* spread throughout the country and into socialist "brother states," where local variants developed, but the meaning of the term gradually came to focus on *estrada*'s musical dimension. In contemporary Uzbekistan, *estrada* is used almost exclusively in reference to music, but the originally broader concept is still evident, for example, in the existence of a "College for *Estrada* and Circus Arts" in Tashkent, and in the English translation "Variety Arts Association" for the Uzbek "*Estrada* Association" O'zbeknavo. Moreover, at *estrada* concerts, musical performances are often interrupted by short comedy acts. Some proponents of *estrada* in its broader sense advocate for a distinction between *estrada* and *estrada* music—the latter term referring specifically to the musical dimension of *estrada*.

classificatory systems, however, categories often overlap and resist efforts to define them through mutually exclusive and universally valid sets of criteria. Here are some of the terms that you can find in musical discourse in Uzbekistan:

Estrada, or *estrada* music, is a widely used term (see insert, "Estrada") that typically refers to mainstream popular music—what in the West would simply be called "pop." Sometimes the term *estrada* is further particularized by adding modifiers in Uzbek or Russian such as "national" (*milliy*), "Europeanized" (*yevrolashgan*), "foreign" (*zarubezhnaya*), "world" (*mirovaya*), "Eastern" (*vostochnaya*), "Western" (*zapadnaya*), "wedding" (*toy*), "composers" (*kompozitorskaya*), "commercial" (*kommercheskaya*), or by naming its place of origin: Uzbek, Russian, Italian, etc. Very often public performances of *estrada* are only partially live or not live at all: singers either sing to an instrumental playback or use a full playback and just pretend to sing with the microphone switched off.

Popsa has a derogatory meaning, and commonly refers to a part of the *estrada* repertoire. Whoever uses this term wants to express that he or she considers this music of low quality, quickly and badly produced, aesthetically unappealing, or created simply for commercial gain. Some people may even dismiss all *estrada* music as *popsa.*

Another category, alternative music, encompasses styles such as rap, rock, punk, and electronic music. For people who are active in this sphere—musicians, fans, organizers—alternative music represents the opposite of *popsa:* Its image is that of self-made music with a message and artistic sincerity that is best demonstrated in live concerts. Even though rock, rap, and punk musicians might agree that they all perform a kind of alternative music, they rarely mix, but rather have separate musical scenes. Fans of *estrada* often regard alternative music as unappealingly rough and harsh, although tamer versions of rock and rap have actually become fashionable in *estrada,* too.

Jazz is a category difficult to grasp: Some people in Uzbekistan define it as a subcategory of *estrada,* while others—mostly those who practice it themselves—see it as a separate genre with a higher artistic value and in this respect closer to Western classical music.

Since *estrada* music is by far the most prominent form of popular music in contemporary Uzbekistan, the following paragraphs will focus on the historical development and present-day setting of Uzbek *estrada* productions.

STUDY QUESTIONS

1. Which terms do you know to classify styles in the field of popular music?

2. What criteria do you use to differentiate styles?

3. Are the criteria only musical, or do you consider other factors, too?

ESTRADA IN SOVIET UZBEKISTAN

A poster for the Estrada Orchestra of Uzbekistan depicts early stars of Uzbek *estrada*.

Courtesy of Yunus Turaev.

A local *estrada* scene developed in Uzbekistan—then known as the Uzbek Soviet Socialist Republic (Uzbek SSR)—at the end of the 1950s. Important influences in this formative period were Russian *estrada* and official Soviet releases of Western pop and rock, "underground" records and tapes that were smuggled into the country as well as Western and Asian radio stations such as Voice of America or Radio Kabul that people listened to secretly.

In addition to these external stimuli on the development of *estrada* music in the mid-twentieth century, local predecessors also existed, including various forms of street theater or entertainment at weddings and in bazaars as well as brigades of artists that played for troops during the civil war following the October Revolution, and during the Second World War. A particularly influential figure was a dancer and singer known as Tamara Khanum. She was the star of a so-called ethnographic ensemble that in the 1920s and 1930s became famous for performing stage versions of Uzbek, Arab, Persian, and other Asian folk music and dance traditions. The troupe not only toured throughout the Soviet Union but also in Eastern and Western Europe.

Similarly international was the repertoire of early *estrada* artists in the Uzbek SSR such as Botyr Zakirov (1936–1985), who is generally considered to be the founder of Uzbek *estrada* and reached the peak of his career in the 1960s. Botyr Zakirov sang in Russian, Uzbek, and French as well as in the original languages of songs that he arranged from different parts of Asia. He was usually accompanied by a mixture of big band and symphony orchestra, which produced a sound that was very fashionable at that time throughout Europe and America.

LISTEN

Example 33.1. "Arabskoe Tango" (Arabian Tango), music and lyrics by Farid Al-Atrash, recording by Botyr Zakirov and the Estrada Orchestra of Uzbekistan, conductor Aleksandr Dvoskin, 1959. A link to this example is available on the companion website.

Many Uzbeks regard Botyr Zakirov's song "Arabskoe Tango" (Arabian tango) as the essence of his art. The song is a cover of "Ya Zahratan Fi Khayali" (Flower of my dreams) by then-popular Syrian singer Farid Al-Atrash. Botyr Zakirov sang it in the original Arabic and performed it at the World Festival of Youth and Students (1957) in Moscow for the first time.

STUDY QUESTIONS

1. Listen to the song, and describe the music and the quality of the voice. Do you know pieces similar to this one?

2. Who, in your own music culture, is generally known to be the first pop star in history?

3. Was his or her music similar to this song of Botyr Zakirov?

In the 1970s and 1980s, one of the best known Uzbek *estrada* acts was Yalla, a vocal-instrumental ensemble (VIA), as *estrada* groups were officially called in the Soviet era. Yalla, featuring Botyr Zakirov's brother Farrukh (b. 1946) as lead singer, mostly sang in Russian. But through their lyrics, musical ornamentation, and costumes they, too, often integrated diverse Asian influences and images into their music, in their case, into a pop-rock setting. One song that illustrates this approach particularly well is the 1986 production "The Musical Teahouse." Yalla became famous throughout and beyond the Soviet Union and they still continue to perform, but it is their old repertoire from the 1980s that they are most famous for and that now makes them sought after for retro, i.e., oldie shows in Russia.

Botyr Zakirov's "Arabian Tango" and Yalla's "The Musical Teahouse" are just two examples drawn from more than thirty years of *estrada* music in the Uzbek SSR, but they illustrate a general trend. On the one hand, Soviet-era Uzbek *estrada* was based on models from Euro-American popular music and Russian *estrada;* on the other, artists integrated older Uzbek traditions as well as other Asian or Arab sources into their musical creations. At first sight, this international take on Uzbek *estrada* seems to fit well into the internationalist maxim of the Soviet Union. But on closer inspection, the issue becomes more complex: The cultures to which Uzbek *estrada* artists turned for musical inspiration were overwhelmingly not those of the officially sanctioned "brother nations" of the Soviet Union, which were mostly in socialist Eastern Europe. Rather, they represented cultural connections that predated the founding of the Soviet Union and transcended the ideological frame and geographical space of socialism. These cultural connections could be viewed as a subversive alternative to the officially promulgated ideology of "friendship among peoples"—which implicitly meant "friendship among socialist peoples." But the musical appropriations and fusions that characterized Soviet Uzbek *estrada* can also be understood in a politically more affirmative way: By integrating a variety of Asian and Arab musical sources and references into their music, Uzbek *estrada* artists created a diffuse and imaginary oriental soundscape. And through this soundscape they served and nourished the orientalist fantasies and clichés of many Russians, who viewed the Soviet Union's southern republics in Central Asia and the Caucasus as a kind of internal Orient.

WATCH

Example 33.2. "Muzykal'naya Chaykhana" (The musical teahouse), performed by Yalla, music by Farrukh Zakirov, lyrics by Yevgenii Berezikov, arrangement by Rustam Il'yasov, 1986. A link to this example is available on the companion website.

With this song Yalla reached the finals of the pan-Soviet song competition "Pesnia–88," as you can see in the video. Passages omitted in the following transcription and translation of the lyrics consist of repetitions and embellishments on the word *chaykhana.* These sections are marked [. . .].

Nalivai chaykhanchik chaiu	Pour tea, *chaykhanchik,*[1]
Vmesto krepkogo vina.	instead of strong wine.
Ya vam muzyku sygrayu,	I will play music for you,
Zdes' vsem nravitsya ona.	here everybody likes it.
Na Vostoke, na Vostoke—	In the East,[2] in the East—
Chto za nebo bez luny?	what would the sky be without the moon?
Na Vostoke, na Vostoke—	In the East, in the East—
Chto za zhizn' bez chaykhany?	what would life be without the teahouse?
Chto za zhizn' bez chaykhany?	what would life be without the teahouse?

Piala idyot po krugu,	The teacup is going round in the circle,
Aksakaly smotryat v mir.	the *aksakals*[3] are looking into the world.
Rady gostyu, rady drugu.	Glad about a guest, glad about a friend.
Zdes' zastol'e, no ne pir.	Here the table is set, but there is no feast.
[. . .]	[. . .]
Khot' byvaet zdes' i tesno,	Even if it is packed here sometimes,
Chaykhana, ty chudo-rai.	teahouse, you are a wonderful paradise.
Chtoby pesnya stala pesnei,	For the song to become a song,
S nami vmeste napevai.	sing together with us.
[. . .]	[. . .]

STUDY QUESTIONS

1. Which elements of the music, the lyrics, and the performance could be described as oriental clichés?

2. Compare this song to Botyr Zakirov's "Arabian Tango."

Whatever explanation for these oriental connections you follow, Soviet Uzbekistan's *estrada* musicians were very successful with their art. They toured frequently, mostly through the Soviet Union and other countries of the Eastern Bloc, but sometimes also beyond the socialist world. On the whole, however, Soviet-era Uzbek *estrada* remained a relatively small scene that was in various ways closely controlled and organized by state cultural authorities.

ESTRADA IN INDEPENDENT UZBEKISTAN

In 1991 Uzbekistan became an independent state. Most *estrada* musicians agree that the early 1990s were an unruly time, in culture as well as in politics. The breakup of the Soviet Union marked the end of pan-Soviet institutions, among them government structures responsible for managing musical life. Previously established mechanisms of control and organizational routines ceased to function as before, and new ones were just beginning to be installed. At the same time that Uzbekistan was experiencing a fundamental ideological transformation, considerably more music from all over the world was becoming available. *Estrada* musicians differ in their judgments about these first years of independence: Some regard them as a period of unwanted chaos, while for others, they were a time of much-wanted freedom.

A concert in a Tashkent park on the occasion of Independence Day, 2008.

Istiqlol Saroyi (Independence Palace), formerly known as the Palace of the Friendship of Peoples (Xalqlar Do'stligi Saroyi), provides a venue for major *estrada* concerts.

A gala concert at Istiqlol Saroyi presenting winners of the 2008 Nihol Prize, a state award for young artists in various categories of music and dance. Winners are offered free higher education in a field linked to their artistic endeavors.

What is undisputed, however, is that the *estrada* scene began to grow considerably after independence, and that in the mid-1990s *estrada* was granted a prominent position in Uzbek cultural politics that it continues to occupy today.

Under President Islam Karimov, a central goal of government initiatives in the domain of music is the development of so-called *milliy estrada*: "national" *estrada*. An important agent in this process is an institution called O'zbeknavo. O'zbeknavo was founded in 1996 by decree of the Cabinet, and after some alterations in its structure and responsibilities, it became known as the official Uzbek Estrada Association. Presently it focuses on two areas of activity: allocating licenses to *estrada* musicians and concert producers, and organizing an *estrada* program as a part of state celebrations on national holidays such as Independence Day and Nowruz (Uzbek: Navro'z), the beginning of spring. Both activities are of crucial importance to the *estrada* scene. In order to perform in public (for example, at weddings, concerts, on radio and television), *estrada* musicians officially need a license. They apply for it at O'zbeknavo by giving their songs, video clips, and lyrics to a review committee. If their materials are approved, artists are granted a license for up to a year. There are several categories of licenses, which differ in the scope of activity they permit and in the official price musicians are required to pay to obtain them. A license from O'zbeknavo exempts *estrada* musicians from paying income tax on earnings from their musical activities. Licences can be renewed, but they can also be withdrawn at short notice. Part of the licensing agreement between artists and O'zbeknavo is the obligation to perform for free at state-organized concerts, especially at official celebrations on national holidays. Before these events, O'zbeknavo organizes large auditions, where artists are supposed to present songs that fit the occasion. To be selected is considered prestigious, especially for younger singers, whose careers benefit from participation in state festivities. But such commitments also mean long weeks of often daily rehearsals that allow little time for financially profitable musical activities.

Other institutions involved in the development of *estrada* are located in the educational sector, such as the *estrada* faculty in the Uzbekistan National Conservatory in Tashkent or *estrada* departments in music or art colleges and at specialized music schools. In addition, music competitions on topics such as "My Motherland" (*Vatanim menim*) or its successors, "The Motherland Is Incomparable, The Motherland Is Unique" (*Vatan yagonadir, vatan bittadir*) and "You Are Unique, Sacred Motherland!" (*Yagonasan, muqaddas vatan!*) usually organized by O'zbeknavo and the Ministry of Culture and Sport jointly with other institutions, are meant to promote the development of *estrada*. Meanwhile, radio and television stations maintain formal or informal artistic councils (*khudsovety*) charged with ensuring that their music programming follows governmental guidelines.

This constellation of institutions, initiatives, and ideas might seem like the perfect instrument to create exactly the kind of *estrada* the Uzbek government wants to develop. And of course, state institutions and officials have considerable power, and their activities and discussions influence the *estrada* scene, its productions, and consequently the Uzbek soundscape. But the reality is more complex, and not everything that happens in Uzbek *estrada* is congruent with how official policies look on paper.

One fundamental but simple reason for this is that directives from above often leave room for interpretation; the ambiguity can be used unintentionally or strategically. A good example is the notion of "national *estrada*" described earlier, which currently is central to debates about *estrada* in Uzbekistan yet does not have a clear definition.

Most people involved in *estrada* agree that "national *estrada*" should have lyrics in Uzbek, but they are less in agreement with regard to other distinctive features. Among those frequently mentioned are the use of Uzbek musical instruments, the integration of older Uzbek musical and poetic traditions, the use of Uzbek vocal styles, and the treatment of specifically Uzbek topics. Yet even these criteria leave room for ambiguity: many musical traditions and instruments that are common in Uzbekistan may also be found beyond its borders; regional diversity and representativeness is an issue; and the historical depth and ethnic inclusivity of the very term Uzbek are a matter of interpretation and dispute.

Ongoing debates about what constitutes "national *estrada*" notwithstanding, songs that are considered to fit this category are typically performed at state celebrations and can be heard on radio and television programs during the time surrounding these events. At least the lyrics of these songs are usually "national" in that they feature patriotic content. "About the motherland" (*vatan haqida* [Uzbek], or *o rodine* [Russian]) is the term commonly used to characterize this specific sub-category of "national *estrada*." Almost all *estrada* artists have at least one such song "about the motherland" in their repertoire, and some artists compose new ones nearly every year.

Example 33.3. "Hech Kimga Bermaymiz Seni O'zbekiston" (We will not give you to anyone, Uzbekistan), music and arrangement by Yulduz Usmanova, lyrics by Muhammad Yusuf, adaptation by Yulduz Usmanova, 1999. A link to this example is available on the companion website.

WATCH

Performer Profile: Yulduz Usmanova

Many Uzbeks regard Yulduz Usmanova as the country's most famous *estrada* star and often speak of her as "our prima donna," "our diva," or "our queen." Born in 1963 to parents who worked in a silk factory in the city of Margilan, in the Ferghana Valley, Yulduz Usmanova studied vocal arts at the conservatory in Tashkent and launched her career as an *estrada* singer in the 1990s. Her relationship with the Uzbek government has oscillated widely since then, and shaped her artistic biography. At times she has played the role of a de facto court singer to the Uzbek leadership, while at other times, she has been regarded as persona non grata—periods that she has mostly spent living outside Uzbekistan. In the 1990s, she became the first Uzbek to successfully enter the Euro-American "world music" scene, while the dawn of the new millennium saw her shifting most of her musical activities to Turkey. Yulduz Usmanova is known for her untiring musical productivity, resulting in a continuous output of albums. Many Uzbeks value her not only for her vocal abilities and the poetic tone of her lyrics but also for her candor with regard to social topics. Women in particular appreciate her attention to gender issues. In June 2010 Yulduz Usmanova composed a song, "Qirg'izlarga," about the bloody

Photo by Mukhiddin A Lee.

conflicts between Uzbeks and Kyrgyz in the south of Kyrgyzstan. The song lyrics implicitly took the Uzbek side in the conflict, producing strong reactions in listeners that ranged from approbation to resentment to outrage.

The title of this song also served as the headline of several military-patriotic shows in Uzbekistan in the year 1999, which were meant to draw the country's youth toward the official project of nation-building.

Oq yo'rgakka o'ragansan o'zing bizni.	You yourself wrapped us in a white napkin.
Oq yuvib oq taragansan o'zing bizni.	You yourself washed and combed us clean.
Beshigimiz uzra bedor ona bo'lib.	You were a vigilant mother over our cradle.
Kunimizga yaragansan o'zing bizni.	You yourself were at our daily life's service.
[. . .]	[. . .]
Adoying bo'lgaymiz seni, O'zbekiston!	We will do everything for you, Uzbekistan!
Hech kimga bermaymiz seni, O'zbekiston!	We will not give you to anyone, Uzbekistan!

Fidoying bo'lgaymiz seni, O'zbekiston!	We will be ready to sacrifice ourselves for you, Uzbekistan!
Hech kimga bermaymiz seni, O'zbekiston!	We will not give you to anyone, Uzbekistan!
Qalqoningmiz, qasd qilsa kim gar joningga.	We are your shield, if anybody should try to kill you.
Alpomishlar ruhi yor har o'g'loningga.	The spirit of Alpamysh[4] is dear to your every son.
Gulday o'pib asragaymiz ostonangni.	We will guard your gate, as we cherish a flower.
Yovlar yaqin yo'lolmagay qo'rg'oningga.	Enemies will not be able to get close to your fortress.
[. . .]	[. . .]
Tuzing totib, unutganlar xor bo'ladi.	Those who tasted your food and forgot it will be despised.
Ko'zlariga ikki dunyo tor bo'ladi.	The world will become small for their two eyes.
Tinch kuningni ko'rolmagan yurtfurushtlar,	Those traitors that envied your peaceful life,
bir kun bir kaft tuprog'ingga zor bo'ladi.	Will one day be desperate for one handful of your soil.
[. . .]	[. . .]

WATCH **Example 33.4.** "Ajdodlar Ruhi" (The spirit of ancestors), performed by Se'Tanho (formerly Setora), music and arrangement by Vitalii Zolotarev, lyrics by Shahnoz. A link to this example is available on the companion website.

Se'Tanho (formerly Setora) used to be a three-girl group from Tashkent that was sometimes dubbed the "Uzbek Spice Girls." They—Feruza, Kamila, and Laylo—became famous at the end of the 1990s, successfully continued their career together for about ten years, and then split up to embark on solo projects. In 2005 they were forced to give up the name Setora and had problems with the rights to their former repertoire after a break with Tarona Records, their producing company. Tarona Records almost immediately installed a new three-girl band that also used the name Setora, with similar-looking girls who took over the former

Setora's songs. For some time, this issue sparked discussions in Uzbekistan about copyright laws.

The story in the clip is based on the historical figure of Jalal-al-din Manguberdi, the last ruler of the Khorezmian Empire, who fought the Mongols under Genghis Khan for more than a decade until he was killed, in 1231. Jalal-al-din Manguberdi has been chosen as one of the national heroes and moral role models by the Uzbek government. The original full-length version of the clip, which is hard to find now, ends with a switch to independent Uzbekistan. In this version, the three young warrior women appear at the end in contemporary clothing, laying flowers at a statue of Manguberdi. When they turn, they—and the viewer—see Manguberdi himself standing in modern and modest everyday dress. The sound track for this part of the clip features acoustic instrumental music without singing, but there are some headings in the video, which are included in the following translation of the lyrics.

Girl:	*Shoshmakir! Bu nima?*	Wait! What's that?
Narrator:	*Bir ming ikki yuz o'n to'qqizinchi yil. Chingiz Xon boshchiligida yov qo'shinlar Movaro'nnahr va Xorezm yerlari bosib bordilar.*	It is the year 1219. Troops under the command of Genghis Khan went out to conquer the lands of Transoxania and Khorezm.
	Dovonlar osha o'zib g'animlar kelar to'zib.	Crossing mountain passes, the enemy came from all sides.
	Qilichdan o'tib har jon, ariqlardan oqdi qon.	They killed all life, they killed with their swords, rivers of blood ran.
	Tinchliging bo'ldi vayron, yovlarga to'ldi har yon.	Your peace was ruined, every flank fell to the enemy.
	Tinchlik bermadi senga xalqing ohu fig'oni.	The loud cry of your people did not leave you undisturbed.
	Qaddingni bukmay bording elimning mard o'g'loni.	Without lowering your head you went, my country's brave royal sons.
	Kurashding g'anim bilan chiqquncha qora joni.	You fought with the enemy until their evil souls left them.
	Olishding g'anim bilan chiqquncha qora joni.	You wrestled with the enemy until their evil souls left them.
	Bor begunoh xalqing faryodi, azobli go'dak nolasi.	It is there, the wailing of your innocent people, the painful cry of infants.

Bor sen uchun qalqon bo'lguvchi, zabardast farzandlaring bor.	It is there, a future shield for you, your powerful children, they are there.
Bor ona tuprog'ing bag'rida asrlar uzra beg'ubor,	It is there, at the bosom of your motherland, unsullied over the centuries,
ajdodlar ruhi madadkor, zafar senga bo'ldi yor.	the spirit of ancestors as protectors, their victory was happiness for you.
Tomiringdan oqadi sadoqat vafo qoni.	In your veins runs the blood of devotion and loyalty.
Qalbingdan o'chmas sening xo'rlangan ayol dodi.	In your heart the never-ending cries of abused women.
Adovating bor sening, sendan xalqning umidi.	There is an urge for retribution in you, in you lies your people's hope.
Mangu zulmatga ketar ayanch qayg'uli kunlar.	These pitiful days of grief shall be forever banished.
Batamom o'tmas endi biz vahshiy yovlar.	Never again will brutal enemies cross our borders.
Tabarruk ona yerim bag'rida yayrar elim.	At the bosom of my sacred motherland, my people will rejoice.
Tabarruk ona yerim bag'rida yayrar elim.	At the bosom of my sacred motherland, my people will rejoice.

Text:	*18 yildan so'ng*	18 years later
	[. . .]	[. . .]
Text:	*Bizning kunlar*	In our days
Text and narrator:	*Vatan sajdagohdek muqaddas!*	The homeland is as sacred as a place of prayer!

STUDY QUESTIONS

1. What, in your opinion, is patriotic about these songs and videoclips?

2. What are differences and similarities between them?

3. Do you know patriotic pop songs from other music cultures? If so, how are they similar or different from the Uzbek songs presented in examples 33.3 and 33.4?

4. Do you think that patriotic songs actually make people love their country more?

Patriotic songs do not make up the majority of *estrada* artists' repertoire, however. As is true in popular music throughout the world, the principal theme of Uzbek *estrada* is love between women and men, or between teenage girls and boys. These are the songs whose lyrics and accompanying video clips most often lead to disputes between Uzbek singers and government representatives on issues of morality and permissiveness. Artists usually hold more liberal views in these confrontations and may be asked to change content and visual dramatization; or broadcast of the song in question may be forbidden; or singers might even lose their license to perform. This ultimate sanction within the *estrada* bureaucracy is usually imposed only when artists are accused of more severe deviance from official directives, but it has been imposed and severely curbed the careers of some performers.

Not all songs about love are potentially problematic, though, and many are even considered very suitable for "national *estrada,*" for example, those in which love results in a marriage accepted by both parents. Other aspects of family life also represent common subjects in *estrada*—in particular, those that conform to state-sanctioned social ideals by depicting respect towards elders, typical gender models, social responsibility, and so on. In contrast to other Muslim-majority countries—Egypt and Indonesia, for example—where Islamic themes permeate recent pop music, in Uzbekistan, culture authorities regard Islam and religion in general as inappropriate topics for *estrada,* and they are conspicuously absent from the repertoire.

With regard to sound and musical structure, proponents of the ideal of "national *estrada*" advocate the rejection of foreign musical influences for the sake of a presumed musical purity. Artists who infuse *estrada* with influences from neighboring or closely related music cultures such as Turkey, Iran, Azerbaijan, the Arab countries, and India are regularly criticized. Similar disapproval is directed toward artists whose work is closely modeled on Russian or Anglo-American popular music. This situation could be understood to mean that such *estrada* musicians are not following government plans for the development of a "national *estrada.*" Such a conclusion, however, is both true and false: Many artists like to integrate older Uzbek musical traditions or use poems by famous poets as song lyrics and generally support government plans for the development of a "national *estrada.*" Yet they—and their listeners—do not want to be musically confined to one style. On the contrary, many artists are eager to experiment and play with a variety of musical traditions. Their reasons may be aesthetic or commercial or both. Offering a varied repertoire has the potential to enlarge one's audience—within Uzbekistan and beyond its borders. Some *estrada* artists with international ambitions aim at other Asian markets, e.g., Turkey, while others try to appeal to listeners in Russia or Western Europe. A few permanently relocate to pursue a career abroad, such as Oksana Nechitaylo, from Tashkent, who now lives in Russia and has managed to establish herself firmly in the Russian pop scene under the name "Sogdiana."

One contemporary Uzbek *estrada* artist who has been particularly successful in moving into and maneuvering within various European and North American music circuits is Sevara Nazarkhan (b. 1978). UK label Real World Records released two of her albums (*Yol Bolsin* 2003; *Sen* 2007). The first features mostly trip hop-like modulations of Uzbek folk and classical pieces, while the second primarily showcases her own compositions in a similarly electronic but more beat-laden style. These CDs helped her navigate the "world music" scene and, in the case of *Yol Bolsin,* win a prestigious BBC Radio 3 Award for World Music in 2004. In addition to productions of Uzbek-language *estrada* for the domestic market during the past several years (for example, *Bu Sevgi,* 2006), Sevara Nazarkhan's activities have also focused on Russia, including a Russian-language pop album (*Sevara and Ėl'f: Tak Legko,* 2010). Geographical expansion is clearly linked to stylistic diversity in this artist's case—and with consequences that are quite typical for some "world music" artists. Many Uzbeks greatly admire Sevara Nazarkhan for her talent, individuality, innovative explorations, and international success. The same people, however, often admit that they do not understand or like her experiments for the "world music" scene. Conversely, irritated "world music" fans often dismiss her productions for the Russian and Uzbek markets—if these reach their ears at all—as astonishingly straight mainstream pop. A 2011 release, *Tortadur*, which is devoted to acoustic renditions of Uzbek classical traditions, has appealed to listeners both within and outside Uzbekistan, and is far from the genre of *estrada*.

WATCH **Example 33.5.** "Yol Bolsin," performed by Sevara Nazarkhan, 2003. Promotional clip for *Yol Bolsin* (2002). A link to this example is available on the companion website.

Yol bolsin is actually spelled *yo'l bo'lsin* in Uzbek and literally means "may there be a path." In this translation it is common as a farewell phrase wishing someone a safe trip or luck. *Yo'l bo'lsin* is also, but more rarely, used in the sense of the question "Where are you going?" The track is an arrangement by Sevara Nazarkhan and Hector Zazou of an old Uzbek song that has been interpreted and recorded by several Uzbek artists.

WATCH **Example 33.6.** "Sen bilasan," performed by Sevara Nazarkhan, music by Sevara Nazarkhan, lyrics by Nurmukhamad Isroil. From *Bu Sevgi* (This love), Real World Records, 2006. A link to this example is available on the companion website.

Example 33.7. "On ne prishyol" (He didn't come), performed by Sevara Nazarkhan, music and lyrics by Sergei Mikhalok. Clip from 2009 of a track on the Russian album *Sevara and Ėl'f: Tak Legko* (Sevara and the elf: So easy) (2010). A link to this example is available on the companion website.

STUDY QUESTIONS

1. Compare the music and the singer's image in the three video clips.

2. Do you know other artists who work for different markets? Is their repertoire similarly diverse? If yes, how would you describe the various styles?

3. What is meant by "world music"? Try to find out more about the history and concept of this scene. What is problematic about the notion of "world music"?

While their stylistic variety and international reach might not be as extensive as Sevara Nazarkhan's, many Uzbek *estrada* stars are very mobile. Most of them regularly travel within Uzbekistan or cross borders to neighboring countries such as Kyrgyzstan and Kazakhstan to perform at concerts or weddings. In general, Uzbek *estrada* musicians earn their living predominantly by performing at private or business celebrations, especially at weddings, and thus are keen to match the diverse tastes of the people who hire them. In their quest for variety and expansion of their audience, they are usually backed by another important player in the world of Uzbek *estrada*: show business. While state institutions exert mechanisms of control and have ideological power, they do not command the extensive financial resources that would allow them to create their own market. Economic power rests with Uzbek show business, which is continuously expanding its reach, both locally and internationally, and includes production companies, recording studios, radio

Poster for a series of concerts by singer Shahzoda. On the right are the logos of the companies that sponsored this event, which included a furniture shop in addition to several media enterprises.

and television stations, image companies, and journals. Some of these enterprises work like large-scale entertainment businesses, but the majority of activity is conducted by small, semi-professional firms, or even individuals who may sponsor a single artist of their choice. Of course, show business cannot work completely independently of government culture policy, but its considerable financial resources enable it to push the boundaries of what is possible in Uzbek *estrada* beyond what government policies envisage and permit.

A very simplified model of Uzbek *estrada* as a socially and politically contextualized musical phenomenon would show two prominent forces that work in opposite directions. One of these, which to a large extent represents the efforts of the government, works to focus the creative potential of Uzbek musicians on "uzbekicizing" *estrada* music through the concept of "national *estrada*" and to create a truly national popular art form—whatever this is supposed to be. The other force represents the more outward-oriented aspirations of artists and show business to "internationalize" *estrada*. At times these forces achieve a temporary equilibrium, yet there is a continuing tension between them, which gives the *estrada* scene a diverse and continually changing quality. This scene, however, cannot be neatly divided into two opposing and consistent positions that represent the interests of the government versus the interests of artists. For example, while some *estrada* musicians liken current musical policies in Uzbekistan to Stalinist approaches to censorship, others actually support an even tighter government grip on the *estrada* scene. At the same time, there are government officials who bemoan the lack of stylistic variety and criticize the high level of state control. Furthermore, show business in Uzbekistan is currently undergoing substantial transformations. Until 2013, President Islam Karimov's eldest daughter, Gulnora Karimova, was one of the key players in this domain, overseeing the media company *Terra Group* as well as the NGO *Fund Forum Uz*. Since her business conduct has become the subject of legal investigations, the activities of this company and NGO have been halted. The long-term consequences for the Uzbek *estrada* scene are unknown, but a significant reorganization is all but inevitable.

REGIONAL VARIETY IN *ESTRADA*

Like other aspects of Uzbek culture and cultural administration, the *estrada* scene is centralized in Tashkent. Tashkent offers the largest concert halls, the best recording technology, the greatest variety of radio stations, and the highest number of *estrada* stars. This concentration of activity in the capital does not mean, however, that in the rest of the country *estrada* is nonexistent. On the contrary, thriving regional varieties of *estrada* within Uzbekistan reflect the strong regional identities that are expressed through language, material culture, food, and music. Regional *estrada* styles often draw musical ideas from folk traditions particular to their locale, and mostly circulate within their own region. Some of these traditions, however, are popular across regions or have entered the nationwide *estrada* circuit. A good example of such mobility is *estrada* from Khorezm, a province in the west of Uzbekistan, which in recent years has become popular in the mainstream *estrada* of Tashkent. Musical migration also takes place in the opposite direction when major *estrada* stars tour or perform at weddings across the country.

One could rightfully ask whether the Tashkent scene is not just one of the regional variants of *estrada*. On the one hand there are indeed *estrada* artists who create a regionally specific *estrada* by drawing on folk traditions that are unique to this area. On the other, the Tashkent scene is made up of such a great variety of people from different regions and backgrounds and is so ample in its stylistic scope, that its very diversity is one of its major regional characteristics.

Two cities in Uzbekistan where musical style and content are closely linked to ethnicity and language are Bukhara and Samarkand, whose populations are predominantly Tajik-speaking. *Estrada* artists in Bukhara and Samarkand have close ties to Tajikistan but are all but absent from the Tashkent media and *estrada* scene. This situation can be partially explained by the Uzbek government's strong advocacy for art forms representing the nation's titular ethnicity and language— Uzbek—in contrast to far lesser efforts to represent the cultures of Uzbekistan's ethnic minorities.

WATCH

Example 33.8. "Surxonlik Qiz," music by Mahmud Namozov, lyrics by Abdugaffor Mansurov, 2012. A link to this example is available on the companion website.

Mahmud Namozov (b. 1960) is an *estrada* musician from the province of Surkhondaryo in the southeast of Uzbekistan. He is famous for working with or representing folk music from his home region, which Uzbeks usually characterize as being particularly lively and colorful, and which is known for its vigorous style of dancing.

STUDY QUESTIONS

1. What, in your opinion, links this song and video to folk music?

2. Are there artists from your own music culture with a similar approach to regional music traditions?

BEYOND *ESTRADA*: ALTERNATIVE MUSIC

Beyond *estrada,* popular music in Uzbekistan encompasses a variety of genres, in-cluding those discussed earlier in this article under the label "alternative music": rock, punk, rap, and electronic music. Of these, rock has the longest history in Uz-bekistan—a history that started in the 1960s, with groups playing covers of famous

Western bands—and still makes up the largest part of alternative music. On the whole, however, alternative music has little public visibility and audibility compared to *estrada*. One reason for this is that culture policies and administrative practices are unfavorable for or even work against the proliferation of this scene. Cultural authorities typically consider the musical style and sound, content, language, dress code, and habitus of alternative music to contradict or even harm the cultural values and ideals of the Uzbek nation. Applying to O'zbeknavo for a license to perform such music is usually hopeless but would, even in the unlikely case of success, definitely be unprofitable. Opportunities to earn back the money that performers would have to spend for a license are rare. Not many people hire rock bands or hip hop acts for weddings, and live music clubs in Tashkent are scarce—as are fans who could afford to pay expensive ticket prices. In addition, the record market runs mostly on piracy, and mediated forms of distribution for alternative music are also problematic. Most radio stations play Uzbek *estrada* and other Asian or Arab pop music, and those whose programs include rock and rap have almost exclusively Western and Russian bands on their playlists.

Important events for promoting alternative music in Uzbekistan are festivals. While some of them focus just on music produced within the country, others include foreign bands in their lineup, mostly from neighboring states. The British Council in Tashkent was influential in organizing two editions of their festival of alternative music, "Creating Legends," in 2004 and 2006. Recently the rock scene in particular has been active in this respect, establishing, among others, the Uz-Fest, Iosis Fest, and the Ilkhom Rock Fest. The existence of these events should not distract from the fact, however, that activities in the field of alternative music are often obstructed by state authorities by means ranging from verbal criticism to physical force.

Top: Young *estrada* performers await their turn to perform at a wedding.

Above: A rock band performs at a Tashkent nightclub as part of the 2008 Rock Fest.

WATCH **Example 33.9.** "10 grammov LSD" (10 grams of LSD), performed by Slyozy Solntsa (Tears of the sun), music and lyrics by Nikita Makarenko, arrangement by Slyozy Solntsa. 2010. A link to this example is available on the companion website.

Slyozy Solntsa calls itself a "funky rock-group from Tashkent." Founded in 2002 and featuring a lineup of six, Slyozy Solntsa is a prominent act in the Tashkent rock scene and also active in forging links with rock bands from other Central Asian states.

In order to understand the song "10 Grammov LSD," you might need some information about its context: It refers to the demolition and lavish construction works in Tashkent that have considerably altered the city's appearance and outlook in the years since independence. Part of the re-shaping of the urban landscape has involved cutting down old plane trees, in whose place small fir trees were planted.

Ya bredu plyvu v bredu kuda-to	I'm wandering and drifting in delirium somewhere.
Ulits i farvatera ne uznayu	I don't recognize the streets and waterways.
Vot stoit ogromnyĭ ėkskavator	There's a huge excavator
Chërnuyu vypustil struyu	That's emitting black smoke.
Mozhet byt' ėto kit? A mozhet byt' os'minog?	Maybe it's a whale? Or maybe an octopus?
Ya begu begu begu so vsekh nog	I'm running, running at full speed.
Ya begu begu begu so vsekh nog	I'm running, running at full speed.
Eli, eli smotryu na nikh i grushchu	Fir trees, fir trees—I look at them and become sad.
Gde moi lokhmatye chinary?	Where are my bushy plane trees?
Ya pod ëlkoĭ iakor' ne spushu	I won't drop anchor under a fir tree,
Pod neyu ne budu igrat' na gitare	I won't play the guitar under it.
El'–neudachnaya gavan' nashemu korablyu	Fir trees are an unfavorable harbor for our ship.
Vsplyvayut prizraki goroda, kotorogo ya lyublyu	Emerging are the ghosts of the city that I love,
Goroda, kotorogo ya lyublyu	Of the city that I love.
Esli by ya byla ėkstrasensom	If I were a spirit medium
Ya ekskavatory zaslala by na Mars	I would send the excavator to Mars.
Tam vodu ishchut svetila progressa	There, luminaries of progress search for water.

Tam tozhe tsarit kopatel'nyi fars	There, the farce of excavation also reigns.
Eto pustaya bor'ba, no ya znayu ver-noe sredstvo	It is a futile fight, but I know the right means
Chtoby vyzvat' prizrakov goroda svoego detstva	To call forth the ghosts of the city of my childhood.
Lish' 10 grammov, 10 grammov LSD	Only 10 grams of LSD, 10 grams of LSD
Vernut na mesto zhizni ostrova	Will bring back islands of life.
Na podokonnike –trava	There's weed on the windowsill[5]
A pod oknom bratva iz ROVD	And under the window are the brothers from the ROVD.[6]
Lish' 10 grammov, 10 grammov LSD	Only 10 grams of LSD, 10 grams of LSD
Vernut na mesto zhizni ostrova	Will bring back islands of life.
I snitsya snitsya snitsya nam trava	And we dream and dream about weed.
A inogda rebyata iz ROVD	And sometimes about the brothers from the ROVD.
Ėto udachnaya gavan' nashemu korablyu	This is a safe harbor for our ship.
Vsplyvayut prizraki goroda, kotorogo ya lyublyu	Emerging are the ghosts of the city that I love,
Goroda, kotorogo ya lyublyu	Of the city that I love.

STUDY QUESTIONS

1. Do you know rock bands from your own music culture? Describe the music, lyrics, and performance of Slyozy Solntsa and compare them with other rock bands you know.

2. What makes Slyozy Solntsa "alternative" in the Uzbek context? How would you describe their attitude?

3. Are there also musical styles that are considered "alternative" in your culture? Which ones?

4. What are their characteristics, and how does their way of "being alternative" compare to the Uzbek concept of "being alternative"?

NOTES

1. *Chaykhanchik:* person who runs a teahouse.

2. *Vostok:* "the East" is the more general translation; the word is also used to denote "the Orient."

3. *Aksakal:* "the white bearded"; an old man.

4. Alpamysh is the hero of an oral epic known among many Turkic peoples. The fact that his name appears in the plural here (Alpamysh-lar) does not mean that the poet who wrote the lyrics wants to refer to several Alpamyshs. To pluralize a name is a standard way in Uzbek to express respect toward a person.

5. *Trava:* "grass"; here: marijuana.

6. ROVD (Rayonnyi Otdel' Vnutrennykh Del): lit. District Department of Internal Affairs, a district police station. For many Uzbeks ROVDs are emblematic habitats of lawlessness and corruption. "Brothers from the ROVD" is an ironically polite form for saying something like "goddamn cops."

Chapter 34

Innovation in Tradition

SOME EXAMPLES FROM MUSIC AND THEATER IN UZBEKISTAN

Aleksandr Djumaev

CENTRAL ASIA'S SOUNDSCAPE IN THE 1990S: THE RISE OF ECLECTICISM

In the early 1990s, during the so-called transition period that followed the breakup of the Soviet Union, Central Asia's soundscape was enriched by an eclectic variety of cultural influences both Western and Eastern: Soviet *estrada,* new Russian hits, local pop, American jazz and rap, traditional "national" folk and classical music, Russian and European classics, and other kinds of music from around the world. Musical styles and repertoires that at first glance seemed wholly incompatible not only coexisted in the same social space but were melded into a variety of new forms of musical fusion by composers, performers, and arrangers. These fusion forms drew on sound sources both familiar and exotic to the ears of most Central Asians. Sonic exotica included not only various forms of contemporary music but also traditional music—the colorful cacophony of avant-garde composers as well as the subtle sonic arabesques of Islamic sacred chant, which, during the Soviet era, were all but absent from Central Asia's soundscape.

The musical avant-garde first emerged in Uzbekistan as a result of international festivals of contemporary music held in the country. These festivals aimed to expose audiences in the post-Soviet era—primarily professional performers and composers as well as students in music schools—to styles of contemporary music that were all but unknown to them. Most such music was imported from Europe and the United States and complemented the more familiar music of Russian composers. Audience response varied, depending on the age and professional focus of the listener: young people with an interest in arts enthusiastically welcomed it; innovative composers, regardless of their age, listened attentively, yet with certain reservations ("well, it's interesting, but . . ."). For most of Uzbekistan's conservative-minded listeners, however, contemporary music appeared strange and impenetrable. Nonetheless, it stimulated musical thinking and helped musicians in Uzbekistan understand their own place on the world musical stage.

By comparison with the sounds of the avant-garde, the "new" sounds of sacred music and chant rooted in Islamic tradition were much more readily embraced by listeners in Uzbekistan. Welcomed as the "forgotten tradition of ancestors," these sounds were imbued with a symbolic importance that contributed to an unofficial mass revival of pre-Soviet customs and traditions. Many contemporary painters, composers, theater directors, poets, and writers in Central Asia understood intuitively that Islamic spiritual and artistic heritage represented a vast, unexplored artistic resource with a huge potential for artistic reinterpretation and innovation.

The striking contrasts among the many different kinds of sound and music that comprised Uzbekistan's soundscape in the 1990s were readily apparent to listeners, yet at the time, even professional music and art critics had difficulty making sense of the situation intellectually. Indeed, they had plenty of other issues to think about. Together with the breakup of the USSR, norms and aesthetic concepts intrinsic to Soviet culture also ruptured. Ideological and artistic censorship weakened, and artists were no longer required to observe Soviet aesthetic principles of style, content, and form in their works. As these Soviet-inspired aesthetic principles withered, new languages of artistic expression proliferated. For decades, Soviet cultural politics had supported artistic work that consciously synthesized Eastern and Western artistic systems. Suddenly, the "problem" of East-West artistic synthesis that had been a central focus of Russian and Soviet theoretical thought in music and musical aesthetics was summarily resolved by musical practice itself, without any need for theoretical discourse or directives.

The expansion and increasing diversity of Uzbekistan's soundscape affected traditional music as well. Like other musical styles and repertoires, traditional music had to adapt to the omnivorous taste of audiences and, in particular, to the taste of a younger generation whose immersion in the world of global audio and video accessed through the Internet distanced them from canonical forms and performance styles of traditional music. At the same time, alienation from canonical representations of tradition nourished an openness to new forms of artistic collaboration. Indeed, the "socio-acoustic" environment of Uzbekistan in the 1990s, with its blend of openness and permissiveness, was highly conducive to artistic experimentalism. An early model of such experimentalism is the music of Tashkent-born composer Dmitri Yanov-Yanovsky.

Yanov-Yanovsky composed prolifically in many different musical styles and genres, among them, film soundtracks. His 1996 soundtrack for the documentary film *The End of an Era: Tashkent*, directed by Mark Weil traces the clash of Eastern

Dmitri Yanov-Yanovsky.
Photo by Alexander Shepelin.

and Western cultures in the multicultural megalopolis of Tashkent, from their initial collision and confrontation in the time of the Russian Empire to their eventual integration and unification in the Soviet era, to the tragic collapse of this Central Asian "Babylon" in the post-Soviet era of independence. From the film's very first scenes, Yanov-Yanovsky's music immerses viewers in the inexpressible clash of two different cultural worlds. The daily routine of readying a mosque for worshippers—covering the floor with carpets and rugs—is accompanied by the episodic convergence and divergence of electronic sonorities with the sound of the Call to Prayer (*adhān*) being chanted in the distance. The effect is as unexpected as it is mesmerizing, and the episode instantly gains a symbolic meaning in the film—as if summing up the entire message of the documentary. Excerpt 34.1 is an excerpt from Yanov-Yanovsky's soundtrack.

WATCH **Example 34.1.** Excerpts from *The End of an Era: Tashkent,* directed by Mark Weil. Soundtrack composed by Dmitri Yanov-Yanovsky. Video courtesy of the composer.

PIONEERS OF ARTISTIC EXPERIMENTALISM

Theater was the first artistic domain to react to the social changes of the post-Soviet era. In a similar way, theater had served as a bellwether of social change in the 1920s and 1950s, when it became an arena for experiments that blended traditional forms and styles of music—including classical vocal and instrumental repertoire—with the principles of new theatrical dramaturgy. At the end of perestroika, in the early 1990s, it was theater again where bold innovation and experimentation took place.

Studio theaters with an experimental focus appeared across Central Asia. Examples include the Avara (Vagrant) Theater in Turkmenistan, where the peripatetic theater director Ovlyakuli Hojakuli began his career; the Eski Masjid (Old Mosque) theater-studio in the city of Karshi in Uzbekistan; and the experimental theater-studio Ilhom (Inspiration) in Tashkent, directed by Mark Weil. Among these, it was the Ilhom Theater that put the most emphasis on the experimental use of live music. In Bishkek, Kyrgyzstan, Kyrgyz director Nurlan Asanbekov created his own space for theatrical and musical experimentalism based on lost archetypes of traditional life depicted in the rich Kyrgyz legacy of oral epics. All of these theaters and directors incorporated a broad range of traditional expressive culture into their productions, including different kinds of local folk and classical music, Sufi rituals, and archaic, shamanistic ceremonial practices. By removing these traditions from their original functional setting and presenting them in an aesthetically refined form on a theatrical stage, the directors aimed to expose and amplify their artistic qualities and sensibility.

Theater scholars and professionals acknowledge Farroukh Qasimov (1948–2010), a well-known theater director from Tajikistan, as the founder of this new artistic and aesthetic trend in Central Asia. In 1990, Qasimov directed the production *Lost Joseph Will Return to Canaan* (Yusufi gumgashta boz oyad ba Kan'on) in Dushanbe. In this production, as well as in *Sheikh San'on* (1996), the director shares the results of his immersion in Sufi philosophy, aesthetics, and musical expression, and suggests that new aesthetic principles be applied to interpretations of the spiritual and artistic legacy of the East. Sufi poetry as well as traditional music, dance, and the Sufi ritual of *zikr* (remembrance of God) are fully present on stage, and have a strong emotional and aesthetic impact on the audience. Qasimov's theater provided a brilliant example for other theatrical experimentalists in Central Asia of how cultural heritage can be reinterpreted and recast within the frame of contemporary languages of art. In the mid-1990s, Qasimov brought his theater to Uzbekistan, staging *The Lost Joseph* in Tashkent and *Sheikh San'on* in Karshi to a strong critical reception.

THE MUSICAL AND THEATRICAL INNOVATIONS OF OVLYAKULI HOJAKULI

Theater director Ovlyakuli Hojakuli.
Photo by Galina Vinogradova.

The most successful and faithful follower of the artistic path pioneered by Farroukh Qasimov is the much-acclaimed theater director Ovlyakuli Hojakuli (Hodjakuliev) (b. 1959). A core principle of Hojakuli's creative method is the appropriation of older forms of expressive culture and their transformation into new forms of artistic representation. For Hojakuli, a music-lover, the "old" includes classical music (*maqoms*), folk melodies, Islamic and Sufi rituals and chants, and other forms of traditional cultural expression. In the process of assimilating traditional music into his work, he progressed from the concept of "music in theater" to the idea of "theater in music." Accordingly, in productions such as *Cain and Abel, The Mystery of a Chinese Woman,* and *Dance of the Heavens,* music plays a role no less important than movement or speech. Eventually, Hojakuli completely separated music from dramatic plot and action, and presented it as a performance art whose aesthetic power emanates from its own kinetic and visual energy. This is the approach to music and movement that reached maturity in Hojakuli's production "Mavrigi," a contemporary take on traditional Bukharan wedding entertainment, and "Rapshee," which fused the guttural vocal style of epic singers with rap music.

Hojakuli's first experience with the reinterpretation of traditional music was in his production of *Cain and Abel* (2000). In this production as well as in the two that followed—*The Mystery of a Chinese Woman* and *Dance of the Heavens* (Raksu Samo), music served as a dynamic element of the show's dramaturgy.[1]

Dance of the Heavens (2002), based on Alisher Navo'i's poem, "Seven Planets," has two subtitles that help clarify its meaning—one in Uzbek, "*Sufiyona*"

(Sufi), and the other in Russian, "*Nebesnyi Tanets*" (Heavenly dance). The performance includes an artistic reconstruction of a Sufi *zikr* infused with shamanistic elements. Performed as a kind of ritualized music theater, the stylized *zikr* competes with the dramatic plot and becomes a "performance within a performance" while remaining subordinate to the work as a whole. *Dance of the Heavens* mesmerizes audiences with its ecstatic frame drum rhythms. The nuances of these rhythmic patterns, which range from passionate and erotic to mysterious and spiritually elevated, are perhaps the most active musical element in the work. Hojakuli employed this same mastery of frame drum language in later works, in particular, *Mavrigi*.

Hojakuli's 2005 production of *Conference of the Birds* at the Uzbek National Academic Drama Theater represented the culmination of the first major period in his work, which he called "music in theater." Characteristically for Hojakuli, the piece is subtitled "A theatrical version of Sufi chants in the style and rhythm of classical *maqom*s." *Conference of the Birds* incorporates extensive dance and movement, and features traditional vocal music sung by professional traditional singers (in the show, their characters are named First Hafiz and Second Hafiz).

In 2006, Hojakuli carried out his first large-scale experiment in fusing two radically different kinds of performing arts: rap music and the traditional oral poetry performed by singer-reciters called *bakhshi* (thus "Rapshee"). Where most listeners and critics perceived the forms as diametrical opposites, Hojakuli, drawing on a keen and quirky artistic intuition, found points of contact. In the eclectic cultural

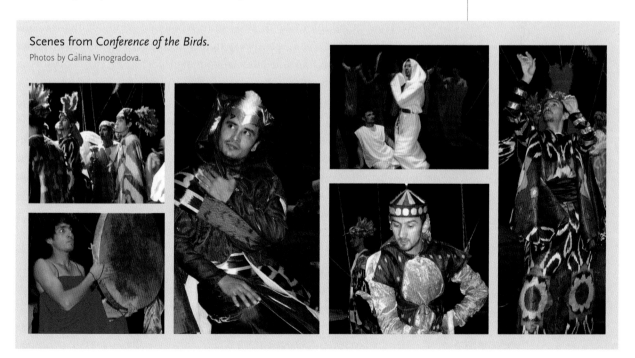

Scenes from *Conference of the Birds*.
Photos by Galina Vinogradova.

conditions of turn-of-the-century Uzbekistan, these two artistic traditions had coexisted but never intersected. Fusing them together, Hojakuli created a unique form of artistic dialogue filled with vigorous musical improvisation and a variety of stylistic intersections. The intersection at the center of Hojakuli's fusion arose from his realization that rap and *bakhshi* music share a similar declamatory style of oral recitative. Moreover, both rap and *bakhshi* music embrace a kind of "anarchy" in which stylistic norms can be challenged and overturned. The dance and movement in *Rapshee* also drew on similarities between the virtuosic physical movements and gestural language of traditional dance from Khorezm and the energetic body language characteristic of rap performers. In the course of a performance of *Rapshee,* both performers and audiences may discover more parallels between rap and *bakhshi* music—parallels that lend themselves to improvisational elaboration and development by the performers. Hojakuli's *Rapshee* suggests the potential of artistic fusion projects not only to attract young people to traditional music but to increase tolerance for other forms of art and culture and build cross-cultural understanding. Unfortunately, the challenging logistics of producing *Rapshee,* with its large and multicultural cast, made it impossible to sustain as a regular part of a theatrical repertoire. Created as an experiment in organized improvisation, it continues to live in mediated form, as a DVD produced by the Swiss Agency for Development and Cooperation. In the future, the director hopes to produce and further develop *Rapshee* in other venues.

For Hojakuli, the process of "combining the uncombinable" is the most vital part of his work. "First we worked on each component separately," the director recounted, "but the most exciting part was when we got together, looked in one another's eyes, and realized what we were doing. That was the real beginning. The moment when fusion actually happens is amazing. At first the participants either resist or don't understand, but eventually they get it, and this becomes a thrilling moment of discovery. Then they come up with new ideas and desires, they feel inspired, and things move ahead fairly quickly. This process is what is key. The concert itself is just an opportunity to share our work and see whether it has an effect. From the feedback we got after the concerts in Tashkent and Navoi, I can say that yes, it did work, maybe even better than we expected. The audiences responded wonderfully, with great excitement."[2]

WATCH **Example 34.2.** Excerpt of *Rapshee* concert. From DVD produced by the Swiss Agency for Development and Cooperation, Arts & Culture Programme Uzbekistan.

The positive response to *Rapshee* inspired Hojakuli to pursue other musical fusion experiments. In April 2009, in the main concert hall of Uzbekistan's national conservatory—a prestigious venue that reflected Hojakuli's high artistic status—the director presented his next innovative project, a multimedia music-video composition called *Jyrau-Rock: 21st Century.* For *Jyrau-Rock,* Hojakuli collaborated with Tashkent composer and conductor Artyom Kim. As in *Rapshee,* Hojakuli brought together two groups of musicians representing different musical worlds—the world of rock and the world of traditional oral poetry performed by bards called *jyrau* or *baqsy.* Hojakuli's *jyrau*s and *baqsy*s came from Karakalpakstan, an arid region in the northwest of Uzbekistan whose cultural traditions reflect the Karakalpaks' nomadic origins. The video component of *Jyrau-Rock* is projected on a large screen placed on the stage, and music and video become an organic whole. In the video, archival film footage depicting Karakalpak cultural traditions is interspersed with contemporary footage that chronicles the death of the Aral Sea, which borders Karakalpakstan, and whose desiccation became an environmental catastrophe for the region in the late twentieth century. The multimedia element represented by video montage playing as a backdrop against the theatrically presented melding of the two groups of musicians exemplifies what Hojakuli meant by "theater in music."

A rehearsal for *Jyrau-Rock: 21st Century.*

Another example of Hojakuli's innovative "theater in music" is his song and dance cycle *Mavrigi,* which premiered in Tashkent in 2007. In *Mavrigi,* Hojakuli resituated a traditional genre of song and dance performance by presenting it in a contemporary theatrical context.

In its traditional form, *mavrigi* is a song and dance cycle closely associated with the city of Bukhara that is performed by an ensemble of male singers, called *mavrigikhon*s, who accompany themselves on frame drums (*doira*s). *Mavrigi* means "from Merv"—the oasis city (now called Mary) in present-day Turkmenistan that was once a principal cultural center of Khorasan. Parts of the *mavrigi,* in particular the opening section, "Shahd," preserve a vocal style that local listeners readily identify as Persian.

An abbreviated version of a "Shahd" is presented in Example 34.3, in a performance by Mahdi Ibadov (1932–2006) and his ensemble. Following the opening a cappella section, with the "Persian" sound of its nasalized vibrato, high vocal tessitura (vocal register), and free rhythm, "Shahd" progresses to a series of *bukharchas*—Bukharan folk songs sung in the local Bukharan dialect of Persian-Tajik.

Example 34.3. "Shahd," performed by Mahdi Ibadov and his ensemble. Recorded by Theodore Levin and Otanazar Matyakubov. From *Bukhara: Musical Crossroads of Asia* (SFR, 1991), track 2.

"Shahd" is the first of four or five distinct and contrasting musical sections in *mavrigi*. A performance of *mavrigi* builds slowly, from the improvised, contemplative introduction to the furious tempo and pulsating rhythms of the conclusion.

In its original social context, *mavrigi* was usually performed as a part of life-cycle events such as weddings and other festivities. During the late Soviet era, *mavrigi*s were transformed into folklore performed in concerts of "national cultural heritage" by professional singers and folk ensembles. Yet even as folklore, performances of *mavrigi* remained faithful to their original musical structure and performance style.

Hojakuli and his artistic team radically changed both the concept and the structure of the traditional *mavrigi* cycle as they transformed it into contemporary musical theater. They collapsed the traditional sequence of four or five sections into three sections ("Shahd," "Taraqqiyot," and "Pirovard") and lengthened each of these through the addition of numerous traditional Bukharan songs. In this new format, a *mavrigi* that originally lasted twenty to thirty minutes now filled an entire concert program.

Hojakuli's concert version preserves original features of *mavrigi* and other kinds of Bukharan folk music, such as call-and-response between soloist and chorus, and the presence of interpolated narrative episodes. It also adds new features such as metrically free singing with an ostinato-like choral performance of folk songs in the background. The aesthetic quality of the sound is the main focus. Contrasting combinations of vocal timbres are complemented by the rich sound palette of the *doira* with its low, dark colors—all but forgotten in contemporary concert music. The dance part, choreographed by Viloyat Akilova, first appears in the "Shahd" and accompanies the vocal part throughout the entire concert. Indeed, it develops in parallel to the music and poetry, and significantly increases the sensuality of traditional Bukharan female dance. Its choreography is modified in accordance with Hojakuli's overall concept, so that dance becomes music in motion—a visual representation of music that reveals and highlights the idea of the passionate yet impossible love between the divine "him" and earthly "her" that is such a ubiquitous and evocative image in Sufi poetry.

Hojakuli's *Mavrigi* offers an aesthetically refined and nuanced depiction of humanity through the prism of traditional Central Asian social life and spirituality: love and humor (the latter illustrated, for example, by the popular Bukharan song "Murghak" [Hen]); Sufi motifs represented by the exclamations "Ha," "Hu,"

"Yo haqq" (references to God that typically occur during the performance of *zikr*); and contemplative praise hymns recited in a Qur'anic style. Heavenly and earthly images merge in the music to create a large-scale artistic landscape of Bukhara— multidimensional and multifaceted, spiritually rich and culturally nuanced. The meaning and message of Hojakuli's *Mavrigi* can perhaps be best conveyed by an aphorism that is popular in Bukhara: "*Goh Khudoyu rasul, goh nagmayu usul*" (Once for God and the Prophet, once for music and dance—or to paraphrase, "Be pious, but enjoy life!").

WATCH **Example 34.4.** Excerpt from a performance of Ovlyakuli Hojakuli's *Mavrigi*. From DVD produced by the Swiss Agency for Development and Cooperation, Arts & Culture Programme Uzbekistan.

STUDY QUESTIONS

1. In your view, did Ovlyakuli Hojakuli succeed in achieving his goal of creating an artistic fusion between rap and *bakhshi* music? What is the basis for your judgment?

2. What about Hojakuli's *Mavrigi*? In your view, how successful is it as an example of innovation in tradition?

3. Based on your own experience, how do you view "innovation in tradition" as a sphere of artistic activity? Should traditional arts be preserved in a pure form, as a record of the past for the benefit of future generations? Or should traditional arts be available, like any other domain of art or culture, for appropriation, experimentation, and creative recycling by contemporary artists?

4. Ovlyakuli Hojakuli's *Rapshee* project developed from the premise that despite their obvious differences, rap and *bakhshi* music share salient musical and rhetorical characteristics. Can you think of other examples of traditional and contemporary art forms that are linked by similarities of performance style, melodic development, sound production, rhythm, or other characteristics? Can you think of contemporary parallels to Hojakuli's theatricalization of traditional music and dance?

5. Are you familiar with the musical traditions of ethnic minorities in your country or region? How do they interact with mainstream music?

NOTES

1. *Cain and Abel* was staged by actors of the Eski Masjid Theater in Karshi, Uzbekistan, and premiered at Tashkent's Ilhom Theater. It was subsequently presented in cities throughout Uzbekistan. *Cain and Abel* and *Dance of the Heavens* were produced with support from the Arts and Culture Program of the Open Society Institute/Uzbekistan.

2. From Ovlyakuli Hojakuli's comments in the DVD *"Rapshee" Concert* (Tashkent: Arts & Culture Programme Uzbekistan, Swiss Agency for Development and Cooperation).

CHAPTER 35 # Tradition-Based Popular Music in Contemporary Tajikistan

FEDERICO SPINETTI

In Tajikistan, as in other parts of Central Asia, popular music has a highly visible and audible role in cultural life. Learning about popular music is vital to an understanding of collective musical experience and popular culture in contemporary Tajik society. But how should Tajik popular music (*estradai Tojik*) be defined, and how should it be distinguished from music that Tajiks commonly refer to as "traditional" or "folk" (*musiqii sunnatī* or *an'anavī, musiqii khalqī, folklor*)? Although current official culture policy and, to a lesser extent, common discourse maintain a distinction between "popular" and "traditional" music, the many ways in which they intersect and combine in Tajik musical life pose a challenge to conventional musical categories. This chapter provides a few examples of contemporary music that straddles the not-so-clear boundaries between these categories, underscoring the need to understand them as flexible and porous, rather than fixed and impermeable.

From a broad perspective, Tajik popular music can be described as locally produced music that is receptive to transnational popular music idioms, such as rock and its offshoots, electronic dance music, and the prominent use of electric or electrified instruments. Though originating for the most part in the Anglo-American world, these transnational idioms have been locally adopted and reworked by musicians in Tajikistan (and of course in many other countries as well). The process of local appropriation began in the Soviet era and developed through a dialogue with similar practices that were ongoing in Russia and in other parts of the former Soviet Union. During the Soviet era, Tajik musicians had little opportunity for direct contact with the musical worlds of Europe and the United States, but official cultural exchanges between the Soviet Central Asian republics, Afghanistan, and the nations of South Asia, along with radio broadcasts from beyond the borders of the USSR, offered a readily available source for many different kinds of popular music. Since the breakup of the Soviet Union, popular music has also flowed into Tajikistan from Iran, Turkey, and the Arab world. These transnational popular music influences span a broad range of styles and idioms. Some of them make little or no reference to local musical traditions, while others actively incorporate traditional instruments, genres, or song lyrics, and represent a creative continuity of traditional sensibilities expressed in contemporary musical styles.

Popular music and traditional music in Tajikistan share still another important attribute: a long-standing reliance on technological mediation—for example, recordings, radio, television, film—as a form of dissemination. Conventional views of "traditional music" often emphasize oral transmission and face-to-face master-disciple (*ustod-shogird*) pedagogy as defining characteristics, in contrast to the central role of technological mediation in the transmission of popular music. Indeed, technological mediation was integral to the development of Tajik popular music in the Soviet era, with its vast state-sponsored entertainment industry consisting of radio and television stations, the world's largest record company (Melodiya), prolific local film studios, and concert and festival programming that reached the most remote regions of the country. But at the behest of Soviet culture policy, this entertainment industry also devoted considerable resources to the dissemination of traditional music. Technological mediation of both popular and traditional music has continued to play a major role in post-Soviet Tajikistan through a burgeoning local independent recording industry. Conversely, oral transmission has facilitated the dissemination not only of traditional music but of popular music in the form of live performances at community social events. Both kinds of music are often performed on festive occasions such as wedding parties and other community or family celebrations (*toy*), and these grassroots contexts provide the primary venue for forging connections between popular and traditional idioms.

The important role of popular music in community life, especially at *toy*s, is evident not only in urban settings but also in rural ones. Urban-based professional

A record shop in Dushanbe.
Photo by Stefano Triulzi.

Both traditional and popular music are performed at weddings and other community and family celebrations (*toy*).
Photo by Stefano Triulzi.

musicians are frequently hired at rural *toy*s, leading to a musical cross-fertilization between urban and rural locales. While popular music is predominantly the product of urban centers—especially Dushanbe, Tajikistan's capital—many of its exponents are migrants from the periphery who often infuse their music with distinctive regional features. At the same time, these urban-based musicians serve as a stimulus to rural musical life and have a considerable influence on rural performers, both professional and amateur (for purposes of this discussion, "professional" refers to musicians who earn their livelihood primarily from performing music, whereas "amateurs," though they may be excellent musicians, earn their livelihood primarily by other means). This situation contributes in no small part to the cultural and social significance of popular music in Tajikistan, especially in relation to identity formation. For example, it is not uncommon for musicians and audiences alike to associate different aesthetic preferences in popular music with different regional affiliations, in this way contributing to politically and socially significant discourses concerning regional or ethnic identity that are not dissimilar to those surrounding traditional music.

While popular music emerged in Soviet Tajikistan with the support and under the supervision of state institutions and media, and only gradually penetrated unofficial performance contexts, such as wedding parties, its current proliferation is very much a post-Soviet phenomenon. The driving force of this proliferation is the exponential growth of a local private recording industry of audiocassettes and, lately, VCDs (Video CDs), DVDs, and other digital media, as well as the central role of *toy*s in the activities of most professional musicians. Drastic changes in the economy of music since the end of the Soviet Union have been influential factors in these developments. Strong centralized support for the arts in the Soviet Union made commercial viability a marginal concern for professional musicians, whether their focus was traditional music, Western classical music, or popular music. In the post-Soviet era, however, state support for the arts is typically uneven and more narrowly focused, while non-governmental and privately funded cultural initiatives are expanding. In these conditions, the viability of music professionalism has come to depend largely on self-management in a marketplace where commercial projects, private patronage, and bookings for *toy* performances represent the primary sources of income for musicians.

In this new scenario, repertoires that synthesize elements of popular and traditional music offer the most reliable option for most musicians to participate actively and profitably in the *toy* circuit, the recording industry, or both. By contrast, music that lies firmly in the domain of tradition offers limited income-generating opportunities within Tajikistan itself (performers of traditional music who represent Tajik culture at state occasions are often expected to provide their services free of charge). Ironically, the largest paying audience for Tajik traditional music is beyond Tajikistan's borders, in the international marketplace for "world music." This marketplace, however, is no substitute for the vastly diminished support for traditional arts that was a core element of Soviet culture policy. As a consequence, musicians who perform traditional music have increasingly gravitated towards the domain of popular music. Their dual proficiency and expertise have facilitated a rich variety of artistic fusions created from an amalgam of local and imported musical instruments, and traditional and popular musical styles.

THREE SONGS

As a first example of tradition-based popular music, I discuss a song by Gulchehra Sodiqova titled "Zi durī," which was published in Tajikistan in 2005 (example 35.1). Gulchehra has long been a major exponent of traditional music of the Kulob region of southwestern Tajikistan. Over the last decade, in collaboration with her sons, she has developed an electrified repertoire suitable for their performances on the wedding circuits of Dushanbe and Kulob, as well as for studio recordings. "Zi durī" is an example of how traditional tunes and forms can be arranged in a popular music style. The piece introduces elements of harmony, a Western musical concept that does not exist in traditional Tajik music, into a melodic and rhythmic framework that adheres closely to traditional models. The song is arranged for a mixed instrumental ensemble that includes local lutes, percussions, and flute (*dumbra*, Kashgar *rubab, tablak, doira, nay*) along with violin and synthesizer. The lyrics are drawn from both classical and folk poetry, with a *ghazal* by the Persian poet Badruddin Hiloli (1470–1529) featured in the first part of the song. The sequence of melodic phrases in Gulchehra's vocals reflects the rhyme pattern of the

poem, recapturing a correspondence between poetic and musical forms that is customary in musical settings of *ghazal*s, especially in Kulobi regional traditions. Each half-line of poetry is set to one melodic statement in the vocal part. The sequence of rhymed and non-rhymed half-lines is echoed through melodic repetition and contrast, the only exception being the last statement, which serves as a transition to the second part of the piece.

The traditional role of poetry as a vehicle for the propagation of social, religious, and ethical values in Tajik expressive culture is perpetuated

Gulchehra Sodiqova.
Photo by Stefano Triulzi.

in Tajik popular music by the frequent use of poems drawn from the corpus of classical Persian poetry, or from contemporary Tajik authors for whom this corpus serves as an expressive model. As in "Zi durī," a major theme is love, which may interchangeably be interpreted as mundane or devotional, particularly in relation to the mystical theme of longing for the Divine. Although newly composed lyrics that depart from the conventions of classical poetry figure in the repertoire of several Tajik popular music artists, classical poetry continues to be perceived as an indicator of artistic excellence, and its traditional, eminent position in Tajik musical aesthetics permeates the popular music domain.

The piece closes with two folk quatrains on the theme of separation, performed in the typical style of the genre known as *falak* (see chapter 30). Here also the musical vocabulary is strongly receptive to Kulobi traditional idioms, complemented by a popular music sonic texture and by quotations of a symphonic reworking of *falak* by Tajik composer Abdufattoh Odinaev that was first performed in 1973 and remains in circulation today.

LISTEN

Example 35.1. "Zi durī" (Far away), performed by Gulchehra Sodiqova, based on a *ghazal* by Badruddin Hiloli (1470–1529).

	Rhyme	Melody Type
Zi durī to ba kay moro chunin mahjur medorī	X	A
Agar nazdi tu meoyam tu khudro dur medorī.	X	A
Tabibi man tuī ammo maro bemor mekhohī	—	B
Davoi man tuī ammo maro ranjur medorī.	X	A
Ba nuri khud shabe ravshan nakardī majlisi moro	—	C
Charoghi oshnoīro charo be nur medorī.	X	A
Magar kayfiyati ranji khumor ey jon namedonī	—	B
Ki moro be sharobi lahmi khud makhmur medorī.	X	A
Ba bazmi vasl hozir mekunī arbobi khashmatro	—	C
Hamin miskin Hiloliro zi khud mahjur medorī.	X	D

How long will you keep me far away from you?
If I come close to you, you stay away from me.
You are my healer, but you want me to be ill
You are my remedy, but you make me suffer.
You have not turned the night into daylight for us to meet
Why do you keep our friendship in the dark?
Could it be that you do not know the pain of longing, my love,
Since you inebriate me without the sweet wine of your presence?
You exclude me from the banquet of reunion
And keep this poor Hiloli far away from you.

FALAK QUATRAINS

[e] Shinam shinam [e] az tu shirin yod oyad
[e] Ohe mekasham az falak dod oyad [jon]
[e] Rozi dilma [e] agar ba sangho guyam [joni]
[e] Sang az tagi daryo ba faryod oyad [e]

I sit for hours, the sweet memory of you comes to me
I sigh and a cry for help comes from the sky
If I reveal the secrets of my heart to the rocks
From the riverbed the rocks will answer my call.

[e] Shinam ba balandiho turo yod kunam [e]
[e] Oyam ba guzargohi tu faryod kunam [jon]
[e] Faryod kunam kase javobam nadihad [joni]
[e] Umram ba tamoshoi tu bar bod kunam [e]

I sit on the heights and think of you
I come where you used to pass and I call you
I call out and if no one answers
I shall give my life away for you.

STUDY QUESTIONS

1. What influences from contemporary pop styles and idioms do you hear in the performance of "Zi Durī"?

2. How does the sound of the music change at the point where the *falak* quatrains begin?

3. How successful is "Zi Durī" as a work of tradition-based popular music?

Another musician from Kulob is Manija Davlatova, a young singer now based in Dushanbe, who enjoys celebrity in the Tajik popular music scene and is active in the recording industry as well as on the wedding circuit in Dushanbe and Kulob. Compared with Gulchehra Sodiqova, her repertoire places less emphasis on traditional material, and combines traditional elements with a wider range of musical influences.

Manija Davlatova's performance style is illustrated by the song "To hastam," composed by another prominent popular music artist, D. Zuhuriyon, and recorded by Manija in 2002 (example 35.2). Two features of this song represent continuity with traditional practice: one is the use of a seven-beat rhythm, which is particularly common in the traditional music of southern Tajikistan and has been widely adopted in Tajik popular music; the second is the use of classical poetry—specifically,

Manija Davlatova.
Photo by Stefano Triulzi.

a *ghazal* by the renowned contemporary Tajik poet, Loiq Sherali. Here too the sequence of melodic lines mirrors the rhyme structure of the poem. In the first section of the song, with the exception of the first half-line, rhymed half-lines are set to the same melody (melody B in the transcription in example 35.2). In the remainder of the song, melodic lines shift back and forth between higher and lower vocal registers. Throughout the song, however, the recurrence of the rhyme is marked by repetition of the melody (melody [E] in the transcription).

Alongside these elements of local tradition, the influence of Indian film music reverberates in "To hastam" through the use of a sitar and the string and choral arrangements that undergird the song. Iranian popular music has also had a considerable influence on Manija's vocal style, especially singer Leilā Foruhar, one of Manija's major sources of inspiration. Manija Davlatova's music reflects the appeal of Indian, Iranian, and Afghan popular music to Tajik audiences. At the same time, her music is popular across the Tajik border, in Afghanistan, where many people speak Dari, the local version of Persian. Through Manija's songs, listeners throughout the Persian-speaking world are brought together into a transnational music community. Meanwhile, within Tajikistan, Manija's cosmopolitanism allows her music to cross regional boundaries that are both culturally and politically significant. And in Dushanbe, the varied cultural influences in her music resonate with urban audiences who are themselves from diverse cultural and geographic backgrounds. Nonetheless, some listeners from Kulob, Manija's birthplace, persist in hearing her music as "Kulobi," and it is Kulobi audiences that continue to form the majority of her patrons on the *toy* circuit.

LISTEN

Example 35.2. "To hastam" (As long as I live), Manija Davlatova, based on a *ghazal* by Loiq Sherali.

	Rhyme	Melody Type
Section 1		
To hastam bud to hastī hamroz-i tu khoham bud	X	A
To soz-i dame doram damsoz-i tu khoham bud.	X	B
Andar dil-i purshūram to nash'ai darde hast	—	C
Maftun-i tabu sūzi ovoz-i tu khoham bud.	X	B

Section 2

Chun jona baroi tan shoista-i jonon ast	—	D
To jon-u jahon doram jonboz-i tu khoham bud.	X	E
Bar qasd-i hama qahr-u shūr-u shar-i taqdiram	—	F
Qurbon-i yak-i mo-yu yak noz-i tu khoham bud.	X	E

[Section 1 repeats]

Section 3

To nola kunad jonam to shikva kunad rūhat	—	D
Bo bol-u par-i she'ram parvoz-i tu khoham bud	X	E
Orom namejuyam anjom namekhoham	—	F
To okhir-i umr-i did oghoz-i tu khoham bud	X	E

Section 1

As long as you and I live, I will be your intimate friend
As long as I breathe, I will accompany you.
As long as joy and pain dwell in my restless heart
I will be enchanted by your voice, and burn with passion.

Section 2

As long as the body elects the soul as its beloved
As long as my soul is in this world, I will be your devotee.
Against all the fury, the troubles and the bitterness of my destiny
I will surrender myself to our union, and to a single whim of yours.

Section 3

As long as your soul cries and revolts, my dear
I will give you wings with the wings of my poems.
I do not seek rest, I am not waiting for the end
Until I see the end of life, I will be your beginning.

STUDY QUESTIONS

1. How successful is Manija at blending the various cultural influences that she drew on to create her arrangement of "To hastam"?

2. Do you find the style of tradition-based pop represented by Manija's arrangement appealing? Why or why not?

Nobovar Chanorov and
Shams.
Photo by Stefano Triulzi.

A final example of tradition-based popular music is the song "Dunyoi fonī" drawn from the repertoire of singer and musician Nobovar Chanorov and his band, Shams. Originally from the southeastern province of Badakhshan and currently based in Dushanbe, Nobovar and other members of Shams are well versed in Badakhshani traditional music, which they occasionally perform as part of their professional activity at concerts and other initiatives meant to showcase local culture and music, both on national and international stages. Concurrently, they are well placed in the popular music market, continuing the lineage of Badakhshani pop-rock that, since the 1970s, has yielded influential figures such as Daler Nazarov and Muboraksho. Shams exemplifies the way that musicians with multiple musical skills in contemporary Tajikistan play out their creativity and expertise in different musical contexts and balance the needs and interests of different audiences.

In "Dunyoi fonī," instrumentation and music vocabulary are firmly positioned in the popular music sphere, though a few tradition-based features are discernible, especially in the vocal line. The relationship between musical and poetic forms is vague: while each melody corresponds to a poetic half-line, the distribution of melodic repetition and contrast largely disregards the rhyme structure (see example 35.3). However, the piece recaptures traditional aesthetic and cultural sensibilities by employing a poem attributed locally to the mystic Jalal ad-Din Rumi (commonly known in Tajikistan as Shams-i Tabrizi, Shams, or Mavlana). This choice establishes a particularly strong connection with the ritual, spiritual, and musical traditions of Nobovar's religious and regional community, the Shi'a Ismailis of Badakhshan. Indeed, this poem, with its sapiential theme focusing on the transient nature of worldly achievements, is deemed particularly appropriate for a worship context among Tajik Ismailis and, as such, it appears frequently in the Badakhshani devotional performance genre known as *maddoh* (see chapter 28). By virtue of such references to traditional practices, artists like Nobovar may come to be perceived as knowledgeable bearers and upholders of local aesthetic and spiritual values, though their explorations of devotional themes in a popular music format are not always uncontroversial, and play into debates within the Ismaili community about the legitimacy of innovation and modernization in their religious music traditions.

Example 35.3. "Dunyoi fonī" (Transient world), performed by Nobovar Chanorov and Shams, based on a *ghazal* attributed to Jalal ad-Din Rumi.

	Rhyme	Melody Type
Dil ba in dunyo maband dunyo-i fonī bigzarad	X	A
Navbat-i pirī daroyad navjavonī bigzarad.	X	A
Tu ki dorī uzru noz dar jahoni komron	—	A
Uzru nozat bar sar oyad komronī bigzarad.	X	A
Tu ki dorī zūr-i bozu dar jahon ey pahlavon	—	B
Zūr-i bozuyat namonad pahlavonī bigzarad.	X	B
Tu ki dorī bogh-u buston khushsaro bo mamlakat	—	A
Bogh-i tu vayrona gardad boghbonī bigzarad.	X	A
Shams-i Tabrizi buzurgonand biraftand zeri khok	X	A
In hama kore tu donī kordonī bigzarad.	X	A

Do not bind your heart to this world, the transient world shall pass away
Old age shall gain its turn, youth shall pass away.
You who have playful excuses in a joyful world
Your caprices and excuses shall come to an end, joy shall pass away.
You with strength in your arms, in the world you are a hero
Strength in your arms shall not last, heroes shall pass away.
You who have gardens and orchards, prosperous and magnificent
Your garden shall be destroyed, your gardening shall pass away.
Shams-i Tabrizi, great men lie beneath the ground
You know all this, but knowledge shall pass away.

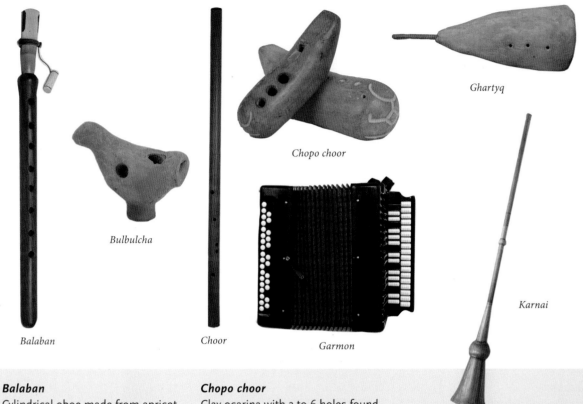

Ghartyq

Chopo choor

Bulbulcha

Karnai

Balaban

Choor

Garmon

Balaban
Cylindrical oboe made from apricot, mulberry, or nut wood played with a large double reed that produces a soft, breathy, and often mournful sound.

Bulbulcha
Tajik name for clay ocarina, played mostly by children, and found in all Tajik regions.

Choor (also *kurai, tsuur*)
End-blown flute made from reed or wood with 4 or 5 holes. Under various names and in various sizes, end-blown flutes—e.g., *tsuur* (Mongolian), *chuur* (Tuvan), *sybyz-ghy* (Kazakh), *kurai* (Bashkir)—are widespread among Inner Asian pastoralists.

Chopo choor
Clay ocarina with 3 to 6 holes found in southern Kyrgyzstan and most commonly played by children.

There is evidence that horse herders used ocarinas as signaling instruments in thick forests, where they would often graze their horses at night.

Garmon (also *saz, syrnai*)
Small accordion played in the Caucasus by female entertainers (*khalfas*) in the Khorezm region of northwest Uzbekistan, and by Kazakhs, who call it 'syrnai.'

Ghartyq
Clay ocarina played by blowing on a detachable single reed inserted into the flue of the instrument; traditionally used by Karakalpak pastoralists.

Karnai (also *karnay*)
Long, straight trumpet consisting of conjoined sections of a cylindrical brass tube ending in a flared bell. Typically played by urban musicians for ceremonial events, weddings, fanfares, and to accompany circus arts.

Saz syrnai

Karnak saz syrnai

Koshnai   Nai   Pamiri nai

Surnai

Sybyzghy

Koshnai

Single-reed wind instrument consisting of two short reed pipes tied together, both of which are typically played in unison.

Nai

Wooden side-blown flute used in many styles of Tajik and Uzbek music, including in ensembles that perform Shashmaqom.

Pamiri *nai*

Wooden fipple flute made from apricot wood with six finger holes and a thumbhole, used particularly for festive occasions.

Saz syrnai

Clay ocarina with four to six holes used by Kazakh and Karakalpak pastoralists.

Surnai (also *surnay, sunay*)

Loud oboe or shawm, traditionally played at weddings, funerals, and other outdoor ceremonies; widespread in folk music traditions of West and Central Asia, southeastern Europe, parts of North Africa, and, as *suona*, in parts of China.

Sybyzghy (see glossary of terms for alternative spellings)

Side-blown or end-blown flute that figures in nomadic musical traditions and can be made from wood, reed, or the wood of mountain bushes as well as from metal.

Üshpelek

Clay whistle traditionally used by Karakalpak pastoralists.

Üshpelek

Afghan rubab

Badakhshani rubab

Balandmaqom

Balandzikom

Afghan *rubab*

Double-chambered lute with 3 main strings (originally made of animal gut, now nylon), 4 frets, 2–3 long drone strings, and up to 15 sympathetic strings (made of copper and steel).

Badakhshani *rubab*

Long-necked partially fretted lute with animal skin covering the lower part of the resonating chamber; 5 main strings and 6 sympathetic strings.

Balandmaqom

Nineteen-stringed lute devised by Sufi poet, astronomer, and musician Muborak Wakhoni (d. 1903) used to accompany the singing of *qasoid-khonī*.

Balandzikom

Local version of the Pamiri *tanbur* used in the Wakhan Valley region of Tajik Badakhshan to accompany performances of *qasoid-khonī* (cf.

long-necked lute depicted in miniature painting of Persian artist Farrukh Beg, dated 1588, reproduced in Bonnie C. Wade, *Imagining Sound*, figure 88; op. cit. chapter 2, n 1).

Dilrabo

Diltar

Dombyra

Dumbrak

Dilrabo

Two-stringed spike fiddle 19–24 inches in length used in Tajik and Afghan Badakhshan, typically to play lyrical melodies. (Cognate with *dilruba*, an Indian bowed lute with four main strings and 19 sympathetic strings.)

Diltar

One-of-a-kind double-necked instrument created by Uyghur musician Abdulla Mäjnun that combines the plucked *tämbur* with the bowed *satar*.

Dombyra (also *dombra*)

A name for various types of fretted, long-necked lutes typically strung with 2 gut or silk strings. The Kazakh *dombyra* is strummed or plucked.

Ivory and ebony inlay at the base of the *diltar*.

The Kalmyk *dombra* has a larger body and produces a louder sound.

Dumbrak (also *dombrak, dombra, dumbra*)

Unfretted two-stringed long-necked lute played in the south of Tajikistan as well as among Tajiks and Uzbeks in northern Afghanistan and adjacent regions of Uzbekistan.

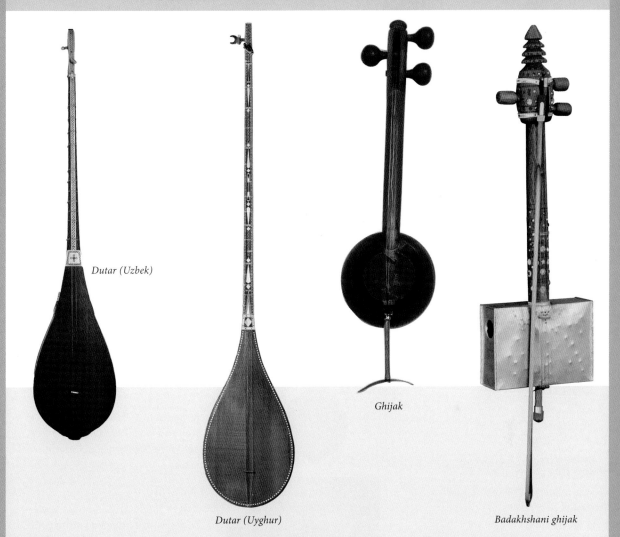

Dutar (Uzbek)

Dutar (Uyghur)

Ghijak

Badakhshani ghijak

Dutar
Designates different kinds of two-stringed long-necked fretted lutes among Uzbeks, Tajiks, Turkmen, Karakalpaks, Uyghurs, and other groups.

Dutar (Uyghur)
The longest of the *dutars*, like all Uyghur lutes, beautifully decorated with settings in horn or bone.

Ghijak (also *Ghirjek*)
A round-bodied spike fiddle with 3 or 4 metal strings and a short, fretless neck used by Uzbeks, Tajiks, Turkmen, and Karakalpaks.

Badakhshani *ghijak*
In Badakhshan, *ghijaks* often use a tin can as a resonator.

Kamancha

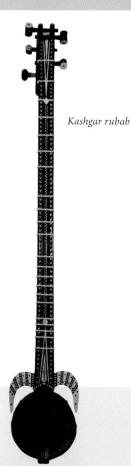

Kashgar rubab

Kyl-kiyak

Kamancha

Spherical spike fiddle with a cylindrical neck fitted with 4 steel strings. The resonating chamber is traditionally covered with catfish skin. To play different strings, performers turn the instrument left or right on its spike instead of changing the angle of the bow.

Kashgar *rubab*

Uzbek appropriation of one of the many regional forms of Uyghur *rawap*, a plucked, long-necked lute with a membrane-covered resonating chamber. The Uzbek version has 5 strings, and fixed frets. In Uzbekistan, the Kashgar *rubab* was

Kyrgyz musician Bakyt Chytyrbaev plays a *kyl-kiyak*.

Photo by Katherine Vincent. Courtesy of Aga Khan Music Initiative.

a mainstay of Soviet-era folk orchestras and is still produced with frets set to the Western equally tempered scale.

Kyl-kiyak

Kyrgyz variant of an upright bowl fiddle, with 2 horsehair strings. Kazakhs call an almost identical instrument *qyl-qobyz*. The deck is usually made from the hide of a camel or a cow, and the body is carved from a single piece of wood, typically apricot. The instrument's repertory is programmatic; that is, melodies narrate stories and often imitate different sounds. In the past, the instrument had a strong connection to shamanism and the recitation of oral poetry.

Komuz

Pamiri rubab

Badakhshani tanbur

Pipa

Komuz
Main folk instrument of the Kyrgyz—a 3-stringed long-necked fretless lute, typically made from apricot wood, nut wood, or juniper. Playing techniques include plucking, strumming, and striking strings with the fingernails, as well as the use of stylized hand and arm gestures, which add an additional narrative component to the *komuz*'s typically programmatic repertory.

Pamiri *rubab*
Unfretted long-necked lute with skin-covered resonating chamber strung with 6 gut or nylon strings.

Pamiri *tanbur*
Long-necked partially fretted lute with animal skin covering the lower part of the resonating chamber; 3 melody strings and 4 or 6 sympathetic strings.

Pipa
Short-necked plucked lute that came to China from Central Asia around the 7th century. It has 4 metal strings and 6 wedge-shaped frets, as well as 26 smaller bamboo frets.

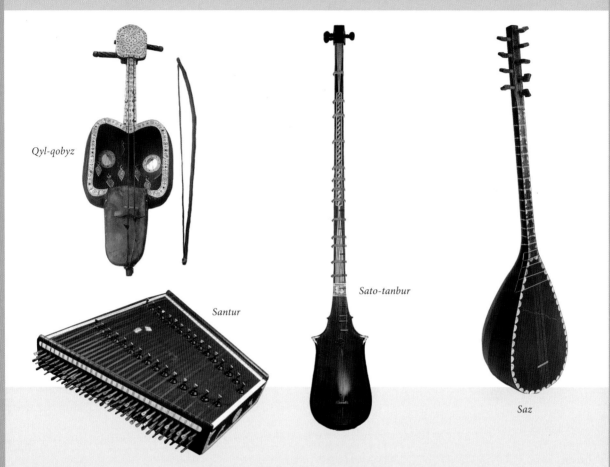

Qyl-qobyz

Santur

Sato-tanbur

Saz

Qobyz (also *qyl-qobyz*)
Two-stringed bowed lute hollowed out from a whole piece of wood, played by Kazakhs and Karakalpaks. Known among Kyrgyz as *kyl-kiyak*.

Santur
Trapezoidal zither whose strings are struck with light wooden mallets. The *santur* has ancient roots in Iranian culture and is also played in Iraq and other parts of the Middle East, as well as in Kashmir. Struck zithers exist in many cultures under a variety of names, and with different numbers of strings configured in a variety of tuning systems. Well-known examples include the American hammer dulcimer, Hungarian *cimbalom*, and Chinese *yangqin*.

Sato-tanbur
Long-necked lute with 5 strings that may be bowed (*sato*) or played with a plectrum (*tanbur*). The top string is fingered to provide the melody while the other strings serve as drones. Used principally by performers of Tajik-Uzbek classical music (*maqom*).

Satar
Uyghur bowed *tanbur*. See also *sato-tanbur*

Saz (also *choghur*)
Long-necked fretted lute with metal strings identified with the *ashiq*s of Turkey and Azerbaijan.

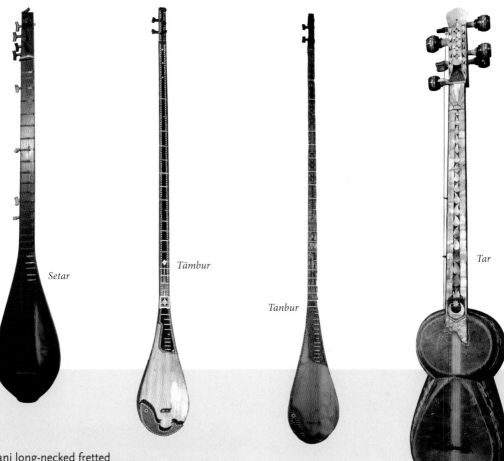

Setar

Tämbur

Tanbur

Tar

Setar

Badakhshani long-necked fretted lute with wood-covered deck, 3 steel melody strings, and a variable number of sympathetic strings that provide a drone background to the melody strings.

Tämbur

Uyghur long-necked plucked lute, similar to Uzbek-Tajik *tanbur*. The Uyghur *tämbur* is probably the longest of all Central Asian lutes, at around 150 cm, with 5 metal strings plucked with a tiny metal pick (*na-khala*) strapped to the index finger.

Tanbur

Long-necked plucked lute with raised frets used in Uzbek-Tajik and Uyghur classical music traditions. The fundamental accompanying instrument for vocal performances of Shash-maqom. One string is plucked, while the others serve as drones.

Tar

Double-chested plucked lute used in urban music from the Caucasus and Iran. In Azerbaijan, the *tar* is widely considered the national instrument. Iranian and Azeri *tar*s are distinguished by number of strings, quantity and position of frets, playing position, and type of plectrum. The skin-like cover of the resonating chamber is traditionally made from the pericardial membrane that englobes a cow heart.

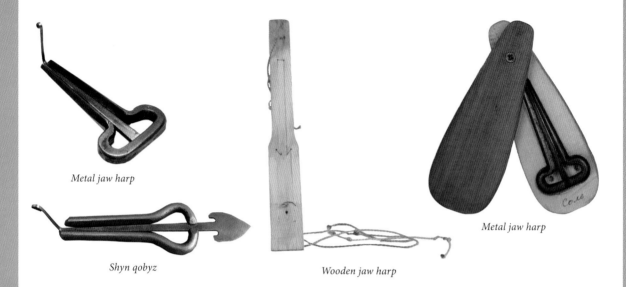

Metal jaw harp

Shyn qobyz

Wooden jaw harp

Metal jaw harp

Matrasul Matyakubov plays the *surnai* with accompanying musicians on *doira* and *qairaq*. Khiva, Uzbekistan, 1994.
Photo by Theodore Levin.

Jaw harp (also *chang kobuz, jygach ooz komuz, shang qobyz, shyn qobyz, temir ooz komuz*)
Called by a variety of local names, jaw harps belong to the traditional instrumentarium of pastoralists throughout Inner Asia. The specifics of instrument construction and performance styles vary, but jaw harps in Inner Asia are made either from wood or metal, the latter representing an early and sophisticated use of metallurgy by nomadic peoples. A magical or spiritual dimension has been attached to jaw harps in many cultures.

Qairaq
Clappers; a pair of stone castanets found in Afghanistan and Transoxania.

Qairaq

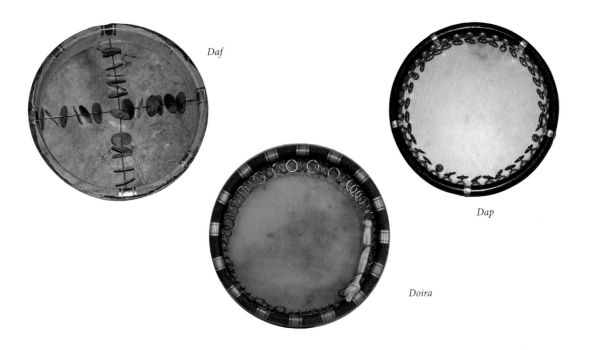

Daf

Dap

Doira

Daf
Frame drum of different sizes that is the principal percussion instrument of Badakhshan. Small frame drums called *daf* or *gaval* (*qaval*) are also widely used in Azerbaijan, both in folk music and in the classical *mugham*. Jingling metal rings are sometimes attached to the inside of the frame.

Dap
Uyghur frame drum, similar to the Uzbek or Tajik *doira;* normally covered with donkey hide, set with metal rings. The smaller *dap* is a virtually indispensable instrument for the Twelve Muqam, marking out

Alim Qasimov playing the *daf*.
Photo by Sebastian Schutyser. Courtesy of Aga Khan Music Initiative.

the complex rhythmic cycles. A larger version is used in folk contexts to accompany dancing at *mäshräp* festivities and in shamanic-style healing rituals.

Doira
Frame drum with jingles commonly played by both men and women among sedentary (i.e., non-nomadic) populations in Central Asia.

Kosh naghora
A pair of small kettle drums played with sticks, typically as part of an ensemble that includes *karnai* and *surnai;* used on festive and ceremonial occasions.

Kosh naghora

Tabla

Naghara

Naghora

Zerbaghali

Naghara

Cylindrical double-sided frame drum held under the arm and played with hands rather than sticks. *Naghara* is typically played at festive celebrations, especially weddings.

Naghora

Single ceramic kettle drum used as a military signaling instrument or, together with *karnai* and *surnai,* on festive and ceremonial occasions.

Tabla

Pair of hand-played, tunable drums that is the principal percussion instrument in North Indian classical music, also used since the middle of the 19th century in the Kabuli art music tradition. The *bayan* (*right*) is a metal kettle drum whose pitch is modulated by pressure from the heel of the hand on the drum skin. The tabla or *dahina* (*left*) is a wooden drum whose skin can be tuned to a precise pitch.

Zerbaghali

Goblet drum commonly used in small ensembles that perform Pashtun folk music.

Adhān: Muslim call to prayer.

Aerophone: musical instrument whose sound is produced by the vibration of a body of air, as in brass and wind instruments.

Aitys. See *Aitysh*.

Aitysh (also Kazakh: *aitys*): Kyrgyz term for an oral poetry competition.

Alti-yarim Maqom: "six and a half *maqoms*"; also known as Khorezm Maqom. One of the three principal traditions of Central Asian *maqom*. Alti-yarim Maqom is associated with the city of Khiva, the historical seat of the Khivan Khanate.

Ambitus: pitch range of a mode or musical instrument.

Än: Kazakh term for lyrical song.

Änshi: Kazakh composer-performer of lyrical songs.

Änshilik: the art of performing lyrical songs among the Kazakhs.

Aqsaq (also *aqsak*): "limping" rhythm, usually transcribed as 7/8, which is common in the music of sedentary dwellers in Transoxania.

Aqyn: specialized performer of oral poetry in Kazakh, Kyrgyz, and other historically nomadic cultures.

Aqyndyq: the art of *aqyn*s.

Aruz (also ʻ*arud*): system of quantitative prosody that is the basis of classical poetry in Arabic, Persian, and Turkic languages.

As (also Kyrgyz *ash*): memorial feast (the one-year anniversary of the dead) among the Kazakhs.

Ash (also *osh*): among Uzbeks and Tajiks, early-morning quasi-religious gathering of men given separately by the fathers of both bride and groom before a marriage.

Ashiq (also *ashig, ashug*): name given to troubadours or bardic singer-instrumentalists in Turkey, Azerbaijan, Armenia, Georgia, Iran, and among the Uyghurs of western China.

Äuen (also *saz, saryn*): Kazakh term for melody, tune, motif in singing or instrumental music.

Auyl (also *ayil, awil, awul, aal*): among historically nomadic peoples of Inner Asia, a rural settlement or community.

Awj: melodic and emotional apogee of a song.

Azanchi: in Transoxania, the local term for *muezzin*—the person who performs the *adhān*.

Bacha: in pre-Soviet urban Transoxania, a boy dancer who dressed as a woman.

Balaman (also *balaban*): single-reed clarinet that figures in the musical traditions of the Azerbaijanis, Karakalpaks, Tajiks, and Uzbeks.

Balandmaqom: nineteen-stringed lute devised by Sufi poet, astronomer, and musician Muborak Wakhoni (d. 1903) and used to accompany the singing of *qasoid-khonī*.

Balandzikom: local version of the Pamiri *tanbur* used in the Wakhan Valley region of Tajik Badakhshan to accompany performances of *qasoid-khonī*. Similar to long-necked lutes depicted in 16th-century Persian miniature painting, thus affirming the continuity of this form of long-necked lute and its historical connection to Iran.

Baqsy (also *bagshy, bakhshi, bakshy*): reciter of oral epic; may also refer to a shamanic healer.

Baraka: spiritual power.

Barbat: short-necked lute that was popular in the courts of Sassanid Persia, which included parts of Central Asia. Generally considered to be the ancestor of the oud, which developed in Arab lands, and the *pipa*, which developed in China.

Barmaq (also *barmak*): a traditional scheme of poetic verse organization in Turkic languages that is based on the number of syllables per line—usually seven, eight or eleven.

Bastakor: composer or singer-songwriter. The term was applied both to artists who wrote music using conventional Western notation and to traditional singer-songwriters who composed orally and memorized their songs.

Bastakorlik: the art of *bastakor*s.

Bazm: feast; the culminating feast of a wedding.

Beat: regular rhythmic pulse.

Bel canto: Italian vocal style of the 18th and early 19th centuries, the qualities of which include perfect legato production throughout the range, the use of a light tone in the higher registers, and agile and flexible delivery.

Bukharcha: Bukharan folk songs sung in the local Bukharan dialect of Persian-Tajik.

Bulbulcha: Tajik name for clay ocarina, played mostly by children, and found in all Tajik regions.

Buyn: in Kazakh *dombyra* music, a specific pitch area or register.

Cadence: conclusion of a phrase, movement, or piece based on a recognizable melodic formula, harmonic progression, or dissonance resolution; the formula on which such a conclusion is based.

Cadenza: in Western classical music, a section near the end of a concerto in which the orchestra stops playing, leaving the soloist to perform alone in a display of virtuosity.

Chang kobuz. *See* jaw harp.

Choor: Kyrgyz name for an end-blown flute made from reed or wood with four or five holes.

Chopo choor: ocarina; a vessel flute with a hollow body, originally in the shape of a large, elongated egg.

Chordophone: general term for instruments that produce their sound by setting up vibrations in a stretched string by plucking, bowing, or striking.

Chormaqom: four *maqom*s. One of the classical musical repertories of Central Asia, also known as the Fergana-Tashkent *maqom*. See also *maqom*.

Chromatic: based on an octave of twelve semitones, as opposed to a seven-note diatonic scale; a chromatic scale consists of an ascending or descending line that advances by semitones.

Contrafactum: in vocal music, the substitution of one text for another without substantial change to the music.

Daf: frame drum used in musical traditions of Azerbaijan and Badakhshan.

Dafsoz: a form of male singing to the accompaniment of the Badakhshani frame drum (*daf*).

Dap: Uyghur term for a frame drum.

Dastan (also *dästan, dessan*): heroic or lyrical epic poem.

Dastanchi (also *dessanchy*): performer of *dastan*s.

Dervish: member of a Sufi religious order who has taken vows of poverty and austerity; an itinerant religious mendicant.

Diatonic: based on or derived from an octave of seven pitches (five wholetones and two semitones) arranged in a particular configuration, as opposed to chromatic and other forms of scales.

Dilrabo: two-stringed spike fiddle 19–24 inches in length used in Tajik and Afghan Badakhshan, typically to play lyrical melodies. (Cognate with *dilruba,* an Indian bowed lute with four main strings and 19 sympathetic strings.)

Diltar: one-of-a-kind bowed and plucked double-necked lute invented by Uyghur musician Abdulla Mäjnun.

Dobulbas: Kyrgyz single-headed drum with a membrane made of camel skin.

Doira (also *dayra*): tambourine or frame drum, usually with metal rings attached to the wooden rim.

Dombyra (Russified as *dombra*): Kazakh two-stringed long-necked fretted lute played by bards to accompany the performance of oral poetry or lyrical songs, or in instrumental music.

Drone: steady or constantly reiterated pitch performed synchronically with a melody—the simplest of all accompaniments. Drones are commonly produced by wind instruments, bowed strings, or by a vocalist holding a steady pitch.

Dumbrak (also *dombrak, dombra, dumbra*): unfretted two-stringed long-necked lute played in the south of Tajikistan as well as among Tajiks and Uzbeks in northern Afghanistan and adjacent regions of Uzbekistan.

Dumbra. See *dumbrak.*

Dutar (also *duwtar, dutor*): two-stringed long-necked fretted lute that occurs in local variant forms and sizes among Uzbeks, Tajiks, Turkmen, Karakalpaks, Uyghurs, and other groups.

Dutarchy: virtuosic solo *dutar* player.

Duwtar: in Karakalpakstan, the local variety of long-necked two-stringed lute. See also *dutar.*

Electrophone: general term for instruments that produce vibrations that must be passed through a loudspeaker before they are heard as sound.

Epic: long narrative poem, often transmitted orally through performance by specialized bards, that typically recounts the life history of a great figure using a combination of history, legend, and myth.

Equal temperament: division of an octave into twelve equal semitones that facilitates modulation between different keys.

Estrada: in the former Soviet Union, a widely used term that typically refers to mainstream popular music. *Estrada* ensembles use a combination of European and indigenous instruments to turn local songs and tunes into vaudeville-like popular music.

Falak: musical genre whose strongest cultural associations are with the mountain-dwelling populations of southeastern and southwestern Tajikistan. *Falak*s are typically sober, lament-like songs that many singers and listeners believe to possess healing qualities, and whose texts typically address philosophical themes.

Fiqh: Islamic law.

Frame drum: circular drum with one or two heads stretched over a frame or hoop. In Central Asia, frame drums typically have one head and are played with the hands, rather than with sticks.

Gaval: frame drum. See also *daf.*

Ghartyq: clay ocarina played by blowing on a detachable single reed inserted into the flue of the instrument; traditionally used by Karakalpak pastoralists.

Ghazal: poetic form consisting of rhyming couplets and a refrain, with each line sharing the same meter. The first *ghazal*s were composed in Arabic, and the form was subsequently adopted by poets writing in Persian, Turkish, Urdu, and other languages.

Ghijak (also *giyjak, gyjak*): round-bodied spike fiddle with three or four metal strings and a short,

GLOSSARY OF TERMS

fretless neck used by Uzbeks, Tajiks, Turkmen, and Karakalpaks. In Badakhshan, *ghijak*s often use a tin can as a resonator.

Girjek: among the Karakalpaks, a spike fiddle. See also *ghijak*.

Gopuz: Turkmen jaw harp.

Hadith: collection of traditions containing sayings of the Prophet Muhammad, which, together with accounts of his daily practice (*sunna*), constitutes the major source of guidance for Muslims along with the Qur'an.

Hafiz: male classical singer.

Halal: religiously acceptable according to Islamic law.

Halypa: master (in Turkmen).

Haram: forbidden or proscribed by Islamic law.

Harmonic: pitch whose frequency is an integral multiple (2x, 3x, 4x. . . .) of the frequency of any fundamental pitch (1x).

Harmonium: small keyboard instrument that operates like a reed organ with air supplied by hand-operated bellows; popular in Indian music as a drone instrument.

Hazzan: Hebrew term for cantor.

Horde: historical socio-political and military structure found on the Eurasian steppe, usually associated with the Mongols. See also *jüz*.

Idiophone: general term for instruments whose sound is produced by the instrument itself without the use of strings or membranes. Common playing techniques include striking, shaking, scraping, rubbing, and plucking (as in plucking the tongue of a jaw harp).

Igil: two-stringed upright fiddle played in Tuva.

Jamakchy: amateur oral poet among the Kyrgyz.

Jar-jar: type of Kazakh or Kyrgyz wedding song traditionally sung by female performers among women,

and later, among mixed audiences or in alternation by groups of men and women. Among Tajiks and Uzbeks similar songs are called *yor-yor* (also *yār-yār*).

Jaw harp (also *chang kobuz, jygach ooz komuz, komus, shang qobyz, shyn qobyz, temir ooz komuz*): generic term for a type of mouth-resonated instrument consisting of a flexible tongue, or lamella, fixed at one end to a surrounding frame.

Jinn (also *jin*): a spirit or fury.

Joqtau: Kazakh funeral lament.

Jüz: Kazakh term for one of the three major tribal confederations, or hordes.

Jygach ooz komuz: Kyrgyz wooden jaw harp.

Jyr (also Kyrgyz: *yr*): Kazakh term for oral epic poem.

Jyrau: in Kazakhstan and Karakalpakstan, a reciter of oral poetry who accompanies himself (or herself) on the *dombyra* or *qobyz*.

Jyraulyq: the art of *jyrau*s.

Jyrshy (also Kyrgryz: *yrshy*): in former times, an individual who both performed and composed epic texts. Nowadays, a performer of pre-composed poetry in a variety of lyric and smaller epic genres.

Kamancha (also *kamancheh, kemanche*): term applied to various types of spike fiddle found mainly in Iran, the Caucasus, and Turkey.

Karnai (also *karnay*): long, straight trumpet consisting of conjoined sections of a cylindrical brass tube ending in a flared bell. Typically played by urban musicians for ceremonial events, weddings, fanfares, and to accompany circus arts.

Kashgar rubab: plucked long-necked fretted lute, adopted in Uzbekistan from the Uyghur *rawap*.

Katta ashula: literally "great song"; a song genre, traditionally performed a cappella, whose origins are associated with the practice of *zikr* in the Ferghana Valley.

Khalfa: in the Khorezm region of northwestern Uzbekistan, a female wedding entertainer.

Khalipe: in Uyghur, a teacher or leader.

Khanaqa (also *khaniqa*): a meeting place of a Sufi order or brotherhood to perform religious rituals.

Khushtar: in Uyghur musical culture, a spike fiddle.

Khuur: Mongolian fiddles with the generic name *khuur* comprise a variety of spike, box-, bowl-, and tube-bodied lutes sounded by bowing. These occur among all Mongol groups, but their modes of construction, styles, and tunings differ. Most common is the *morin khuur*.

Komuz: three-stringed unfretted Kyrgyz lute.

Kosh naghora: a pair of small kettle drums played with sticks, typically as part of an ensemble that includes *karnai* and *surnai;* used on festive and ceremonial occasions.

Koshnai: single-reed wind instrument consisting of two short reed pipes tied together, both of which are typically played in unison.

Koshok (also *joktoo*): Kyrgyz song form sung in the context of weddings and funerals.

Koshokchu: Kyrgyz professional lamenter.

Küi: Kazakh term for a narrative instrumental piece traditionally performed by a solo player.

Küishi: Kazakh composer-performer of *küi*.

Küü: Kyrgyz term for a narrative instrumental piece traditionally performed by a solo player.

Kyl-Kiyak: Kyrgyz spike fiddle.

Lalaik: in Badakhshan, female ritual music for memorial gatherings.

Libretto: the literary text, both sung and spoken, of an opera or other musical work.

Limping rhythm. See *aqsaq*.

Lively notes: in Uyghur *muqam*, unstable tones that change in pitch depending on the direction of melodic movement.

Lyrical: the musical expression of emotion in an imaginative and beautiful way.

Maddoh (also *maddāh, maddo, madāh, madh*): reciter-performer of lyrical poems and devotional odes.

Madrasah: Muslim theological college.

Manaschy: reciter of the Kyrgyz epic *Manas*.

Maqom (also *makam, maqām, mugham, mukam, muqam*): the modal principle in Uzbek and Tajik art music. Cognate terms that refer to analogous modally organized art music traditions include *makam* (Turkish), *maqām* (Arabic), *mugham* (Azerbaijani), and *muqam* (Uyghur). Non-cognate terms that refer to analogous modally organized art music traditions include *dastgah* (Iran) and *nubah* (Arabo-Andalusian). In Kazakh music, *maqam* refers more generally to a recurrent vocal tune or melody in vocal music. In Turkmen music, *mukam* refers to a small set of formally coherent instrumental compositions as well as, more loosely, to any instrumental composition. *Maqom* (and its cognates) may also designate a suite consisting of a succession of melodic types and metro-rhythmic genres. *See also* mode.

Maqomat: plural form of *maqom* in Arabic.

Mavrigi: "from Merv"; a vocal suite performed at men's *bazms* by a *mavrigikhon*.

Mavrigikhon: performer of *mavrigi*.

Melismatic: a passage containing a melisma is said to be melismatic. A melisma is a group of notes sung to a single syllable of text.

Glossary of Terms

Membranophone: general term for musical instruments that produce their sound through the vibration of a stretched membrane.

Meter: the pattern of stressed and unstressed beats in a measure or other temporal unit of music.

Microtone: any musical interval or difference of pitch distinctly smaller than a semitone.

Mimetic rhythm: representation or imitation of rhythmic patterns imported from the real world, whether of natural or human origin.

Mode: musicological concept used cross-culturally in a variety of local traditions of music theory to describe hierarchical features of pitch organization within a melody. Specific modal entities are conceptualized along a continuum that extends from a generalized tune to a particularized scale. In oral tradition music, mode typically provides the basis for melodic improvisation, extemporization, and composition.

Morin khuur: Mongolian two-stringed horse-head fiddle.

Mugham: the Azerbaijani tradition of modally organized vocal and instrumental art music.

Mukam: in Turkmen music, a small set of specialized musical compositions revered by Turkmen *dutar* players. In a more general sense, *mukam* can mean "melody," or it may be used loosely to refer to any instrumental composition.

Mullah: Muslim religious leader.

Muqam: in Uyghur culture, a group of distinct but related regional repertories consisting of large suites that include sung poetry and instrumental sections, and may also include dance and stories.

Muqamchi: lead singer in a Uyghur *muqam* ensemble.

Mutrib (also *motreb*): in Iran and the Iranian cultural sphere, groups of professional entertainers, both male and female, who perform at festivities.

Naghara (also *naghora, nagora, naqqara, nakarre*): cylindrical double-sided frame drum held under the arm and played with hands rather than sticks. Also, a single ceramic kettle drum or pair of kettledrums used as a military signaling instrument, or together with *karnai* and *surnai,* on festive and ceremonial occasions.

Nai (also *nay, ney*): various forms of flutes that may be transverse or end-blown, and may be made from wood, reed, or bamboo.

Non-diatonic: opposite of *diatonic*. See also *diatonic*.

Octave: For any pitch of frequency x, an octave is the interval between x and 2x, or between x and 0.5x. In European solfège, pitches an octave apart have identical names, e.g., do-do$_1$, re-re$_1$.

Öleng: Kazakh term for recited or sung verse. See also *qara öleng*.

Olonkho: Sakha (Yakut) epic.

Ostinato: musical device in which a rhythmic, melodic, or harmonic motif or pattern is repeated while other musical elements undergo variation or development.

Otin-oy (also *otin-oyi*): Uzbek term to designate women who are spiritual leaders within communities of women, usually in rural areas.

Oud (also ud): short-necked plucked lute of the Arab world, the direct ancestor of the European lute, whose name derives from *al-ʿūd* (the lute) in Arabic.

Overtone: one of the higher frequency components of a complex sound that contributes to its characteristic timbre, or sound quality.

Pamiri *nai*: wooden fipple flute made from apricot wood with six finger holes and a thumbhole, used particularly for festive occasions.

Pamiri *tanbur*: long-necked partially fretted lute with animal skin covering the lower part of the resonating chamber, three melody strings, and four or six sympathetic strings. See also *tanbur*.

Pipa: Chinese pear-shaped short-necked four-stringed lute.

Popsa: commonly used term to designate a part of the overall repertory of *estrada* music that is considered of low quality, quickly and badly produced, aesthetically unappealing, or created simply for commercial gain.

Pulse: used synonymously with *beat* to refer to regularly recurring articulations in the flow of musical time.

Qabaq: in Karakalpakstan, a drum made out of a hollowed-out gourd.

Qairaq (or *qairyk*): clappers; a pair of stone castanets found in Afghanistan and Transoxania.

Qalandar: wandering dervish who performs didactic spiritual songs for alms. Also, the genre of devotional poetry and songs associated with such singers.

Qamys nay: in Karakalpak culture, a type of clarinet made from a reed.

Qara öleng (literally "black" or "simple song"): Kazakh song genre based on an eleven-syllable verse form.

Qasoid-khonī: in the Wakhan region of Badakhshan, a performance of sung poetry (*qaṣīda*s) accompanied by musical instruments (analogous to *maddoh*).

Qobyz (also *qyl-qobyz*): two-stringed fiddle traditionally used by shamans and epic bards among the Kazakhs and Karakalpaks.

Quatrain: stanza of four lines, especially one having alternate rhymes.

Quray: long, end-blown flute that is considered the national instrument of the Bashkirs. Also used in Karakalpak culture as a generic name for flutes.

Qyssakhan: among the Karakalpaks, a storyteller who recites or sings unaccompanied written and oral literature in verse and prose.

Radif: Persian: "order," "row," "series." A modally organized repertory of vocal and instrumental pieces that serves as a model—often identified with a particular master musician—for teaching, transmission, and performance in the Persian art music tradition.

Raga: Sanskrit: "color," "hue," used figuratively to mean "passion," "affect." In the art music traditions of India, a *raga* is a modal entity that comprises the melodic material and performance procedures necessary for the composition and extemporization of vocal and instrumental music.

Rawap: Uyghur long-necked plucked lute.

Rebec: early medieval European bowed string instrument, probably introduced to Europe through the Crusades, or by earlier contact between European and Asian cultures.

Register: the pitch range of an instrument, singing voice, or composition, or, more commonly, a specific portion of this range, e.g., "high register," "low register."

Rondo: common musical form in which a recurring refrain section alternates with contrasting episodes of differentiated musical material, e.g., abacadaea.

Rubab (also *rebab, robab, rabab*): term for various chordophones, particularly lutes (mainly with a skin-covered deck), both bowed and plucked, and lyres, widely distributed across North Africa, the Middle

Glossary of Terms

East, Iran, Central Asia, South Asia, and Southeast Asia. In Central Asia, local forms of plucked *rubab* play a leading role in the musical traditions of Afghans and Uyghurs, and are also commonly played in Uzbekistan and in Tajik Badakhshan.

Rubā'ī (plural form: *rubā'iyāt*): Persian poetic genre consisting of quatrains composed in quantitative verse meter, typically with end rhyme scheme aaba.

Rubato: performance practice of disregarding strict time for purposes of expressive effect, or to create a sense of spontaneity.

Safail: type of rattle sometimes used in *zikr* ceremony throughout Central Asia. Commonly found among plains and river valley Tajiks and Uzbeks.

Sarangi: short-necked fiddle of South Asia, found both in the art music of North India and Pakistan and, in related forms, in traditional music.

Sarinda: double-chested fiddle from southern Afghanistan and South Asia.

Saryn. See *äuen*.

Satar: Uyghur long-necked bowed lute or *tanbur* with one melodic string and eight to twelve sympathetic metal strings.

Sato: bowed *tanbur* or long-necked lute played by performers of Tajik-Uzbek and Uyghur classical music. The *sato* has five strings of which one is bowed and the others serve as drones.

Saz: Tajik and Uzbek: "harmony"; also a Turkish and Persian term for a musical instrument, most typically one of the long-necked fretted lutes of Turkey, the Caucasus, and northern Iran. *Saz* may also refer to a small accordion played in the Caucasus and by female entertainers (*khalfas*) in the Khorezm region of northwest Uzbekistan.

Saz syrnai: clay ocarina with four to six holes used by Kazakh and Karakalpak pastoralists.

Setar: small, long-necked lute with four steel strings used in Persian classical music (*setar* literally means "three strings," but a fourth string was added later and is now standard). In Badakhshan, *setar* denotes a larger long-necked lute with a wood-covered deck, three steel melody strings, and a variable number of sympathetic strings.

Shah: Persian: "king." A traditional title given to the sovereign of Persia, Iran, and historically Iranian kingdoms in Central Asia (e.g., Khorezm). The last Shah of Iran was deposed in 1979.

Shahada: name of the Muslim declaration of belief in the oneness of God and acceptance of Muhammad as God's prophet.

Shakirt (also *shäkirt*). See *shogird*.

Shakuhachi: Japanese end-blown bamboo flute.

Shaman (also *baqsy, bakshy, porkhan*): person regarded as being able to access and invoke the powers of the spirit world, typically through a ritual practice that in Central Asia involves the use of drumming, chanting, or playing bowed instruments, flutes, or jaw harps.

Shamanism: refers to a range of practices and beliefs regarding communication with the spirit world. *See also* shaman.

Shang qobyz. See jaw harp.

Shari'a: exoteric Muslim religious law.

Shashmaqom: "six *maqoms*"; a compendium of instrumental and vocal pieces comprising six modally organized suites that embody classical Central Asian aesthetic ideals in music and poetry. Shashmaqom is historically associated with the city of Bukhara.

Shehnai (also *shahnai, shenai*): loud oboe widely played in India and Pakistan, similar to the Central Asian *surnai,* Chinese *suona,* and Turkish *zurna.*

Sheikh (also *shaykh*): spiritual leader of a Sufi lineage or brotherhood; also, in Arab culture, the chief or head of a tribe, family, or village.

Shertpe: a style of Kazakh *dombyra* performance associated with eastern Kazakhstan which involves plucking strings with individual fingers.

Shi'a: one of the two main branches of Islam, whose adherents, centered in Iran, comprise around 10 percent of all Muslims. Shi'a doctrine rejects the first three Sunni caliphs as successors of the Prophet, and regards Ali, the fourth caliph, as Muhammad's true successor.

Shogird (also *shakirt, shäkirt*): in music and other professions and trades, an apprentice, student, or disciple of an *ustod (ustoz),* or master.

Shyn qobyz: Karakalpak name for a jaw harp (or Jew's harp).

Sitar: large, long-necked lute with six or seven playing strings and typically thirteen sympathetic strings— the quintessential instrument of the North Indian (Hindustani) classical music tradition.

Sonority: sound defined by a combination of timbres or registers, particularly one that plays an important part in a work; the quality of tone produced by an instrumentalist.

Sorud: bowed fiddle widespread throughout the Indian subcontinent. Related to the *sarangi* and *sarinda,* as well as to the Central Asian *qobyz.*

Soundscape: totality of constituent sounds produced within a particular space, topography, or environment—the aural analogue of landscape.

Sozanda: professional female entertainer in the cities of Bukhara and Samarkand.

Sufism: the mystical dimension of Islam. A Sufi is one who follows the mystical path of Sufism.

Suona: shawm of the Han Chinese, related to the *surnai* of Central Asia. See also *surnai.*

Sura (also *surah*): chapter or section of the Qur'an.

Surnai (also *surnay, sunay*): loud oboe or shawm, traditionally played at weddings, funerals, and other outdoor ceremonies; widespread in folk music traditions of West and Central Asia, Southeastern Europe, parts of North Africa, and parts of China.

Sybysghy (also *sybyzgy, sybyzghy, sybysgy, sybyzyk*): side-blown or end-blown flute that figures in nomadic musical traditions.

Sympathetic strings: on string instruments, strings that are not played (i.e., not bowed or plucked) but are excited by the vibration of physically proximate bowed or plucked strings tuned to the same pitch.

Syngsu: Kazakh bridal lament.

Tabla: pair of hand-played, tuneable drums that is the principal percussion instrument in North Indian classical music.

Tablak: in Tajikistan, a goblet drum.

Tanbur (also *tämbur*): name applied to various long-necked fretted plucked lutes of the Middle East and Central Asia.

Taoist: adept of a Chinese philosophy based on the writings of Lao-tzu, advocating humility and religious piety.

Tar (also *tor*): double-chested plucked lute used in urban music from the Caucasus and Iran. In Azerbaijan the *tar* is widely considered the national

GLOSSARY OF TERMS

instrument. The *tar* is also popular in the Khorezm region of Uzbekistan.

Tariqa(t): Arabic, Persian, Turkish: "path," "way." In Sufism, the mystical path toward ultimate truth; also, a Sufi school or brotherhood.

Tartys: a form of instrumental competition among the Kazakhs.

Tawhid: doctrine of oneness of God; the concept of monotheism in Islam that holds that God (Allah) is one and unique.

Temir ooz komuz: Kyrgyz metal jaw harp. *See also* jaw harp.

Tempo: speed at which a piece of music is performed.

Tengrianism (also Tengrism; Turkic: *Tengrichilik, Tängirshilik*): neologism coined to describe a complex of contemporary beliefs and practices rooted in the indigenous spiritual culture of Inner Asia, in particular, a belief in the power of spirit-deities. Tengrianism takes its name from the ancient Turkic sky deity Tengri.

Terme: genre of didactic and philosophical poetry—an example of what is known as "wisdom literature"—composed and performed as songs by Kazakh and Kyrgyz improvising poets (*aqyn*s, *jyrshy*s).

Tessitura: term used to describe the part of a vocal (or less often instrumental) compass in which a piece of music lies, e.g., "high tessitura," "low tessitura." The tessitura of a piece is not fixed by the extremes of its range, but rather by which part of the range is most used.

Texture: overall quality of sound of a musical piece as determined by the way melodic, harmonic, and rhythmic elements are combined.

Theorbo: large European lute with separate long and short courses of strings that achieved popularity in the late Renaissance and Baroque.

Throat-singing (also "overtone singing"): vocal style indigenous to the Altai region of south Siberia and western Mongolia in which a single vocalist produces two notes simultaneously—a fundamental drone pitch and a reinforced harmonic pitch that sounds louder than the fundamental.

Timbre (adjectival form: timbral): tone color; that which distinguishes the quality of tone or voice of one instrument or singer from another.

Tökpe: a style of Kazakh *dombyra* performance centered in western Kazakhstan that employs strumming across the strings with a wrist movement of the right hand.

Tolghau: genre of didactic and philosophical poetry composed and performed by Kazakh and Karakalpak bards. See also *terme*.

Tonal: term referring to music rooted in the Western system of major and minor keys; contrasts with music that is atonal, modal, or generated by other non-key-based mechanisms for organizing pitch relationships.

Tone: the particular sound of an instrument or voice, as well as a performer's particular coloring of that sound.

Toy (also *tüy*): in Transoxania, a wedding; more broadly, a family ceremony marking life-cycle occasions including marriage, circumcision, the first haircut of a boy, the first placing of a baby in a cradle, first day of school, and so on.

Transoxania (also Transoxiana): "beyond the Oxus." The name is adopted from Arabic *mā warā' al-nahr*, "that which is beyond the river." The region includes the territory that arcs eastward from the Aral Sea between the Amu Darya (the River Oxus of antiquity) and the Syr Darya, comprising most of the present-day nations of Uzbekistan and Tajikistan and portions of Kyrgyzstan and Kazakhstan; in antiquity, Soghdia and Khorezm.

Tremolo: shaking, trembling. On string instruments, the rapid reiteration of a note or chord by back-and-forth strokes of the bow; also, on plucked string instruments as well as other instruments, the very rapid alternation between two notes.

Tsuur (also *choor, shuur*): Mongolian name for end-blown flute with three holes. Performers sometimes produce a breathy vocal drone while simultaneously playing the instrument. See also *choor; sybysghy*.

Tutik: in Badakhshan, the name of a small wooden flute.

Tuyaq: Karakalpak instrument consisting of horseshoes clapped together.

Unison: simultaneous performance of one melodic line by multiple instruments or voices, or by an entire choir or orchestra; unison singing or playing may be at a single pitch or at pitches related by octave equivalence.

Ustod (also *ustad, ustat, ustaz*): honorific title used to designate a master musician.

Usul: regularly recurring metro-rhythmic patterns; also, a general name for the metro-rhythmic dimension of music.

Vibrato: wavering of pitch used to enrich and intensify the tone of a voice or instrument. Vibrato is practiced in particular by vocalists, and by performers of bowed stringed instruments and wind instruments.

Wahhabi: adherent of Wahhabiya, an orthodox Sunni Muslim sect founded by Muhammad ibn 'Abd al-Wahhab (1703–92) that advocates a return to the early Islam of the Qur'an and Sunna, rejecting later innovations.

Yrchy. See *jyrshy*.

Zikr (also *dhikr, zikir, zekr*): Sufi ceremony of remembrance that consists of the repetition of divine names or religious formulas, and that may also include various forms of communal and solo chanting, singing, dancing, and instrumental music.

Zurna: shawm. Cognate term of *surnai*. See also *surnai*.

Audio and video examples were recorded or filmed by a chapter's author or co-author unless otherwise indicated.

Abbreviations

SFR: Smithsonian Folkways Recordings

4. The Kyrgyz Epic *Manas*

Example 4.1. Urkash Mambetaliev recites the episode "Chong Kazat" (The great campaign) from *Manas.* Filmed by Nurlanbek Nyshanov, Bishkek, Kyrgyzstan, 2011.

Example 4.2. Rysbek Jumabaev recites from *Manas.* Filmed by Saodat Ismailova and Carlos Casas, 2004.

Example 4.3. Sayakbay Karala uulu recites excerpts from *Manas.* Filmed by Melis Ubukeev, around 1970.

Example 4.4. Rysbay Isakov recites excerpts from *Manas* with music by Ensemble Ordo-Sakhna. Recording courtesy of Ensemble Ordo-Sakhna.

Example 4.5. Samat Köchörbaev recites the episode "Semetey's Encounter with Sary Taz" from the epic *Semetey* in the *Manas* trilogy. Filmed by Nurlanbek Nyshanov, Bishkek, Kyrgyzstan, 2011.

Example 4.6. Kulmat Sydykov recites the episode "Kanykeydin Taytorunu chapkany" (Kanykey's horse race on Taytoru) from *Manas.* Filmed by Nurlanbek Nyshanov, Bishkek, Kyrgyzstan, 2011.

5. Oral Epic in Kazakhstan

Example 5.1. Uljan Baibosynova with her *ustaz,* Bidas agha Rüstembekov. Filmed by Uljan Baibosynova, 2010.

6. Music of the Karakalpaks

Example 6.1. Excerpt from epic *Alpamys,* performed by Baqbergen jyrau, 2010.

Example 6.2. "Qara jorgha" (Pacer horse), performed by G'ayrat O'temuratov on the *dutar.*

Example 6.3. "Särbinaz" (Cypress), performed by Gülnara Allambergenova (*dutar* and vocal) and Injigül Saburova (*girjek*), 2012.

Example 6.4. "Lullaby," composed by J. Allambergenov, performed by Gülzabira Mambetnazarova to her four-month-old daughter, Hürliman. From Frédéric Léotar, *Karakalpakistan—La Voix des Ancêtres* [Karakalpakistan: The voice of ancestors]. Musique du Monde/Music from the World 3017797. (CD, DVD, PDF file) (Buda Records/Universal, 2008), bonus DVD, chapter 1. Video, text, and translation courtesy of Buda Records.

Example 6.5. "Aman jetker yarymny" (Deliver my lover safe and sound), excerpt from the *dästan Ghärip Ashyq,* performed by Rambergen Khojambergenov, Nukus, 1965. Courtesy of the archive of the Karakalpakstan Television and Radio Broadcasting Company.

Example 6.6. "Dawytköl," composed and performed by Sadyq Nurymbetov, Nukus, 1970. Courtesy of the archive of the Karakalpakstan Television and Radio Broadcasting Company.

Example 6.7. "Körip keldim" (I saw), a *täriyp* composed and performed by Abbaz Dabylov, Nukus, 1968. Courtesy of the archive of the Karakalpakstan Television and Radio Broadcasting Company.

Example 6.8. Excerpt from the *dästan Bahadyr,* composed and performed by Abbaz Dabylov, Nukus, 1959. Courtesy of the archive of the Karakalpakstan Television and Radio Broadcasting Company.

Example 6.9. "Ne körding, qara atym, ne körding?" (What have you seen, my black horse, what have you seen?), excerpt from the *dästan Alpamys,* performed by Biybiraba O'tepbergenova. From Frédéric Léotar, *Karakalpakistan—La Voix des Ancêtres* [Karakalpakstan—The Voice of Ancestors], Musique du Monde/Music from the World 3017797. (CD, DVD, PDF file) (Buda Records/Universal, 2008), track 9.

INVENTORY OF AUDIO AND VIDEO EXAMPLES

Example 6.10. *Geshtek* (Male get-together), excerpt from the *dästan Ghärip Ashyq*, performed by Khalila Dawletnazarov, and conversation with Kärimbai Tynybayev, Nukus, 2013. Film courtesy of Kalmurza Kurbanov.

7. The Art of the Turkmen *Bagshy*

Example 7.1. "Näler görüner" (What will you not see), a folk song on a poem by Magtymguly, performed by Sahy Jepbarow (vocal, *dutar*), accompanied by Ýagmur Nurgeldiýew (*dutar*) and Ata Ablyýew (*gyjak*). Recording from the archives of Turkmen National Conservatory; year of recording unknown.

Example 7.2. "Tä men gelinçäm" (Until I return), performed by Muhammetgeldi Geldinejad, *dutar* and voice. Filmed by George Murer, Istanbul, 2014.

Example 7.3. "Jan jan" (My soul, my soul), performed by Muhammetgeldi Geldinejad, *dutar* and voice. Filmed by George Murer, Istanbul, 2014.

Example 7.4. "Akmeňli" (female name), a folk song set to a poem by Mämmetweli Kemine (1770–1840), performed by Ashyrmämmet Dawudow (vocal, *dutar*), accompanied by Myratdurdy Hajyýew (*dutar*) and S. Garajayýew (*gyjak*). Gazanjyk village, Balkan, 1997.

Example 7.5. "Ýusup soltanym" (My sultan Yusup), a song (*tirme*) from the heroic *dessan Ýusup-Ahmet,* by Magrupy. Performed by Musaguly Ýazmyradow (vocal, *dutar*), accompanied by Hally Begmämmedow (*gyjak*). Halach village, Lebap, 1997.

Example 7.6. "Hatyja" (female name), a folk song (*tirme*) on a poem by Seýdi, performed by Hojamyrat Oraýew (vocal, *dutar*), accompanied by Baky Rejepow (*gyjak*). Tagta town, Dashoguz, 2001.

Example 7.7. "Serwi agajy" (On the cypress), from the epic *Gülpam,* performed by Gurt Ýakupow (vocal, *dutar*) accompanied by Ýazgeldy Kuwwadow and Amannazar Ataýew (*dutar*s). Ashgabat, around 1984.

Video recording from the sound archive of the Center for Folk Music Studies of the Turkmen National Conservatory.

Example 7.8. "Serwi agajy" (On the cypress), from the epic *Gülpam,* followed by a section of narrative prose text, performed by Chary Ýakup. Filmed by George Murer, Mary, Turkmenistan, 2014.

Example 7.9. Chary Ýakup performs on the *dutar* at a *toy*. Filmed by George Murer, Mary, Turkmenistan, 2014.

8. The Turkmen *Dutar*

Example 8.1. "Garry saltyk," performed by Ýazmyrat Rejepow. Video provided by David Fossum.

Example 8.2. "Goňurbaş mukamy" performed by Akmyrat Çaryýew. Video provided by David Fossum.

Example 8.3. "Balsaýat" (Sweet Saýat), performed by Ýazmyrat Rejepow. Video provided by David Fossum.

Example 8.4. "Balsaýat" (Sweet Saýat), perfomed by Akmyrat Çaryýew. Video provided by David Fossum.

9. Kyrgyz Wisdom Songs

Example 9.1. "Jalgan düynö" (False world) performed by Elmira Köchümkulova.

Example 9.2. *Terme* of Arstanbek, performed by Maksat Kuluev.

Example 9.3. "Dünüyö" (World), performed by Roza Amanova.

Example 9.4. "Kalk armany" (The people's lament/misfortune), performed by Jengishbek Toktobekov.

10. *Aqyns* and Improvised Poetry Competitions among the Kazakhs and Kyrgyz

Example 10.1. *Alym sabak aitysh* between senior master *aqyn* Tuuganbay and his pupil, Aaly *aqyn*.

Example 10.2. *Tabyshmak aitysh,* a riddle *aitysh* performed by Azamat Bolgonbaev.

Example 10.3. *Süre aitys* between Köken Shäkeev and Qonysbai Äbilov (excerpt). Almaty, Kazakhstan, 1985. From Jürsin Erman, *Aitys* 4. *Torghai— Kökshetau oblystary aqyn-jyrshylarynyng öner saiysy* [Competition between the art of *aqyn*s and *jyrshy*s from the Torghai and Kökshetau regions] (Almaty: Studiya Dastan, 2006).

Example 10.4. *Aitys* between Amanjol Ältaev and Mels Qosymbaev (excerpt). Almaty, Kazakhstan, 1990. From Jürsin Erman, *Aitys* 5 (VHS cassette) (Almaty: Center Records, 2002).

Example 10.5. *Aitys* between Didar Qamiev and Ainur Tursunbaeva (excerpt). Shieli, Qyzylorda region, Kazakhstan, 2009. Video courtesy of Didar Qamiev.

Example 10.6. *Aitysh* between Aaly Tutkuchev and Qanysha Raisova (excerpt). Bishkek, Kyrgyzstan, 2008.

11. Singing Traditions of the Kazakhs

Example 11.1. Excerpt from *Syngsu* (Bridal lament), performed by Aitughan. Settlement of Senek, Manghystau region, Kazakhstan, 1997. From János Sipos, *Kazakh Folksongs from the Two Ends of the Steppe* (book and CD) (Budapest: Akadémiai Kiadó, 2001), track 11 (music notation on p. 162).

Example 11.2. "Ädemi qyz" (A beautiful girl), performed by Indira Rasylkhan, vocal and *dombyra*. *Musical Heritage of Kazakhstan,* disc 2, track 10. Produced by PanTerra (Sound Light Stages) and EL Producer Centre.

Example 11.3. "Ükili qamshat" (The girl with a beaver fur hat adorned with eagle-owl feathers), performed by Ardaq Balajanova, vocal and *dombyra*. Recorded by Michael Church, *Songs from the Steppes: Kazakh Music Today* (Topic Records, 2005), track 17.

Example 11.4. "Balqadisha" (A girl's name), composed by Aqan seri, performed by Tileules Qurmanghali, vocal and *dombyra*. *Musical Heritage of Kazakhstan,* disc 2, track 16. Produced by PanTerra (Sound Light Stages) and EL Producer Centre.

Example 11.5. "Aq qaiyn" (White birch), composed by Shäshubai Qoshqarbaev (1865–1952), performed by Qurmash Ibishev, vocal and *dombyra*. Recorded by Michael Church, *Songs from the Steppes: Kazakh Music Today* (Topic Records, 2005), track 8.

Example 11.6. "Jienbaidyng termesi" (Jienbai's *terme*), performed by Bidas Rüstembekov, vocal and *dombyra*. Words and music by Jienbai, grandfather of Bidas. Qarmaqshy, Qyzylorda region, 2001. From *Journey to Epic Qyzylorda: Three Kazakh Jyraus* (DVD), vol. 4 of *Musical Treasures of The Silk Road House* (Silk Road House, 2013), scene 10. English translation by Scott Bartling.

Example 11.7. "Nurtughannyng termesi" (Nurtughan's *terme*), composed by Nurtughan Kenjeghululy on a text by Mysabai, performed by Rysbek Ashimov, vocal and *dombyra*. Qarmaqshy, Qyzylorda region, 2001. From *A Journey to Epic Qyzylorda: Three Kazakh Jyraus* (DVD), vol. 4 of *Musical Treasures of The Silk Road House* (Silk Road House, 2013), track 27. English translation by Scott Bartling.

12. Kyrgyz Funeral Laments

Example 12.1. *Koshok* sung at a Kyrgyz memorial feast in Aksy region, 2003. Performed by Anash Andeleyeva.

Example 12.2. "Chyngyz ölbös bolsochu" (If only Chingiz were immortal), composed and performed by Elmirbek Imanaliev. Film footage compiled by Aytysh Film Co., Bishkek, Kyrgyzstan.

13. Kyrgyz Wedding Songs

Example 13.1. Bridal *koshok* performed by Kynatai Tashybekova at author Elmira Köchümkulova's wedding, Aksy District of Jalal-Abad Province, southern Kyrgyzstan, 1999.

Example 13.2. *Koshok* recited by Kunduz Toktomambetova, 2001.

Example 13.3. The same *koshok* as in example 13.2, sung instead of recited.

14. Narrative Instrumental Music

Example 14.1. "Aqsaq qulan" (Lame wild horse), folk legend *küi,* performed by Rüstembek Omarov. Courtesy of Central State Archive of Film, Photography, and Sound Recordings of the Republic of Kazakhstan.

Example 14.2. "Alatau" (Many-colored mountain), composed by Qurmanghazy Saghyrbaiuly, performed by Qali Jantileuov. Fragment from the film *Shabyt,* 1980s. Courtesy of the archive of the Kazakhstan Republic Television and Radio Corporation.

Example 14.3. "Töremurat," composed by Qurmanghazy Saghyrbaiuly, performed by Rysbai Ghabdiev. Fragment from a film, 1983. Courtesy of Central State Archive of Film, Photography, and Sound Recordings of the Republic of Kazakhstan.

Example 14.4. "Nauysqy," attributed to Qurmanghazy Saghyrbaiuly or Dina Nurpeisova, performed by Dina Nurpeisova. Documentary film, 1947. Courtesy of Central State Archive of Film, Photography, and Sound Recordings of the Republic of Kazakhstan.

Example 14.5. "Kerbez Aqjeleng" (Graceful Aqjeleng), attributed to Qazanghap Tilepbergenuly, performed by Säduaqas Balmaghambetov. Courtesy of Central State Archive of Film, Photography, and Sound Recordings of the Republic of Kazakhstan.

Example 14.6. "Qaqpaly Nauai" (Nauai with finger strokes), folk *küi,* performed by Murat Öskenbaev. Fragment from a film, 1978. Courtesy of Central State

Archive of Film, Photography, and Sound Recordings of the Republic of Kazakhstan.

Example 14.7. "Sylqyldaq" (Tinkling), composed by Tättimbet Qazanghapuly, performed by Äpike Äbenova. Fragment from a film, 1980. Courtesy of Central State Archive of Film, Photography, and Sound Recordings of the Republic of Kazakhstan.

Example 14.8. "Qyrmyzy Qosbasar" (Scarlet Qosbasar), composed by Tättimbet Qazanghapuly, performed by Äbiken Khasenov. Courtesy of Central State Archive of Film, Photography, and Sound Recordings of the Republic of Kazakhstan.

Example 14.9. "Saryjailau" (Golden summer settlement), composed by Tättimbet Qazanghapuly, performed by Äbiken Khasenov. Courtesy of Central State Archive of Film, Photography, and Sound Recordings of the Republic of Kazakhstan.

Example 14.10. "Toghyz tarau" (Nine branches), composed by Sügir Äliuly, performed by Jappas Qalambaev. Courtesy of Central State Archive of Film, Photography, and Sound Recordings of the Republic of Kazakhstan.

Example 14.11. "Saltanat," composed and performed by Tölegen Mombekov. Fragment from a film, 1980s. Courtesy of the archive of the Kazakhstan Republic Television and Radio Corporation.

Example 14.12. "Jänibek, Jänibek, shap" (Jänibek, Jänibek, strike), or "Kök dönen," folk *küi,* performed by Qabykei Aqmeruly. Aqjar, Taldyqorghan region, Kazakhstan, 2004.

Example 14.13. "Buqtym, buqtym, saira buqtym" (I'm ducking, I'm ducking, I'm ducking in a ditch), composed by Qurmanghazy Saghyrbaiuly, performed by Abdulhamit Raiymbergenov. Almaty, Kazakhstan, 2005.

Example 14.14. "Qongyr" (Deep-brown), composed and performed by Äbiken Khasenov. Courtesy of

Central State Archive of Film, Photography, and Sound Recordings of the Republic of Kazakhstan.

Example 14.15. "Äbikendi jubatu" (Consolation of Äbiken), composed and performed by Talasbek Äsemqulov. Courtesy of Zira Naurzbaeva.

Example 14.16. "Kara özgöy" (Impudent one), composed by Niyazaaly Boroshev, performed by Emilbek Ishenbek uulu. Filmed by Nurlanbek Nyshanov, Bishkek, Kyrgyzstan, 2011.

Example 14.17. "Ak-Tamak—Kök-Tamak" (White-throat—gray-throat), composed by Atay Ogonbaev, performed by Namazbek Uraliev. Filmed by Theodore Levin, Semenovka, Kyrgyzstan, 2003.

Example 14.18. "Toguz kayryk" (Nine variations) composed by Toktogul Satylganov, performed by Ruslan Jumabaev. Filmed by Theodore Levin, Bishkek, Kyrgyzstan, 2003.

Example 14.19. "Kambarkan," composed by Karamoldo, performed by Nurak Abdyrakhmanov. From *Tengir-Too: Mountain Music of Kyrgyzstan,* vol. 1 of *Music of Central Asia* (SFR, 2005), track 17.

Example 14.20. "Jol jürüsh" (On the road), composed and arranged by Nurlanbek Nyshanov, performed by members of Ensemble Tengir-Too. From *Tengir-Too: Mountain Music of Kyrgyzstan,* vol. 1 of *Music of Central Asia* (SFR, 2005), track 12.

Example 14.21. "Song of Attila Khan," performed by Nurak Abdyrakhmanov, *komuz* and vocal. Filmed by Saodat Ismailova and Carlos Casas, Kyrgyzstan, 2003.

15. Kyrgyz Jaw Harps

Example 15.1. "Kükük" (Cuckoo), traditional *küü,* performed by Nurlanbek Nyshanov (wooden jaw harp).

Example 15.2. "Ala too jazy" (Spring in the Ala Too mountains) and "Erkin too" (Free mountain), performed by Nurlanbek Nyshanov (metal jaw harp).

Example 15.3. "Tagyldyr too" (Mountain where an orphan baby deer lives), composed by Adamkaliy Baybatyrov, performed by Gülbara Baigashkaeva (metal jaw harp).

Example 15.4. "Jangylyk" (Novelty), composed by Nurlanbek Nyshanov, performed by Kambar Kalendarov (metal jaw harp in A), Kutmanaaly Sultanbekov (wooden jaw harp in A), and Gülbara Baigashkaeva (metal jaw harp in E).

16. The Kazakh *Qobyz*

Example 16.1. "Qongyr," (Deep-brown), attributed to Qorqyt, performed by Jappas Qalambaev. Courtesy of Kündiz Qalambaeva.

Example 16.2. "Aqqu" (White swan), folk *küi,* performed by Raushan Orazbaeva. Filmed by Saodat Ismailova, 2014.

Example 16.3. "Erden," composed by Yqylas Dükenuly, performed by Smatai Umbetbaev. From Xavier and Saoulé Hallez, *Kazakhstan: The Kobyz, The Ancient Viol of the Shamans* (France: INEDIT Maison des Cultures du Monde, 2004), track 1.

Example 16.4. "Aria" for *prima-qobyz* and piano accompaniment, composed by Akhmet Jubanov, performed by Ghaliya Moldakarimova. Courtesy of Ghaliya Moldakarimova.

Examples 16.5. "Qongyr" (Deep-brown), attributed to Qorqyt, performed by Däulet Myqtybaev. Fragment from film, 1970s. Courtesy of the archive of the Kazakhstan Republic Television and Radio Corporation.

Example 16.6. "Qorqyt," attributed to Qorqyt, performed by Bazarkhan Qosbasarov. Fragment from film, 1970s. Courtesy of the archive of the Kazakhstan Republic Television and Radio Corporation.

Example 16.7. "Oyanu" (Awakening), composed and performed by Güljan Amanjol. Recorded by Bakhtiyar Amanjol.

INVENTORY OF AUDIO AND VIDEO EXAMPLES

17. *Dombyra* Performance, Migration, and Memory among Mongolian Kazakhs

Example 17.1. "Zar zaman" (The time of sorrow), composed by Berdibai Mataiuly, performed by Öserkhan Saghynbaiuly. Ulaankhus, Bayan-Ölgii, Mongolia, 1978. Courtesy of Mels Öserkhanuly.

Example 17.2. "Beijin sary atan" (The golden camel of Beijing), performed by Näsiretkhan Qambaruly. Ölgii, Bayan-Ölgii, Mongolia, 2004.

Example 17.3. "Beibitshilik" (Peace), composed and performed by Öserkhan Saghynbaiuly. Ulaankhus, Bayan-Ölgii, Mongolia, 1978. Courtesy of Mels Öserkhanuly.

Example 17.4. "Beibitshilik qusy" (The bird of peace), composed by Öserkhan Saghynbaiuly, performed by Turymtai Müsirbaiuly. Qalbatau, Semei region, Kazakhstan, 2006.

Example 17.5. "Mereke tolghau" (Celebratory contemplation), composed and performed by Raikhan Mukhambetuly, Saryözek. Qaraghandy region, Kazakhstan, 2006.

18. *Maqom* Traditions of the Tajiks and Uzbeks

Example 18.1. "Navruzi Sabo," performed by Domla Halim Ibadov, vocal and *dutar,* Shohnazar Sohibov, *tanbur,* and unknown *doira* player. Recording made in 1935. Record pressed in Noginsk record factory, Noginsk, Russia.

Example 18.2. "Talqincha-i sabo," performed by the Academy of Maqom. From *Invisible Face of the Beloved: Classical Music of the Tajiks and Uzbeks,* vol. 2 of *Music of Central Asia* (SFR, 2006), track 15.

Example 18.3. "Muqaddima-i segoh," performed by Farhod Davletov (vocal and *tar*), accompanied by Shuhrat Razzaqov (*dutar*), Habibulla Kurambaev (*doira*), and Murod Norkuziev (*ghijak*). From *In the Shrine of the Heart: Popular Classics from Bukhara and Beyond,* vol. 7 of *Music of Central Asia* (SFR, 2010), track 7.

Example 18.4. "Nasr-i segoh," arranged and performed by Turgun Alimatov. Tashkent, Uzbekistan, 1993.

19. The Uyghur *Muqam*

Example 19.1. *Nawa muqäddimä,* performed by Abliz Shakir, 1997.

Example 19.2. Muqam Ensemble musicians perform a short suite-within-a-suite from Öjal Muqam. Filmed at the Bath International Festival, 2003.

Example 19.3. Chahargah Muqam *mäshräp,* performed by Abdulla Mäjnun. From *Borderlands: Wu Man and Master Musicians from the Silk Route,* vol. 10 of *Music of Central Asia* (SFR, 2011), track 14.

Example 19.4. Musicians from Mäkit play Dolan Muqam, 2000.

Example 19.5. Mäkit *mäshräp,* clowning, 2000.

20. New Images of Azerbaijani *Mugham* in the Twentieth Century

Example 20.1. "Shabih-Hijran" (Parting night) from *Leyli and Majnun,* composed by Uzeyir Hajibeyli. Performed by the orchestra and choir of the Azerbaijan State Opera and Ballet Theater, Kazim Aliverdibeyov, conductor. From Uzeyir Hajibeyov, *Leyli and Majnun,* AICD 1301 (STATOIL and *Azerbaijan International,* 2001). Courtesy of Betty Blair and *Azerbaijan International.*

Examples 20.2 and 20.3. Uzeyir Hajibeyli, *Layla and Majnun,* adapted and arranged by Jonathan Gandelsman and Colin Jacobsen for the Silk Road Ensemble and performed by the Silk Road Ensemble, Artistic Director Yo-Yo Ma. Harvard University New College Theater, November 29, 2007. Courtesy of the Silk Road Project.

Example 20.4. Excerpt from documentary film about Alim and Fargana Qasimov by Saodat Ismailova and Carlos Casas in *Alim and Fargana Qasimov: Spiritual Music of Azerbaijan* (DVD), vol. 6 of *Music of Central Asia* (SFR, 2007).

Example 20.5. Mugham Chargah: "Bardasht," performed by Alim and Fargana Qasimov (vocal) on a text by Seyyid Azim Shirvani (1835–1888), with Rafael Asgarov (*balaban*), Rauf Islamov (*kamancha*), Ali Asgar Mammadov (*tar*), and Natiq Shirinov (percussion). From *Alim and Fargana Qasimov: Spiritual Music of Azerbaijan,* vol. 6 of *Music of Central Asia* (SFR, 2007), track 1.

Example 20.6. "Kurd Ovshari," composed by Fikrat Amirov and performed by the Azerbaijan State Symphony Orchestra, conductor Yalchin Adigozalov. From *Symphonic,* vol. 1 of *Classical Music of Azerbaijan* (*Azerbaijan International,* 1997), track 1. Courtesy of *Azerbaijan International* magazine editor-in-chief Betty Blair.

Example 20.7. "Composition-2," composed by Vagif Mustafazade. From *Vagif Mustafazade* (2-DVD set) (*Azerbaijan International,* 2007). Sponsored by the Ministry of Communication & Informational Technologies of the Republic of Azerbaijan. Courtesy of *Azerbaijan International* magazine editor-in-chief Betty Blair.

21. Popular Classics

Example 21.1. "Dilhiroj" (Tormented heart), composed by Sodir Khan Baba Sharifov on a text of Hafez, performed by Nasiba Omonboeva (vocal), accompanied by Sirojiddin Juraev (*dutar*). From *In the Shrine of the Heart: Popular Classics from Bukhara and Beyond,* vol. 7 of *Music of Central Asia* (SFR, 2010), track 10.

Example 21.2. "Galdir" (Fool of God), composer of music unknown, performed by Nodira Pirmatova (vocal and *dutar*). Lyrics by Abdulhamit Cho'lpon (d. 1938). From *In the Shrine of the Heart: Popular Classics from Bukhara and Beyond,* vol. 7 of *Music of Central Asia* (SFR, 2010), track 1.

Example 21.3. "Ranoni Gördim" (I saw Rano), composed by Komiljon Otaniyozov, performed by Farhod Davletov (vocal and *tar*), accompanied by Shuhrat Razzaqov (*dutar*), Habibulla Kurambaev (*doira*), and Murod Norkuziev (*ghijak*). Author of lyrics unknown. From *In the Shrine of the Heart: Popular Classics from Bukhara and Beyond,* vol. 7 of *Music of Central Asia* (SFR 2010), track 2.

Example 21.4. Profile of Farhod Davletov. Excerpt from documentary film by Saodat Ismailova and Carlos Casas in *In the Shrine of the Heart: Popular Classics from Bukhara and Beyond* (DVD), vol. 7 of *Music of Central Asia* (SFR, 2010).

Example 21.5. "Ufor-i Iroq," composer of music unknown, performed by Nodira Pirmatova (vocal), accompanied by Mahmudjon Tojibaev (*tar*). Text by Hajji Husaini Kangurti (1880–1916). From *In the Shrine of the Heart: Popular Classics from Bukhara and Beyond,* vol. 7 of *Music of Central Asia* (SFR, 2010), track 14.

Example 21.6. Profile of Nodira Pirmatova. Excerpt from documentary film by Saodat Ismailova and Carlos Casas in *In the Shrine of the Heart: Popular Classics from Bukhara and Beyond* (DVD), vol. 7 of *Music of Central Asia* (SFR, 2010).

Example 21.7. "Qushtar" (Double strings), composer of music unknown, performed by Sirojiddin Juraev (*dutar*). Performance version of Kuzikhon Madrahimov (1888–1954). From *In the Shrine of the Heart: Popular Classics from Bukhara and Beyond,* vol. 7 of *Music of Central Asia* (SFR, 2010), track 4.

Example 21.8. "Qushtar," composer of music unknown, performed by Sirojiddin Juraev (*dutar*).

Performance version of Kuzikhon Madrahimov (1888–1954). Unreleased studio recording, Joel Gordon, sound engineer, 2014.

Example 21.9. "Mehri Vatan" (Love of my homeland), composed and performed by Sirojiddin Juraev, *dutar.* Unreleased studio recording, Joel Gordon, sound engineer, 2014.

Example 21.10. "Zavq-i Javoni" (Interest of youth), composed and performed by Sirojiddin Juraev, *dutar.* Unreleased studio recording, Joel Gordon, sound engineer, 2014.

22. Religious Music and Chant in the Culture of Sedentary Dwellers

Example 22.1. Call to Prayer (*Adhān*), performed by Saifullajan Musaev at the Hoja Zainiddin Mosque, Bukhara, Uzbekistan. Recorded by Theodore Levin and Otanazar Matyakubov in Bukhara, 1990. From *Bukhara: Musical Crossroads of Asia* (SFR, 1991), track 7.

Example 22.2. Call to Prayer (*Adhān*) in Dushanbe,Tajikistan. Filmed by Saodat Ismailova and Carlos Casas, 2012.

Example 22.3. *Na'at,* performed by Dervish Orif Bobo Hamro Ogli. Recorded by Theodore Levin and Otanazar Matyakubov in Bukhara, 1990. From *Bukhara: Musical Crossroads of Asia* (SFR, 1991), track 8.

Example 22.4. Excerpt from a Yassawi *zikr* in the city of Turkestan, southern Kazakhstan. Filmed by Saodat Ismailova, 2004.

Example 22.5. "Qoilman" *Katta ashula,* composed by Hamroqulqori Turaqulov, performed by Mahmudjon Tojibaev. Lyrics by Muqimiy. From *In the Shrine of the Heart: Popular Classics from Bukhara and Beyond,* vol. 7 of *Music of Central Asia* (SFR, 2010), track 9.

Example 22.6. Bobo Raykhon and companion perform *Katta Ashula* in Isfara, Tajikistan. Filmed by Saodat Ismailova and Carlos Casas, 2012.

Example 22.7. *Qalandar* song, performed by Muhammad Aminjon Nasriddinov. Recorded by Theodore Levin and Otanazar Matyakubov in Bukhara, 1990. From *Bukhara: Musical Crossroads of Asia* (SFR, 1991), track 12.

23. Sufism and the Ceremony of Zikr in Ghulja

Example 23.1. Excerpts from the ceremony of *zikr.* Ghulja (Yining), Xinjiang Uyghur Autonomous Region, China, 2007.

24. *Dastan* Performance among the Uyghurs

Example 24.1. Introduction to *Abdurakhman Pasha,* performed by Ubulhäsän Muhämmät. Filmed by Rahile Dawut, Aynur Kadir, Nijat Niyaz, and Aysajan Yusup, Khotan, Xinjiang Uyghur Autonomous Region, China, 2009.

Example 24.2. Introduction to *Yüsüp-Ähmäd,* performed by Turdimämät Nasir. Filmed by Rahile Dawut and Mutallip Iqbal, Khotan, Xinjiang Uyghur Autonomous Region, China, 2010.

Example 24.3. Excerpt from the *dastan Patimämning wapatnamisi* (The death of Fatima), performed by Mämättokhti Yasin. Filmed by Aynur Kadir, Khotan, Xinjiang Uyghur Autonomous Region, China, 2010.

Example 24.4. Excerpt from the *dastan Häwzikhan,* performed by Mämättokhti Tokhti Daka. Filmed by Mutallip Iqbal, Kashgar, Xinjiang Uyghur Autonomous Region, China, 2010.

Example 24.5. Excerpt from the *dastan Yachibäg,* performed by Ibrahim Yaqup (vocals, *ghijäk*) and Säydul Nursha (*rawap*). Recorded by Rahile Dawut, Qomul, Xinjiang Uyghur Autonomous Region, China, 2009.

Example 24.6. Excerpt from the *dastan Siyit Nochi,* performed by Mämättokhti Yasin. Filmed by

Rahile Dawut and Aynur Kadir, Khotan, Xinjiang Uyghur Autonomous Region, China, 2009. Subtitles translated by Joshua L. Freeman and Zulpiye Zumretshah.

25. Female Musicians in Uzbekistan

Example 25.1. Excerpt from the "Diwan-i Hikmat" of Hoja Ahmad Yassawi (d. 1166), performed by *otin-oy* Malika Asqarova (b. 1955).

Example 25.2. "Nolish" (Groan, lament) from the repertoire of Kamiljon Jabarov, performed by Malika Ziyoyeva and her *dutar* ensemble: Dilfuza Yulchieva, Dilorom Turgunova, and Malika Zufarova. From *Uzbekistan: Instrumental Art Music,* VDE CD 974 (Geneva, Switzerland: VDE-Gallo, 1998).

Example 25.3. "Kelmadi" (He didn't come) performed by Munojat Yulchieva on a text by Alisher Navo'i (1441–1501). From *Uzbekistan: Munodjat Yulchieva & Ensemble Shavkat Mirzaev* (Frankfurt: WDR and World Network, 1997).

26. Music in the City of Bukhara

Example 26.1. Tohfakhon Pinkhasova and members of her ensemble entertain at a *toy* in the outskirts of Bukhara, 1990.

Example 26.2. "Bukharcha," performed by Tohfakhon Pinkhasova and Nozanin. Recorded by Theodore Levin and Otanazar Matyakubov. From *Bukhara: Musical Crossroads of Asia* (SFR, 1991), track 3.

Example 26.3. "Mavrigi," performed by Mahdi Ibadov. Recorded by Theodore Levin and Otanazar Matyakubov. From *Bukhara: Musical Crossroads of Asia* (SFR, 1991), track 2.

Example 26.4. Reading from the Torah by Yakub Meer Ochildiev. Recorded by Theodore Levin and Otanazar Matyakubov. From *Bukhara: Musical Crossroads of Asia* (SFR, 1991), track 10.

Example 26.5. "Dror Yikra" (Proclaim freedom) performed by Ezra Malakov and Roshel Rubinov. From Ezra Malakov, *Musical Treasure of the Bukharian Jewish Community* (Tel-Aviv: World Bukharian Jewish Congress, 2007), disc 1, track 7.

Example 26.6. *The Bukharan Jews of Queens, New York: Ezra Malakov, Avrom Tolmasov.* Filmed by Saodat Ismailova and Carlos Casas in Queens, New York, 2011.

Example 26.7. "Katta ashula," performed by Ezra Malakov and Abukhai Aminov (vocal), Matat Barayev (*doira*), David Davidov (*tar*), and Ochil Ibragimov (violin). Queens, New York, 2011.

Example 26.8. "Haqqoni," performed by Ezra Malakov and Abukhai Aminov. Queens, New York, 2011.

Example 26.9. "Surnai navosi," performed by Ari Babakhanov on the Kashgar *rubab,* 2002.

Example 26.10. "Gardun-i Dugoh," performed by Ari Babakhanov on the Kashgar *rubab.*

Example 26.11. "Khurram," performed by Ari Babakhanov on the Kashgar *rubab.*

Example 26.12. "Tarje-i Navo," performed by Ari Babakhanov on the Kashgar *rubab,* accompanied by Tolib Temirov (*doira*).

Example 26.13. "Talqincha-i Mashq-i Chorgoh" and "Nagora Chorgoh," performed by Ari Babakhanov on the Kashgar *rubab* and Tolib Temirov (*doira*).

27. Music and Culture in Badakhshan

Example 27.1. "Lalaik," performed by Azatmo Munchoeva and companions. Filmed by Saodat Ismailova and Carlos Casas in the village of Khichigh, 2009.

Example 27.2. "Rapo," performed by Jonboz Dushanbiev (*ghijak*), Ghulomsho Safarov (Pamiri *tanbur*), and Shodi Mabatqulov (*daf*). From *The Badakhshan Ensemble: Song and Dance from the Pamir Mountains,* vol. 5 of *Music of Central Asia* (SFR, 2007), track 7.

Example 27.3. Excerpt from "Rapo" Dance, performed by Ghulomsho Safarov and members of his family with Jonboz Dushanbiev, *ghijak* and vocal. Filmed by Saodat Ismailova and Carlos Casas, 2005.

Example 27.4. "Kholatro Banda" (I'm a slave of your mole), performed by Mukhtor Muborakqadamov (*setar*) and Shodi Mabatqulov (*daf*). *The Badakhshan Ensemble: Song and Dance from the Pamir Mountains, Music of Central Asia,* vol. 5 of *Music of Central Asia* (SFR, 2007), track 8.

Example 27.5. Shodi Mabatqulov demonstrates frame drum (*daf*) rhythms. Filmed by Saodat Ismailova and Carlos Casas near Khorog, Badakhshan, 2006.

Example 27.6. "Dafsoz," performed in Suchon by Abdulakim Abdurakhimov (*sarbaytkhon*), Aliyar Bakhtiyarov, Shanbe Oshurmamadov, Sultonsaid Dodmamadov, Asadbek Shodmonbekov, and Shirinjon Olamov. Video courtesy of Haydar Tawakkalov.

Example 27.7. Badakhshan Ensemble performing at a teenager's birthday party. Filmed by Saodat Ismailova and Carlos Casas, Badakhshan, 2006.

Example 27.8. "Zohidi Pokizasirisht" (The virtuous puritan), composed by Mukhtor Muborakqadamov (2000) on a text by Hafez and performed by the Badakhshan Ensemble. Vocal solo by Aqnazar Alovatov. *The Badakhshan Ensemble: Song and Dance from the Pamir Mountains,* vol. 5 of *Music of Central Asia* (SFR, 2007), track 3.

28. The *Maddoh* Tradition of Badakhshan

Example 28.1. "Maddoh" (Praise), arranged by Aqnazar Alovatov, performed by Aqnazar Alovatov (vocal), Shodi Mabatqulov (*daf* and vocal), Olucha Mualibshoev (vocal), Mukhtor Muborakqadamov (*setar*), and Ghulomsho Safarov (Pamiri *rubab,* Pamiri *tanbur,* vocal). From *The Badakhshan Ensemble: Song and Dance from the Pamir Mountains,* vol. 5 of *Music of Central Asia* (SFR, 2007), track 6. English translations by Saghi Ghazerani.

29. *Qasoid-khonī* in the Wakhan Valley of Badakhshan

Example 29.1. Fragments from the *qaṣīda* "Risola-yi Chihil Dunyo" (Treatise of the forty worlds) and a *qaṣīda* known as "Naqsh-i dolon" (Corridor decoration), by Muborak Wakhoni, performed by Khalifa Mamadbek on the *balandmaqom.* Wakhan, November 2011.

Example 29.2. "Panj Kishti" (Five ships), a *qaṣīda* by Forighī, performed by Zaimkhon Muborakqadamov (*rubab*) and Aslamkhon Muborakqadamov (*tablak*). Village of Shitkharv, Wakhan, November 2011.

Example 29.3. "Qasoid-khonī," performed by Zaimkhon Muborakqadamov (*rubab*) and Aslamkhon Muborakqadamov (*tablak*), on texts by Shams-i Tabrizi (1185–1248), Farid ud-Din Attar (1145–1221), and anonymous poets. Village of Shitkharv, Wakhan, November 2011.

30. *Falak*

Example 30.1. "Falak-i Badakhshani," performed by Soheba Davlatshoeva. From *Badakhshan Ensemble: Song and Dance from the Pamir Mountains,* vol. 5 of *Music of Central Asia* (SFR, 2007), track 1.

Example 30.2. "Falak-i sūzi," performed by Olucha Mualibshoev and the Badakhshan Ensemble. From *Badakhshan Ensemble: Song and Dance from the Pamir Mountains,* vol. 5 of *Music of Central Asia* (SFR, 2007), track 5.

Example 30.3. "Falak-i dashti," performed by Gulchehra Sodiqova. Filmed by Kirill Kuzmin, Kulob, 2014.

Example 30.4. "Ay pari" (Oh fairy) performed by the Badakhshan Ensemble. From *Badakhshan Ensemble: Song and Dance from the Pamir Mountains,* vol. 5 of *Music of Central Asia* (SFR, 2007), track 2.

Example 30.5. "Navo-i kuhiston" (Melody from the mountains), composed by Dosti Orzuyev, performed by Muhammadvali Orzuyev. Recording courtesy of Muhammadvali Orzuyev.

31. Revitalizing Musical Traditions

Example 31.1. Improvisation of "Qushtar," performed by Sirojddin Juraev (Tajikistan, *dutar*), Rebal Alkhodri (Syria, vocal), and Badiaa Bou Hreizi (Tunisia, vocal). Performance at Remix interregional music workshop, Al Ganaina Theater, Al Azhar Park, Cairo, co-produced by Al Mawred Al Thaqafy (Cultural Resource) and the Aga Khan Music Initiative. Filmed by Ahmed Zeidan, 2011.

Example 31.2. Homayun Sakhi (Afghanistan/USA, Afghan *rubab*) leads an arrangement of the Indian raga *madhuvanti* at Remix interregional music workshop, Al Ganaina Theater, Al Azhar Park, Cairo, co-produced by Al Mawred Al Thaqafy (Cultural Resource) and the Aga Khan Music Initiative. Filmed by Ahmed Zeidan, 2011.

Example 31.3. Kronos Quartet and Alim Qasimov. Excerpt from documentary film by Saodat Ismailova and Carlos Casas in *Rainbow: Kronos Quartet with Alim & Fargana Qasimov and Homayun Sakhi* (DVD), vol. 8 of *Music of Central Asia* (SFR, 2010).

Example 31.4. "Mehriban Olaq" (Let's be kind). Music and lyrics by Shafiqa Akhundova. String quartet parts arranged for Kronos by Jacob Garchik. Performed by the Kronos Quartet (David Harrington, violin;

John Sherba, violin; Hank Dutt, viola; and Jeffrey Zeigler, cello) and the Alim Qasimov Ensemble (Alim Qasimov, vocal; Fargana Qasimova, vocal and *daf*; Rafael Asgarov, *balaban*; Rauf Islamov, *kamancha*; Ali Asgar Mammadov, *tar*; and Vugar Sharifzadeh, *naghara*). From *Rainbow: Kronos Quartet with Alim & Fargana Qasimov and Homayun Sakhi*, vol. 8 of *Music of Central Asia* (SFR, 2010), track 3.

Example 31.5. Excerpt from "Rangin Kaman" (Rainbow). Composed by Homayun Sakhi (2008). Arranged by Stephen Prutsman. Performed by Kronos Quartet (David Harrington, violin; John Sherba, violin; Hank Dutt, viola; and Jeffrey Zeigler, cello) and Homayun Sakhi, (Afghan *rubab*), Salar Nader (tabla), and Abbos Kosimov (*doira* and *qairaq*). From *Rainbow: Kronos Quartet with Alim & Fargana Qasimov and Homayun Sakhi*, vol. 8 of *Music of Central Asia* (SFR, 2010), track 1.

32. Cultural Renewal in Kyrgyzstan

Example 32.1. "Ak Kepter" (White doves) arranged by Nurlanbek Nyshanov, performed by Ordo-Sakhna Ensemble with Damyra Niyazbekova. Recording courtesy of Ordo-Sakhna.

Example 32.2. "Ordo," (Nomadic campsite) composed by Nurlanbek Nyshanov, performed by Ordo-Sakhna Ensemble. Recording courtesy of Ordo-Sakhna.

Example 32.3. "Erke Sary" (Darling redhead younger brother), composed by Ruslan Jumabaev, performed by Ordo-Sakhna Ensemble.

Example 32.4. "Echo of Time" (*Mezgil jangyrygy*), composed and arranged by Kambar Kalendarov, performed by Ensemble Ustatshakirt Plus. Filmed by television station Pyatyi kanal, program "Kvartira No. 5," Bishkek, 2014.

Example 32.5. "Vocalese," by Askat Jetigen uulu, performed by Ensemble Ustatshakirt Plus and the

Manas Presidential Chamber Orchestra. Filmed by television station Pyatyi kanal, program "Kvartira No. 5," Bishkek, 2014.

Example 32.6. "Emotional Tango," composed by Askat Jetigen uulu, performed by Ensemble Ustatshakirt Plus and Manas Presidential Chamber Orchestra. Filmed by television station Pyatyi canal, program "Kvartira No. 5," Bishkek, 2014.

33. Popular Music in Uzbekistan

Example 33.1. "Arabskoe Tango" (Arabian Tango), music and lyrics by Farid Al-Atrash, recording by Botyr Zakirov and the Estrada Orchestra of Uzbekistan, conductor Aleksandr Dvoskin, 1959.

Example 33.2. "Muzykal'naya Chaykhana" (The musical teahouse), performed by Yalla, music by Farrukh Zakirov, lyrics by Yevgenii Berezikov, arrangement by Rustam Il'yasov, 1986.

Example 33.3. "Hech Kimga Bermaymiz Seni O'zbekiston" (We will not give you to anyone, Uzbekistan), music and arrangement by Yulduz Usmanova, lyrics by Muhammad Yusuf, adaptation by Yulduz Usmanova, 1999.

Example 33.4. "Ajdodlar Ruhi" (The spirit of ancestors), performed by Se'Tanho (formerly Setora), music and arrangement by Vitalii Zolotarev, lyrics by Shahnoz.

Example 33.5. "Yol Bolsin," performed by Sevara Nazarkhan, 2003.

Example 33.6. "Sen bilasan," performed by Sevara Nazarkhan, music by Sevara Nazarkhan, lyrics by Nurmukhamad Isroil. From *Bu Sevgi* (This love), Real World Records, 2006.

Example 33.7. "On ne prishyol" (He didn't come), performed by Sevara Nazarkhan, music and lyrics by Sergei Mikhalok.

Example 33.8. "Surxonlik Qiz," music by Mahmud Namozov, lyrics by Abdugaffor Mansurov, 2012.

Example 33.9. "10 grammov LSD" (10 grams of LSD), performed by Slyozy Solntsa (Tears of the sun), music and lyrics by Nikita Makarenko, arrangement by Slyozy Solntsa. 2010.

34. Innovation in Tradition

Example 34.1. Excerpts from *The End of an Era: Tashkent*, directed by Mark Weil. Soundtrack composed by Dmitri Yanov-Yanovsky. Video courtesy of the composer.

Example 34.2. Excerpt of *Rapshee* concert. From DVD produced by the Swiss Agency for Development and Cooperation, Arts & Culture Programme Uzbekistan.

Example 34.3. "Shahd," performed by Mahdi Ibadov and his ensemble. Recorded by Theodore Levin and Otanazar Matyakubov. From *Bukhara: Musical Crossroads of Asia* (SFR, 1991), track 2.

Example 34.4. Excerpt from a performance of Ovlyakuli Hojakuli's *Mavrigi*. From DVD produced by the Swiss Agency for Development and Cooperation, Arts & Culture Programme Uzbekistan.

35. Tradition-Based Popular Music in Contemporary Tajikistan

Example 35.1. "Zi durī" (Far away), performed by Gulchehra Sodiqova, based on a *ghazal* by Badruddin Hiloli.

Example 35.2. "To hastam" (As long as I live), Manija Davlatova, based on a *ghazal* by Loiq Sherali.

Example 35.3. "Dunyoi fonī" (Transient world), performed by Nobovar Chanorov and Shams; *Ghazal* attributed to Jalal ad-Din Rumi.

SAIDA DAUKEYEVA

is a Kazakh music researcher and musician whose areas of expertise include medieval Middle Eastern music theory, early European performance, and Central Asian traditional and modern music. While a student of musicology and harpsichord at the Moscow Tchaikovsky Conservatory, she became interested in the musical writings of the Arab-Muslim philosopher al-Farabi and traveled to Syria to pursue field and archival research that became the basis of her Candidate of Science dissertation, later published as a book, *Philosophy of Music by Abu Nasr Muhammad al-Farabi* (Soros Foundation-Kazakhstan, 2002). Her exposure to Western ethnomusicology at the School of Oriental and African Studies in London and her discovery of a Kazakh hereditary community of players on the two-stringed lute, *dombyra*, in western Mongolia led her to conduct several periods of fieldwork in Mongolia and Kazakhstan and complete a doctoral dissertation that explores *dombyra* performance among Mongolian Kazakhs in relation to issues of migration, transnationalism, social memory, and identity. As part of her study of Kazakh and Central Asian music, she has initiated and organized conferences, workshops, and concerts that bring musicians from the region to the attention of Western audiences. She has headed the Folklore Research Laboratory at the Kurmangazy Kazakh National Conservatory in Almaty and is presently a Georg Forster Research Fellow (HERMES) at Humboldt University in Berlin.

EDITORS

ELMIRA KÖCHÜMKULOVA

is a Kyrgyz scholar whose research focuses on the nomadic cultures and oral traditions of Central Asia. She grew up in the mountains of Kyrgyzstan, and both her parents come from families with a long tradition of nomadism. In 1994, not long after Kyrgyzstan gained its independence from the Soviet Union, she went to study in the United States, receiving BA and MA degrees in Near Eastern Languages and Civilizations and a PhD in Near and Middle Eastern Studies from the University of Washington. Köchümkulova is also a self-taught musician who sings and composes Kyrgyz traditional songs accompanied by *komuz,* the three-stringed lute that Kyrgyz consider their national instrument. Currently she is Senior Research Fellow and Head of the Cultural Heritage and Humanities Unit at the University of Central Asia in Bishkek, Kyrgyzstan. Her books *Respect Graces the Living, Lamentation Graces the Dead*: *Kyrgyz Funeral Lamentations* (in Kyrgyz) and *Kyrgyz Herders of Soviet Uzbekistan: Historical and Ethnographic Narratives,* authored with her father (in Kyrgyz and English), were published in 2014.

THEODORE LEVIN

first visited Central Asia in 1974 and has been traveling there ever since. As an advocate for music and musicians from other cultures, he has written books, produced recordings, curated concerts and festivals, and contributed to international arts initiatives. He currently serves as Senior Project Consultant to the Aga Khan Music Initiative and Senior Research Fellow in the Humanities at the University of Central Asia. Levin is the author of *The Hundred Thousand Fools of God: Musical Travels in Central Asia (and Queens, New York)* (IUP, 1996) and *Where Rivers and Mountains Sing: Sound, Music, and Nomadism in Tuva and Beyond* (IUP, 2006). Over the past four decades, his ethnographic research and documentation projects have received support from the Ford, Mellon, Rockefeller, and Watson Foundations; the National Geographic Committee for Research and Exploration; National Endowment for the Humanities; Smithsonian Institution; International Research and Exchanges Board; US Fulbright Commission; Social Science Research Council; and Aga Khan Music Initiative, a program of the Aga Khan Trust for Culture. He lives in Vermont and is on the faculty of Dartmouth College, where he is Arthur R. Virgin Professor of Music. Levin received a BA *magna cum laude* from Amherst College and a PhD from Princeton University.

ABDUVALI ABDURASHIDOV

a leading performer and scholar of Shashmaqom, is artistic director of the Academy of Maqom, in Dushanbe, Tajikistan, which he founded in 2003 in collaboration with the Aga Khan Music Initiative. He studied *sato-tanbur* with the great Uzbek master Turgun Alimatov (1922–2008) and has been at the forefront of the current Shashmaqom revival in Tajikistan. Working with a small group of graduate students in the Academy of Maqom, Abdurashidov re-created a historically informed performance version of the six Shashmaqom suites that he transcribed, recorded, and annotated with the aim of publishing a new critical edition of the Shashmaqom. The results of this work are also presented on *Music of Central Asia*, vol. 2, *Invisible Face of the Beloved: Classical Music of the Tajiks and Uzbeks* (Smithsonian Folkways Recordings 2006).

ELISE ANDERSON

is an ethnomusicologist and student of Central Asian music and folklore who has been conducting research in Xinjiang since 2007. A native Oklahoman, she became interested in the region as a college student, when she taught English for one summer at Xinjiang University. She knows Uyghur and Mandarin and has also studied a smattering of other Eurasian languages. She is a trained vocalist and wind instrumentalist and is now learning to sing *muqam* and play folksong and classical repertories on the *dutar* and *tämbur*. She enjoys taking part in Uyghur dance and finds that some of her most rewarding moments in the field come from "being artistic" with others.

FAROGHAT AZIZI

is a Tajik musicologist whose scholarly research has embraced a broad range of musical styles and genres with the aim of understanding their historical interrelationship. As an undergraduate student at Tashkent State Conservatory, Azizi studied the links between Central Asian *maqom* and Indian *raga*. Later, she studied the *falak* traditions of the mountain Tajiks and published a monograph, for which she was awarded a Doctor of Science degree from the Highest Russian Council of Scientific Degrees (Moscow), in which she examines the relationship between *falak* and *maqom*. In 2006, Dr. Azizi was named Deputy Minister of Culture of Tajikistan, and in 2013 she was named rector of the National Conservatory, a post that she continues to occupy while she pursues her own scholarly research.

CONTRIBUTORS

ULJAN BAIBOSYNOVA

is a musician, scholar, and teacher based in Almaty Kazakhstan. Her special interest is the repertoire of oral poetry performed by Kazakh bards known as *jyrau*. As a performer, she has participated in international theatrical and multimedia works including Peter Sellars's production of Euripedes's *Children of Herakles,* and a docu-fictional musical theater production for orchestra, vocals, movement, and video by composer Marc Sinan based on the early Turkic epic *The Book of Dede Korkut.* Her riveting performances of Kazakh oral poetry are featured on *Bardic Divas: Women's Voices in Central Asia*, volume 4 of *Music of Central Asia* (Smithsonian Folkways Recordings, 2007).

RAHILE DAWUT (CHINESE NAME: REYILA DAWUTI)

was born and raised in Urumqi, China. She is acting Director of the Xinjiang Folklore Research Center and Professor in the College of Humanities, Xinjiang University. Her research focuses on the folklore and Islamic rituals of Uyghurs in Xinjiang, and is born out of a lifelong desire to introduce her people and their traditions to the outside world. She has received various international grants for research and is widely published in the Uyghur, Mandarin, and English languages. She has been a visiting scholar at universities in the United States and the United Kingdom and uses every opportunity to introduce Uyghur music, culture, and hospitality customs to those who are unfamiliar with them.

ALEKSANDR DJUMAEV (LEFT)

lives and works in Tashkent, Uzbekistan, where, for three decades, he has produced prolific scholarship on Central Asian music and its role in social history and contemporary cultural life. Djumaev's scholarship links the methodology of music ethnography, which is rooted in field research, with the skills of music historians who work with original source materials such as manuscripts, books, letters, photos, and recordings. A recurring focus of Djumaev's work is the role of music and musicians in the history of Bukhara, one of Central Asia's oldest cities. As a cultural advocate and activist, Djumaev has been instrumental in helping bring outstanding musicians from Uzbekistan to the attention of worldwide audiences.

DAVID FOSSUM

had been playing guitar for ten years when he picked up a Turkmen *dutar* for the first time. He encountered the instrument while serving as a Peace Corps Volunteer in Turkmenistan from 2004 to 2006. In his free time after teaching English at the school in the small Turkmen town where he had been assigned to work, he studied the instrument under a local *dutar* teacher. The experience inspired him to go on to earn an MA in ethnomusicology from Wesleyan University, where he wrote a master's thesis about Turkmen *dutar* performance. He is currently pursuing a PhD in ethnomusicology at Brown University.

CHORSHANBE GOIBNAZAROV

is a Tajik scholar and ethnographer whose research concerns the interrelation of music and Islam in Badakhshan. Growing up in the Ishkashim district of Badakhshan's Wakhan valley, he was surrounded by musical instruments and singing in a family where music was an active part of everyday life. As a student at Khorog State University, he developed an interest in the local poetic tradition among women of the Wakhan region. Later, at the Aga Khan University, he studied the role of music in Muslim cultures and societies, and explored performance of *qasoid-khonī* as an expression of religious identity. Since 2011, he has been conducting ethnographic fieldwork in Badakhshan, which provides the source material for his doctoral dissertation on *qasoid-khonī* and its relation to Islam and identity at Berlin Graduate School of Muslim Cultures and Societies.

JAMILYA GURBANOVA

was born in Ashgabat, Turkmenistan, to a family of Turkmen intellectuals and artists. Following studies of music history and theory at Owezow State Music College, she graduated from Kurmangazy Kazakh National Conservatory in Almaty, Kazakhstan, where she wrote a thesis on the Turkmen *dutar* and later received a *Kandidat* degree for a dissertation on the twentieth-century Turkmen composer Nury Halmämmedow, who combined Turkmen and European elements in his music. Jamilya Gurbanova lectures on Turkmen music in the Department of Music History at Turkmen National Conservatory and is currently involved in digitizing the audio-video archive of the conservatory's Center for Folk Music Studies. For her contribution to the development of music education and scholarship in Turkmenistan, she received the prestigious state award *Gaýrat* (Zeal).

CONTRIBUTORS

RACHEL HARRIS

is Reader in the Music of China and Central Asia at SOAS, University of London. In addition to journal articles and book chapters, she is the author of *Singing the Village: Memories, Music and Ritual amongst the Sibe of Xinjiang* (2004) and *The Making of a Musical Canon in Chinese Central Asia* (2008). She has co-edited two volumes: *Situating the Uyghurs between China and Central Asia* (2007) and *Gender in Chinese Music* (2013). Her research interests include global musical flows, identity politics, and Islamic soundscapes, and she currently leads the AHRC research network *Sounding Islam in China*. She is actively engaged with outreach projects relating to Central Asian and Chinese music, including recordings, musical performance, and consultancy.

AIDA HUSEYNOVA

a native of Baku, Azerbaijan, is a pianist and musicologist whose research and performance activities link the worlds of Western classical music and Eastern musical traditions. She earned her PhD at the Saint Petersburg Conservatory and has taught music history classes at Baku Music Academy and, since 2008, at Indiana University's Jacobs School of Music, where she offers courses in music theory and on the music of the Silk Road. Fluent in Azerbaijani, Russian, and English, she has served as a research advisor and interpreter for the Aga Khan Music Initiative and for the Silk Road Project, founded by cellist Yo-Yo Ma. She is the author of *Music of Azerbaijan: From* Mugham *to Opera* (IUP, 2016).

KERSTIN KLENKE

embarked on a PhD project that would merge her academic training in ethnomusicology and social anthropology with her interest in theater, film, and television studies after graduating from the University of Cologne. This background, together with a regional interest in post-Soviet space, brought her to Tashkent to study popular music and politics in Uzbekistan. Since 2011, she has been affiliated with the Center for World Music at the University of Hildesheim, Germany. Outside academia, she is actively involved in the world music scene, working to give musicians from Central Asia and the Caucasus more exposure in Europe.

BENJAMIN D. KOEN (*FRONT RIGHT, HOLDING CHILD*)
conducted extensive musical fieldwork in Tajik Badakhshan, where he explored the relationship between music, spiritual practice, and healing. He is the author of *Beyond the Roof of the World: Music, Prayer, and Healing in the Pamir Mountains* (2009), from which his chapter is adapted. He has also edited the *Oxford Handbook of Medical Ethnomusicology* (2008). Koen teaches medical ethnomusicology, music, and anthropology at Xiamen University in Xiamen, China, and is also an accomplished jazz musician.

ALMA KUNANBAEVA
grew up in Almaty, Kazakhstan, and began playing piano as a child. Later she studied in Russia, where she obtained a *Kandidat* degree from the State Institute of Theatre, Music, and Cinematography in Leningrad (now St. Petersburg) with a dissertation on the music of Kazakh epics. She has conducted extensive ethnographic fieldwork in the Qyzylorda, Aralsk, and Atyrau regions of south and west Kazakhstan. In 1993, she immigrated to the United States, where she has taught courses at leading universities focusing on the music, languages, and peoples of Central Asia. She is presently Lecturer in Anthropology at Stanford University and has published widely on Kazakh music in English, Russian, and Kazakh languages. Together with her husband, Russian music specialist Izaly Zemtsovsky, she founded and currently directs Silk Road House, a non-profit cultural and educational center in Berkeley, California.

KALMURZA KURBANOV
is an ethnomusicologist specializing in epic performance traditions among the Karakalpaks. A graduate of the Uzbekistan State Conservatory, he is currently teaching courses in ethnomusicology and ethnographic practice there and supervising students' field trips to various regions of Uzbekistan. He also works as a research fellow at the Institute for Arts Studies of the Uzbekistan Academy of Sciences, where he is involved in documenting the collection of the Institute's sound archive. In addition to his academic activities, he plays the Karakalpak two-stringed lute, *dutar*, following in the footsteps of his father, *baqsy* Turghanbai Kurbanov, who gained wide acclaim and was awarded the title People's Artist of Karakalpakstan.

CONTRIBUTORS

FRÉDÉRIC LÉOTAR

is an ethnomusicologist trained at the Université de Montréal whose research interests focus on the musical repertories of nomads and agro-pastoralists in Central Asia and the Altai Region of South Siberia. With the aim of developing a broad comparative framework for these repertories, Léotar has collected and documented music in Tuva, Kyrgyzstan, Kazakhstan, and Uzbekistan. In recent years, he has been particularly drawn to the musical culture of the Karakalpaks. He has inventoried the intangible heritage of Karakalpakstan for UNESCO, helped digitize local musical archives, and produced an authoritative CD-DVD of Karakalpak music. His book, *La Steppe musicienne: analyses et modélisation du patrimoine musical turcique* [The Steppe musician: analyses and modelization of Turkic musical heritage], was published in 2014 and has a companion website at http://lasteppemusicienne.oicrm.org.

MUKADDAS MIJIT

was born in Urumchi, China. She started to play piano at the age of six and attended a dance conservatory where she studied both Western classical ballet and traditional Uyghur dance. In the same conservatory, she received her undergraduate degree in classical piano, and at age 21 came to Paris with the idea of promoting Uyghur culture by studying ethnomusicology. She received a master's degree from the Sorbonne and a doctoral degree from the University of Paris-Ouest Nanterre—both in ethnomusicology—for her research on Uyghur music. She plays *dutar* and *dap* and is currently making documentary films about Uyghur music.

FAIROUZ NISHANOVA

is a cultural development specialist with a lifelong love of music and dance that embraces the many styles and traditions of the lands where she has lived, worked, and traveled. Born in Sri Lanka to Uzbek parents, she grew up in Amman, Jordan, and studied economics and international relations at Moscow State University and the London School of Economics and Political Science. After working at the United Nations, she joined the Aga Khan Trust for Culture, where, since 2005, she has served as director of the Music Initiative, based in Geneva, Switzerland.

NURLANBEK NYSHANOV

was born in the Jumgal region of Naryn province in northern Kyrgyzstan. He took his first music lessons from a skilled *komuz* player in his village and from his grandmother, who played the metal jaw harp. Through his work as a composer, arranger, performer, luthier, and artistic director, he has dedicated his professional life to reconstructing and developing Kyrgyz traditional music. Nyshanov is the musical director of the ensembles Ordo-Sakhna and Ustsatshakirt Plus and was the founder and artistic director of Ensemble Tengir-Too.

JANGÜL QOJAKHMETOVA

is a Kazakh musicologist whose research has focused on the art of *aqyn*s and *jyrshy*s and the tradition of improvised poetry contests, *aitys,* among the Kazakhs. A native of the city of Qaraghandy in central Kazakhstan, she studied musicology and *dombyra* performance at the Qaraghandy Arts College named after Tättimbet before entering the Kurmangazy Kazakh National Conservatory in Almaty where she later defended a Candidate of Science dissertation on the topic of Kazakh *aitys*. She has led a *dombyra* circle at the Kazakh-American University in Almaty and is currently teaching courses in musicology at the Qaraghandy Arts College and State University named after Buketov. Her publications include a teaching guide on music theory, *Qarapaiym muzyka teoriyasy* [Basic music theory] (2006), and a book on *aitys,* entitled *Muzyka kazakhskogo aitysa* [Music of the Kazakh *aitys*] (2012).

FEDERICO SPINETTI

is professor of ethnomusicology at the University of Cologne, Germany, and adjunct professor of music at the University of Alberta, Canada. A native of Italy, he developed an interest in the music of Tajikistan thanks to his friendship with Milan-based Tajik tenor and *falak* singer Rustam Duloev. Spinetti lived and researched in Tajikistan in 2002 and 2003, and since then has continued to travel there and collaborate with musicians from various parts of the country. Since 2006 he has also undertaken research in Iran, especially on the music and traditional martial arts of the Zurkhaneh. His main research interests include the political economy of music, music and architecture, and ethnographic filmmaking.

CONTRIBUTORS

RAZIA SULTANOVA

grew up in the Ferghana Valley region of Uzbekistan. She studied both Uzbek and Western music at the Tashkent State Conservatory and later received a *Kandidat* degree in musicology from the Moscow Conservatory. In 1992, she moved to Europe, living in France and Germany before settling in the United Kingdom, where she has held research and teaching appointments at Goldsmith's College, the School of Oriental and African Studies, and the University of Cambridge. She has conducted extensive field research in Central Asia and the Middle East, focusing on the relationship between music and poetry, religion, gender, and society. Her publications include the monograph *From Shamanism to Sufism: Women and Islam in Central Asian Culture* and an edited volume, *Sacred Knowledge: Schools or Revelation? Master-Apprentice System of Oral Transmission in the Music of the Turkic-Speaking World.* She is currently working on a book on popular culture in Afghanistan.

WILL SUMITS

is an ethnomusicologist and linguist whose musical interests revolve around the classical musical traditions of Central Asia and extend to other areas of the Near East, North Africa, and South Asia. His initial exposure to various musical traditions as a teenager led him to his current interests, and while his scholarly activities have focused on uncovering the musical history of Central Asia, he is also an active musician who performs Afghan, Tajik, Uzbek, and Greek music on a variety of stringed instruments and has lived for extended periods among the musical communities from which he has learned. Sumits holds a PhD degree in ethnomusicology from the School of Oriental and African Studies of London University.

RAZIYA SYRDYBAEVA

graduated in 1995 from the Kyrgyz National Conservatory in Bishkek, Kyrgyzstan, where she studied both Western and Central Asian music and musicology. In 2015 she received a *Kandidat* degree from the Chingiz Aitmatov Institute of Language and Literature for a dissertation on Kyrgyz writer Aitmatov's prose poetics. Since 2005, she has served as the Director of Centre Ustatshakirt, a Bishkek-based non-governmental organization whose mission is to support the revitalization and further development of Kyrgyz music. Within Kyrgyzstan, she is active as a cultural entrepreneur, educator, concert producer, and cultural development specialist.

NOTE: Page numbers in *italics* refer to illustrations.

Aaly aqyn, 159, 177n22
"Abai" (opera), 167
'Abbasid Dynasty, 17
"Abbaz hawazy-Qaratereng yrghaqlary" (festival), 107
Abdiyev, Tuuganbay, 159, 174
Abdullaeva, Mehro, 428
Abdurakhimov, Abdulakim, 466
Abdurakhman Pasha (*dastan*), 409, 413–415
Abdurashidov, Abduvali, *16*, 328, 368, 376
Abdusamadov, Abdughafar, *30*
Abdykalykov, Aktan, 542
Abdyrakhmanov, Nurak, *274*, *275*, *276*; on "grandfather Gambar" legend, 26–27; "Kambarkan," 272; and Kambarkan ensemble, 543; and Kazakh *küi*s, 236; and Kyrgyz cultural renewal, 543; and Kyrgyz *küüi*s, 267, 272, 274–278
Äbenova, Äpike, *253*, 253
"Äbikendi jubatu" (*dombyra küi*), 264
Äbilov, Qonysbai, 161
Ablyýew, Ata, 118, 119
Abu-Bakir Kerderi, 92
*abysyn*s, 208, 216n24
Academy of Maqom, *319*, *320*; and Aga Khan Music Initiative, 526; objectives of, *328*, 328–329; and "Talqincha-i sabo," 330
accordion: and *aqyn*s, 150; *garmon*, 597; and Kyrgyz *küüi*s, 265, 277; and nomadic/sedentary cultural divide, 34; *sal* and *seri* songs, 187; *saz*, 616; and Soviet influence, 307
"Ädemi qyz" (Kazakh *qara öleng* song), 183

adhān (Call to Prayer), 10–11, 24n2, 385–386, 579
Adigozalov, Yalchin, 363
Adil Baba (Attila the Hun), 278
advice songs: and improvised poetry competitions, 154–155; and Kyrgyz wisdom songs, 139, 146; and wedding *koshok*s, 223–224, 228–230. See also *terme*
Aeneid (Virgil), 43
aerophones, 30
Afghanistan: and Aga Khan Music Initiative, 531, 532; and geography of Central Asia, 4; master-apprentice programs in, 526, *533*; popular music of, 592
Afghan *rubab*, 599, *599*. See also *rubab* (long-necked lute)
Afrasiyab, Emil, 365
Aga Khan Development Network (AKDN), 523–524, *524*, 531
Aga Khan Historic Cities program, 533
Aga Khan IV, *462*, 494, 523, 530
Aga Khan Music Initiative (AKMI), 521–540; achievements of, 532–533; under Aga Khan Development Network, *524*; and Centre Ustatshakirt, 553; and concerts, 526, *526*, *530*, *532*, 532; and cultural awareness/appreciation, 532–533; development principles of, 533; integrated revitalization model of, 533; and Kronos Quartet collaboration, 528, 535; launch of, 524, 531; objectives of, 525, 531; poster for, *23*; programs/projects of, 524–525, 531–532; scope of mission, 529; and Soviet cultural policies, 525; and tradition-bearers, 525, 526
Aga Khan Trust for Culture, 523, *524*, 524, 531, 533, 540n2

agha, 78n1
Agzamova, Mavluda, 428
Ahal (Ahal-Teke) school of epic performance: and Turkmen *bagshy*, 116–117, 117–122, *118*, 123; and Turkmen *dutar*, 131–132, 137
ahangsoz, 367
Ahmedova, Kimsanhan, 427, *428*
Ahmedova, Sharopat, 427
Aidyraliev, Suragan, 545
Aimaqtyq dombyrashy title, 307–308
Aishuaquly, Esir, 250
Aitkul uulu, Sovetaly, *227*
Aitmatov, Chingiz, 45, 60, 178n26, 213–215, *214*
Aitughan, 180
aitysh/aitys: contemporary forms, 168–176; description of, 156–158; form of, 162–164; and gender roles in music, 14; *jumbaq-aitys*, 94; and Karakalpak *qyssakhan*, 92; and Kazakh singing traditions, 181; poetic/musical structure of, 164–165; and repertory of *yrchy*, 56; types of, 158–161
"Ajdodlar Ruhi" (The spirit of ancestors), 565–566
Akaev, Askar, 62, 145–147
Akbalta, 54
Akbarov, Ilyas, 428
Akhlaq-e Nasiri (Tusi), *323*
ākhūn, 176n1
Akhun, Turdi, 347, *347*, 350
Akhundova, Shafiqa, 536
Akilova, Viloyat, 584
"Ak Kepter" (White doves), 546, 547
Akmeňli, 123
aksak ("limping" rhythms), 331
Aksu, Sezen, 555
"Ak-Tamak-Kök-Tamak," 268–269
Akunov, Turatbek, 545

INDEX

"Alatau," 241, 242

"Ala too jazy," 285

Alexander the Great, 130n7

Alexiou, Margaret, 200

Algara, 57

Ali (first Shi'a Imam): and "Five Ships" story, 495–497; and *maddoh*s, 462; and Pamiri houses, 488; and *qasoid-khonī*, 494

Alim and Fargana Qasimov (2007), 362

Alimatov, Turgun, 339, 340, *341*, 341–342

Alim Khan, Said Mir Mohammad, Emir of Bukhara, *19*

Alim Qasimov Ensemble, 536–537

Äliuly, Sügir, 255–257

Aliyev, Ilham, 366

Alkhodri, Rebal, 534

Allambergenova, Gulnara, *84*, 84–85

allegory: and *bastakor*s, 368, 370; and female musicians in Uzbekistan, 433; and Islamic art, 15; and Kazakh *küi*s, 238; and Kazakh singing traditions, 189; and *maddohkhon*s, 463; and *qasoid-khonī*, 490

All-Kazakhstan Rally of Folk Art Workers, 246

All-Union Competition of Performers on Folk Instruments, 246

Almaty Conservatory, 263, 308

Alovatov, Aqnazar, 463, 467, 475, 479, *480*

Alpamys (*Alpamysh*) epic: authorship of, 318; and Central Asian epic traditions, 45, 47; and Karakalpak music, 81–82, 104–105; name treatment in Uzbek, 576n4; and Uzbek popular music, 565

Alshynbai uly, Ötesh, 90

Ältaev, Amanjol, 165, 172, 173

Altai region: and geography of Central Asia, 5; and Kazakh *küi*s, 260; and

Manas epic, *54*, 55; and Mongolian Kazakhs, 304, 313

Altai Uriankhai minority, 307

alternative music in Uzbekistan, 557–558, 572–575, *573*

Alti-yarim Maqom (six and a half *maqom*s), 321, 324, *325*, 335–338, *336*

alto-qobyz, 295

Altymysh, 155

Alykulov, Barpy, 154, 176, 178n26

alym sabak aitysh, 158, 159

Amanjol, Güljan, 299

Amanova, Roza, *143*, 143–144

Aminov, Abukhai, 453–454

Amirov, Fikrat, 359, *363*, 363

Amirov, Jamil, 365

Amirov, Meshadi Jamil, 359

Amu Darya (literary journal), 106

än, 164–165

"Ana buiryghy" (Nurpeisova), 246

Anahita, 488

Anarkül, 228

ancestor veneration: and *aqyn*s, 154, 172, 174; and avant-garde music, 578; and *bagshy* music, 110; and cultural revival, 529, 530, 551, 567; and epic traditions, 46; and *jyraulyq*, 70, 77; and lameness symbolism, 279n6; and *La Voix des Ancêtres*, 107n2; and nomadic/sedentary cultures, 34, 36, 41; and *qobyz* music, 287, 289–290; and settlement patterns in Central Asia, 7; and Sufism, 380; and Twelve Muqam, 347

Andalib, 114, 115

Andeleyeva, Anash, 202

Andijani, 322

ängime, 152

animals of Central Asia: animal spirit-patrons, 69–70; and Kazakh legends, 279n6; and Kyrgyz *küi*s, 283, 284;

and musical styles, 36; and wedding *koshok*s, 224

animist-shamanist practices, 380

Annaýew, Ilaman, 112

"Another Country" (Bhabha), 521

än salu, 189

änshilik, 179, 190

Appiah, Kwame Anthony, 528–529

apprenticeship: and Aga Khan Music Initiative, 526, 527, *533*; and Alimatov, 342; and *aqyn*s, 154–156; and *bagshychylyk*, 111; and Centre Ustatshakirt, 553, *553*; and construction of musical instruments, *30*; and *dastan* performance, 409–410, 413; erosion of practice, 328; and female musicians in Uzbekistan, 423; and improvised poetry competitions, 174; and Jetigen uulu, 552; and Kazakh *qobyz*, 297; and Kyrgyz *küi*s, 267–268, 274; and luthiers, *545*; and *maddoh* tradition, 473; and *manaschy*, 56–57; and *maqom*s, 319, 324; and oral epic in Kazakhstan, 69; and revitalization of musical traditions, 526–527, 531; and sedentary dwellers, 319; as traditional practice, 22; of traditional singer-songwriters, 368, 372, 375, 376; and Turkmen *dutar*, 137

Apylov, Shaiymbek, 546

Aqanai, 75

Aqan seri, 176n3

"Aqjeleng," 245

Aqmeruly, Qabykei, *260*, 260–261

"Aq qaiyn," 187–188

"Aqsaq qulan," 237–238

Aqymbet, 84

Aqymbetova, Gülbähär, 84, *85*

aqyndyq, 172, 190

*aqyn*s: and apprenticeship, 154–156; and contemporary *aitysh/aitys*, *168*,

168–176; and description of *aitysh/*
aitys, 156–158; and form of an
aitysh/aitys, 162–164; and funeral
*koshok*s, 198–199, 213–214; and
improvised poetry competitions,
157; and Karakalpak *qyssakhan*, 92;
and Kazakh singing traditions, 179;
and *küis*, 236; master performers,
150–151, *151*; and nomadic culture,
149–150; and poetic/musical
structure of *aitysh/aitys*, 164–165;
repertory of *aqyn*s, 152–154; social
role of, 152–154, 166–168; and *terme*,
139–140, 142–143, 145–146; and
types of *aitysh/aitys*, 158–161
Arabic culture and language: and *estrada*
of Uzbekistan, 568; and geography
of Central Asia, 5; and improvised
poetry, 151; and Karakalpak
qyssakhan, 88, 89; and Soviet-era
music, 21
Arabo-Persian culture, 80
"Arabskoe Tango" (Arabian Tango), 559
Aral Sea, 80
archery, 156
argymak: defined, 216n19; and
improvised poetry, 152; and Kyrgyz
funeral laments, 205, 207; and Kyrgyz
wisdom songs, 144; and *Manas* epic, 61
"Aria," 295
Ari Roland Jazz Quartet, *527*
Aristotle, 17
arnau, 191
Aronuly, Süiinbai, 155
Arqa *dombyra* tradition, 256
Arqa region, 252
"Arsar *küi*s," 267
Arstanbek, 143, 152–153, 160
Arts and Culture Program of the Open
Society Institute, 584n1
aruz meter, 89, 90, 322–323, 332,
416–417

Asanbekov, Nurlan, 543, 579
Asan qaighy, 235, 255
Äsemqulov, Talasbek, 262–264, *263*,
280n30
Asgarov, Rafael, *319*, 362
ash, 49, 152, 200, *401*
Ashig Garib (Hajibeyli), 358
Ashimov, Rysbek, 195
Ashiq (troubadour) songs, 349, *350*,
355, 528
*ashug*s, 360
ashyq dawys, 85
ashyqlyq dästanlary, 90
Ashyrowa, Bibinur, 111
Asqarova, Malika, 425
Ata Hoja, 125
Atanazar ogly, 125
Ata ogly, Pälwan bagshy, 125
Ataýew, Amannazar, 127
Atrash, Farid Al-, 559
Attar, Farid ud-Din, 499
Äuezov, Mukhtar, 172
Aura folk jazz group, 542
ayash, 68n21
aýdym, 115
Aydyn Pir, Ashyk, *111*, 111–112
"Ay pari" (Oh fairy), 513–516
Aytaliev, Ashyraaly, 174
azanchi, 385
Azerbaijan: ensembles in, *319*;
and *estrada* of Uzbekistan, 568;
geography of, *354*, 355; and jazz
mugham, 364–366; and *mugham*
opera, 356–359; and popular song
writing, 536; and power of *mugham*,
355–356; and Soviet era, 354, 355;
and symphonic *mugham*, 359–360;
and Westernization, 355. See also
mugham (Azerbaijani)
Azerbaijan State Jazz Orchestra, 364
Azerbaijan State Opera and Ballet
Theater, 357

Azerbaijan State Symphony
Orchestra, 363
äzil aitysh, 160
Äzirbaev, Kenen, 167, *167*
Äzizi, Säypidin, 347
Azizova, Muhtaram, 427

Babakhanov, Ari, 454–459, *455*, *456*
Babakhanov, Moshe, 454, *455*
Babaly, 75–76
Baba Raushan, 89
Babayev, Rafig, 365
*bacha*s, 15, *15*
Badakhshan (autonomous region),
461–469; and Aga Khan, *462*, 462;
and Chanorov, 594; cultural isolation
in, 461; and "Dafsoz," 466; and
dance, 464; devotional songs of,
462; drumming in, *465*, 465–466;
and *falak*, 463, 504; gender divisions
in, 463; instrumental music of,
463–466; and Islamic culture, 380,
487; Ismailis of, 462, 470, 485; and
"Kholatro Banda," 465; and "Lalaik,"
463; languages in, 461, 485–486;
and "Maddoh" (Praise), 475–483;
and *maddoh*s, 462–463, 470–484;
map of, *462*, *504*; Pamiri culture
in, 461, 462, 470; and "Panj Kishti"
("Five Ships"), 495–497; and poetry,
461, 467, 479; and "Qasoid-khonī,"
499–502; and "Rapo," 464–465;
rhythms of, 465–466; and "Risola-yi
Chihil Dunyo," 492; and Soviet era,
467; Wakhan Valley of, 485–487, *486*;
and "Zohidi Pokizasirisht," 467–469.
See also *qasoid-khonī*
Badakhshan Ensemble, *466*, 466–467;
and "Ay pari" (Oh fairy), 513–514;
and *falak* performances, 508; and
*maddoh*s, 483; repertory of, 467; and
"Zohidi Pokizasirisht," 467–469

Badakhshan Ensemble (2007): "Ay pari" (Oh fairy), 513–516; "Falak-i Badakhshani," 506–507; "Falak-i sūzi," 509–511; *falak* performances, 509; "Kholatro Banda," 465; *maddoh*s, 475; "Rapo," 464; "Zohidi Pokizasirisht," 467–469

Badakhshani *ghijak*, 601, *601*

Badakhshani *rubab*s, 599, *599*. See also *rubab* (long-necked lute)

bagshy: Ahal school, 117–122; Balkan school, 122–123; Dashoguz school, 125–126; description and origins, 109–111; learning, 111–112; Lebap school, 123–125; local styles and schools, 116–117; Mary school, 126–129; performances by, 113–114; and *tökpe küi*s, 250

Bahadyr (Dabylov), 102–103

Baibosynova, Uljan, *72*

Baigashkaeva, Gülbara, 265, 285, 286

Baijanova, Nazira, *397*

Baijanuly, Jayau Musa, 185

Baijigit, 252, 262, 263

Baijuma, 246

Baishubar, 82

Baituov, Jäken, 172

Baizakov, Isa, 151

Bakay, 58

bakhshi, 49, 50, 82, 109, 110, 581–582, 609. See also *baqsy*

Bakhtiyarov, Aliyar, 466

Bakiev, Kurmanbek, 145–147, 170

bakshy: and *Manas* epic, 58; and *terme*, 140

Baku, Azerbaijan, 364

Baku Music Academy, *366*

balaban, 361, 362, *597*, 597

Balajanova, Ardaq, 184–185

Balamaisan, 246

balaman (clarinet), 84

balandmaqom, 492, *492*, *493*, 599, *599*

balandzikom, 490, 599, *599*

Balgyzyl, Döwletmämmet, 122

Baliq, 278

Balkan school of epic performance, 122–123

Balkh, 438

Balmaghambetov, Säduaqas, 245, 248

"Balqadisha," 186–187, 189

"Balsaýat," 136

Bang on a Can, 551

Bäpiuly, Mädi, 185

baqsy: and epic tradition of Central Asia, 49, 50; and Hojakuli, 583; and Karakalpak epic poetry, 81; and Karakalpak music, 82–85, *83*, *84*; and Karakalpak *qyssakhan*, 105, 106; from Karakalpakstan, 583; and Kazakh *qobyz*, 288, *288*–289, 290–291, *291*–292, 294; and musical and theatrical innovation, 583; and Turkmen *bagshy*, 109; and Turkmen *dutar*, 131; types of, 114–116. See also *bagshy*; *bakshy*

baraka, 463, 472–473

Barayev, Matat, 454

"Barbar City" (*Shahri Barbar*), 497

barbat, 32, 34, 38n2

barcha, 207, 216n21

"Bardasht," 362

Bardic Divas, *526*

barmaq meter, 89, 90, 101–102, 104, 416–418

bas buyn, 241, 244, 249

bass-qobyz, *295*, 295, 297

bastakor tradition, 367–372, 378, 457–458

bastau, 191, 192, 195

Bath International Festival (2003), 348

Battle of Talas, 9

battue tradition, 189

Bayan-Ölgii, *302*, 302–303, 305–306, 307–312, *309*

bayāz, 324

Baybatyrov, Adamkaliy, 285

Bayqara, Husayn, 28, 128, 130n10, 323, 436

Baýramow, Nurýagdy, 118

baytal, 207, 216n23

bazaars: connotations of, 216n12; and *dastan*s, 410, 412; in Dushanbe, *317*; and *estrada* scene, 558; and improvised poetry competitions, 175; and Karakalpak *qyssakhan*, 100; and Kazakh singing traditions, 180; and *Körughly* epic, 74–75; and Kyrgyz funeral laments, 204–205; and "Mavrigi," 447; and Muslim holidays, 386; and predecessors of *estrada*, 558; and *qalandar*s, 394; in Tajikistan, *317*; and Tajik spiritual songs, 510

Bazarov, Jumabay, *43*

Bäzirgen, 90

Bedil, 322, 395

Begmämmedow, Hally, 124

Behbudov, Rashid, 556

"Beibitshilik," 308–309, 313

"Beibitshilik qusy," 309

"Beijin sary atan," 306

Beirut, Lebanon, 530

Beliaev, Viktor, 18, 19, 113

Beowulf, 46

Berezikov, Yevgenii, 560

Berikbaev, Maratbek, 545

Berikbaev, Ulukbek, *545*

Berkenbaiuly, Estai, 186

Beshik-toy ritual, *423*

Beshkempir (1998), 542, 546

betashar, 93

Beysheev, Taalay, 542

beyshembilik, 200

Bhabha, Homi, 521, 522

bidda'h, 201

biographical *küi*s, 258

birinshi sagha, 244, 259

Birjan-sal, 14, 167, 185, 241

"Birjan-Sara," 167, *167*

Bishkek City Drama Theater, 542

Bismillah, 204, 216n5

biwa, 34

Bökei Orda (Horde), 241, 279n11

böket öleng songs, 182

Bökönbaev, Joomart, 167

Bola bakhshy, *45*

Bolgonbaev, Azamat, 160

Bolshevik Revolution, 354, 383, 457, 557

Borderlands: Wu Man and Master Musicians from the Silk Route, 350

Boroshev, Niyazaaly, *267*, 267, 268

bóshi, 110

boş kakuw, 133

botoy, 269

bowing technique, 30, 35, 256, 287, 297

bowl fiddle (*kyl-kiyak*), 36–37, 265–266, 545, 547, 613

Bozpu, 207, 216n15

bridal *koshok*s, 226

bridal laments, 180

bride price (*kalyng*), 219, 229

Brigades of Art and Propaganda, 307

British National Sound Archive, 427

"broken" rhythms (*zarb-i shikasta*), 505

Brusilovskii, Evgenii, 167

Buddhism, 9, 111, 380

Bukhara, Uzbekistan, 435–460; and Ari Babakhanov's performer profile, 454–459, *455*, *456*; and *Bukharan Jews of Queens, New York: Ezra Malakov, Avrom Tolmasov* (2011), 453; and "Bukharcha," 444–445; and *bukharcha* (folk songs), 437–438, 444, 583; as "dome of Islam," 15; and "Dror Yikra," 450–451; emergence as musical center, *436*, 436–437, *437*; and *estrada*, 572; female musicians in, 438; festivity and celebration in, 437–440;

and "Gardun-i Dugoh," 457; gender divisions in, 441; and geography of Central Asia, 8; and "Haqqoni," 454; and Islam, 379, 380, 435–436, 437; Jewish musical traditions of, 448–453; Jewish population of, 438–440, *439*; and "Katta ashula," 454; and "Khurram," 458; location of, *435*; and *maqom* tradition, 321, *321*, 322, 436–437, 455–456; and "Mavrigi," 446–448; and *mavrigikhon*, 445–448; and Mir-i Arab madrasah, *384*, 384; and Ramadan, 386; and Shashmaqom, 321, 329, 456, 457, *457*; and Soviet era, 437, 438; *sozanda*s of, *440*, 440–445, 448; and "Surnai navosi," 455–456; and "Tarje-i Navo," 459; and Torah recitation, 449–450; and *zikr*s, 390

Bukhara: Musical Crossroads of Asia (1991), 396, 446, 449, 579

Bukharan Emirate, 321

Bukharan Jews: assimilation of Muslim practice, 448–449; in Bukhara, 438–440, 448–453; and diaspora communities, 24; and gender associations in music, 14; and Islamic cultural influences, 379, 380; and *maqom* traditions, 450; and Torah recitation, 449–450

Bukharan Jews of Queens, New York: Ezra Malakov, Avrom Tolmasov, The (2011), 453

Bukharan State Philharmonia, 456

"Bukharcha," 444–445

bukharcha, 437–438, 444, 583

Bukhari, Mavlana Nadjm al-Din Kawkabi, 436–437

bulbulcha, *597*, 597

"Buqtym, buqtym," 262

"Buranbel Aqjeleng," 245

burap-style, 192

Burkhanov, Mutavaqqil, 25n6

Bu Sevgi (This love) (2006), 569

buyn, 241, 245, 312

"Byla lyubov" (There was love) (Valeriya), 555

Cain and Abel (2000), 580, 584n1

call-and-response in *sozanda* style, 444

calligraphy, 17

Call to Prayer (*Adhān*), 10–11, 24n2, 385–386, 579

canonical performance traditions, practices, and repertories: and artistic hybridity, 528; and *bagshy*'s apprenticeship, 112; of Islamic worship, 383, 384–386; and Kyrgyz jaw harps, 286; and *maqom*s, 319, 327, 345; and Masterpieces of the Oral and Intangible Heritage of Humanity (UNESCO), 23; and *mugham*, 355; and musical innovations in Uzbekistan, 578; and *rubā'ī* (*rubā'īyat*), 331

caravans, 9, 34

carved fiddles, 34

Çaryýew, Akmyrat, 133–134, *134*

Casas, Carlos, 362, 373, 375, 536

çekimli, 136

censorship, 146, 166, 292, 542, 571, 578

Central Asian Music (Beliaev), 19

Centre Ustatshakirt: and Aga Khan Music Initiative, 526–527, 553; education programs of, 526–527, *527*, *529*, *550*; master-apprentice programs of, *545*, *550*, 553, *553*; mission of, 553

ceremonial music, 179–185; in Bukhara, 437–440; and Kazakh singing traditions, 179–185; and nomadic culture, 35; Shi'a ceremonies, 389. See also *aitysh/aitys*; *aqyndyq*; funeral ceremonies; life-cycle events; *maddoh*; Qyssakhan; weddings and wedding songs; *zikr chachpak*, 207, 216n18

Chagatai language, 90

chahor shadd (four suites), 324, 329

chang, 123

Changi, Darvish Ali, 17

chang kobuz, 606, *606. See also* jaw harps

Chanorov, Nobovar, *594*, 594–595

Charyýew, Akmyrat, 136, 137

chechendik aitysh, 158

"Chijik-Pyjik," 247

children and Kazakh singing traditions, 191

China: and architectural influences, *9*; cultural heritage lists in, 420n2; Cultural Revolution of, 344, 346, 400; and *Manas* epic, 55; and Uyghurs, 400, 407; and Wakhan Corridor, 486, *486*; and *zikr* ceremony, 399–405

choghur (also *saz*), *604*, 604

Cho'lpon, Abdulhamid, 370–371, 427

Chongdu, 160

"Chong Kazat," 56–57

choor (*tsuur*), 266, 306, 545, 551, 597, *597*, 610, 619

Choorchu (*Choor* Player), 546

chopo choor (ocarina), 266, 545, 547, *553*, 597, *597*

chordophones, 30

Chormaqom (four *maqom*s), 322

choros (of Manas), 44

chorzarb (chanting), 391

Chowdur, 125

Christianity, 9, 379, 380, 381

chromatic: frets, 311; scales, 309, 610; tones, 260

Chyiyrdy, 63–66

"Chyngyz ölbös bolsochu" (Imanaliev), 214

Chytyrbaev, Bakyt, 545

clan-based society, 218, 303

classification of instruments, 30–32

clay ocarina, 266

Clubs and Houses of Culture, 21, 161, 307, 311, 522

communism, 19, 166. *See also* Soviet era

Communist Party Brigade of Art and Propaganda, 307

competitions, 107; and Kazakh *dombyra*, 312; and Kazakh singing traditions, 182; and Kyrgyz *küü*s, 274; and *Manas* epic, 62, 63; and *tökpe küü*s, 250. See also *aitysh/aitys*

composers (*bastakor*s), 367–372, 378

"Composition-2" (composition of Vagif Mustafazade), 364, 365

Conference of the Birds (2005), *581*, 581

Conover, Willis, 365

construction of instruments. *See* instrument making/reconstruction

cosmopolitanism, 528–529; and the Aga Khan Music Initiative, 525, 528–529, 533; and Bukhara, 435; and Central Asian cities, 8; and *falak*, 517; and globalization, 355; and Kyrgyz neotraditionalism, 547, 553, 554; and Oglan bagshy, 120; and Tajik popular music, 592

Cosmopolitanism: Ethics in a World of Strangers (Appiah), 528–529

"Creating legends" music festival, 573

cultural boundaries of Central Asia, 3, 3–6

"cultural enlightenment" programs, 307

cultural heritage: and the Aga Khan Music Initiative, 522–523, 525, 528, 531, 533; and artistic experimentalism, 580, 584; and Central Asian Islam, 379; and *dastan*s, 406; intangible cultural heritage lists, 420n2; and Kyrgyz cultural renewal, 543; and neo-tradition, 298; and Soviet cultural policies, 327

cultural strategies (Soviet), 18–21, 522

dabyl, 188

Dabylov, Abbaz, 95, 100–103, *101*, *102*, 106–107

daf (frame drum), *35*, *607*, 607; in Badakhshan, *464*, 466, *469*, 486; and *dafsoz*, 466, 486; and *falak*, 505; in "Kholatro Banda" (Badakhshan song), 465; in *maddoh*s, 474, 475, 478, 482; in *mugham*, 356; and *qasoid-khonī*, 490–491; in "Rapo" (Badakhshani dance), 464; in Wakhan Valley, 491

dafsoz, 466, 486

Daka, Mämättokhti Tokhti, 418

Damana school of epic performance, 116, 117

Dance of the Heavens (2002), 580–581, 584n1

dap (frame drum), 348, 350, 351, *607*, 607. See also *daf* (frame drum)

Darapshah, 90

Dashoguz school of epic performance, 125–126

dastan (*dästan*, *dessan*), 406–420; and *Abdurakhman Pasha*, 409, 413–415; and *bagshy*, 114–116, 125, 128; characteristics of, 412–420; and cultural spaces, 410–412, *411*, *412*; and *dastanchi*s, 406, 409, 410, 412, 419, 420n1; duration of, 411, 412; and epic singers, 49; five types of, 408–409, 410; and *Häwzikhan*, 418; and improvised poetry, 152; and Karakalpak *jyrau* and *baqsy*, 80; and Karakalpak *qyssakhan*, 90, 104–105, 106; and Kazakh oral epics, 72–73; and Kyrgyz *küü*s, 267; learning to perform, 409–410; of *maddoh*s, 395; and *Manas* epic, 56; meter and musical accompaniment of, 407; narratives of, 408; and *Patimämning wapatnamisi* (The death of Fatima),

417–418; and poetry, 409; repertory of, 407–409; and *Siyit Nochi*, 419; skills required for, 410; and *terme*, 140; two traditions of, 407; and *Yachibäg*, 418; and *Yüsüp-Ähmäd*, 414, 415–416

Däurenbekov, Tanash, 292

Davidov, David, 454

Davlatova, Manija, 591–592, *592*

Davlatshoeva, Soheba, *506*; and "Ay pari" (Oh fairy), 513–514; and Badakhshan Ensemble, 466–467, 508; and "Falak-i Badakhshani," 506, 513

Davletov, Farhod: and "Muqaddima-i segoh," 336, 337; performer profile of, 372, *372*, 373; and "Ranoni Gördim," 372

Davydova, Berta, 430, *430*

Dawletnazarov, Khalila, 105, 106, *106*

Dawudow, Ashyrmämmet, 123, *123*

"Dawytköl," 98–99

Day Lasts Longer than a Hundred Years, A (Aitmatov), 178n26

Dede Korkut Kitabi, 287–288

dervishes: defined, 610; and *hal*, 361; and Islam in Central Asia, 10; and Kyrgyz wisdom songs, 140; and literary genres, 89; and Muslim holidays, 387; and oral epics of Kazakhstan, 75; and Sufi *zikr*s, 389–390; and Turkmen *bagshy*, 113; and Uyghur *muqam*, 349; wandering dervishes (*qalandar*s), 381–383, *382*, 389–390, 394, *395*, 396, 436, 438

dessan. See *dastan* (*dästan, dessan*)

Dhul-Qarnayn, 130n7

dialogue songs, 180, 181, 389, 422

diatonic intervals, 33, 260

didactic *dastan*s, 409, 410

didor (vision), 494–495

Dilaram, 89

"Dilhiroj" (Tormented heart), 368–369

dilli tuýduk, 127

"Dilrabo" (Babakhanov), 458

dilrabo spike fiddle, *600*, 600

diltar, 348–349, *349*, *600*, 600. *See also* Mäjnun, Abdulla

dini aitysh, 160

"Diwan-i Hikmat," *391*, 425

dobulbas (tuned goblet drums), 551

Dodmamadov, Sultonsaid, 466

doira (frame drum), 35, *607*, 607; and gender associations in music, 14; and Karakalpak *jyrau* and *baqsy*, 84; in "Katta ashula," 454; in *Mavrigi*, 583; and *mavrigikhon*, 446; in "Muqaddima-i segoh," 336; in "Nagora Chorgoh," 459; in "Navruzi Sabo" recording, 326; in "Rangin Kaman," 537, 539; in "Ranoni Gördim," 372; in small ensembles of sedentary dwellers, *319*; in "Talqincha-i Mashq-i Chorgoh," 459; in "Talqincha-i sabo," 330; in "Tarje-i Navo," 459; and Turkmen *bagshy*, 123; women playing, *397*; in "Zi durī," 589; and *zikr*s, 390

Dolan Muqam, 351–353, *353*

"Domalatbai Aqjeleng," 245

dombyra (*dombra*), *600*, *600*; and Aga Khan Music Initiative, 532; and *aitysh/aitys*, 156, 158, 160, 164–165, 172–173, 177n11; and *aqyn*s, 150, 154; and cultural esteem, 32; and diaspora communities, 303–306; "*Dombyra* Community" (*Qalaqshanyng auyly*), 303–305, 307, 310, 312; of eastern Kazakhstan, *241*; frets, 186, 260, 305, 309, 311, *600*, 600; and *jyrau*s, 190–191; and Kazakh *küi*s, 235, 237–238, 239–250, *250*, 251–256, 261–262; and Kazakh singing traditions, 192–193; and *küi* performance style, 239–250, 313;

and nomadic Kazakhs, 302–303; and nomadic vs. sedentary music, 37; and oral epic in Kazakhstan, 71, 72; and post-Soviet independence, 309–313; societal perceptions of, 532; and Soviet era, 307–309; and *terme*, 139; three-stringed, 279n12; of western Kazakhstan, *240*. *See also* Äsemqulov, Talasbek; Nurpeisova, Dina; Qazanghapuly, Tättimbet; Qurmanghazy Saghyrbaiuly; Raiymbergenov, Abdulhamit; Tilepbergenuly, Qazanghap

"dome of Islam," 15

domestic music, 223, 422, 423–426

Dönenbaiuly, Beisenbi, 304

Döölötbakova, Jumakan, *215*

Dostmukhamedova, Kizlarkhon, 458

Dos uulu, Korgol, 140

double bass-qobyz, 295, *296*

Döwletnazarow, Oraznepes, 118

dowries, 219–220, 226, 229

dream motifs, 46–47

drone-overtone music, 306

drone strings: and *dutar*, 136; and Kazakh *dombyra*, 305, 308, 309; and Kazakh *küi*s, 238, 256, 257, 260; and "Kholatro Banda," 465; and lutes of sedentary dwellers, 33; and *Rainbow*, 539

"Dror Yikra," 450–451

Düken (father of Yqylas), 292

Dükenuly, Yqylas, 239, 256, 296–297, 298

dumbra, 589

dumbrak (also *dombrak, dombra, dumbra*), *600*, *600*

Dungan Muslims, *9*

dunggur, *7*

"Dünüyö," 143–144

"Dunyoi fonī," 594–595

du'o, 471

Durdyýew, Dörtguly, 118

Index

Durdyýew, Jumadurdy, 112

Dushanbe, Tajikistan, *317*, 327, *462*, *464*, 588

Dushanbiev, Jonboz, 464, 467, 508

dutar, 601, *601*; and Aga Khan Music Initiative, 532; and Alimatov, 341, 342; and *baqsy*, 82–83; in Bukhara, 437; in "Dilhiroj" (Tormented heart), 369; and *dutar maqomlari*, 336; and *falak*, 505; female players of, 426–429, *427*; frets, 132, 133, 135, 376–377, 601, *601*; and gender issues in music, 14; legendary origins of, 26; in "Mehri Vatan" (Love of my homeland), 377; in "Muqaddima-i segoh," 336; in "Navruzi Sabo" recording, 326; "neotraditional," 377; in "Nolish" (Groan, lament), 429; and nomadic vs. sedentary music, 37; origins of, 27; in "Qushtar," 376, 534; in "Ranoni Gördim," 372; societal perceptions of, 532; string names, 138n1; in "Talqincha-i sabo," 330; and *tökpe küü*s, 250; and traditional singer-songwriters, 375–376; and Turkmen *bagshy*, 113, *114*, 114–116, *117*, 117, *118*, 119–120, 123–124, 125–126, 126–129, 131–132, *132*, 132–137; Uyghur *dutar*, *601*, 601; in Uyghur *muqam*, 344, 349, 350. *See also* Alimatov, Turgun; Çaryýew, Akmyrat; Juraev, Sirojiddin; O'temuratov, G'ayrat; Rejepow, Ýazmyrat; Ýakup, Chary

Dutarchi Kizlar (*Dutar* Girls) ensemble, 428–429

Dutt, Hank, 539

Dvoskin, Aleksandr, 559

"Echo of Time" (*Mezgil jangyrygy*), 550–551

Edige epic, 81

Edige ibn Tükli Aziz, 90

education: and Abdyrakhmanov, 274; and the Aga Khan Music Initiative, 523–527, *524*, *529*, 530–533; and *aitys*, 169; and Alim and Fargana Qasimov, 360–362; and *aqyn*s, 151, 174; and Äsemqulov, 263; and *bagshy*, 112, 120; and Centre Ustatshakirt, 553; and Davletov, 372; and *estrada* musicians, 562; European models, 21; and instrument construction, 545; and *küü*s, 297; and Kyrgyz *küü*s, 274; and *maddoh*s, 471; and *maqom*s, 327–328; and Nyshanov, 550; and Orozov, 272; and Osmonbek kyzy, 283; and *Otin-oy*, 423–424; and post-Soviet era, 542; and *qobyz* training, 297; and Qur'an recitation, 384–385; and *qyssakhan*, 89–90, 93; and Raiymbergenov, Abdulhamit, 261–262; and the Russian Empire, 382; and the Silk Road Project, 358; and Soviet era, 22; and *sozanda*s, 440; in Turkmenistan, 112. *See also* apprenticeship

Egen, Nurbek, 63

Egypt, 533

ekinshi sagha, 244, 245, 259

Elebekov, Jüsüpbek, 186

electrophones, 30

emigration, 24, 311. *See also* nomadic culture

"Emotional Tango" (Jetigen uulu), 554

"Empty Head" (*Kallai pusidasar*), 497

end-blown reed flute, 266

End of an Era: Tashkent, The (1996), 578–579

"Engbek eri" (Nurpeisova), 246

English language studies, 553

Ensemble Ordo-Sakhna, 63, *63*

ensembles: and epic recitations, 50; and *Manas* epic, *63*, 63; and *maqom* tradition, *319*, 319; and modern *komuz* music, 273; and nomadic/sedentary dwelling patterns, 33, 318, *319*

Ensemble Tengir-Too, 273, *546*, 546

Ensemble Ustatshakirt Plus, 550, 552

epics and epic recitation: and *aitysh*/*aitys*, 169, 172, 175, 177n17, 178n26; and *aqyn*s, 150, 152–153, 156; authorship of, 318; decline of, 291; defined, 43; heroes of, 44–46; and *jyrau*, 190–196; and Karakalpak music, 80; and Kazakh *küü*s, 244; and Kazakh *qobyz*, 287, 288; and Kazakh singing traditions, 179, 196; language of, 48–49; and nomadic cultures, 42; and nomadic/sedentary cultural divide, 37; performance of, 49; and settlement patterns in Central Asia, 7; singers, 49–51; themes of, 46–48. *See also specific titles*

epithets, 48, 156

"Erden," 293, 298

Erjanov, Manarbek, 186

Erkekshora, 252

"Erke Sary" (Darling redhead younger brother), 546, 548–549, 551

"Erkin too," 284, 285

Ersary school of epic performance, 116, 117, 123

"Eselbai," 284

Esenaman, 162

Eshmanbetov, Asylbek, 277

Eski Masjid (Old Mosque) theater-studio, 579, 584n1

Esshan, 246

estrada ensembles, 21

estradai Tojik (popular music of Tajikistan), 586–595; "Dunyoi fonī," 594–595; and poetry, 589–590, 591–592, 594; role of, in community life, 587–588; and Soviet era, 586,

588; technological mediation in transmission of, 587; and "To hastam" (As long as I live), 591–593; and traditional music, 588–589, 591–592; transnational influences on, 586–587; and "Zi durī" (Far away), 589–591

estrada of Uzbekistan, 555–576; and "Ajdodlar Ruhi" (The spirit of ancestors), 565–566; and alternative music, 557–558, 572–575, *573*; and "Arabskoe Tango" (Arabian Tango), 559; diversity of, 556; economics of, 570; and educational sector, 562; governmental involvement in, 562, 568, 570–571; and "Hech Kimga Bermaymiz Seni O'zbekiston" (We will not give you to anyone, Uzbekistan), 563–565; in independent Uzbekistan, 561–571; and international influences, 568; licenses issued for, 562, 568, 573; and mobility of musicians, 570; and musical competitions, 562–563; and musical performances, *561*, *562*; music stores, *555*, *556*; and "Muzykal'naya Chaykhana" (The musical teahouse), 559, 560–561; "national" *estrada*, 562, 563–565, 568, 571; and "On ne prishyol" (He didn't come), 570; and *popsa*, 557; predecessors of, 558–559; public performances of, 557; regional variety in, 571–572; and "Sen bilasan," 569; in Soviet era, 557, 558–561; and "Surxonlik Qiz" (Namozov), 572; and "10 grammov LSD" (10 grams of LSD), 573–575; term, 557; themes of, 568; and "Yol Bolsin," 569

Estrada Orchestra, *558*, 559

"Eternal Melody," 298

Ethics of Nasir (Tusi), *323*

ethnicity and ethnic diversity, 8

ethnography: and *bagshy* performance, 113; and documentation of the *Manas* epic, 55; and shamanic rituals, 288; and Soviet era, 18–21

European cultural influences: and geography of Central Asia, 6; and Kazakh *qobyz*, 296, 297; and Kyrgyz *küüs*, 276; and Soviet era, 20

experimentalism, 578–580

fable (*ötirik*) *aitysh*, 160

falak, 504–517; "Ay pari" (Oh fairy), 513–516; in Badakhshan, 463; contexts for performances of, 505; cultural influences on, 319; emotional power of, 517; "Falak-i Badakhshani," 506–507, 513; *falak-i dashti*, 512–513; "Falak-i sūzi," 509–511; and "fate" theme, 463; and funeral ceremonies, 489; and *ghazal*, 509; and *maddoh* performances, 471–472, 482, 505; "Navo-i kuhiston" (Melody from the Mountains), 516; and Pamiri houses, 489; and poetry, 471; popular song and dance arrangements, 505, 513–514; and *qasoid-khonī*, 499; regions associated with, 504; *rubā'ī* template for, 506, 517; and Soviet era, 505; styles of, 504; term, 504; variety in, 516–517; vocal music with accompaniment, 508–510; and "Zi durī" (Far away), 590, 591

Farabi, Abu Nasr Muhammad al-, 17

farewell songs, 180

Faruqi, Lois al-, 11

Fatima, 397, 488, 489

Feast of the Sacrifice (*Kurban bayram* or *Kurban khayit*), 388, 388–389

Ferdowsi, 88, 89, 107n3

Ferghana-Tashkent Maqom (Chormaqom), 338–340

fiddles: and *baqsy* bards, 84; *dilrabo*, *600*, 610; and European influences, 38n2; *ghijak*, *26*, 344, 348, 352, 422, 463–464, 474, 505, *601*, 611; *girjek*, 84, 612; *gyjak*, 118–119, 123–126, 131; iconography of, *29*; *igil*, 36, *36*, 612; and *jyrau* bards, 81–82; *kamancha*, 356, 474, *602*, 612; *khushtar*, 348, 613; *kyl-kiyak*, 36–37, 265–266, 545, 547, 613; *morin khuur*, 32, 36, *36*, 613; and nomadic people, 33–35, 36; *sarangi*, 34, 616; *sarinda*, 34, 616; *sorud*, 34, 617. *See also qobyz* (also *qyl-qobyz*)

fingering techniques: and classification of musical instruments, 31; and iconography of musical instruments, *29*; and improvised poetry competitions, 165; and Kazakh *küis*, 240–242, 245, 247, 250, 251, 260; and Kazakh *qobyz*, 289, 293–295, 297; and Kyrgyz jaw harps, 282–283, 285; and Kyrgyz *küüs*, 269, 274–277; and Mongolian Kazakhs, 305; and nomadic/sedentary cultural divide, 33, 35; and Turkmen *dutar*, *132*, 132–133, 136. *See also* plucking technique

finger strokes (*qaghys*), 240

fiqh (Islamic jurisprudence), 11

"Five Ships" (*Panj Kishti*), 490, 495–497

flutes: *choor* (*tsuur*), 266, 306, 545, 551, *597*, *597*, 610, 619; and ensembles, 361; and *falak* performance, 505, 512; *kagutu* flute, 35; and Kazakh *küis*, 265; *nai*, 128, *598*, *598*, 614, 615; and post-neo-traditional music, 551; *quray*, 615; restoration and reconstruction, 545; *shakuhachi* (Japanese bamboo flute), 358, 616; and shamans, 616; *sybyzghy*, 235, 266, 279n6, 306, *598*, *598*, 617; and tradition-based popular music, 589; *tutik*, 619; *tuyduk*, 114, 127

folk legend *küis*, 236, 238

folk orchestras, 309–311, 527, 531

Foreseeing the Birth of Manas (2010), 63

Forighi, 495

Foruhar, Leilā, 592

frame drums, 35, *607*, 607; in Badakhshan, *465*, 466; and *Dance of the Heavens* (2002), 581; in *Mavrigi*, 583; in "Navruzi Sabo," 326; and nomadic vs. sedentary music, 33, 35, 37, 318; in *qalandar* song, 396; and *Rainbow*, 539; in "Talqincha-i sabo," 330. See also *daf* (frame drum); *dap* (frame drum); *doira* (frame drum)

frets and fretted instruments: and al-Farabi's influence, 17; *dombyra*, 186, 240, 260, 305, 309, 311, *600*, 600; *dutar*, 132, 133, 135, 376–377, *601*, 601; and instruments of sedentary dwellers, 33, 34; intermediate movable frets, 240, 280n13; and *küi* performance, 264; and nomadic vs. sedentary music, 34; *pipa*, 603, *603*; *rubab*, 457, 599, *599*, 602, *602*; *saz*, *604*, 604; *setar*, 465, 605, *605*; *tanbur*, 330, *603*, 603, 605, *605*; *tar*, 605, *605*

Fund Forum Uz, 571

funeral ceremonies: and *aqyn*s, 152; and *falak*, 471–472, 505, 506; and gender divisions, 489; *koshok*s (funeral laments), 198–215; and *maddoh* performances, 471–472; and Pamiri houses, 489; and *qasoid-khonī*, 489; and *rubab*s (long-necked lutes), 494; and Sufi *khelipe*, 400; and Sufi ritual music and chant, 383

fusion experimentation: and Ari Babakhanov, 459; in Azerbaijan, 355; East-West fusion, 527, 577; and Kyrgyz neo-traditionalism, 549–550; *mugham* and jazz, 364–366; and *mugham* opera, 356; and Soviet Uzbek *estrada*, 560; and symphonic *mugham*, 359; and theatrical innovations, 581–583

"future of the past," 22–23

Fuzuli, 322, 356, 431

"Galdir" (Fool of God), 367, 370–371

Gambar, Baba, 111, 112

Gambarov, Salman, 365

Gandelsman, Jonathan, 358, 359

garaöÿ, 116

Garchik, Jacob, 535, 536–537

"Gardun-i Dugoh," 457

gargy tuýduk, 114, 127

Garlyÿew, Magtymguly, 112, *113*

garmon (also *saz*, *syrnai*), 597, 597

"Garry saltyk," 133, 137

gaval (frame drum), 356

Geldinejad, Abdolghaffar, 119–120, *120*

Geldinejad, Muhammetgeldi (Oglan bagshy), 119–120

gender issues/divisions: and *aqyn*s, 171; in Badakhshan, 463; and *bagshychylyk*, 111; in Bukhara, 441; and *dombyra* performance, 246–247; and funeral ceremonies, 199, 206–207, 208, 489; influences on gender roles in music, 13–15; and Islam, 319, 422; and jaw harps, 283; and Kazakh singing traditions, 179–180, 181, 190, 191–192; and *Manas* epic, 56; and musical performances, 319; and nomadic vs. sedentary music, 33, 35–37; and Pamiri houses, 489; and popularity of musicians, 422; and religious music and chant, 397, *397*; and sedentary dwellers, 318–319; in Shi'a ceremonies, 389; and Soviet era, 430–431; and *sozanda*s, 441–442; and Uyghur *muqam*, 348; in wedding celebrations, 441; and wedding

*koshok*s, 218, 219, 221; and *zikr*s, 390, 400–401

Genghis Khan, 42–44, 54, 68n24, 237

geographical boundaries of Central Asia, 3, 3–6, 22, 55

"Geri Dön" (Come back), 555

geshtek, 94, 105, 106

gestural movements, 35, 267–269, *271*, 285

Ghabdiev, Rysbai, *244*, 244

Ghajdenbek, 73–74

Gharghabai uly, Berdaq, 84, 90

Ghärip (pen name), 94

Ghärip Ashyq: and Karakalpak epic poetry, 80, 84; and Karakalpak *qyssakhan*, 90, 94, 96–97, 100, 105, 106

ghartyq, 597, *597*

ghazal: and *bagshy* singing, 116; and *bastakor*s, 368; in Bukhara, 436; and "Dunyoi fonī," 595; and *falak* performances, 509–511; and "Kelmadi" (He didn't come), 431; and *maddoh* performances, 471, 475, 478, 479, 482; and *maqom* tradition, 322, 337; as spiritual allegories, 433; and "Zi durī" (Far away), 589, 590

ghijak (also *ghirjek*), 26, 601, *601*; Badakhshani *ghijak*, 601, *601*; in Badakhshan instrumental music, 463–464, *464*; and *bagshy*, 114–115; and Dushanbiev, Jonboz, 467; and *falak*, 505; and *maddoh* performances, 474; in "Muqaddima-i segoh," 336; and nomadic/ sedentary cultural divide, 34, 37; and Parpishoev, Qimmatshah, 465; in "Ranoni Gördim," 372; in "Rapo" (Badakhshani dance), 464; in Uyghur *muqam*, 344, 348, 352; in *Yachibäg*, 418. See also fiddles

Ghirat, 77

Ghiyosi, 479

Ghulja and *zikr* ceremony, 399–405

girjek (spike fiddle), 84, 612

Glass, Philip, 551

globalization, 21–24, 107, 521, 527–528

Goch bagshy, 125

Göklen tribe, 122

Golden Age of Islam, 17

Golden Horde, 237

Golden Steppe, 185. *See also* Saryarqa region

Gönibek, Amangeldi, 117

"Goñurbaş mukamy," 133–134, *135*

Görogly, 77, 113, 115–116. See also *Görughly* epic; *Körughly* epic

Görughly epic, 80, 90

goshgy form, 116

Gramophone Company, 325

Greater Central Asia, *4*

Greater Khorasan, 109

Great Horde (*Uly jüz*), 240

Great Patriotic War, 173. *See also* World War II

Greek Homeric epic, 45

gülazyk, 68n15

Gul-Bilbil (Shabende), 115

Gulistan and Bustan (Sa'adi), 88

Guliyev, Tofig, 364

Gullyev, Shahym, 138n2

Gülpam epic, 127, 128

Gül-Sänewber, 90. See also *Gul-Senuber* (Sheýdaýy)

Gul-Senuber (Sheýdaýy), 115. See also *Gül-Sänewber*

"Gulustan Bayati Shiraz," 359

Gutlymyradow, Begmyrat, 118

gyjak: and *bagshy*, 118–119, 123–126; and Turkmen *dutar*, 131. See also *ghijak* (also *ghirjek*); *girjek* (spike fiddle)

gyruw, *132*, 133

hadiths, 10, 11, 471

Hafez: and "Ay pari" (Oh fairy), 515–516; and Badakhshan, 461, 467; and "Dilhiroj" (Tormented heart), 369; and *falak* performances, 509, 510–511; gatherings devoted to work of, 395–396; and *maddoh*s, 471, 476, 482; and *maqom*s, 322; and music of Muslim holidays, 387; and music of sedentary dwellers, 318; and "Talqincha-i sabo," 331

Hajibeyli, Uzeyir, *356*, 356–358, 359, 362, 366n1

Hajibeyli, Zulfugar, 358

Hajiyev, Rauf, 364

Hajj pilgrimage, 25n3

hal (state of spiritual awakening), 341, 361

Halilova, Mukkaram, *423*, 424

halypa, 137

handasat al-ṣawt, 11

haqqoni, 453, 454

harmonic series, 306

Harrington, David: on improvisation, 536; and Qasimov, Alim, *534*, 534–535; and *Rainbow*, 534–536; and Sakhi, Homayun, 538, 539

Hasan, Imam, 389, 488–489

Hasidism, 139

"Hatyja," 126

Häwzikhan, 418

healers and healing ceremonies: among women, 422; *bakshy*s, 58; and epic traditions of Central Asia, 50; and *falak*, 463, 504; and Kazakh *dombyra küi*s, 241; and Kazakh *qobyz*, 289, 290, 292; and Kazakh singing traditions, 190; and *maddoh*, 471, 472, 473–474; and Sufi *zikr*s, 383, 390, 397

"Hech Kimga Bermaymiz Seni O'zbekiston" (We will not give you to anyone, Uzbekistan), 563–565

heroic epics: and epic tradition of Central Asia, 43–46, 48, 53, 54, 62, 76, 77, 89, 110, 115, 190, 199; and funeral *koshok*s, 198; and Karakalpak epic poetry, 81; and Karakalpak *qyssakhan*, 90, 93, 104; and Uyghur *dastan*s, 408, 410. See also *Manas* epic

hikmät (prayers), 350

Hiloli, Badruddin, 322, 461, 471, 589, 590

historical *dastan*s (Uyghur), 409, 410

Historic Cities Preservation program, 540n2

Hojaeva, Bashorat, 428

Hojakuli, Ovlyakuli, 579, *580*, 580–585

holiday-related music and chant, 386–389

Homeric epic, 45, 47

Hordes (*jüz*), 237, 239–240, 252, 279n11, 291, 300n13, 302, 612

Hornbostel, Erich von, 30–31

Hornbostel-Sachs system, 30–31

horsehead fiddle (*igil, morin khuur*), *36*

Houses of Culture, 166, 311

Hreizi, Badiaa Bou, 534

Hui Muslims, 9

Humboldt, Alexander von, 3–6

*Husayniya-khona*s, 389

Husein, 389, 488–489

Huseini, Shah Karim al- (Aga Khan IV), 494

Huvaido, 397

Ibadov, Domla Halim, *325*, 326

Ibadov, Mahdi, *445*, 445–448, 583, 584

Ibn Sina (Avicenna), 17

Ibragimov, Ochil, 454

Ibraiym uly, Künkhoja, 90

iconography of musical instruments, *28–29*, 28–29

'Id al-Fiṭr, 12

idiophones, 30, 612

Index

igil, *36*, 36, 612

Ikramov, Imamjon, 430

Ilhom (Inspiration) theater-studio in Tashkent, 579

Iliad, The (Homer), 43, 46, 48, 52

Ilkhom Rock Fest, 573

Ilýasov, Orazgeldi, 118

Il'yasov, Rustam, 560

Imam Asim shrine in Khotan, *411*, *412*, 412

Imanaliev, Elmirbek, *154*, 156, *213*, 214–215

Imanaliev, Zainidin, *22*, 552

improvisation: and Aga Khan Music Initiative, 534; and *aitysh/aitys*, 157; and *aqyn*s, 151, 154, 172, 174, 175; and Hojakuli, 582; and Kazakh singing traditions, 179, 182; and Kronos Quartet collaboration, 536; and Kyrgyz *küü*s, 265, 271; and *Manas* epic, 53, 56–57; and musical and theatrical innovation, 582; and nomadic cultures, 42; and *Rainbow*, 535–536, 539

independence movements, 62, 309–313, 313n3

India: and Aga Khan Music Initiative, 533; and Davlatova's music, 592; and *estrada* of Uzbekistan, 568; and origins of the *komuz*, 27; popular music of, 592; and raga *madhuvanti*, 534; *sitar* of, 465; and tabla, 537

Inner Asia, 34, 41, 55. *See also specific countries and regions*

innovation in tradition, 577–585

Institute of Arts in Dushanbe, 466

instrument making/reconstruction, 30–32; and Abdyrakhmanov, Nurak, 277; decline in, *30*, 531; and Kambarkan, 543; in Kyrgyzstan, 543, 545, *545*; and Soviet era, 294, 531, 543

insult *aitysh*, 170–171

intangible cultural heritage: and the Aga Khan Music Initiative, 533; in China, 420n2; and Convention for the Safeguarding of the Intangible Cultural Heritage, 23; and governmental cultural organizations, 523; and Kyrgyz *tökmölük*, 174; and *Manas* epic, 67n1; nominations for, 23; and Nowruz, 24; and Pasar'akhu, Shamämät, 413; and Shashmaqom, 327; and Uyghur *muqam*, 347

intergovernmental organizations, 13, 22–23

international *aitysh*, 171

International Women's Day, 247

In the Shrine of the Heart (2010): and Davletov profile, 373; and "Dilhiroj," 369; and "Muqaddima-i segoh," 336; and Pirmatova profile, 375; and "Qoilman," 393; and "Qushtar," 376; and "Ranoni Gördim," 372; and "Ufor-i Iroq," 373

Invisible Face of the Beloved (2006), 330

Iosis Fest, 573

Isabaev, Chalagyz, 542, 543

Isakov, Rysbay, 62–63, *63*

Isfendiyar, Khan of Khiva, *19*

Is'hakova, Barno, *327*, 327, 373

*ishan*s, 205, 216n9, 390

Ishenbek uulu, Emilbek, 268

Iskendar (Alexander the Great), 130n7

Islam and Muslims: and *adhān* (Call to Prayer), 10–11, 24n2, 385–386, 579; and Aga Khan Development Network, 523, 531; and *aqyn*s, 150–151; and Badakhshan, 487; and Bukhara, 435–436, 437; and chanting, 10–11; in cities, 379; and civilizational axes of Central Asia, 8; cultural adaptations of, 379; and *dastan*s, 408–409; and *estrada* of Uzbekistan, 568; and gender

issues/divisions, 13, 14, 319, 422; and geography of Central Asia, 5; Golden Age of, 17; and holiday-related music and chant, 383, 386–389; importance of sacred music and chant to, 379; influence of, 8–10, 524; Islamic art, 15–18, *16*; Islamic jurisprudence, 11; Islamization process in Central Asia, 10; Jewish assimilation of practices, 448–449; and Karakalpak music, 88; and Kazakh *qobyz*, 291–292; and mullahs, 92, 111, 140, 176n1, 423; non-Islamic influences in, 380; and other religions, 379; and patronage, 324; and *qasoid-khonī*, 487; and Qur'anic recitation, 10–11, 384–385, 391; and Ramadan, 386–389, *387*, 397; revivalism of, 397; and Russian Empire, 382; and *shabih*, 357; and Soviet era, 301n20, 382–383, 397, 531; spiritual and artistic heritage of, 578; and *terme*, 139–140, 145, 146; in Uzbekistan, 578; Wahhabis, 201. *See also* Ismailism; Shi'a Islam; Sufism; Sunni Islam

Islamov, Rauf, *319*, 362, 535

Ismaghul, 176n3

Ismailism: and Aga Khan Development Network, 523; and *didor* (vision), 494–495; and *estradai Tojik* (popular music of Tajikistan), 594; and *falak*, 505; and "Five Ships" story, 495–497; history of, 5; and Imamat Day, *495*; and Islamic tradition in Central Asia, 5; and *maddoh*s, 462–463, 470, 505; and Pamiri houses, 488–489; in Pamir Mountains, 462; and *qasoid-khonī*, 489, 494, 497–499; religious expression in, 462–463; and *rubab* (long-necked lute), 493–494; and Shah Karim al-Huseini (Aga Khan IV), 494, 502, 503n11

Ismailova, Kommuna, 430, 458

Ismailova, Saodat, 362, 373, 375, 392, 536

Isroil, Nurmukhamad, 569

Issyk-Kul Kyrgyz, 55

iyash khomus (Tuvan wooden jaw harp), 282. See also *jygach ooz komuz* (Kyrgyz wooden jaw harp)

Jabaev, Jambyl, 155, *156*, 167

Jabarov, Kamiljon, 429

Jacobsen, Colin, 358, 359

Jakyp (father of Manas), 47, 54

"Jalgan düynö," 140–142

Jalol, Ata, 450, 456

jamakchy, 154

Jami, 322, 471

Jamshid, 130n8

Janat, 172

"Jangylyk," 285, 286

"Jänibek, Jänibek, shap," 260–261

"Jan jan," 121–122

Jantileuov, Qali, 242

Janysh-Baiysh epic, 47

Japaqov, Mayasar, 151

Japarov, Shamil, 63

japsar, 220, 233n4

jar-jar, 156, 180, 233n1

Jaw (2011), 551

jaw harps, 606, *606*; and classification of musical instruments, 31; and "Echo of Time" (*Mezgil jangyrygy*), 551; and ensemble performance, *286*; and gender roles in music, 14; and Kyrgyz cultural renewal, 551; and Kyrgyz küüs, 265, 266, 278; metal (*temir komuz*), *31*, 266, *282*, 282–283, *284*, 300n2, 545, 551; wooden (*jygach ooz komuz*), 266, *282*, 282–286, *284*, 300n2, 545

jayloo (pasturelands of Kyrgyzstan), 157, 204, 274, 548

Jaysang yrchy, 46

*jazgych/jazba aqyn*s, 140, 151, 176n3

jazz: Jazz Bishkek Autumn Festival, *527*; jazz *mugham* of Azerbaijan, *364*, 364–366, *366*; in Uzbekistan, 558

jeen, 205, 216n12

jele, 207, 216n22

Jelmaya, 288

Jengijok, 152–153

"Jengis" (Nurpeisova), 246

Jepbarow, Sahy, 118, *118*, 119, 137

Jetigen uulu, Askat, 550, *552*, 552–554

Jetisu region, 260

Jienbai, 69–72, 192–193

"Jienbaidyng termesi," 193

Jilani, Abdulqadir, 389

Jochi Khan, 237

joke (*äzil*) *aitysh*, 160

joktoo, 152, 198, 214, 217. See also *koshok*

"Jol jürüsh," 273

jomok, 49, 152

jomokchu, 49, 56

Jorobekova, Shaken, 545

journey motif (in oral epic), 47

Jubanov, Akhmet, 167, 294, 295, 301n15

Jubari Kalon madrasah, 424–425

Judaism and Jews. *See* Bukharan Jews

Jugi (Gypsies), 436

jük, 210, 216n27, 220, 233n6

juk-juk, 123

Julgaýew, Amangeldi, 118

Jumabaev, Ruslan, *271*; and "Erke Sary," 548, 549, 551; and Kyrgyz cultural renewal, 546, 548, 549, 551; and Kyrgyz küüs, 270; and neo-traditionalism, *546*, 546

Jumabaev, Rysbek, 7, 58, *59*

Jumaev, Murod, *319*

Jumaniyazov, Qädirbai, 106

Jumatova, Miyasar, 84

jumbaq-aitys, 94, 160

jumbaq öleng songs, 182

Jung, Angelika, 456

Jungars, 260, 302

Juraev, Sirojiddin: and "Dilhiroj" (Tormented heart), 369; *dutar* improvisation, 534; and "Mehri Vatan" (Love of my homeland), 377; and neotraditional *dutar* music, 377; performer profile of, 376, *376*; and "Qushtar" (Double strings), 376; and Remix workshop, 534; and "Zavq-i Javoni" (Interest of youth), 377

Jüsip, Kete, 176n3

Jüsip, Qanly, 176n3

Jusupov, Sabyt, 181

jygach ooz komuz (Kyrgyz wooden jaw harp), *282*, 282–286, *284*, *606*; described, 606; and Kyrgyz küüs, 266; neo-traditional reconstruction of, 545; and "*qobyz*" term, 300n2. *See also* jaw harps

jyldyk, 200, 202

jyr: and Kazakh *jyraulyq*, 192; poetic meter of, 300n12; and structure of *aitysh/aitys*, 164–165; and *tökpe dombyra* style, 245; and types of epic singers, 49

jyraulyq, 70, 179, 190–196

Jyrau-Rock: 21st Century, 583, *583*

*jyrau*s: and epic recitations, *43*, 49–50; and improvised poetry competitions, 150–151; and Karakalpak music, 81–82, 93, 104, 106; and Kazakh *qobyz*, 291; and Kazakh singing traditions, 190; and *Körughly* epic, 69–77; and *maqam*s, 78n4; and *terme*, 139. *See also* Baibosynova, Uljan; Rüstembekov, Bidas

jyrshy (*yrchy*): and *aitysh/aitys*, 160; of Hojakuli, 583; and improvised poetry competitions, 150–151, 152; and recitation styles of the *Manas* epic, 56; social role of, 152–154; and *terme*, 139 *kagutu*, 35

kaiyn jurt, 208, 216n25

kakuw, 133, *135*

Kalendarov, Kambar, 286, 550, *551*, 551, 553

Kalila wa Dimna (Ibn al-Muqaffaʻ), 88

kalima shahada, 216n5

"Kalk armany," 146

Kalmyks and epic traditions, 45

Kalyk (Kyrgyz *ayn*), 154

kamancha, 602, *602*; in "Bardasht," 362; and iconography of musical instruments, 29; in *Leyli and Majnun*, 358; in *maddoh*, 474; in *mugham*, 356, 361, 362; and nomadic vs. sedentary music, 34; in small ensembles of sedentary dwellers, *319*

kamancha (spike fiddle), 356, 474, *602*, 612

Kambar, 26–27, 269, 271–272

"Kambarkan," 272

Kambarkan folk ensemble, 542, 543

Kambarkan *küü*s, 267, 269, 271

kanat, 210, 216n28

Kangurti, Hajji Husaini, 373

kanjyga, 222, 233n11

"Kanykey's Long-distance Horse Race on Taytoru," 63–67

"Karacha torgoi," 284

Karakalpakistan-La Voix des Ancêtres (Léotar), 104

Karakalpak Research Institute, 101

Karakalpaks: and Abbaz Dabylov, 100–103; and *baqsy* bards, 82–85; and decline of *qyssakhan*, 103–107; described, 79–81; and epic traditions, 49, 50; and folk songs, 86–87; hybrid sedentary/nomadic culture of, 317; and *jyrau*s, *43*, 81–82; and music of Muslim holidays, 387; and oral epic in Kazakhstan, 72; and origin of

qyssakhan, 88–89; and performance of *qyssakhan*, 93–94; and *qyssakhan* in Soviet era, 95–96; and Ram Shaiyr, 96–98; and repertory of *qyssakhan*, 89–93; and Sadyq Nurymbetov, 98–100; and *tökpe küü*s, 244, 250

Karakalpakstan, *79*, 79–80, 583

*kara küü*s, 269–272

Karala uulu, Sayakbay, 49, 56–61, *60*

Karamoldo (Toktomambet Orozov), 236, 277

"Kara özgöy," 267, 268

Karimov, Asanbay, 545

Karimov, Azizkhon, 487, 494

Karimov, Islam, 562, 571

Karimova, Gulnora, 571

Kärmenov, Jänibek, 186

karnai (also *karnay*), 597, *597*

karnai players, *533*

Kashgar, *8*, 339, 345, 347, 418

Kashgar *rubab*s, 457, 602, *602. See also* Babakhanov, Ari

kassam (storytellers), 395

Katta ashula (Great song), 393–394, 453, 454

Kawkabi, Najm al-Din al-, 17

kayni, 202, 215n2

Kazakh National Conservatory, 297

Kazakhs: and *aitysh/aitys*, 161; and *baqsy* bards, 82; and epic traditions, 45, 49, 50, 291–292; folklore of, 14; and iconography of musical instruments, 32; and improvised poetry competitions, 149–176; and *küi* performance, 235–264, *236*, 292–293; Mongolian Kazakhs, 302–303, *303*–306, 307–313; and narrative instrumental music, 234; and *qobyz* neo-tradition, 298–299; and revival of *qobyz* performance,

296–297; and sacred status of the *qobyz*, 287–291; and *shertpe küi*s, 260; and Soviet-era suppression, 294–296; and wedding *koshok*s, 229. *See also* Kazakhstan

Kazakh Soviet Socialist Republic, 167

Kazakhstan, *239*; and Aga Khan Music Initiative, 526, 531, 532; autonomy of cultural sector in, 523; and *dastan*s, 406; and *estrada* of Uzbekistan, 570; and geography of Central Asia, 5; independence, 149–150; Kökil College, 526; and *Manas* epic, *54*, 55; and Mausoleum of Khoja Ahmad Yassawi, *381*; oral epic in, 69–77; and Ramadan, 387; role of music in, 380; and Soviet era influences, 19, 21; and *zikr*s, 392. *See also* Kazakhs

Kazakh State Philharmonic Society, 296

Kecha va kunduz (Choʻlpon), 427

"Kelmadi" (He didn't come), 431–433

kendir, 202–203, 215n2

"Kenges," 304

Kenjeghululy, Nurtughan, 195

kepich, 233n17

"Kerbez Aqjeleng," 245, 248, 249

*kerbez küü*s, 269

kerege, 220, 233n5

Kerei tribal group, 302–303, 305, 310–311

"Ker özön," 284

"Kertolghau," 256

"Ker tolgoo," 267

Ket, 283

Ketbugha (Kerbuqa), 235, 279n7

"Ket Buka," 267

Khakas shaman, *7*

khalfa, 14, 397, 438

Khamdamov, Kamoliddin, *319*

Khamidi, Latyf, 167

Khamsa (Nizami), 88
Khan, Amanissa, 345
Khan, Feruz, 337
*khanaqa*s, 381–382, 387, 390
Khan-Tengiri ensemble, 546
Khasenov, Äbiken, 254, *255*, 255, 264
khat, 191
Khiva, Khorezm, Uzbekistan, 244, 321, *321*, 322, 336
Khoja, Niyozjon, 335, 339
Khojambergenov, Rambergen (Ram shaiyr), 96–98, 100, 102, 106
"Kholatro Banda" (I'm a slave of your mole), 465
Khorezm: and *aitys*, 92; and *bagshy* performance, 117, 250; and epic tradition of Central Asia, 45; and female entertainers, 14, 397, 426, 438, 613, 616; and the *garmon*, 597; Khorezmian civilizations, 80, 88; Khorezm oasis, 244; and *maqom*s, 321, 335–338, 339, 609; and Middle Eastern religious literature, 89, 89; and musical innovation, 582; and *otin-oy* rituals, 423; principal cultural centers, 371–372; and religious music influences, 380; and "shah" title, 616; and Sufi *zikr*s, 389–390; and the *tar*, 618; Uzbek and Tajik popular music, 375, 555, 566, 571; and *Uzbek Folk Music*, 20
Khorezmname, 89, 89
Khorezm oasis, 244
Khunar Centre, Tajikistan, 526
"Khurram" (Babakhanov), 458
khushtar spike fiddle, 348, 613
Khusraw, Nasir: and Ismaili Muslims of Badakhshan, 462; and *maddoh*s, 471, 478, 482; and Pamir Mountains, 472; and *qaṣīda*, 487
Khwarizmi, Muhammad al-, 17

Khyrmandäli, 90
Kildebaki, Hadi, 382
Kim, Artyom, 583
Kino, 555
Kipchak *dastan*s, 407–408
Kirghizia, 19
Kitāb al-adwār (Urmawi), 17
Kitāb al-mūsīqī al-kabīr (al-Farabi), 17
Köbök, 159
köch, 205–207, 216n7
Köchörbaev, Samat, *50*, 62–63, *64*
Köchörbay uulu, Kasymkul, 274
Köchümkulova, Elmira: with *komuz*, *140*; and Kyrgyz wisdom songs, 140; Tutkuchev interview, 174–176; wedding of, *226*, 226, *227*
Koen, Benjamin D., 27
Kojojash, 175
"Kojojash mergen," 284
"Kök dönen," 261
Kökil College, Kazakhstan, 261, 526
Komsomol evening, 229
komuz, *603*, 603; and Aga Khan Music Initiative, 532; and *aitysh/aitys*, 158, 163, 164, 174, 176, 177n11; and *aqyn*s, 150–151, 153, 154, 178n26; and Centre Ustatshakirt, *527*, 553; and epic recitation, 50; and epic singers, 56; instruction in public schools, *527*; and Jetigen uulu, Askat, 552; and Jumabaev, Ruslan, 546; and Kyrgyz cultural renewal, 546; and Kyrgyz *küü*s, 265–267, *267*, 269–272, 273–278; legendary origins of, 26–27; and modern popular music, 273–278; neo-traditional reconstruction of, 545, *545*; and nomadic vs. sedentary music, 37; societal perceptions of, 532; and *terme*, 139, 140, 143, 146. *See also* Abdyrakhmanov, Nurak;

Jumabaev, Ruslan; Ogonbaev, Atay; Satylganov, Toktogul; Uraliev, Namazbek
köngil qos, 191
Kongurbay Khan, 57
kordoo aitysh, 158, 170–171
Korgol, 155
"Körip keldim" (Dabylov), 101–102
Korkut, Dede, 110
Koroğlu, 77. *See also* *Görogly*
Körughly epic, 45, 71–72, 75–77, 318. *See also* *Görughly* epic
kosh naghora, 608, *608*
koshnai, 598, *598*
koshok: for Chingiz Aitmatov, 213–215; core themes of wedding songs, 219–232; for a daughter, 208–209; described, 198–200; and epic traditions, 46; for a father, 206–208; features and poetic structure, 201–203; for funerals, 198–215; at grave site, 212–213; and improvised poetry competitions, 152; and Kazakh singing traditions, 180; *koshokchu*s (professional lamenters), 199, 202, 215, 222, 226; and *Manas* epic, 52; poetic structure, 219; preservation and transmission of, 201; sociocultural context, 218; for weddings, 217–232; for a younger man, 209–212
Kosimov, Abbos, *537*, 539, *539*
koumiss, 41, 204–205, 207, 216n22, 274
Kozlovsky, Alexei, 25n6
Kronos Quartet: and Aga Khan Music Initiative, 528, 535; and Qasimov, Alim, *535*, 535, 536–537; and "Rangin Kaman," 537–539; and Sakhi, Homayun, *537*, 537–539, *539*
Kubat, Aktan Arym, 546
kudagyi, 224–225, 227

Index

küi: and cosmology, 241; and *dombyra* performance style, 239–250; historical development of, 235–238; and Kazakh *dombyra*, 310; and mythology, 236; and *shertpe* style, 251–264; and *tökpe* style, 240–250; variety of, 237. *See also* Äsemqulov, Talasbek; Khasenov, Äbiken; Nurpeisova, Dina; Qazanghapuly, Tättimbet; Qurmanghazy Saghyrbaiuly; Raiymbergenov, Abdulhamit; Tilepbergenuly, Qazanghap

"*Küi* basy Aqjeleng," 245

Kuikuro people, 35

*küishi*s, 235, *236*

"Kükük," 283

Küläiim, 75–76

Kuluev, Maksat, *142*, 143

külük (race horse): and improvised poetry competitions, 152; and Kyrgyz funeral laments, 203, 205, 207; and Kyrgyz wedding songs, 228; and *Manas* epic, 61

Kunanbaeva, Alma, 181

Kurambaev, Habibulla, 336, 372

"Kurd Ovshari" (Amirov), 359–360, 363

Küshikbai, 253

Kutmanaliev, Amantay, 156

küü: classical, 269–272; core tunings for, 270; current popularity of, 273–278; described, 265–267; and epic poems, 267; and "Erke Sary" (Darling redhead younger brother), 546; gestural elements, 267–269; and jaw harps, 283–284; and Kyrgyz cultural renewal, 546. *See also* Abdyrakhmanov, Nurak; Jumabaev, Ruslan; Karamoldo (Toktomambet Orozov); Ogonbaev, Atay; Satylganov, Toktogul; Uraliev, Namazbek

Kuwwadow, Ýazgeldy, 127

kyjym, 208, 216n26

kyl-kiyak (bowl fiddle), 36–37, 265–266, 545, 547, *602*, 602, 613

Kynatai, 226–227

Kyrgyz: and *bakshy* bards, 82; and *dastan*s, 406; and epic traditions, 45, 49, 50; and funeral *koshok*s, 201; and horse racing, 67; and improvised poetry competitions, 149–176; and interethnic conflict, 145; and jaw harps, *282*, 282–286, *284*; and narrative instrumental music, 234; and Ramadan, 387; and terms for mountains, 233n13; and wedding *koshok*s, 217–232; and *zikr*s, 390. *See also* Kyrgyzstan; *Manas* epic

Kyrgyz National Conservatory, 550

Kyrgyzstan, 541–554; and Aga Khan Music Initiative, 531, 532; and "Ak Kepter" (White doves), 546, 547; autonomy of cultural sector in, 523; and Centre Ustatshakirt, 526–527, *527*, 529, 550, *553*, 553; and cultural revitalization, 546; and "Echo of Time" (*Mezgil jangyrygy*), 550–551; and "Emotional Tango" (Jetigen uulu), 554; and "Erke Sary" (Darling redhead younger brother), 546, 548–549, 551; and *estrada* of Uzbekistan, 570; independence, 149–150; instruments of, 543, 545, *545*; and *jayloo* (pasturelands of Kyrgyzstan), 548; Kyrgyz Ministry of Culture, 62; and liberalization, 542–543; and *Manas* epic, *54*, 55; national awakening of, 541–542; neotraditionalism in, 543, *544*, 545, 546–550; and "Ordo" (Yurt camp), 546, 548, 549; post-neo-traditionalist composers of, 550–554; role of music in, 380; and Soviet era influences, 19, 21; stylistic pluralism embraced

by, 542; and "Vocalese" (Jetigen uulu), 552. *See also* Kyrgyz

kyrky, 200

Kyzyl-Jar, 230

Labrat, Dunash ha-Levi ben, 450

lalaik, 463

lapyzy bar, 85

Laylat al-Qadr, 484n2

Lebap school of epic performance, 123–125

"Legend of Kambar, The," *27*

Léotar, Frédéric, 104

Levicha (Levi Babakhanov), 454, 455

Leýli-Mejnun, 115, 356–359, *358*, 366n2

life-cycle events, 12, 264, 280n30. *See also* funeral ceremonies; weddings and wedding songs

"limping" rhythms (*aksak*), 331, 351

linguistic diversity of Central Asia, 5, 8, 46

literacy, 88–89, 94

Little Horde (*Kishi jüz*), 239

Lord, Albert Bates, 45

Lost Joseph Will Return to Canaan (1990), 580

lullabies (in Karakalpak music), 86–87

lutes. *See barbat*; *dombyra* (*dombra*); *dutar*; *komuz*; *pipa* (Chinese plucked lute); *tanbur*

luthiers, 30, 31, 277, 294

Ma, Yo-Yo, 36, 358, 359

maasy, 233n16

Mabatqulov, Shodi, 464, *464*, 465, 466, 475

madaqtau, 191

mäddah, 49, 406, 420n1

maddoh: in Badakhshan, 462–463, 470–484; and *baraka*, 472–473; in Bukhara, 436, 438; cultural influences on, 319; distinctiveness of, 471;

duration of, 471–472; and *falak*, 471–472, 482, 505; functions of, 471–472; as healing ceremony, 473–474; and Ismailism, 505; "Maddoh" (Alovatov's arrangement), 475–483; and *maddohkhon* (musician), 463, 470, 471, 474, 475; and *maddohkhona* (ceremonial space), *472*, 472–473; medical applications of, 471; poetry of, 395, 470–471, 475; and *rubab*, *474*, 474–475; in Samarkand, *382*; and Soviet era, 471; term, 470, 485, 487; variety in, 461. See also *qasoid-khonī*

maddohkhona (ceremonial space), *472*, 472–473

madhiya, 436

Madrahimov, Kuzikhon, 376

madrasahs: in Bukhara, *8*, *384*, 436; and domestic music, 424; and Middle Eastern literary traditions, 88; and Qur'an recitation, 384–385; and *qyssakhan*s, 88, 93–94; and sedentary dwellers, 379; and Sufism, 399

maghulbozī, 486

Magomayev, Muslim, 358

Magtymguly, Pyragy, 113, 118

Mahabharata, 43, 46, 52

Majitov, Seifulghabit, 94

mäjnun, *349*, 349–351

Mäjnun, Abdulla, 349–350

makam (Ottoman art music tradition), 320, 331

Makarenko, Nikita, 573

Makhambet (Kazakh revolutionary leader), 262

Malakov, Ezra, 450–452, *452*, 453, 454

Mali, 533

Malika Ziyoyeva Dutar Group, *428*

Mamadbek, Khalifa, 492, *493*

Mambetaliev, Urkash, *57*, 57, 68n13

Mammadov, Ali Asgar, *319*, 362, 535

*manaschy*s: and epic tradition of Central Asia, 49, *50*; and improvised poetry competitions, 153; and national identity, 62; and recitation styles of the *Manas* epic, 56–57; Sayakbay Karala uulu, 60–61; and visionary dreams, 57–59

Manas Encyclopedia, 54, 58

Manas epic: and *aqyn*s, 169; authorship of, 318; and contemporary Kyrgyzstan, 62–67; documenting, 55–56; and epic themes, 46–47; and epic tradition of Central Asia, 43, 45, 46, 49–50, *50*; and funeral *koshok*s, 214; hero figure, *53*, 53–54; historical significance, 54–55; and Kyrgyz wedding songs, 233n15; and language of epics, 48; and *mankurtchuluk* term, 178n26; and nomadic/sedentary cultural divide, 37; recitation of, 56–57; and Sayakbay uulu, 60–61; and spirit animals, *44*; statue of Manas, *62*; structure of, 53; and *terme*, 147; trilogy, 52–53; and UNESCO Intangible Cultural Heritage Convention, 23; and visionary dreams, 57–59. *See also* Karala uulu, Sayakbay

Manas Presidential Chamber Orchestra, 552, 554

Manghystau *dombyra* players, 250

Manguberdi, Jalal-al-din, 566

Manichaeism, 9, 380

mankurtchuluk, 174, 178n26

Mansurov, Abdugaffor, 572

maqām: and *aitysh/aitys*, 164; etymology of, 177n17; and Islamic art, 15; and Kazakh oral epics, 71–72; and oral epic in Kazakhstan, 72, 74n4; term, 320; and Turkmen *dutar* music, 134. See also *maqom*; *mugham* (Azerbaijani); *muqam*

maqom, 320–342; Academy of Maqom, *319*, *320*, *328*, 328–329, 330, 526; and Alimatov, *341*, 341–342; Alti-yarim Maqom (six and a half *maqom*s), 321, 324, *325*, 335–338, *336*; and Babakhanov, Ari, 455–456, 457, 458–459; in Bukhara, 368, 436–437, 455–456; Bukharan Jewish assimilation of, 450; cognates of, 320; and *Conference of the Birds* (2005), 581; Davletov, Farhod on, 372; and diaspora communities of Bukharan Jews, 24; female players of, 429–433; Ferghana-Tashkent Maqom (Chormaqom), 338–340; geography of, *321*, 321–323; historical development of, 323–327; and Islamic art, 15–18, *16*; meanings of, 320–321; and nomadic vs. sedentary music, 37; Omonboeva, Nasiba, performance of, 368; and poetry, 322–323, 431; and "popular classics," 373; principal forms of, 321–322; and sedentary dwellers, 319; in Sufi rituals, *382*; and *tanbur*, 14; theory, 17; and traditional singer-songwriters, 368, 372; transcribing and publication of, 327. See also *mugham* (Azerbaijani); *on ikki muqam* (Twelve Muqam); Shashmaqom (six *maqom*s)

maqtau, 90, 191

Maraghi, Abd al-Qadir al-, 17

Marghulan, Älkei, 300n13

marionette theater (nomadic), 42

Marxism-Leninism, 19–20. *See also* Soviet era

Mary region. *See* Merv (now called Mary)

Mary school of epic performance, 126–129

Mashakow, Baky, *127*

Mashrab, 395, 397, 431

INDEX

mäshräp (section of Uyghur *muqam* suite), 345, 350–351

mäshräp (Uyghur secular festivity), 12, *353*, 353, 410

masnavi, 471

master-apprentice relationships. *See* apprenticeship

Masterpiece of Intangible Cultural Heritage (UNESCO), 174. *See also* intangible cultural heritage

Masterpieces of the Oral and Intangible Heritage of Humanity (UNESCO), 23, 347. *See also* intangible cultural heritage

Mataiuly, Berdibai, 304–305

mathnawikhon, 436, 438

Matyakubov, Otanazar, *45*

mavrigi: in Bukhara, 445, 446–448; Hojakuli's *Mavrigi*, 580, 581, 583–585; and *mavrigikhon*, 15, 445–448

Mawlik, Qazy, 94, 100

Maymyl (2001), 542

medieval science of music, 17

"Mehriban Olaq" (Let's be kind), 536–537

"Mehri Vatan" (Love of my homeland), 377

Melodiya, 385

melody: and *aitysh*, 164, 177n17; in Alti-Yarim Maqom, 338; in Badakhshani *maddoh*s, 471; compared to Arabic calligraphy, 17; embellishment and ornamentation of in *maqom*, 16; formulaic approaches to in Kazakh ritual songs, 181; and Islamic aesthetic sensibility, 15; in *katta ashula*, 393; and Kazakh *dombyra*s, 305–306; and Kazakh *küi*s, 238, 243, 245; in Kazakh *qara öleng* songs, 182, 184; in Kazakh *sal-seri* repertoire, 187; and Kyrgyz *aqyn*s, 176; in Kyrgyz funeral *koshok*s, 199,

214; and Kyrgyz *terme*, 140, 146; melodic contour in Shashmaqom, 330, 334; melodic mode (type) *sabo*, 331; melodic modes (melodic type) in Shashmaqom, 320–321; melodic structure in Shashmaqom, 333, *334*, 334; melodic superimposition in Shashmaqom, 459; and metrical scheme of texts in Shashmaqom, 322; and *qyssakhan*, 98; *segoh*, 337, 340; in *shertpe küi*s, 251, 256, 260; in Tajik *falak*, 505, 506, 513; in Tajik popular music, 594; in *tökpe küi*s, 250; and Turkmen *dutar*, 131, 134–136; in Uyghur *dastan*s, 418; in Uyghur *muqam*, 346, 348, 352; in Uyghur *zikr*s, 402, 403; in wedding *koshok*s, 217, 226, 229–230

membranophones, 30

memorial gatherings and feasts, 158, 180, 200, 204

Merv (now called Mary): and "Iskendar" folk legends, 130n7; Jewish population of, 438; and *mavrigi*, 445, 583; and Shi'a minority, 436; and Turkmen *bagshy*, 117, 123, 126–127, 128; and Turkmen *dutar*, 131, *131*

metal jaw harps (*temir komuz*), *31*, 266, *282*, 282–283, *284*, 300n2, 545, 551

metal strings, 34

metaphor: in Bukharan *mavrigi*, 448; and falak, 512; and funeral *koshok*s, 201–202, 204, 208–209, 210, 212, 215; and inner spiritual realities, 473; and Kazakh *küi*s, 236, 242, 305; and Kazakh singing traditions, 189; and Pamiri *qasoid-khonī*, 487; and Pamiri *rubab*, 474, 493; in Sufi-inspired poetic texts, 333, 433; and wedding *koshok*s, 217, 218, 220, 224–225

meter (poetic and musical): and *aqyn*s, 164, 165, 170, 173; *aruz* meter, 89, 90, 322–323, 332, 335, 368, 416–417; in Badakhshani *maddoh*s, 478; and *baqsy* bards, 83–84; *barmaq* meter, 89–90, 98, 101–102, 104, 416–418; in *bukharcha*, 444; in *falak*, 463, 504, 508, 517; in *katta ashula*, 393; in Kazakh *jyr*, 300n12; and Kazakh *küi*s, 251; in *qasoid-khonī*, 499; and *qyssakhan*, 90, 98, 104; theorization of meter and rhythm, 35, 318; and Turkmen epic, 116; in Uyghur *dastan*s, 407; in Uyghur *on ikki muqam*, 345, 346, 349, 351

microtones, 33

Middle East: and Aga Khan Music Initiative, 529, 533; and Arabic linguistic cohesion, 5; and interregional creative collaboration, 534; and Karakalpak music, 88–89, 96; and Remix workshop, 534

Middle Horde (*Orta jüz*), 240, 252, 291, 300n13, 302

migration. *See* nomadic culture

Mikhalok, Sergei, 570

mimetic music, 35

minimalism, 551, 552

Minstrel Poetry from the Pamir Mountains (Van den Berg), 479, 482

Mirbek (Kyrgyz clairvoyant), 59

Mir-i-Arab Madrasah, *8*, *384*, 384

Mironov, Nikolai, 18

Mirza, Ibrahim, 29

Mirzaev, Muhammadjon, 431, 457

Mirzaev, Shavkat, 430–431

Misgingylych (Turkmen poet), 122

"mobile pastoralists," 6. *See also* nomadic culture

modernization: and decline of *qyssakhan*s, 103–107; and Ismaili religious music traditions, 594;

and Karakalpak music, 80–81; and Kazakh *qobyz*, 296; and Soviet rule, 382, 531

Moldakarimova, Ghaliya, 295

Mombekov, Tölegen, 257–258, *258*

Mongolian culture: and civilizational axes of Central Asia, 8; and epic traditions, 45; heroic epics, 81; and iconography of musical instruments, 32; *khuur*, 287; Mongolian Kazakhs, 302–303, *303*–306, 307–313; and nomadic vs. sedentary music, 34; Oirat Mongols, 302–303

Mongolian People's Republic, 302–304

morin khuur, 32, 36, *36*, 613

Mosolov, Alexander, 25n6

Mualibshoev, Olucha, 475, 479, 509

Muborakqadamov, Aslamkhon, 496, 499

Muborakqadamov, Mukhtor, *464*, 465, 467

Muborakqadamov, Zaimkhon, 495, 496, *496*, 497–499

Muboraksho, 594

muezzin, 385. See also *adhān* (Call to Prayer)

Mughal dynasty and iconography of musical instruments, 28

mugham (Azerbaijani), 354–366; and *Alim and Fargana Qasimov*, 358, 359, *360*, 360–362, *361*; and "Bardasht," 362; and "Composition-2" (of Vagif Mustafazade), 364, 365; and *hal* (state of spiritual awakening), 361; instruments of, 356; jazz *mugham*, *364*, 364–366, *366*; and "Kurd Ovshari," 359–360, 363; and *Leyli and Majnun*, 356–359, *358*, 366n2; *mugham* opera, 356–359, 366n2; *mugham* singers, *318*; power of, 355–356; "Shabih-Hijran" (Parting night), 357; symphonic *mugham*, 359–360, 363–364; *zarbi-mugham*,

360. *See also* Qasimov, Alim; Qasimova, Fargana

Muhammad, Prophet: eulogies for, 25n3; and Islamization in Central Asia, 9–10, 11; and Kyrgyz *terme* poetry, 145; and *na'at* performances, 387; and Pamiri houses, 488, 489; and religious *dastan*s, 408–409; and *rubab* (long-necked lute), 493; *zikr*s in honor of, 400

Muhämmät, Ubulhäsän, *413*, 413, 414

Mujitova, Muhiniso, *12*

mukam (in Turkmen *dutar* music), 134

Mukhambetuly, Raikhan, 310–312, *312*

mukhammas, 96, 442–443, 471

Mukimy, Aminkhudja, 428

mullahs, 92, 111, 140, 176n1, 423

Muller, Frank, 546

Munchoeva, Azatmo, 463

"Muqaddima-i segoh," 336–338, *338*

muqam (Uyghur), 344–353; asymmetrical rhythmic patterns in, 331; Dolan Muqam, 351–353, *353*; and *mäjnun*s, *349*, 349–351; necessity of playing, 344–345; regional genres, 345; Twelve Muqam (*on ikki*), 345–349, *349*–351

muqamchi, 344

Muqam Ensemble, 345, 347, 348, *348*

Muqam Research Committee, 347

Muqimiy, 393

murabba' form, 116

Muradow, Durdy, *114*

Musaev, Saifullajan, 385

Musa uly, Ayapbergen, 90–92, *94*, 102

musical revitalizers, 522–523

Musical Treasures of the Bukharian Jewish Community (Malakov), 451, 452

Music and Islam (Kildebaki), 382

Music of Central Asia (CD-DVD anthology): and Aga Khan Music

Initiative, 526; *Alim and Fargana Qasimov* (excerpt), 362; "Ay pari," 514; "Bardasht," 362; Chahargah Muqam *mäshräp*, 350; Davletov profile, 373; "Dilhiroj" (Tormented heart), 369; "Falak-i Badakhshani," 506; "Falak-i süzi," 509; "Galdir" (Fool of God), 370; *In the Shrine of the Heart* (excerpt), 373, 375; "Jol jürüsh," 273; "Kambarkan," 272; "Kholatro Banda," 465; and Kronos Quartet, 528, 536; "Maddoh" (Alovatov's arrangement), 475; "Mehriban Olaq," 536; "Muqaddima-i segoh," 336; Pirmatova, Nodira profile, 375; production of, 526; "Qoilman," 393; "Qushtar," 376; *Rainbow* (excerpt), 536; "Rangin Kaman," 539; "Ranoni Gördim," 372; "Rapo," 464; "Talqincha-i sabo," 330; "Ufor-i Iroq," 373; "Zohidi Pokizasirisht," 467

Mustafazade, Aziza, 365–366

Mustafazade, Vagif, 364, *364*, 365

Musulmankulov, Moldobasan, 46

Muzaffar-khan, Emir, 437

"Muzykal'naya Chaykhana" (The musical teahouse), 559, 560–561

Myqtybaev, Däulet, 296, *297*, 297, 298

Myradowa, Akjagul, *111*

Myrzabaeva, Meyilkan, *215*

Mysabai, 195

na'at, 25n3, 387

Nabiev, Jurabek, 368

"Nabor" (Nurpeisova), 246

Nader, Salar, *537*, 539, 539

naghara, 319, 608, *608*

naghora, 608, *608*

"Nagora Chorgoh" (Babakhanov), 459

nai, 128, *598*, 598

Naiman (Kazakh tribal group), 302

Naimanbaiuly, Äset, 186

Index

"Näler görüner," 118–119

Namozov, Mahmud, 572

Naqshband, Bahauddin, 10, 148n2, 387, *390*

Naqshbandi Sufi order (Naqshbandiyya), 10, 148n2, *390*, 390–391

"Naqsh-i dolon," 492

naqyl söz, 191

narrative instrumental music. See *küi; küü*

Nasir, Turdimämät, 415

Nasriddinov, Muhammad Aminjon, 396, *396*, 396

Nasriddinov, Najmiddin, 455

"Nasr-i segoh," 339–340, *341*

Nasyrova, Halima, 375

national identity: and *aqyn*s, 146, 168, 171; and intangible cultural heritage, 23; and Kazakh *küi*s, 235; in Kyrgyzstan, 541, 549; and *Manas* epic, 62; and musical instruments, 32, 265; and tradition, 522

"Nauai" melodies, 250

"Nauysqy" (Qurmanghazy), 247, 248

Navo'i, Ali Shir: and Bukhara, 436; and *Dance of the Heavens* (2002), 580; and "Kelmadi" (He didn't come), 431–433; and *maqom*s, 322, 323, 436; as Mirali (in Turkmen epic *Gülpam*), 128, 130n10; and repertoire of Munojat, Yulchieva, 431

"Navo-i kuhiston" (Melody from the Mountains), 516

"Navruzi Sabo," 326

Nawa muqäddimä, 345

nay, 589. See also *nai; ney*

Nazarbaev, Nursultan, 168

Nazarkhan, Sevara, 23, 421, 569, 570

Nazarov, Daler, 594

Nazarowa, Almagül, 111

Nechitaylo, Oksana, 568

negizgi buyn, 241, 243, 245, 249, 259

neotraditionalism, 522, 543, *544*, 545

Nestorian Christianity, 9

ney, 505

Nibelungenlied, 45

Nihol Prize, *562*

Nivkh, 283

"Niyazaaly's Kambarkan," 267, 268

Niyazbekova, Damyra, 547

Niyazi (Niyazi Tagizade-Gajibekov), 364

Nobatow, Ödeniyaz, *118*

"Nolish" (Groan, lament), 429

nomadic culture: described, 41–42; and epic traditions, 45; and funeral *koshok*s, 201, 215; and gender issues in music, 13–14; and geography of Central Asia, 5; and Karakalpak music, 79, 88; and Kazakh *dombyra*, 302–303, 305, 307; and Kazakh *küi*s, 236, 264; and Kazakh singing traditions, 181; and lameness theme, 279n6; and musical instruments, 26, *31*, 32–37, *33*; and music composition, 42; and narrative instrumental music, 234; and percussion instruments, 318; and sedentary dwellers, 317; and settlement patterns in Central Asia, 6; and wedding *koshok*s, 218, 229, 233n13

non-diatonic intervals, 33

non-governmental organizations (NGOs), 13, 22, 523, 542–543

"non-music," 10–11, 25n3

Norkuziev, Murod, 336, 372

North Africa, 5, 529, 533, 534

notation systems: and Alti-yarim Maqom suites, 324; and European cultural models, 20–21; and improvised poetry competitions, 158; and Kazakh *dombyra*, 310; and Kyrgyz jaw harp, 285–286;

and Kyrgyz *küü*s, 265, 273, 276–277; and post-Soviet-era Kazakhs, 310, 313; and *tanbur*, 324, *325*, 325; and Turkmen *bagshy*, 112; and Turkmen *dutar*, 134, 137

Novrasli, Shahin, 365

Nowruz (New Year's), 12, *24*, 397, *433*, 462

Nozanin (Bukharan music ensemble), 444

Nozanin, 444

Nurgeldiýew, Ýagmur, 117, 118

Nurjan Hapiz, *401*, 401–403, 405

Nurpeisova, Dina, *246*, 246–247, *247*, 248

Nursha, Säydul, 418

"Nurtughannyng termesi," 195

Nurymbetov, Sadyq, *95*, 99; and "Dawytköl," 99; and Karakalpak *qyssakhan*, 95, 98–100, 102, 106

Nyshanov, Nurlanbek, *546*; and "Ak Kepter" (White doves), 547; and Bishkek City Drama Theater, 542; and current *komuz* music, 273; and educational programs, *550*; and "Jangylyk," 286; Jetigen uulu, Askat as *shakirt* of, 552; and "Jol jürüsh," 273; and Kambarkan ensemble, 543; and "Kükük," 283; at Kyrgyz National Conservatory, *550*; and neotraditional revitalization efforts, 545, 546–550; and "Ordo" (Yurt camp), 548; and Saamal, 542; students of, *273*

obon, 176

obon küülör, 267

Ochildiev, Yakub Meer, *449*, 449

October Revolution, 166

Odinaev, Abdufattoh, 590

Odyssey, The (Homer), 43, 45, 46, 47, 52

Oghuz *dastan*s, 407–408

Oghuz Khanate, 77, 110, 287–288

Ogli, Orif Bobo Hamro, 387

Ogonbaev, Atay, 268, *268*

Oirat Mongols, 302–303

Öjal Muqam, 348

Olamov, Shirinjon, 466

olonkho, 49

Omarov, Rüstembek, 238

Omonboeva, Nasiba, 368, *368*, 369

"On altynshy jyl" (Nurpeisova), 246

"1000 Traditional Kazakh *Küi*," 298

on ikki muqam (Twelve Muqam), 345–349, 349–351, 416

"On ne prishyol" (He didn't come), 570

orality and oral tradition: and *aqyn*s, 173; in Badakhshan, 461; and *dastan*s, 413–414; and documentation of epics, 55–56; and epic performance traditions, 49; and epic recitation, 44–46; and Karakalpak music, 89; and Kazakh singing traditions, 190; and *maqom* traditions, 324; and music during Soviet era, 20–21; and nomadic cultures, 42, 318; and Soviet era, 531; and Tajikistan, 587

Oraýew, Hojamyrat, 125–126

Oraz, 489

Orchestra of Folk Instruments, 296

"Ordo" (Yurt camp), 546, 548, 549

Ordo-Sakhna Ensemble, 273, 546, 547, 548, 549

Orientalism, 21

Orkhon script, 7

Ormon Khan, 175

"Orom" (Babakhanov), 458

Orozbak uulu, Sagymbay, 55–56

Orozov, Toktomambet (Karamoldo), 236

orta buyn, 241, 243, 245, 249, 259

Orta jüz (Middle Horde), 302

Orzuyev, Dosti, 516

Orzuyev, Muhammadvali, 516

Oshurmamadov, Shanbe, 466

ösiet (in repertoire of Kazakh *jyrau*), 191

Öskenbaev, Murat, *250*, 250

Osmonbek kyzy, Burulcha, 283

Osmonov, Alykul, 151

Otaniyazov, Komiljon, 372

Otarbayev, Rawaj, 106

Ötemisuly, Makhambet, *240*

O'temuratov, G'ayrat, 83, *83*

O'tepbergenova, Biybiraba, 104

otin-oy, 423–426

ötirik aitysh, 160

O'tkan kunlar (Qadiry), 426–427

ovozi khonaqoī, 437

"Oyanu," 299

oyku-kayky, 170

O'zbeknavo, 562, 573

"Pakhtachilik yashnasin," 20

Pakistan, 533

Pamir Ethnographic Ensemble, 513

Pamiri homes, *472*; architecture of, *488*, 488–489; and *maddoh* performances, 472–473; and *rubab* (long-necked lute), 493

Pamiri *nai*, 598, *598*

Pamiri *rubab*, 474–483, 493–494, 603, *603*

Pamiri *tanbur*, *603*, 603

Pamir Mountains, 472

Panj Kishti ("Five Ships"), 490, 495–497

Parpishoev, Qimmatshah, 465

Parry, Milman, 45

Pasar'akhu, Shamämät, *413*, 413

Pashino, Petr, 149

pastoralism, 14, 26, 380. *See also* nomadic culture

Path Brothers Company, 325

Patimämning wapatnamisi (The death of Fatima), 417–418

patronage, 12–13, 15, 323, 324. *See also* state support for musicians

Päyghämbär äläyhissalamning täwällutnamisi (*dastan*), 408–409

Pazi, Vladimir, 542

pedagogy. *See* apprenticeship

People's Artist of the Republic title, 246, 277–278

People's Commissariat of Enlightenment of the Kazakh SSR, 246

People's Republic of China (PRC), 67n1, 347, 348, 407

percussion instruments: and Kazakh *küi*s, 240; and Kazakh *qobyz*, 295; and nomadic/sedentary cultures, 33, 34–35, 37, 318; and Turkmen *dutar*, 132. *See also* frame drums

perestroika, 284

Persian culture and language: and *aruz*, 90, 323, 393; and *bayāz* (handwritten collections of song texts), 490; and Central Asia as "double periphery," 6; and Central Asian *maqom*s, 329, 331, 336; and *dastan*s, 406; and influence on oral epic, 49; and Karakalpak culture and music, 80, 88, 89, 94, 107n3; and Khorasan (Persianate geocultural region), 109; and *maddoh*s, 470, 471; and Manija Davlatova, 592; and medieval histories, 53; and medieval science of music, 17; and mystical poetry, 322; and Naqshbandi Sufi order, 391; Oghuz *dastan*s, 408, 416, 417; and old musical scales, 21; and origins of Bukharan Jews, 436, 439; and origins of female entertainers, 438; and Pamiri languages, 461, 463; Persianate civilizational axis of Central Asia, 8; "Persian" sound in *mavrigi*, 583; poetry circulated among sedentary dwellers, 318; and *qaṣīda*, 487; and Qyzylbas, 73; and Soviet-era influences, 21; and Tajik language, 77; and Turkmen epic, 115, 122; and *ustod-shogird* (master-apprentice) system, 22, 52

philosophical *küü*s, 269

Index

pilgrimages, 111

Pinkhasova, Tohfakhon, 14, *440*, 440–443, *441*, 444

pipa (Chinese plucked lute), *32*, 34, 358, 603, *603*

Pirimov, Gurban, 359

Pirmatova, Nodira, *421*; and "Galdir" (Fool of God), 370; international audience of, 421; performer profile of, 375, *375*; and "Ufor-i Iroq," 373

Plato, 17

plectrum, 35

plucking technique: and classification of musical instruments, 30; and epic tradition of Central Asia, 50; and iconography of musical instruments, 29; and improvised poetry competitions, 165; and Kazakh *küi*s, 251, 258, 260; and Kazakh *qobyz*, 291; and Kazakh singing traditions, 186; and Kyrgyz jaw harps, 282–283, 285; and Mongolian Kazakhs, 303, 305; and nomadic/sedentary cultural divide, 33–35; and *shertpe küi*s, 252, 260; and Turkmen *bagshy*, 123. *See also* fingering techniques

pluralism, 529, 530, 531

poetry and poets: authorship of, 318; in Badakhshan, 461, 467, 479; competitions, 42, 149–176; and *dastan*s, 409, 414; and *estradai Tojik* (Tajikistan), 589–590, 591–592, 594; and *falak*, 471; and Karakalpak music, 90; and *maddoh*s, 395, 470–471, 475; and *maqom* tradition, 322–323, 324, 431; and religious music and chant, 380, 397; and sedentary dwellers, 318, 319; and Shashmaqom (six *maqom*s), 329, 331–333; and Soviet era, 428; Sufi poets, 395–396, 403, 425, 489, 580, 584; and *terme*, 142–145; and traditional singer-songwriters, 368,

372; and Uyghur *muqam*, 344; and women's performances, 397, 428; and *zikr*s, 403. *See also* epics and epic recitation; *qasoid-khonī*; *specific poets*

political boundaries of Central Asia, *3*, 3–6

popular music and culture, 10, 23, 394–396, 505. See also *estradai Tojik* (popular music of Tajikistan); *estrada* of Uzbekistan

porkhan, 82

prima-qobyz, *294*, 294–295, *296*, 299

professional oral tradition music, 320

program music, 234, 239, 292

Prutsman, Stephen, 538, 539

Pyragy, Magtymguly, 84, 114

Qabulova, Saodat, 375

Qaderi, Abdul Azim, *30*

Qadiry, Abdulla, 426–427

Qalambaev, Jappas, 256–257, *294*, 296

qalandar. *See* wandering dervishes (*qalandars*)

qalaqsha (type of *dombyra*), 305, 308–309, 311

Qalaqshanyng auyly ("*Dombyra* Community"), 303–305, 307, 310, 312

Qalmambetuly, Öskenbai, 249

qalon (Uyghur plucked zither), 348, 352

Qalqamanuly, Bukhar jyrau, 291

Qambaruly, Näsiretkhan, 306

Qamiev, Didar, 169, *170*, *172*, 172–173

Qamiev, Ulanghasyr, 172

"Qaneki, tilim, söileshi," 195

"Qaqpaly Nauai," 250

"Qara jorgha," 83

qara öleng songs, 181–185, 186–187

qara qaghys (rapid strumming technique), 238

Qaratau *dombyra* tradition, 255–256

Qaratau *shertpe* tradition, 257–258

qashaghan perne (intermediate movable frets), 240, 280n13

Qashaubaiuly, Ämre, 186

qaśīda, 471, 487, 489

Qasimov, Alim, *318*, *525*; and apprenticeship, 22; and Harrington, David, *534*, 535–536; and Kronos Quartet, *535*, 535, 536–537; and *Leyli and Majnun*, 358, 359; performer profile of, *360*, 360–362, *361*; and *Rainbow*, 528

Qasimov, Farroukh, 580

Qasimova, Fargana: and Kronos Quartet, *535*, 536; and *Leyli and Majnun*, 358, 359; performer profile of, 360–362, *361*; and *Rainbow*, 528

Qasimov Ensemble, 535

qasoid-khonī, 485–503; categories of, 489; and "Dafsoz," 466; and *didor* (vision), 494–495; instruments of, *490*, 490–494, *491*, *492*; and "Kholatro Banda," 465; and "Lalaik," 463; language of, 490; and "Maddoh" (Praise), 475–483; and *maddoh*s, 463, 485; and Pamiri homes, *488*, 488–489; and "Panj Kishti" ("Five Ships"), 495–497; and *qasoid-khon*, 489; and "Qasoid-khonī," 499–502; and "Rapo" (dance), 464–465; as religious ceremony, 489–490, 494; and "Risola-yi Chihil Dunyo," 492; sections of, 498–499; spiritual and structural aspects of, 494–499; term, 487, 503n1; themes of, 490, 494; and Wakhan Valley, 485–487, *486*; and "Zohidi Pokizasirisht," 467–469

Qäwender bala, 94, 95, 100

qayraq (clappers), 537, 539, 606, *606*

Qazanghapuly, Tättimbet, *252*, 252–253, 253–255, 262, 311

Qing dynasty, 303–304, 313n3

"Qirg'izlarga" (Usmanova), 564

qissa, 152

qiyan, 438

Qoblan epic, 81

qobyz (also qyl-qobyz), *32*, 602, 604, *604*; and childbirth, 301n15; and decline of epic tradition, 291–292; and etymology of instrument names, 300n2; and improvised poetry competitions, 150; and inventor of, 27; and *jyrau*s, 190; and Karakalpak music, *81*, 81; and *küi* performance, 235, 292–293; and Myqtybaev, Däulet, 297; neo-tradition, 298–299; origins of, 27, 36, 287–291; and Qurmanghazy Orchestra, *295*; revival of, 296–297; and *shertpe küi*s, 256; and Soviet-era suppression, 294–296, 301n20; widespread use of, 301n14

"Qoilman," 393

Qojaghululy, Birjan sal, 167, 185, *241*

"Qongyr," 264, 296, 298

Qoqand, 321, *321*, 322, 338

Qoramsauly, Aqan seri, 185, 186–187

Qorqyt (Qorqyt-ata), 27, 235, 287–288, 297, 298

"Qosbasar," 253

Qosbasarov, Bazarkhan, 298

Qoshqarbaev, Shashubai, 187–188

Qosybai uly, Äjiniyaz, 84, 90

Qosymbaev, Mels, 165

Qozy-Körpesh-Bayan-Sulu, 169

Qulbai (Turkmen *bagshy*), 250

Qulymbet (Karakalpak poet), 92

Qunanbaev, Abai, 162

Qur'an: and funeral *koshok*s, 212–213; and Karakalpak music, 88; and *Laylat al-Qadr*, 484n2; and *maddoh* performances, 471; and "non-music," 10–11; Qur'anic recitation, 10–11, 384–385, 391; and *süre aitys* term, 177n12

quray, 615

Qurbonsho (Wakhi poet and singer), 490

Qurmanghali, Tileules, 186–187, 245

Qurmanghazy Orchestra, *295*, *296*, 308, 310, 311

Qurmanghazy Saghyrbaiuly, *242*; and Kazakh *küi*s, 241–242, 244, 246–248, 261–262; and Kazakh *qobyz*, 294; and *tökpe* style, 310–311

"Qushtar" (Double strings), 376, 534

qyl-qobyz. See *qobyz* (also *qyl-qobyz*)

"Qyrmyzy Qosbasar," 253–254

Qyryq qyz epic, 81

qyssa (prose-narrative), 94, 115

qyssa joly, 104

Qyssakhan: and Abbaz Dabylov, 100–103; decline of, 103–107; and Khalila Dawletnazarov, 106; origins of, 88–89; performance and transmission, 93–94; and *qyssa*, 94; and *Qyssakhanlar* (documentary film), 107; and Ram shaiyr, 96–98; repertory of, 89–93; and Sadyq Nurymbetov, 98–100; in Soviet era, 95–96; and types of epic singers, 49

Qyssakhanlar, 107

qyssakhanshylyq, 88, 90

Qyzylbas, 73, 75–76, 78n6

Qyzylqurt tribe, 262

rabab, 36, 38n2

radif, 116

Radio Kabul, 558

Radlov, Vasily, 18, 55

Raev, Sultan, 543

Rahimov, Kahar, *48*

Rahmon, Emomali, 328

Rainbow: Kronos Quartet with Alim & Fargana Qasimov and Homayun Sakhi (CD), 528, 534–539, *539*

Raisova, Qanysha, 171

Raiymbergenov, Abdulhamit, *261*, 261–262

Ramadan, *387*, 397, 484n2

Ramayana, 43, 46

Ram shaiyr (Rambergen Khojambergenov), 95, 96–98, 100, 102, 106

"Rangin Kaman" (Homayun Sakhi), 528, 537–539, *539*

"Ranoni Gördim," 372–373

rap music, 581–582

"Rapo" (dance), 464–465

Rapshee, 580, 581–583

Rasylkhan, Indira, 183–184

Raushanbek (in *Körughly* epic), 73–74

rawap, 352, 353, 413, 418, 602

rawzakhon (in Shi'a ceremonies), 389

Raykhon, Bobo, 394

Razbek uly, Qorazbek (Ghärip), 94, 101

Razzaqov, Shuhrat, 336, 372

rebab, 34, 36

rebec, 36, 38n2

recitation: Qur'anic recitation, 10–11, 384–385, 391; recitation styles, 56–57; Torah recitation, 449–450. *See also* epics and epic recitation

Reich, Steve, 551

Rejepow, Ýazmyrat, 126, 133, 136–137, *137*

Rejepowa, Soltanbagt, 111

religious music and chant, 379–398; among Bukharan Jews, 448–454; canonical performance traditions, 383, 384–386; development of, 380–383; and funeral *koshok*s, 212–213; importance of, to Uzbeks and Tajiks, 379; *maddoh*s, 470–484; for Muslim holidays, 383; popular religious music and chant, 383, 394–396; *qasoid-khonī*, 485–503; religious (*dini*) *aitysh*, 160; religious *dastan*s (Uyghurs), 408–409, 410; Sufi music and chant, 383, 389–394, 399–405; and *terme*, 145–147; themes of, 145–147, 212–213; by women, *397*, 397, 423–425. *See also maddoh*; *qasoid-khonī*; Sufism; *zikr*

Index

Remix workshop, 534

Representative List of the Intangible Cultural Heritage of Humanity, *24*, 67n1, 327. *See also* intangible cultural heritage

rhythm and rhythmic patterns: and *aitysh/aitys*, 149; and Azerbaijani *mugham*, 360, 362–363; and Badakhshani music, 463, 465–467; and creative collaboration, 538–539; and Dashoguz *dessanchy bagshys*, 125; and *dastan* performance, 415–416, 419; and *dombyra* styles, 305; and epic recitation, 191–192; and European influences, 20; and *falak*, 504–505, 508, 513–514, 517; and female musicians in Uzbekistan, 424, 429; and funeral *koshok*s, 206, 213, 230; and heroic epics, 104; and Islamic art, 15, 17; and the Kashgar *rubab*, 459; and Kazakh *küü*s, 238, 240, 244, 250, 251, 260, 262; and *maddoh* tradition, 471, 475–476, 478, 482–483; and *maqom*s, 320–321, 322–323, 330–331, 335, 338–339; and musical memory, 530, 533; and neo-traditional music, 549, 551–552, 554; nomads and sedentary dwellers contrasted, 34–35, 318; and popular music, 368, 373, 375, 377; and *qasoid-khonī*, 498–499; and *qobyz* styles, 292; and religious music and chant, 384, 386, 391; ritual and ceremonial songs, 181; and "*shahd*," 456; and *sozanda*s of Bukhara, 444; and structure of "Garry saltyk," 133; and Sufi *zikr*s, 401–403, 403–405; and *terme* poetry, 142, 146; and theatrical innovations, 581, 583–584; and tradition-based popular music, 589, 591; and Uyghur *muqam*, 345, 350–353

Richthofen, Ferdinand von, 9

riddle *aitysh/aitys*, 160, 182

Riley, Terry, 551

"ringing" *küü*s, 269

Risāla al-sharafiyya (al-Urmawi), 17

"Risola-yi Chihil Dunyo" (Treatise of the forty worlds), 492

Roksanaki (Kazakh rock group), 23

Romanovskaya, Yelena, 18

romantic *dastan*s, 408, 410

romantic epics, 90

Roslavets, Nikolai, 25n6

rubab (long-necked lute), 599, *599*; and Babakhanov, Ari, 454, 455, 456, 457, 458, *458*, 459; construction of, *30*, 491, 492; and *falak*, 505; frets, 457, 599, *599*, 602, *602*; in "Gardun-i Dugoh," 457; in Indian raga *madhuvanti*, 534; Kashgar *rubab*, 457, *602*, 602; in "Khurram," 458; in *maddoh*, *474*, 474–475, 476, 478; mythical origins, 27–30; in "Nagora Chorgoh," 459; in Pamiri Ismaili community, 493–494; Pamiri *rubab*, 474–483, 493–494, 603, *603*; and *qasoid-khonī*, 490, 491, *492*, 492, 499; in *Rainbow*, 537–538; in "Rangin Kaman," 537–538, *538*, 539; as sacred instrument, 493, 498; and Sakhi, Homayun, 528; societal perceptions of, 532; in "Surnai navosi," 456; as symbol and metaphor, 474–475; in "Talqincha-i Mashq-i Chorgoh," 459; in "Tarje-i Navo," 459; in "Zi durī," 589

rubā'ī (*rubā'iyat*), 332, 471, 482, 506, 517

Rubinov, Roshel, 450–452

Rudaki, 107n3

Rumi, Jalal ad-Din: and Badakhshan, 461; and "Dunyoi fonī," 594, 595; and *falak* performances, 509–510; and *maddoh* performances, 471, 481; and

maqom, 322; pen name of, 517; and *qasoid-khonī*, 489; in Tajikistan, 594; and transmission among sedentary dwellers, 318

Russia: and *aqyn*s, 166–168; and geography of Central Asia, 5, 6; and Kazakh *dombyra*, 261–262, 302–303; Russian Empire, 382; Russian language, 6; Russian Revolution, 99, 325; and wedding traditions, 229. *See also* Soviet era

Russian Geographical Society, 55

Rüstembekov, Bidas, 69, *72*, 77, 181, 191, *192*, 193, 195

Saamal folk ensemble, 542

sabo melodic type, 330, 331. See also *maqom*

Sabri, 322

Saburova, Injigül, *85*

Sachs, Curt, 30–31

Sa'di, 322, 471

Sadykov, Fahriddin, 431

Sadykova, Salamat, 543

Sadyq Nurymbetov, 98–100

safail (rattle), 390, 394

Safarov, Ghulomsho, 464, 475, 479

Safavid dynasty, 28–29, 78n6

Safaviyeh Sufi order, 78n6

sagha, 245, 249

sagha buyn, 241

Saghynbaiuly, Mukhambet, *312*

Saghynbaiuly, Öserkhan, 305, 307, 308, 309

Sakha (Yakut) people, 49

Sakhi, Homayun: and Harrington, David, 535; and Indian raga *madhuvanti*, 534; and Kronos Quartet collaboration, *537*, 537–539, *539*; and "Rangin Kaman," 537–539, *539*

Sakhna Theater, 543

sal, 181, 185–189, 189–190. See also *seri*

"Saltanat," 257–259

Saltuu muzyka borboru (Center for [Kyrgyz] Traditional Music), 143. *See also* Centre Ustatshakirt

Salyr-Saryk school of epic performance, 116, 117

Samarkand, Uzbekistan: and *estrada*, 572; and Islam, 379, 380; Jewish population of, 438; and Shashmaqom, 321; and *zikr*, 390

Sanai, 471

sanat aitysh, 158

Sandybaiuly, Ybyrai, 185

santur, 604, *604*

Sarabsky, Isfar, 366

sarangi, 34, 616

*sarbaytkhon*s, 466

"Särbinaz," 85

sarinda, 34, 616

Saryarqa region, 185, 252, 262

"Saryjailau," 255

Sarymsakova, Lutfihonim, 428

saryn (recurrent motif): etymology of, 177n17; and improvised poetry competitions, 164–165, 173; and Kazakh *qobyz*, 290, 292–293, 298

"Sary-Özök," 276

Saryýew, Pürli, *117*, 117, 118, 137

Sassanian dynasty, 9, 38n2

satar (long-necked lute), 344, 604, *604*

sato-tanbur, 330, 341, 604, *604*

Satybaldieva, Büsaadat, *214*

Satylganov, Toktogul, 143, 268, *270*, 270–271, 281n41

Sayakbay Karala uulu. *See* Karala uulu, Sayakbay

Sayatkhan Hämire epic, 80, 90

Saýatly Hemra (Turkmen epic tale), 136

Sayatölekov, Baghanaly, 263

Sayyido (poet), 322

saz (long-necked lute), 360, *597*, 597, 604, *604*

sazanda (Turkmen term for musician), 109. See also *sozanda*

saz syrnai, 598, *598*

Secret History of the Mongols, The (Cleaves, tr. and ed.), 43, 44, 46, 54

sedentary culture and dwellers: ensembles of, 318; and geography of Central Asia, 5; Islamic influence on, 15, 319; and Karakalpak music, 79, 80, 88; and *maqom*, 319; and musical instruments, 26, 32–37, *33*; and nomads, 5, 317; and orality, 318; and patterns of settlement, 6–8; and percussion instruments, 318; poetry recorded by, 318; religious music of (*see* religious music and chant); role of gender in performances of, 318–319; and sedentarization, 317, *317*; spiritual culture of, 8; term, 317; and wedding *koshok*s, 229

"Segizinshi mart" (Nurpeisova, Dina), 246

segoh melodic type, 337, 340. See also *maqom*

Seifullin, Säken, 293

Selkinchek (1993), 542

Semetey, 52, 53, 60, 63–67, 68n12

"Sen bilasan," 569

seri, 181, 185–189, *189*–190, 197n1

"Serwi agajy," 127

Se'Tanho (formerly Setora), 565–566

setar, 605, *605*; in Badakhshan, *464*, *465*, 465; and *falak*, 505; frets, 465, *605*, 605; and Muborakqadamov, Mukhtor, 467

settlement. *See* sedentary culture and dwellers

Sevara and Ėl'f: Tak Legko (Sevara and the elf: So easy) (2010), 570

"Seven Planets" (Navo'i'), 580

Seytek, 52, 53, 60

Shabahrem (Shabende), 115

Shabende, 114, 115

shabih (*taziyeh*), 357

"Shabih-Hijran" (Parting night), 357

Shaghdat, Shah, 73

shahada, 140

"Shahd," 583–584

shahd, 446, 456

"Shahd-i gardon," 446–448

Shah Ismayil (Magomayev), 358

shahnai, 34

Shahname (Ferdowsi), 88, 89

Shahzoda (Uzbek singer), *570*

shaiyr-qyssakhan, 94

Shäkeev, Köken, 161, *164*, 164

Shakir, Abliz, 345–346, *346*

shakuhachi (Japanese bamboo flute), 358

shamanic practices: and *aqyn*s, 153; and *baqsy* bards, 82, 109; drums used in, 318; and epic traditions, 50; and Islamic influence in Central Asia, 10, 380; and *jyrau*s, 190–191; and Kazakh *qobyz*, 287–294, *288*, 298–299; and Kazakh singing traditions, 188, 190; and Kyrgyz *küü*s, 281n30; and *Manas* epic, 7; and musical instruments, 26; and musical styles, 36; and *tökpe küü*s, 241; and traditional knowledge, 7; and visionary dreams, 58

Shams, *594*, 594–595

Shams-i Tabrizi, 322, 471, 489, 499, 500, 501, 517, 594, 595, 630

shang qobyz, 606, *606*. See also jaw harps

shari'a, 11

Sharifov, Sodir Khan Baba, 368–369

Shäryar epic, 81, 90

Shashmaqom (six *maqom*s): and Academy of Maqom, 526; and Aga Khan Music Initiative, 526; asymmetrical rhythmic patterns in, 331; and Babakhanov, Ari, 458–459; and *bayāz* references, 324; and

INDEX

Bukhara, 321, 329, 456, 457, *457*; and cultural politics, 23; first mention of, 329–335; and Ishakova, Barno, 327; and Islamic influences, 16, *16*; Jewish assimilation of, 450, 452, *452*; and Jewish population, 440; Omonboeva, Nasiba's performance of, 368; and poetic texts, 331–333; and "popular classics," 373; regions associated with, 321; "Talqincha-i sabo," 330–335, *334*; and *tanbur*, *324*, 329; and UNESCO recognition, 327; Uspensky's edition of, *327*. *See also* Abdurashidov, Abduvali

Shashmaqom Ensemble, *452*, 452

Shatenov, Bakyt, 543

Sheikh Antahur Mosque, 386, *387*

Sheikh San'on (1996), 580

Sherali, Loiq, 592

Sherba, John, 539

Sheripova, Ziyada, 84, *85*

shertpe style: and improvised poetry competitions, 165; and Kazakh *küi*s, 239–240, 251–264; and Mongolian Kazakhs, 305–306, 311–312; and three-string *dombyra*, 279n12

Sheýdaýy, 114, 115

Shi'a Islam: and Ashura (Ashuro), 383, 389; in Azerbaijan, 354; in Bukhara, 389, 436, 445, 446; and geography of Central Asia, 5; and Ismaili Muslims, 462, 523, 594; and Pamiri houses, 488; and *qyzylbas* term, 78n6; and *shabih* (*taziyeh*), 357; Shi'a populations, 380; and Uyghur *dastan*s, 408. *See also* Ali (first Shi'a Imam)

Shirazi, Qutb al-Din al-, 17

Shirinov, Natiq, *319*

shiru shakar (milk and sugar), 448

Shirvani, Seyyid Azim, 362

Shodmonbekov, Asadbek, 466

Shoqan Valikhanov monument, *18*

Shüdüngüt *küü*s, 267

"Shur" (Amirov), 359–360, 363

Shushinski, Khan, 359

Shygaev, Yuristanbek, 542

Shyghaiuly, Däuletkerei, 241, 245, 246–247

*shyngyrama küü*s, 269

"Shyngyrau," 293

shyn qobyz, 606, *606*. *See also* jaw harps

Silk Road: and Islamic influence in Central Asia, 9; and Kashgar, 8; and nomadic vs. sedentary music, 33–34; and settlement patterns in Central Asia, 8; and spread of religions, 9; and Wakhan Corridor, 486

Silk Road Ensemble, 36, 358, 359

sitar of India, 465, 592

Siyit Nochi (*dastan*), 419

sky deity, 7. *See also* Tengrism (Tengrianism)

Smithsonian Folkways Recordings, 421, 526

socialism, 19, 95, 307, 560. *See also* Soviet era

social role of musicians: and *aqyn*s, 152–154, 166–168; and funeral *koshok*s, 208; and Karakalpak music, 102; and Kyrgyz *terme* poetry, 145–146; and marginalization of musicians, 14–15; social justice, 166–168; and *toy*, 12–13

Sodiqova, Gulchehra, 512, 516, *516*, 589, *589*

Sodir Khan. *See* Sharifov, Sodir Khan Baba

Sogdiana (Oksana Nechitaylo), 568

Sohibov, Shohnazar, 326

Solntsa, Slyozy, 573–574

soloists: and Karakalpak epic poetry, 84; and Kyrgyz wisdom songs, 143; and *Manas* epic, 63; and modern *komuz* music, 273; and nomadic/

sedentary cultures, 33–34, 42; and Turkmen *bagshy*, 114, 118, 125, 127; and Turkmen *dutar*, 131–132; and wedding *koshok*s, 233n1. *See also* virtuosic pieces and performances

Soltansoýun Baýkara, 128

"Song of Attila Khan," 278

sorud, 34, 617

South Slavic epic, 45

Soviet era: and *aitysh/aitys*, 151, 158; and Alimatov, Turgun, 342; and *aqyn*s, *150*, 166–167, 174; and Azerbaijan, 354, 355; and Badakhshan, 467; and Bukhara, 437, 438; cultural influence in Central Asia, 6; and cultural policies, 326–327, 328, 459, 522, 523, 525, 543, 578, 587; and documentation of the *Manas* epic, 55–56; and epic traditions, 49; and *estrada* (Uzbekistan), 557, 558–561; and *estradai Tojik* (Tajikistan), 586, 588; and European–indigenous music fusions, 527, 543, 545; and *falak*, 505, 508; and female musicians, 428, 430–431; and folk orchestras, 527, 531; and gender issues in music, 14, 37, 430–431; and iconography of musical instruments, 28; influence on Central Asian music, 18–21; and instrument reconstruction, 543; and internationalist emphasis, 560; and Islam, 382–383, 397; and jazz *mugham*, 364; and Karakalpak music, 80, 95–96; and *katta ashula*, 453; and Kazakh *qobyz*, 287, 292, 294, 296–298; and Kyrgyz folk music, 56; and Kyrgyz *komuz* music, 277; and *maddoh* tradition, 471; and Manas epic, 62; and *Manas* epic, 68n11; and *mankurtchuluk* term, 178n26; and *maqom* tradition, 326–327, 455; and master-apprentice programs, 553;

and modernization of indigenous traditions, 531; and nomadic cultures, 42; and orally transmitted repertories, 531; and *otin-oy*, 423; and patronage, 13; and persecution of kulaks, 177n22; and poetry, 428; and *qyssakhan*, 95–96, 101; and settlement patterns in Central Asia, 6–7; and *shertpe küi*s, 263; and Sufi music, 391, 392, 393; and support of the arts, 307–308, 588, 589; and Tajikistan, 586–587, 588; and *terme*, 146; and Toktogul's exile, 281n41; and traditional singer-songwriters, 367; and traditional songs, 370; and Turkmen *bagshy*, 111, 117; in Uzbekistan, 557, 558–561, 578; and wedding *koshok*s, 229; and *zikr*, 391

Soviet Ministry of Culture, 20

Söyünow, Baÿrammyrat, *134*

sozanda: in Bukhara, 438, *440*, 448; cultural role of, 448; and gender associations in music, *14*, 14; profile of Pinkhasova, Tohfakhon, *440*, 440–443, *441*; repertory of, 443–445

spike fiddles, *26*, *29*, 34

Stalin, Joseph, 20, 177n22, 371

Stalin Prize, 167

Stambaev, Jünisbai, 263

State Radio of Uzbekistan, 428

state support for musicians, 246, 277–278, 307–308, 588, 589. *See also* patronage

steppe region, 6–8, 36

storytellers and storytelling, 152, 237, 381. *See also* epics and epic recitation

strophic form: and *dafsoz*, 466; and Kazakh *aitys*, 164–165; and Kazakh *küi*s, 254, 258, 260; and musical collaboration, 536; and *qyssakhan*, 93, 101–102; and Sufi *zikr*s, 391; and texts of epic songs, 116

strumming technique, 34, *132*, 132–133, 238, 245, 260. *See also* plucking technique

Sufism: brotherhoods of, 399; in Bukhara, 436; and China's Cultural Revolution, 400; and *Conference of the Birds* (2005), 581; and *hal*, 361; and Hojakuli's *Mavrigi*, 584; influence of, on Islam, 380; and Islamic art, 15; and Islamic influence in Central Asia, 10, 11; and Karakalpak music, 89, 96–97; and Kashgar *rubab*, 457; and Kazakh *qobyz*, 292; *khanaqa*s of, 387; and *khelipe*, 399–400; "limping" rhythms used in, 351; and oral epic in Kazakhstan, 78n6; and poetry, 344, 395, 489; and Qasimov, Alim, 580; religious music and chant, 381, 389–394; and Soviet era, 391, 392, 393; spiritual chain continuity (*silsila*), 430; and *terme*, 139–140, 148n2; and Uyghur *muqam*, 344, 351; and *zikr* ceremony, 382, 389–392, *391*, 399–405, 580, 581. *See also* Hafez; Naqshbandi Sufi order (Naqshbandiyya); Rumi, Jalal ad-Din; Yassawiyya (also Yassawi order); *zikr*

Suhangulyevw, Tächmämmet, 117, *118*

Sultanbekov, Kutmanaaly, *284*, 286, 551, *553*

Sultanov, Jurahon, 431

sumalak (ritual meal), *433*

sunna, 11

Sunni Islam, 5, 380, 436, 446

suona, 34

süre aitysh, 160–161, 177n12

surnai (*surnay*, *sunay*), 14, 34, 266, 336, 598, *598*

"Surnai navosi," 455–456

"Surxonlik Qiz" (Namozov), 572

Suusar, 204

Süyew baqsy, 84

Süyirbek uly, Omar, 90

*suyryp salma aqyn*s, 151, 154, 172

Swiss Agency for Development and Cooperation, 584

sybyzghy, 235, 266, 279n6, 306, 598, *598*

Sydykov, Kulmat, *66*, 66

"Sylqyldaq," 252, 253

symbolism in music: and Badakhshani music and dance, 464; and Bukharan Jewish musical tradition, 453; cultural significance of *maqom* music, 327; and funeral *koshok*s, 200, 204, 209, 215; and *jyrau*s, 194; and Kazakh singing traditions, 180, 183, 188; and Kyrgyz *küi*s, 280n30; and *maddoh* poetry, 471, 473; and musical eclecticism, 578–579; numeral "twelve" in Uyghur culture, 345; and Pamiri *rubab*, 473–483, 493; and Persian mystical poetry, 322; and *qasoid-khonī*, 490–492, 498–499; and social identity, 529; and Sufism, 401, 431

sympathetic strings, 33, 352, 465, 539

symphonic *mugham*, 359–360, 363–364

synchy, 177n4

synsu, 180

Syrdybaeva, Raziya, 527

syrnai (button accordion), 150, *597*, 597

Syrnev, Victor, 543

Syrymbetov, Baqbergen, 82

Systematists, 17

tabla, 608, *608*; and master-apprentice programs, *533*; and Nader, Salar, 539, *539*; in *Rainbow*, 537; in "Rangin Kaman," 539

tablak, 499, 589

Tabrizi, Shams-i, 322, 471, 489, 499

Tabyn, 240

tabyshmaktuu aitysh, 158, 159–160

Tächmämmedow, Chary, 117, *118*, 137

INDEX

Tächmyradow, Mylly, 117

Tagizade-Gajibekov, Niyazi, 364

"Tagyldyr too," 285

Tahir-Zöhrä (*dastan*), 408

Tahmasp I, 29

Täjibaev, Äbdilda, 169

Tajiki Persian (language), 490

Tajikistan, 504–517, 586–595; and Aga
    Khan Music Initiative, 526, 531, 532;
    autonomy of cultural sector in, 523;
    bazaar in, *317*; and *dastan*, 406; and
    gender divisions, 319; and geography
    of Central Asia, 5; importance of
    sacred music and chant in, 379;
    Jewish population of, 440; and
    Khunar Centre, 526; location of,
    504; and *maddoh*s, 470; and *maqom*
    tradition, 327, 328, 338; and poetry,
    589–590; popular music of (see
    estradai Tojik [popular music of
    Tajikistan]); and religious music and
    chant, *397*, 397; singer-songwriters
    of, 367–378; and small ensembles,
    319; and Soviet era, 19, 21, 586–587,
    588; technological mediation in
    transmission of music in, 587; *toy*
    (celebrations) in, *587*, 587–588;
    traditional music of, 367–378, 587,
    588–589, 594; urban and rural locales
    of, 587–588; and *yakkakhoni*, 392;
    zikr in, *391*

Tajiniso (female *dutar* performer), 427

tajwīd (chanting of the Qur'an), 10–11

tala, 35

Talasbaeva, Burulay, *215*

Talas region, *54*, 64–67, 67n2

Taliban, 11, 526

talqin, 331

talqincha, 330

"Talqincha-i Mashq-i Chorgoh"
    (Babakhanov, Ari), 459

"Talqincha-i sabo," 330–335, *334*

Tama (tribe of Little Horde), 240

tamalashaluu aytys, 158

Tamara Khanum, 430, 558

tämbur in Uyghur *muqam*, 344, 348,
    350, 605, *605*

"Ta men gelinçäm," 120–121

tanbur, 605, *605*; and Alimatov, Turgun,
    341, 342; in Badakhshan instrumental
    music, 464; and *falak*, 505; frets,
    330, *603*, 603, 605, *605*; and gender
    issues in music, 14; and *maddoh*
    performances, 474, 475; in "Navruzi
    Sabo" recording, 326; and nomadic
    vs. sedentary music, 37; and notation
    system, 324; Pamiri *tanbur*, *603*, 603;
    in "Rapo" (Badakhshani dance), 464;
    and Shashmaqom (six *maqom*s),
    324, 329; societal perceptions of, 532;
    in "Talqincha-i sabo," 330. *See also*
    Abdurashidov, Abduvali; Alimatov,
    Turgun

Tang dynasty, 9

Taoism, 139

tar, *605*, 605; in "Bardasht," 362; frets,
    605, 605; in "Katta ashula," 454; in
    Leyli and Majnun, 358; in *mugham*,
    356, 361, 362; in "Muqaddima-i
    segoh," 336; and Pirimov, Gurban,
    359; in "Ranoni Gördim," 372;
    in small ensembles of sedentary
    dwellers, *319*; in "Ufor-i Iroq," 373

Taraquly, Abyl, 250

täriyp, 90, 94, 100–101

"Tarje-i Navo," 458, 459

tarona, 330

taronasoz, 367

tartys, 250

tasawwuf, 10

Tashkent, Uzbekistan: and cities of
    Central Asia, 8; and documentary
    film "The End of an Era: Tashkent,"
    578; estrada music in, 555–574; and

Farroukh Qasimov, 580; and female
    entertainers, 438, 441; and Hojakuli,
    Ovlyakuli, 582–583; and Ilhom
    Theater, 609n1; and Jewish musical
    traditions, 449, 452; and *maqom*
    tradition, 322, 327, 338–340, 341–
    342; as multicultural megalopolis,
    579; and *otin-oy*s, 423; and Ramadan
    observances, 386–387, *387*; and
    Soviet influence, 437; and state
    supported cultural events, 246; and
    Sufi *zikr*s, *383*, 389–390, 391, 393; and
    Uyghur population, 344; wandering
    dervishes in, *382*

Tashpulatov, Maarufjon, 455

Tashybekova, Kynatai, *226*, 226

Tatarstan, 5

taziyah, 357, 389

"tea bowl" dance, 349

Teke (Turkmen tribal group), 77

temir komuz (jaw harps), *31*, 551

temir ooz komuz (metal jaw harp), 266,
    282, 282, 300n2, 345, 606, *606*. *See
    also* jaw harps

Temirov, Tolib, 459

Temüjin, 46–47. *See also* Genghis Khan

Ten Days of Music of the Republics of
    Central Asia, 246

"10 grammov LSD" (10 grams of LSD),
    573–575

tengeu, 90

Tengir-Too (Kyrgyz music ensemble), *6*,
    273, *286*, 549

Tengrism (Tengrianism), 7, 181,
    262–264

"Tengri's Whisper" (name for *küi*
    performance), 262–264

terme, 139–147; contemporary *terme*
    songs, 145–147; described, 139–142;
    and *jyrau*s, 191; poetic structure and
    melody, 142–145

theorbo, 38n2

"throat-singing," 306

Tilepbergenuly, Qazanghap, 245, 248, 261

Timur (Tamerlane), 68n24, 128, 439

Timurid dynasty, 28, 323, 381, 436, 439

"Tinchlik diyori" (Country of peace), 458

tirade tunes, 164–165

tirme and *bagshy*, 114–116, 118, 122–123, 125–126

"Toghyz tarau," 256–257

"Toguz kayryk" (nine variations), 270

"To hastam" (As long as I live), 591–593

Tohfakhon. *See* Pinkhasova, Tohfakhon

Tojibaev, Mahmudjon, 373, 393, *395*

Tokhti, Häkhät, 353

*tökmö aqyn*s, 56, 151, 154, 175. See also *tökpe* style

tökmölük, 174–175, 265

Tokombaev, Aaly, 151

tökpe style, 240–250; and apprenticeship, 154; and categories of *aqyn*s, 151, 165; and Kazakh *dombyra*, 310–311; and Kazakh *küi*, 239–240, 240–250, 251, 253, 256–258, 264, 280n28

Toktakhunova, Samarbubu, 543

Toktobekov, Jengishbek, *146*, 146–147, 156, 168

Toktogul. *See* Satylganov, Toktogul

Toktomambetova, Kunduz, 230

Tölebaev, Muqan, *167*, 167

Tölek clan, 303, 307

tolghau: function of, 81; and *jyrau*s, 81, 191; and Kazakh *küi*, 237, 256; "Mereke tolghau," 312; and philosophical reflections, 191; and Qamiev, Didar, 173; and wisdom poetry, 152

Tolmasov, Avrom, 453

Tolybai, Khan, 73

"Top shengel," 182–183

Torah recitation, 449–450

"Töremurat" (*küi* composed by Qurmanghazy), 241, 244

Tortadur (Nazarkhan, Sevara) (2011), 569

Toshmatov, Ganijon, 428

toy (festive gathering): and *aqyn*s, 152; in Bukhara, Uzbekistan, 442, *442*; *bukharcha*s performed at, 438; and Kazakh singing traditions, 180; *mavrigikhon*s at, 446; and social context of musical performance, *12*, 12–13; *sozanda*s at, 441, *442*; in Tajikistan, *587*, 587–588; and *tökpe küi*, 250; and Turkmen *bagshy*, 113–114, 129; and wedding *koshok*s, 226

"Toy bastar" (Nurpeisova, Dina), 246

trade, 8, 9, 33–34. *See also* Silk Road

tradition: and authenticity in *qobyz* performance, 299; as cultural and social construct, 522; discussed by Turgun Alimatov, 342; and the "future of the past," 521; and innovation, discussed by Nurak Abdyrakhmanov, 276; innovation in, 577–585; and neotraditionalism, 546–550; and post-neotraditionalists, 550–554; revitalization of, 521–533; traditional singer-songwriters, 367–378; and tradition-based popular music, 23, 466, 586–595; tradition-based vs. traditional, 525, 527, 528

traditional singer-songwriters, 367–378; and Davletov, Farhod, *372*, 372, 373; and "Dilhiroj" (Tormented heart), 368–369; and "Galdir" (Fool of God), 367, 370–371; and instrumental music, 375–377; Juraev, Sirojiddin, *376*, 376; and *Katta ashula*, 393–394; lyrics of, 368, 370; and "Mehri Vatan" (Love of my homeland), 377; and *na'at*, 387; Omonboeva, Nasiba,

368, *368*, 369; Pirmatova, Nodira, 375, *375*; and "Qushtar" (Double strings), 376; and "Ranoni Gördim," 372–373; themes of, 368; and "Ufor-i Iroq," 373–374; and "Zavq-i Javoni" (Interest of youth), 377

Transoxania, *321*

Tulpar, 191

tümön, 68n14

tündük, 147, 205, 216n11

tunings and Kyrgyz *küü*s, 269–270, 277

Turaqulov, Hamroqulqori, 393

türe aitysh, 160–161, 177n12

Turgunova, Dilorom, 429

Turkestan, Kazakhstan, *381*, 390, 392, 457

Turkey, 331, 355, 361, 392, 568, 587

Turkic culture and languages: and civilizational axes of Central Asia, 8; and epic traditions, 44, *44*, 46, 50; and funeral *koshok*s, 198; and geography of Central Asia, 5–6; heroic epics, 81; and Karakalpak music, 88, 89, 90, 107n3; and *Körughly* epic, 77; and nomadic vs. sedentary music, 34; and oral epic in Kazakhstan, 70; and "Turkmen" identity, 109

Turkmen: and *bagshy* music, 109–129; and *baqsy* bards, 82; and *dutar*, 131–137; and epic traditions, 49; language, 90; and music of Muslim holidays, 387; and oral epic in Kazakhstan, 72–74, 77; and Ramadan, 387; and *tökpe küi*, 244, 250; and "Yaremezan," 387

Turkmenia, 19

Turkmenistan: and musical and theatrical innovation, 583; music education in, 112; provinces, *110*; role of music in, 380; and Soviet era influences, 19, 21; state influence on culture in, 523; and "Turkmen" identity, 109

Turkmenskaya Muzyka (*Turkmen Music*) (Uspenskii and Beliaev), 18, 113

Turkmen Soviet Socialist Republic, 117

Tursunaliev, Estebes (Esteke), *167*, 167, 174

Tursunbaeva, Ainur, 169

Tusi, Nasir al-Din, *323*

tutik (Badakhshani flute), 505, 619

Tutkuchev, Aaly, 163, 168, 171, *174*, 174–176

Tuuganbay, 155

Tuva, *41*, 282, *317*, *522*

tuýduk (Turkmen flute), 124, 127–128

Twelve Muqam (Uyghur), 345–349, 349–351, 416

two-stringed fiddles, 36

Tynybayev, Kärimbai, 105, 106

typologies of musical instruments, 32–37

Ufor (dance genre), 373

"Ufor-i Iroq," 367, 373–374

"Ükili qamshat," 184–185

ulak, 156, 205, 216n8

Ulibibi, Khalfa, *397*

Umbetbaev, Smatai, 293, 298

umma, 8–9

Umuraliev, Arsen, 542

UNESCO: and China's cultural heritage lists, 420n2; and cultural preservation efforts, 23, *24*; and improvised poetry competitions, 174; on "intangible cultural heritage," 523; and *Manas* epic, 67nn1–2; and patronage of cultural institutions, 13; and Shashmaqom music, 327; and Uyghur *muqam*, 347. *See also* intangible cultural heritage; Representative List of the Intangible Cultural Heritage of Humanity

Union of Composers, 523

Uraliev, Namazbek, 269, *269*

urbanization: and Kazakh *qobyz*, 296; and nomadic cultures of Central Asia, 42; and *qyssakhan* tradition, 107. *See also* sedentary culture and dwellers

Urgench, Khorezm, Uzbekistan, 321

Urmawi, Safi al-Din al-, 17

üshpelek, *598*, 598

Usmanova, Yulduz, 23, 421, 563, 564, *564*

Üsönbaev, Alymkul, 167, 175

Üsönbaev, Zamirbek, 174

Uspensky, Viktor, 18, 113, *327*

ustat-shakirt/ustaz-shäkirt, 22, 146, 154. See also *ustod-shogird* (master-apprentice)

ustat/ustaz, 69–70, 154

ustod-shogird (master-apprentice), 22, 527. *See also* Centre Ustatshakirt; *ustat-shakirt/ustaz-shäkirt*

Ustod-Shogird Centre in Kabul, Afghanistan, *533*

usul, 35, 318, 330, 331, 335, 391, 459

Uyghurs and Uyghur culture: and *bagshychylyk*, 111, 112; and *baqsy* bards, 82; and China, 347, 407; compared to Turkmen *dutar*, 132; and epic traditions, 49; and geography of Central Asia, 4; and Kazakh *dombyra*, 303; and *mäjnun*s, *349*, 349–351; region of, *344*, 347; and Sufism, 399. See also *dastan* (*dästan*, *dessan*); *muqam* (Uyghur)

Uzaq (Kazakh *küishi*), 241, 245, 246

Uzbek Estrada Association, 562

Uzbek Folk Music (*Özbek khalq muzikasi*), 20

Uzbekistan, 555–576, 577–585; Academy of Sciences, 101; and alternative music, 557–558, 572–575; avant-garde music in, 577–578; celebration of Bukhara's founding, *523*; diversity of, 578; *dutar* players, 426–429, *427*, *428*; and *The End of an Era: Tashkent* (1996), 578–579; experimentalism in, 578–580; female musicians in, 421–433, *423*, *424*, *427*, *428*, *430*, *433*; and gender divisions, 319; and geography of Central Asia, 5; and Hojakuli, Ovlyakuli, *580*, 580–585; and Independence Palace, *562*; Islamic influence in, 568, 578; jazz in, 558; Jewish population of, 440; and Karakalpak *jyrau*s and *baqsy*, 79; *karnai* players from, *533*; and *katta ashula*, 453; and *maqom* tradition, 321–322, 327, *430*; and *Mavrigi*, 581, 583–585; and Nihol Prize, *562*; and *otin-oy*s, *423*, 423–425, *424*; popular music of, 557–558 (see also *estrada* of Uzbekistan); and Ramadan, 387; and *Rapshee*, 581–583; and religious music and chant, 379, *397*; and "Shahd," 583–584; show business industry of, 570; and Soviet era, 19, 21, 557, 558–561, 578; state influence on culture in, 523; State Radio of Uzbekistan, 428; and theater innovations, 579–585; traditional singer-songwriters of, 367–378; and *yakkakhonlik*, 392; *zikr* ceremony in, *383*. *See also* Karakalpaks; Uzbeks

Uzbekistan: Munodjat Yulchieva & Ensemble Shavkat Mirzaev (1997), 431–432

Uzbekistan National Conservatory, 562

Uzbek National Academic Drama Theater, 581

Uzbeks: and *baqsy* bards, 82; and epic traditions, 49, 50; and interethnic conflict, 145; and oral epic in Kazakhstan, 72; and *tökpe küi*s, 244;

and Uzbek language, 90. *See also*
  Uzbekistan
Uzbek State Philharmonic
  Ensemble, 431
Uzbek State Radio, 431
Uzbek Television and Radio
  Company, 428
Uz-Fest, 573

Vagif Mustafazade (2-DVD set), 363, 365
Valikhanov, Shoqan, *18*, 18, 55
Vámbéry, Arminius (Ármin), 113
Van den Berg, Gabrielle, 479, 482
"vanity" *küü*s, 269
verse forms: and *bagshy* music, 116; and
  epic traditions, 49; and Karakalpak
  music, 96; and *qara öleng* songs,
  182, 615; and *qyssakhan*s, 104;
  and sedentary dwellers, 331; and
  terme, 192
Veselovskii, A. N., 45
Vinogradov, Viktor, 18
Virgil, 43
virtuosic pieces and performances: and
  improvised poetry competitions,
  156; and jazz *mugham*, 364; and
  Karakalpak *qyssakhan*, 93; and
  Kashgar *rubab*s, 454; and Kazakh
  *küü*s, 242, 247, 252, 261; and Kazakh
  singing traditions, 191; and Kyrgyz
  jaw harps, 282; and Kyrgyz *küü*s,
  265, 274; and Mongolian Kazakhs,
  310; and *mugham* composition,
  356; and neo-traditional music, 546,
  549; and nomadic cultures, 42; and
  Rainbow, 535; and sedentary dwellers,
  318; and social context of musical
  performance, 12; and theatrical
  performance, 582; and Turkmen
  bagshy, 125; and Turkmen *dutar*,
  131–132, 136; and Uzbek-Tajik *dutar*,
  375–377, 428, 534

visionary dreams, 57–59
"Vocalese" (Jetigen uulu), 552
Voice of America, 558
Vorotnikova, Tatyana, *544*
vowel elongation (in Uyghur *dastan*s),
  415–416

Wahhabi Islam, 201
Wakhan Valley, 485–487, *486*, 491
Wakhi-language poems, 490
Wakhoni, Muborak, 492, *492*
wandering dervishes (*qalandar*s), *382*;
  in Bukhara, 436, 438; culture of, 394;
  and dissemination of Islamic values,
  381; and *qalandarkhane*s, 394, *395*;
  and *Qalandar* song, 396; widespread
  presence of, 389
weddings and wedding songs: and
  alternative music, 573; and *aqyn*s,
  152; in Bukhara, 441; and *falak*, 505;
  and gender roles in music, 15, 441;
  and improvised poetry competitions,
  156; and Karakalpak music, 80; and
  Kazakh singing traditions, 179–180;
  and mourning customs, 491; and
  Pamiri houses, 489; and *sozanda*s,
  441–442; in Tajikistan, *13*; in Wakhan
  Valley, 491
Weil, Mark, 578, 579
Western Mongols, 302
Where Rivers and Mountains Sing (Levin
  and Süzükei), 68n17
Where the Sky Meets the Land
  (Muller), 546
wisdom songs. See *terme*
women: of Badakhshan, 463, *465*;
  of Bukhara, 438; and "Diwan-i
  Hikmat," 425; domestic music of,
  422, 423–426; *dutar* players, 426–429,
  427, *428*; female musicians in
  Uzbekistan, 421–433, *433*; and gender
  segregation, 422 (*see also* gender

issues/divisions); and International
  Women's Day, 247; and "Kelmadi"
  (He didn't come), 431–433; and
  lalaik, 463; and madrasahs, 424–425;
  and *maqom* tradition, 429–433, *430*;
  and "Nolish" (Groan, lament), 430;
  and *otin-oy*s, *423*, 423–426, *424*;
  religious music and chant by, 397,
  397; and Soviet era, 428, 430–431;
  subordination of, 422; of Uzbekistan,
  421–433, *423*, *424*, *427*, *428*, *430*, *433*.
  See also gender issues/divisions
wooden jaw harps (*jygach ooz komuz*),
  266, *282*, 282–286, *284*, 300n2, 545
"wordless language" (*sözsiz tili*), 236
world music, 352, 532, 554, 557, 564,
  569, 589
World War II, 96, 166, 246, 364, 430,
  445, 558. *See also* Great Patriotic War
Writers and Composers Unions of the
  Kazakh SSR, 167
Writers Union of Karakalpakstan, 101

Xinjiang Uyghur Autonomous Region:
  and *dastan*s, 406, 407–408, 412,
  413–414; and Dolan Muqam, *353*;
  and geography of Central Asia, 4;
  and Kazakh *küü*s, 260; and *Manas*
  epic, 67n1; and Mongolian Kazakhs,
  302, 304; shrine festival in, *350*; and
  Sufis, 400; and Twelve Muqam, 347;
  and UNESCO Convention, 23; and
  Uyghur population, 344

Yachibäg, 418
yakkakhoni/yakkakhonlik, 392
Ýakup, Chary, 127, 128, *128*
Ýakupow, Gurt, 127, 128, *128*
Ýakupow family, 128
Yakut people, 49, 284
Yalla (ensemble), 559, 560
yalla (song genre), 438

INDEX

yallachi, 438

yanama bagshy, *114*, 114–115

Yanov-Yanovsky, Dmitri, *578*, 578–579

Yaqup, Ibrahim, 418

Yaqup, Yasin, 350

Yärkänd Khanate, 345

Yasin, Mämättokhti, 417, 419

Yassawi, Khoja Ahmad: *Diwan-i Hikmat*, 391; gatherings devoted to work of, 396; mausoleum of, *381*; and *otin-oy*s, 425; poetry of, 395; and women's performances, 397; and Yassawi order, 10, 391

Yassawiyya (also Yassawi order), 10, 387, 390, 391, 392

"Ya Zahratan Fi Khayali" (Flower of my dreams), 559

Yazdahum, 389

Ýazmyradow, Musaguly, 123, 124

Yesügin, 47

"Yol Bolsin" (Nazarkhan, Sevara), 569

Yol Bolsin (Nazarkhan, Sevara) (2003), 569

Yomut school of epic performance: key figures, 130n9; and *Körughly* epic, 77; and Turkmen *bagshy*, 111, 116, 117, 122–123, 125–126

Yomut *ýoly*, 125

Yormamadov, Abdulmamad, 491

Young, La Monte, 551

yrchy. See *jyrshy* (*yrchy*)

Yrchy uul, Yramandyn, 46, 52

yrghaq (vocal undulations), 85

Yulchieva, Dilfuza, 429

Yulchieva, Munojat, 421, *430*, 430–431, 432

yurts: collapsible side wings, 216n28, 233n5; and cultural revival, 546, 548; and *dessan* narratives, 116; exterior coverings, 233n3; and funeral *koshok*s, *199*, 200–202, 204–205, 207–211, 215; and jaw harp songs, 283; and *jyrau*s, 70–71; in Karakalpak, *80*; and Kazakh *küi*, 253, 280n30; and Kyrgyz *küü*, 266; and Kyrgyz wisdom songs, 142; and *Manas* epic, 58, 60; and nomads, 37, 42, *42*; and norms of hospitality, 189; and *qara öleng* songs, 182–183; and *qobyz*, 301n15; Red Yurts, 307; roof structure, 216n11; sleeping mats, 216n27; Tuvan, *41*; and wedding *koshok*s, 218, 220, 223, 225–229, *226*

Yusuf, Muhammad, 563

Yusuf-Zuleikha (Jami), 88, 89

Yüsüp-Ähmäd (also *Ýusip-Akhmet* epic), 80, 90, 124, 414, 415–416

Yusupov, Ibraiym, 84

"Yusup soltanym," 124–125

Yusup-Zuleýha (Andalib), 115

Zakirov, Botyr, 556, 558–559

Zakirov, Farrukh, 559, 560

*zalkar küü*s, 269–272

*zamanachy aqyn*s, 176n3

Zaraboev, Lutfulloh, 492

zarbi-mugham, 360

"Zar zaman," 304–305, 313

Zatayevich, Aleksandr, 18, 294, 301n19

"Zavq-i Javoni" (Interest of youth), 377

Zäwre-Taiyr, 90

Zazou, Hector, 569

Zeigler, Jeffrey, 539

Zen Buddhism, 139

Zengi-Ata, Sheikh, 387

zerbaghali, 608, *608*

Zeynel-Arab, 89

"Zi durï" (Far away), 516, 589–591

zikr, 389–392; attendance at, 400–401; breath and rhythm in, 403–405; circumcision ceremony, 401–403; female *zikr*, 397; and gender divisions, 390, 400–401, 403; integrated into mosques, 382; and Kazakh *qobyz* music, 292; as religious ceremony, 383, *383*; ritual circumcision ceremony, 400, *402*; and Rumi, 322; and Shiʻa ceremonies, 389; significance of, 400; and Sufi poets, 403; in Tajikistan, *391*; types of, 390–391, 392; of Uyghur Sufis of Ghulja, 399–405; in Uzbekistan, *383*

zithers, 34, 123

Ziwidä qara köz (*dastan*), 409

Ziyoda (Uzbek *estrada* star), 556

Ziyoyeva, Malika, 428, 429, 430

"Zohidi Pokizasirisht" (The virtuous puritan), 467–469

Zolotarev, Vitalii, 565

Zoroastrianism, 9, 380, 488

Zoy, Viktor, 555

Zufarova, Malika, 429

Zufunun, 89

Zuhuriyon, D., 591

zurna, 34